CATHOLIC COMMUNITY
HYMNAL

G-5000H

CATHOLIC COMMUNITY HYMNAL

GIA PUBLICATIONS, INC.
CHICAGO

PREFACE

Ever since 1971, when GIA published *Worship,* its first post-Vatican II hardcover hymnal, we have sustained a strong commitment to providing the Church with permanent alternatives to disposable worship aids. The *Catholic Community Hymnal* is the newest and completes the present range of offerings.

Using the same editorial standards, typography, and quality materials of our previous editions— *Worship* (three editions), *Gather* (two editions), *RitualSong,* and *Gather Comprehensive*—this new offering is especially designed for parishes looking to make the transition from a disposable worship aid to a permanent hymnal for the first time. While it is the smallest of our collections, it still remains a complete hymnal/service book designed to provide the parish with that full, comprehensive repertoire of hymns, psalms, songs, and service music, that has become common to a majority of Catholic parishes today. The beauty of its paper, typography, and binding, along with the familiarity and facility that comes from using a book that is unchanging, makes it a book worthy of use by any worshiping community. The *Catholic Community Hymnal* also seeks to provide a more affordable option than that of endless yearly subscription and shipping expenses.

Special recognition for this project goes to editorial consultants Michael A. Cymbala, Kelly Dobbs Mickus, and Sarah Griffith; project coordinator Jeffry Mickus; music engraver Philip Roberts; proofreaders Victoria Krstansky and Clarence Reiels; copyright permission editor Laura Cacciattolo; and the world's most experienced and competent hymnal indexer, Robert H. Oldershaw.

Robert J. Batastini
      Project Director and Senior Editor
Edward J. Harris
      Publisher

Contents

Lectionary

Prayers of the Individual and Household

Indexes

* These indexes only appear in the choir and accompaniment editions.

Morning Praise

The Church's sense for how to pray in the morning comes from our Jewish heritage. Whatever the day, whatever the difficulties, the tradition has been to begin the day with praise for the creator. The sign of the cross, first traced on the Christian at baptism, is again made to begin the new day and its prayer. In the hymn and the psalms, in the scripture and intercessions, each one who prays and the community together finds what it is to stand at the beginning of a new day as a Christian. The morning's prayer gives the day its meaning when, through the years, these prayers become one's own.

INVITATORY

All make the sign of the cross on their lips.

Presider: Lord, open my lips.
Assembly: **And my mouth will proclaim your praise.**

MORNING HYMN

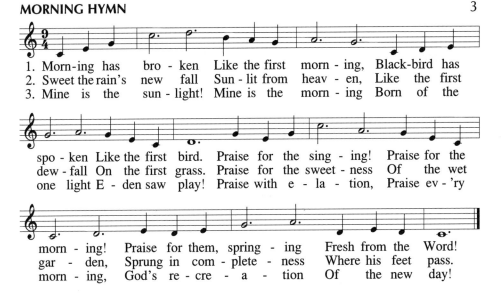

1. Morn-ing has bro-ken Like the first morn-ing, Black-bird has
2. Sweet the rain's new fall Sun-lit from heav-en, Like the first
3. Mine is the sun-light! Mine is the morn-ing Born of the

spo-ken Like the first bird. Praise for the sing-ing! Praise for the
dew-fall On the first grass. Praise for the sweet-ness Of the wet
one light E-den saw play! Praise with e-la-tion, Praise ev-'ry

morn-ing! Praise for them, spring-ing Fresh from the Word!
gar-den, Sprung in com-plete-ness Where his feet pass.
morn-ing, God's re-cre-a-tion Of the new day!

Text: Eleanor Farjeon, 1881-1965, *The Children's Bells,* © David Higham Assoc., Ltd.
Music: BUNESSAN, 5 5 5 4 D; Gaelic; acc. by Robert J. Batastini, © 1998, GIA Publications, Inc.

PSALMODY

The singing of one or more psalms is a central part of Morning Praise. Psalm 63, given below, is one of the premier morning psalms. Psalm 51 is commonly substituted for Psalm 63 on Wednesday and Friday, as well as during Lent. Other appropriate psalms for morning are Psalms 8, 66, 80, 85, 95, 98, 100, 118, and 150.

4   PSALM 63

Sit

Antiphon

In the morn - ing I will sing, will sing glad songs of praise to you.

Text: *Praise God in Song*
Music: David Clark Isele
© 1979, GIA Publications, Inc.

Verses

1. O   God, you are my God, for   you   I   long;
            My body   pines   for   you
            So I gaze on you in   the   sanc - tu - ary
2. For your love is bet   -   ter   than   life,
            So I will bless you   all   my   life,
            My soul shall be filled as with   a   ban   -   quet,
3. On my   bed I   re - mem - ber   you.
            for you have   been   my   help;
            My soul   clings   to   you;
4. Give   praise to the Father   Al - might   -   y,
            to the Spirit who dwells   in   our   hearts,

1. for you   my   soul   is   thirst - ing.
   like a dry, weary   land   with - out wa   - ter.
   to see your   strength and   your   glo - ry. ℟.
2. my lips   will   speak   your   praise.
   in your name I will lift   up   my   hands.
   my mouth shall   praise you   with   joy. ℟.
3. On you I   muse   through the   night
   in the shadow of your wings   I   re - joice.
   your right   hand   holds   me   fast. ℟.
4. to his Son, Je   - sus   Christ, the   Lord,
   both now and for   ev   - er.   A   - men. ℟.

Text: Psalm 63; © 1963, 1993, The Grail, GIA Publications, Inc., agent
Music: Tone 6f; acc. by Robert J. Batastini, © 1975, GIA Publications, Inc.

PSALM PRAYER

Stand

All respond: **Amen.**

WORD OF GOD   5

Sit

Reader concludes: The word of the Lord.
        Assembly: **Thanks be to God.**

GOSPEL CANTICLE   6

Stand. All make the sign of the cross as the canticle begins.

1. Now ✠ bless the God of Is - ra - el, Who
2. Re - mem - ber - ing the cov - e - nant, God
3. In ten - der mer - cy, God will send The

comes in love and pow'r, Who rais - es from the
res - cues us from fear, That we might serve in
day - spring from on high, Our ris - ing sun, the

roy - al house De - liv - 'rance in this hour. Through
ho - li - ness And peace from year to year; And
light of life For those who sit and sigh. God

ho - ly proph - ets God has sworn To
you, my child, shall go be - fore To
comes to guide our way to peace, That

free us from a - larm, To save us from the
preach, to proph - e - sy, That all may know the
death shall reign no more. Sing prais - es to the

heav - y hand Of all who wish us harm.
ten - der love, The grace of God most high.
Ho - ly One! O wor - ship and a - dore!

Text: *Benedictus*, Luke 1:68-79; Ruth Duck, © 1992, GIA Publications, Inc.
Music: FOREST GREEN, CMD; English, harm. by Ralph Vaughan Williams, 1872-1958, © Oxford University Press

7 INTERCESSIONS

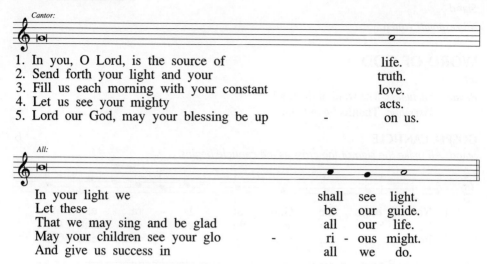

Cantor:

1. In you, O Lord, is the source of   life.
2. Send forth your light and your   truth.
3. Fill us each morning with your constant   love.
4. Let us see your mighty   acts.
5. Lord our God, may your blessing be up -   on us.

All:

In your light we   shall see light.
Let these   be our guide.
That we may sing and be glad   all our life.
May your children see your glo -   ri - ous might.
And give us success in   all we do.

Praise God in Song, © 1979, GIA Publications, Inc.

8 LORD'S PRAYER

All: **Our Father, who art in heaven,**
    hallowed be thy name;
    thy kingdom come;
    thy will be done on earth as it is in heaven.
    Give us this day our daily bread;
    and forgive us our trespasses
    as we forgive those who trespass against us;
    and lead us not into temptation,
    but deliver us from evil.
    For the kingdom, the power,
    and the glory are yours,
    now and for ever. Amen.

The concluding prayer follows.

9 DISMISSAL

Presider: Let us bless the Lord.
Assembly: **And give him thanks.**
Presider: May the Lord bless us,
           protect us from all evil
           and bring us to everlasting life.
    All: **Amen.**

Evensong

The Church gathers in the evening to give thanks for the day that is ending. In the earliest tradition, this began with the lighting of the lamps as darkness fell and the hymn of praise of Christ who is "radiant Light . . . of God the Father's deathless face." The evening psalms and the Magnificat bring the day just past to focus for the Christian: "God has cast down the mighty from their thrones, and has lifted up the lowly"; "God has remembered the promise of mercy, the promise made to our ancestors." Prayers of intercession are almost always part of the church's liturgy, but those which conclude evening prayer are especially important. As day ends, the church again and again lifts up to God the needs and sorrows and failures of all the world. Such intercession is the daily task and joy of the baptized.

LIGHT PROCLAMATION 11

Stand

Presiding minister or assistant: *Assembly:*

Light and peace in Je - sus Christ our Lord.   Thanks be to God.

EVENING HYMN 12

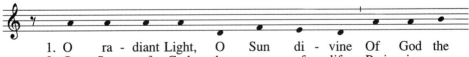

1. O ra - diant Light, O Sun di - vine Of God the
2. O Son of God, the source of life, Praise is your
3. Lord Je - sus Christ, as day - light fades, As shine the

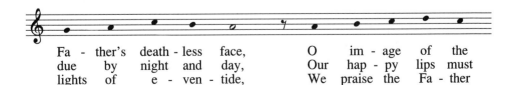

Fa - ther's death - less face, O im - age of the
due by night and day, Our hap - py lips must
lights of e - ven - tide, We praise the Fa - ther

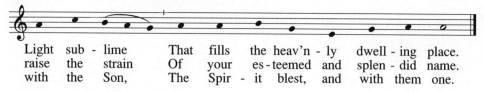

Light	sub - lime	That	fills	the heav'n - ly	dwell - ing place.
raise	the strain	Of	your	es - teemed and	splen - did name.
with	the Son,	The	Spir - it	blest, and	with them one.

Text: *Phos Hilaron,* Greek, c.200; tr. by William G. Storey, ©
Music: JESU DULCIS MEMORIA, LM; Mode I; acc. by Richard Proulx, © 1975, GIA Publications, Inc.

PSALMODY

The singing of one or more psalms is a central part of Evensong. Psalm 141, given below, is one of the premier evening psalms. It is customary to use incense as it is sung. Other appropriate psalms for evening are Psalms 19, 23, 27, 91, 104, 117, 118, 121, 130, 136, and 145.

13   PSALM 141 / INCENSE PSALM

Antiphon

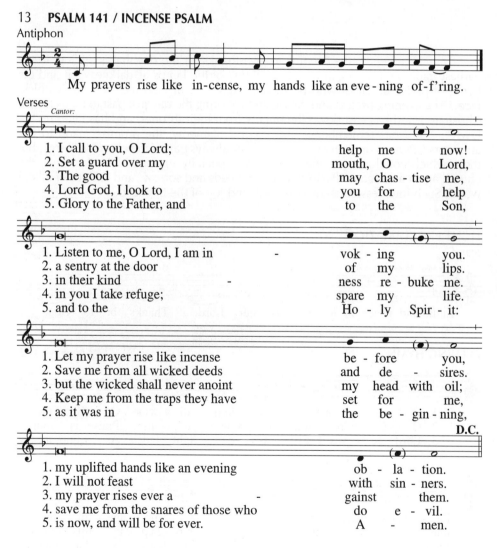

My prayers rise like in-cense, my hands like an eve - ning of-f'ring.

Verses

Cantor:

1. I call to you, O Lord;	help me now!
2. Set a guard over my	mouth, O Lord,
3. The good	may chas - tise me,
4. Lord God, I look to	you for help
5. Glory to the Father, and	to the Son,

1. Listen to me, O Lord, I am in -	vok - ing you.
2. a sentry at the door	of my lips.
3. in their kind -	ness re - buke me.
4. in you I take refuge;	spare my life.
5. and to the	Ho - ly Spir - it:

1. Let my prayer rise like incense	be - fore you,
2. Save me from all wicked deeds	and de - sires.
3. but the wicked shall never anoint	my head with oil;
4. Keep me from the traps they have	set for me,
5. as it was in	the be - gin - ning,

D.C.

1. my uplifted hands like an evening	ob - la - tion.
2. I will not feast	with sin - ners.
3. my prayer rises ever a -	gainst them.
4. save me from the snares of those who	do e - vil.
5. is now, and will be for ever.	A - men.

Text: Psalm 141; Howard Hughes, SM
Music: Howard Hughes, SM
© 1979, GIA Publications, Inc.

PSALM PRAYER

Stand

All respond: **Amen.**

WORD OF GOD 14

Sit

Reader concludes: The word of the Lord.
      Assembly: **Thanks be to God.**

GOSPEL CANTICLE 15

Stand. All make the sign of the cross as the canticle begins.

1. My ✠ soul gives glo - ry to the Lord, In God my
2. His mer - cy goes to all who fear, From age to
3. He raised his ser - vant Is - ra - el, Re - mem - b'ring

Sav - ior I re - joice. My low - li - ness he did re -
age and to all parts. His arm of strength to all is
his e - ter - nal grace, As from of old he did fore -

gard, Ex - alt - ing me by his own choice. From this day
near; He scat - ters those who have proud hearts. He casts the
tell To A - bra - ham and all his race. O Fa - ther,

all shall call me blest, For he has done great
might - y from their throne And rais - es those of
Son and Spir - it blest, In three - fold Name are

things for me, Of all great names his is the
low de - gree; He feeds the hun - gry as his
you a - dored, To you be ev - 'ry prayer ad -

best, For it is ho - ly; strong is he.
own, The rich de - part in pov - er - ty.
dressed, From age to age the on - ly Lord.

Text: Luke 1:46-55; J.T. Mueller, 1885-1967, alt.
Music: MAGNIFICAT, LMD; Michael Joncas, © 1979, 1988, GIA Publications, Inc.

16   GENERAL INTERCESSIONS

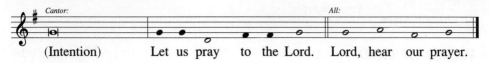

Cantor: *All:*

(Intention)   Let us pray   to the Lord.   Lord, hear our prayer.

Music: Byzantine chant

17   LORD'S PRAYER

All: **Our Father, who art in heaven,**
    hallowed be thy name;
    thy kingdom come;
    thy will be done on earth as it is in heaven.
    Give us this day our daily bread;
    and forgive us our trespasses
    as we forgive those who trespass against us;
    and lead us not into temptation,
    but deliver us from evil.
    For the kingdom, the power,
    and the glory are yours,
    now and for ever. Amen.

The concluding prayer follows.

18   DISMISSAL

Presider: Let us bless the Lord.
Assembly: **And give him thanks.**
Presider: May the Lord bless us,
        protect us from all evil
        and bring us to everlasting life.
All: **Amen.**

Psalm 8: How Great Is Your Name   19

Antiphon I

How great   is your name, O   Lord our God,   through all the earth!

Antiphon II

From the voic-es of chil - dren,   Lord, comes the sound of your   praise.

Text: The Grail
Music: A. Gregory Murray, OSB
© 1963, The Grail, GIA Publications, Inc., agent

Psalm Tone

Music: Chant tone 5; acc. by Robert J. Batastini, © 1975, GIA Publications, Inc.

Gelineau Tone

*2 How **great** is your **name**, O Lòrd our **God**,
   throúgh **all** the **earth!**

   Your **majesty is praised** above the **hèav**ens;
3 on the **lips** of **chíl**dren and of **babes**
   you have found **praise** to **foil** your **èn**emy,
   to **si**lence the **fóe** and the **reb**el.

4 When I see the **heav**ens, the **work** of
      yòur **hands,**
   the **moon** and the **stárs** which you
      ar**ranged,**
5 what are **we** that you should **keep** us
      in **mìnd,**
   mere **mor**tals thát you **care** for **us?**

6 Yet you have **made** us little **less** than **gòds;**
   and **crowned** us with **glór**y and **hon**or,
7 you gave us **pow**er over the **work** of
      yòur **hands,**
   put **all** things **ún**der our **feet.**

Omitted when Antiphon I is used.

8 **All** of them, **sheep** and **càt**tle,
   yes, **even** thé **savage beasts,**
9 **birds** of the **air**, and **fish**
   that **make** their **way** throúgh the **wa**ters.

*10 How **great** is your **name**, O Lòrd our **God**,
   throúgh **all** the **earth!**

   Give **glor**y to the **Fa**ther Al**mìgh**ty,
   to his **Son**, Jésus **Christ,** the **Lord,**
   to the **Spir**it who **dwells** in òur **hearts,**
   both **now** and for **év**er. **Amen.**

Text: Psalm 8; The Grail
Music: Joseph Gelineau, SJ
© 1963, 1993, The Grail, GIA Publications, Inc., agent

20 Psalm 19: Lord, You Have the Words

Refrain

Lord, you have the words of ev-er-last-ing life.

Verses

1. The law of the Lord is perfect, refreshing the soul;
   the Lord's rule is to be trusted, the simple find wisdom.

2. The fear of the Lord is holy, abiding for ever;
   the decrees of the Lord are true, all of them just.

3. The precepts of the Lord are right, they gladden the heart,
   the command of the Lord is clear, giving light to the eye.

4. They are worth more than gold, than the finest gold,
   sweeter than honey, than honey from the comb.

Text: Psalm 19:8, 9, 10, 11; David Haas, © 1983, GIA Publications, Inc.; refrain trans. © 1969, ICEL
Music: David Haas, © 1983, GIA Publications, Inc.

21 Psalm 22: My God, My God

Refrain

My God, my God, O why have you a - ban-doned me?

Verses

1. All who see me laugh at me, they mock me and they shake their heads:
   "He relied on the Lord, let the Lord be his refuge."

2. As dogs around me, they circle me about.
   Wounded me and pierced me, I can number all my bones.

3. My clothing they divided, for my garments casting lots,
   O Lord, do not desert me, but hasten to my aid.

4. I will praise you to my people, and proclaim you in their midst,
   O fear the Lord, my people, give glory to God's name.

Text: Psalm 22:8-9, 17-18; 19-20; 23-24; Marty Haugen, © 1983, GIA Publications, Inc.; refrain trans. © 1969, ICEL
Music: Marty Haugen, © 1983, GIA Publications, Inc.

Psalm 23: My Shepherd Is the Lord   22

Antiphon I

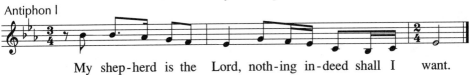

My shep-herd is the Lord, noth-ing in-deed shall I want.

Text: Psalm 23; The Grail
Music: Joseph Gelineau, SJ
© 1963, The Grail, GIA Publications, Inc., agent

Antiphon II

The Lord is my shep-herd, noth-ing shall I want: he leads me by safe paths, noth-ing shall I fear.

Text: Psalm 23; The Grail
Music: A. Gregory Murray, OSB
© 1963, The Grail, GIA Publications, Inc., agent

Psalm Tone

Omit for 4-line stanzas

Music: Richard Proulx, © 1975, GIA Publications, Inc.

Gelineau Tone

Omit for 4-line stanzas

¹ **Lord, you** are mỳ **shep**herd;
there is **noth**ing Í shall **want.**

² **Fresh** and **green** are thè **pas**tures
where you **give** me ré**pose.**
Near **rest**ful **wa**ters yòu **lead** me,

³ to re**vive** my droop**íng spirit.**

You **guide** me a**long** the rìght **path;**
You are **true** tó your **name.**

⁴ If I should **walk** in the **val**ley òf **dark**ness
no evil would Í **fear.**
You are **there** with your **crook** and yòur
staff;
with **these** you give mé **comfort.**

⁵ You have pre**pared** a **ban**quet fòr **me**
in the **sight** óf my **foes.**
My **head** you have a**noint**ed wìth **oil;**
my **cup** is ové**rflowing.**

⁶ Surely **good**ness and **kind**ness shàll
follow me
all the **days** óf my **life.**
In the **Lord's** own **house** shall Ì **dwell**
for **ever** ánd **ever.**

To the **Fa**ther and **Son** gìve **glo**ry,
give **glo**ry tó the **Spir**it.
To God who **is,** who **was,** and whò **will**
be
for **ever** ánd **ever.**

Text: Psalm 23; The Grail
Music: Joseph Gelineau, SJ
© 1963, 1993, The Grail, GIA Publications, Inc., agent

23 Psalm 25: To You, O Lord

Refrain

To you, O Lord, I lift my soul, to you, I lift my soul.

Verses

1. Lord, make me know your ways, teach me your paths
   and keep me in the way of your truth, for you are God, my Savior.

2. For the Lord is good and righteous, revealing the way to those who wander,
   gently leading the poor and the humble.

3. To the ones who seek the Lord, who look to God's word, who live God's love,
   God will always be near, and will show them mercy.

Text: Psalm 25:4-5, 8-9, 12-14; Marty Haugen, © 1982, GIA Publications, Inc.; refrain trans. © 1969, ICEL
Music: Marty Haugen, © 1982, GIA Publications, Inc.

24 Psalm 27: The Lord Is My Light

Refrain

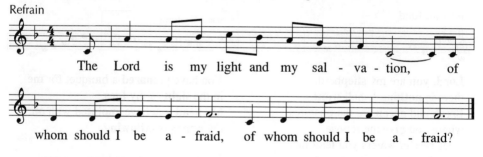

The Lord is my light and my sal - va - tion, of whom should I be a - fraid, of whom should I be a - fraid?

Verses

1. The Lord is my light and my help; whom should I fear?
   The Lord is the stronghold of my life; before whom should I shrink?

2. There is one thing I ask of the Lord; for this I long:
   to live in the house of the Lord all the days of my life.

3. I believe I shall see the goodness of the Lord in the land of the living;
   hope in God, and take heart. Hope in the Lord!

Text: Psalm 27:1-2, 4, 13-14; David Haas
Music: David Haas
© 1983, GIA Publications, Inc.

Psalm 30: I Will Praise You, Lord   25

Refrain

I will praise you, Lord, you have res - cued me,
I will praise you, Lord, for your mer-cy. I will praise you, Lord,
you have res - cued me: I will praise you, Lord.

Verses

1. I will praise you, Lord, you have rescued me
   and have not let my enemies rejoice over me.
   O Lord, you have raised my soul from the dead,
   restored me to life from those who sink into the grave.

2. Sing psalms to the Lord, all you faithful, give thanks to his holy name.
   God's anger lasts but a moment; God's favor through life.
   At night there are tears, but joy comes with dawn.

3. The Lord listened and had pity. The Lord came to my help.
   For me you have changed my mourning into dancing;
   O Lord my God, I will thank you for ever.

Text: Psalm 30:2, 4, 5-6, 11-13; © 1963, 1993, The Grail, GIA Publications, Inc., agent; refrain, Paul Inwood, © 1985, alt.
Music: Paul Inwood, © 1985
Published by OCP Publications

26 Psalm 34: Taste and See

Refrain

Taste and see the good-ness of the Lord, the good - ness of the Lord.

Verses

1. I will bless the Lord at all times, God's praise ever in my mouth.
   Glory in the Lord for ever, and the lowly will hear and be glad.

2. Glory in the Lord with me, let us together extol God's name.
   I sought the Lord, who answered me and delivered me from all my fears.

3. Look to God that you might be radiant with joy,
   and your faces free from all shame.
   The Lord hears the suffering souls, and saves them from all distress.

Text: Psalm 34:2-3, 4-5, 6-7; Marty Haugen, © 1980, GIA Publications, Inc.; refrain trans. © 1969, ICEL
Music: Marty Haugen, © 1980, GIA Publications, Inc.

27 Psalm 34: The Cry of the Poor

Refrain

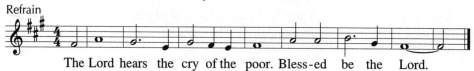

The Lord hears the cry of the poor. Bless-ed be the Lord.

Verses

1. I will bless the Lord at all times, with praise ever in my mouth.
   Let my soul glory in the Lord, who will hear the cry of the poor.

2. Let the lowly hear and be glad: the Lord listens to their pleas;
   and to hearts broken God is near, who will hear the cry of the poor.

3. Ev'ry spirit crushed God will save; will be ransom for their lives;
   will be safe shelter for their fears, and will hear the cry of the poor.

4. We proclaim your greatness, O God, your praise ever in our mouth;
   ev'ry face brightened in your light, for you hear the cry of the poor.

Text: Psalm 34:2-3, 6-7, 18-19, 23; John Foley, SJ
Music: John Foley, SJ
© 1978, 1991, John B. Foley, SJ, and New Dawn Music

Psalm 51: Be Merciful, O Lord   28

Refrain

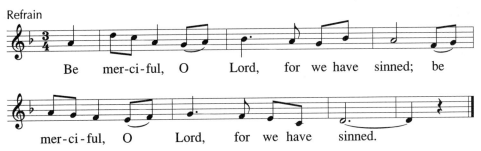

Be mer-ci-ful, O Lord, for we have sinned; be
mer-ci-ful, O Lord, for we have sinned.

Verses

1. Have mercy on me, God, in your kindness,
   in your compassion, blot out my offense.
   O wash me more and more from my guilt and my sorrow,
   and cleanse me from all of my sin.

2. My offenses, truly I know them, and my sins are always before me;
   against you alone have I sinned, O Lord, what is evil in your sight I have done.

3. Create in me a clean heart, O God, put your steadfast spirit in my soul.
   Cast me not away from your presence, O Lord, and take not your spirit from me.

4. Give back to me the joy of your salvation, let your willing spirit bear me up
   and I shall teach your way to the ones who have wandered,
   and bring them all home to your side.

Text: Psalm 51:3-4, 5-6, 12-13, 14-15; Marty Haugen, © 1983, GIA Publications, Inc.; refrain trans. © 1969, ICEL
Music: Marty Haugen, © 1983, GIA Publications, Inc.

29 Psalm 63: Your Love Is Finer Than Life

Refrain

O God, I seek you, my soul thirsts for
you, your love is fin-er than life.

Verses

1. As a dry and weary desert land, so my soul is thirsting for my God,
   and my flesh is faint for the God I seek, for your love is more to me than life.

2. I think of you when at night I rest, I reflect upon your steadfast love,
   I will cling to you, O Lord my God, in the shadow of your wings I sing.

3. I will bless your name all the days I live, I will raise my hands and call on you,
   my joyful lips shall sing your praise, you alone have filled my hungry soul.

Text: Psalm 63; Marty Haugen
Music: Marty Haugen
© 1982, GIA Publications, Inc.

30 Psalm 66: Let All the Earth

Refrain

Let all the earth cry out in joy to the Lord;
Let all the earth cry out in joy to the

1.-3. *To verses* | *Last time*

Lord! Lord! to the Lord!

Verses

1. Cry out in joy to the Lord, all peoples on earth,
   sing to the praise of God's name, proclaiming for ever,
   "tremendous your deeds for us."

2. Leading your people safe through fire and water,
   bringing their souls to life, we sing of your glory, your love is eternal.

3. Hearken to me as I sing my love of the Lord,
   who answers the prayer of my heart. God leads me in safety, from death unto life.

Text: Psalm 66:1-3, 12, 16; Marty Haugen
Music: Marty Haugen
© 1982, GIA Publications, Inc.

Psalm 80/85/Luke 1: Lord, Make Us Turn to You   31

Refrain

Lord, make us turn to you, show us your face, and we shall be saved.

Verses

1. Shepherd of Israel, hearken from your throne and shine forth,
   O rouse your power, and come to save us.

2. We are your chosen vine, only by your care do we live,
   reach out your hand, O Lord, unto your people.

3. If you will dwell with us, we shall live anew in your love,
   O shine upon us, great Lord of life.

4. Lord, we are present here, show us your kindness and love,
   O speak your word of peace unto your people.

5. Lord, let salvation rain, shower down your justice and peace,
   the earth shall bring forth truth, the skies your love.

6. See, Lord, we look to you, you alone can bring us to life,
   O walk before us to light our pathways.

7. You have done wondrous things, holy is your name for all time,
   your mercy and your love are with your people.

8. You are my joy and song, I would have my life speak your praise,
   on me your love has shown, your blessings given.

9. You fill all hungry hearts, sending the rich empty forth,
   and holding up in love the meek and lowly.

Text: Psalm 80:2-3, 15-16, 18-20; Psalm 85:9-14; Luke 1:46-55; Marty Haugen
Music: Marty Haugen
© 1982, GIA Publications, Inc.

32 Psalm 91: Be with Me

Refrain

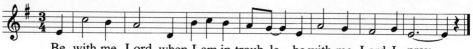

Be with me, Lord, when I am in trouble, be with me, Lord, I pray.

Verses

1. You who dwell in the shelter of the Lord, Most High,
   who abide in the shadow of our God,
   say to the Lord: "My refuge and fortress, the God in whom I trust."

2. No evil shall befall you, no pain come near,
   for the angels stand close by your side,
   guarding you always and bearing you gently, watching over your life.

3. Those who cling to the Lord live secure in God's love,
   lifted high, those who trust in God's name,
   call on the Lord, who will never forsake you.
   God will bring you salvation and joy.

Text: Psalm 91:1-2, 10-11, 14-15; Marty Haugen
Music: Marty Haugen
© 1980, GIA Publications, Inc.

33 Psalm 95: If Today You Hear God's Voice

Refrain

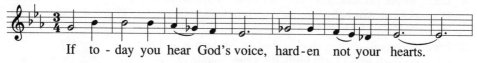

If to - day you hear God's voice, hard-en not your hearts.

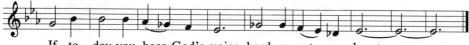

If to - day you hear God's voice, hard-en not your hearts.

Verses

1. Come, ring out our joy to the Lord, hail the rock who saves us,
   let us come now before our God, with songs let us hail the Lord.

2. Come, let us bow and bend low, let us kneel before God who made us,
   for here is our God; we the people, the flock that is led by God's hand.

3. O that today you would hear God's voice, "Harden not your hearts,
as on that day in the desert, when your parents put me to the test."

Text: Psalm 95:1-2, 6-7, 8-9; David Haas
Music: David Haas
© 1983, 1994, GIA Publications, Inc.

Psalm 98: All the Ends of the Earth   34

Refrain

All the ends of the earth have seen the pow-er of God;

all the ends of the earth have seen the pow-er of God.

Verses

1. Sing to the Lord a new song, for God has done wondrous deeds;
whose right hand has won the vict'ry for us, God's holy arm.

2. The Lord has made salvation known, and justice revealed to all,
remembering kindness and faithfulness to Israel.

3. All of the ends of earth have seen salvation by our God.
Joyfully sing out all you lands, break forth in song.

4. Sing to the Lord with harp and song, with trumpet and with horn.
Sing in your joy before the king, the king, our Lord.

Text: Psalm 98:1, 2-3, 3-4, 5-6; David Haas, Marty Haugen
Music: David Haas, Marty Haugen
© 1983, GIA Publications, Inc.

35 Psalm 100: Arise, Come to Your God

Antiphon I

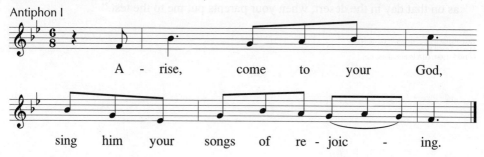

A - rise, come to your God,

sing him your songs of re - joic - ing.

Text: Joseph Gelineau, SJ
Music: Joseph Gelineau, SJ
© 1963, The Grail, GIA Publications, Inc., agent

Antiphon II

Al - le - lu - ia, al - le - lu - ia, al - le - lu - ia.

Music: A. Gregory Murray, OSB, © 1963, The Grail, GIA Publications, Inc., agent

Psalm Tone

Music: Chant tone 8-g; acc. by Richard Proulx, © 1975, GIA Publications, Inc.

Gelineau Tone

¹ Cry out with **joy** to the **Lord,** all the
  ēarth.
² **Serve** the **Lord** with glàdness.
  Come before God, **síng**ing for **joy**.

³ **Know** that the **Lord** is **Gōd,**
  our **Mak**er, to **whom** we belòng.
  We are God's **peo**ple, **shéep** of the
  flock.

⁴ **En**ter the **gates** with thanks**giv**ing,
  God's **courts** with **sòngs** of **praise**.
  Give **thanks** to Gód and **bless** his
  name.

⁵ **Indeed**, how **good** is the **Lōrd,**
  whose **mer**ciful **love** is etèrnal;
  whose **faith**fulness **lásts** for **ev**er.

  Give **glo**ry to the **Fa**ther Al**might**ȳ,
  to his **Son**, Jesus **Chrìst**, the **Lord,**
  to the **Spir**it who **dwélls** in our **hearts**.

Text: Psalm 100; The Grail
Music: Joseph Gelineau, SJ
© 1963, 1993, The Grail, GIA Publications, Inc., agent

Psalm 100: We Are God's People 36

Ostinato Refrain

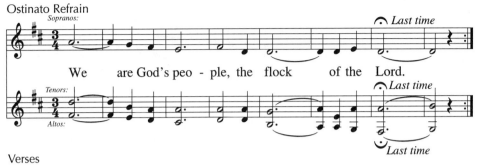

We are God's peo - ple, the flock of the Lord.

Verses

1. Cry out with joy to the Lord, all you lands, all you lands.
   Serve the Lord now with gladness, come before God singing for joy!

2. Know that the Lord is God! Know that the Lord is God,
   who made us, to God we belong, God's people, the sheep of the flock!

3. Go, now within the gates giving thanks, giving thanks.
   Enter the courts singing praise, give thanks and bless God's name!

4. Indeed, how good is the Lord, whose mercy endures for ever,
   for the Lord is faithful, is faithful from age to age!

Text: Psalm 100:1-2, 3, 4, 5; David Haas
Music: David Haas
© 1983, GIA Publications, Inc.

Psalm 103: The Lord Is Kind and Merciful 37

Refrain

The Lord is kind and mer-ci-ful,   the Lord is kind and mer-ci-ful.

Verses

1. Bless the Lord, O my soul, and all my being bless God's name;
   bless the Lord, and forget not God's benefits.

2. God pardons all your iniquities, and comforts your sorrows,
   redeems your life from destruction and crowns you with kindness.

3. Merciful, merciful, and gracious is our God;
   slow to anger, abounding in kindness.

Text: Psalm 103:1-2, 3-4, 8; para. by Marty Haugen, © 1983, GIA Publications, Inc.; refrain trans. © 1969, ICEL
Music: Marty Haugen, © 1983, GIA Publications, Inc.

38 Psalm 104: Lord, Send Out Your Spirit

Refrain

Lord, send out your Spir-it, and re-new the face of the earth!

Verses

1. Bless the Lord, O my soul; O Lord, my God, you are great indeed!
   How manifold are your works, O Lord! The earth is full of your creatures!

2. If you take away their breath, they die and they return to their dust.
   When you send forth your Spirit of life, they are created in your sight!

3. May his glory last for all time; may the Lord be glad in his works.
   Pleasing to him will be my theme; I will be glad in the Lord!

*May be sung as a canon.

Text: Psalm 104:1, 24, 29-30, 31, 34; Paul Lisicky, © 1985, GIA Publications, Inc.; refrain trans. © 1969, ICEL
Music: Paul Lisicky, © 1985, GIA Publications, Inc.

39 Psalm 113: Praise God's Name

Refrain

Al - le - lu - ia! Al - le - lu - ia! Al - le - lu - ia!

Verses

1. You servants of the Lord, bless the Lord: Blessed be the name for ever!
   From east to west, praised be the name of the Lord our God!

2. High above the nations the Lord is God;
   high above the heavens God's glory!
   Who is like God, enthroned on the stars above earth and sky?

3. Raising up the lowly and the poor from the dust,
   God gives them a home among rulers:
   blessing the barren, giving them children singing for joy!

4. Glory to the Father and glory to the Son; glory to the Holy Spirit:
   glory and honor, wisdom and power for evermore!

Text: Psalm 113; Michael Joncas, alt.
Music: Michael Joncas
© 1979, New Dawn Music

Psalm 117: Holy Is God, Holy and Strong 40

Refrain

Ho - ly is God! Ho - ly and strong!

Ho-ly is God! Ho-ly and strong! Ho-ly and liv-ing for ev-er!

Verses

1. O praise the Lord, all you nations, acclaim God, all you peoples!
   Strong is God's love for us, the Lord is faithful for ever!

2. Give glory to the Father Almighty, to his Son Jesus Christ the Lord,
   to the Spirit who dwells in our hearts, both now and for ever. Amen!

Text: Psalm 117; © 1963, 1993, The Grail, GIA Publications, Inc., agent; refrain trans. © 1969, ICEL
Music: Michael Joncas, © 1979, GIA Publications, Inc.

Psalm 118: Let Us Rejoice 41

Refrain

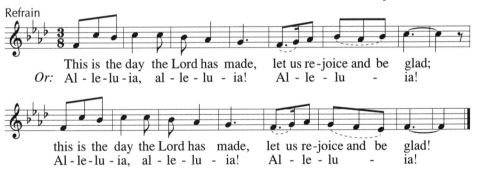

This is the day the Lord has made, let us re-joice and be glad;
Or: Al - le-lu-ia, al - le - lu - ia! Al - le - lu - ia!

this is the day the Lord has made, let us re-joice and be glad!
Al - le-lu - ia, al - le - lu - ia! Al - le - lu - ia!

Verses

1. Give thanks to the Lord, for God is good; God's mercy endures for ever;
   Let the house of Israel say: "God's mercy endures for ever."

2. The hand of the Lord has struck with power, God's right hand is exalted,
   I shall not die, but live anew, declaring the works of the Lord.

3. The stone which the builders rejected has become the cornerstone,
   the Lord of love and mercy has brought wonder to our eyes!

Text: Psalm 118:1-2, 16-17, 22-23; Marty Haugen, © 1983, GIA Publications, Inc.; refrain trans. © 1969, ICEL
Music: Marty Haugen, © 1983, GIA Publications, Inc.

42 Psalm 121: Our Help Comes from the Lord

Refrain

Our help comes from the Lord, the mak-er of heav-en and earth.

Verses

1. I lift up my eyes to the mountains: from where shall come my help?
   My help shall come from the Lord who made heaven and earth.

2. May God never allow you to stumble! Let God sleep not, your guard.
   Neither sleeping nor slumbering, God, Israel's guard.

3. The Lord is your guard and your shade: and at your right side stands,
   By day the sun shall not smite you nor the moon in the night.

4. The Lord will guard you from evil: God will guard your soul.
   The Lord will guard your going and coming both now and for ever.

5. Glory to the Father, and to the Son, and to the Holy Spirit:
   as it was in the beginning, is now, and will be for ever. Amen.

Text: Psalm 121; © 1963, 1993, The Grail, GIA Publications, Inc., agent; refrain by Michael Joncas, © 1979, GIA Publications, Inc.
Music: Michael Joncas, © 1979, GIA Publications, Inc.

43 Psalm 128: Blest Are Those Who Love You

Refrain

Blest are those who love you, hap - py those who fol - low you, blest are those who seek you, O God.

Verses

1. Happy all those who fear the Lord, and walk in God's pathway;
   you will find what you long for: the riches of our God.

2. Your spouse shall be like a fruitful vine in the midst of your home,
   your children flourish like olive plants rejoicing at your table.

3. May the blessings of God be yours all the days of your life,
   may the peace and the love of God live always in your heart.

Text: Psalm 128:1-2, 3, 5; Marty Haugen
Music: Marty Haugen
© 1987, GIA Publications, Inc.

Psalm 130: With the Lord There Is Mercy   44

Refrain

With the Lord there is mer-cy, and full-ness of re-demp-tion.

Verses

1. From out of the depths, I cry unto you,
   Lord, hear my voice, come hear my prayer;
   O let your ear be open to my pleading.

2. If you, O Lord, should mark our guilt,
   then who could stand within your sight?
   But in you is found forgiveness for our failings.

3. Just as those who wait for the morning light,
   even more I long for the Lord, my God,
   whose word to me shall ever be my comfort.

Text: Psalm 130:1-2, 3-4, 5-6; Marty Haugen, © 1983, GIA Publications, Inc.; refrain trans. © 1969, ICEL
Music: Marty Haugen, © 1983, GIA Publications, Inc.

45 Psalm 136: Love Is Never Ending

Cantor:

1. We give thanks un - to you, O God of might:
2. In your wis - dom and love you shaped the skies:
3. You have filled all the skies with glo - ry and light:
4. From of old you have led your peo - ple in faith:
5. You de - liv - ered the ones who called un - to you:
6. You have o - pened the sea and brought your peo - ple through:
7. You re - mem - ber your prom - ise age to age:
8. You give food and life to all liv - ing things:

All:

for your love is nev - er end - ing,

Cantor:

We give thanks un - to you, the God of gods:
You spread out the earth up - on the sea:
The sun for the day and moon for night:
You have shown your com - pas - sion, strength and love:
From bond - age to free-dom, you brought them forth:
Brought them in - to a land that flows with life:
You show mer - cy on those of low de - gree:
We give thanks un - to you, the God of all:

All:

for your love is nev - er end - ing.

Text: Psalm 136; Marty Haugen
Music: Marty Haugen
© 1987, GIA Publications, Inc.

Psalm 145: I Will Praise Your Name   46

Refrain

I will praise your name, my King and my God.

I will praise your name, my King and my God.

Verses

1. I will give you glory, my God above, and I will bless your name for ever.
   Ev'ry day I will bless and praise your name for ever.

2. The Lord is full of grace and mercy, who is kind and slow to anger.
   God is good in ev'ry way, and full of compassion.

3. Let all your works give you thanks, O Lord,
   and let all the faithful bless you.
   Let them speak of your might, O Lord, the glory of your kingdom.

4. The Lord is faithful in word and deed,
   and always near, his name is holy.
   Lifting up all those who fall, God raises up the lowly.

Text: Psalm 145:1-2, 8-9, 10-11, 13b-14; David Haas
Music: David Haas
© 1983, GIA Publications, Inc.

47 Psalm 150: Praise God in This Holy Dwelling

Al-le - lu - ia! Al - le - lu - ia! Al -le - lu - ia!

1. Praise God in this ho - ly dwell-ing; Praise God on the
2. Praise God with the blast of trum - pet; Bring praise now with
3. Praise God with re - sound - ing cym - bals; With cym - bals that
4. Praise God, the al - might - y Fa - ther; Praise Christ, the be -

might - y throne; Prais - ing for all won - der-ful
lyre and harp; Prais - ing with the tim - brel and
crash, give praise; O let ev - 'ry-thing that has
lov - ed Son; Give praise to the Spir - it of

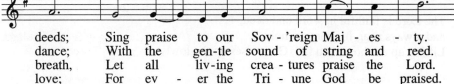

deeds; Sing praise to our Sov - 'reign Maj - es - ty.
dance; With the gen-tle sound of string and reed.
breath, Let all liv-ing crea - tures praise the Lord.
love; For ev - er the Tri - une God be praised.

Al - le - lu - ia! Al - le - lu - ia!

1.-3.
Al - le - lu - ia!

4.
lu - ia!

Text: Psalm 150:1-2, 3-4, 5-6; adapt. by Omer Westendorf
Music: Jan M. Vermulst; arr. by Charles G. Frischmann
© 1964, World Library Publications, Inc.

Canticle of Mary / Luke 1:46-55   48

Antiphon

My soul re - joic - es, my soul re - joic - es in my God.

Text: Luke 1:46; Robert J. Batastini
Music: Robert J. Batastini
© 1972, GIA Publications, Inc.

Psalm Tone

Music: *Lutheran Worship,* © 1982, Concordia Publishing House

Gelineau Tone

Stanzas 1, 2, 9, 10   Stanzas 3-8

1. My **soul glori**fies the **Lord,**
   my **spir**it re**joic**es in **Gód,** my **Sa**vior.

2. He **looks** on his **ser**vant
   ìn her **noth**ingness;
   hence**forth** all **ag**es will
   cáll me **bless**ed.

3. The Al**mighty** works **mar**vèls for **me.**
   Holy his name!

4. His **mer**cy is from **àge** to **age,**
   on **thóse** who **fear** him.

5. He **puts** forth his **àrm** in **strength**
   and **scat**ters thé proud**heart**ed.

6. He **casts** the **might**y fròm their
   thrones
   and **rais**és the **low**ly.

7. He **fills** the **starv**ing wìth good **things,**
   sends the **rich** áway **emp**ty.

8. He pro**tects** Isra**èl** his **ser**vant,
   remem**beríng** his **mer**cy,

9. the **mer**cy **prom**ised tò our **fathers,**
   for **Abra**ham and his **sóns** for **ev**er.

10. Praise the **Fa**ther, the **Son**
    and **Hòly Spir**it,
    both **now** and for **ag**es unend**íng. Amen.**

Text: Luke 1:46-55; The Grail
Music: Joseph Gelineau, SJ
© 1963, The Grail, GIA Publications, Inc., agent

Christian Initiation of Adults

49

The passage of an adult into the Christian community takes place over an extended period of time. The members of the local church, the catechists and sponsors, the clergy and the diocesan bishop take part in the journey from inquiry through the catechumenate to baptism, confirmation and eucharist. The candidates are invited by example to pray, reflect on the scriptures, to fast and to join in the community's practice of charity. They are to learn the way of Jesus from the members of the church.

This journey of the candidates and community is marked by liturgical rites; thus the community publicly acknowledges, encourages and strengthens the candidates. The first of these is the rite of becoming catechumens. It concludes the sometimes lengthy period during which those who have come to ask about the way of the church and the life of a Christian have heard the gospel proclaimed and seen it practiced. Those who then feel called to walk in this way of Christ's church ask to begin the journey toward baptism. If the church judges the inquirers ready, they are accepted into the order of catechumens.

Those who have entered the catechumenate are already part of the household of Christ. During this time the catechumens are to hear and reflect on God's word, to learn the teachings and practices of the church, to become gradually accustomed to the ways of prayer and discipline in the church, to observe and to join in the good works of Christians. Ordinarily the catechumens are present on Sunday for the liturgy of the word and may be dismissed after the homily—to continue prayer and study with their catechists—since they cannot join in the eucharist.

Rites of exorcism and blessing may be celebrated during the catechumenate. Through such rites the church prays that the catechumens will be purified, strengthened against all evil and thus eagerly grow in faith and good works. The very presence of the catechumens—at the Sunday liturgy, in these special rites and in everyday life—is itself a source of strength and blessing to the faithful.

Each year as Lent begins, the bishop, with the help of the local pastor and others involved with the catechumens, is to call those catechumens who are judged ready to prepare themselves for baptism at the Easter Vigil. Thus the catechumens become the "elect", the chosen, and for the forty days of Lent they make preparations: praying, fasting, doing good works. All the faithful join them in this. On several Sundays in Lent the rites of scrutiny take place when the assembled church prays over the elect. During Lent also the catechumens may publicly receive the words of the church's creed and of the Lord's Prayer. (The Rite of Election is found with the First Sunday of Lent, no. 502; the scrutiny rites are found with the Third, Fourth and Fifth Sundays of Lent, nos. 508, 511, and 514.)

Good Friday and Holy Saturday are days of prayer, fasting and preparation for the rites of the Easter Vigil. On the night between Saturday and Sunday, the church assembles to keep vigil and listen to many readings from scripture. Then the catechumens are called forward for baptism and confirmation. (These rites are found in the Easter Vigil, no. 533 and following.)

The newly baptized, now called neophytes, take a special place in the Sunday eucharist throughout the fifty days of Eastertime. This is a time for their full incorporation into the local community.

All of these stages of initiation take place in the midst of the community. In various rites, the faithful show the Christian life to the inquirers and catechumens. In turn, the faithful are strengthened and challenged in their faith by the presence of the catechumens.

Those who seek to belong to the Roman Catholic church and who are already baptized may take some part in the catechumenate but they are not baptized again. Rather, they are received into the full communion of the Roman Catholic Church.

ACCEPTANCE INTO THE ORDER OF CATECHUMENS 50

INTRODUCTORY RITES
The presider greets the assembly: candidates, sponsors, members of the parish. The candidates are asked what it is that they seek and each replies. After each candidate has responded, the following may be sung:

51

We stand with you,   we pray for you,   O   ho-ly child of God!

Text: David Haas
Music: David Haas
© 1988, GIA Publications, Inc.

CANDIDATES' FIRST ACCEPTANCE OF THE GOSPEL
The presider solemnly asks if the candidates are ready to begin walking this way of the gospel. The sponsors and all present are asked if they stand ready to assist the candidates as they strive to know and follow Christ. All respond: **We are.**

SIGNING OF THE CANDIDATES WITH THE CROSS
The sign of the cross marks the candidates for their new way of life. The presider signs each on the forehead saying:

N., receive the cross on your forehead.
It is Christ himself who now strengthens you
with this sign of his love.
Learn now to know him and follow him.

Sponsors and others also sign the candidates. Ears and eyes and other senses may also be signed. The presider prays that the catechumens may share in the saving power of the cross.

INVITATION TO THE CELEBRATION OF THE WORD OF GOD

The assembly may go into the church for the liturgy of the word singing an appropriate psalm (for example, Psalm 34, no. 26 and 27).

52 LITURGY OF THE WORD

There may be one or more readings from scripture, together with a responsorial psalm. After the homily, a book containing the scriptures may be given to the new catechumens for their study and prayer throughout the time of the catechumenate.

INTERCESSIONS

All join in prayer for the new catechumens.

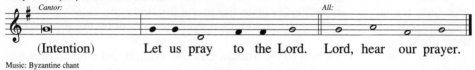

(Intention)   Let us pray   to the Lord.   Lord, hear   our prayer.

Music: Byzantine chant

53 RITES OF THE CATECHUMENATE

DISMISSAL OF THE CATECHUMENS

When the catechumens are present at Mass, they are usually dismissed after the homily. Only when they have been baptized are they able to join the faithful in the reception of the eucharist. After their dismissal, the catechumens remain together and are joined by their catechists or others to pray and reflect on the scripture.

54   *The following may be sung to accompany the dismissal:*

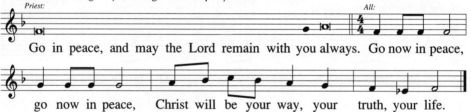

Go in peace, and may the Lord remain with you always. Go now in peace,

go now in peace,   Christ will be your way, your   truth, your life.

Text: *Rite of Christian Initiation of Adults,* © 1985, ICEL
Music: Lynn Trapp, © 1991, Morning Star Music Publishers

CELEBRATIONS OF THE WORD OF GOD

On Sundays, after the catechetical sessions, before the liturgical seasons and at other times the catechumens and others may join for liturgy: song, reading of scripture, psalmody, prayer and silence are normally part of such a service.

MINOR EXORCISMS

At appropriate times during the catechumenate, the catechists or other ministers may lead the community in prayers of exorcism over the catechumens. These prayers acknowledge the struggle against evil and ask that God strengthen the catechumens.

BLESSINGS OF THE CATECHUMENS

Prayers of blessing and the laying on of hands may take place whenever the catechumens gather for instruction of other purposes. Catechists or other ministers ask these blessings over the catechumens.

ANOINTINGS AND PRESENTATIONS

During the catechumenate or during Lent, the candidates may be anointed with the oil of catechumens as a sign of strength given for their struggle to live the gospel. At some point in this time they are publicly presented with the church's treasury of prayer and faith, the Our Father and the Creed.

RITE OF ELECTION OR ENROLLMENT OF NAMES

See First Sunday of Lent, no. 502.

SCRUTINIES   55

The scrutinies occur on the Third, Fourth and Fifth Sundays of Lent. The elect are called before the community for exorcism and prayer. This rite may conclude with the following song, sung prior to dismissal of the elect:

Refrain

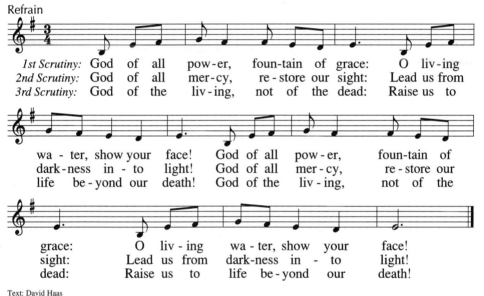

1st Scrutiny: God of all pow-er, foun-tain of grace: O liv-ing
2nd Scrutiny: God of all mer-cy, re-store our sight: Lead us from
3rd Scrutiny: God of the liv-ing, not of the dead: Raise us to

wa-ter, show your face! God of all pow-er, foun-tain of
dark-ness in-to light! God of all mer-cy, re-store our
life be-yond our death! God of the liv-ing, not of the

grace: O liv-ing wa-ter, show your face!
sight: Lead us from dark-ness in-to light!
dead: Raise us to life be-yond our death!

Text: David Haas
Music: David Haas
© 1988, GIA Publications, Inc.

PREPARATORY RITES

Various preparation rites take place during the day on Holy Saturday. These include prayer, recitation of the Creed, and the rite of Ephpheta (opening of ears and mouth).

SACRAMENTS OF INITIATION

See the Easter Vigil, no. 533.

PERIOD OF MYSTAGOGIA

"Mystagogia" refers to the fifty-day period of postbaptismal celebration when the newly baptized are gradually drawn by the community into the fullness of Christian life and prayer. The newly baptized retain a special place in the assembly and are mentioned in the prayers of intercession. A special celebration, on Pentecost or just before, may mark the conclusion of the whole period of initiation.

The Baptism of Children

56

Children are baptized in the faith of the church: of parents, godparents, the local parish, the church throughout the world, the saints. Bringing their children for baptism, the parents profess their commitment to make a home where the gospel is lived. And the godparents and all members of the community promise to support the parents in this. Thus the children enter the waters of baptism and so are joined to this people, all baptized into the death and resurrection of Christ.

Baptism is celebrated above all at the Easter Vigil, but also on other Sundays, for Sunday is the Lord's day, the day when the church gathers to proclaim the paschal mystery. Although baptism may take place at the Sunday Mass, it is always to be celebrated in an assembly of members of the church.

57 RECEPTION OF THE CHILDREN

The parents and godparents are welcomed by all. The priest/deacon asks the names of the children and questions the parents about their own expectations and willingness to take on the responsibilities this baptism brings. The godparents are asked if they are ready to assist the parents to become Christian mothers and fathers.

With joy, then, the priest/deacon, the parents and godparents make the sign of the cross on the child's forehead: "I claim you for Christ our Savior by the sign of his cross."

All then go in procession to the place where the scriptures will be read. The following antiphon, or a hymn, may be sung during this procession:

The assembly repeats each phrase after the cantor.

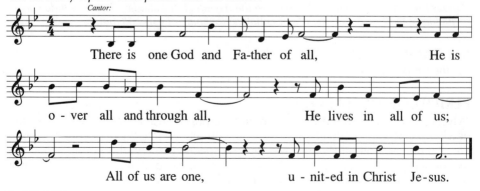

Text: ICEL, © 1969
Music: Marty Haugen, © 1995, GIA Publications, Inc.

LITURGY OF THE WORD

FIRST READINGS

One or more passages from scripture are read. At the conclusion of each:

Reader: The word of the Lord.
Assembly: **Thanks be to God.**

RESPONSORIAL PSALM

The following psalm may follow the first reading:

Refrain

The Lord is my light and my sal - va - tion.

Text: *Lectionary for Mass,* © 1969, ICEL
Music: Anthony E. Jackson, © 1984

Verses

The Lord is my light and my help;
whom shall I fear?
The Lord is the stronghold of my life:
before whom shall I shrink? .

I am sure I shall see the Lord's goodness
in the land of the living.
Hope in him, hold firm and take heart.
Hope in the Lord! ℟.

There is one thing I ask of the Lord,
    for this I long,
to live in the house of the Lord,
    all the days of my life,
to savor the sweetness of the Lord,
to behold his temple. ℟.

Text: Psalm 27:1, 4, 13-14, © 1963, The Grail, GIA Publications, Inc., agent
Music: Cyril Baker, © The Antilles Episcopal Conference

GOSPEL

Before the gospel reading, this acclamation is sung:

Cantor, then all:

Al - le - lu - ia, al - le - lu - ia, al - le - lu - ia.

Music: Chant Mode VI; acc. by Richard Proulx, © 1985, GIA Publications, Inc.

During Lent:

Cantor, then all:

Praise to you, Lord Je - sus Christ, king of end - less glo - ry!

Music: Frank Schoen, © 1970, GIA Publications, Inc.

Deacon (or priest): The Lord be with you.
    Assembly: **And also with you.**
      Deacon: A reading from the holy gospel according to N.
    Assembly: **Glory to you, Lord.**

After the reading:

     Deacon: The gospel of the Lord.
    Assembly: **Praise to you, Lord Jesus Christ.**

60 GENERAL INTERCESSIONS

All join in prayer for the church, the needs of the world, the poor, the children to be baptized and their parents.

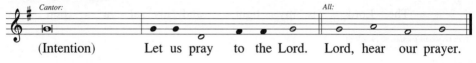

(Intention)   Let us pray   to the Lord.   Lord, hear our prayer.

Music: Byzantine chant

This prayer concludes with the litany of the saints which may include the patron saints of the children and of the local church.

61

1. Holy Mary, Mother of   God,   pray   for us.
2. Saint John the   Bap - tist,   pray   for us.
3. Saint   Jo - seph,   pray   for us.
4. Saint Peter and Saint   Paul,   pray   for us.

The names of other saints may be added here. The litany concludes:

5. All you saints of   God,   pray   for us.

62 PRAYER OF EXORCISM AND ANOINTING

The priest/deacon stands before the parents with their infants and prays that God deliver these children from the power of evil. The children may be anointed with the oil of catechumens, an anointing which makes them strong for their struggle against evil in their lives or the priest/deacon may lay hands on each child. The priest/deacon lays hands on each child to show the love and concern the Church has for them. If there is a procession to the baptistry, the following may be sung:

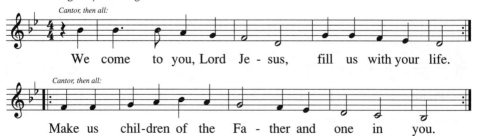

We come to you, Lord Je - sus, fill us with your life.

Make us chil-dren of the Fa - ther and one in you.

Music: Ronald Arnatt, © 1984, GIA Publications, Inc.

SACRAMENT OF BAPTISM 63

BLESSING AND INVOCATION OF GOD OVER BAPTISMAL WATER
When all are gathered at the font, the priest/deacon leads a blessing of the water, unless the baptismal water has already been blessed.

RENUNCIATION OF SIN AND PROFESSION OF FAITH
The priest/deacon then questions the parents and godparents, and they make a renunciation of sin and evil and profess their faith. The assembly listens to their responses. The priest/deacon then invites all to give their assent to this profession of faith:

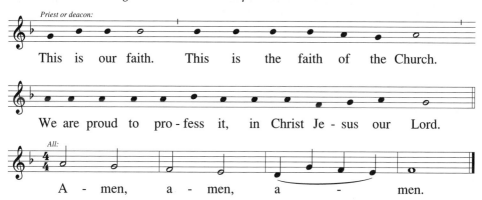

Priest or deacon:
This is our faith. This is the faith of the Church.
We are proud to pro-fess it, in Christ Je-sus our Lord.
All:
A - men, a - men, a - men.

Music: Danish Amen

BAPTISM 64
One by one, the infants are brought to the font by their parents. There the parents express their desire to have their child baptized in the faith of the church which they have professed. The infant is then immersed in the water three times (or water is poured over the infant's head three times) as the priest/deacon says: "N., I baptize you in the name of the Father, and of the Son, and of the Holy Spirit." All may respond to each baptism with an acclamation.

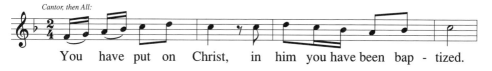

Cantor, then All:
You have put on Christ, in him you have been bap - tized.

Al - le - lu - ia, al - le - lu - ia.

Music: Howard Hughes, SM, © 1977, ICEL

ANOINTING WITH CHRISM 65
The priest/deacon anoints each child on the crown of the head with holy chrism, a mixture of oil and perfume. The word "Christ" means "anointed." The baptized child has been "Christ-ed" and the sweet smell of the anointing reminds all of this.

CLOTHING WITH THE BAPTISMAL GARMENT AND GIVING OF THE CANDLE

The infants are then clothed in baptismal garments and a candle for each of the newly baptized is lighted from the paschal candle.

| Optional | *The priest/deacon may touch the ears and mouth of each child: "May Jesus soon touch your ears to receive his word, and your mouth to proclaim his faith."* |

CONCLUSION AND BLESSING

If baptism is celebrated at Mass, the liturgy continues with the eucharist. Otherwise, all process to the altar, carrying lighted candles. The above acclamation may be sung again during this procession. All then pray the Lord's Prayer, the parents are blessed and the liturgy concludes with a hymn of praise and thanksgiving.

Reconciliation of Several Penitents

The sacrament of penance, also called the sacrament of reconciliation, may be celebrated with one penitent or with many. The latter form, the communal penance service, is a gathering of a few or a large number of Christians. Together they listen to the scriptures, sing psalms and hymns, pray, individually confess their sins and receive absolution, then praise God whose mercy and love are greater than our evil. In the rite of penance, the members of the church confront the struggle that was entered at baptism. There has been failure, evil done and good undone, but the penitent church comes again and again to name and renounce its sins and to return to the way of the Lord.

INTRODUCTORY RITES   67
An appropriate hymn or psalm may be sung.

GREETING
The priest and people greet each other in these or other words:

    Priest: Grace, mercy, and peace be with you
              from God the Father and Christ Jesus our Savior.
Assembly: **And also with you.**

OPENING PRAYER
After silent prayer, the priest concludes the gathering rite with a solemn prayer.

CELEBRATION OF THE WORD OF GOD   68

FIRST READINGS
One or more passages from scripture are read. At the conclusion of each:

    Reader: The word of the Lord.
Assembly: **Thanks be to God.**

RESPONSORIAL PSALM

The following psalm may follow the first reading:

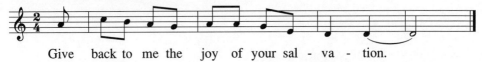

Give back to me the joy of your sal - va - tion.

Text: ICEL, © 1974
Music: Howard Hughes, SM, © 1986, GIA Publications, Inc.

Have mercy on me, God, in your kindness.
In your compassion blot out my offense.
O wash me more and more from my guilt
and cleanse me from my sin. ℟.

My offenses truly I know them;
my sin is always before me.
Against you, you alone, have I sinned;
what is evil in your sight I have done. ℟.

A pure heart create for me, O God,
Put a steadfast spirit within me.
Do not cast me away from your presence,
nor deprive me of your holy spirit. ℟.

Give me again the joy of your help;
with a spirit of fervor sustain me,
that I may teach transgressors your ways
and sinners may return to you. ℟.

Text: Psalm 51:3-4, 5-6, 12-13, 14-15
Music: Joseph Gelineau, SJ
© 1963, The Grail, GIA Publications, Inc., agent

69 GOSPEL

Before the gospel reading, this acclamation is sung:

Cantor, then all:

Al - le - lu - ia,   al - le - lu - ia,   al - le - lu - ia.

Music: Chant Mode VI; acc. by Richard Proulx, © 1985, GIA Publications, Inc.

During Lent:

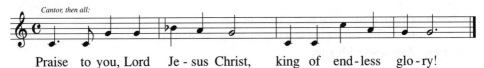

Cantor, then all:

Praise to you, Lord Je - sus Christ,   king of end - less glo - ry!

Music: Frank Schoen, © 1970, GIA Publications, Inc.

Deacon (or priest): The Lord be with you.
    Assembly: **And also with you.**
      Deacon: A reading from the holy gospel according to N.
    Assembly: **Glory to you, Lord.**

After the reading:

    Deacon: The gospel of the Lord.
    Assembly: **Praise to you, Lord Jesus Christ.**

HOMILY

EXAMINATION OF CONSCIENCE
In silence or through some other manner all reflect on their lives with sorrow for their sins.

SACRAMENT OF PENANCE 70

GENERAL CONFESSION OF SINS
*Kneeling (or with another posture that expresses sorrow,) all join in confession.
This form may be used:*

**I confess to almighty God,
and to you, my brothers and sisters,
that I have sinned through my own fault
in my thoughts and in my words,
in what I have done,
and in what I have failed to do;
and I ask blessed Mary, ever virgin,
all the angels and saints,
and you, my brothers and sisters,
to pray for me to the Lord our God.**

71

*Standing, all join in a litany using one of the following responses, or a song asking God's
mercy. The Lord's Prayer is then recited or sung (see no. 106, 120, and 156).*

| A | **We pray you, hear us.** |

| B | **Lord, be merciful to me, a sinner.** |

| C | **Lord, have mercy.** |

INDIVIDUAL CONFESSION AND ABSOLUTION 72
*One by one the penitents approach the priest confessors. All confess their sins, accept some
fitting act of satisfaction and the counsel of the confessor. Then the priest extends his hands
over the penitent's head and speaks the prayer of absolution, concluding: "Through the ministry of the church may God give you pardon and peace, and I absolve you from your sins in
the name of the Father, and of the Son, and of the Holy Spirit." The penitent responds,
"Amen." (Note: On those occasions when general absolution is permitted, the rest of the rite
remains the same.)*

PROCLAMATION OF PRAISE FOR GOD'S MERCY
*The priest invites all to give thanks and to show by their lives—and in the life of the whole
community—the grace of repentance. A psalm, canticle or hymn may be sung to proclaim
God's mercy.*

CONCLUDING PRAYER OF THANKSGIVING
This prayer is spoken by the priest.

BLESSING AND DISMISSAL
The priest blesses all present and the deacon or other minister dismisses the assembly.
All respond: **Thanks be to God.**

Funeral Mass

73

The rites which surround the death of a Christian extend from the Viaticum (last communion) and final prayers before death through the wake service and funeral Mass to the burial of the body or ashes. In all of this the community affirms its faith in the communion of saints and the resurrection of the dead. The family and friends are helped in their time of sorrow with prayer and song. Thus they express present grief even as they hold to the church's lasting hope. Following is the rite of the funeral Mass.

INTRODUCTORY RITES

74 GREETING

The priest greets the assembly at the door, using these or similar words.

> *Priest:* The grace and peace of God our Father and the Lord Jesus Christ be with you.
> *Assembly:* **And also with you.**

The body is sprinkled with holy water.

SONG

As the procession enters the church, an appropriate song is sung.

The Mass continues as usual with the Opening Prayer, no. 95.

75 FINAL COMMENDATION

Following the prayer after Communion, the commendation begins with an invitation to silent prayer.

76 SONG OF FAREWELL

The following or another appropriate responsory or song may be sung.

Refrain

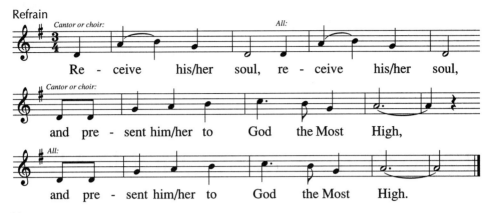

Re - ceive his/her soul, re - ceive his/her soul,

and pre - sent him/her to God the Most High,

and pre - sent him/her to God the Most High.

Verses

1. Saints of God, come to his/her aid!
   Hasten to meet him/her, angels of the Lord!

2. May Christ, who called you, take you to himself;
   may angels lead you to the bosom of Abraham.

3. Eternal rest grant unto him/her, O Lord, and let
   perpetual light shine upon him/her.

Text: *Order of Christian Funerals,* © 1985, ICEL
Music: Steven R. Janco, © 1990, GIA Publications, Inc.

PRAYER OF COMMENDATION   77

At the conclusion of the prayer all respond: **Amen.**

PROCESSION TO THE PLACE OF COMMITTAL

The deacon or priest says: In peace let us take our brother/sister to his/her place of rest.

SONG   78

As the assembly leaves the church, the following or another appropriate responsory or song may be sung.

May the an - gels lead you in - to par - a - dise; may the

mar - tyrs come to wel - come you and take you to the ho - ly

cit - y, the new and e - ter - nal Je - ru - sa - lem.

Text: *Order of Christian Funerals,* © 1985, ICEL
Music: Steven R. Janco, © 1990, GIA Publications, Inc.

Holy Communion Outside Mass

79

When for good reason communion cannot be received at Mass, the faithful may share in the paschal mystery through the liturgy of the word and the reception of holy communion.

INTRODUCTORY RITES

An appropriate hymn or psalm may be sung.

80   GREETING

If the minister is a priest or deacon, the usual form of greeting is used:

Assembly: **And also with you.**

If the minister is not a priest or deacon, another form of greeting may be used:

Assembly: **Blessed be God forever.**

PENITENTIAL RITE

The minister invites silent reflection and repentance. After some silence:

Assembly: **I confess to almighty God,**
               and to you, my brothers and sisters,
               that I have sinned through my own fault
               in my thoughts and in my words,
               in what I have done,
               and in what I have failed to do;
               and I ask blessed Mary, ever virgin,
               all the angels and saints,
               and you, my brothers and sisters,
               to pray for me to the Lord our God.

The forms found at no. 92 may also be used.

CELEBRATION OF THE WORD OF GOD 81

FIRST READINGS
One or more passages from scripture are read. At the conclusion of each:

Reader: The word of the Lord.
Assembly: **Thanks be to God.**

RESPONSORIAL PSALM
An appropriate psalm may follow the first reading.

GOSPEL 82
Before the gospel reading, the alleluia or Lenten acclamation is sung.

⌈*Deacon (or priest):* The Lord be with you.⌉
⌊ *Assembly:* **And also with you.** ⌋
Reader: A reading from the holy gospel according to N.
Assembly: **Glory to you, Lord.**

After the reading:

Reader: The gospel of the Lord.
Assembly: **Praise to you, Lord Jesus Christ.**

GENERAL INTERCESSIONS 83
The assembly joins in prayer for the needs of the world, of the poor, and of the church.

HOLY COMMUNION 84
The minister invites all to join in the Lord's Prayer, then to exchange a sign of peace. The minister then raises the eucharistic bread and all respond to the invitation.

Assembly: **Lord, I am not worthy to receive you,**
but only say the word and I shall be healed.

A psalm or hymn may be sung during communion. Afterwards, there may be a period of silence or the singing of a psalm or hymn. The minister then recites a concluding prayer.

CONCLUDING RITE
All are blessed and dismissed.

Presiding minister: Go in the peace of Christ.
Assembly: **Thanks be to God.**

Eucharistic Exposition and Benediction

85

"Exposition of the holy eucharist . . . is intended to acknowledge Christ's marvelous presence in the sacrament. Exposition invites us to the spiritual union with him that culminates in sacramental communion. Thus it fosters very well the worship which is due to Christ in spirit and in truth.

This kind of exposition must clearly express the cult of the blessed sacrament in its relationship to the Mass. The plan of the exposition should carefully avoid anything which might somehow obscure the principal desire of Christ in instituting the eucharist, namely, to be with us as food, medicine, and comfort" (Holy Communion and Worship of the Eucharist outside of Mass, #82).

86 EXPOSITION

As the priest or deacon prepares the holy eucharist for adoration, the following or another suitable song is sung:

```
1. O        Sav - ing   Vic - tim,    o - p'ning  wide  The
2. To       your  great name  be      end - less  praise, Im -
1. O        sa - lu - tá - ris  hó - sti - a,  Quae
2. U - ni   tri - nó - que  Dó - mi - no  Sit

gate  of  heav'n to   us   be - low! Our  foes  press  on  from
mor - tal  God-head,  One  in  Three; O  grant  us   end - less
cae - li  pan - dis   ó - sti - um:  Bel - la  pre - munt  ho -
sem - pi - tér - na   gló - ri - a:  Qui  vi - tam  si - ne
```

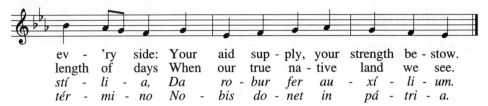

ev - 'ry side: Your aid sup - ply, your strength be - stow.
length of days When our true na - tive land we see.
stí - li - a, Da ro - bur fer au - xí - li - um.
tér - mi - no No - bis do - net in pá - tri - a.

Text: Thomas Aquinas, 1227-1275; tr. by Edward Caswall, 1814-1878, alt.
Music: DUGUET, LM; Dieu donne Duguet, d.1767

ADORATION   87

During the adoration there are prayers, songs, Scripture readings, and possibly a homily to develop a better understanding of the eucharistic mystery. Silent prayer is also encouraged. If time allows, the Liturgy of the Hours may be celebrated here.

BENEDICTION   88

As the priest or deacon incenses the Blessed Sacrament, the following or another appropriate hymn or song may be sung:

1. Come a - dore this won - drous pres - ence, Bow to Christ the
2. Glo - ry be to God the Fa - ther, Praise to his co -
1. Tan - tum er - go Sa - cra - mén - tum Ve - ne - ré - mur
2. Ge - ni - tó - ri, Ge - ni - tó - que Laus et ju - bi -

source of grace. Here is kept the an - cient prom - ise
e - qual Son, Ad - o - ra - tion to the Spir - it,
cér - nu - i: Et an - tí - quum do - cu - mén - tum
lá - ti - o, Sa - lus, ho - nor, vir - tus quo - que

Of God's earth - ly dwell - ing - place. Sight is blind be -
Bond of love, in God - head one. Blest be God by
No - vo ce - dat rí - tu - i: Prae - stet fi - des
Sit et be - ne - dí - cti - o: Pro - ce - dén - ti

fore God's glo - ry, Faith a - lone may see his face.
all cre - a - tion Joy - ous - ly while a - ges run.
sup - ple - mén - tum Sén - su - um de - fé - ctu - i.
ab u - tró - que Com - par sit lau - dá - ti - o.

Text: Thomas Aquinas, 1227-1274; tr. by James Quinn, SJ, © 1969. Used by permission of Selah Publishing Co., Inc.
Music: ST. THOMAS, 8 7 8 7 8 7; John F. Wade, 1711-1786

After a prayer, the priest or deacon blesses the assembly with the Blessed Sacrament.

89 REPOSITION

As the priest or deacon replaces the Sacrament in the tabernacle, the assembly sings or says the following acclamations:

Blessed be God.
Blessed be his holy name.
Blessed be Jesus Christ, true God and true man.
Blessed be the name of Jesus.
Blessed be his most sacred heart.
Blessed be his most precious blood.
Blessed be Jesus in the most holy sacrament of the altar.
Blessed be the Holy Spirit, Consoler.
Blessed be the great Mother of God, Mary most holy.
Blessed be her holy and immaculate conception.
Blessed be her glorious assumption.
Blessed be the name of Mary, virgin and mother.
Blessed be Saint Joseph, her most chaste spouse.
Blessed be God in his angels and in his saints.

The Order of Mass

Each church gathers on the Lord's Day to listen to the Scriptures, to offer prayers, to give thanks and praise to God while recalling God's gifts in creation and saving deeds in Jesus, and to share in holy communion.

In these rites of word and eucharist, the Church keeps Sunday as the Lord's Day, the day of creation and resurrection, the "eighth day" when the fullness of God's kingdom is anticipated. The Mass or eucharistic celebration of the Christian community has rites of gathering, of word, of eucharist, of dismissal. All those who gather constitute the assembly. One member of this assembly who has been ordained to the presbyterate or episcopate, the priesthood, leads the opening and closing prayers and the eucharistic prayer, and presides over the whole assembly. A member ordained to the diaconate may assist, read the gospel, and preach. Other members of the assembly are chosen and trained for various ministries: These are the readers, servers, ushers, musicians, communion ministers. All of these assist the assembly. It is the assembly itself, all those present, that does the liturgy.

The Order of Mass which follows is familiar to all who regularly join in this assembly. It is learned through repetition. This Order of Mass leaves many decisions to the local community and others are determined by the various seasons of the liturgical year.

INTRODUCTORY RITES

The rites which precede the liturgy of the word assist the assembly to gather as a community. They prepare that community to listen to the Scriptures and to celebrate the eucharist together. The procession and entrance song are ways of expressing the unity and spirit of the assembly.

GREETING

All make the sign of the cross.

Priest: In the name of the Father, and of the Son, and of the Holy Spirit.

Assembly: **Amen.**

After the sign of the cross one of the greetings is given.

A
> *Priest:* The grace of our Lord Jesus Christ and the love of God
> and the fellowship of the Holy Spirit be with you all.
>
> *Assembly:* **And also with you.**

B
> *Priest:* The grace and peace of God our Father
> and the Lord Jesus Christ be with you.
>
> *Assembly:* **Blessed be God, the Father of our Lord Jesus Christ.**
> *or:* **And also with you.**

C
> *Priest:* The Lord be with you. (*Bishop:* Peace be with you.)
>
> *Assembly:* **And also with you.**

91 BLESSING AND SPRINKLING OF HOLY WATER

On Sundays, especially during the season of Easter, instead of the penitential rite below, the blessing and sprinkling of holy water may be done. The following or another appropriate song is sung as the water is sprinkled.

Refrain

If we have died to our-selves in Je-sus, then we shall a - rise to new life in him. Al - le - lu - ia, al - le - lu - ia!

Verses

1. We are fire and wa - ter, we are sym - bol and
2. In the wa - ter we seek him, in the well-spring of
3. In the fire we seek him, in the hun - gers and
4. In our dy - ing and ris - ing, we shall fol - low where
5. Flow-ing out of the des - ert, roll - ing down from the
6. Rain - ing down from the heav-ens, spring-ing up from the
7. Gift of love and of mer-cy, giv - en free - ly to

sign of grace, we are the mys - t'ry,
all that lives, all who are thirst - y,
pains we bear, hope for the hope - less,
he has gone, pil - grims and lov - ers,
moun - tain side, up from with - in you,
dri - est earth, sim - ple and ho - ly,
all who thirst, gen - tle and yield - ing,

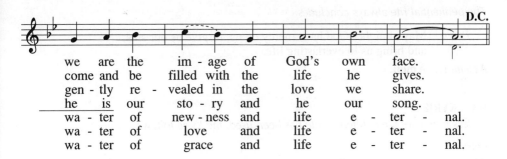

we	are	the	im - age	of	God's	own	face.	
come and	be	filled with	the	life	he	gives.	
gen - tly	re -	vealed in	the	love	we	share.	
he	is	our	sto - ry	and	he	our	song.	
wa - ter	of	new - ness	and	life	e - ter - nal.
wa - ter	of	love	and	life	e - ter - nal.
wa - ter	of	grace	and	life	e - ter - nal.

Text: *Mass of Creation*, Marty Haugen
Music: *Mass of Creation*, Marty Haugen
© 1984, GIA Publications, Inc.

PENITENTIAL RITE 92

The priest invites all to be mindful of their sins and of the great mercy of God. After a time of silence, one of the following forms is used.

A *Assembly:* **I confess to almighty God,**
and to you, my brothers and sisters,
that I have sinned through my own fault
in my thoughts and in my words,
in what I have done,
and in what I have failed to do;
and I ask blessed Mary, ever virgin,
all the angels and saints,
and you, my brothers and sisters,
to pray for me to the Lord our God.

B *Priest:* Lord, we have sinned against you: Lord, have mercy.
Assembly: **Lord, have mercy.**
Priest: Lord, show us your mercy and love.
Assembly: **And grant us your salvation.**

C *The priest or another minister makes a series of invocations according to the following pattern.*

Priest: (Invocation)
Lord, have mercy.
Assembly: **Lord, have mercy.**

Priest: (Invocation)
Christ, have mercy.
Assembly: **Christ, have mercy.**

Priest: (Invocation)
Lord, have mercy.
Assembly: **Lord, have mercy.**

The penitential rite always concludes:

> *Priest:* May almighty God have mercy on us, forgive us our sins,
> and bring us to everlasting life.

Assembly: **Amen.**

93 KYRIE

Unless form C of the penitential rite has been used, the Kyrie follows.

Refrain

Lord, have mer - cy. Christ, have mer - cy.

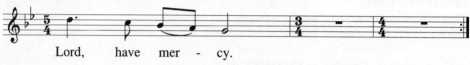

Lord, have mer - cy.

Music: *Mass of Creation*, Marty Haugen, © 1984, GIA Publications, Inc.

94 GLORIA

The Gloria is omitted during Advent, Lent, and most weekdays.

Refrain

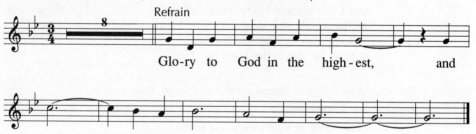

Glo-ry to God in the high-est, and

peace to his peo - ple on earth.

Verses

1. Lord God, heavenly King, almighty God and Father,
   we worship you, we give you thanks,
   we praise you for your glory.

2. Lord Jesus Christ, only Son of the Father,
   Lord God, Lamb of God,
   you take away the sin of the world: have mercy on us;
   you are seated at the right hand of the Father:
   receive our prayer.

3. For you alone are the Holy One,
   you alone are the Lord,
   you alone are the Most High, Jesus Christ,
   with the Holy Spirit,
   in the glory of God, the Father. Amen! Amen!

Music: *Mass of Creation,* Marty Haugen, © 1984, GIA Publications, Inc.

OPENING PRAYER   95
After the invitation from the priest, all pray for a while. The introductory rites conclude with the proper opening prayer and the Amen of the assembly.

LITURGY OF THE WORD   96
When the Church assembles, the book containing the Scriptures (Lectionary) is opened and all listen as the readers and deacon (or priest) read from the places assigned. The first reading is normally from the Hebrew Scriptures (Old Testament), the second from the letters of the New Testament, and the third from the Book of Gospels. Over a three-year cycle, the Church reads through the letters and gospels and a portion of the Hebrew Scriptures. During the Sundays of Ordinary Time, the letters and gospels are read in order, each Sunday continuing near the place where the previous Sunday's readings ended. During Advent/Christmas and Lent/Easter, the readings are those which are traditional and appropriate to these seasons.

The Church listens to and—through the weeks and years—is shaped by the Scriptures. Those who have gathered for the Sunday liturgy are to give their full attention to the words of the reader. A time of silence and reflection follows each of the two readings. After the first reading, this reflection continues in the singing of the psalm. A homily, bringing together the Scriptures and the life of the community, follows the gospel. The liturgy of the word concludes with the creed, the dismissal of the catechumens and the prayers of intercession. In the latter, the assembly continues its constant work of recalling and praying for the universal Church and all those in need.

This reading and hearing of the word—simple things that they are—are the foundation of the liturgical celebration. The public reading of the Scriptures and the rituals which surround this—silence and psalm and acclamation, posture and gesture, preaching and litany of intercession—gather the Church generation after generation. They gather and sustain and gradually make of us the image of Christ.

READING I
In conclusion:

   Reader: The word of the Lord.
   Assembly: **Thanks be to God.**

After a period of silence, the responsorial psalm is sung.

READING II
In conclusion:

   Reader: The word of the Lord.
   Assembly: **Thanks be to God.**

A time of silence follows the reading.

97 GOSPEL

Before the gospel, an acclamation is sung.

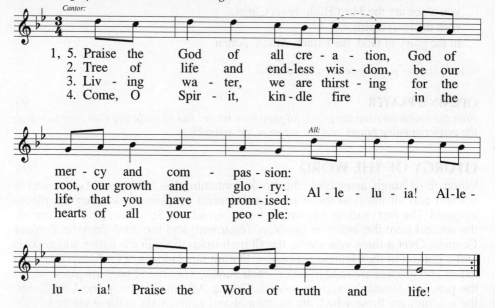

Text: *Mass of Creation*, Marty Haugen
Music: *Mass of Creation*, Marty Haugen
© 1984, GIA Publications, Inc.

During Lent one of the following acclamations replaces the alleluia.

Music: *Mass of Creation*, Marty Haugen, © 1984, GIA Publications, Inc.

Or:

| B | **Praise and honor to you, Lord Jesus Christ!** |

| C | **Glory and praise to you, Lord Jesus Christ!** |

| D | **Glory to you, Word of God, Lord Jesus Christ!** |

Deacon (or priest): The Lord be with you.
    Assembly: **And also with you.**
      Deacon: A reading from the holy gospel according to N.
    Assembly: **Glory to you, Lord.**

After the reading:

Deacon: The gospel of the Lord.
Assembly: **Praise to you, Lord Jesus Christ.**

HOMILY

PROFESSION OF FAITH 98

We believe in one God,
the Father, the Almighty,
maker of heaven and earth,
of all that is seen and unseen.

We believe in one Lord, Jesus Christ,
the only Son of God,
eternally begotten of the Father,
God from God, Light from Light,
true God from true God,
begotten, not made, one in Being with the Father.
Through him all things were made.
For us men and for our salvation he came down from heaven:

All bow at the following words up to: and became man.

by the power of the Holy Spirit
he was born of the Virgin Mary, and became man.
For our sake he was crucified under Pontius Pilate;
he suffered, died, and was buried.
On the third day he rose again
in fulfillment of the Scriptures;
he ascended into heaven
and is seated at the right hand of the Father.
He will come again in glory to judge the living and the dead,
and his kingdom will have no end.

We believe in the Holy Spirit, the Lord, the giver of life,
who proceeds from the Father and the Son.
With the Father and the Son he is worshiped and glorified.
He has spoken through the Prophets.
We believe in one holy catholic and apostolic Church.
We acknowledge one baptism for the forgiveness of sins.
We look for the resurrection of the dead,
and the life of the world to come. Amen.

99 *At Masses with children, the Apostles' Creed may be used:*

We believe in God, the Father almighty,
creator of heaven and earth.

We believe in Jesus Christ, his only Son, our Lord.
He was conceived by the power of the Holy Spirit
and born of the Virgin Mary.
He suffered under Pontius Pilate,
was crucified, died, and was buried.
He descended to the dead.
On the third day he arose again.
He ascended into heaven,
and is seated at the right hand of the Father.
He will come again to judge the living and the dead.

We believe in the Holy Spirit,
the holy catholic Church,
the communion of saints,
the forgiveness of sins,
the resurrection of the body,
and the life everlasting. Amen.

100 GENERAL INTERCESSIONS

The people respond to each petition as follows, or according to local practice.

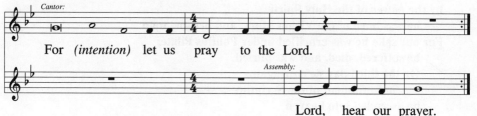

For *(intention)* let us pray to the Lord.

Lord, hear our prayer.

Music: *Mass of Creation*, Marty Haugen, © 1984, GIA Publications, Inc.

LITURGY OF THE EUCHARIST 101

To celebrate the eucharist means to give God thanks and praise. When the table has been prepared with the bread and wine, the assembly joins the priest in remembering the gracious gifts of God in creation and God's saving deeds. The center of this is the paschal mystery, the death of our Lord Jesus Christ which destroyed the power of death and his rising which brings us life. That mystery into which we were baptized we proclaim each Sunday at the eucharist. It is the very shape of Christian life. We find this in the simple bread and wine which stir our remembering and draw forth our prayer of thanksgiving. "Fruit of the earth and work of human hands," the bread and wine become our holy communion in the body and blood of the Lord. We eat and drink and so proclaim that we belong to one another and to the Lord.

The members of the assembly quietly prepare themselves even as the table is prepared. The priest then invites all to lift up their hearts and join in the eucharistic prayer. All do this by giving their full attention and by singing the acclamations from the "Holy, holy" to the great "Amen." Then the assembly joins in the Lord's Prayer, the sign of peace and the "Lamb of God" litany which accompanies the breaking of bread. Ministers of communion assist the assembly to share the body and blood of Christ. A time of silence and prayer concludes the liturgy of the eucharist.

PREPARATION OF THE ALTAR AND THE GIFTS
Bread and wine are brought to the table and the deacon or priest prepares these gifts. If there is no music, the prayers may be said aloud, and all may respond: **"Blessed be God for ever."** *The priest then invites all to pray.*

Assembly: **May the Lord accept the sacrifice at your hands**
for the praise and glory of his name,
for our good, and the good of all his Church.

The priest says the prayer over the gifts and all respond: **Amen.**

EUCHARISTIC PRAYER 102

The central prayer of the Mass begins with this greeting and invitation between priest and assembly.

The Lord be with you. And al - so with you. Lift up your hearts.

We lift them up to the Lord. Let us give thanks to the Lord, our God.

It is right to give him thanks and praise.

Music: *Mass of Creation*, Marty Haugen, © 1984, GIA Publications, Inc.

103 *The Sanctus acclamation is sung to conclude the introduction to the eucharistic prayer.*

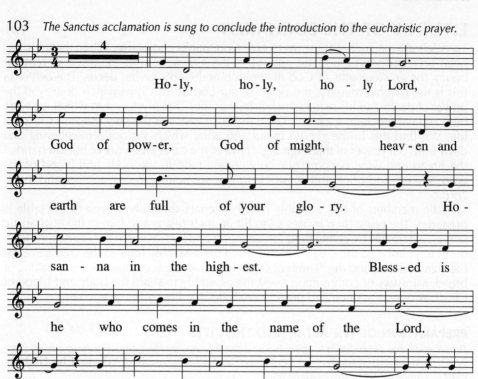

Ho-ly, ho-ly, holy Lord,
God of pow-er, God of might, heav-en and
earth are full of your glo-ry. Ho-
san-na in the high-est. Bless-ed is
he who comes in the name of the Lord.
Ho-san-na in the high-est, ho-
san-na in the high - est.

Music: *Mass of Creation*, Marty Haugen, © 1984, GIA Publications, Inc.

104 *One of the following acclamations follows the priest's invitation: "Let us proclaim the mystery of faith."*

A

Priest:
Let us pro-claim the mys-ter-y of faith:

All:
Christ has died, Christ is ris-en, Christ will come a - gain.

Christ has died, Christ is ris-en, Christ will come a - gain!

Music: *Mass of Creation*, Marty Haugen, © 1984, GIA Publications, Inc.

Music: *Mass of Creation,* Marty Haugen, © 1990, GIA Publications, Inc.

C

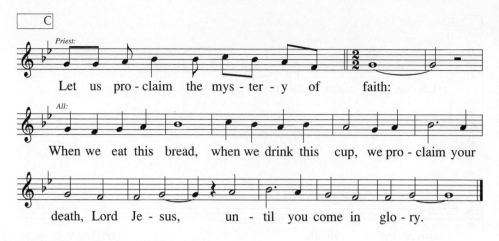

Priest: Let us pro-claim the mys-ter-y of faith:

All: When we eat this bread, when we drink this cup, we pro-claim your death, Lord Je-sus, un-til you come in glo-ry.

Music: *Mass of Creation,* Marty Haugen, © 1993, GIA Publications, Inc.

D

Priest: Let us pro-claim the mys-ter-y of faith:

All: Lord, by your cross and res-ur-rec-tion you have set us free. You are the Sav-ior of the world. You are the Sav-ior of the world.

Music: *Mass of Creation,* Marty Haugen, © 1993, GIA Publications, Inc.

105 *The eucharistic prayer concludes:*

Priest: Through him, with him, in him, in the unity of the Holy Spirit, all glory and honor is yours, almighty Father, for ever and ever.

A - men, a - men, a - men!

A - men, a - men, a - men!

Music: *Mass of Creation,* Marty Haugen, © 1984, GIA Publications, Inc.

COMMUNION RITE

The priest invites all to join in the Lord's Prayer.

Our Fa - ther, who art in heav-en,

hal - low-ed be thy name; thy king-dom come; thy

will be done on earth as it is in heav-en.

Give us this day our dai - ly bread; and for -

give us our tres-pass-es as we for-give those who

tres - pass a - gainst us; and lead us not in - to temp -

ta - tion, but de - liv - er us from e - vil.

Priest: Deliver us, Lord. . . for the coming of our Savior, Jesus Christ.

All:

For the king-dom, the pow - er, and the glo - ry are yours,

now and for ev - er - more. A - men.

Music: *Mass of Creation*, Marty Haugen, © 1984, GIA Publications, Inc.

107 *Following the prayer "Lord, Jesus Christ," the priest invites all to exchange the sign of peace.*

Priest: The peace of the Lord be with you always.
Assembly: And also with you.

All exchange a sign of peace.

108 *Then the eucharistic bread is solemnly broken and the consecrated bread and wine are prepared for holy communion. The litany "Lamb of God" is sung during the breaking of the bread.*

1. Je-sus, Lamb of
2. Je-sus, Bread of
3. Je-sus, Prince of

God,
Life,   you   take a-way the   sins of the   world: have
Peace,

mer-cy on   us.   Je-sus, Lamb of   God;   you

take a-way the sins of the   world: grant us your peace.

Music: *Mass of Creation*, Marty Haugen, © 1984, GIA Publications, Inc.

109 *The priest then invites all to share in holy communion.*

Priest: This is the Lamb of God...his supper.
Assembly: **Lord, I am not worthy to receive you,**
but only say the word and I shall be healed.

Minister of communion: The body (blood) of Christ.
Communicant: **Amen.**

A song or psalm is ordinarily sung during communion. After communion, a time of silence is observed or a song of thanksgiving is sung. The rite concludes with the prayer after communion to which all respond: **Amen.**

CONCLUDING RITE 110

The liturgy of word and eucharist ends very simply. There may be announcements of events and concerns for the community, then the priest gives a blessing and the assembly is dismissed.

GREETING AND BLESSING

Priest: The Lord be with you.
Assembly: **And also with you.**

Optional

When the bishop blesses the people he adds the following:

Bishop: Blessed be the name of the Lord.
Assembly: **Now and for ever.**

Bishop: Our help is in the name of the Lord.
Assembly: **Who made heaven and earth.**

The blessing may be in a simple or solemn form. All respond to the blessing or to each part of the blessing: **Amen.**

DISMISSAL

The deacon or priest then dismisses the assembly:

Go in the peace of Christ. Thanks be to God.
or: The Mass is end - ed, go in peace.
or: Go in peace to love and serve the Lord.

EASTER DISMISSAL

The deacon or priest then dismisses the assembly:

Go in the peace of Christ, al-le-lu - ia, al-le - lu - ia.
Thanks be to God, al-le-lu - ia, al-le - lu - ia.

Composite Setting

111 CLEANSE US, O LORD

Cantor, then all:

Cleanse us, O Lord, from all our sins; wash us, and we

shall be clean, clean as new snow. *1. and last time* snow. *2.* *Cantor:* I will

pour clean wa - ter o - ver you and wash a - way all your sins. *D.C. al %*

Cantor: snow. A new heart will I give you, says the Lord. *D.C.*

Music: Joseph Roff, © 1985, GIA Publications, Inc.

112 KYRIE ELEISON

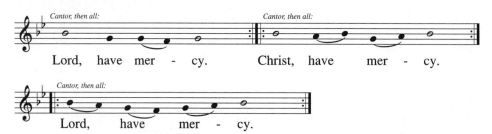

Cantor, then all:

Lord, have mer - cy. *Cantor, then all:* Christ, have mer - cy.

Cantor, then all:

Lord, have mer - cy.

Music: *Litany of the Saints;* adapt. by Richard Proulx, © 1971, GIA Publications, Inc.

Or:

Ky - ri - e   e - le - i - son.   Chri - ste e - le - i - son.

Ky - ri - e   e - le - i - son.

Music: *Litany of the Saints;* adapt. by Richard Proulx, © 1971, GIA Publications, Inc.

GLORIA 113

Glo - ry to God in the high - est, and peace to his peo-ple on earth. Lord God, heav - en - ly King, al - might - y God and Fa - ther, we wor - ship you, we give you thanks, we praise you for your glo - ry.

Choir (Congr. ad lib):

Lord Je - sus Christ, on - ly Son of the Fa - ther, Lord God, Lamb of God, you take a - way the sin of the world: have mer - cy on us; you are seat - ed at the right hand of the Fa - ther: re - ceive our prayer.

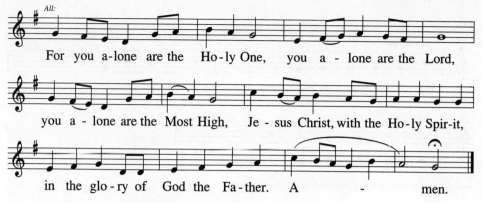

For you a-lone are the Ho-ly One, you a - lone are the Lord, you a - lone are the Most High, Je - sus Christ, with the Ho-ly Spir-it, in the glo - ry of God the Fa - ther. A - men.

Music: *A New Mass for Congregations,* Carroll T. Andrews, © 1970, GIA Publications, Inc.

114 GOSPEL ACCLAMATION

Al - le - lu - ia, al - le - lu - ia, al - le - lu - ia.

Music: Chant Mode VI; acc. by Richard Proulx, © 1985, GIA Publications, Inc.

Lenten Acclamation

Praise to you, Lord Je - sus Christ, king of end-less glo-ry!

Music: Frank Schoen, © 1970, GIA Publications, Inc.

115 GENERAL INTERCESSIONS

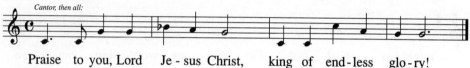

(Intention) Let us pray to the Lord. Lord, hear our prayer.

Music: Byzantine chant

116 PREFACE DIALOG

The Lord be with you. And al - so with you.

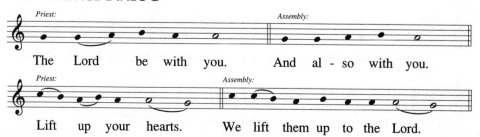

Lift up your hearts. We lift them up to the Lord.

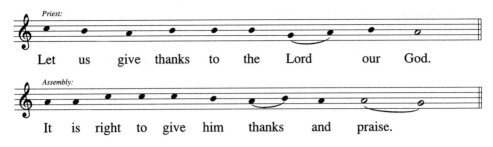

Let us give thanks to the Lord our God.

It is right to give him thanks and praise.

Music: Sacramentary, 1974

SANCTUS 117

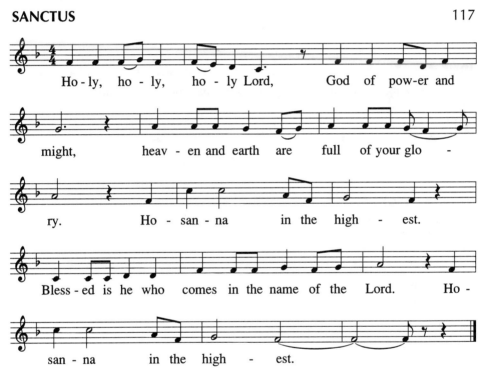

Ho - ly, ho - ly, ho - ly Lord, God of pow-er and might, heav - en and earth are full of your glo - ry. Ho - san - na in the high - est. Bless - ed is he who comes in the name of the Lord. Ho - san - na in the high - est.

Music: *People's Mass,* Jan Vermulst, 1925-1994, acc. by Richard Proulx, © 1970, World Library Publications

MEMORIAL ACCLAMATION 118

Christ has died, Christ is ris-en, Christ will come a - gain.

Music: *Danish Amen Mass,* Charles George Frischmann and David Kraehenbuehl, © 1970, J. S. Paluch Company, Inc.

119 AMEN

A - men,   a - men,   a -   men.

Music: Danish Amen

120 COMMUNION RITE

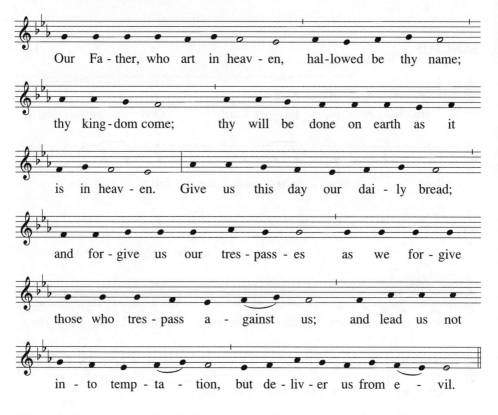

Our Fa - ther, who art in heav - en,   hal - lowed be thy name;

thy king - dom come;   thy will be done on earth as it

is in heav - en.   Give us this day our dai - ly bread;

and for - give us our tres - pass - es   as we for - give

those who tres - pass a - gainst us;   and lead us not

in - to temp - ta - tion, but de - liv - er us from e - vil.

Priest: Deliver us, Lord…
for the coming of our Savior, Jesus Christ.

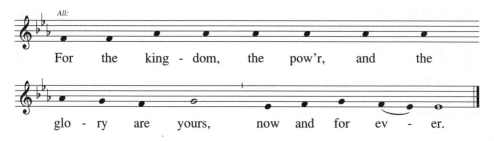

All:

For   the   king - dom,   the   pow'r,   and   the

glo - ry   are   yours,   now   and   for   ev -   er.

Music: Traditional chant, adapt. by Robert Snow, 1964; acc. by Robert J. Batastini, © 1975, 1993, GIA Publications, Inc.

AGNUS DEI

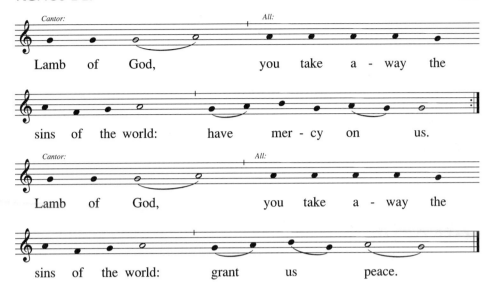

Cantor: Lamb of God, *All:* you take a - way the sins of the world: have mer - cy on us.

Cantor: Lamb of God, *All:* you take a - way the sins of the world: grant us peace.

Music: Agnus Dei XVIII, Vatican Edition; acc. by Robert J. Batastini, © 1993, GIA Publications, Inc.

Setting One

MASS OF LIGHT

122 KYRIE ELEISON

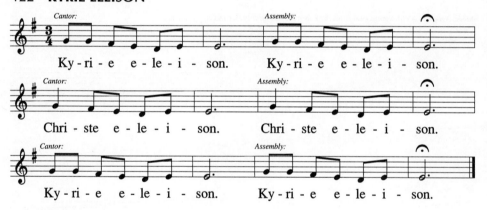

Ky - ri - e e - le - i - son. Ky - ri - e e - le - i - son.

Chri - ste e - le - i - son. Chri - ste e - le - i - son.

Ky - ri - e e - le - i - son. Ky - ri - e e - le - i - son.

Music: *Mass of Light,* David Haas, © 1988, GIA Publications, Inc.

123 GLORIA

Refrain

Glo-ry to God in the high - est, Sing! Glo-ry to

God! Glo - ry to God in the high - est, and

peace to his peo - ple on earth!

Verses

1. Lord God, heavenly King, almighty God and Father,
   we worship you, we give you thanks, we praise you for your glory.

2. Lord Jesus Christ, only Son of the Father, Lord God, Lamb of God,
   you take away the sin of the world: have mercy on us;
   you are seated at the right hand of the Father: receive our prayer.

3. For you alone are the Holy One, you alone are the Lord,
   the Most High, Jesus Christ, with the Holy Spirit, in the glory of God the Father.

Music: *Mass of Light,* David Haas, © 1988, GIA Publications, Inc.

ALLELUIA   124

Al - le - lu - ia! Al - le - lu - ia! Al - le - lu - ia!

Music: *Mass of Light,* David Haas, © 1988, GIA Publications, Inc.

LENTEN GOSPEL ACCLAMATION   125

Glo-ry to you, O Word of God, Lord Je - sus Christ!

Music: *Mass of Light,* David Haas, © 1988, GIA Publications, Inc.

PREFACE DIALOG   126

The Lord be with you. And al - so with you.

Lift up your hearts. We lift them

up to the Lord. Let us give thanks to the Lord our

God. It is right to give him thanks and praise.

Music: *Mass of Light,* David Haas, © 1988, GIA Publications, Inc.

127 SANCTUS

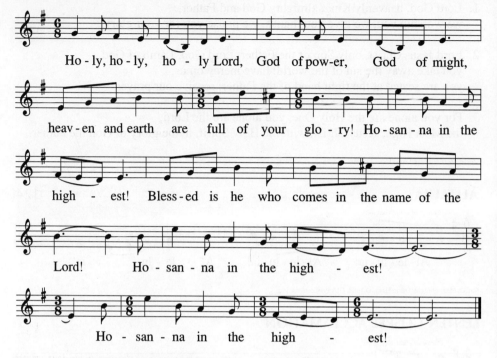

Ho - ly, ho - ly, ho - ly Lord, God of pow-er, God of might,

heav - en and earth are full of your glo - ry! Ho - san - na in the

high - est! Bless-ed is he who comes in the name of the

Lord! Ho - san - na in the high - est!

Ho - san - na in the high - est!

Music: *Mass of Light,* David Haas, © 1988, GIA Publications, Inc.

128 EUCHARISTIC ACCLAMATION I (OPTIONAL)*

Ho - san - na in the high - est!

Music: *Mass of Light,* David Haas, © 1988, GIA Publications, Inc.

*As in the Eucharistic Prayers for Masses with Children.

129 MEMORIAL ACCLAMATION

Dy - ing you de - stroyed our death, ris - ing you re - stored our life.

Lord Je - sus come! Lord Je - sus come in glo - ry!

Music: *Mass of Light,* David Haas, © 1988, GIA Publications, Inc.

EUCHARISTIC ACCLAMATION II (OPTIONAL) 130

Hear us, hear us. Hear us, hear us.

Music: *Mass of Light,* David Haas, © 1988, GIA Publications, Inc.

AMEN 131

A - men, a - men! A - men, a - men!

Music: *Mass of Light,* David Haas, © 1988, GIA Publications, Inc.

AGNUS DEI 132

Cantor: All:

*Lamb of God,
Bread of Life, you take a - way the sins of the world:
Son of God,

have mer - cy on us.

Last time

Cantor: All:

Lamb of God, you take a - way the sins of the

world grant us your peace.

"Lamb of God" is sung the first and last times. Alternate intervening invocations include: "Saving Cup," "Hope for all," "Prince of Peace," "Wine of Peace," etc.

Music: *Mass of Light,* David Haas, © 1988, GIA Publications, Inc.

Setting Two

MASS OF THE ANGELS AND SAINTS

133 SPRINKLING RITE

Each verse concludes:

1. Faith - ful - ly now God's praise we sing.

Faith - ful - ly now God's praise we sing.

2. Thankfully now... 3. Joyfully now...

Text: Michael A. Saward, © 1982, Hope Publishing Co.
Music: *Mass of the Angels and Saints,* Steven R. Janco, © 1996, GIA Publications, Inc.

134 KYRIE ELEISON

Lord, have mer - cy. Christ, have mer - cy.

Lord, have mer - cy.

Priest: May almighty God...everlasting life.

A - men.

Music: *Mass of the Angels and Saints,* Steven R. Janco, © 1996, GIA Publications, Inc.

GLORIA

Refrain

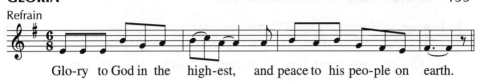

Glo-ry to God in the high-est, and peace to his peo-ple on earth.

Verses

1. Lord God, heavenly King, almighty God and Father,
   we worship you, we give you thanks, we praise you for your glory. *(To refrain)*

2. Lord Jesus Christ, only Son of the Father, Lord God, Lamb of God,
   you take away the sin of the world: have mercy on us;
   you are seated at the right hand of the Father: receive our prayer. *(To refrain)*

3. For you alone are the Holy One, you alone are the Lord,
   you alone are the Most High, Jesus Christ,
   with the Holy Spirit, in the glory of God the Father. *(To refrain)*

Cantor, then all:

A - men.

Music: *Mass of the Angels and Saints,* Steven R. Janco, © 1996, GIA Publications, Inc.

ALLELUIA

136

Al - le - lu - ia, al - le - lu - ia, al - le - lu - ia.

Al - le - lu - ia, al - le - lu - ia, al - le - lu - ia.

Optional Verse Response

After first phrase:

After second phrase:

D.C.

Al - le - lu - ia. Al - le - lu - ia.

Music: *Mass of the Angels and Saints,* Steven R. Janco, © 1996, GIA Publications, Inc.

137 LENTEN GOSPEL ACCLAMATION

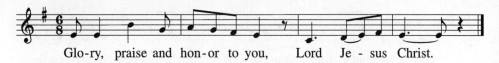

Glo-ry, praise and hon-or to you, Lord Je-sus Christ.

Music: *Mass of the Angels and Saints,* Steven R. Janco, © 1996, GIA Publications, Inc.

138 GENERAL INTERCESSIONS

We pray to the Lord: Lord, hear our prayer.

Alternate Responses

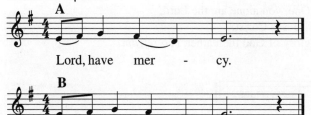

A

Lord, have mer - cy.

B

Gra-cious-ly hear us.

Music: *Mass of the Angels and Saints,* Steven R. Janco, © 1996, GIA Publications, Inc.

139 PREFACE DIALOG

The Lord be with you. And al - so with you.

Lift up your hearts. We lift them up to the Lord.

Let us give thanks to the Lord our God.

It is right to give him thanks and praise.

Music: *Mass of the Angels and Saints,* Steven R. Janco, © 1996, GIA Publications, Inc.

SANCTUS

Ho - ly, ho - ly, ho - ly Lord, God of pow - er and might, heav'n and earth are full of your glo - ry. Ho - san - na, ho - san - na, ho - san - na in the high - est. Ho - san - na, ho - san - na, ho - san - na in the high - est. Bless - ed is he who comes in the name of the Lord. Ho - san - na, ho - san - na, ho - san - na, in the high - est. Ho - san - na, ho - san - na, ho - san - na in the high - est.

Music: *Mass of the Angels and Saints,* Steven R. Janco, © 1996, GIA Publications, Inc.

141 MEMORIAL ACCLAMATION A

Christ has died, Christ is ris - en, Christ will come a - gain.

Christ has died, Christ is ris - en, Christ will come a - gain.

Music: *Mass of the Angels and Saints,* Steven R. Janco, © 1996, GIA Publications, Inc.

142 MEMORIAL ACCLAMATION B

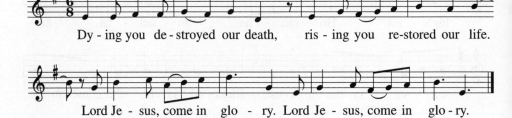

Dy - ing you de - stroyed our death, ris - ing you re-stored our life.

Lord Je - sus, come in glo - ry. Lord Je - sus, come in glo - ry.

Music: *Mass of the Angels and Saints,* Steven R. Janco, © 1996, GIA Publications, Inc.

143 MEMORIAL ACCLAMATION C

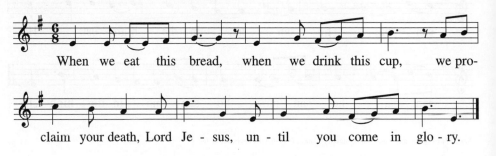

When we eat this bread, when we drink this cup, we pro-

claim your death, Lord Je - sus, un - til you come in glo - ry.

Music: *Mass of the Angels and Saints,* Steven R. Janco, © 1996, GIA Publications, Inc.

MEMORIAL ACCLAMATION D 144

Lord, by your cross and res - ur - rec - tion you have set us free.

You are the Sav - ior of the world, the Sav - ior of the world.

Music: *Mass of the Angels and Saints,* Steven R. Janco, © 1996, GIA Publications, Inc.

AMEN 145

A - men, a - men, a - men.

A - men, a - men, a - men.

Music: *Mass of the Angels and Saints,* Steven R. Janco, © 1996, GIA Publications, Inc.

AGNUS DEI 146

Cantor, then all: Repeat ad lib.

Have mer - cy on us.

Cantor: All:

Grant us peace. Grant us peace.

Music: *Mass of the Angels and Saints,* Steven R. Janco, © 1996, GIA Publications, Inc.

Setting Three

SING PRAISE AND THANKSGIVING

147 CLEANSE US, LORD

Refrain

Cleanse us, Lord, from all our sins; wash us and we shall be clean as new snow. Cleanse us, Lord, from all our sins; wash us and we shall be clean as new snow.

Verses

1. Springs of water, bless the Lord; give God glory, glory and praise!
   Seas and rivers, bless the Lord; give God glory and praise!

2. I will pour clean water over you; I will wash you from all your sin.
   I will place a new heart within you: You are my people and I am your God!

3. You are a people God calls to be born, calls to be born as an off'ring of praise,
   praise that God called you from darkness to light,
   praise that God called you from death into life!

4. I saw water, I saw water flowing from the temple; it brought God's life,
   it brought God's life, it brought God's life and salvation.

KYRIE ELEISON

Lord, have mer-cy. Lord, have mer-cy.
Ky - ri-e e - le-i-son. *Ky - ri-e e - le-i-son.*

Christ, have mer-cy. Christ, have mer-cy.
Chri - ste e - le-i-son. *Chri - ste e - le-i-son.*

Lord, have mer-cy. Lord, have
Ky - ri-e e - le-i-son. *Ky - ri-e e -*

mer-cy, have mer-cy, have mer-cy.
le-i-son, e - le-i-son, e - le-i-son.

Music: *Sing Praise and Thanksgiving,* J. Michael Joncas, © 1989, World Library Publications, Inc.

GLORIA

Refrain

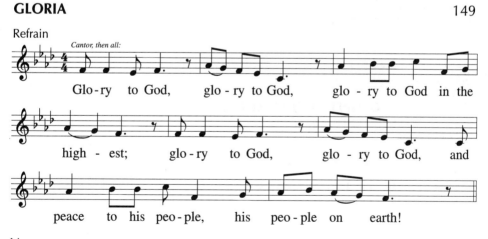

Glo-ry to God, glo-ry to God, glo-ry to God in the

high - est; glo-ry to God, glo-ry to God, and

peace to his peo-ple, his peo-ple on earth!

Verses

1. Lord God, heavenly King, almighty God and Father,
   we worship you, we give you thanks, we praise you for your glory. *(To refrain)*

2. Lord Jesus Christ, only Son of the Father, Lord God, Lamb of God,
   Lord Jesus Christ, you take away the sin of the world: have mercy on us;
   you are seated at the right hand of the Father: receive our prayer. *(To refrain)*

3. For you alone are the Holy One, you alone are the Lord,
   you alone are the Most High, Jesus Christ,

All:

with the Ho - ly Spir - it, in the glo - ry of God, the

glo - ry of God the Fa - ther. A - men.

A - men. A - men. A - men. A - men.

Music: *Sing Praise and Thanksgiving,* J. Michael Joncas, © 1989, World Library Publications, Inc.

150 ALLELUIA

Refrain

Cantor, then all:

Al - le - lu - ia, al - le - lu - ia,

al - le - lu - ia, al - le - lu - ia, al - le - lu - ia.

Music: *Sing Praise and Thanksgiving,* J. Michael Joncas, © 1989, World Library Publications, Inc.

151 LENTEN GOSPEL ACCLAMATION

Refrain

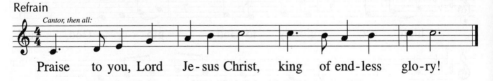

Cantor, then all:

Praise to you, Lord Je - sus Christ, king of end - less glo - ry!

Music: *Sing Praise and Thanksgiving,* J. Michael Joncas, © 1989, World Library Publications, Inc.

152 GENERAL INTERCESSIONS

Lord, in your mer - cy, hear our prayer.

Music: *Sing Praise and Thanksgiving,* J. Michael Joncas, © 1989, World Library Publications, Inc.

SANCTUS 153

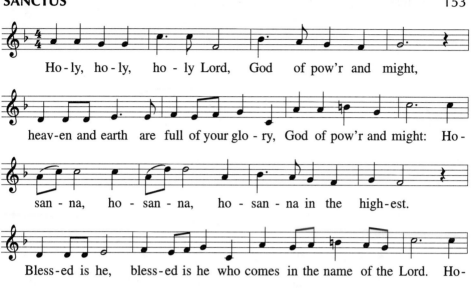

Ho - ly, ho - ly, ho - ly Lord, God of pow'r and might,

heav-en and earth are full of your glo - ry, God of pow'r and might: Ho -

san - na, ho - san - na, ho - san - na in the high-est.

Bless-ed is he, bless-ed is he who comes in the name of the Lord. Ho-

san - na, ho - san - na, ho - san - na in the high-est. Ho -

san - na, ho - san - na, ho - san - na in the high-est!

Music: *Sing Praise and Thanksgiving,* J. Michael Joncas, © 1989, World Library Publications, Inc.

MEMORIAL ACCLAMATION 154

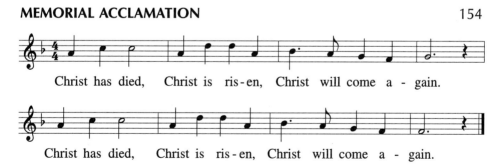

Christ has died, Christ is ris-en, Christ will come a - gain.

Christ has died, Christ is ris-en, Christ will come a - gain.

Music: *Sing Praise and Thanksgiving,* J. Michael Joncas, © 1989, World Library Publications, Inc.

155 AMEN

A - men, a - men, a - men.

Music: *Sing Praise and Thanksgiving,* J. Michael Joncas, © 1989, World Library Publications, Inc.

156 LORD'S PRAYER

Our Fa - ther, who art in heav-en, hal-low - ed be thy

name; thy king-dom come, thy will be done on

earth as it is in heav-en. Give us this day our

dai - ly bread; give us this day our dai - ly bread; and for-

give us our tres-pass-es as we for-give those who tres - pass a-

gainst us. And lead us not in - to temp-ta - tion, but de-

liv - er us from e - vil.

Priest: Deliver us, Lord...coming of our Savior, Jesus Christ.

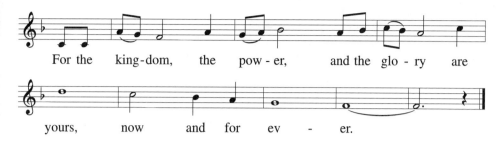

For the king-dom, the pow - er, and the glo - ry are yours, now and for ev - er.

Music: *Sing Praise and Thanksgiving,* J. Michael Joncas, © 1989, World Library Publications, Inc.

AGNUS DEI 157

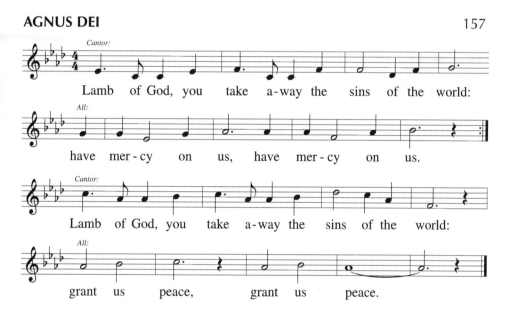

Cantor:
Lamb of God, you take a-way the sins of the world:

All:
have mer - cy on us, have mer - cy on us.

Cantor:
Lamb of God, you take a-way the sins of the world:

All:
grant us peace, grant us peace.

Music: *Sing Praise and Thanksgiving,* J. Michael Joncas, © 1989, World Library Publications, Inc.

Service Music

158 RITE OF SPRINKLING

Refrain

Springs of wa-ter, bless the Lord! Give him glo-ry and praise for ev-er!

Verses

Cantor:

1. O - ceans of earth, sing glo-ry to God! Praise to the one who
2. Riv - ers and lakes, sing glo-ry to God! Praise, all you ponds and
3. Brooks of the hills, sing glo-ry to God! Praise to the source of
4. Show - ers and springs, sing glo-ry to God! Praise, all you liv - ing

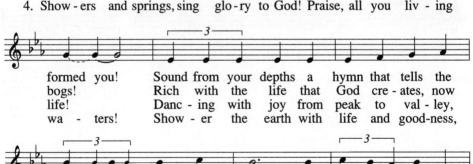

formed you! Sound from your depths a hymn that tells the
bogs! Rich with the life that God cre - ates, now
life! Danc - ing with joy from peak to val - ley,
wa - ters! Show - er the earth with life and good-ness,

won - ders God has done!
let your song be heard!
laugh-ing and clear your song! Oh Bless-ed be God for
show - er the grace of God!

D.C.

All:

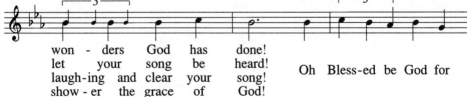

ev - er! Bless - ed be God for ev - er!

Text: Refrain trans. © 1973, ICEL; additional text by Marty Haugen, © 1994, GIA Publications, Inc.
Music: Marty Haugen, © 1994, GIA Publications, Inc.

GLORIA

All:

Glo-ry to God in the high-est, and peace to his peo-ple on earth.

Glo-ry to God in the high-est, and peace to his peo-ple on earth.

Cantor or T. B.:

Lord God, heav-en - ly King, al-might-y God and Fa - ther.

All:

Glo-ry to God in the high-est, and peace to his peo-ple on earth.

Cantor or S. A.:

We wor-ship you, we give you thanks, we praise you for your

All:

glo - ry. Glo-ry to God in the high - est, and

Cantor or T. B.:

peace to his peo-ple on earth. Lord Je - sus Christ, on - ly

All:

Son of the Fa - ther. Glo-ry to God in the high-est, and

T. B.:

peace to his peo-ple on earth. Lord God, Lamb of God,

you take a-way the sin of the world; have mer-cy on us;

S. A.:

you are seat - ed at the right hand of the Fa-ther:

Music: *Mass of the Bells*, Alexander Peloquin, © 1972, 1973, GIA Publications, Inc.

GLORIA

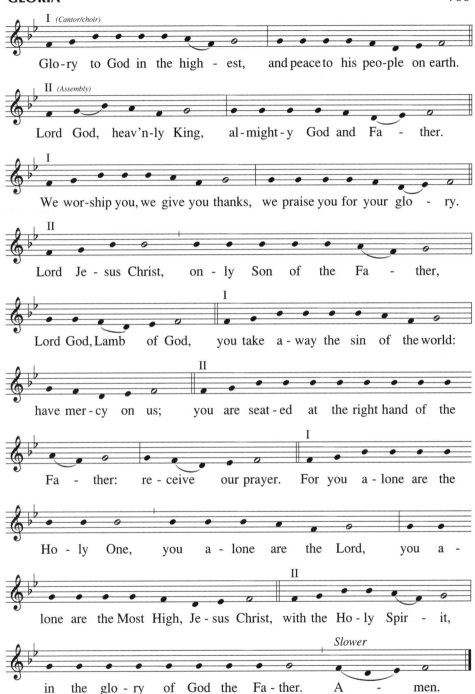

Glo-ry to God in the high - est, and peace to his peo-ple on earth.

Lord God, heav'n-ly King, al-might-y God and Fa - ther.

We wor-ship you, we give you thanks, we praise you for your glo - ry.

Lord Je - sus Christ, on - ly Son of the Fa - ther,

Lord God, Lamb of God, you take a - way the sin of the world:

have mer - cy on us; you are seat - ed at the right hand of the

Fa - ther: re - ceive our prayer. For you a - lone are the

Ho - ly One, you a - lone are the Lord, you a -

lone are the Most High, Je - sus Christ, with the Ho - ly Spir - it,

in the glo - ry of God the Fa - ther. A - men.

Music: *Congregational Mass,* John Lee, © 1970, GIA Publications, Inc.

161 GLORIA

Gló-ri - a in ex-cél-sis De - o. Et in ter-ra pax ho-mí-ni-bus

bo-nae vo-lun-tá - tis. Lau-dá - mus te.

Be-ne-dí-ci-mus te. A-do-rá - mus te.

Glo-ri-fi-cá-mus te. Grá-ti-as á-gi-mus ti-bi

pro-pter ma-gnam gló-ri-am tu-am. Dó-mi-ne De-us, Rex cae-

lé-stis, De-us Pa-ter om-ní-po-tens.

Dó-mi-ne Fi-li u-ni-gé-ni-te, Je-su Chri-ste.

Dó-mi-ne De-us, A-gnus De-i, Fí-li-us Pa-tris.

Qui tol-lis pec-cá-ta mun - di, mi-se-ré - re no-bis.

Qui tol-lis pec-cá-ta mun - di, sú-sci-pe de-pre-ca-ti-ó-

nem no - stram. Qui se-des ad déx-te-ram Pa-tris,

mi-se-ré-re no - bis. Quó - ni - am tu so - lus San - ctus.

Tu so-lus Dó - mi - nus. Tu so-lus Al - tís - si-mus,

Je - su Chri-ste. Cum San - cto Spí - ri - tu,

in gló-ri-a De-i Pa - tris. A - men.

Music: Vatican Edition VIII, acc. by Richard Proulx, © 1995, GIA Publications, Inc.

GLORIA

162

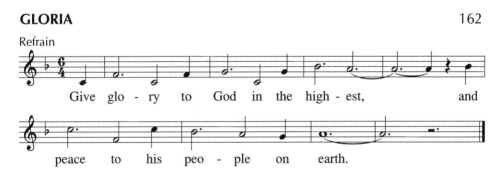

Refrain

Give glo - ry to God in the high - est, and

peace to his peo - ple on earth.

Verses

1. Lord God, heavenly King, almighty God and Father,
   we worship you, we give you thanks, we praise you for your glory.

2. Lord Jesus Christ, only Son of the Father, Lord God, Lamb of God,
   you take away the sin of the world: have mercy upon us;
   you are seated at the right hand of the Father: receive our prayer.

3. You alone are the Holy One, you alone are the Lord,
   you alone are the Most High, Jesus Christ,
   with the Holy Spirit, in the glory of God the Father.

Music: John B. Foley, SJ, © 1978, John B. Foley, SJ, and New Dawn Music

163 GLORIA

Refrain

Glo - ry to God in the high - est, and peace to his peo - ple on earth.

Verses

1. Lord God, heavenly King, almighty God and Father,
   we worship you, we give you thanks, we praise you for your glory.

2. Lord Jesus Christ, only Son of the Father, Lord God, Lamb of God,
   you take away the sin of the world: have mercy on us;
   you are seated at the right hand of the Father: receive our prayer.

3. For you alone are the Holy One, you alone are the Lord,
   you alone are the Most High, Jesus Christ,
   with the Holy Spirit, in the glory of God the Father. Amen.

Music: *Mass of Hope,* Becket Senchur, OSB, © 1992, GIA Publications, Inc.

164 ALLELUIA

Al - le - lu - ia, al - le - lu - ia, al - le - lu - ia, al-le - lu-ia, al - le - lu - ia.

Music: Joe Wise; acc. by Kelly Dobbs Mickus, © 1966, 1973, 1986, GIA Publications, Inc.

165 ALLELUIA

Al - le - lu - ia, al - le - lu - ia, al - le - lu - ia.

Music: A. Gregory Murray, OSB, © 1958, The Grail, GIA Publications, Inc., agent

ALLELUIA 166

Al - le - lu - ia, al - le - lu - ia, al - le - lu - ia.

Al - le - lu - ia, al - le - lu - ia, al - le - lu - ia!

Music: Alleluia 7; Jacques Berthier, © 1984, Les Presses de Taizé, GIA Publications, Inc., agent

ALLELUIA 167

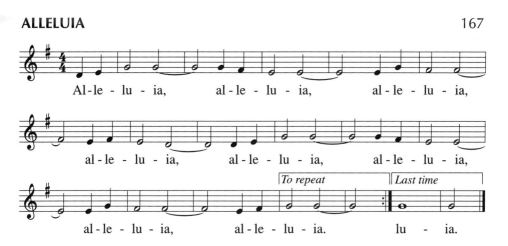

Al - le - lu - ia, al - le - lu - ia, al - le - lu - ia,

al - le - lu - ia, al - le - lu - ia, al - le - lu - ia,

To repeat ‖ *Last time*

al - le - lu - ia, al - le - lu - ia. lu - ia.

Music: Jerry Sinclair, © 1972, Manna Music, Inc.; arr. by Betty C. Pulkingham, © 1971, 1975, Celebration

ALLELUIA 168

Al - le - lu - ia, al - le - lu - ia!

Al - le - lu - ia, al - le - lu - ia!

Text: *Celtic Alleluia;* Christopher Walker
Music: Fintan O'Carroll and Christopher Walker
© 1985, Fintan O'Carroll and Christopher Walker, published by OCP Publications

169 ALLELUIA

Music: *Alleluia in C*, Howard Hughes, SM, © 1973, 1982, GIA Publications, Inc.

170 LENTEN GOSPEL ACCLAMATION

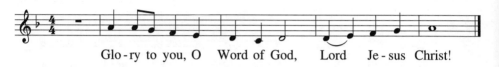

Glo-ry to you, O Word of God, Lord Je-sus Christ!

Music: Richard Proulx, © 1975, GIA Publications, Inc.

171 GENERAL INTERCESSIONS

Gra-cious Lord, hear us we pray.

Music: Ronald F. Krisman, © 1977, GIA Publications, Inc.

172 SANCTUS—A COMMUNITY MASS

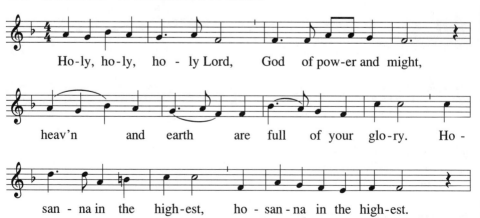

Ho-ly, ho-ly, ho - ly Lord, God of pow-er and might,

heav'n and earth are full of your glo-ry. Ho -

san - na in the high-est, ho - san-na in the high-est.

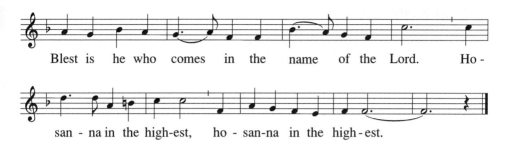

Blest is he who comes in the name of the Lord. Ho-
san - na in the high-est, ho - san-na in the high-est.

MEMORIAL ACCLAMATION A 173

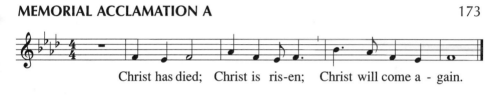

Christ has died; Christ is ris-en; Christ will come a - gain.

MEMORIAL ACCLAMATION B 174

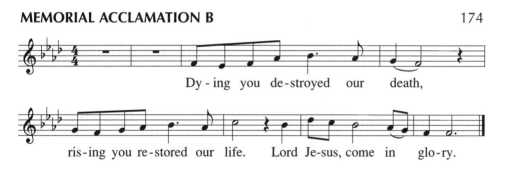

Dy - ing you de-stroyed our death,
ris-ing you re-stored our life. Lord Je-sus, come in glo-ry.

MEMORIAL ACCLAMATION C 175

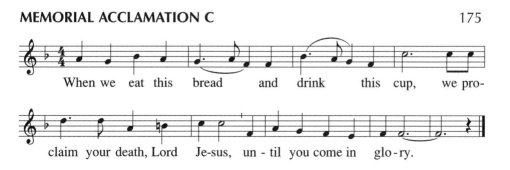

When we eat this bread and drink this cup, we proclaim your death, Lord Je-sus, un - til you come in glo-ry.

176 MEMORIAL ACCLAMATION D

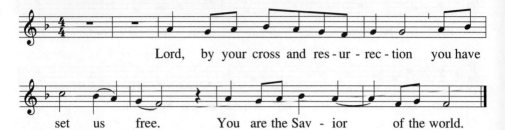

Lord, by your cross and res-ur-rec-tion you have set us free. You are the Sav-ior of the world.

Music: *A Community Mass,* Richard Proulx, © 1998, GIA Publications, Inc.

177 AMEN

A - men, a - men, a - men.

Music: *A Community Mass,* Richard Proulx, © 1971, 1977, GIA Publications, Inc.

178 AGNUS DEI

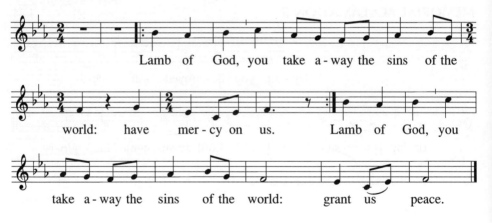

Lamb of God, you take a-way the sins of the world: have mer-cy on us. Lamb of God, you take a-way the sins of the world: grant us peace.

Music: *A Community Mass,* Richard Proulx, © 1971, 1977, GIA Publications, Inc.

179 SANCTUS—ST. LOUIS JESUITS MASS

Ho-ly, ho-ly, ho-ly Lord, God of pow'r and might, heav-en and earth are full of your glo -

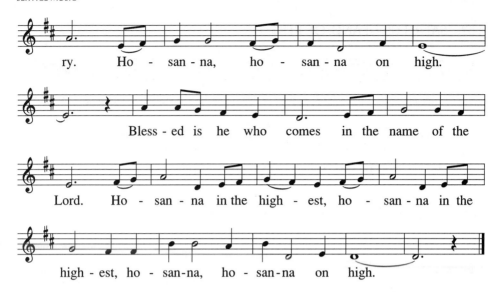

ry. Ho - san - na, ho - san - na on high.

Bless - ed is he who comes in the name of the

Lord. Ho - san - na in the high - est, ho - san - na in the

high - est, ho - san - na, ho - san - na on high.

Music: *St. Louis Jesuits Mass,* Robert J. Dufford, SJ, and Daniel L. Schutte, © 1973, Robert J. Dufford, SJ, and Daniel L. Schutte. Administered by New Dawn Music; acc. by Diana Kodner

WHEN WE EAT THIS BREAD 180

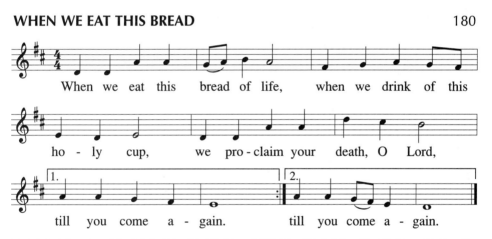

When we eat this bread of life, when we drink of this

ho - ly cup, we pro - claim your death, O Lord,

1. till you come a - gain. 2. till you come a - gain.

Music: *St. Louis Jesuits Mass,* Robert J. Dufford, SJ, and Daniel L. Schutte, © 1979, Robert J. Dufford, SJ, and Daniel L. Schutte. Administered by New Dawn Music

AMEN 181

A - men, al - le - lu - ia, for ev - er and ev - er, for

ev - er, al - le - lu - ia, for ev - er and ev - er. A - men.

Music: *St. Louis Jesuits Mass,* Robert J. Dufford, SJ, and Daniel L. Schutte, © 1973, Robert J. Dufford, SJ, and Daniel L. Schutte. Administered by New Dawn Music; acc. by Diana Kodner

182 SANCTUS—LAND OF REST

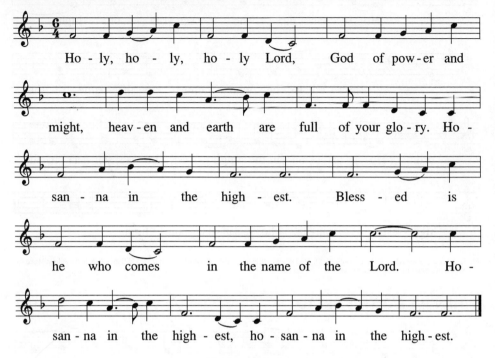

Ho - ly, ho - ly, ho - ly Lord, God of pow-er and might, heav-en and earth are full of your glo - ry. Ho - san - na in the high - est. Bless - ed is he who comes in the name of the Lord. Ho - san - na in the high - est, ho - san - na in the high - est.

Music: *Land of Rest,* adapt. by Marcia Pruner, © 1980, Church Pension Fund; acc. by Richard Proulx, © 1986, GIA Publications, Inc.

183 MEMORIAL ACCLAMATION

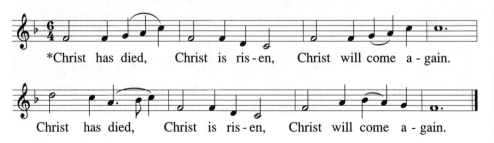

*Christ has died, Christ is ris - en, Christ will come a - gain.
Christ has died, Christ is ris - en, Christ will come a - gain.

For a shorter version of this acclamation, sing the first two measures and the last two measures.

Music: *Land of Rest,* adapt. by Richard Proulx, © 1986, GIA Publications, Inc.

184 AMEN

A - men, a - men, a - men.

Music: *Land of Rest,* adapt. by Richard Proulx, © 1986, GIA Publications, Inc.

SANCTUS 185

San - ctus, San - ctus, San - ctus Do - mi - nus De - us Sa - ba - oth.

Ple - ni sunt cae - li et ter - ra glo - ri - a tu - a. Ho - san - na

in ex - cel - sis. Be - ne - di - ctus qui ve - nit in no - mi - ne

Do - mi - ni. Ho - san - na in ex - cel - sis.

Music: *Sanctus XVIII, Vatican Edition;* acc. by Gerard Farrell, OSB © 1986, GIA Publications, Inc.

MEMORIAL ACCLAMATION 186

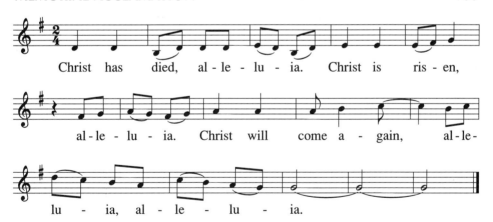

Christ has died, al - le - lu - ia. Christ is ris - en,

al - le - lu - ia. Christ will come a - gain, al - le -

lu - ia, al - le - lu - ia.

Music: Joe Wise; acc. by T.F. and R.P., © 1971, 1972, GIA Publications, Inc.

187 AGNUS DEI

Cantor: / *All:*

A-gnus De - i, qui tol-lis pec-ca-ta mun-di: mi-se-re-re no - bis.

Cantor: / *All:*

A-gnus De - i, qui tol-lis pec-ca-ta mun-di: do-na no-bis pa - cem.

Music: Agnus Dei XVIII, Vatican Edition; acc. by Robert J. Batastini, © 1993, GIA Publications, Inc.

188 AGNUS DEI

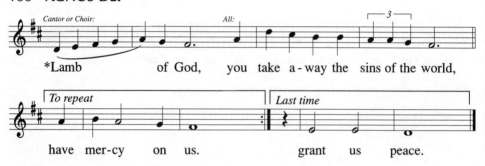

Cantor or Choir: / *All:* / 3

*Lamb of God, you take a-way the sins of the world,

To repeat / Last time

have mer-cy on us. grant us peace.

*Alternates: 1. Emmanuel, 2. Prince of peace, 3. Son of God, 4. Word made flesh,
5. Paschal Lamb, 6. Bread of Life, 7. Lord Jesus Christ, 8. Lord of Love,
9. Christ the Lord, 10. King of kings.*

Music: *Holy Cross Mass,* David Clark Isele, © 1979, GIA Publications, Inc.

189 AGNUS DEI

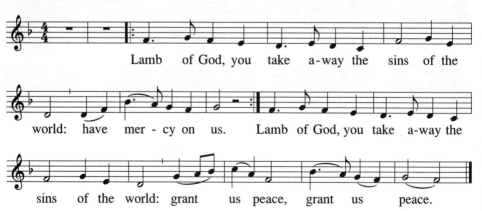

Lamb of God, you take a-way the sins of the

world: have mer-cy on us. Lamb of God, you take a-way the

sins of the world: grant us peace, grant us peace.

Music: Richard Proulx, © 1975, GIA Publications, Inc.

O Come, O Come, Emmanuel 190

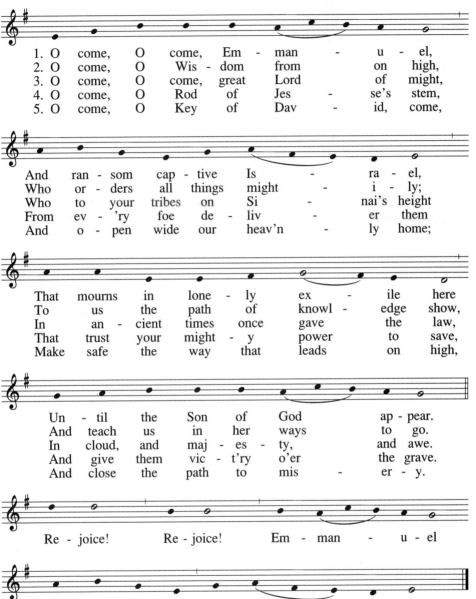

1. O come, O come, Emmanuel,
2. O come, O Wisdom from on high,
3. O come, O come, great Lord of might,
4. O come, O Rod of Jesse's stem,
5. O come, O Key of David, come,

And ransom captive Israel,
Who orders all things mightily;
Who to your tribes on Sinai's height
From ev'ry foe deliver them
And open wide our heav'nly home;

That mourns in lonely exile here
To us the path of knowledge show,
In ancient times once gave the law,
That trust your mighty power to save,
Make safe the way that leads on high,

Until the Son of God appear.
And teach us in her ways to go.
In cloud, and majesty, and awe.
And give them vic'try o'er the grave.
And close the path to misery.

Re - joice! Re - joice! Emmanuel

Shall come to you, O Israel.

6. O come, O Dayspring from on high
And cheer us by your drawing nigh;
Disperse the gloomy clouds of night,
And death's dark shadow put to flight.

7. O come, Desire of nations, bind
In one the hearts of humankind;
O bid our sad divisions cease,
And be for us our King of Peace.

Text: *Veni, veni Emmanuel;* Latin 9th C.; tr. by John M. Neale, 1818-1866, alt.
Tune: VENI VENI EMMANUEL, LM with refrain; Mode I; adapt. by Thomas Helmore, 1811-1890; acc. by Richard Proulx, b.1937, © 1975,
   GIA Publications, Inc.

191 People, Look East

1. Peo - ple, look East. The time is near
2. Fur - rows, be glad. Though earth is bare.
3. Birds, though you long have ceased to build,
4. Stars, keep the watch. When night is dim
5. An - gels an - nounce with shouts of mirth

Of the crown - ing of the year.
One more seed is plant - ed there:
Guard the nest that must be filled.
One more light the bowl shall brim,
Him who brings new life to earth.

Make your house fair as you are a - ble,
Give up your strength the seed to nour - ish,
E - ven the hour when wings are fro - zen
Shin - ing be - yond the frost - y weath - er,
Set ev - 'ry peak and val - ley hum - ming

Trim the hearth and set the ta - ble.
That in course the flow'r may flour - ish.
He for fledg - ing time has cho - sen.
Bright as sun and moon to - geth - er.
With the word, the Lord is com - ing.

Peo - ple look East and sing to - day:

Love the Guest is on the way.
Love the Rose is on the way.
Love the Bird is on the way.
Love the Star is on the way.
Love the Lord is on the way.

Text: Eleanor Farjeon, 1881-1965, © David Higham Assoc. Ltd.
Tune: BESANCON, 87 98 87; French Traditional; harm. by Martin Shaw, 1875-1958, © Oxford University Press

Like a Shepherd 192

Refrain

Like a shep-herd he feeds his flock and gath-ers the
lambs in his arms, hold-ing them care-ful-ly
close to his heart, lead-ing them home.

Verses 1, 2

1. Say to the cit-ies of Ju - dah: Pre-pare the
2. I my-self will shep-herd them, for oth-ers have

way of the Lord. Go to the moun-tain top,
led them a - stray. The lost I will res-cue and

D.C.

lift your voice; Je-ru-sa-lem, here is your God.
heal their wounds and pas-ture them, giv-ing them rest.

Verse 3

3. Come un-to me if you are

heav-i-ly bur-dened, and take my yoke up-

D.C.

on your shoul-ders, I will give you rest.

Text: Isaiah 40:9ff, Ezekiel 34:11, Matthew 11:28ff; Bob Dufford, SJ, b.1943
Tune: Bob Dufford, SJ, b.1943; acc. by Sr. Theophane Hytrek, OSF, 1915-1992, alt.
© 1976, Robert J. Dufford, SJ, and New Dawn Music

193 The King Shall Come When Morning Dawns

1. The King shall come when morn - ing dawns And
2. Not, as of old, a lit - tle child, To
3. The King shall come when morn - ing dawns And
4. And let the end - less bliss be - gin, By
5. The King shall come when morn - ing dawns And

light tri - um - phant breaks. When beau - ty gilds the
suf - fer and to die, But crowned with glo - ry
earth's dark night is past; O haste the ris - ing
wea - ry saints fore - told, When right shall tri - umph
light and beau - ty brings. Hail, Christ, the Lord! Your

east - ern hills And life to joy a - wakes.
like the sun That lights the morn - ing sky.
of that morn Whose day shall ev - er last.
o - ver wrong, And truth shall be ex - tolled.
peo - ple pray: Come quick - ly, King of kings.

Text: John Brownlie, 1857-1925
Tune: MORNING SONG, CM; John Wyeth, 1770-1858; arr. by Robert J. Batastini, b.1942, © 1994, GIA Publications, Inc.

194 On Jordan's Bank

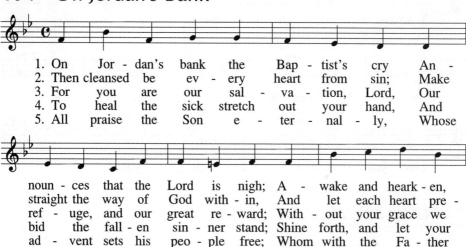

1. On Jor - dan's bank the Bap - tist's cry An -
2. Then cleansed be ev - ery heart from sin; Make
3. For you are our sal - va - tion, Lord, Our
4. To heal the sick stretch out your hand, And
5. All praise the Son e - ter - nal - ly, Whose

noun - ces that the Lord is nigh; A - wake and heark - en,
straight the way of God with - in, And let each heart pre -
ref - uge, and our great re - ward; With - out your grace we
bid the fall - en sin - ner stand; Shine forth, and let your
ad - vent sets his peo - ple free; Whom with the Fa - ther

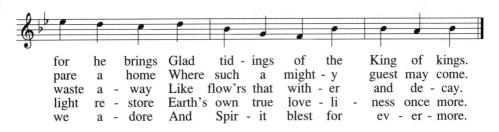

for	he	brings	Glad	tid - ings	of	the	King	of	kings.
pare	a	home	Where	such a	might - y		guest may come.		
waste	a - way		Like	flow'rs that	with - er		and	de - cay.	
light	re - store		Earth's	own true	love - li -	ness once more.			
we	a - dore		And	Spir - it	blest for		ev - er - more.		

Text: *Jordanis oras praevia;* Charles Coffin, 1676-1749; tr. by John Chandler, 1806-1876
Tune: WINCHESTER NEW, LM; adapt. from *Musikalisches Handbuch,* Hamburg, 1690

Creator of the Stars of Night 195

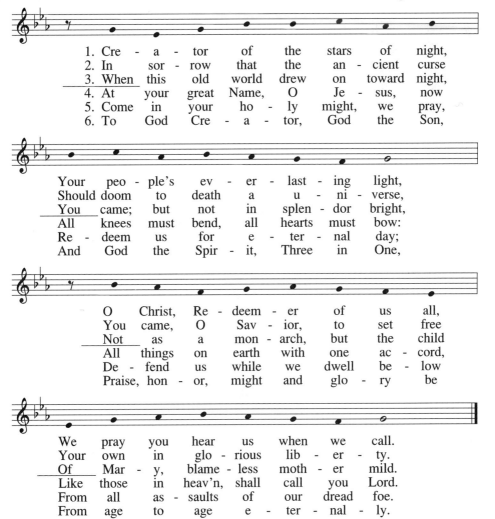

1. Cre - a - tor of the stars of night,
2. In sor - row that the an - cient curse
3. When this old world drew on toward night,
4. At your great Name, O Je - sus, now
5. Come in your ho - ly might, we pray,
6. To God Cre - a - tor, God the Son,

Your peo - ple's ev - er - last - ing light,
Should doom to death a u - ni - verse,
You came; but not in splen - dor bright,
All knees must bend, all hearts must bow:
Re - deem us for e - ter - nal day;
And God the Spir - it, Three in One,

O Christ, Re - deem - er of us all,
You came, O Sav - ior, to set free
Not as a mon - arch, but the child
All things on earth with one ac - cord,
De - fend us while we dwell be - low
Praise, hon - or, might and glo - ry be

We pray you hear us when we call.
Your own in glo - rious lib - er - ty.
Of Mar - y, blame - less moth - er mild.
Like those in heav'n, shall call you Lord.
From all as - saults of our dread foe.
From age to age e - ter - nal - ly.

Text: *Conditor alme siderum,* Latin 9th. C.; tr. *The Hymnal 1982,* © 1985, The Church Pension Fund
Tune: CONDITOR ALME SIDERUM, LM; Mode IV; acc. by Gerard Farrell, OSB, b. 1919, © 1986, GIA Publications, Inc.

196 O Come, Divine Messiah

1. O come, Di-vine Mes-si-ah, The world in si-lence
2. O come De-sired of na-tions, Whom priest and proph-et
3. O come in peace and meek-ness, For low-ly will your

waits the day When hope shall sing its tri-umph, And
long fore-told, Will break the cap-tive fet-ters, Re-
cra-dle be: Though clothed in hu-man weak-ness We

sad-ness flee a-way.
deem the long-lost fold. Dear Sav-ior,
shall your God-head see.

haste! Come, come to earth. Dis-pel the

night and show your face, And bid us hail the dawn of

grace. O come, Di-vine Mes-si-ah, The

world in si-lence waits the day When hope shall sing its

tri-umph, And sad-ness flee a-way.

Text: *Venez, divin Messie;* Abbé Simon-Joseph Pellegrin, 1663-1745; tr. by S. Mary of St. Philip, 1877
Tune: VENEZ, DIVIN MESSIE, 7 8 7 6 with refrain; French Noël, 16th C.; harm. by Healey Willan, 1880-1968, © 1958, The Basilian Fathers, assigned to Ralph Jusko Publications, Inc.

My Soul in Stillness Waits 197

Refrain

For you, O Lord, my soul in still - ness waits, tru - ly my hope is in you.

Verses

1. O Lord of Light, our on - ly hope of
2. O Spring of Joy, rain down up - on our
3. O Root of Life, im - plant your seed with -
4. O Key of Knowl - edge, guide us in our
5. Come, let us bow be - fore the God who
6. Here we shall meet the Mak - er of the

glo - ry, your ra - diance shines in all who look to
spir - its, our thirst - y hearts are yearn - ing for your
in us, and in your ad - vent, draw us all to
pil - grim-age, we ev - er seek, yet un - ful - filled re -
made us, let ev - 'ry heart be o - pened to the
heav - ens, Cre - a - tor of the moun-tains and the

you, come, light the hearts of all in dark and
Word, come, make us whole, be com - fort to our
you, our hope re - born in dy - ing and in
main, o - pen to us the path-way of your
Lord, for we are all the peo - ple of his
seas, Lord of the stars, and pres - ent to us

D.C.

shad - ow.
hearts.
ris - ing.
peace.
hand.
now.

Text: Psalm 95 and "O" Antiphons; Marty Haugen, b.1950
Tune: Marty Haugen, b.1950
© 1982, GIA Publications, Inc.

198 Come, O Long Expected Jesus

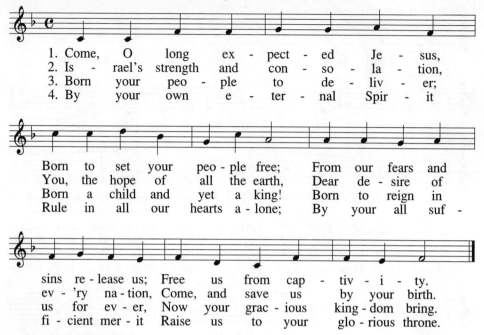

1. Come, O long ex - pect - ed Je - sus,
2. Is - rael's strength and con - so - la - tion,
3. Born your peo - ple to de - liv - er;
4. By your own e - ter - nal Spir - it

Born to set your peo - ple free; From our fears and
You, the hope of all the earth, Dear de - sire of
Born a child and yet a king! Born to reign in
Rule in all our hearts a - lone; By your all suf -

sins re - lease us; Free us from cap - tiv - i - ty.
ev - 'ry na - tion, Come, and save us by your birth.
us for ev - er, Now your grac - ious king - dom bring.
fi - cient mer - it Raise us to your glo - rious throne.

Text: Haggai 2:7; Charles Wesley, 1707-1788, alt.
Tune: STUTTGART, 8 7 8 7; Christian F. Witt, 1660-1716; adapt. by Henry J. Gauntlett, 1805-1876

199 Wait for the Lord

Wait for the Lord, whose day is near.

Wait for the Lord: be strong, take heart!

Text: Isaiah 40, Philippians 4, Matthew 6-7; Taizé Community, 1984
Tune: Jacques Berthier, 1923-1994

Savior of the Nations, Come   200

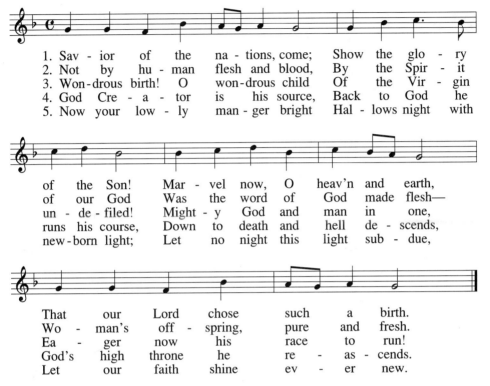

1. Sav - ior of the na - tions, come; Show the glo - ry
2. Not by hu - man flesh and blood, By the Spir - it
3. Won-drous birth! O won-drous child Of the Vir - gin
4. God Cre - a - tor is his source, Back to God he
5. Now your low - ly man - ger bright Hal - lows night with

of the Son! Mar - vel now, O heav'n and earth,
of our God Was the word of God made flesh—
un - de - filed! Might - y God and man in one,
runs his course, Down to death and hell de - scends,
new - born light; Let no night this light sub - due,

That our Lord chose such a birth.
Wo - man's off - spring, pure and fresh.
Ea - ger now his race to run!
God's high throne he re - as - cends.
Let our faith shine ev - er new.

Text: *Veni, Redemptor gentium;* ascr. to St. Ambrose, 340-397; tr. sts. 1-3a, William Reynolds, 1812-1876; sts. 3b-5, Martin L. Seltz, 1909-1967, alt.
Tune: NUN KOMM DER HEIDEN HEILAND, 77 77; *Geystliche gesangk Buchleyn,* Wittenberg, 1524

Gloria, Gloria   201

Canon—*4 voices*

Glo - ri - a,   glo - ri - a,   in ex - cel - sis De - o!

Glo - ri - a,   glo - ri - a,   al - le - lu - ia,   al - le - lu - ia!

Tune: Jacques Berthier, © 1979, 1988, Les Presses de Taizé, GIA Publications, Inc., agent

202 O Come, All Ye Faithful / Adeste Fideles

1. O come, all ye faith-ful, joy-ful and tri-um-phant, O
2. God of God, Light of Light,
3. Sing, choirs of an-gels, sing in ex-ul-ta-tion,
4. Yea, Lord, we greet thee, born this hap-py morn-ing,
1. *Ad - é - ste fi - dé - les, laé - ti, tri-um-phán - tes, Ve -*
2. *De - um de De - o, Lu - men de Lú – mi - ne*
3. *Can - tet nunc i - o, cho - rus an - ge - lo - rum,*
4. *Er - go qui na - tus Di - e ho - di - ér - na,*

come ye, O come ye to Beth - le - hem;
Lo! He comes forth from the Vir - gin's womb.
Sing, all ye cit-i-zens of heav'n a - bove!
Je - sus, to thee be all glo - ry giv'n;
ní - te, ve - ní - te in Béth - le - hem.
Ge - stant pu - él - lae ví - sce - ra.
Can - tet nunc au - la cae - lés - ti - um.
Je - su___ ti - bi sit gló - ri - a.

Come and be - hold him, born the King of an - gels;
Our ver - y God, be - got - ten not cre - a - ted,
Glo - ry to God, all glo - ry in the high - est;
Word of the Fa - ther, now in flesh ap - pear - ing;
Na - tum vi - dé - te, Re - gem an - ge - ló - rum.
De - um ve - rum, Gé - ni - tum, non fa - ctum.
Gló - ri - a, gló - ria, in ex - cél - sis De - o.
Pa - tris ae - ter - nae ver - bum ca - ro fa - ctum.

O come, let us a - dore him, O come, let us a - dore him,
Ve - ní - te a - do - ré - mus, ve - ní - te a - do - ré - mus,

O come, let us a - dore him, Christ, the Lord!
ve - ní - te a - do - ré - mus Dó - mi - num.

Text: *Adeste fideles;* John F. Wade, c.1711-1786; tr. by Frederick Oakeley, 1802-1880, alt.
Tune: ADESTE FIDELES, Irregular with refrain; John F. Wade, c.1711-1786

Joy to the World   203

1. Joy to the world! the Lord is come: Let
2. Joy to the world! the Sav - ior reigns: Let
3. No more let sin and sor - rows grow, Nor
4. He rules the world with truth and grace, And

earth re - ceive her King; Let ev - 'ry
us, our songs em - ploy; While fields and
thorns in - fest the ground; He comes to
makes the na - tions prove The glo - ries

heart pre - pare him room, And
floods, rocks, hills and plains Re -
make his bless - ings flow Far
of his right - eous - ness, And

heav'n and na - ture sing, And heav'n and na - ture
peat the sound - ing joy, Re - peat the sound - ing
as the curse is found, Far as the curse is
won - ders of his love, And won - ders of his

sing, And heav'n, and heav'n and na - ture sing.
joy, Re - peat, re - peat the sound-ing joy.
found, Far as, far as the curse is found.
love, And won - ders, won - ders of his love.

Text: Psalm 98; Isaac Watts, 1674-1748
Tune: ANTIOCH, CM; arr. from George F. Handel, 1685-1759, in T. Hawkes' *Collection of Tunes,* 1833

204 Silent Night, Holy Night

1. Si - lent night, ho - ly night, All is calm,
2. Si - lent night, ho - ly night, Shep - herds quake
3. Si - lent night, ho - ly night, Son of God,

all is bright Round yon Vir - gin Moth - er and Child,
at the sight; Glo - ries stream from heav - en a - far,
love's pure light Ra - diant beams from thy ho - ly face,

Ho - ly In - fant so ten - der and mild, Sleep in heav - en - ly
Heav'n - ly hosts sing al - le - lu - ia; Christ, the Sav - ior, is
With the dawn of re - deem - ing grace, Je - sus, Lord, at thy

peace, Sleep in heav - en - ly peace.
born! Christ, the Sav - ior, is born!
birth, Je - sus, Lord, at thy birth.

Text: *Stille Nacht, heilige Nacht;* Joseph Mohr, 1792-1849; tr. John F. Young, 1820-1885
Tune: STILLE NACHT, 66 89 66; Franz X. Gruber, 1787-1863

205 Night of Silence

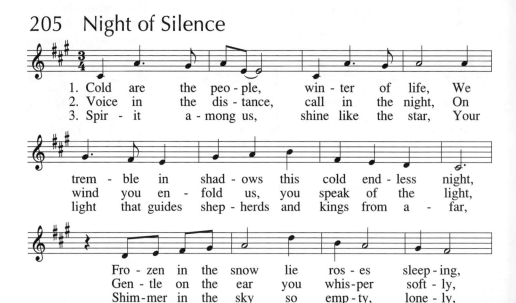

1. Cold are the peo - ple, win - ter of life, We
2. Voice in the dis - tance, call in the night, On
3. Spir - it a - mong us, shine like the star, Your

trem - ble in shad - ows this cold end - less night,
wind you en - fold us, you speak of the light,
light that guides shep - herds and kings from a - far,

Fro - zen in the snow lie ros - es sleep - ing,
Gen - tle on the ear you whis - per soft - ly,
Shim - mer in the sky so emp - ty, lone - ly,

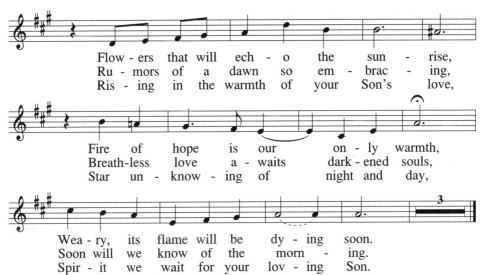

Flow - ers that will ech - o the sun - rise,
Ru - mors of a dawn so em - brac - ing,
Ris - ing in the warmth of your Son's love,

Fire of hope is our on - ly warmth,
Breath-less love a - waits dark - ened souls,
Star un - know - ing of night and day,

Wea - ry, its flame will be dy - ing soon.
Soon will we know of the morn - ing.
Spir - it we wait for your lov - ing Son.

Text: Daniel Kantor, b.1960
Tune: Daniel Kantor, b.1960
© 1984, GIA Publications, Inc.

Away in a Manger 206

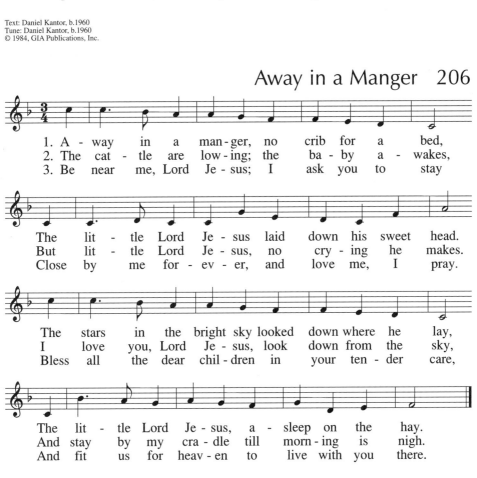

1. A - way in a man-ger, no crib for a bed,
2. The cat - tle are low-ing; the ba - by a - wakes,
3. Be near me, Lord Je - sus; I ask you to stay

The lit - tle Lord Je - sus laid down his sweet head.
But lit - tle Lord Je - sus, no cry - ing he makes.
Close by me for - ev - er, and love me, I pray.

The stars in the bright sky looked down where he lay,
I love you, Lord Je - sus, look down from the sky,
Bless all the dear chil - dren in your ten - der care,

The lit - tle Lord Je - sus, a - sleep on the hay.
And stay by my cra - dle till morn - ing is nigh.
And fit us for heav - en to live with you there.

Text: St. 1-2, anonymous, st. 3, John T. McFarland, 1851-1913
Tune: MUELLER, 11 11 11 11; James R. Murray, 1841-1905; harm. by Robert J. Batastini, b. 1942, © 1994, GIA Publications, Inc.

207 Awake! Awake, and Greet the New Morn

1. A - wake! a - wake, and greet the new morn, For
2. To us, to all in sor - row and fear, Em -
3. In dark - est night his com - ing shall be, When
4. Re - joice, re - joice, take heart in the night, Though

an - gels her - ald its dawn - ing, Sing out your joy, for
man - u - el comes a - sing - ing, His hum - ble song is
all the world is de - spair - ing, As morn - ing light so
dark the win - ter and cheer - less, The ris - ing sun shall

now he is born, Be - hold! the Child of our long - ing.
qui - et and near, Yet fills the earth with its ring - ing;
qui - et and free, So warm and gen - tle and car - ing.
crown you with light, Be strong and lov - ing and fear - less;

Come as a ba - by weak and poor, To bring all hearts to -
Mu - sic to heal the bro - ken soul And hymns of lov - ing
Then shall the mute break forth in song, The lame shall leap in
Love be our song and love our prayer, And love, our end - less

geth - er, He o - pens wide the heav'n - ly door And
kind - ness, The thun - der of his an - thems roll To
won - der, The weak be raised a - bove the strong, And
sto - ry, May God fill ev - 'ry day we share, And

lives now in - side us for ev - er.
shat - ter all ha - tred and blind - ness.
weap - ons be bro - ken a - sun - der.
bring us at last in - to glo - ry.

Text: Marty Haugen, b.1950
Tune: REJOICE, REJOICE, 9 8 9 8 8 7 8 9; Marty Haugen, b.1950
© 1983, GIA Publications, Inc.

Angels We Have Heard on High   208

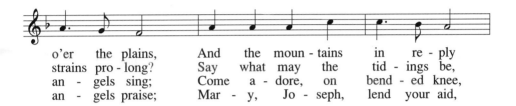

1. An - gels   we   have   heard   on high   Sweet - ly   sing - ing
2. Shep-herds,   why   this   ju - bi - lee?   Why   your   joy - ous
3. Come   to   Beth - le - hem   and see   Him   whose   birth   the
4. See   him   in   a   man - ger laid,   Whom the   choirs   of

o'er   the   plains,   And   the   moun - tains   in   re - ply
strains pro - long?   Say   what   may   the   tid - ings   be,
an - gels sing;   Come   a - dore,   on   bend - ed   knee,
an - gels praise;   Mar - y,   Jo - seph,   lend   your   aid,

Ech - o   back   their   joy - ous   strains.
Which   in - spire   your   heav'n - ly   song.
Christ,   the   Lord,   the   new - born   King.
While   our   hearts   in   love   we   raise.

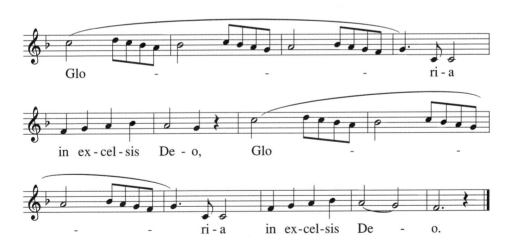

Glo   -   -   -   ri - a

in ex - cel - sis De - o,   Glo   -   -

-    -   ri - a   in ex - cel - sis De   -   o.

Text: *Les anges dans nos campagnes;* French, c. 18th C.; tr. from *Crown of Jesus Music,* London, 1862
Tune: GLORIA, 7 7 7 7 with refrain; French traditional

209 Hark! The Herald Angels Sing

1. Hark! the her - ald an - gels sing, "Glo - ry to the
2. Christ, by high - est heaven a - dored, Christ the ev - er -
3. Hail the heav'n - born Prince of Peace! Hail the Sun of

new - born King; Peace on earth, and mer - cy mild
last - ing Lord: Late in time be - hold him come,
Right - eous - ness! Light and life to all he brings,

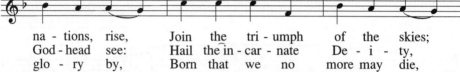

God and sin - ners rec - on - ciled!" Joy - ful, all you
Off - spring of the Vir - gin's womb. Veiled in flesh the
Ris'n with heal - ing in his wings. Mild he lays his

na - tions, rise, Join the tri - umph of the skies;
God - head see: Hail the in - car - nate De - i - ty,
glo - ry by, Born that we no more may die,

With the an - gel - ic host pro - claim, "Christ is born in Beth - le - hem!"
Pleased as man with us to dwell, Je - sus, our Em - man - u - el.
Born to raise us from the earth, Born to give us sec - ond birth.

Hark! the her - ald an - gels sing, "Glo - ry to the new - born King!"

Text: Charles Wesley, 1707-1788, alt.
Tune: MENDELSSOHN, 77 77 D with refrain; Felix Mendelssohn, 1809-1847

O Little Town of Bethlehem 210

1. O lit - tle town of Beth - le - hem, How
2. For Christ is born of Mar - y, And
3. How si - lent - ly, how si - lent - ly, The
4. O ho - ly Child of Beth - le - hem! De -

still we see thee lie! A - bove thy deep and
gath - ered all a - bove, While mor - tals sleep, the
won - drous gift is giv'n! So God im - parts to
scend to us we pray; Cast out our sin and

dream - less sleep The si - lent stars go by;
an - gels keep Their watch of won - d'ring love.
hu - man hearts The bless - ings of his heav'n.
en - ter in, Be born in us to - day.

Yet in the dark streets shin - eth The ev - er -
O morn - ing stars, to - geth - er Pro - claim the
No ear may hear his com - ing, But in this
We hear the Christ - mas an - gels The great glad

last - ing Light; The hopes and fears of
ho - ly birth! And prais - es sing to
world of sin, Where meek souls will re -
tid - ings tell; O come to us, a -

all the years Are met in thee to - night.
God the King, And peace to all on earth.
ceive him, still The dear Christ en - ters in.
bide with us, Our Lord Em - man - u - el!

Text: Phillips Brooks, 1835-1893
Tune: ST. LOUIS, 8 6 8 6 7 6 8 6; Lewis H. Redner, 1831-1908

211 Of the Father's Love Begotten

1. Of the Fa - ther's love be - got - ten,
2. O that birth for ev - er bless - ed,
3. Let the heights of heav'n a - dore him;
4. Christ, to you with God the Fa - ther,

Ere the worlds be - gan to be,
When the Vir - gin, full of grace,
An - gel hosts, his prais - es sing;
Spir - it blest e - ter - nal - ly,

He is Al - pha and O - me - ga,
By the Spir - it blest con - ceiv - ing,
Pow'rs, do - min - ions, bow be - fore him,
Hymn and chant and high thanks - giv - ing,

He the source, the end - ing he,
Bore the Sav - ior of our race;
And ex - tol our God and King;
And un - end - ing prais - es be:

Of the things that are, that have been,
And the Babe, the world's Re - deem - er,
Let no tongue on earth be si - lent,
Hon - or, glo - ry, and do - min - ion,

And that fu - ture years shall see,
First re - vealed his sa - cred face,
Ev - 'ry voice in con - cert ring,
And e - ter - nal vic - to - ry,

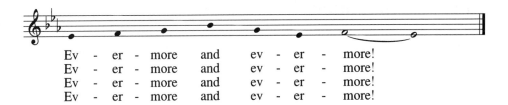

Ev - er - more and ev - er - more!
Ev - er - more and ev - er - more!
Ev - er - more and ev - er - more!
Ev - er - more and ev - er - more!

Text: *Corde natus ex Parentis;* Aurelius Prudentius, 348-413; tr. by John M. Neale, 1818-1866 and Henry W. Baker, 1821-1877
Tune: DIVINUM MYSTERIUM, 8 7 8 7 8 7 7; 12th C.; Mode V; acc. by Richard Proulx, b. 1937, © 1985, GIA Publications, Inc.

He Came Down 212

He came down that we may have *love; He
came down that we may have love; He came down that we may
have love, Hal-le-lu-jah for ev-er-more.

Cantor: Why did he come?

Substitute peace, joy, hope, life, etc.

Text: Cameroon traditional
Tune: Cameroon traditional; transcribed and arr. by John L. Bell, b.1949, © 1990, Iona Community, GIA Publications, Inc., agent

213 It Came upon the Midnight Clear

1. It came up - on the mid - night clear, That
2. Still through the clo - ven skies they come, With
3. Yet with the woes of sin and strife, The
4. For, lo, the days are has - tening on, By

glo - rious song of old, From an - gels bend - ing
peace - ful wings un - furled, And still their heav'n - ly
world has suf - fered long; Be - neath the heav'n - ly
proph - ets seen of old, When with the ev - er -

near the earth To touch their harps of gold: "Peace
mu - sic floats O'er all the wea - ry world: A -
hymn have rolled Two thou - sand years of wrong; And
cir - cling years Shall come the time fore - told, When

on the earth, good will to all From
bove its sad and low - ly plains They
war - ring hu - man - kind hears not The
peace shall o - ver all the earth Its

heaven's all gra - cious King"; The world in sol - emn
bend on hov - 'ring wing, And ev - er o'er its
tid - ings which they bring; O hush the noise and
an - cient splen - dors fling, And all the world give

still - ness lay, To hear the an - gels sing.
Ba - bel sounds The bless - ed an - gels sing.
cease your strife And hear the an - gels sing.
back the song Which now the an - gels sing.

Text: Edmund H. Sears, 1810-1876, alt.
Tune: CAROL, CMD; Richard S. Willis, 1819-1900

Rise Up, Shepherd, and Follow 214

Verses

Leader:

1. There's a star in the East on Christ-mas morn,
2. If you take good heed to the an - gel's words,

All:

Rise up, shep - herd, and fol - low, It will
Rise up, shep - herd, and fol - low, You'll for -

Leader:

lead to the place where the Christ was born,
get your flocks, you'll for - get your herds,

All:

Rise up, shep - herd, and fol - low.
Rise up, shep - herd, and fol - low.

Refrain

Fol - low, fol - low, Rise up, shep-herd, and

fol - low, Fol - low the Star of Beth - le - hem,

Rise up, shep-herd, and fol - low.

Text: Traditional
Tune: African-American spiritual

215 Good Christian Friends, Rejoice

1. Good Christian friends, re-joice With heart and soul and voice; O give heed to what we say: Jesus Christ is born to-day! Ox and ass before him bow, And he is in the manger now. Christ is born to-day! Christ is born to-day!

2. Good Christian friends, re-joice With heart and soul and voice; Now you hear of end-less bliss: Jesus Christ was born for this! He has o-pened heaven's door, And we are blest for ev-er-more. Christ was born for this! Christ was born for this!

3. Good Christian friends, re-joice With heart and soul and voice; Now you need not fear the grave: Jesus Christ was born to save! Calls you one and all To gain his ev-er-last-ing hall. Christ was born to save! Christ was born to save!

1. *Good Christian friends, re-joice With heart and soul and voice! Raise your wea-ry hearts and see: Jesus Christ has come to free! When the cap-tives find re-lease, In feet that bring the word of peace, Christ has come to free! Christ has come to free!*

2. *Good Christian friends, re-joice With heart and soul and voice! In the kind and just and true Jesus Christ is born a-new! In the low-ly, weak and poor, The hum-ble stran-ger at our door, Christ is born a-new! Christ is born a-new!*

3. *Good Christian friends, re-joice With heart and soul and voice! Still be-fore us on the way, Jesus Christ is here to-day! In the break-ing of the bread, In life that cries out to the dead, Christ is born to-day! Christ is born to-day!*

Text: *In dulci jubilo;* Latin and German, 14th C.; tr. by John M. Neale, 1818-1866; alt. verses, Marty Haugen, b.1950, © 1992, GIA Publications, Inc.
Tune: IN DULCI JUBILO; 66 77 78 55; Klug's *Geistliche Lieder,* Wittenberg, 1535; harm. by Robert L. Pearsall, 1795-1856

God Rest You Merry, Gentlemen 216

1. God   rest you mer - ry, gen - tle-men, Let noth-ing you dis - may,
2. In   Beth - le - hem in   Ju - dah This bless-ed babe was born,
3. From   God   our great Cre - a - tor A   bless-ed an - gel came,
4. The   shep-herds at those   tid - ings Re - joic-ed much in mind,
5. Now   to   the Lord sing   prais - es, All you with - in this place,

For   Je - sus Christ our Sav - ior Was   born up - on   this day,
And   laid with - in   a   man - ger Up - on   this bless - ed morn:
And   un - to   cer - tain shep - herds Brought tid - ings   of   the same,
And   left their flocks a - feed - ing In   tem - pest, storm, and wind,
And   with true love and char-i - ty Each   oth - er   now em -brace;

To   save us   all from Sa - tan's power When we were gone a - stray.
For   which his moth - er   Mar - y Did   noth-ing take in scorn.
How   that in   Beth - le - hem was born The Son of   God by name.
And   went to   Beth - le - hem straight-way, The bless - ed babe to find.
This ho - ly tide of   Christ - mas All   oth - ers shall re - place.

O   tid - ings of   com - fort and   joy,   com - fort and

joy;   O   tid - ings of   com - fort and   joy!

Text: English carol, 18th C.
Tune: GOD REST YOU MERRY, 8 6 8 6 8 6 with refrain; English 18th C.; harm. by John Stainer, 1840-1901

217 Lo, How a Rose E'er Blooming

1. Lo, how a Rose e'er bloom-ing From
2. I - sa - iah 'twas for - told it, The
3. O Flower, whose fra-grance ten - der With

ten - der stem hath sprung! Of Jes - se's lin - eage
Rose I have in mind, With Mar - y we be -
sweet-ness fills the air, Dis - pel in glo - rious

com - ing As seers of old have sung. It
hold it, The Vir - gin Moth - er kind. To
splen - dor The dark-ness ev - 'ry - where; True

came, a blos - som bright, A - mid the cold of
show God's love a - right, She bore to us a
man, yet ver - y God, From sin and death now

win - ter, When half spent was the night.
Sav - ior, When half spent was the night.
save us, And share our ev - 'ry load.

Text: Isaiah 11:1; *Es ist ein' Ros' entsprungen; Speier Gesangbuch,* 1599; tr. sts. 1-2 by Theodore Baker, 1851-1934; st. 3, *The Hymnal, 1940*
Tune: ES IST EIN' ROS' ENTSPRUNGEN, 7 6 7 6 6 7 6; *Geistliche Kirchengesang,* Cologne, 1599; harm. by Michael Praetorius, 1571-1621

218 Infant Holy, Infant Lowly

1. In - fant ho - ly, In - fant low - ly, For his bed a
2. Flocks were sleep - ing: Shep-herds keep - ing Vi - gil till the

cat - tle stall; Ox - en low - ing, Lit - tle know - ing
morn-ing new. Saw the glo - ry, Heard the sto - ry,

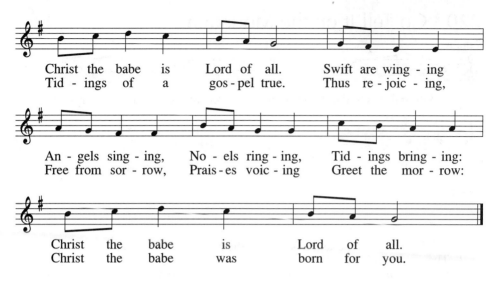

Christ the babe is Lord of all. Swift are wing - ing
Tid - ings of a gos - pel true. Thus re - joic - ing,

An - gels sing - ing, No - els ring - ing, Tid - ings bring - ing:
Free from sor - row, Prais - es voic - ing Greet the mor - row:

Christ the babe is Lord of all.
Christ the babe was born for you.

Text: Polish carol; para. by Edith M.G. Reed, 1885-1933
Tune: W ZLOBIE LEZY, 44 7 44 7 4444 7; Polish carol; harm. by A.E. Rusbridge, 1917-1969, © Horfield Baptist Housing Assoc. Ltd.

Angels, from the Realms of Glory   219

1. An - gels, from the realms of glo - ry, Wing your flight o'er
2. Shep - herds, in the fields a - bid - ing, Watch-ing o'er your
3. Sag - es, leave your con - tem - pla - tions, Bright - er vi - sions
4. Though an in - fant now we view him, He shall fill his

all the earth; You who sang cre - a - tion's sto - ry,
flocks by night, God on earth is now re - sid - ing,
beam a - far; Seek the great De - sire of na - tions,
heav'n - ly throne, Gath - er all the na - tions to him;

Now pro - claim Mes - si - ah's birth:
Yon - der shines the in - fant light: Come   and wor-ship,
You have seen his morn - ing star:
Ev - 'ry knee shall then bow down:

come and wor - ship, Wor - ship Christ, the new-born King.

Text: Sts. 1-3, James Montgomery, 1771-1854; st. 4, *Christmas Box,* 1825
Tune: REGENT SQUARE, 8 7 8 7 8 7; Henry Smart, 1813-1879

220 Go Tell It on the Mountain

Refrain

Go tell it on the moun-tain, O-ver the hills and ev-'ry-where;

Go tell it on the moun - tain That Je - sus Christ is born!

Verses

1. While shep - herds kept their watch - ing O'er
2. The shep - herds feared and trem - bled When
3. Down in a low - ly man - ger The

si - lent flocks by night, Be - hold through-out the
lo! a - bove the earth Rang out the an - gel
hum - ble Christ was born, And God sent us sal -

D.C.

heav - ens There shone a ho - ly light.
cho - rus That hailed our Sav - ior's birth.
va - tion That bless - ed Christ - mas morn.

Text: African-American spiritual; adapt. by John W. Work, Jr., 1871-1925, © Mrs. John W. Work, III
Tune: GO TELL IT ON THE MOUNTAIN, 7 6 7 6 with refrain; African-American spiritual; harm. by Robert J. Batastini, b.1942, © 1995, GIA
    Publications, Inc.

221 What Child Is This

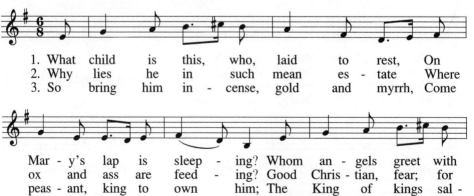

1. What child is this, who, laid to rest, On
2. Why lies he in such mean es - tate Where
3. So bring him in - cense, gold and myrrh, Come

Mar - y's lap is sleep - ing? Whom an - gels greet with
ox and ass are feed - ing? Good Chris - tian, fear; for
peas - ant, king to own him; The King of kings sal -

an - thems sweet, While shep - herds watch are keep - ing?
sin - ners here The si - lent Word is plead - ing.
va - tion brings, Let lov - ing hearts en - throne him.

This, this is Christ the King, Whom shep-herds guard and an-gels sing;

Haste, haste to bring him laud, The babe, the son of Mar - y.

Text: William C. Dix, 1827-1898
Tune: GREENSLEEVES, 8 7 8 7 with refrain; English melody, 16th C.; harm. by John Stainer, 1840-1901

What Star Is This 222

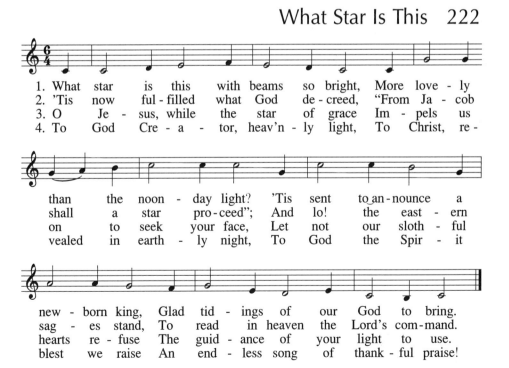

1. What star is this with beams so bright, More love - ly
2. 'Tis now ful - filled what God de - creed, "From Ja - cob
3. O Je - sus, while the star of grace Im - pels us
4. To God Cre - a - tor, heav'n - ly light, To Christ, re -

than the noon - day light? 'Tis sent to an - nounce a
shall a star pro - ceed"; And lo! the east - ern
on to seek your face, Let not our sloth - ful
vealed in earth - ly night, To God the Spir - it

new - born king, Glad tid - ings of our God to bring.
sag - es stand, To read in heaven the Lord's com - mand.
hearts re - fuse The guid - ance of your light to use.
blest we raise An end - less song of thank - ful praise!

Text: *Quem stella sole pulchrior*, Charles Coffin, 1676-1749; tr. by John Chandler, 1806-1876, alt.
Tune: PUER NOBIS, LM; adapt. by Michael Praetorius, 1571-1621

223　The First Nowell

1. The first Now - ell, the an - gel did say, Was to
2. They look - ed up and saw a star Shin-ing
3. And by the light of that same star Three
4. This star drew nigh to the north - west, O'er
5. Then en - tered in those wise men three, Full
6. Then let us all with one ac - cord Sing

cer - tain poor shep-herds in fields as they lay; In
in the east, be - yond them far, And
wise men came from coun - try far; To
Beth - le - hem it took its rest; And
rev - 'rent - ly up - on their knee, And
prais - es to our heav - 'nly Lord; Who

fields where they lay keep-ing their sheep, On a
to the earth it gave great light, And
seek for a king was their in - tent, And to
there it did both stop and stay, Right
of - fered there, in his pres - ence, Their
with the Fa - ther we a - dore And

cold win - ter's night that was so deep.
so it con - tin - ued both day and night.
fol - low the star where - ev - er it went.
o - ver the place where Je - sus lay.
gold and myrrh and frank - in - cense.
Spir - it blest for ev - er - more.

Now - ell, Now - ell, Now - ell, Now - ell,

Born is the King of Is - ra - el.

Text: English Carol, 17th C.
Tune: THE FIRST NOWELL, Irregular; English Melody; harm. from *Christmas Carols New and Old,* 1871

We Three Kings of Orient Are 224

1. We three kings of O - ri - ent are, Bear - ing
2. Born a babe on Beth - le - hem's plain, Gold we
3. Frank - in - cense to of - fer have I; In - cense
4. Myrrh is mine: its bit - ter per - fume Breathes a
5. Glo - rious now be - hold him rise, King and

gifts we trav - erse a - far Field and foun - tain,
bring to crown him a - gain; King for - ev - er,
owns a De - i - ty nigh, Prayer and prais - ing
life of gath - 'ring gloom; Sor - rowing, sigh - ing,
God and sac - ri - fice: Heav'n sings, "Hal - le -

Moor and moun - tain, Fol - low - ing yon - der star.
Ceas - ing nev - er, O - ver us all to reign.
Glad - ly rais - ing, Wor - ship - ing God on high.
Bleed - ing, dy - ing, Sealed in the stone cold tomb.
lu - jah!" "Hal - le - lu - jah!" earth re - plies.

O star of won - der, star of night, Star with

roy - al beau - ty bright, West - ward lead - ing, still pro -

ceed - ing, Guide us to the per - fect Light.

Text: Matthew 2:1-11; John H. Hopkins, Jr., 1820-1891
Tune: KINGS OF ORIENT, 88 44 6 with refrain; John H. Hopkins, Jr., 1820-1891

225 As with Gladness Men of Old

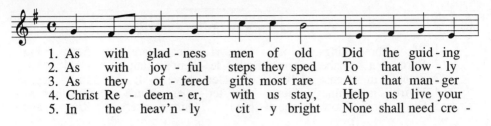

1. As with glad - ness men of old Did the guid - ing
2. As with joy - ful steps they sped To that low - ly
3. As they of - fered gifts most rare At that man - ger
4. Christ Re - deem - er, with us stay, Help us live your
5. In the heav'n - ly cit - y bright None shall need cre -

star be - hold; As with joy they hailed its light,
man - ger - bed, There to bend the knee be - fore
crude and bare; So may we this ho - ly day,
ho - ly way; And when earth - ly things are past,
a - ted light; You, its light, its joy, its crown,

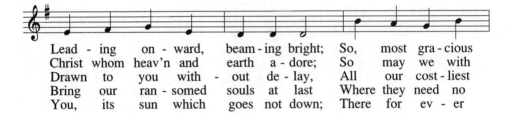

Lead - ing on - ward, beam - ing bright; So, most gra - cious
Christ whom heav'n and earth a - dore; So may we with
Drawn to you with - out de - lay, All our cost - liest
Bring our ran - somed souls at last Where they need no
You, its sun which goes not down; There for ev - er

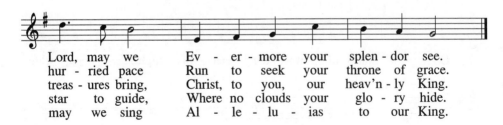

Lord, may we Ev - er - more your splen - dor see.
hur - ried pace Run to seek your throne of grace.
treas - ures bring, Christ, to you, our heav'n - ly King.
star to guide, Where no clouds your glo - ry hide.
may we sing Al - le - lu - ias to our King.

Text: William C. Dix, 1837-1898
Tune: DIX, 77 77 77; arr. from Conrad Kocher, 1786-1872, by William H. Monk, 1823-1889

Lord, Today 226

Refrain

Lord, to - day we have seen your glo - ry, dawn fol - lows the night. We, your peo - ple who walked in dark - ness now have seen a great light.

Verses

1. A child is born, a Son giv - en us, on him do - min - ion shall rest. His name shall be Won - der - ful God,
2. The Lord is king, the na - tions re - joice, let all God's peo - ple be glad. The heav - ens pro - claim jus - tice for all.
3. O Beth - le - hem, you are from of old, too small a - mong Ju - dah's clans. From you shall come a rul - er this day,
4. The days will come, the Lord prom - ised us, when God would raise up a shoot to rule the land, reign as a king,
5. New light has dawned up - on all the just, glad - ness for up - right of heart. Re - joice in the Lord, you faith - ful ones.

Coun - sel - or, Prince of Peace.
Glo - ry has filled the land.
shep - herd to guide the land.
whose name is Lord the Just.
Give thanks to God's great name.

D.C.

Text: Mike Balhoff, b.1946
Tune: Darryl Ducote, b.1945, Gary Daigle, b.1957
© 1978, Damean Music. Distributed by GIA Publications, Inc.

227 Songs of Thankfulness and Praise

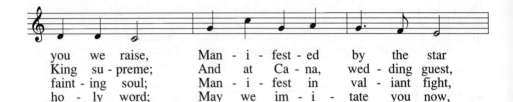

1. Songs of thank - ful - ness and praise, Je - sus, Lord, to
2. Man - i - fest at Jor - dan's stream, Proph - et, Priest, and
3. Man - i - fest in mak - ing whole Pal - sied limbs and
4. Grant us grace to see you, Lord, Mir - rored in your

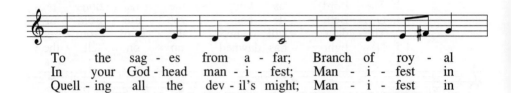

you we raise, Man - i - fest - ed by the star
King su - preme; And at Ca - na, wed - ding guest,
faint - ing soul; Man - i - fest in val - iant fight,
ho - ly word; May we im - i - tate you now,

To the sag - es from a - far; Branch of roy - al
In your God - head man - i - fest; Man - i - fest in
Quell - ing all the dev - il's might; Man - i - fest in
And on us your grace en - dow; That we like to

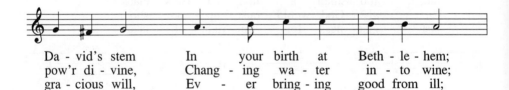

Da - vid's stem In your birth at Beth - le - hem;
pow'r di - vine, Chang - ing wa - ter in - to wine;
gra - cious will, Ev - er bring - ing good from ill;
you may be At your great e - piph - a - ny;

An - thems be to you ad - drest, God in flesh made man - i - fest.
An - thems be to you ad - drest, God in flesh made man - i - fest.
An - thems be to you ad - drest, God in flesh made man - i - fest.
And may praise you ev - er blest, God in flesh made man - i - fest.

Text: Christopher Wordsworth, 1807-1885
Tune: SALZBURG, 77 77 D; Jakob Hintze, 1622-1702, alt.; harm. by J.S. Bach, 1685-1750

At the Cross Her Station Keeping 228

1. At the cross her sta - tion keep-ing, Mar - y stood in
2. While she wait - ed in her an-guish, See - ing Christ in
3. With what pain and des - o - la - tion, With what no - ble
4. Ev - er pa - tient in her yearn-ing, Though her tear - filled

sor - row, weep - ing, When her Son was cru - ci - fied.
tor - ment lan - guish, Bit - ter sor - row pierced her heart.
res - ig - na - tion, Mar - y watched her dy - ing Son.
eyes were burn - ing, Mar - y gazed up - on her Son.

5. Who, that sorrow contemplating,
On that passion meditating,
   Would not share the Virgin's grief?

6. Christ she saw, for our salvation,
Scourged with cruel acclamation,
   Bruised and beaten by the rod.

7. Christ she saw with life-blood failing,
All her anguish unavailing,
   Saw him breathe his very last.

8. Mary, fount of love's devotion,
Let me share with true emotion
   All the sorrow you endured.

9. Virgin, ever interceding,
Hear me in my fervent pleading:
   Fire me with your love of Christ.

10. Mother, may this prayer be granted:
That Christ's love may be implanted
   In the depths of my poor soul.

11. At the cross, your sorrow sharing,
All your grief and torment bearing,
   Let me stand and mourn with you.

12. Fairest maid of all creation,
Queen of hope and consolation,
   Let me feel your grief sublime.

13. Virgin, in your love befriend me,
At the Judgment day defend me.
   Help me by your constant prayer.

14. Savior, when my life shall leave me,
Through your mother's prayers receive me
   With the fruits of victory.

15. Let me to your love be taken,
Let my soul in death awaken
   To the joys of Paradise.

Text: *Stabat mater dolorosa*; Jacopone da Todi, 1230-1306; trans. by Anthony G. Petti, 1932-1985, © 1971, Faber Music, Ltd.
Tune: STABAT MATER, 88 7; *Mainz Gesangbuch*, 1661; harm. by Richard Proulx, b.1937, © 1986, GIA Publications, Inc.

229 Hear Us, Almighty Lord / Attende Domine

Hear us, al - might - y Lord, show us your
At - tén - de Dó - mi - ne, et mi - se -

mer - cy Sin - ners we stand here be - fore you.
ré - re, Qui - a pec - cá - vi - mus ti - bi.

1. Je - sus our Sav - ior, Lord of all the na - tions,
2. Word of the Fa - ther, key-stone of God's build - ing,
3. God of com - pas - sion, Lord of might and splen - dor,
1. *Ad te Rex sum - me, óm - ni - um re - dém - ptor,*
2. *Déx - te - ra Pa - tris, la - pis an - gu - lá - ris,*
3. *Ro - gá - mus, De - us, tu - am ma - je - stá - tem:*

Christ our Re - deem - er, hear the prayers we of - fer,
Source of our glad - ness, gate - way to the King - dom,
Gra - cious - ly lis - ten, hear our cries of an - guish.
Ó - cu - los nó - stros sub - le - vá - mus flen - tes:
Vi - a sa - lú - tis já - nu - a cae - lé - stis,
Áu - ri - bus sa - cris gé - mi - tus ex - aú - di:

D.C.

Spare us and save us, com - fort us in sor - row.
Free us in mer - cy from the sins that bind us.
Touch us and heal us where our sins have wound - ed.
Ex - aú - di, Chri - ste, sup - pli - cán - tum pre - ces.
Áb - lu - e no - stri má - cu - las de - lí - cti.
Crí - mi - na no - stra plá - ci - dus in - dúl - ge.

4. Humbly confessing that we have offended,
   Stripped of illusions, naked in our sorrow,
   Pardon, Lord Jesus, those your blood has ransomed.

5. Innocent captive, you were led to slaughter,
   Sentenced by sinners when they brought false witness.
   Keep from damnation those your death has rescued.

4. *Tibi fatémur, crímina admíssa:*
   Contríto corde pándimus occúlta:
   Túa redémptor, píetas ignóscat.

5. *Innocens captus, nec repúgnans ductus,*
   Téstibus falsis, pro ímpiis damnátus:
   Quos redemísti, tu consérva, Christe.

Text: Latin, 10th C.; tr. by Ralph Wright, OSB, b.1938, © 1980, ICEL
Tune: ATTENDE DOMINE, 11 11 11 with refrain; Mode V; acc. by Richard Proulx, b.1937, © 1975, GIA Publications, Inc.

Earthen Vessels 230

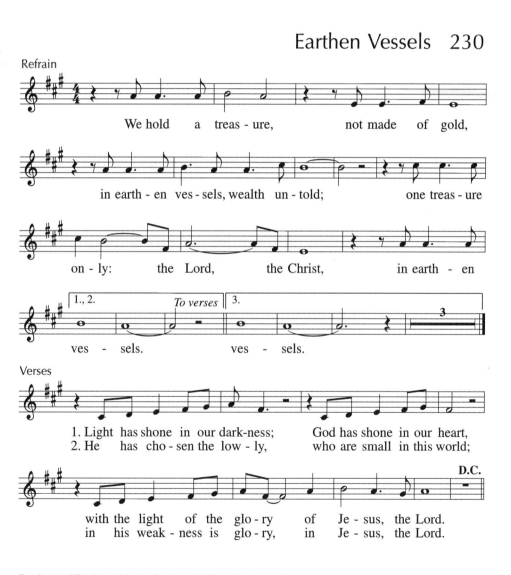

Text: Based on 2 Corinthians 4:6-7, and 1 Corinthians 1:27-28; John Foley, SJ, b.1939
Tune: John Foley, SJ, b.1939
© 1975, John B. Foley, SJ and New Dawn Music

231 Jerusalem, My Destiny

Refrain

I have fixed my eyes on your hills, Je - ru - sa - lem, my des - ti - ny! Though I can - not see the end for me, I can - not turn a - way. We have set our hearts for the way; this jour - ney is our des - ti - ny. Let no-one walk a - lone. The jour - ney makes us one.

Verses

1. Oth - er spir - its, less - er gods, have court - ed me with lies.
2. See, I leave the past be - hind; a new land calls to me.
3. In my thirst, you let me drink the wa - ters of your life.
4. All the worlds I have not seen you o - pen to my view.
5. To the tombs I went to mourn the hope I thought was gone.

D.C.

Here a - mong you I have found a truth which bids me rise.
Here a - mong you now I find a glimpse of what might be.
Here a - mong you I have met the sav - ior, Je - sus Christ.
Here a - mong you I have found a vi - sion, bright and new.
Here a - mong you I a - woke to un - ex - pect - ed dawn.

Text: Rory Cooney, b.1952
Tune: Rory Cooney, b.1952
© 1990, GIA Publications, Inc.

Somebody's Knockin' at Your Door 232

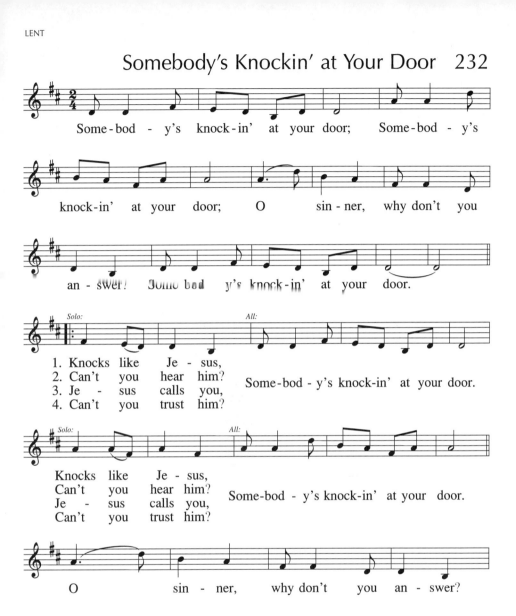

Some-bod - y's knock-in' at your door; Some-bod - y's
knock-in' at your door; O sin - ner, why don't you
an - swer! Some-bod - y's knock-in' at your door.

Solo: | All:
1. Knocks like Je - sus,
2. Can't you hear him?
3. Je - sus calls you,
4. Can't you trust him?

Some-bod - y's knock-in' at your door.

Solo: | All:
Knocks like Je - sus,
Can't you hear him?
Je - sus calls you,
Can't you trust him?

Some-bod - y's knock-in' at your door.

O sin - ner, why don't you an - swer?

Some-bod - y's knock-in' at your door.

Text: African-American spiritual
Tune: SOMEBODY'S KNOCKIN', Irregular; African-American spiritual; harm. by Richard Proulx, b.1937, © 1986, GIA Publications, Inc.

233 Deep Within

Refrain

Deep with-in I will plant my law,
not on stone, but in your heart.
Fol-low me, I will bring you back, you will
be my own, and I will be your God.

Verses

1. I will give you a new heart, a new spir-it with-
2. Seek my face, and see your
3. Re-turn to me, with all your

D.C.

in you, for I will be your strength.
God, for I will be your hope.
heart, and I will bring you back.

Text: Jeremiah 31:33, Ezekiel 36:26, Joel 2:12; David Haas, b.1957
Tune: David Haas, b.1957; acc. by Jeanne Cotter, b.1964
© 1987, GIA Publications, Inc.

234 Parce Domine

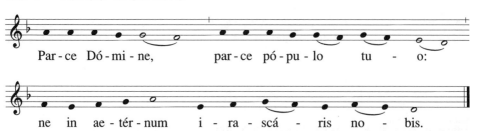

Par-ce Dó-mi-ne, par-ce pó-pu-lo tu - o:
ne in ae-tér-num i-ra-scá - ris no - bis.

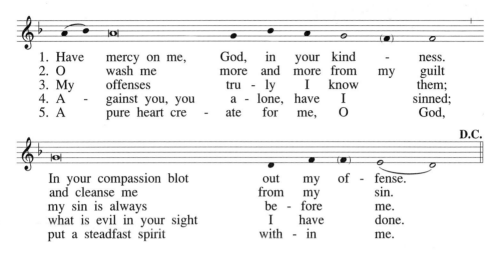

1. Have mercy on me, God, in your kind - ness.
2. O wash me more and more from my guilt
3. My offenses tru - ly I know them;
4. A - gainst you, you a - lone, have I sinned;
5. A pure heart cre - ate for me, O God,

D.C.

In your compassion blot out my of - fense.
and cleanse me from my sin.
my sin is always be - fore me.
what is evil in your sight I have done.
put a steadfast spirit with - in me.

Text: *Spare your people, Lord, lest you be angry for ever,* Joel 2:17, Psalm 51:3-6, 12; tr. The Grail, © 1963, The Grail, GIA Publications, Inc., agent
Tune: PARCE DOMINE, Irregular; Mode I with Tonus Peregrinus; acc. by Robert LeBlanc, OSB, b.1948, © 1986, GIA Publications, Inc.

Jesus Walked This Lonesome Valley   235

1. Je - sus walked this lone - some val - ley;
2. We must walk this lone - some val - ley;
3. You must go and stand your tri - al;

He had to walk it by him - self.
We have to walk it by our - selves.
You have to stand it by your - self.

Oh, no - bod - y else could walk it for him;
Oh, no - bod - y else can walk it for us;
Oh, no - bod - y else can stand it for you;

He had to walk it by him - self.
We have to walk it by our - selves.
You have to stand it by your - self.

Text: American Folk Hymn
Tune: LONESOME VALLEY, 8 8 10 8; American folk hymn; harm. by Richard Proulx, b.1937, © 1975, GIA Publications, Inc.

236 Seek the Lord

Refrain

Seek the Lord while he may be found;
call to him while he is still near.

Verses 1, 2

1. To-day is the day and now the pro-per hour
2. As high as the sky is a-bove the earth,

to for-sake our sin-ful lives and turn to the Lord.
so high a-bove our ways, the ways of the Lord.

Verse 3

3. Find-ing the Lord, let us cling to him. His

words, his ways lead us to life.

Verse 4

4. Some day we'll live in the house of God;

gaze on his face and praise his name.

Text: Isaiah 55:6-9; Roc O'Connor, SJ, b.1949
Tune: Roc O'Connor, SJ, b.1949; arr. by Peter Felice, alt.
© 1975, 1996, Robert F. O'Connor, SJ, and New Dawn Music

From Ashes to the Living Font   237

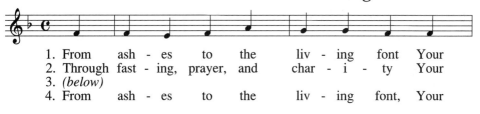

1. From ash - es to the liv - ing font Your
2. Through fast - ing, prayer, and char - i - ty Your
3. *(below)*
4. From ash - es to the liv - ing font, Your

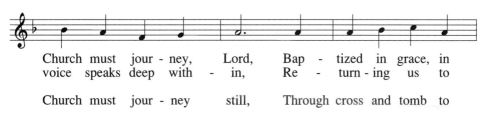

Church must jour - ney, Lord, Bap - tized in grace, in
voice speaks deep with - in, Re - turn - ing us to

Church must jour - ney still, Through cross and tomb to

grace re - newed By your most ho - ly word.
ways of truth And turn - ing us from sin.

Eas - ter joy, In Spir - it - fire ful - filled.

Sundays I & II

3. From desert to the mountaintop
   In Christ our way we see,
   So, tempered by temptation's might
   We might transfigured be.

Sunday III

3. For thirsting hearts let waters flow
   Our fainting souls revive;
   And at the well your waters give
   Our everlasting life.

Sunday IV

3. We sit beside the road and plead,
   "Come, save us, David's son!"
   Now with your vision heal our eyes,
   The world's true Light alone.

Sunday V

3. Our graves split open, bring us back,
   Your promise to proclaim;
   To darkened tombs call out, "Arise!"
   And glorify your name.

Text: Alan J. Hommerding, b.1956, © 1994, World Library Publications, Inc.
Tune: ST. FLAVIAN, CM; *John's Day Psalter,* 1562; harm. based on the original *faux-bourdon* setting

238 Lord, Who throughout These Forty Days

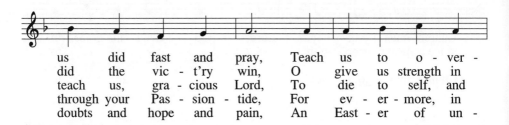

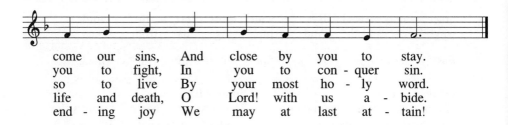

1. Lord, who through - out these for - ty days, For
2. As you with Sa - tan did con - tend, And
3. As you did hun - ger and did thirst, So
4. And through these days of pen - i - tence, And
5. A - bide with us, that through this life Of

us did fast and pray, Teach us to o - ver -
did the vic - t'ry win, O give us strength in
teach us, gra - cious Lord, To die to self, and
through your Pas - sion - tide, For ev - er - more, in
doubts and hope and pain, An East - er of un -

come our sins, And close by you to stay.
you to fight, In you to con - quer sin.
so to live By your most ho - ly word.
life and death, O Lord! with us a - bide.
end - ing joy We may at last at - tain!

Text: Claudia F. Hernaman, 1838-1898, alt.
Tune: ST. FLAVIAN, CM; *John's Day Psalter*, 1562; harm. based on the original *faux-bourdon* setting

239 The Glory of These Forty Days

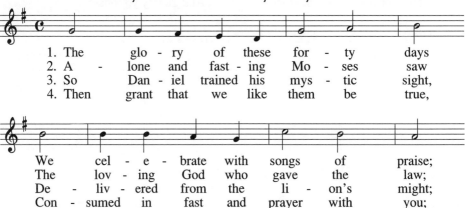

1. The glo - ry of these for - ty days
2. A - lone and fast - ing Mo - ses saw
3. So Dan - iel trained his mys - tic sight,
4. Then grant that we like them be true,

We cel - e - brate with songs of praise;
The lov - ing God who gave the law;
De - liv - ered from the li - on's might;
Con - sumed in fast and prayer with you;

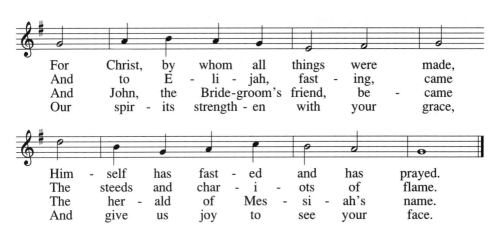

For Christ, by whom all things were made,
And to E - li - jah, fast - ing, came
And John, the Bride-groom's friend, be - came
Our spir - its strength - en with your grace,

Him - self has fast - ed and has prayed.
The steeds and char - i - ots of flame.
The her - ald of Mes - si - ah's name.
And give us joy to see your face.

Text: Ominium ... Pope Gregory the Great, c. 540-604; tr. by Maurice F. Bell, 1862-1947, © Oxford University Press
Tune: OLD HUNDREDTH, LM; Louis Bourgeois, c.1510-1561

Hosea 240

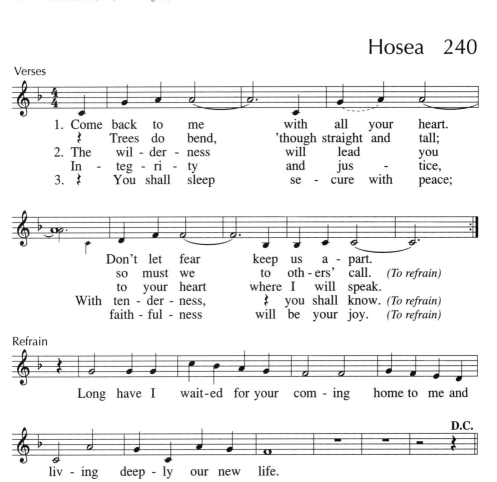

Verses

1. Come back to me with all your heart.
   Trees do bend, 'though straight and tall;
2. The wil - der - ness will lead you
   In - teg - ri - ty and jus - tice,
3. You shall sleep se - cure with peace;

Don't let fear keep us a - part.
so must we to oth - ers' call. *(To refrain)*
to your heart where I will speak.
With ten - der - ness, you shall know. *(To refrain)*
faith - ful - ness will be your joy. *(To refrain)*

Refrain

Long have I wait-ed for your com - ing home to me and

D.C.

liv - ing deep - ly our new life.

Text: Based on Hosea 6:1, 3:3, 2:16,21; Joel 2:12; Gregory Norbet, b.1940
Tune: Gregory Norbet, b.1940; arr. by Mary David Callahan, b.1923
© 1972, 1980, The Benedictine Foundation of the State of Vermont, Inc.

241 Again We Keep This Solemn Fast

1. A - gain we keep this sol - emn fast
2. The law and proph - ets from of old
3. More spar - ing, there - fore, let us make
4. Let us a - void each harm - ful way
5. We pray, O bless - ed Three in One,

A gift of faith from a - ges past,
In fig - ured ways this Lent fore - told,
The words we speak, the food we take,
That lures the care - less mind a - stray;
Our God while end - less a - ges run,

This Lent which binds us lov - ing - ly
Which Christ, all a - ges' Lord and Guide,
Our sleep, our laugh - ter, ev - 'ry sense;
By watch - ful prayer our spir - its free
That this, our Lent of for - ty days,

To faith and hope and char - i - ty.
In these last days has sanc - ti - fied.
Learn peace through ho - ly pen - i - tence.
From schem - ing of the En - e - my.
May bring us growth and give you praise.

Text: *Ex more docti mystico;* ascr. to Gregory the Great, c. 540-604, tr. by Peter J. Scagnelli, b. 1949, ©
Tune: OLD HUNDREDTH, LM; Louis Bourgeois, c.1510-1561

242 Tree of Life

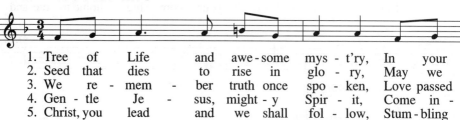

1. Tree of Life and awe - some mys - t'ry, In your
2. Seed that dies to rise in glo - ry, May we
3. We re - mem - ber truth once spo - ken, Love passed
4. Gen - tle Je - sus, might - y Spir - it, Come in -
5. Christ, you lead and we shall fol - low, Stum - bling

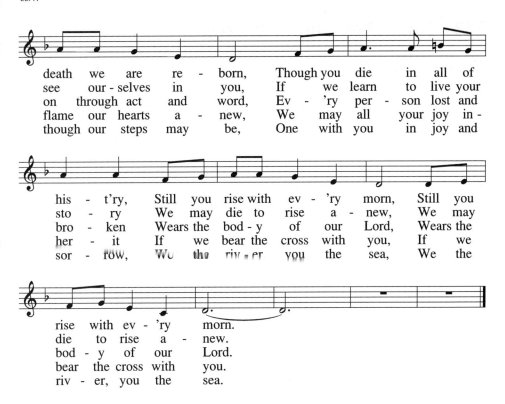

death	we	are	re -	born,	Though you	die	in	all	of
see	our - selves	in		you,	If	we	learn	to	live	your
on	through act	and		word,	Ev -	'ry	per -	son	lost	and
flame	our hearts	a -		new,	We	may	all	your	joy	in -
though our	steps	may		be,	One	with	you	in	joy	and

his -	t'ry,	Still	you	rise with	ev -	'ry	morn,	Still	you
sto -	ry	We	may	die to	rise	a -	new,	We	may
bro -	ken	Wears the	bod - y	of	our	Lord,	Wears the
her -	it	If	we	bear the	cross	with	you,	If	we
sor -	row,	We	the	riv - er	you	the	sea,	We	the

rise	with	ev -	'ry	morn.
die	to	rise	a -	new.
bod -	y	of	our	Lord.
bear	the	cross with		you.
riv -	er,	you	the	sea.

Lenten Verses:

General: Light of life beyond conceiving, Mighty Spirit of our Lord;
Give new strength to our believing, Give us faith to live your word.

1st Sunday: From the dawning of creation, You have loved us as your own;
Stay with us through all temptation, Make us turn to you alone.

2nd Sunday: In our call to be a blessing, May we be a blessing true;
May we live and die confessing Christ as Lord of all we do.

3rd Sunday: Living Water of salvation, Be the fountain of each soul;
Springing up in new creation, Flow in us and make us whole.

4th Sunday: Give us eyes to see you clearly, Make us children of your light;
Give us hearts to live more nearly As your gospel shining bright.

5th Sunday: God of all our fear and sorrow, God who lives beyond our death;
Hold us close through each tomorrow, Love as near as every breath.

Text: Marty Haugen, b.1950
Tune: THOMAS, 8 7 8 77; Marty Haugen, b.1950
© 1984, GIA Publications, Inc.

243 Forty Days and Forty Nights

1. For - ty days and for - ty nights You were fast - ing in the wild;
2. Shall not we your sor - row share And from world - ly joys ab - stain,
3. Then if Sa - tan on us press, Flesh or spir - it to as - sail,
4. So shall we have peace di - vine: Ho - lier glad - ness ours shall be;
5. Keep, O keep us, Sav - ior dear, Ev - er con - stant by your side;

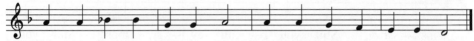

For - ty days and for - ty nights Tempt - ed and yet un - de - filed.
Fast - ing with un - ceas - ing prayer, Strong with you to suf - fer pain?
Vic - tor in the wil - der - ness, Grant we may not faint nor fail!
Round us, too, shall an - gels shine, Such as served you faith - ful - ly.
That with you we may ap - pear At the e - ter - nal East - er - tide.

Text: George H. Smyttan, 1822-1870, alt.
Tune: HEINLEIN, 7 7 7 7; attr. to Martin Herbst, 1654-1681, *Nürnbergisches Gesangbuch,* 1676

244 All Glory, Laud, and Honor

All glo - ry, laud, and hon - or To you, Re - deem - er, King!

To whom the lips of chil - dren Made sweet ho - san - nas ring.

1. You are the King of Is - ra - el, And Da - vid's roy - al Son,
2. The com - pa - ny of an - gels Are prais - ing you on high;
3. The peo - ple of the He - brews With palms be - fore you went:
4. To you be - fore your pas - sion They sang their hymns of praise:
5. Their prais - es you ac - cept - ed, Ac - cept the prayers we bring,

D.C.

Now in the Lord's Name com - ing, Our King and Bless - ed One.
And mor - tals, joined with all things Cre - a - ted, make re - ply.
Our praise and prayers and an - thems Be - fore you we pre - sent.
To you, now high ex - alt - ed, Our mel - o - dy we raise.
Great source of love and good - ness, Our Sav - ior and our King.

Text: *Gloria, laus et honor;* Theodulph of Orleans, c.760-821; tr. by John M. Neale, 1818-1866, alt.
Tune: ST. THEODULPH, 7 6 7 6 D; Melchior Teschner, 1584-1635

Hosanna 245

Refrain

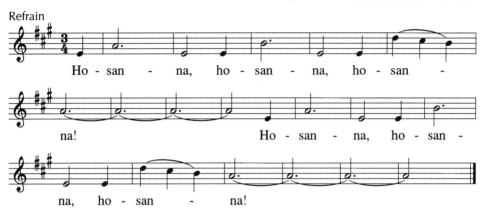

Ho - san - na, ho - san - na, ho - san -

na! Ho - san - na, ho - san -

na, ho - san - na!

Verses

1. Blessed is he, blessed is he who comes in the name of the Lord!
   Blessed is he, blessed is he who comes in the name of the Lord!

2. Blessed is the reign of our father, David.
   Blessed is the reign of our father, David, to come!

Text: Mark 11:9-10; David Haas, b.1957
Tune: David Haas, b.1957
© 1988, GIA Publications, Inc.

Jesus, Remember Me 246

Ostinato Refrain

Je-sus, re-mem-ber me   when you come in-to your   King-dom.

Je-sus, re-mem-ber me   when you come in-to your King-dom.

Text: Luke 23:42; Taizé Community, 1981
Tune: Jacques Berthier, 1923-1994
© 1981, Les Presses de Taizé, GIA Publications, Inc., agent

247 Ubi Caritas

Refrain

U - bi ca - ri - tas et a - mor,
Live in char - i - ty and stead - fast love,

u - bi ca - ri - tas De - us i - bi est.
live in char - i - ty; God will dwell with you.

Text: 1 Corinthians 13:2-8; *Where charity and love are found, God is there;* Taizé Community, 1978
Tune: Jacques Berthier, 1923-1994
© 1979, Les Presses de Taizé, GIA Publications, Inc., agent

248 Jesu, Jesu

Refrain

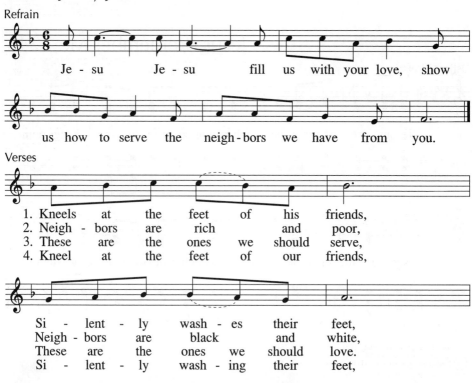

Je - su Je - su fill us with your love, show

us how to serve the neigh - bors we have from you.

Verses

1. Kneels at the feet of his friends,
2. Neigh - bors are rich and poor,
3. These are the ones we should serve,
4. Kneel at the feet of our friends,

Si - lent - ly wash - es their feet,
Neigh - bors are black and white,
These are the ones we should love.
Si - lent - ly wash - ing their feet,

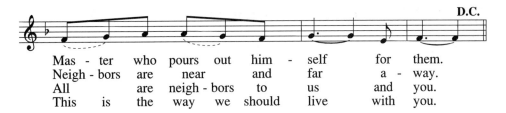

Mas - ter who pours out him - self for them.
Neigh - bors are near and far a - way.
All are neigh - bors to us and you.
This is the way we should live with you.

Text: John 13:3-5; Ghana folk song; tr. by Tom Colvin, b.1925
Tune: CHEREPONI, Irregular; Ghana folk song; Tom Colvin, b.1925; acc. by Jane M. Marshall, b.1924, © 1982, Hope Publishing Co.

Jesus, the Lord 249

Refrain

Je - sus. Je - sus. Let all cre-

a - tion bend the knee to the Lord.

Verse 1

1. In him we live, we move and have our be-ing; in

him the Christ, in him the King. Je - sus, the Lord.

Verses 2, 3

2. Though Son, he did not cling to
3. He lived o - be - dient - ly his

god - li - ness; but emp - tied him - self, be -
Fa - ther's will ac - cept - ing his death,

came a slave! Je - sus, the Lord.
death on a tree!

Text: *Jesus Prayer*, Philippians 2:5-11; Acts 17:28; Roc O'Connor, SJ, b.1949
Tune: Roc O'Connor, SJ, b.1949; arr. by Rick Modlin
© 1981, 1994, Robert F. O'Connor, SJ, and New Dawn Music

250 O Sacred Head Surrounded

1. O   Sa - cred Head sur - round - ed By crown of pierc - ing
2. I   see your strength and vig - or All fad - ing in   the
3. In   this, your bit - ter pas - sion, Good Shep-herd, think of

thorn!   O   bleed - ing Head, so   wound - ed, Re -
strife,   And death with cru - el   rig - or, Be -
me   With your most sweet com - pas - sion, Un -

viled and put   to   scorn! The pow'r of death comes
reav - ing you of   life;   O   ag - o - ny and
worth - y though I   be: Be - neath your cross a -

o'er   you,   The glow of   life de - cays, Yet
dy - ing! O   love to   sin - ners free! Je -
bid - ing For   ev - er would I   rest,   In

an - gel hosts a - dore you, And trem - ble as they gaze.
sus, all grace sup - ply - ing, O   turn your face on   me.
your dear love con - fid - ing, And with your pres - ence blest.

Text: *Salve caput cruentatum;* ascr. to Bernard of Clairvaux, 1091-1153; tr. by Henry Baker, 1821-1877
Tune: PASSION CHORALE, 7 6 7 6 D; Hans Leo Hassler, 1564-1612; harm. by J. S. Bach, 1685-1750

Were You There 251

1. Were you there when they cru - ci - fied my Lord?
2. Were you there when they nailed him to the tree?
3. Were you there when they pierced him in the side?
4. Were you there when the sun re - fused to shine?
5. Were you there when they laid him in the tomb?
6. Were you there when they rolled the stone a - way?

Were you there when they cru - ci - fied my Lord?
Were you there when they nailed him to the tree?
Were you there when they pierced him in the side?
Were you there when the sun re - fused to shine?
Were you there when they laid him in the tomb?
Were you there when they rolled the stone a - way?

Oh! Some - times it caus - es me to

trem - ble, trem - ble, trem - ble, Were you

there when they cru - ci - fied my Lord?
there when they nailed him to the tree?
there when they pierced him in the side?
there when the sun re - fused to shine?
there when they laid him in the tomb?
there when they rolled the stone a - way?

Text: African-American spiritual
Tune: WERE YOU THERE, 10 10 with refrain; African-American spiritual; harm. by Robert J. Batastini, b.1942, © 1987, GIA Publications, Inc.

252 Come, Ye Faithful, Raise the Strain

1. Come, ye faith - ful raise the strain Of tri - um - phant glad - ness; God has brought his Is - ra - el In - to joy from sad - ness; Led them with un - moist - ened foot Through the Red Sea wa - ters.

2. 'Tis the spring of souls to - day; Christ has burst the pris - on, And from three days' sleep in death As a sun has ris - en; All the win - ter of our sins, Long and dark is fly - ing From his light, to whom we give Laud and praise un - dy - ing.

3. Now the queen of sea - sons, bright With the day of splen - dor, With the roy - al feast of feasts, Comes its joy to ren - der; Comes to glad - den faith - ful hearts Who with true af - fec - tion Wel - come in un - wea - ried strains Je - sus' res - ur - rec - tion.

4. Nei - ther could the gates of death, Nor the tomb's dark por - tal, Nor the watch - ers, nor the seal Hold him as a mor - tal; For to - day a - mong the Twelve Christ ap - peared be - stow - ing Last - ing peace which hu - man know - ing. ev - er - more Pass - es hu - man know - ing.

5. "Al - le - lu - ia!" now we cry To our King im - mor - tal, Who, tri - um - phant, burst the bars Of the tomb's dark por - tal; "Al - le - lu - ia!" with the Son, God the Fa - ther prais - ing; "Al - le - lu - ia!" yet a - gain To the Spir - it rais - ing.

Text: Exodus 15; Ασωμεν παντεζ λαοι; John of Damascus, c.675-c.749; tr. by John M. Neale, 1818-1886, alt.
Tune: GAUDEAMUS PARITER, 7 6 7 6 D; Johann Horn, c.1495-1547

Christ the Lord Is Risen 253

1. Christ the Lord is ris'n! Christ the Lord is ris'n!
2. He has con-quered death. He has con-quered death.
3. Sin has done its worst. Sin has done its worst.
4. He is King of kings. He is King of kings.
5. He is Lord of lords. He is Lord of lords.
6. All the world is his. All the world is his.
7. Come and wor-ship him. Come and wor-ship him.
8. Christ our Lord is ris'n! Christ our Lord is ris'n!
9. Hal-le-lu-jah! Hal-le-lu-jah!

Je-su. Christ the Lord is ris'n!
Je-su. He has con-quered death.
Je-su. Sin has done its worst.
Je-su. He is King of kings.
Je-su. He is Lord of lords.
Je-su. All the world is his.
Je-su. Come and wor-ship him.
Je-su. Christ our Lord is ris'n!
Je-su. Hal-le-lu-jah!

Christ the Lord is ris'n! Je-su.
He has con-quered death. Je-su.
Sin has done its worst. Je-su.
He is King of kings. Je-su.
He is Lord of lords. Je-su.
All the world is his. Je-su.
Come and wor-ship him. Je-su.
Christ our Lord is ris'n! Je-su.
Hal-le-lu-jah! Je-su.

Text: Tom Colvin, b.1925
Tune: GARU, 55 2 55 2; Ghanian folk song, adapt. by Tom Colvin, b.1925, arr. by Kevin R. Hackett
© 1969, Hope Publishing Company

254 Sing to the Mountains

Refrain

Sing to the moun-tains, sing to the sea. Raise your

voic - es, lift your hearts. This is the day the

Lord has made. Let all the earth re - joice.

Verse 1

1. I will give thanks to you, my Lord. You have

an - swered my plea. You have saved my

soul from death. You are my strength and my song.

Verse 2

2. Ho - ly, ho - ly, ho - ly Lord,

heav - en and earth are full of your glo - ry.

Verse 3

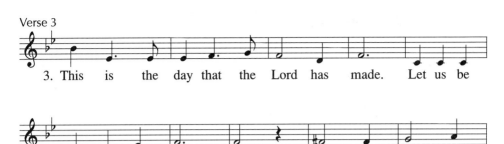

3. This is the day that the Lord has made. Let us be

glad and re - joice. He has turned all

D.C.

death to life. Sing of the glo - ry of God.

Text: Psalm 118; Bob Dufford, SJ, b.1943
Tune: Bob Dufford, SJ, b.1943; acc. by Randall DeBruyn
© 1975, 1979, Robert J. Dufford, SJ and New Dawn Music

Be Joyful, Mary 255

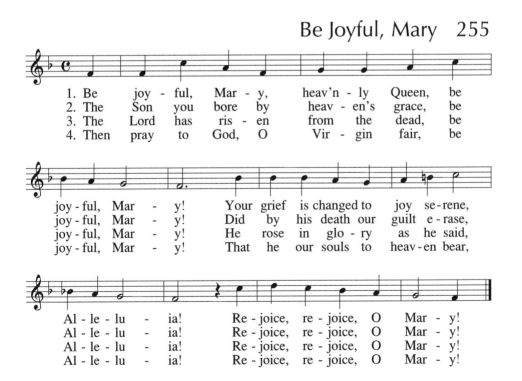

1. Be joy - ful, Mar - y, heav'n - ly Queen, be
2. The Son you bore by heav - en's grace, be
3. The Lord has ris - en from the dead, be
4. Then pray to God, O Vir - gin fair, be

joy - ful, Mar - y! Your grief is changed to joy se - rene,
joy - ful, Mar - y! Did by his death our guilt e - rase,
joy - ful, Mar - y! He rose in glo - ry as he said,
joy - ful, Mar - y! That he our souls to heav - en bear,

Al - le - lu - ia! Re - joice, re - joice, O Mar - y!
Al - le - lu - ia! Re - joice, re - joice, O Mar - y!
Al - le - lu - ia! Re - joice, re - joice, O Mar - y!
Al - le - lu - ia! Re - joice, re - joice, O Mar - y!

Text: *Regina caeli, jubila;* Latin, 17th C.; tr. anon. in *Psallite,* 1901
Tune: REGINA CAELI, 8 5 8 4 7; Leisentritt's *Gesangbuch,* 1584, alt.

256 At the Lamb's High Feast We Sing

1. At the Lamb's high feast we sing Praise to our vic-
2. Where the Pas-chal blood is poured, Death's dark an-gel
3. Might-y vic-tim from the sky, Hell's fierce powers be-
4. East-er tri-umph, East-er joy, This a-lone can

to-rious King. Who has washed us in the tide
sheathes his sword; Is-rael's hosts tri-umph-ant go
neath you lie; You have con-quered in the fight,
sin de-stroy; From sin's power, Lord, set us free

Flow-ing from his pierc-ed side; Praise we him, whose
Through the wave that drowns the foe. Praise we Christ, whose
You have brought us life and light: Now no more can
New-born souls in you to be. Fa-ther, who the

love di-vine Gives his sa-cred Blood for wine,
blood was shed, Pas-chal vic-tim, Pas-chal bread;
death ap-pall, Now no more the grave en-thrall;
crown shall give, Sav-ior, by whose death we live,

Gives his Bod-y for the feast,
With sin-cer-i-ty and love
You have o-pened par-a-dise,
Spir-it, guide through all our days,

Christ the vic-tim, Christ the priest.
Eat we man-na from a-bove.
And in you your saints shall rise.
Three in One, your name we praise.

Text: *Ad regias agni dapes;* Latin, 4th C.; tr. by Robert Campbell, 1814-1868
Tune: SALZBURG, 77 77 D; Jakob Hintze, 1622-1702; harm. by J.S. Bach, 1685-1750

Christ the Lord Is Risen Today 257

1. Christ the Lord is ris'n to - day, Al - le -
2. Lives a - gain our glo - rious King; Al - le -
3. Love's re - deem - ing work is done, Al - le -
4. Soar we now where Christ has led, Al - le -

lu - ia! All on earth with an - gels say,
lu - ia! Where, O death, is now your sting?
lu - ia! Fought the fight, the bat - tle won.
lu - ia! Fol - l'wing our ex - alt - ed head;

Al - le - lu - ia! Raise your joys and
Al - le - lu - ia! Once he died our
Al - le - lu - ia! Death in vain for -
Al - le - lu - ia! Made like him, like

tri - umphs high, Al - le - lu - ia!
souls to save, Al - le - lu - ia!
bids him rise; Al - le - lu - ia!
him we rise, Al - le - lu - ia!

Sing, O heav'ns, and earth re - ply,
Where your vic - to - ry, O grave?
Christ has o - pened par - a - dise.
Ours the cross, the grave, the skies.

Al - le - lu - ia!

Text: Charles Wesley, 1707-1788
Tune: LLANFAIR, 77 77 with alleluias; Robert Williams, 1781-1821

258 Alleluia! Alleluia! Let the Holy Anthem Rise

1. Al - le - lu - ia! Al - le - lu - ia! Let the
2. Al - le - lu - ia! Al - le - lu - ia! He en -
3. Al - le - lu - ia! Al - le - lu - ia! Like the
4. Al - le - lu - ia! Al - le - lu - ia! He has
5. Al - le - lu - ia! Al - le - lu - ia! Bless - ed

ho - ly an - them rise, And the choirs of heav-en
dured the knot - ted whips, And the jeer - ing of the
sun from out the wave He has ris - en up in
burst our pris - on bars; He has lift - ed up the
Je - sus, make us rise From the life of this cor -

chant it In the tem - ple of the skies; Let the
rab - ble, And the scorn of mock-ing lips, And the
tri - umph From the dark - ness of the grave. He's the
por - tals Of our home be-yond the stars; He has
rup - tion To the life that nev - er dies. May we

moun - tains skip with glad - ness And the
ter - rors of the gib - bet Up - on
splen - dor of the na - tions; He's the
won for us our free - dom— 'Neath his
share with you your glo - ry When the

joy - ful val - leys ring With ho - san - nas in the
which he would be slain, But his death was on - ly
lamp of end - less day; He's the ver - y Lord of
feet our foes are trod; He has pur - chased back our
days of time are past, And the dead shall be a -

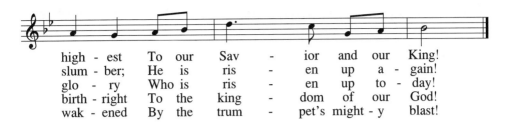

high - est   To   our   Sav   -   ior   and   our   King!
slum - ber;   He   is   ris   -   en   up   a -   gain!
glo - ry   Who is   ris   -   en   up   to -   day!
birth - right To   the   king -   dom   of   our   God!
wak - ened   By   the   trum -   pet's might - y   blast!

Text: Edward Caswall, 1814-1878
Tune: HOLY ANTHEM, 8 7 8 7 D; traditional melody; harm. Jerry R. Brubaker, © 1975, Romda Ltd.

I Know That My Redeemer Lives   259

1. I   know that   my   Re - deem - er   lives;
2. He   lives, to   bless me   with   his   love;
3. He   lives, and grants me   dai -   ly   breath;
4. He   lives, all glo - ry   to   his   name;

What   joy   the   blest as - sur - ance   gives!
He   lives, to   plead for   me   a -   bove;
He   lives, and I   shall   con - quer death;
He   lives, my   Sav - ior   still   the   same;

He   lives, he   lives, who   once was   dead;
He   lives, my   hun - gry   soul to   feed;
He   lives, my   man - sion   to   pre - pare;
What   joy   the   blest as -   sur - ance gives;

He   lives, my   ev   -   er - last - ing   Head!
He   lives, to   help   in   time of   need.
He   lives, to   bring   me   safe - ly   there.
I   know that   my   Re - deem - er   lives!

Text: Samuel Medley, 1738-1799
Tune: DUKE STREET, LM; John Hatton, c.1710-1793

260 O Sons and Daughters

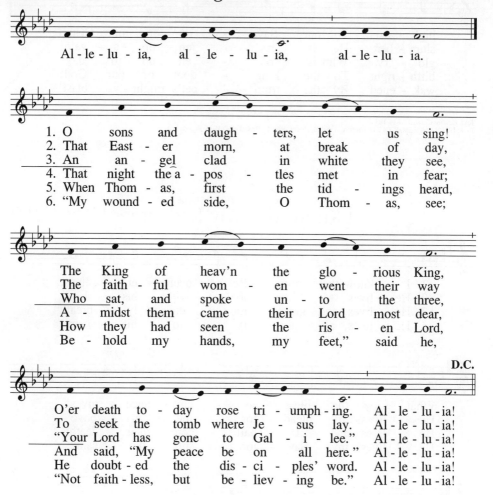

Al - le - lu - ia,   al - le - lu - ia,   al - le - lu - ia.

1. O sons and daugh - ters, let us sing!
2. That East - er morn, at break of day,
3. An an - gel clad in white they see,
4. That night the a - pos - tles met in fear;
5. When Thom - as, first the tid - ings heard,
6. "My wound - ed side, O Thom - as, see;

The King of heav'n the glo - rious King,
The faith - ful wom - en went their way
Who sat, and spoke un - to the three,
A - midst them came their Lord most dear,
How they had seen the ris - en Lord,
Be - hold my hands, my feet," said he,

O'er death to - day rose tri - umph - ing. Al - le - lu - ia!
To seek the tomb where Je - sus lay. Al - le - lu - ia!
"Your Lord has gone to Gal - i - lee." Al - le - lu - ia!
And said, "My peace be on all here." Al - le - lu - ia!
He doubt - ed the dis - ci - ples' word. Al - le - lu - ia!
"Not faith - less, but be - liev - ing be." Al - le - lu - ia!

7. No longer Thomas then denied,
   He saw the feet, the hands, the side;
   "You are my Lord and God," he cried. Alleluia!

8. How blest are they who have not seen,
   And yet whose faith has constant been,
   For they eternal life shall win. Alleluia!

9. On this most holy day of days,
   To God your hearts and voices raise,
   In laud, and jubilee and praise. Alleluia!

Text: *O filii et filiae;* Jean Tisserand, d.1494; tr. by John M. Neale, 1818-1866, alt.
Tune: O FILII ET FILIAE, 888 with alleluias; Mode II; acc. by Richard Proulx, b.1937, © 1975, GIA Publications, Inc.

Jesus Christ Is Risen Today 261

1. Je - sus Christ is ris'n to - day, Al - le - lu - ia!
2. Hymns of praise then let us sing, Al - le - lu - ia!
3. But the pains which he en - dured, Al - le - lu - ia!
4. Sing we to our God a - bove, Al - le - lu - ia!

Our tri - um-phant ho - ly day, Al - le - lu - ia!
Un - to Christ, our heav'n-ly King, Al - le - lu - ia!
Our sal - va - tion have pro - cured; Al - le - lu - ia!
Praise o for nul us his love, Al - le - lu - ia!

Who did once up - on the cross, Al - le - lu - ia!
Who en - dured the cross and grave, Al - le - lu - ia!
Now a - bove the sky he's King, Al - le - lu - ia!
Praise him, now his might con - fess, Al - le - lu - ia!

Suf - fer to re - deem our loss. Al - le - lu - ia!
Sin - ners to re - deem and save. Al - le - lu - ia!
Where the an - gels ev - er sing. Al - le - lu - ia!
Fa - ther, Son, and Spir - it blest. Al - le - lu - ia!

Text: St. 1, *Surrexit Christus hodie,* Latin, 14th C.; para. in *Lyra Davidica,* 1708, alt.; st. 2, 3, *The Compleat Psalmodist,* c.1750, alt.; st. 4, Charles
Wesley, 1707-1788
Tune: EASTER HYMN, 77 77 with alleluias; *Lyra Davidica,* 1708

262 Sing with All the Saints in Glory

1. Sing with all the saints in glo - ry, Sing the res - ur -
2. O what glo - ry, far ex - ceed - ing All that eye has
3. Life e - ter - nal! heav'n re - joic - es: Je - sus lives who
4. Life e - ter - nal! O what won - ders Crowd on faith; what

rec - tion song! Death and sor - row, earth's dark sto - ry,
yet per - ceived! Ho - liest hearts for a - ges plead - ing,
once was dead; Shout with joy, O death - less voic - es!
joy un - known, When, a - midst earth's clos - ing thun - ders,

To the for - mer days be - long. All a - round the
Nev - er that full joy con - ceived. God has prom - ised,
Child of God, lift up your head! Pa - tri - archs from
Saints shall stand be - fore the throne! O to en - ter

clouds are break - ing, Soon the storms of time shall cease;
Christ pre - pares it, There on high our wel - come waits;
dis - tant a - ges, Saints all long - ing for their heav'n,
that bright por - tal, See that glow - ing fir - ma - ment,

In God's like - ness, we a - wak - en,
Ev - 'ry hum - ble spir - it shares it,
Proph - ets, psalm - ists, seers, and sag - es,
Know, with you, O God im - mor - tal,

Know - ing ev - er - last - ing peace.
Christ has passed the e - ter - nal gates.
All a - wait the glo - ry giv'n.
Je - sus Christ whom you have sent!

Text: 1 Corinthians 15:20; William J. Irons, 1812-1883, alt.
Tune: HYMN TO JOY, 8 7 8 7 D; arr. from Ludwig van Beethoven, 1770-1827, by Edward Hodges, 1796-1867

That Easter Day with Joy Was Bright   263

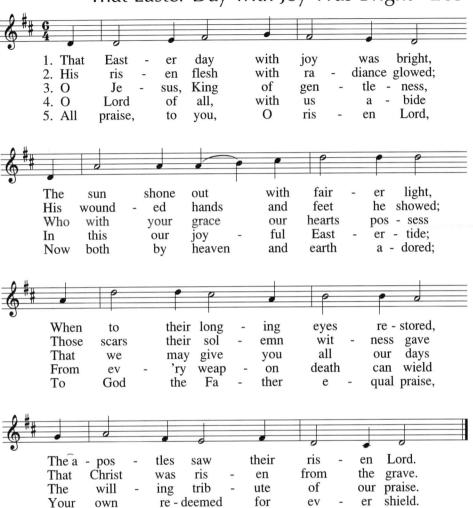

1. That East - er day with joy was bright,
2. His ris - en flesh with ra - diance glowed;
3. O Je - sus, King of gen - tle - ness,
4. O Lord of all, with us a - bide
5. All praise, to you, O ris - en Lord,

The sun shone out with fair - er light,
His wound - ed hands and feet he showed;
Who with your grace our hearts pos - sess
In this our joy - ful East - er - tide;
Now both by heaven and earth a - dored;

When to their long - ing eyes re - stored,
Those scars their sol - emn wit - ness gave
That we may give you all our days
From ev - 'ry weap - on death can wield
To God the Fa - ther e - qual praise,

The a - pos - tles saw their ris - en Lord.
That Christ was ris - en from the grave.
The will - ing trib - ute of our praise.
Your own re - deemed for ev - er shield.
And Spir - it blest, our songs we raise.

Text: *Claro paschali gaudio;* Latin 5th C.; tr. by John M. Neale, 1818-1866, alt.
Tune: PUER NOBIS, LM; adapt. by Michael Praetorius, 1571-1621

264 Alleluia, Alleluia, Give Thanks

Refrain

Al - le - lu - ia, al - le - lu - ia, give thanks to the ris - en Lord.

Al - le - lu - ia, al - le - lu - ia, give praise to his Name.

Verses

1. Je - sus is Lord of all the earth.
2. Spread the good news o'er all the earth:
3. We have been cru - ci - fied with Christ.
4. God has pro - claimed his gra - cious gift:
5. Come, let us praise the liv - ing God,

D.C.

He is the King of cre - a - tion.
Je - sus has died and has ris - en.
Now we shall live for ev - er.
Life e - ter - nal for all who be - lieve.
Joy - ful - ly sing to our Sav - ior.

Text: Donald Fishel, b.1950, © 1973, Word of God Music
Tune: ALLELUIA NO. 1, 8 8 with refrain; Donald Fishel, b.1950, © 1973, Word of God Music; descant harm. by Betty Pulkingham, b.1929,
    Charles Mallory, b.1953, and George Mims, b.1938, © 1979, Celebration

265 Regina Caeli / O Queen of Heaven

Re - gí - na cae - li, lae - tá - re, al - le - lú - ia,
O Queen of heav - en, be joy - ful, al - le - lu - ia,

Qui - a quem me - ru - í - sti por - tá - re, al - le - lú - ia,
For he whom you have hum - bly borne for us, al - le - lu - ia,

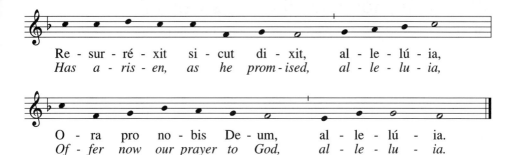

Re - sur - ré - xit si - cut di - xit, al - le - lú - ia,
Has a - ris - en, as he prom - ised, al - le - lu - ia,

O - ra pro no - bis De - um, al - le - lú - ia.
Of - fer now our prayer to God, al - le - lu - ia.

Text: Latin, 12th C.; tr. by C. Winfred Douglas, 1867-1944, alt.
Tune: REGINA CAELI, Irregular; Mode VI; acc. by Robert LeBlanc, OSB, b.1948, © 1986, GIA Publications, Inc.

The Strife Is O'er 266

Al - le - lu - ia! Al - le - lu - ia! Al - le - lu - ia!

1. The strife is o'er, the bat - tle done; Now is the
2. Death's might - iest pow'rs have done their worst, And Je - sus
3. He closed the yawn - ing gates of hell; The bars from
4. On the third morn he rose a - gain, Glo - rious in

Vic - tor's tri - umph won; Now be the song of
has his foes dis - persed; Let shouts of praise and
heav'n's high por - tals fell; Let hymns of praise his
maj - es - ty to reign; O let us swell the

D.C.

praise be - gun: Al - le - lu - ia!
joy out - burst: Al - le - lu - ia!
tri - umph tell: Al - le - lu - ia!
joy - ful strain: Al - le - lu - ia!

Text: *Finita iam sunt praelia;* Latin, 12th C.; tr. by Francis Pott, 1832-1909, alt.
Tune: VICTORY, 888 with alleluias; Giovanni da Palestrina, 1525-1594; adapt. by William H. Monk, 1823-1889

267 Lord, You Give the Great Commission

1. Lord, you give the great com-mis-sion: "Heal the sick and preach the word." Lest the Church ne-glect its mis-sion, And the Gos-pel go un-heard, Help us wit-ness to your pur-pose With re-newed in-teg-ri-ty;

2. Lord, you call us to your serv-ice: "In my name bap-tize and teach." That the world may trust your prom-ise, Life a-bun-dant meant for each, Give us all new fer-vor, draw us Clos-er in com-mun-i-ty;

3. Lord, you make the com-mon ho-ly: "This my bod-y, this my blood." Let us all, for earth's true glo-ry, Dai-ly lift life heav-en-ward, Ask-ing that the world a-round us Share your chil-dren's lib-er-ty;

4. Lord, you show us love's true meas-ure: "Fa-ther, what they do, for-give." Yet we hoard as pri-vate treas-ure All that you so free-ly give. May your care and mer-cy lead us To a just so-ci-e-ty;

5. Lord, you bless with words as-sur-ing: "I am with you to the end." Faith and hope and love re-stor-ing, May we serve as you in-tend, And, a-mid the cares that claim us, Hold in mind e-ter-ni-ty;

With the Spir-it's gifts em-power us For the work of min-is-try.

Text: Jeffery Rowthorn, b.1934, © 1978, Hope Publishing Co.
Tune: ABBOT'S LEIGH, 8 7 8 7 D; Cyril V. Taylor, 1907-1991, © 1942, 1970, Hope Publishing Co.

May also be sung to HYMN TO JOY.

A Hymn of Glory Let Us Sing 268

1. A hymn of glo - ry let us sing! New
2. The ho - ly ap - os - tol - ic band Up -
3. To whom the shin - ing an - gels cry, "Why
4. O ris - en Christ, as - cend - ed Lord, All

hymns through - out the world shall ring: Al - le - lu - ia! Al - le -
on the Mount of Ol - ives stand. Al - le - lu - ia! Al - le -
stand and gaze up on the sky?" Al - le - lu - ia! Al - le -
praise to you let earth ac - cord: Al - le - lu - ia! Al - le -

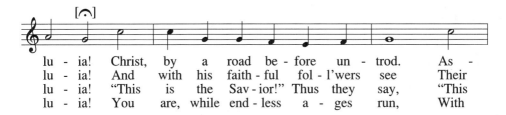

lu - ia! Christ, by a road be - fore un - trod. As -
lu - ia! And with his faith - ful fol - l'wers see Their
lu - ia! "This is the Sav - ior!" Thus they say, "This
lu - ia! You are, while end - less a - ges run, With

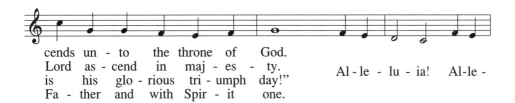

cends un - to the throne of God.
Lord as - cend in maj - es - ty.   Al - le - lu - ia! Al - le -
is his glo - rious tri - umph day!"
Fa - ther and with Spir - it one.

lu - ia! Al - le - lu - ia! Al - le - lu - ia! Al - le - lu - ia!

Text: *Hymnum canamus gloria;* Venerable Bede, 673-735; tr. *Lutheran Book of Worship,* © 1978
Tune: LASST UNS ERFREUEN, LM with alleluias; *Geistliche Kirchengasange,* Cologne, 1623; harm. by Ralph Vaughan Williams, 1872-1958,
© Oxford University Press

269 Hail the Day That Sees Him Rise

1. Hail the day that sees him rise
2. There for him high tri - umph waits;
3. High - est heav'n its Lord re - ceives,
4. See, he lifts his hands a - bove.
5. Still for us he in - ter - cedes,
6. There we shall with him re - main,
Al - le - lu - ia!

To his throne a - bove the skies;
Lift your heads, e - ter - nal gates;
Yet he loves the earth he leaves:
See, he shows the prints of love.
His pre - vail - ing death he pleads,
Part - ners of his end - less reign;
Al - le - lu - ia!

Christ, a - while to mor - tals given,
He has con - quered death and sin;
Though re - turn - ing to his throne,
Hark, his gra - cious lips be - stow,
Near him - self pre - pares our place,
There his face un - cloud - ed see,
Al - le - lu - ia!

Re - as - cends his na - tive heav'n.
Take the King of glo - ry in.
Still he calls the world his own.
Bless - ings on his church be - low.
He the first fruits of our race.
Live with him e - ter - nal - ly.
Al - le - lu - ia!

Text: Charles Wesley, 1707-1788, alt.
Tune: LLANFAIR, 77 77 with alleluias; Robert Williams, 1781-1821

Go   270

1. Go ye there-fore and teach all na - tions, go,
2. If you love me, real - ly love me, feed

go, go. Go ye there-fore and teach all
my sheep. If you love me, real - ly

na - tions, go, go, go. Bap-tiz - ing
love me, feed my sheep. And lo, I'll be

them in the name of the Fa-ther and Son and Ho - ly
with you for ev - er and ev - er un - til the ends of the

Ghost. Go, go, go.
world, go, go, go.

Text: Leon Patillo
Tune: Leon Patillo
© 1984, Word Music, Inc.

Veni Sancte Spiritus   271

Ostinato Refrain

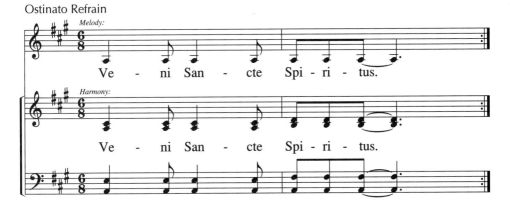

Melody:

Ve - ni San - cte Spi - ri - tus.

Harmony:

Ve - ni San - cte Spi - ri - tus.

Text: *Come Holy Spirit;* Verses drawn from the Pentecost Sequence; Taizé Community, 1978
Tune: Jacques Berthier, 1923-1994
© 1979, Les Presses de Taizé, GIA Publications, Inc., agent

272 O Holy Spirit, by Whose Breath

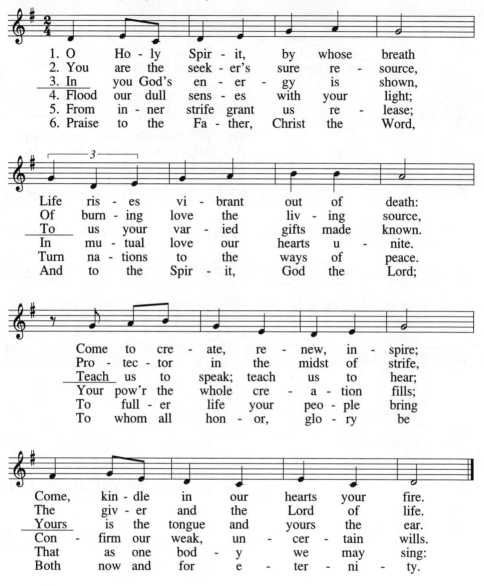

1. O Ho - ly Spir - it, by whose breath
2. You are the seek - er's sure re - source,
3. In you God's en - er - gy is shown,
4. Flood our dull sens - es with your light;
5. From in - ner strife grant us re - lease;
6. Praise to the Fa - ther, Christ the Word,

Life ris - es vi - brant out of death:
Of burn - ing love the liv - ing source,
To us your var - ied gifts made known.
In mu - tual love our hearts u - nite.
Turn na - tions to the ways of peace.
And to the Spir - it, God the Lord;

Come to cre - ate, re - new, in - spire;
Pro - tec - tor in the midst of strife,
Teach us to speak; teach us to hear;
Your pow'r the whole cre - a - tion fills;
To full - er life your peo - ple bring
To whom all hon - or, glo - ry be

Come, kin - dle in our hearts your fire.
The giv - er and the Lord of life.
Yours is the tongue and yours the ear.
Con - firm our weak, un - cer - tain wills.
That as one bod - y we may sing:
Both now and for e - ter - ni - ty.

Text: *Veni, Creator Spiritus;* attr. to Rabanus Maurus, 776-865; tr. by John W. Grant, b.1919, © 1971
Tune: VENI CREATOR SPIRITUS, LM; Mode VIII; setting by Richard J. Wojcik, b.1923, © 1975, GIA Publications, Inc.

Veni Creator Spiritus 273

1. Ve - ni Cre - á - tor Spí - ri - tus,
2. Qui dí - ce - ris Pa - rá - cli - tus,
3. Tu se - pti - fór - mis mú - ne - re,
4. Ac - cén - de lu - men sén - si - bus,
5. Hó - stem re - pél - las lón - gi - us,
6. Per te sci - á - mus da Pa - trem,
7. De - o Pa - tri sit gló - ri - a,

Men - tes tu - ó - rum ví - si - ta:
Al - tís - si - mi dó - num De - i,
Di - gi - tus pa - tér - nae déx - te - rae,
In - fun - de - a - mó - rem cór - di - bus,
Pa - cém - que do - nes pró - ti - nus:
No - scá - mus at - que Fí - li - um
Et Fí - li - o, qui a mór - tu - is

Im - ple - su - pér - na grá - ti - a
Fons vi - vus, i - gnis, cá - ri - tas,
Tu ri - te pro - mís - sum Pa - tris,
In - fír - ma no - stri cór - po - ris
Du - ctó - re sic te práe - vi - o,
Te - que u - tri - ús - que Spí - ri - tum
Sur - ré - xit, ac Pa - rá - cli - to,

Quae tu cre - á - sti pé - cto - ra.
Et spi - ri - tá - lis ún - cti - o.
Ser - mó - ne di - tans gút - tu - ra.
Vir - tú - te fír - mans pér - pe - ti.
Vi - té - mus om - ne nó - xi - um.
Cre - dá - mus om - ni tém - po - re.
In sae - cu - ló - rum sáe - cu - la. A - men.

Text: Attr. to Rabanus Maurus, 776-856
Tune: VENI CREATOR SPIRITUS, LM; Mode VIII; acc. by Richard Proulx, b.1937, © 1975, GIA Publications, Inc.

274 The Spirit of God

Refrain

The Spir-it of God rests up-on me, The Spir-it of God con-se-crates me, The Spir-it of God bids me go forth to pro-claim God's peace and joy.

Verses

1.-5. The Spir-it of God sends me forth, Called to wit-ness the king-dom of Christ a-mong all the na-tions;

1. Called to pro-claim the good news of Christ to the
2. Called to con-sole the hearts o-ver-come with great
3. Called to com-fort the poor who mourn and who
4. Called to an-nounce the grace of sal-va-tion to
5. Called to re-veal God's glo-ry a-mong all the

D.C.

poor.
sor - row.
weep. My spir-it re-joic-es in God, my Sav - ior.
all.
peo - ple.

Text: Isaiah 61:1, 2; Luke 4:18-19; Lucien Deiss, C S Sp, b.1921
Tune: Lucien Deiss, C S Sp, b.1921
© 1970, 1973, World Library Publications, Inc.

Send Us Your Spirit 275

Refrain

Come Lord Je-sus, send us your Spir-it, re-new the face of the earth. Come Lord Je-sus, send us your Spir-it, re-new the face of the earth.

Verses

1. Come to us, Spir-it of God, breathe in us now, we sing to-geth-er. Spir-it of God hope and of light, fill our lives, come to us, Spir-it of God.
2. Fill us with the fire of your love, burn in us now, bring us to-geth-er. Come to us, dwell in us, change our lives, O Lord, come to us, Spir-it of God.
3. Send us the wings of new birth, fill all the earth with the love you have taught us. Let all cre-a-tion now be shak-en with love, come to us, Spir-it of God.

D.C.

May be sung in canon.

Text: David Haas, b.1957
Tune: David Haas, b.1957; acc. by Jeanne Cotter, b.1964
© 1981, 1982, 1987, GIA Publications, Inc.

276 Come, Holy Ghost

1. Come, Ho - ly Ghost, Cre - a - tor blest,
2. O Com - fort - er, to thee we cry,
3. O Ho - ly Ghost, Through thee a - lone,
4. Praise we the Lord, Fa - ther and Son,

And in our hearts take up thy rest;
Thou heav'n - ly gift of God most high;
Know we the Fa - ther and the Son;
And Ho - ly Spir - it with them one;

Come with thy grace and heav'n - ly aid
Thou fount of life, and fire of love,
Be this our firm un - chang - ing creed,
And may the Son on us be - stow

To fill the hearts which thou hast made,
And sweet a - noint - ing from a - bove,
That thou dost from them both pro - ceed,
All gifts that from the Spir - it flow,

To fill the hearts which thou hast made.
And sweet a - noint - ing from a - bove.
That thou dost from them both pro - ceed.
All gifts that from the Spir - it flow.

Text: *Veni, Creator Spiritus;* attr. to Rabanus Maurus, 776-856; tr. by Edward Caswall, 1814-1878, alt.
Tune: LAMBILLOTTE, LM with repeat; Louis Lambillotte, SJ, 1796-1855, harm. by Richard Proulx, b.1937, © 1986, GIA Publications, Inc.

Everyone Moved by the Spirit 277

Refrain

Ev - 'ry - one moved by the Spir - it is a

son and daugh-ter of God. Led by the

fire of his love we will live in the light of the

Lord. We will live in the light of the Lord.

Verses

1. Come, O Spir - it of Je - sus.
2. Come, O Spir - it of Je - sus.

Come in the pow - er of his name.
Send forth the pow - er of your love.

D.C.

Re - new the depths of our hearts.
Re - new the face of the earth.

278 How Wonderful the Three-in-One

1. How won - der - ful the Three - in - One,
2. Be - fore the flow of dawn and dark,
3. The Lov - er's own Be - lov'd, in time,
4. Their E - qual Friend all life sus - tains
5. How won - der - ful the Liv - ing God:

Whose en - er - gies of danc - ing light
Cre - a - tion's Lov - er dreamed of earth,
Be - tween a cra - dle and a cross,
With green - ing pow'r and lov - ing care,
Di - vine Be - lov'd Em - pow'r - ing Friend,

Are un - di - vid - ed, pure and good,
And with a car - ing deep and wise,
At home in flesh, gave love and life
And calls us, born a - gain by grace,
E - ter - nal Lov - er, Three - in - One,

Com - mun - ing love in shared de - light.
All things con - ceived and brought to birth.
To heal our bro - ken - ness and loss.
In Love's com - mun - ing life to share.
Our hope's be - gin - ning, way and end.

Text: Brian Wren, b.1936, © 1989, 1996, Hope Publishing Co.
Tune: PUER NOBIS, LM; adapt. by Michael Praetorius, 1571-1621

279 O God, Almighty Father

1. O God, al - might-y Fa - ther, Cre - a - tor of all things, The
2. O Je - sus, Word in - car - nate, Re - deem - er most a - dored, All
3. O God, the Ho - ly Spir - it, Who lives with-in our soul, Send

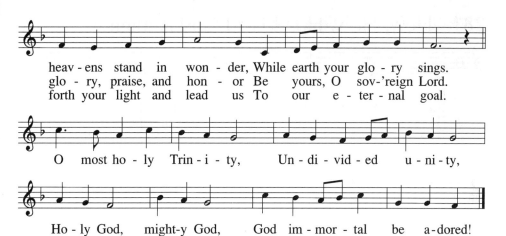

heav - ens stand in won - der, While earth your glo - ry sings.
glo - ry, praise, and hon - or Be yours, O sov-'reign Lord.
forth your light and lead us To our e - ter - nal goal.

O most ho - ly Trin - i - ty, Un - di - vid - ed u - ni - ty,

Ho - ly God, might-y God, God im - mor - tal be a-dored!

Text: *Gott Vater sei gepriesen;* anon; tr. by Irvin Udulutsch, OFM Cap., fl. 1959, alt. © 1959, The Liturgical Press
Tune: GOTT VATER SEI GEPRIESEN, 7 6 7 6 with refrain; *Limburg Gesangbuch,*1838; harm. by Healey Willan, 1880-1968, © 1958, The
Basilian Fathers, assigned to Ralph Jusko Publications, Inc.

Come, Now Almighty King   280

1. Come, now al - might - y King, Help us your
2. Come, now In - car - nate Son, Your life in
3. Come, ho - ly Com - fort - er, Your sa - cred
4. To the great One in Three E - ter - nal

name to sing, Help us to praise.
us be - gun, Our prayer at - tend.
wit - ness bear In this glad hour.
prais - es be For ev - er - more!

Fa - ther all glo - ri - ous, Ev - er vic - to - ri - ous,
Come and your peo - ple bless And give your Word suc - cess;
Your grace to us im - part, Now rule in ev - 'ry heart
Your sov-'reign maj - es - ty May we in glo - ry see

Come and reign o - ver us, An - cient of Days.
Strength-en your right - eous-ness, Sav - ior and Friend!
Nev - er from us de - part, Spir - it of Pow'r!
And to e - ter - ni - ty Love and a - dore!

Text: Anon. c.1757
Tune: ITALIAN HYMN, 66 4 666 4; Felice de Giardini, 1716-1796

281 Holy, Holy, Holy! Lord God Almighty

1. Ho - ly, Ho - ly, Ho - ly! Lord God Al - might - y! Ear - ly in the morn - ing our song shall rise to thee: Ho - ly, Ho - ly, Ho - ly! mer - ci - ful and might - y, God in three Per - sons, bless - ed Trin - i - ty.

2. Ho - ly, Ho - ly, Ho - ly! all the saints a - dore thee, Cast - ing down their gold - en crowns a - round the glass - y sea; Cher - u - bim and ser - a - phim fall - ing down be - fore thee, God ev - er - last - ing through e - ter - ni - ty.

3. Ho - ly, Ho - ly, Ho - ly! though the dark - ness hide thee, Though the eye made blind by sin thy glo - ry may not see, On - ly thou art ho - ly; there is none be - side thee, Per - fect in power, in love, and pu - ri - ty.

4. Ho - ly, Ho - ly, Ho - ly! Lord God Al - might - y! All thy works shall praise thy Name in earth, and sky, and sea; Ho - ly, Ho - ly, Ho - ly! mer - ci - ful and might - y, God in three Per - sons, bless - ed Trin - i - ty.

Text: Reginald Heber, 1783-1826, alt.
Tune: NICAEA, 11 12 12 10; John Bacchus Dykes, 1823-1876

Jesus, My Lord, My God, My All   282

1. Je - sus, my Lord, my God, my All,
2. Had I but Mar - y's sin - less heart,
3. O! see up - on the al - tar placed

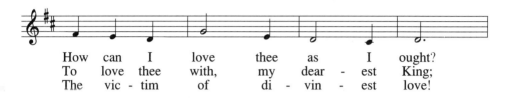

How can I love thee as I ought?
To love thee with, my dear - est King;
The vic - tim of di - vin - est love!

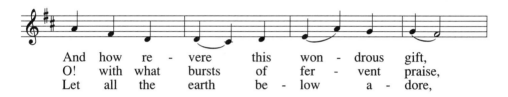

And how re - vere this won - drous gift,
O! with what bursts of fer - vent praise,
Let all the earth be - low a - dore,

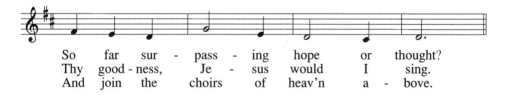

So far sur - pass - ing hope or thought?
Thy good - ness, Je - sus would I sing.
And join the choirs of heav'n a - bove.

Sweet Sac - ra - ment, we thee a - dore! O make us love thee

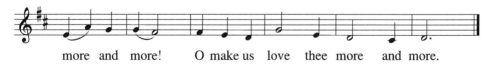

more and more! O make us love thee more and more.

Text: St. 1-2, Frederick W. Faber, 1814-1863; st. 3, *Mediator Dei Hymnal,* 1955, © 1955, GIA Publications, Inc.
Tune: SWEET SACRAMENT, LM with refrain; *Romischkatholisches Gesangbuchlein,* 1826

283 Crown Him with Many Crowns

1. Crown him with man - y crowns, The Lamb up - on his
2. Crown him the Lord of life, Who tri - umphed o'er the
3. Crown him the Lord of love, Be - hold his hands and
4. Crown him the Lord of peace, Whose power a scep - ter
5. Crown him the Lord of years, The ris - en Lord sub -

throne; Hark! how the heav'n - ly an - them drowns All
grave, And rose vic - to - rious in the strife For
side, Rich wounds yet vis - i - ble a - bove In
sways From pole to pole, that wars may cease, Ab -
lime, Cre - a - tor of the roll - ing spheres, The

mu - sic but its own. A - wake, my soul, and sing Of
those he came to save. His glo - ries now we sing, Who
beau - ty glo - ri - fied. No an - gel in the sky Can
sorbed in prayer and praise. His reign shall know no end, And
Mas - ter of all time. All hail, Re - deem - er, hail! For

him who set us free, And hail him as your
died and rose on high, Who died, e - ter - nal
ful - ly bear that sight, But down - ward bends his
round his pierc - ed feet Fair flow'rs of Par - a -
you have died for me; Your praise and glo - ry

heav'n - ly King Through all e - ter - ni - ty.
life to bring, And lives that death may die.
burn - ing eye At mys - ter - ies so bright.
dise ex - tend Their fra - grance ev - er sweet.
shall not fail Through - out e - ter - ni - ty.

Text: Revelation 19:12; St. 1, 3-5, Matthew Bridges, 1800-1894; St. 2, Godfrey Thring, 1823-1903
Tune: DIADEMATA, SMD.; George J. Elvey, 1816-1893

Christ Is the King   284

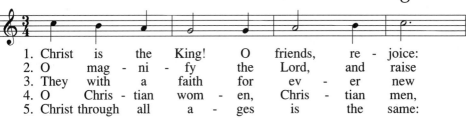

1. Christ is   the King!   O   friends,   re - joice:
2. O   mag - ni - fy   the   Lord,   and   raise
3. They with a   faith for   ev - er   new
4. O   Chris - tian wom - en, Chris - tian men,
5. Christ through all   a - ges   is   the   same:

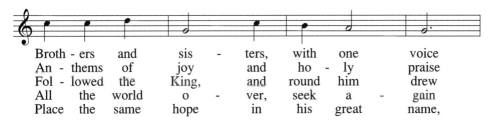

Broth - ers   and   sis - ters,   with one   voice
An - thems   of   joy   and   ho - ly   praise
Fol - lowed the   King,   and   round him   drew
All   the world   o - ver,   seek a - gain
Place the same hope   in   his   great name,

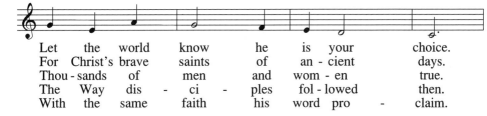

Let   the world know   he   is your   choice.
For Christ's brave saints of   an - cient days.
Thou - sands of   men   and wom - en   true.
The Way dis - ci - ples fol - lowed   then.
With the same faith   his   word pro - claim.

Al - le - lu - ia,   al - le - lu - ia,   al - le - lu - ia.

6. Let love's all reconciling might
   Your scattered companies unite
   In service to the Lord of light.
   Alleluia, alleluia, alleluia.

7. So shall God's will on earth be done,
   New lamps be lit, new tasks begun,
   And the whole Church at last be one.
   Alleluia, alleluia, alleluia.

Text: George K. A. Bell, 1883-1958, alt., © Oxford University Press
Tune: GELOBT SEI GOTT, 888 with alleluias; Melchior Vulpius, c.1560-1616

285 All Hail the Power of Jesus' Name

1. All hail the pow'r of Je - sus' name! Let
2. Crown him, ye mar - tyrs of our God, Who
3. Ye cho - sen seed of Is - rael's race, A
4. O that, with yon - der sa - cred throng, We

an - gels pros - trate fall; Bring forth the roy - al
from his al - tar call; Ex - tol the stem of
rem - nant weak and small, Hail him who saved you
at his feet may fall, Join in the ev - er -

di - a - dem, And crown him Lord of
Jes - se's rod, And crown him Lord of
by his grace, And crown him Lord of
last - ing song, And crown him Lord of

all, And crown him Lord of all, And
all, And crown him Lord of all, And
all, And crown him Lord of all, And
all, And crown him Lord of all, And

crown him Lord of all. Bring forth the roy - al
crown him Lord of all. Ex - tol the stem of
crown him Lord of all. Hail him who saved you
crown him Lord of all. Join in the ev - er -

di - a - dem, And crown him Lord of all.
Jes - se's rod, And crown him Lord of all.
by his grace, And crown him Lord of all.
last - ing song, And crown him Lord of all.

Edward Perronet, 1726-1792; alt. by John Rippon, 1751-1836, alt.
DIADEM, CM with repeats; from the *Primitive Baptist Hymn and Tune Book*, 1902; harm. by Robert J. Batastini, b.1942, © 1995,
Publications, Inc.

Jesus Shall Reign 286

1. Je - sus shall reign wher - e'er the sun
2. To him shall end - less prayer be made,
3. Peo - ple and realms of ev - 'ry tongue
4. Bless - ings a - bound wher - e'er he reigns;
5. Let ev - 'ry crea - ture rise and bring

Does his suc - ces - sive jour - neys run;
And prais - es throng to crown his head;
Dwell on his love with sweet - est song;
The pris - 'ner leaps to lose his chains;
Bless - ing and hon - or to our King;

His king - dom stretch from shore to shore,
His Name like sweet per - fume shall rise
And in - fant voic - es shall pro - claim
The wea - ry find e - ter - nal rest,
An - gels de - scend with songs a - gain,

Till moons shall wax and wane no more.
With ev - 'ry morn - ing sac - ri - fice.
Their ear - ly bless - ings on his Name.
And all who suf - fer want are blest.
And earth re - peat the loud A - men.

Text: Isaac Watts, 1674-1748, alt.
Tune: DUKE STREET, LM; John Hatton, c.1710-1793

287 To Jesus Christ, Our Sovereign King

1. To Jesus Christ, our sov-'reign King, Who is the
2. Your reign ex-tend, O King be-nign, To ev-'ry
3. To you, and to your church, great King, We pledge our

world's sal-va-tion, All praise and hom-age do we bring And
land and na-tion; For in your King-dom, Lord di-vine, A-
heart's ob-la-tion; Un-til be-fore your throne we sing In

thanks and ad-o-ra-tion.
lone we find sal-va-tion. Christ Je-sus, Vic-tor!
end-less ju-bi-la-tion.

Christ Je-sus, Rul-er! Christ Je-sus, Lord and Re-deem-er!

Text: Martin B. Hellriegel, 1891-1981, alt., © 1941, Irene C. Mueller
Tune: ICH GLAUB AN GOTT, 8 7 8 7 with refrain; *Mainz Gesangbuch*, 1870; harm. by Richard Proulx, b.1937, © 1986, GIA Publications, Inc.

288 The King of Glory

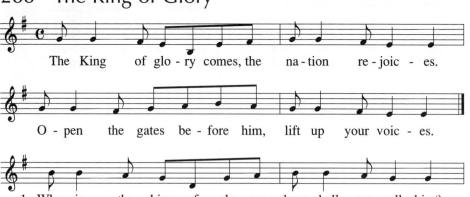

The King of glo-ry comes, the na-tion re-joic-es.

O-pen the gates be-fore him, lift up your voic-es.

1. Who is the king of glo-ry; how shall we call him?
2. In all of Gal-i-lee, in cit-y or vil-lage,
3. Sing then of Da-vid's Son, our Sav-ior and broth-er;
4. He gave his life for us, the pledge of sal-va-tion,
5. He con-quered sin and death; he tru-ly has ris-en.

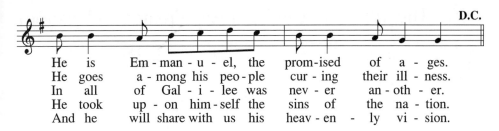

He is Em - man - u - el, the prom-ised of a - ges.
He goes a - mong his peo - ple cur - ing their ill - ness.
In all of Gal - i - lee was nev - er an - oth - er.
He took up - on him - self the sins of the na - tion.
And he will share with us his heav - en - ly vi - sion.

Text: Willard F. Jabusch, b.1930, © 1966, 1982. Administered by OCP Publications
Tune: KING OF GLORY, 12 12 with refrain; Israeli; harm. by Richard Proulx, b.1937

Sing Out, Earth and Skies 289

Verses

1. Come, O God of all the earth: Come to us, O
2. Come, O God of wind and flame: Fill the earth with
3. Come, O God of flash-ing light: Twin-kling star and
4. Come, O God of snow and rain: Show - er down up -
5. Come, O Jus - tice, Come, O Peace: Come and shape our

Right - eous One; Come, and bring our love to birth:
right - eous - ness; Teach us all to sing your name:
burn - ing sun; God of day and God of night:
on the earth; Come, O God of joy and pain:
hearts a - new; Come and make op - pres - sion cease:

In the glo - ry of your Son.
May our lives your love con - fess.
In your light we all are one.
God of sor - row, God of mirth.
Bring us all to life in you.

Refrain

Sing out, earth and skies! Sing of the God who loves you!

Raise your joy-ful cries! Dance to the life a - round you!

Text: Marty Haugen, b.1950
Tune: SING OUT, 7 7 7 7 with refrain; Marty Haugen, b.1950
© 1985, GIA Publications, Inc.

290 The Works of the Lord Are Created in Wisdom

1. The works of the Lord are cre - a - ted in wis - dom!
2. Not e - ven the an - gels have ev - er been grant - ed
3. The sun ev - 'ry morn - ing lights up all cre - a - tion,
4. The wind is his breath and the clouds are his sig - nal,
5. The song is un - fin - ished; how shall we com - plete it,

We view the earth's won - ders and call him to mind;
To tell the full sto - ry of na - ture and grace;
The moon marks the rhy - thm of months in their turn;
The rain and the snow are the robes of his choice;
And where find the skill to per - fect all his praise?

We hear what he says in the world we dis - cov - er,
But o - pen to God is all hu - man per - cep - tion,
The glit - ter - ing stars are ar - rayed in God's hon - or,
The storm and the light - ning, his stan - dards and her - alds,
At work in all plac - es, he cares for all peo - ples—

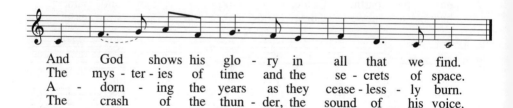

And God shows his glo - ry in all that we find.
The mys - ter - ies of time and the se - crets of space.
A - dorn - ing the years as they cease - less - ly burn.
The crash of the thun - der, the sound of his voice.
How great is the Lord to the end of all days!

Text: Sirach 42-43; Christopher Idle, b.1938, © 1982, Hope Publishing Co.
Tune: KREMSER, 12 11 12 11; *Neder-landtsch Gedanckclank*, 1626; harm. by Edward Kremser, 1838-1914

How Great Thou Art 291

1. O Lord my God, when I in awe-some won-der
2. When thru the woods and for-est glades I wan-der
3. And when I think that God, His Son not spar-ing,
4. When Christ shall come with shout of ac-cla-ma-tion

Con-sid-er all the worlds Thy hands have made,
And hear the birds sing sweet-ly in the trees,
Sent Him to die, I scarce can take it in
And take me home, what joy shall fill my heart!

I see the stars, I hear the roll-ing thun-der,
When I look down from loft-y moun-tain gran-deur
That on the cross, my bur-den glad-ly bear-ing,
Then I shall bow in hum-ble ad-o-ra-tion

Thy pow'r thru-out the un-i-verse dis-played!
And hear the brook and feel the gen-tle breeze.
He bled and died to take a-way my sin!
And there pro-claim, my God, how great Thou art!

Then sings my soul, my Sav-ior God, to Thee;
How great Thou art, how great Thou art! Then sings my soul, my Sav-ior God, to Thee;
How great Thou art, How great Thou art!

Text: Stuart K. Hine, 1899-1989
Tune: O STORE GUD, 11 10 11 10 with refrain; Stuart K. Hine, 1899-1989
© 1953, 1981, Manna Music, Inc.

292 Canticle of the Sun

Refrain

The heav-ens are tell-ing the glo-ry of God,

and all cre-a-tion is shout-ing for joy. Come,

dance in the for-est, come, play in the field, and

sing, sing to the glo-ry of the Lord.

Verses

1. Praise for the sun, the bring-er of day, He car-ries the
2. Praise for the wind that blows through the trees, The seas might-y
3. Praise for the rain that wa-ters our fields, And bless-es our
4. Praise for the fire who gives us his light, The warmth of the
5. Praise for the earth who makes life to grow, The crea-tures you
6. Praise for our death that makes our life real, The knowl-edge of

light of the Lord in his rays; The moon and the stars who
storms, ⁊ the gen-tl-est breeze; They blow where they will, they
crops ⁊ so all the earth yields; From death un-to life her
sun ⁊ to bright-en our night; He danc-es with joy, his
made ⁊ to let your life show; The flow-ers and trees that
loss ⁊ that helps us to feel; The gift of your-self, your

D.C.

light up the way Un-to your throne.
blow where they please To please the Lord.
mys-t'ry re-vealed Springs forth in joy.
spir-it so bright, He sings of you.
help us to know The heart of love.
pres-ence re-vealed To lead us home.

Text: Marty Haugen, b.1950
Tune: Marty Haugen, b.1950
© 1980, GIA Publications, Inc.

Come to the Water 293

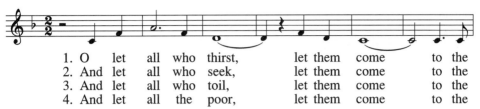

1. O let all who thirst, let them come to the
2. And let all who seek, let them come to the
3. And let all who toil, let them come to the
4. And let all the poor, let them come to the

wa - ter. And let all who have noth - ing,
wa - ter. And let all who have noth - ing,
wa - ter. And let all who are wea - ry,
wa - ter. Bring the ones who are lad - en,

let them come to the Lord: With - out mon - ey,
let them come to the Lord: With - out mon - ey,
let them come to the Lord: All who la - bor,
bring them all to the Lord: Bring the chil - dren

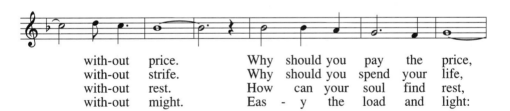

with-out price. Why should you pay the price,
with-out strife. Why should you spend your life,
with-out rest. How can your soul find rest,
with-out might. Eas - y the load and light:

ex - cept for the Lord?
ex - cept for the Lord?
ex - cept for the Lord?
come to the Lord.

Text: Isaiah 55:1, 2, Matthew 11:28-30; John Foley, SJ, b.1939
Tune: John Foley, SJ, b.1939
© 1978, John B. Foley, SJ, and New Dawn Music

294   I Have Loved You

Refrain

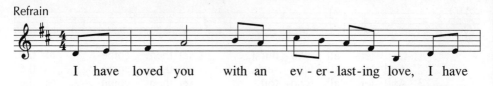

I have loved you   with an   ev - er - last-ing love,   I have

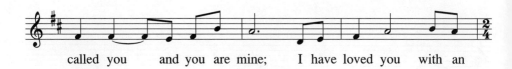

called you   and you are mine;   I have loved you   with an

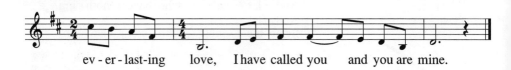

ev - er - last-ing   love,   I have called you   and you are mine.

Verses

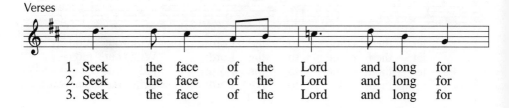

1. Seek   the   face   of   the   Lord   and long   for
2. Seek   the   face   of   the   Lord   and long   for
3. Seek   the   face   of   the   Lord   and long   for

D.C.

him: He will   bring   you his light   and his   peace.
him: He will   bring   you his joy   and his   hope.
him: He will   bring   you his care   and his   love.

Text: Jeremiah 31:3, Psalm 24:3; Michael Joncas, b.1951
Tune: Michael Joncas, b.1951
© 1979, New Dawn Music

We Are the Light of the World   295

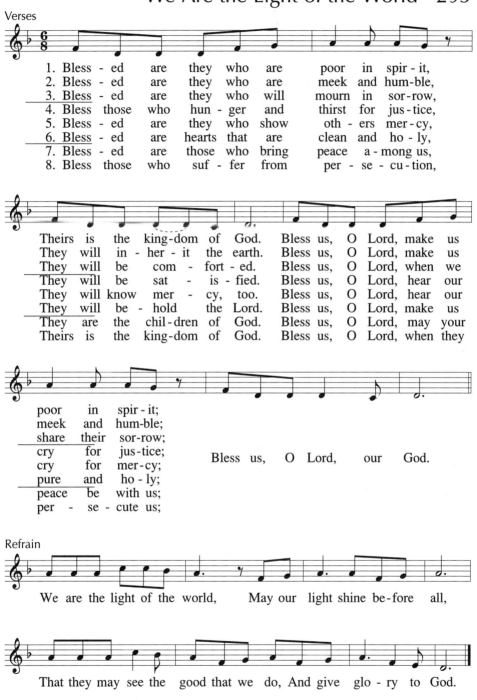

Verses

1. Bless - ed are they who are poor in spir - it,
2. Bless - ed are they who are meek and hum-ble,
3. Bless - ed are they who will mourn in sor-row,
4. Bless those who hun - ger and thirst for jus - tice,
5. Bless - ed are they who show oth - ers mer - cy,
6. Bless - ed are hearts that are clean and ho - ly,
7. Bless - ed are those who bring peace a - mong us,
8. Bless those who suf - fer from per - se - cu - tion,

Theirs is the king-dom of God. Bless us, O Lord, make us
They will in - her - it the earth. Bless us, O Lord, make us
They will be com - fort - ed. Bless us, O Lord, when we
They will be sat - is - fied. Bless us, O Lord, hear our
They will know mer - cy, too. Bless us, O Lord, hear our
They will be - hold the Lord. Bless us, O Lord, make us
They are the chil - dren of God. Bless us, O Lord, may your
Theirs is the king-dom of God. Bless us, O Lord, when they

poor in spir - it;
meek and hum-ble;
share their sor-row;
cry for jus-tice;
cry for mer-cy;
pure and ho - ly;
peace be with us;
per - se - cute us;

Bless us, O Lord, our God.

Refrain

We are the light of the world, May our light shine be-fore all,

That they may see the good that we do, And give glo - ry to God.

Text: Matthew 5:3-11, 14-16; Jean A. Greif, 1898-1981
Tune: Jean A. Greif, 1898-1981
© 1966, Vernacular Hymns Publishing Co.

296 This Little Light of Mine

1. This lit - tle light of mine   I'm gon - na let it shine,
2. Ev - 'ry - where I go,   I'm gon - na let it shine,
3. Je - sus gave it to me,   I'm gon - na let it shine,

This lit - tle light of mine   I'm gon - na let it shine;
Ev - 'ry - where I go,   I'm gon - na let it shine;
Je - sus gave it to me,   I'm gon - na let it shine;

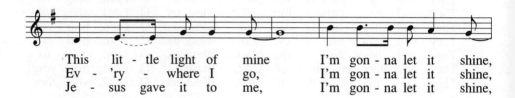

This lit - tle light of mine   I'm gon - na let it shine,
Ev - 'ry - where I go,   I'm gon - na let it shine,
Je - sus gave it to me,   I'm gon - na let it shine,

Let it shine, let it shine, let it shine.
Let it shine, let it shine, let it shine.
Let it shine, let it shine, let it shine.

Text: African-American spiritual
Tune: African-American spiritual; harm. by Horace Clarence Boyer

I Want to Walk as a Child of the Light 297

1. I want to walk as a child of the light.
2. I want to see the bright-ness of God.
3. I'm look-ing for the com-ing of Christ.

I want to fol - low Je - sus.
I want to look at Je - sus.
I want to be with Je - sus.

God set the stars to give light to the world. The
Clear sun of right-eous-ness shine on my path, And
When we have run with pa-tience the race, We

star of my life is Je - sus.
show me the way to the Fa - ther.
shall know the joy of Je - sus.

In him there is no dark - ness at all. The

night and the day are both a - like. The

Lamb is the light of the cit - y of God.

Shine in my heart, Lord Je - sus.

Text: Ephesians 5:8-10, Revelation 21:23, John 12:46, 1 John 1:5, Hebrews 12:1; Kathleen Thomerson, b.1934, © 1970, 1975, Celebration
Tune: HOUSTON, 10 7 10 8 9 9 10 7; Kathleen Thomerson, b.1934, © 1970, 1975, Celebration; acc. by Robert J. Batastini, b.1942, © 1987, GIA
Publications, Inc.

298 Praise to You, O Christ, Our Savior

Refrain

Praise to you, O Christ, our Sav-ior, Word of the Fa-ther, call-ing us to life;

Son of God who leads us to free-dom: glo-ry to you, Lord Je-sus Christ!

Verses

1. You are the Word who calls us out of dark - ness;
2. You are the one whom proph - ets hoped and longed for;
3. You are the Word who calls us to be ser - vants;
4. You are the Word who binds us and u - nites us;

You are the Word who leads us in - to light;
You are the one who speaks to us to - day;
You are the Word whose on - ly law is love;
You are the Word who calls us to be one;

You are the Word who brings us through the des - ert:
You are the one who leads us to our fu - ture:
You are the Word made flesh who lives a - mong us:
You are the Word who teach - es us for - give - ness:

D.C.

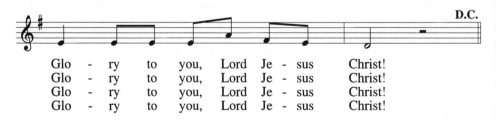

Glo - ry to you, Lord Je - sus Christ!
Glo - ry to you, Lord Je - sus Christ!
Glo - ry to you, Lord Je - sus Christ!
Glo - ry to you, Lord Je - sus Christ!

Text: Bernadette Farrell, b.1957
Tune: Bernadette Farrell, b.1957
© 1986, Bernadette Farrell, published by OCP Publications

Glory and Praise to Our God 299

Refrain

Glo - ry and praise to our God, who a - lone gives

light to our days. Man - y are the

bless-ings he bears to those who trust in his ways.

Verses 1-3

1. We, the daugh - ters and sons of him who built the
2. In his wis - dom he strength - ens us, like gold that's
3. Ev - 'ry mom - ent of ev - 'ry day our God is

val - leys and plains, Praise the won - ders our God has
test - ed in fire. Though the pow - er of sin pre -
wait-ing to save, Al - ways read - y to seek the

D.C.

done in ev - 'ry heart that sings.
vails, our God is there to save.
lost, to an - swer those who pray.

Verse 4

4. God has wa - tered our bar - ren land and spent his

mer - ci - ful rain. Now the riv - ers of life run

D.C.

full for an - y - one to drink.

Text: Psalm 65, 66; Dan Schutte, b. 1947
Tune: Dan Schutte, b. 1947; acc. by Sr. Theophane Hytrek, OSF, 1915-1992, alt.
© 1976, Daniel L. Schutte and New Dawn Music

300 All Creatures of Our God and King

1. All crea-tures of our God and King, Lift
2. O rush-ing wind and breez-es soft, O
3. O flow-ing wa-ters, pure and clear, Make
4. Dear moth-er earth, who day by day Un -
5. O ev-'ry one of ten-der heart, For -

up your voice and with us sing: Al-le-lu-ia! Al-le-
clouds that ride the winds a - loft: Al-le-lu-ia! Al-le-
mu - sic for your Lord to hear. Al-le-lu-ia! Al-le-
folds rich bless-ings on our way, Al-le-lu-ia! Al-le-
giv - ing oth-ers, take your part, Al-le-lu-ia! Al-le-

lu - ia! O burn-ing sun with gold-en beam And
lu - ia! O ris-ing morn, in praise re-joice, O
lu - ia! O fire so mas-ter-ful and bright, Pro -
lu - ia! The fruits and flow'rs that ver-dant grow, Let
lu - ia! All you who pain and sor-row bear, Praise

sil - ver moon with soft-er gleam:
lights of eve-ning, find a voice.
vid - ing us with warmth and light, Al - le -
them God's glo-ry al - so show.
God and cast on God your care.

lu - ia! Al-le-lu - ia! Al-le-lu - ia, al-le-

lu - ia, al-le-lu - ia!

6. And you, most kind and gentle death,
   Waiting to hush our final breath,
   Alleluia! Alleluia!
   You lead to heav'n the child of God,
   Where Christ our Lord the way has trod.
   Alleluia! Alleluia!
   Alleluia, alleluia, alleluia!

7. Let all things their Creator bless,
   And worship God in humbleness,
   Alleluia! Alleluia!
   Oh praise the Father, praise the Son,
   And praise the Spirit, Three in One!
   Alleluia! Alleluia!
   Alleluia, alleluia, alleluia!

Text: *Laudato si, mi Signor;* Francis of Assisi, 1182-1226; tr. by William H. Draper, 1855-1933, alt., © J. Curwen and Sons
Tune: LASST UNS ERFREUEN, LM with alleluias; *Geistliche Kirchengesänge,* 1623; harm. by Ralph Vaughan Williams, 1872-1958, © Oxford
University Press

Praise, My Soul, the King of Heaven 301

1. Praise, my soul, the King of heav - en; To his feet your trib - ute bring; Ran - somed, healed, re - stored, for - giv - en, Ev - er - more his prais - es sing: Al - le - lu - ia! Al - le - lu - ia! Praise the ev - er - last - ing King.
2. Praise him for his grace and fa - vor To his peo - ple in dis - tress; Praise him still the same as ev - er, Slow to chide, and swift to bless: Al - le - lu - ia! Al - le - lu - ia! Glo - rious in his faith - ful - ness.
3. Fa - ther - like he tends and spares us; Well our fee - ble frame he knows; In his hands he gent - ly bears us, Res - cues us from all our foes. Al - le - lu - ia! Al - le - lu - ia! Wide - ly yet his mer - cy flows.
4. Frail as sum-mer's flow'r we flour - ish, Blows the wind and it is gone; But while mor - tals rise and per - ish, God en - dures un - chang - ing on; Al - le - lu - ia! Al - le - lu - ia! Praise the high e - ter - nal one!
5. An - gels, help us to a - dore him; You be - fore him; hold him face to face; Sun and moon, bow down be - fore him, Dwell - ers all in time and space: Al - le - lu - ia! Al - le - lu - ia! Praise with us the God of grace.

Text: Psalm 103; Henry F. Lyte, 1793-1847, alt.
Tune: LAUDA ANIMA, 8 7 8 7 8 7; John Goss, 1800-1880

302 We Praise You

Refrain

We praise you, O Lord, for all your works are won-der-ful.

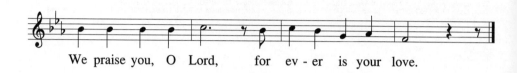

We praise you, O Lord, for ev-er is your love.

Verses

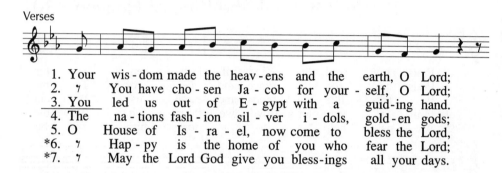

1. Your wis-dom made the heav-ens and the earth, O Lord;
2. ⁊ You have cho-sen Ja-cob for your-self, O Lord;
3. You led us out of E-gypt with a guid-ing hand.
4. The na-tions fash-ion sil-ver i-dols, gold-en gods;
5. O House of Is-ra-el, now come to bless the Lord,
*6. ⁊ Hap-py is the home of you who fear the Lord;
*7. ⁊ May the Lord God give you bless-ings all your days.

You formed the land then set the lights;
So ten-der-ly you spoke his name;
You raised your arm to set us free.
But none have hear-ing, speech or sight.
O House of Aar-on, bless God's name.
So fruit-ful shall your love be - come.
⁊ May you see God fill your land

And like your love the sun will rule the day,
Then called a ho-ly na-tion, Is-ra-el,
And like a ten-der vine you plant-ed us
Their mak-ers shall be like their emp-ty gods,
O bless the Lord, all you who hon-or God,
Your chil-dren flour-ish like the ol-ive plants,
Un - til your chil-dren bring their chil-dren home

italic * wedding verses

D.C.

And	stars	will	grace	the	night.
To	make	them	yours,	you	came.
To	grow	un -	to	the	sea.
The	Lord	a -	lone	brings	life.
And	praise	his	ho -	ly	name.
For	ev - er	are	you	one.
To	show	God's	love	a -	gain.

Text: Mike Balhoff, b.1946
Tune: Darryl Ducote, b.1945, Gary Daigle, b.1957
© 1978, Damean Music. Distributed by GIA Publications, Inc.

All the Earth   303

Refrain

Cantor, then all:

All the earth, pro - claim the Lord; sing your praise to God.

Verses

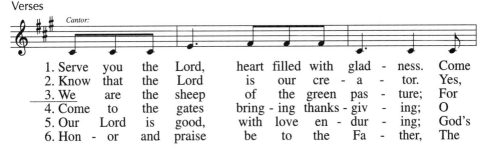

Cantor:

1. Serve	you	the	Lord,	heart	filled	with	glad -	ness.	Come
2. Know	that	the	Lord	is	our	cre -	a -	tor.	Yes,
3. We	are	the	sheep	of	the	green	pas -	ture;	For
4. Come	to	the	gates	bring - ing	thanks - giv -		ing;	O
5. Our	Lord	is	good,	with	love	en -	dur -	ing;	God's
6. Hon -	or	and	praise	be	to	the	Fa -	ther,	The

D.C.

in -	to	God's	pres	-	ence	sing - ing	for	joy!
God	is	our	Fa	-	ther;	we	are	his	own.
we	are	God's	peo	-	ple;	cho - sen	by	God.
en -	ter	the	court	-	yards	sing - ing	in	praise.
word	is	a -	bid	-	ing	now	with	us	all.
Son,	and	the	Spir	-	it,	world	with - out	end.

Text: Lucien Deiss, C S Sp, b.1921
Tune: Lucien Deiss, C S Sp, b.1921
© 1965, World Library Publications, Inc.

304 All the Ends of the Earth

Refrain

All the ends of the earth, all you crea-tures of the sea, lift up your

eyes to the won - ders of the Lord. For the Lord of the earth, the

Mas - ter of the sea, has come with jus - tice for the world.

Verse 1

1. Break in - to song at the deeds of the Lord, the

D.C.

won - ders he has done in ev - 'ry age.

Verse 2

2. Heav - en and earth shall re - joice in his might; ev - 'ry heart,

D.C.

ev - 'ry na - tion call him Lord.

Verse 3

3. The Lord has made sal - va - tion known, faith-ful to the prom-

D.C.

is - es of old. Let the ends of the earth, let the

sea and all it holds make mu - sic be - fore our King!

Text: Psalm 98; Bob Dufford, SJ, b.1943
Tune: Bob Dufford, SJ, b.1943; acc. by Bob Dufford and Chris Morash, alt.
© 1981, Robert J. Dufford, SJ, and New Dawn Music

Praise to the Lord, the Almighty 305

1. Praise to the Lord, the Al - might - y, the king of cre -
2. Praise to the Lord, a - bove all things so might - i - ly
3. Praise to the Lord, who shall pros - per our work and de -
4. Praise to the Lord— O let all that is in us a -

a - tion! O my soul, praise him, for
reign - ing; Keep - ing us safe at his
fend us; Sure - ly his good - ness and
dore him! All that has life and breath

he is your health and sal - va - tion!
side, and so gent - ly sus - tain - ing.
mer - cy shall dai - ly at - tend us.
come now with prais - es be - fore him!

Come, all who hear: Broth - ers and sis - ters, draw near,
Have you not seen All you have need - ed has been
Pon - der a - new What the Al - might - y can do,
Let the "A - men!" Sound from his peo - ple a - gain—

Praise him in glad ad - o - ra - tion!
Met by his gra - cious or - dain - ing?
Who with his love will be - friend us.
Glad - ly with praise we a - dore him!

Text: *Lobe den Herren, den mächtigen König;* Joachim Neander, 1650-1680; tr. by Catherine Winkworth, 1827-1878, alt.
Tune: LOBE DEN HERREN, 14 14 47 8; *Stralsund Gesangbuch,* 1665; descant by C. S. Lang, 1891-1971, © 1953, Novello and Co. Ltd.

306 Holy God, We Praise Thy Name

1. Ho - ly God, we praise thy name! Lord of
2. Hark! the loud ce - les - tial hymn An - gel
3. Ho - ly Fa - ther, Ho - ly Son, Ho - ly

all, we bow be - fore thee; All on earth thy
choirs a - bove are rais - ing; Cher - u - bim and
Spir - it, Three we name thee, While in es - sence

scep - ter claim, All in heav'n a - bove a -
Ser - a - phim In un - ceas - ing cho - rus
on - ly One, Un - di - vid - ed God we

dore thee; In - fi - nite thy vast do - main,
prais - ing, Fill the heav'ns with sweet ac - cord:
claim thee, And a - dor - ing bend the knee,

Repeat ad lib.

Ev - er - last - ing is thy reign.
Ho - ly, ho - ly, ho - ly Lord!
While we own the mys - ter - y.

Text: *Grosser Gott, wir loben dich;* ascr. to Ignaz Franz, 1719-1790; tr. by Clarence Walworth, 1820-1900
Tune: GROSSER GOTT, 7 8 7 8 77; *Katholisches Gesangbuch,* Vienna, c.1774

307 Sing a New Song to the Lord

1. Sing a new song to the Lord, He to whom won - ders be -
2. Now to the ends of the earth See his sal - va - tion is
3. Sing a new song and re - joice, Pub - lish his prais - es a -
4. Join with the hills and the sea Thun - ders of praise to pro -

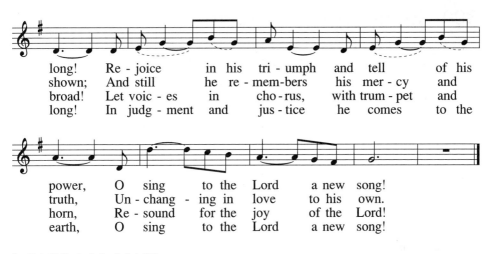

long! Re - joice in his tri - umph and tell of his
shown; And still he re - mem-bers his mer - cy and
broad! Let voic - es in cho - rus, with trum - pet and
long! In judg - ment and jus - tice he comes to the

power, O sing to the Lord a new song!
truth, Un - chang - ing in love to his own.
horn, Re - sound for the joy of the Lord!
earth, O sing to the Lord a new song!

Text: Psalm 98; Timothy Dudley-Smith, b.1926
Tune: CANTATE DOMINO (ONSLOW SQUARE), Irregular; David G. Wilson, b.1940
© 1973, Hope Publishing Co.

Abba! Father!   308

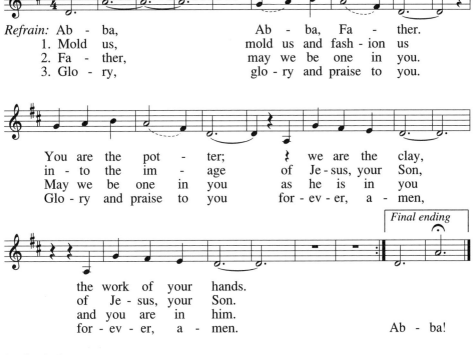

Refrain: Ab - ba, Ab - ba, Fa - ther.
1. Mold us, mold us and fash - ion us
2. Fa - ther, may we be one in you.
3. Glo - ry, glo - ry and praise to you.

You are the pot - ter; we are the clay,
in - to the im - age of Je - sus, your Son,
May we be one in you as he is in you
Glo - ry and praise to you for - ev - er, a - men,

Final ending

the work of your hands.
of Je - sus, your Son.
and you are in him.
for - ev - er, a - men.

Ab - ba!

Text: Carey Landry
Tune: Carey Landry; acc. by Martha Lesinski
© 1977, Carey Landry and North American Liturgy Resources

309 Joyful, Joyful, We Adore You

1. Joy-ful, joy-ful, we a-dore you, God of glo-ry,
2. All your works with joy sur-round you, Earth and heav'n re-
3. Al-ways giv-ing and for-giv-ing, Ev-er bless-ing,
4. Mor-tals join the might-y cho-rus, Which the morn-ing

Lord of love; Hearts un-fold like flowers be-fore you,
flect your rays, Stars and an-gels sing a-round you,
ev-er blest, Well-spring of the joy of liv-ing,
stars be-gan; God's own love is reign-ing o'er us,

Open-ing to the sun a-bove. Melt the clouds of
Cen-ter of un-bro-ken praise; Field and for-est,
O-cean depth of hap-py rest! Lov-ing Fa-ther,
Join-ing peo-ple hand in hand. Ev-er sing-ing,

sin and sad-ness; Drive the dark of doubt a-way;
vale and moun-tain, Flow-ery mead-ow, flash-ing sea,
Christ our broth-er, Let your light up-on us shine;
march we on-ward, Vic-tors in the midst of strife;

Giv-er of im-mor-tal glad-ness, Fill us with the light of day!
Chant-ing bird and flow-ing foun-tain, Prais-ing you e-ter-nal-ly!
Teach us how to love each oth-er, Lift us to the joy di-vine.
Joy-ful mu-sic leads us sun-ward In the tri-umph song of life.

Text: Henry van Dyke, 1852-1933, alt.
Tune: HYMN TO JOY, 8 7 8 7 D; arr. from Ludwig van Beethoven, 1770-1827, by Edward Hodges, 1796-1867

Sing Praise to God Who Reigns Above 310

1. Sing praise to God who reigns a - bove, The
2. What God's al - might - y pow'r has made, God's
3. Then all my glad - some way a - long, I
4. Let all who name Christ's ho - ly name, Give

God of all cre - a - tion, The God of pow'r, the
gra - cious mer - cy's keep - ing; By morn - ing glow or
sing a - loud your prais - es, That all may hear the
God all praise and glo - ry; All you who own his

God of love, The God of our sal - va - tion; With
eve - ning shade God's watch-ful eye ne'er sleep-ing; With-
grate - ful song My voice un - wea - ried rais - es; Be
pow'r, pro - claim A - loud the won - drous sto - ry! Cast

heal - ing balm my soul is filled, And ev - 'ry faith - less
in the king - dom of his might, Lo! all is just and
joy - ful in the Lord, my heart, Both soul and bod - y
each false i - dol from its throne, The Lord is God, the

mur - mur stilled: To God all praise and glo - ry.
all is right: To God all praise and glo - ry.
sing your part: To God all praise and glo - ry.
Lord a - lone: To God all praise and glo - ry.

Text: *Sei Lob und Ehr' dem höchsten Gut;* Johann J. Schütz, 1640-1690; tr. by Frances E. Cox. 1812-1897, alt.
Tune: MIT FREUDEN ZART, 8 7 8 7 88 7; Bohemian Brethren's *Kirchengesange,* 1566

311 Let All Mortal Flesh Keep Silence

1. Let all mor-tal flesh keep si-lence,
2. King of kings, yet born of Mar-y,
3. Rank on rank the host of heav-en
4. At his feet the six-winged ser-aph,

And with fear and trem-bling stand;
As of old on earth he stood,
Spreads its van-guard on the way,
Cher-u-bim with sleep-less eye,

Pon-der noth-ing earth-ly mind-ed,
Lord of lords in hu-man ves-ture,
As the Light of Light de-scend-ing
Veil their fac-es to the Pres-ence,

For with bless-ing in his hand
In the Bod-y and the Blood
From the realms of end-less day,
As with cease-less voice they cry,

Christ our God to earth de-scend-
He will give to all the faith-
That the pow'rs of hell may van-
"Al-le-lu-ia, al-le-lu-

ing, Our full hom-age to de-mand.
ful His own self for heav'n-ly food.
ish As the dark-ness clears a-way.
ia, Al-le-lu-ia, Lord, most high!"

Text: Liturgy of St. James 5th C.; para. by Gerard Moultrie, 1829-1885
Tune: PICARDY, 8 7 8 7 8 7; French Carol; harm. by Richard Proulx, b.1937, © 1986, GIA Publications, Inc.

Sing of the Lord's Goodness 312

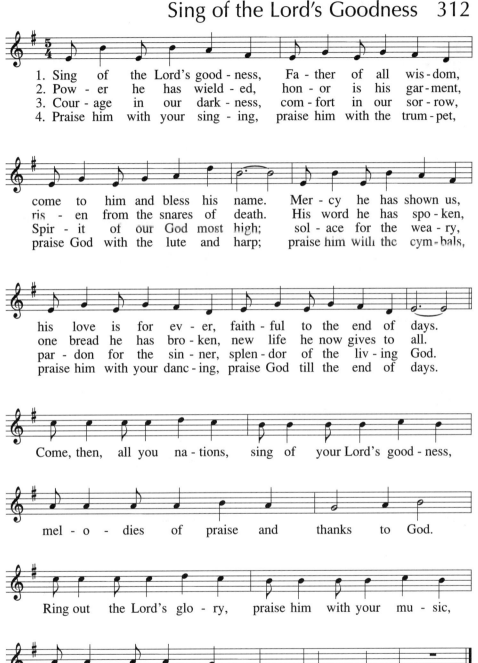

1. Sing of the Lord's good - ness, Fa - ther of all wis - dom,
2. Pow - er he has wield - ed, hon - or is his gar - ment,
3. Cour - age in our dark - ness, com - fort in our sor - row,
4. Praise him with your sing - ing, praise him with the trum - pet,

come to him and bless his name. Mer - cy he has shown us,
ris - en from the snares of death. His word he has spo - ken,
Spir - it of our God most high; sol - ace for the wea - ry,
praise God with the lute and harp; praise him with the cym - bals,

his love is for ev - er, faith - ful to the end of days.
one bread he has bro - ken, new life he now gives to all.
par - don for the sin - ner, splen - dor of the liv - ing God.
praise him with your danc - ing, praise God till the end of days.

Come, then, all you na - tions, sing of your Lord's good - ness,

mel - o - dies of praise and thanks to God.

Ring out the Lord's glo - ry, praise him with your mu - sic,

wor - ship him and bless his name.

Text: Ernest Sands, b.1949, © 1981
Tune: Ernest Sands, b.1949, © 1981; acc. by Paul Inwood, b.1947, © 1986
Published by OCP Publications

313 Joyfully Singing

Verses

1. Joy-ful-ly sing-ing to the Lord,
2. God, in your mer-cy, free our hearts to
3. Gath-er the na-tions to you, Lord,

prais-ing God on high, all of the earth in thank-
praise your ho-ly name, help-ing the poor and low-
draw them to your care, com-ing from all the dis-

ful-ness joins in glad re-ply.
ly ones faith-ful-ly pro-claim.
tant lands glad-ly to de-clare.

Refrain

Bless-ed are your days, ho-ly are your nights,

won-drous is your love all of our lives.

Lord, bring us to-geth-er from east and from

the west. Show us your moun-tain, your

D.C.

dwell-ing place, your life of ho-li-ness.

Text: Mike Balhoff, b. 1946, Gary Daigle, b.1957, Darryl Ducote, b.1945
Tune: Mike Balhoff, b. 1946, Gary Daigle, b.1957, Darryl Ducote, b.1945
© 1985, Damean Music. Distributed by GIA Publications, Inc.

Lift Up Your Hearts 314

Refrain

Lift up your hearts to the Lord, praise God's gra-cious
mer - cy! Sing out your joy to the Lord,
whose love is en - dur - ing.

Verses

1. Shout with joy to the Lord, all the earth!
2. Let the earth wor - ship, sing - ing your praise.
3. God's right hand made a path through the night,
4. Lis - ten now, all you ser - vants of God,

Praise the name a - bove all names! Say to God, "How
Praise the glo - ry of your name! Come and see the
split the wa - ters of the sea. All cre - a - tion,
As I tell of these great works. Bless - ed be the

D.C.

won - drous your works, how glo - rious your name!"
deeds of the Lord, bless God's ho - ly name!
lift up your voice: Our God set us free.
Lord of my life, whose love shall en - dure!

Text: Psalm 66; Roc O'Connor, SJ, b.1949
Tune: Roc O'Connor, SJ, b.1949; acc. by Robert J. Batastini, b.1942
© 1981, 1993, Robert F. O'Connor, SJ, and New Dawn Music

315 Sing a New Song

Refrain

Sing a new song un-to the Lord; let your song be
sung from moun - tains high. Sing a new song
un-to the Lord, sing-ing al - le - lu - ia.

Verses

1. Yah - weh's peo - ple dance for joy. O come be -
2. Rise, O chil - dren, from your sleep; your Sav - ior
3. Glad my soul for I have seen the glo - ry

fore the Lord. And play for him on
now has come. He has turned your
of the Lord. The trum - pet sounds; the

D.C.

glad tam - bou-rines, and let your trum - pet sound.
sor - row to joy, and filled your soul with song.
dead shall be raised. I know my Sav - ior lives.

Text: Psalm 98; Dan Schutte, b.1947
Tune: Dan Schutte, b.1947
© 1972, 1974, Daniel L. Schutte, administered by New Dawn Music

316 Thanks Be to You

1., 3. Praise to you, O God of mer - cy! Thanks be to you for
2. From of old you loved and sought us! Thanks be to you for

ev - er! Rais - ing high the weak and low - ly:
ev - er! Truth and jus - tice you have taught us:

1. **2., 3.**

Thanks be to you for ev - er!
Thanks be to you for ev - er!

Strong is your faith - ful-ness, strong is your love, re -

D.C.

mem - b'ring your cov-e-nant of life with us.

Text: Marty Haugen, b.1950
Tune: Marty Haugen, b.1950
© 1990, GIA Publications, Inc.

We Gather Together 317

1. We gath - er to - geth - er to ask the Lord's bless - ing;
2. Be - side us to guide us, our God with us join - ing,
3. We all do ex - tol you our lead - er tri - um - phant,

He chas - tens and has - tens his will to make known;
Whose king - dom calls all to the love which en - dures.
And pray that you still our de - fend - er will be.

The wick - ed op - press - ing now cease from dis - tress - ing:
So from the be - gin - ning the fight we were win - ning:
Let your con - gre - ga - tion es - cape trib - u - la - tion:

Sing prais - es to his name; he for - gets not his own.
You, Lord, were at our side; all glo - ry be yours!
Your name be ev - er praised! O Lord, make us free!

Text: *Wilt heden nu treden,* Netherlands folk hymn; tr. by Theodore Baker, 1851-1934, alt.
Tune: KREMSER, 12 11 12 11; *Neder-landtsch Gedenckclanck,* 1626; harm. by Edward Kremser, 1838-1914

318 Let All Things Now Living

1. Let all things now liv - ing A song of thanks - giv - ing
2. His law he en - forc - es, The stars in their cours - es,

To God our Cre - a - tor tri - um - phant - ly raise;
The sun in its or - bit o - be - dient - ly shine,

Who fash-ioned and made us, Pro - tect - ed and stayed us,
The hills and the moun-tains, The riv - ers and foun-tains,

By guid - ing us on to the end of our days.
The depths of the o - cean pro - claim God di - vine.

God's ban - ners are o'er us, Pure light goes be - fore us,
We, too, should be voic - ing Our love and re - joic-ing

A pil - lar of fire shin - ing forth in the night:
With glad ad - o - ra - tion, a song let us raise:

Till shad-ows have van - ished And dark - ness is ban-ished,
Till all things now liv - ing U - nite in thanks-giv - ing,

As for - ward we trav - el from light in - to Light.
To God in the high-est, ho - san - na and praise.

Text: Katherine K. Davis, 1892-1980, © 1939, 1966, E.C. Schirmer Music Co.
Tune: ASH GROVE, 66 11 66 11 D; Welsh; harm. by Gerald H. Knight, 1908-1979, © The Royal School of Church Music

Father, We Thank Thee, Who Hast Planted   319

1. Fa - ther, we thank thee, who hast plant - ed
2. Watch o'er thy Church, O Lord, in mer - cy,

Thy ho - ly Name with - in our hearts.
Save it from e - vil, guard it still,

Knowl - edge and faith and life im - mor - tal
Per - fect it in thy love, u - nite it,

Je - sus, thy Son, to us im - parts.
Cleansed and con - formed un - to thy will.

Thou, Lord, didst make all for thy plea - sure,
As grain, once scat - ter'd on the hill - sides,

Didst give us food for all our days,
Was in this bro - ken bread made one,

Giv - ing in Christ the Bread e - ter - nal;
So from all lands thy Church be gath - er'd

Thine is the power, be thine the praise.
In - to thy king - dom by thy Son.

Text: From the *Didache,* c.110; tr. by F. Bland Tucker, 1895-1984, alt., © 1940, The Church Pension Fund
Tune: RENDEZ À DIEU, 9 8 9 8 D; *Genevan Psalter,* 1551; attr. to Louis Bourgeois, c.1510-1561

320 Come, Ye Thankful People, Come

1. Come, ye thank-ful peo-ple, come, Raise the song of
2. All the world is God's own field, Fruit un-to God's
3. For the Lord our God shall come, And shall take the
4. E - ven so, Lord, quick-ly come To your fi - nal

har - vest - home: All is safe-ly gath - ered in,
praise to yield; Wheat and tares to-geth - er sown,
har - vest home; From the field shall in that day
har - vest - home; Gath - er all your peo - ple in,

Ere the win-ter storms be-gin; God, our Mak-er,
Un - to joy or sor-row grown; First the blade, and
All of-fens-es purge a-way, Giv - ing an-gels
Free from sor-row, free from sin; There, for ev-er

does pro-vide For our wants to be sup-plied;
then the ear, Then the full corn shall ap-pear:
charge at last In the fire the tares to cast,
pu - ri-fied, In your pres-ence to a - bide:

Come to God's own tem - ple, come,
Lord of har - vest, grant that we
But the fruit - ful ears to store
Come, with all your an - gels, come,

Raise the song of har - vest - home.
Whole - some grain and pure may be.
In God's gar - ner ev - er - more.
Raise the glo - rious har - vest - home.

Text: Henry Alford, 1810-1871, alt.
Tune: ST. GEORGE'S WINDSOR, 77 77 D; George J. Elvey, 1816-1893

Now Thank We All Our God 321

1. Now thank we all our God With hearts and hands and
2. O may this gra-cious God Through all our life be
3. All praise and thanks to God The Fa-ther now be

voic - es, Who won-drous things has done, In
near us, With ev - er joy - ful hearts And
giv - en, The Son, and Spir - it blest, Who

whom his world re - joic - es; Who, from our moth-ers'
bless - ed peace to cheer us; Pre - serve us in his
reigns in high-est heav - en, E - ter - nal, Tri - une

arms, Hath blest us on our way With
grace, And guide us in dis - tress, And
God, Whom earth and heav'n a - dore; For

count - less gifts of love, And still is ours to - day.
free us from all sin, Till heav - en we pos - sess.
thus it was, is now, And shall be ev - er - more.

Text: *Nun danket alle Gott;* Martin Rinkart, 1586-1649; tr. by Catherine Winkworth, 1827-1878, alt.
Tune: NUN DANKET, 6 7 6 7 6 6 6 6; Johann Crüger, 1598-1662; harm. by A. Gregory Murray, OSB, 1905-1992

322 Give Thanks and Remember

Refrain

Give thanks and re-mem-ber; Here is a liv-ing sign: That one man's dy-ing and ris-ing be-comes our bread and wine.

Verses

1. As long as we are God's peo - ple And earth has fruit to give, So long will God be our Fa - ther; Thank God for all that lives.
2. As long as we live for each oth - er, Plant-ing the words of the Son, So long will God be our Fa - ther; Thank God for all he's done.
3. God tends the pines and the spar - rows, And knows us and all our ways, And God is the source of our life and love; Thank God with sim - ple praise.

D.C.

For the Beauty of the Earth   323

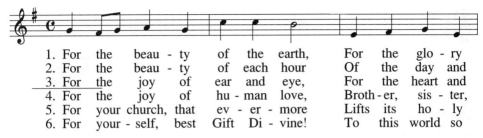

1. For the beau - ty of the earth,   For the glo - ry
2. For the beau - ty of each hour   Of the day and
3. For the joy of ear and eye,   For the heart and
4. For the joy of hu - man love,   Broth - er, sis - ter,
5. For your church, that ev - er - more   Lifts its ho - ly
6. For your - self, best Gift Di - vine!   To this world so

of the skies,   For the love which from our birth
of the night,   Hill and vale, and tree and flow'r,
mind's de - light,   For the mys - tic har - mo - ny
par - ent, child,   Friends on earth, and friends a - bove;
hands a - bove,   Off - 'ring up on ev - 'ry shore
free - ly giv'n;   Word In - car - nate, God's de - sign,

O - ver and a - round us lies:
Sun and moon, and stars of light:
Link - ing sense to sound and sight: Lord of all, to
For all gen - tle thoughts and mild:
Its pure sac - ri - fice of love:
Peace on earth and joy in heav'n:

you we raise This our hymn of grate - ful praise.

Text: Folliot S. Pierpont, 1835-1917
Tune: DIX, 7 7 7 7 77; arr. from Conrad Kocher, 1786-1872, by William H. Monk, 1823-1889

324 Christ Be Beside Me

1. Christ be be - side me, Christ be be - fore me,
2. Christ on my right hand, Christ on my left hand,
3. Christ be in all hearts Think - ing a - bout me;

Christ be be - hind me, King of my heart.
Christ all a - round me, Shield in the strife,
Christ be on all tongues Tell - ing of me.

Christ be with - in me, Christ be be - low me,
Christ in my sleep - ing, Christ in my sit - ting,
Christ be the vis - ion In eyes that see me;

Christ be a - bove me, Nev - er to part.
Christ in my ris - ing, Light of my life.
In ears that hear me, Christ ev - er be.

Text: Ascribed to St. Patrick; James Quinn, SJ, b.1919, © 1969. Used by permission of Selah Publishing Co., Inc., Kingston, N.Y.
Tune: BUNESSAN, 5 5 5 5 4 D; Gaelic; acc. by Robert J. Batastini, b.1942, © 1987, GIA Publications, Inc.

325 Healing River

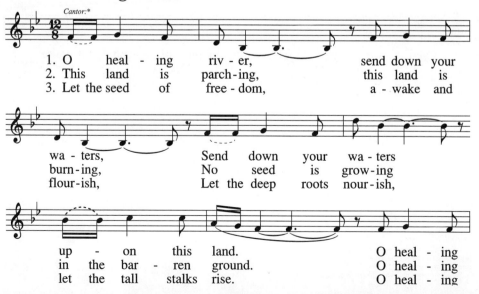

Cantor:*

1. O heal - ing riv - er, send down your
2. This land is parch - ing, this land is
3. Let the seed of free - dom, a - wake and

wa - ters, Send down your wa - ters
burn - ing, No seed is grow - ing
flour - ish, Let the deep roots nour - ish,

up - on this land. O heal - ing
in the bar - ren ground. O heal - ing
let the tall stalks rise. O heal - ing

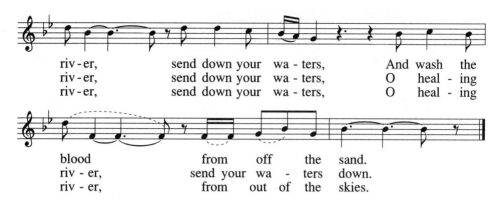

riv - er, send down your wa - ters, And wash the
riv - er, send down your wa - ters, O heal - ing
riv - er, send down your wa - ters, O heal - ing

blood from off the sand.
riv - er, send your wa - ters down.
riv - er, from out of the skies.

The assembly echoes each phrase of the cantor at the interval of one half measure.

Text: Fran Minkoff
Tune: Fred Hellerman; arr. by Michael Joncas, b.1951
© 1964, Appleseed Music, Inc.

O Lord, Hear My Prayer   326

Ostinato Chorale

O Lord, hear my prayer, O Lord, hear my prayer:
*The Lord is my song, the Lord is my praise:

when I call an - swer me. O Lord, hear my prayer, O
all my hope comes from God. The Lord is my song, the

Lord, hear my prayer. Come and lis - ten to me. O
Lord is my praise: God, the well-spring of life. The

*Alternate text

Text: Psalm 102; Taizé Community, 1982
Tune: Jacques Berthier, 1923-1994
© 1982, Les Presses de Taizé, GIA Publications, Inc., agent

327 Lord of All Hopefulness

1. Lord of all hope - ful - ness, Lord of all joy,
2. Lord of all ea - ger - ness, Lord of all faith,
3. Lord of all kind - li - ness, Lord of all grace,
4. Lord of all gen - tle - ness, Lord of all calm,

Whose trust, e - ver child - like, no cares can de - stroy,
Whose strong hands were skilled at the plane and the lathe,
Your hands swift to wel - come, your arms to em - brace,
Whose voice is con - tent - ment, whose pres - ence is balm,

Be there at our wak - ing, and give us, we pray,
Be there at our la - bors, and give us, we pray,
Be there at our hom - ing, and give us, we pray,
Be there at our sleep - ing, and give us, we pray,

Your bliss in our hearts, Lord, at the break of the day.
Your strength in our hearts, Lord, at the noon of the day.
Your love in our hearts, Lord, at the eve of the day.
Your peace in our hearts, Lord, at the end of the day.

Text: Jan Struther, 1901-1953, © Oxford University Press
Tune: SLANE, 10 11 11 12; Gaelic; harm. by Erik Routley, 1917-1982, © 1985, Hope Publishing Co.

328 We Walk by Faith

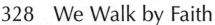

1., 5. We walk by faith, and not by sight: No
2. We may not touch his hands and side, Nor
3. Help then, O Lord, our un - be - lief, And
4. That when our life of faith is done In

gra - cious words we hear Of him who spoke as
fol - low where he trod; Yet in his prom - ise
may our faith a - bound; To call on you when
realms of clear - er light We may be - hold you

none e'er spoke, But we be - lieve him near.
we re - joice, And cry "My Lord and God!"
you are near, And seek where you are found:
as you are In full and end - less sight.

Text: Henry Alford, 1810-1871, alt.
Tune: SHANTI, CM; Marty Haugen, b.1950, © 1984, GIA Publications, Inc.

Beautiful Savior   329

1. Beau - ti - ful Sav - ior, King of cre - a - tion,
2. Fair are the mead - ows, Fair are the wood - lands,
3. Fair is the sun - shine, Fair is the moon - light,
4. Beau - ti - ful Sav - ior, Lord of the na - tions,

Son of God and Son of Man!
Robed in flow'rs of bloom - ing spring;
Bright the spar - kling stars on high;
Son of God and Son of Man!

You will we cher - ish, You will we hon - or,
Je - sus is fair - er, Je - sus is pur - er,
Je - sus shines bright - er, Je - sus shines pur - er
Glo - ry and hon - or, Praise, ad - o - ra - tion,

Light of our souls, their joy and crown.
He makes our sor - r'wing spir - it sing.
Than all the an - gels in the sky.
Now and for - ev - er - more be thine!

Text: Anonymous from *Münster Gesangbuch*, 1977; tr. by Joseph A. Seiss, 1873
Tune: ST. ELIZABETH, 5 5 7 5 5 8; *Schleisische Volkslieder*, 1842; arr. by Richard S. Willis, 1819-1900, alt.

330 We Remember

Refrain

We re - mem-ber how you loved us to your death,

and still we cel - e - brate, for you are with us here;

and we be - lieve that we will see you when you come

in your glo - ry, Lord. We re - mem - ber, we

cel - e - brate, we be - lieve.

Verses

1. Here, a mil - lion wound - ed souls are
2. Now we re - cre - ate your love, we
3. Christ, the Fa - ther's great "A - men" to
4. See the face of Christ re - vealed in

1. yearn - ing just to touch you and be healed.
2. bring the bread and wine to share a meal.
3. all the hopes and dreams of ev - 'ry heart,
4. ev - 'ry per - son stand - ing by your side,

D.C.

1. Gath - er all your peo - ple, and hold them to your heart.
2. Sign of grace and mer - cy, the pres - ence of the Lord.
3. Peace be - yond all tell - ing, and free - dom from all fear.
4. Gift to one an - oth - er, and tem - ples of your love.

Text: Marty Haugen, b.1950
Tune: Marty Haugen, b.1950
© 1980, GIA Publications, Inc.

A Living Faith   331

1. Faith of our fa - thers, liv - ing still
2. Faith of our moth - ers, dar - ing faith,
3. Faith of our broth - ers, sis - ters too,
4. Faith born of God, O call us yet;

In spite of dun - geon, fire and sword;
Your work for Christ is love re - vealed,
Who still must bear op - pres - sion's might,
Bind us with all who fol - low you,

O how our hearts beat high with joy,
Spread-ing God's word from pole to pole,
Rais - ing on high, in pris - ons dark,
Shar - ing the strug - gle of your cross

When - e'er we hear that glo - rious word:
Mak - ing love known and free - dom real:
The cross of Christ still burn - ing bright:
Un - til the world is made a - new,

Faith of our fa - thers, ho - ly faith,
Faith of our moth - ers, ho - ly faith,
Faith for to - day, O liv - ing faith,
Faith born of God, O liv - ing faith,

We will be true to you till death.

Text: St. 1, Frederick W. Faber, 1814-1863, alt.; Sts. 2-4, Joseph R. Alfred, © 1981, alt.
Tune: ST. CATHERINE, LM with refrain; Henry F. Hemy, 1818-1888; adapt. by James G. Walton, 1821-1905

332 I Say "Yes," Lord / Digo "Sí," Señor

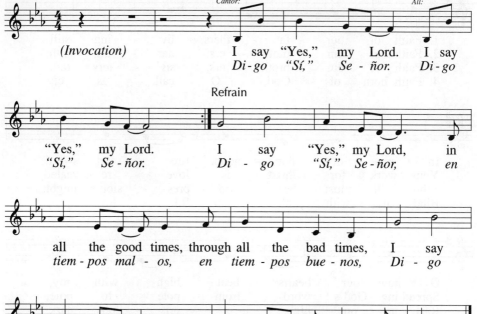

Verses

(Invocation)

Cantor:
I say "Yes," my Lord. I say
Di-go "Sí," Se-ñor. Di-go

Refrain

"Yes," my Lord. I say "Yes," my Lord, in
"Sí," Se-ñor. Di - go "Sí," Se-ñor, en

all the good times, through all the bad times, I say
tiem-pos mal-os, en tiem-pos bue-nos, Di-go

"Yes," my Lord to ev - 'ry word you speak.
"Sí," Se-ñor a to-do lo que ha-blas.

Text: Donna Peña, b.1955
Tune: Donna Peña, b.1955; arr. by Marty Haugen, b.1950
© 1989, GIA Publications, Inc.

333 Blest Be the Lord

Refrain

Blest be the Lord; blest be the Lord, the God of

mer-cy, the God who saves. I shall not fear the dark of

night, nor the ar - row that flies by day.

Verses

1. He will re - lease me from the
2. I need not shrink be - fore the
3. Al - though a thou - sand strong have

nets of all my foes. He will pro -
ter - rors of the night nor stand a -
fall - en at my side, I'll not be

tect me from their wick - ed hands.
lone be - fore the light of day.
shak - en with the Lord at hand.

Be - neath the shad - ow of his wings
No harm shall come to me, no
His faith - ful love is all the

I will re - joice
ar - row strike me down,
ar - mor that I need

D.C.

to find a dwell - ing place se - cure.
no e - vil set - tle in my soul.
to wage my bat - tle with the foe.

Text: Psalm 91; Dan Schutte, b.1947
Tune: Dan Schutte, b.1947; arr. by Sr. Theophane Hytrek, OSF, 1915-1992
© 1976, Daniel L. Schutte and New Dawn Music

334 Only A Shadow

Verses 1, 2

1. The love we have for you, O Lord, is
2. The bread we take and eat, O Lord, is

on - ly a shad - ow of your love for us;
your bod - y bro - ken and shared with us;

on - ly a shad - ow of your love for me, your
your bod - y bro - ken and shared with us, the

deep a - bid - ing love.
gift of your great love.

Refrain

Our lives are in your hands, Our

lives are in your hands. Our love for you will

Last time

grow, O Lord; your light in us will shine.

Verses 3-5

3. Our own be - lief in you, O Lord, is
4. The dreams we have to - day, O Lord, are
5. The joy we share to - day, O Lord, is

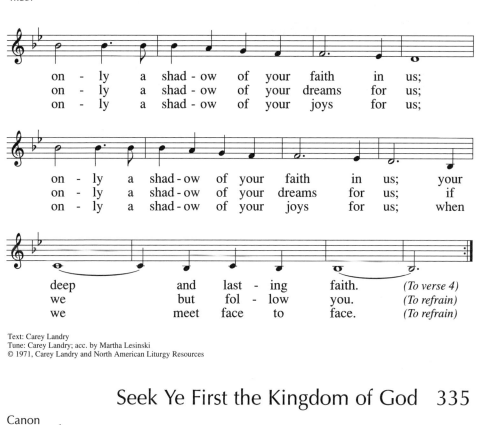

on - ly a shad-ow of your faith in us;
on - ly a shad-ow of your dreams for us;
on - ly a shad-ow of your joys for us;

on - ly a shad-ow of your faith in us; your
on - ly a shad-ow of your dreams for us; if
on - ly a shad-ow of your joys for us; when

deep and last - ing faith. *(To verse 4)*
we but fol - low you. *(To refrain)*
we meet face to face. *(To refrain)*

Text: Carey Landry
Tune: Carey Landry; acc. by Martha Lesinski
© 1971, Carey Landry and North American Liturgy Resources

Seek Ye First the Kingdom of God   335

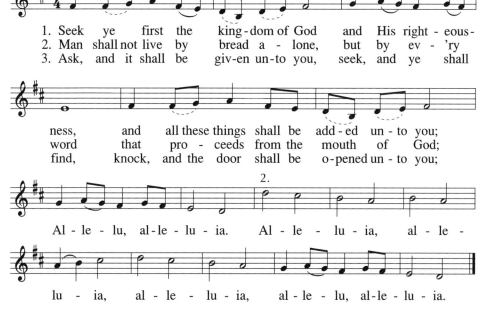

Canon

1. Seek ye first the king-dom of God and His right - eous-
2. Man shall not live by bread a - lone, but by ev - 'ry
3. Ask, and it shall be giv-en un-to you, seek, and ye shall

ness, and all these things shall be add - ed un - to you;
word that pro - ceeds from the mouth of God;
find, knock, and the door shall be o-pened un - to you;

Al - le - lu, al-le - lu - ia. Al - le - lu - ia, al - le -

lu - ia, al - le - lu - ia, al - le - lu, al-le - lu - ia.

Text: Matthew 6:33, 7:7; St. 1, adapt. by Karen Lafferty, b.1948; St. 2, anon.
Tune: SEEK YE FIRST, Irregular; Karen Lafferty, b.1948
© 1972, Maranatha! Music

336 On Eagle's Wings

Verse 1

1. You who dwell in the shel-ter of the Lord, who a-
bide in his shad-ow for life, say to the Lord: "My
ref-uge, my rock in whom I trust!"

Refrain 𝄋

And he will raise you up on ea-gle's wings, bear you on the
breath of dawn, make you to shine like the sun, and

Last time to coda 𝄌 *To verses*

hold you in the palm of his hand. 2. The

Verse 2

snare of the fowl-er will nev-er cap-ture you, and

⌐3⌐

fam-ine will bring you no fear: un-der his wings your

D.S.

ref-uge, his faith-ful-ness your shield.

Text: Psalm 91; Michael Joncas, b.1951
Tune: Michael Joncas, b.1951
© 1979, New Dawn Music

337 All That We Have

Refrain

All that we have and all that we of-fer
Comes from a heart both fright-ened and free.
Take what we bring now and give what we need,
All done in his name.

Verses

1. Some would re - ly on their pow - er,
2. Some - times the road may be lone - some,
3. Some - times when trou - bles are man - y,

Oth - ers put trust in their gold.
Of - ten we may lose our way;
Life can seem emp - ty, it's true,

Some have on - ly their Sav - ior,
Take cour - age and al - ways re - mem - ber
But look at the life of the Mas - ter,

D.C.

Whose faith - ful - ness nev - er grows old.
Love is - n't just for a day.
Who lov - ing - ly suf - fered for you.

Text: Gary Ault, b.1944
Tune: Gary Ault b.1944; acc. by Gary Daigle, b.1957, alt.
© 1969, 1979, Damean Music. Distributed by GIA Publications, Inc.

How Can I Keep from Singing 338

1. My life flows on in end-less song A-
2. Through all the tu-mult and the strife, I
3. What, though my joys and com-fort die, The
4. The peace of Christ makes fresh my heart, A

bove earth's lam - en - ta - tion.   I   hear the real though
hear that mu - sic ring-ing;   It   sounds and ech - oes
Lord, my sav - ior liv - eth.   What though the dark-ness
foun - tain ev - er spring-ing.   All   things are mine since

far - off hymn That hails a new cre - a - tion.
in my soul; How can I keep from sing-ing?
gath-er 'round? Songs in the night it giv - eth.
I am his; How can I keep from sing-ing?

No storm can shake my in-most calm, While to that rock I'm

cling - ing.   Since Christ is Lord of heav-en and earth,

How can I keep from sing-ing?

Text: Robert Lowry, 1826-1899
Tune: HOW CAN I KEEP FROM SINGING, 8 7 8 7 with refrain; Robert Lowry, 1826-1899; harm. by Robert J. Batastini, b.1942, © 1988, GIA
   Publications, Inc.

339 A Mighty Fortress Is Our God

1. A might-y for-tress is our God, A sword and
2. No strength of ours can match his might! We would be
3. Though hordes of dev-ils fill the land All threat-n'ing
4. God's Word for-ev-er shall a-bide, No thanks to

shield vic-to-rious, Who breaks the cruel op-pres-sor's
lost, re-ject-ed. But now a cham-pion comes to
to de-vour us, We trem-ble not, un-moved we
foes, who fear it; For God, our Lord, fights by our

rod And wins sal-va-tion glo-rious. The old sa-
fight, Whom God a-lone e-lect-ed. You ask who
stand; They can-not o-ver-pow'r us. Let this world's
side With weap-ons of the Spir-it. Were they to

tan-ic foe Has sworn to work us woe!
this may be? The Lord of hosts is he!
ty-rant rage; In bat-tle we'll en-gage!
take our house, Goods, hon-or, child, or spouse,

With craft and dread-ful might He arms him-
Christ Je-sus, might-y Lord, God's on-ly
His might is doomed to fail; God's judge-ment
Though life be wrenched a-way, They can-not

self to fight. On earth he has no e-qual.
Son, a-dored. He holds the field vic-to-rious.
must pre-vail! One lit-tle word sub-dues him.
win the day. The King-dom's ours for-ev-er!

Text: Psalm (45) 46; *Ein' feste Burg ins unser Gott;* Martin Luther, 1483-1546; tr. © 1978, *Lutheran Book of Worship*
Tune: EIN' FESTE BURG, 8 7 8 7 66 66 7; Martin Luther, 1483-1546; harm by J.S. Bach, 1685-1750

You Are Near 340

Refrain

Yah-weh, I know you are near, stand-ing al - ways at my side. You guard me from the foe, and you lead me in ways ev er last-ing

Verses

1. Lord, you have searched my heart, and you
2. Where can I run from your love? If I
3. You know my heart and its ways, you who
4. Mar - vel - ous to me are your works; how pro -

know when I sit and when I stand. Your
climb to the heav - ens you are there; if I
formed me be - fore I was born in the
found are your thoughts, my Lord. E - ven

hand is up - on me pro - tect - ing me from death,
fly to the sun - rise or sail be - yond the sea,
se - cret of dark - ness be - fore I saw the sun
if I could count them, they num - ber as the stars,

D.C.

keep - ing me from harm.
still I'd find you there.
in my moth - er's womb.
you would still be there.

Text: Psalm 139; Dan Schutte, b.1947
Tune: Dan Schutte, b.1947; acc. by Sr. Theophane Hytrek, OSF, 1915-1992
© 1971, 1974, Daniel L. Schutte, administered by New Dawn Music

341 For You Are My God

Refrain

For you are my God; you a - lone are my joy.

Last time

De - fend me, O Lord.

Verses 1, 2

1. You give mar - vel-ous com - rades to me: the
2. You are my por - tion and cup; it is

faith - ful who dwell in your land.
you that I claim for my prize. Your

Those who choose a - li-en gods have
her - it - age is my de - light, the

D.C.

cho - sen an a - li - en band.
lot you have giv - en to me.

Verses 3, 4

3. Glad are my heart and my soul;
4. You show me the path for my life;

se - cure - ly my bod - y shall rest.
in your pres - ence the full - ness of joy.

For you will not leave me for dead, nor
To be at your right hand for - ev-er for

lead your be - lov - ed a - stray.
me would be hap - pi-ness al - ways.

Text: Psalm 16; John Foley, SJ, b.1939
Tune: John Foley, SJ, b.1939
© 1970, John B. Foley, SJ, administered by New Dawn Music

Amazing Grace 342

1. A - maz - ing grace! how sweet the
2. 'Twas grace that taught my heart to
3. The Lord has prom - ised good to
4. Through man - y dan - gers, toils, and
5. When we've been there ten thou - sand

sound, That saved a wretch like me!
fear, And grace my fears re - lieved;
me, His word my hope se - cures;
snares, I have al - read - y come;
years, Bright shin - ing as the sun,

I once was lost, but now am
How pre - cious did that grace ap -
He will my shield and por - tion
'Tis grace has brought me safe thus
We've no less days to sing God's

found, Was blind, but now I see.
pear The hour I first be - lieved!
be As long as life en - dures.
far, And grace will lead me home.
praise Than when we'd first be - gun.

Text: St. 1-4, John Newton, 1725-1807; st. 5, attr. to John Rees, fl.1859
Tune: NEW BRITAIN, CM; *Virginia Harmony,* 1831; harm. by Edwin O. Excell, 1851-1921

343 O God, Our Help in Ages Past

1. O God, our help in a - ges past, Our
2. Un - der the shad - ow of your throne Your
3. Be - fore the hills in or - der stood, Or
4. A thou - sand a - ges in your sight Are
5. Time, like an ev - er - roll - ing stream, Soon
6. O God, our help in a - ges past, Our

hope for years to come, Our shel - ter from the
saints have dwelt se - cure; Suf - fi - cient is your
earth re - ceived its frame, From ev - er - last - ing
like an eve - ning gone, Short as the watch that
bears us all a - way; We fly for - got - ten,
hope for years to come, Still be our guard while

storm - y blast, And our e - ter - nal home.
arm a - lone, And our de - fense is sure.
you are God, To end - less years the same.
ends the night Be - fore the ris - ing sun.
as a dream Dies at the op - 'ning day.
trou - bles last, And our e - ter - nal home.

Text: Psalm (89)90; Isaac Watts, 1674-1748
Tune: ST. ANNE, CM; attr. to William Croft, 1678-1727; harm. composite from 18th C. versions

344 Shepherd Me, O God

Refrain

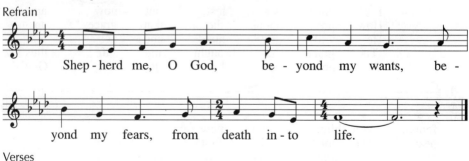

Shep - herd me, O God, be - yond my wants, be -

yond my fears, from death in - to life.

Verses

1. God is my shepherd, so nothing shall I want,
   I rest in the meadows of faithfulness and love,
   I walk by the quiet waters of peace.

2. Gently you raise me and heal my weary soul,
   you lead me by pathways of righteousness and truth,
   my spirit shall sing the music of your name.

3. Though I should wander the valley of death,
   I fear no evil, for you are at my side, your rod and your staff,
   my comfort and my hope.

4. You have set me a banquet of love in the face of hatred,
   crowning me with love beyond my pow'r to hold.

5. Surely your kindness and mercy follow me all the days of my life;
   I will dwell in the house of my God for evermore.

Text: Psalm 23; Marty Haugen, b.1950
Tune: Marty Haugen, b.1950
© 1986, GIA Publications, Inc.

How Firm a Foundation 345

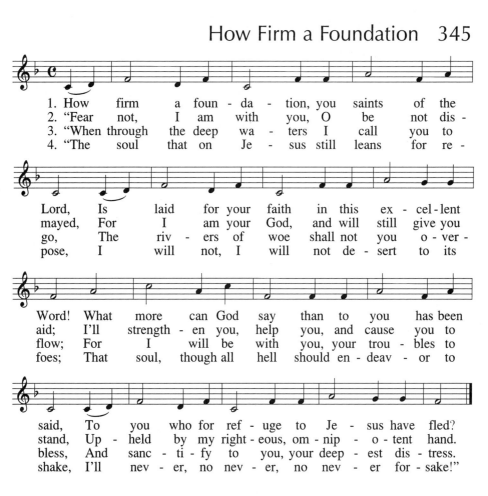

1. How firm a foun - da - tion, you saints of the
2. "Fear not, I am with you, O be not dis -
3. "When through the deep wa - ters I call you to
4. "The soul that on Je - sus still leans for re -

Lord, Is laid for your faith in this ex - cel - lent
mayed, For I am your God, and will still give you
go, The riv - ers of woe shall not you o - ver -
pose, I will not, I will not de - sert to its

Word! What more can God say than to you has been
aid; I'll strength - en you, help you, and cause you to
flow; For I will be with you, your trou - bles to
foes; That soul, though all hell should en - deav - or to

said, To you who for ref - uge to Je - sus have fled?
stand, Up - held by my right - eous, om - nip - o - tent hand.
bless, And sanc - ti - fy to you, your deep - est dis - tress.
shake, I'll nev - er, no nev - er, no nev - er for - sake!"

Text: 2 Peter 1:4; "K" in Rippon's *A Selection of Hymns*, 1787
Tune: FOUNDATION, 11 11 11 11; Funk's *Compilation of Genuine Church Music*, 1832; harm. by Richard Proulx, b.1937,
© 1975, GIA Publications, Inc.

346 Be Not Afraid

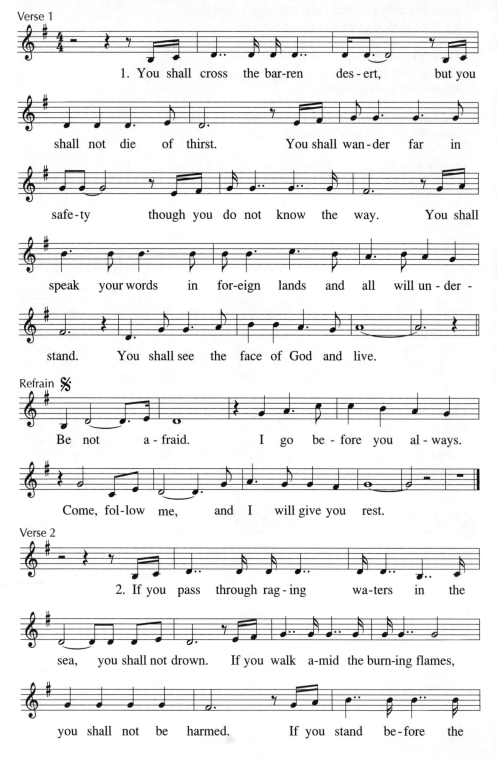

Verse 1

1. You shall cross the bar-ren des-ert, but you shall not die of thirst. You shall wan-der far in safe-ty though you do not know the way. You shall speak your words in for-eign lands and all will un-der-stand. You shall see the face of God and live.

Refrain

Be not a-fraid. I go be-fore you al-ways. Come, fol-low me, and I will give you rest.

Verse 2

2. If you pass through rag-ing wa-ters in the sea, you shall not drown. If you walk a-mid the burn-ing flames, you shall not be harmed. If you stand be-fore the

pow'r of hell and death is at your side,

D.S.

know that I am with you through it all.

Verse 3

3. Bless-ed are your poor, for the king-dom shall be

theirs. Blest are you that weep and mourn, for

one day you shall laugh. And if wick-ed tongues in-

sult and hate you all be-cause of me,

D.S.

bless-ed, bless-ed are you!

Text: Isaiah 43:2-3, Luke 6:20ff; Bob Dufford, SJ, b.1943
Tune: Bob Dufford, SJ, b.1943; acc. by Sr. Theophane Hytrek, OSF, 1915-1992
© 1975, 1978, Robert J. Dufford, SJ, and New Dawn Music

347 Though the Mountains May Fall

Refrain

Though the moun - tains may fall and the hills turn to dust,

yet the love of the Lord will stand

as a shel - ter for all who will call on his name.

Sing the praise and the glo - ry of God.

Verses

1. Could the Lord ev - er leave you? Could the
2. Should you turn and for - sake him, he will
3. Go to him when you're wea - ry; he will
4. As he swore to your fa - thers, when the

Lord for - get his love? Though a moth - er for -
gent - ly call your name. Should you wan - der a -
give you ea - gle's wings. You will run, nev-er
flood de - stroyed the land; He will nev - er for -

D.C.

sake her child, he will not a - ban - don you.
way from him, he will al - ways take you back.
tire, for your God will be your strength.
sake you; he will swear to you a - gain.

Text: Isaiah 54:6-10, 49:15, 40:31-32; Dan Schutte, b.1947
Tune: Dan Schutte, b.1947; acc. by Michael Pope, SJ
© 1975, Daniel L. Schutte and New Dawn Music

There's a Wideness in God's Mercy   348

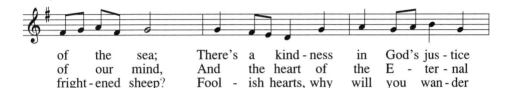

1. There's a wide-ness in God's mer-cy   Like the wide-ness
2. For the love of God is broad-er   Than the meas-ures
3. Trou-bled souls, why will you scat-ter   Like a crowd of

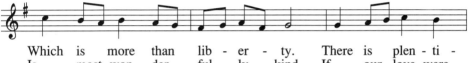

of the sea;   There's a kind-ness in God's jus-tice
of our mind,   And the heart of the E-ter-nal
fright-ened sheep?   Fool-ish hearts, why will you wan-der

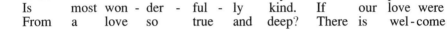

Which is more than lib-er-ty.   There is plen-ti-
Is most won-der-ful-ly kind.   If our love were
From a love so true and deep?   There is wel-come

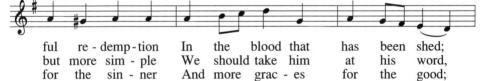

ful re-demp-tion   In the blood that has been shed;
but more sim-ple   We should take him at his word,
for the sin-ner   And more grac-es for the good;

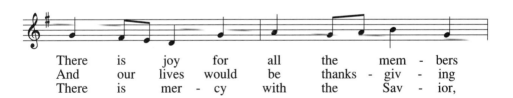

There is joy for all the mem-bers
And our lives would be thanks-giv-ing
There is mer-cy with the Sav-ior,

In the sor-rows of the Head.
For the good-ness of our Lord.
There is heal-ing in his blood.

Text: Frederick W. Faber, 1814-1863, alt.
Tune: IN BABILONE, 8 7 8 7 D; *Oude en Nieuwe Hollanste Boerenlities,* c.1710

349 All I Ask Of You

Refrain

All I ask of you is for-ev-er to re-mem-ber me as lov-ing

1.-5. you.   *To verses*   6. you, for-ev - er as lov - ing you.

Verses

1. Deep the joy of be - ing to - geth-er in one heart and for
2. As we make our way through all the joys and pain, can we
3. Some-one will be call-ing you to be there for a - while. Can you
4. Laugh-ter, joy and pres - ence: the on - ly gifts you are! Have you
5. ⸗ ⸗ Per-sons come in - to the fi - ber of our lives and then their

D.C.

me that's just where it is.
sense our young - er tru - er selves?
hear their cry from deep with - in?
time? I'd like to be with you.
shad - ows fade and dis - ap - pear. But

Text: Gregory Norbet, OSB, and Mary David Callahan, OSB
Tune: Gregory Norbet, OSB, and Mary David Callahan, OSB
© 1973, The Benedictine Foundation of the State of Vermont, Inc. (Western Priory)

350 Lord of All Nations, Grant Me Grace

1. Lord of all na - tions, grant me grace
2. Break down the wall that would di - vide
3. For - give me, Lord, where I have erred
4. Give me your cour - age, Lord, to speak
5. With your own love may I be filled

To love all peo - ple, ev - 'ry race
Your chil - dren, Lord, on ev - 'ry side.
By love - less act and thought - less word.
When - ev - er strong op - press the weak.
And by your Ho - ly Spir - it willed,

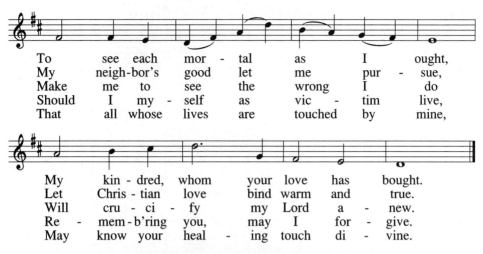

To   see   each   mor - tal   as   I   ought,
My   neigh-bor's good   let   me   pur - sue,
Make   me   to   see   the   wrong   I   do
Should   I   my - self   as   vic - tim   live,
That   all   whose   lives   are   touched by   mine,

My   kin - dred,   whom   your   love   has   bought.
Let   Chris - tian   love   bind   warm   and   true.
Will   cru - ci - fy   my   Lord   a   - new.
Re   - mem - b'ring you,   may   I   for - give.
May   know   your   heal - ing   touch   di   - vine.

Text: Philippians 2:1-18; Olive W. Spannaus, b.1916, © 1969, Concordia Publishing House
Tune: DUKE STREET, LM; John Hatton, c.1710-1793

Where Charity and Love Prevail   351

1. Where   char - i - ty   and   love   pre - vail,
2. With   grate - ful   joy   and   ho - ly   fear
3. For - give   we   now   each   oth - er's   faults
4. Let   strife   a - mong   us   be   un - known,
5. Let   us   re - call   that   in   our   midst
6. No   race   nor   creed   can   love   ex - clude,

There   God   is   ev - er   found;   Brought here   to - geth - er
God's   char - i - ty   we   learn;   Let   us   with   heart and
As   we   our   faults con - fess;   And   let   us   love each
Let   all   con - ten - tion   cease;   Be   God's   the   glo - ry
Dwells God's be - got - ten   Son;   As   mem - bers   of   his
If   hon - ored   be   God's   name;   Our   fam - i - ly   em -

by   Christ's love,   By   love   are   we   thus   bound.
mind and   soul   Now   love   God   in   re - turn.
oth - er   well   In   Chris - tian   ho - li - ness.
that   we   seek,   Be   ours   God's   ho - ly   peace.
bod - y   joined, We   are   in   Christ   made   one.
brac - es   all   Whose   Fa - ther   is   the   same.

Text: *Ubi caritas;* trans. by Omer Westendorf, 1916-1998
Tune: CHRISTIAN LOVE, CM; Paul Benoit, OSB, 1893-1979
© 1960, 1961, World Library Publications, Inc.

352 Love Divine, All Loves Excelling

1. Love di - vine, all loves ex - cel - ling,
2. Come, al - might - y to de - liv - er,
3. Fin - ish then your new cre - a - tion,

Joy of heav'n to earth come down!
Let us all your life re - ceive;
Pure and spot - less, gra - cious Lord,

Fix in us your hum - ble dwell - ing,
Sud - den - ly re - turn and nev - er,
Let us see your great sal - va - tion

All your faith - ful mer - cies crown.
Nev - er more your tem - ples leave.
Per - fect - ly in you re - stored.

Je - sus, source of all com - pas - sion,
Lord, we would be al - ways bless - ing,
Changed from glo - ry in - to glo - ry,

Love un - bound - ed, love all pure;
Serve you as your hosts a - bove,
Till in heav'n we take our place,

Vis - it us with your sal - va - tion,
Pray, and praise you with - out ceas - ing,
Till we sing be - fore the al - might - y

Let your love in us en - dure.
Glo - ry in your pre - cious love.
Lost in won - der, love and praise.

Text: Charles Wesley, 1707-1788, alt.
Tune: HYFRYDOL, 8 7 8 7 D; Rowland H. Prichard, 1811-1887

What Wondrous Love Is This   353

1. What won-drous love is this, O my soul, O my soul?
2. To God and to the Lamb I will sing, I will sing;
3. And when from death I'm free, I'll sing on, I'll sing on;

What won-drous love is this, O my soul?
To God and to the Lamb, I will sing;
And when from death I'm free, I'll sing on;

What won-drous love is this that caused the Lord of bliss
To God and to the Lamb who is the great I Am,
And when from death I'm free, I'll sing and joy-ful be,

To bear the dread-ful curse for my soul, for my soul;
While mil-lions join the theme, I will sing, I will sing;
And through e-ter-ni-ty I'll sing on, I'll sing on!

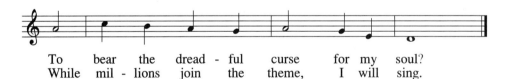

To bear the dread-ful curse for my soul?
While mil-lions join the theme, I will sing.
And through e-ter-ni-ty I'll sing on.

Text: Alexander Means, 1801-1853
Tune: WONDROUS LOVE, 12 9 12 12 9; *Southern Harmony*, 1835; harm. from *Cantate Domino, 1980*, © 1980, World Council of Churches

354 May Love Be Ours

1. Not for tongues of heav-en's an - gels, Not for wis - dom
2. Love is hum - ble, love is gen - tle, Love is ten - der,
3. Nev - er jeal - ous, nev - er self - ish, Love will not re-
4. In the day this world is fad - ing, Faith and hope will

to dis - cern, Not for faith that mas - ters
true, and kind; Love is gra - cious, ev - er
joice in wrong; Nev - er boast - ful nor re -
play their part; But when Christ is seen in

moun - tains, For this bet - ter gift we yearn:
pa - tient, Gen - er - ous of heart and mind—
sent - ful, Love be - lieves and suf - fers long—
glo - ry, Love shall reign in ev - 'ry heart:

May love be ours, Lord; may love be ours.

May love be ours, O Lord.

Text: Timothy Dudley-Smith, b.1926, © 1985, Hope Publishing Co.
Tune: COMFORT, 8 7 8 7 with refrain; Michael Joncas, b.1951, © 1988, GIA Publications, Inc.

355 Eye Has Not Seen

Refrain

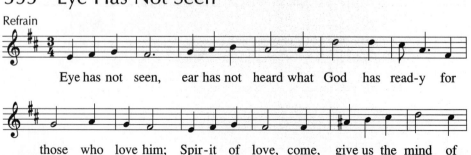

Eye has not seen, ear has not heard what God has read-y for

those who love him; Spir-it of love, come, give us the mind of

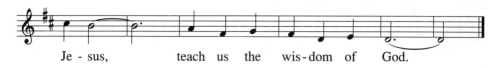

Je - sus, teach us the wis-dom of God.

Verses 1-3

1. When pain and sor - row weigh us down, be near to us, O
2. Our lives are but a sin - gle breath, we flow-er and we
3. To those who see with eyes of faith, the Lord is ev - er

Lord, for - give the weak - ness of our faith, and
fade, yet all our days are in your hands, so
near, re - flect - ed in the fac - es of

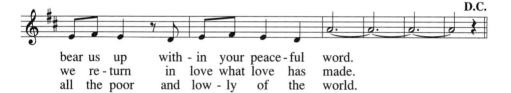

bear us up with - in your peace-ful word.
we re - turn in love what love has made.
all the poor and low - ly of the world.

Verse 4

4. We sing a mys-t'ry from the past in halls where saints have

trod, yet ev - er new the mu - sic rings to

Je - sus, Liv - ing Song of God.

Text: 1 Corinthians 2:9-10; Marty Haugen, b.1950
Tune: Marty Haugen, b.1950
© 1982, GIA Publications, Inc.

356 I Heard the Voice of Jesus Say

1. I heard the voice of Je - sus say, "Come
2. I heard the voice of Je - sus say, "Be -
3. I heard the voice of Je - sus say, "I

un - to me and rest; Lay down, O wea - ry
hold, I free - ly give The liv - ing wa - ter;
am this dark world's light; Look un - to me, your

one, lay down Your head up - on my breast." I
thirst - y one, Stoop down, and drink, and live." I
morn shall rise, And all your day be bright." I

came to Je - sus as I was, So
came to Je - sus, and I drank Of
looked to Je - sus, and I found In

wea - ry, worn, and sad; I found in him a
that life - giv - ing stream; My thirst was quenched, my
him my star, my sun; And in that light of

rest - ing place, And he has made me glad.
soul re - vived, And now I live in him.
life I'll walk Till trav - 'ling days are done.

Text: Horatius Bonar, 1808-1889
Tune: KINGSFOLD, CMD; English; harm. by Ralph Vaughan Williams, 1872-1958, © Oxford University Press

You Are Mine 357

Verses

1. I will come to you in the si - lence,
2. I am hope for all who are hope - less,
3. I am strength for all the des - pair - ing,
4. am the Word that leads all to free - dom, I

I will lift you from all your fear.
I am eyes for all who long to see. In the
heal - ing for the ones who dwell in shame.
am the peace the world can - not give.

You will hear my voice, I claim you as my choice, be
shad - ows of the night, I will be your light,
All the blind will see, the lame will all run free, and
I will call your name, em - brac - ing all your pain, stand

still and know I am here. *(To verse 2)*
come and rest in me. *(To refrain)*
all will know my name. *(To refrain)*
up, now walk, and live! *(To refrain)*

Refrain

Do not be a - fraid, I am with you. I have called you

each by name. Come and fol - low me, I will bring you

D.C.

home; I love you and you are mine.

4. I

Text: David Haas, b.1957
Tune: David Haas, b.1957
© 1991, GIA Publications, Inc.

358 There Is a Balm in Gilead

Refrain

There is a balm in Gil-e-ad To make the wound-ed whole,

There is a balm in Gil-e-ad To heal the sin-sick soul.

Verses

1. Some - times I feel dis - cour - aged And
2. If you can - not preach like Pe - ter, If you
3. Don't ev - er feel dis - cour - aged, For

think my work's in vain, But then the Ho - ly
can - not pray like Paul, You can tell the love of
Je - sus is your friend; And if you lack for

D.C.

Spir - it Re - vives my soul a - gain.
Je - sus, And say, "He died for all!"
knowl - edge He'll ne'er re - fuse to lend.

Text: Jeremiah 8:22, African-American spiritual
Tune: BALM IN GILEAD, Irregular; African-American spiritual; acc. by Robert J. Batastini, b.1942, © 1987, GIA Publications, Inc.

359 Blest Are They

Verses 1-3

1. Blest are they, the poor in spir - it,
2. Blest are they, the low - ly ones,
3. Blest are they who show mer - cy,

theirs is the king - dom of God.
they shall in - her - it the earth.
mer - cy shall be theirs.

Text: Matthew 5:3-12; David Haas, b.1957
Tune: David Haas, b.1957; vocal arr. by David Haas, b.1957, Michael Joncas, b.1951
© 1985, GIA Publications, Inc.

360 Bring Forth the Kingdom

Verses

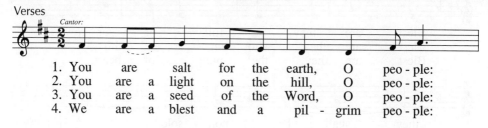

1. You are salt for the earth, O peo-ple:
2. You are a light on the hill, O peo-ple:
3. You are a seed of the Word, O peo-ple:
4. We are a blest and a pil-grim peo-ple:

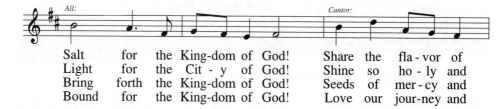

Salt for the King-dom of God! Share the fla-vor of
Light for the Cit-y of God! Shine so ho-ly and
Bring forth the King-dom of God! Seeds of mer-cy and
Bound for the King-dom of God! Love our jour-ney and

life, O peo-ple: Life in the King-dom of God!
bright, O peo-ple: Shine for the King-dom of God!
seeds of jus-tice, Grow in the King-dom of God!
love our home-land: Love is the King-dom of God!

Refrain

Bring forth the King-dom of mer-cy, Bring forth the

King-dom of peace; Bring forth the King-dom of jus-tice,

Bring forth the Cit-y of God!

Text: Marty Haugen, b.1950
Tune: Marty Haugen, b.1950
© 1986, GIA Publications, Inc.

This Is My Body 361

Refrain

This is my bod - y giv - en for your free - dom.

This is my blood which was shed for all my peo - ple.

Take, all, and eat, till the day of my re - turn.

Verses

1. On your jour - ney to the king - dom You will find the
2. Come to me, all you, who la - bor Come, and I will
3. I am Way and Truth and Life, come Fol - low me, be -
4. Hear, my flock, now hear me call - ing For I know you

strength you need At this ta - ble of re - mem - brance
give you rest. Join your fam - 'ly at my ban - quet;
lieve and live. Know that I am al - ways with you,
all by name. Come with me, the bless - ed shep - herd,

D.C.

Of my ris - ing from the dead.
Food and drink are all the best.
Giv - ing all I have to give.
To the new Je - ru - sa - lem.

Text: Anonymous; rev. by Charles G. Frischmann, © 1976, World Library Publications, Inc.
Tune: Anonymous; acc. by Ron Rendek, © 1994, World Library Publications, Inc.

362 The Church's One Foundation

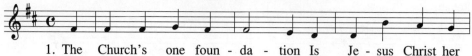

1. The Church's one foun - da - tion Is Je - sus Christ her
2. E - lect from ev - 'ry na - tion, Yet one o'er all the
3. 'Mid toil and trib - u - la - tion, And tu - mult of her
4. Yet she on earth hath un - ion With God, the Three in

Lord; She is his new cre - a - tion By wa - ter and the
earth, Her char - ter of sal - va - tion, One Lord, one faith, one
war, She waits the con - sum - ma - tion Of peace for ev - er -
One, And mys - tic sweet com - mun - ion With those whose rest is

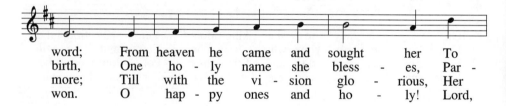

word; From heaven he came and sought her To
birth, One ho - ly name she bless - es, Par -
more; Till with the vi - sion glo - rious, Her
won. O hap - py ones and ho - ly! Lord,

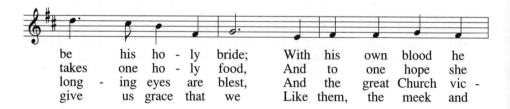

be his ho - ly bride; With his own blood he
takes one ho - ly food, And to one hope she
long - ing eyes are blest, And the great Church vic -
give us grace that we Like them, the meek and

bought her, And for her life he died.
press - es, With ev - 'ry grace en - dued.
to - rious Shall be the Church at rest.
low - ly, On high may dwell with thee.

Text: Samuel J. Stone, 1839-1900
Tune: AURELIA 7 6 7 6 D; Samuel S. Wesley, 1810-1876

Christ Is Made the Sure Foundation 363

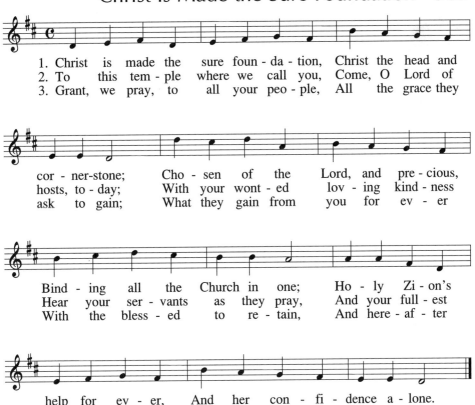

1. Christ is made the sure foun - da - tion, Christ the head and
2. To this tem - ple where we call you, Come, O Lord of
3. Grant, we pray, to all your peo - ple, All the grace they

cor - ner-stone; Cho - sen of the Lord, and pre - cious,
hosts, to - day; With your wont - ed lov - ing kind - ness
ask to gain; What they gain from you for ev - er

Bind - ing all the Church in one; Ho - ly Zi - on's
Hear your ser - vants as they pray, And your full - est
With the bless - ed to re - tain, And here - af - ter

help for ev - er, And her con - fi - dence a - lone.
ben - e - dic - tion Shed in all its bright ar - ray.
in your glo - ry Ev - er - more with you to reign.

Text: *Angularis fundamentum;* 11th C.; tr. by John M. Neale, 1818-1866, alt.
Tune: ST. THOMAS, 8 7 8 7 8 7; John Wade, 1711-1786

364 Church of God

Refrain

Church of God, cho - sen peo - ple, sing your praise to God.

He has called you out of dark-ness in - to his mar - vel-ous light.

Verses

1. Come, peo - ple of God, with joy - ful song, Praise
2. The church is built with liv - ing stones With
3. As heirs of Christ, re - deemed by love We
4. As wa - ter spring - ing from the rock Once
5. We gath - er here to wor - ship God, Our
6. May fra - grant smoke of in - cense rise To
7. The light of Christ has come to us Dis -

God the Fa - ther of all. Bap-tized in Christ, re -
Christ as cor - ner - stone. In him we trust who
wait for his re - turn; A priest - ly peo - ple
brought God's peo - ple life, The liv - ing wa - ter
eu - cha - rist to share. We give him thanks and
fill this house of prayer. May we who gath - er
pel - ling all our fears. His light re - veals the

born in him, Our hearts are filled with joy. He
makes us one, U - nit - ing us in love. We
of - f'ring praise To God, the source of hope. For
giv'n by Christ Cre - ates our lives a - new. So
cel - e - brate The mys - t'ry of his love; The
find true peace, God's pres - ence fill - ing our lives. Our
path of life. We fol - low him with joy, The

cleans - es our sin, Re - new-ing our lives.
build on the rock Of faith in Christ.
Je - sus is Lord, Our Sav - ior and God.
come you who thirst To springs of new life.
Word is made flesh And giv - en for us.
hearts lift with praise, Our lips sing in joy.
glo - ry of God, The light of the world.

Text: Sr. Pamela Stotter
Tune: Margaret Daly
© 1980, International Commission on English in the Liturgy, Inc.

Jesus in the Morning 365

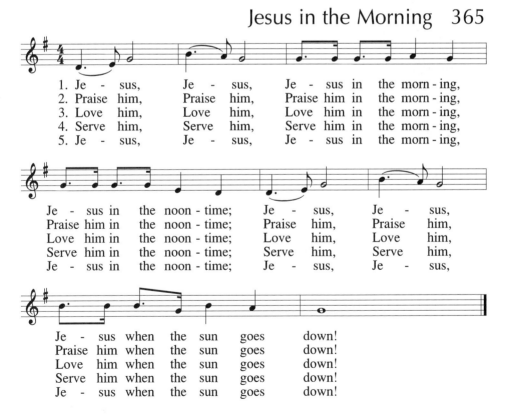

1. Je - sus, Je - sus, Je - sus in the morn - ing,
2. Praise him, Praise him, Praise him in the morn - ing,
3. Love him, Love him, Love him in the morn - ing,
4. Serve him, Serve him, Serve him in the morn - ing,
5. Je - sus, Je - sus, Je - sus in the morn - ing,

Je - sus in the noon - time; Je - sus, Je - sus,
Praise him in the noon - time; Praise him, Praise him,
Love him in the noon - time; Love him, Love him,
Serve him in the noon - time; Serve him, Serve him,
Je - sus in the noon - time; Je - sus, Je - sus,

Je - sus when the sun goes down!
Praise him when the sun goes down!
Love him when the sun goes down!
Serve him when the sun goes down!
Je - sus when the sun goes down!

Text: African-American folk song
Tune: African-American folk song

366 Whatsoever You Do

Refrain

What - so - ev - er you do to the least of my peo-ple, that you do un - to me.

Verses

1. When I was hun - gry, you gave me to eat;
2. When I was home - less, you o - pened your door;
3. When I was wea - ry, you helped me find rest;
4. When I was lit - tle, you taught me to read;
5. When in a pris - on, you came to my cell;
6. In a strange coun - try, you made me at home;
7. Hurt in a bat - tle, you bound up my wounds;
8. When I was Black, or La - ti - no, or white;
9. When I was a - ged, you both - ered to smile;
10. You saw me cov - ered with spit - tle and blood;
11. When I was laughed at, you stood by my side;

When I was thirst - y, you gave me to drink.
When I was na - ked, you gave me your coat.
When I was anx - ious, you calmed all my fears.
When I was lone - ly, you gave me your love.
When on a sick - bed, you cared for my needs.
Seek - ing em - ploy - ment, you found me a job.
Search - ing for kind - ness, you held out your hand.
Mocked and in - sult - ed, you car - ried my cross.
When I was rest - less, you lis - tened and cared.
You knew my fea - tures, though grim - y with sweat.
When I was hap - py, you shared in my joy.

D.C.

Now en - ter in - to the home of my Fa - ther.

Text: Matthew 5:3-12; Willard F. Jabusch, b.1930
Tune: WHATSOEVER YOU DO, 10 10 11 with refrain; Willard F. Jabusch, b.1930; harm. by Robert J. Batastini, b.1942
© 1966, 1982, Willard F. Jabusch. Administered by OCP Publications

'Tis the Gift to Be Simple 367

'Tis the gift to be sim-ple, 'tis the gift to be free, 'tis the

gift to come down where we ought to be, and

when we find our-selves in the place just right, 'twill

be in the val - ley of love and de - light.

When true sim - plic - i - ty is gained to bow and to bend we

shan't be a-shamed, to turn, turn, will be our de-light till by

turn - ing, turn - ing we come round right.

Text: Shaker Song, 18th. C.
Tune: SIMPLE GIFTS; acc. Margaret W. Mealy, © 1984

368 Keep in Mind

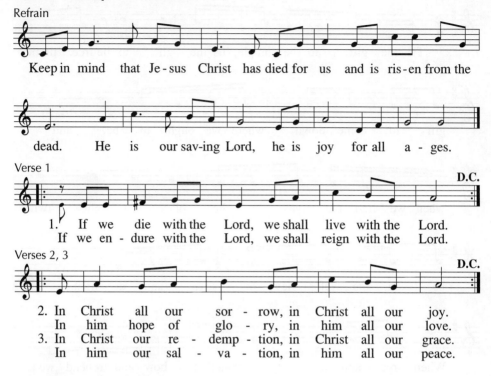

Refrain

Keep in mind that Je-sus Christ has died for us and is ris-en from the
dead. He is our sav-ing Lord, he is joy for all a - ges.

Verse 1
1. If we die with the Lord, we shall live with the Lord.
   If we en - dure with the Lord, we shall reign with the Lord.

Verses 2, 3
2. In Christ all our sor - row, in Christ all our joy.
   In him hope of glo - ry, in him all our love.
3. In Christ our re - demp - tion, in Christ all our grace.
   In him our sal - va - tion, in him all our peace.

Text: 2 Timothy 2:8-12, Lucien Deiss, CSSp, b.1921
Tune: Lucien Deiss, CSSp, b.1921
© 1965, 1966, World Library Publications, Inc.

369 God's Blessing Sends Us Forth

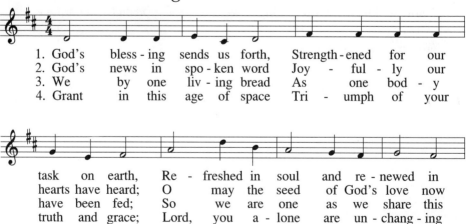

1. God's bless - ing sends us forth, Strength-ened for our
2. God's news in spo - ken word Joy - ful - ly our
3. We by one liv - ing bread As one bod - y
4. Grant in this age of space Tri - umph of your

task on earth, Re - freshed in soul and re - newed in
hearts have heard; O may the seed of God's love now
have been fed; So we are one as we share this
truth and grace; Lord, you a - lone are un - chang - ing

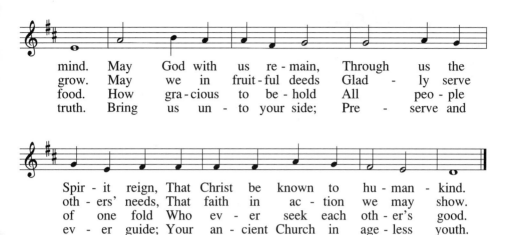

mind. | May | God with | us | re - main, | Through | us | the
grow. | May | we in | fruit - ful deeds | Glad - | ly serve
food. | How | gra - cious | to | be - hold | All | peo - ple
truth. | Bring | us | un - to | your side; | Pre - | serve and

Spir - it reign, That Christ be known to hu - man - kind.
oth - ers' needs, That faith in ac - tion we may show.
of one fold Who ev - er seek each oth - er's good.
ev - er guide; Your an - cient Church in age - less youth.

Text: Omer Westendorf, 1916-1998, © 1964, World Library Publications
Tune: ST. ELIZABETH, 67 9 66 8; *Schlesische Volkslieder,* 1842; harm. by Richard S. Willis, 1819-1900, alt.

We Are Climbing Jacob's Ladder   370

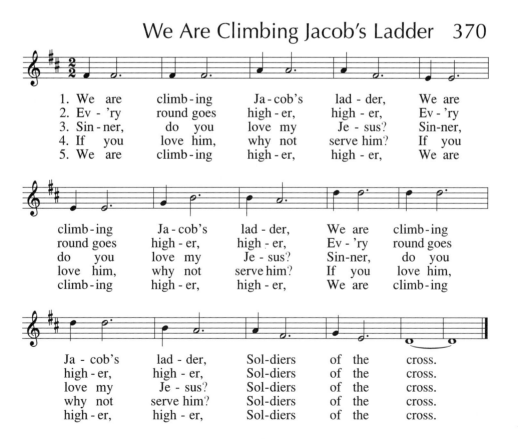

1. We are climb - ing Ja - cob's lad - der, We are
2. Ev - 'ry round goes high - er, high - er, Ev - 'ry
3. Sin - ner, do you love my Je - sus? Sin - ner,
4. If you love him, why not serve him? If you
5. We are climb - ing high - er, high - er, We are

climb - ing Ja - cob's lad - der, We are climb - ing
round goes high - er, high - er, Ev - 'ry round goes
do you love my Je - sus? Sin - ner, do you
love him, why not serve him? If you love him,
climb - ing high - er, high - er, We are climb - ing

Ja - cob's lad - der, Sol - diers of the cross.
high - er, high - er, Sol - diers of the cross.
love my Je - sus? Sol - diers of the cross.
why not serve him? Sol - diers of the cross.
high - er, high - er, Sol - diers of the cross.

Text: African-American spiritual
Tune: JACOB'S LADDER, 8 8 8 5; African-American spiritual

371 City of God

Verses 1, 2

1. A-wake from your slum-ber! A - rise from your
2. We are sons of the morn-ing; we are daugh-ters of

sleep! A new day is dawn - ing
day. The One who has loved us

for all those who weep. The peo - ple in
has bright-ened our way. The Lord of all

dark - ness have seen a great light. The Lord of our
kind - ness has called us to be a light for his

long - ing has con-quered the night.
peo - ple to set their hearts free.

Refrain %

Let us build the cit - y of God. May our tears be

turned in - to danc - ing! For the Lord, our light and our

love, has turned the night in - to day!

Verse 3

3. God is light; in him there is no

dark-ness. Let us walk in his light, his

chil - dren, one and all.

O com-fort my peo - ple; make gen-tle your

words. Pro - claim to my cit-y

D.S.

the day of her birth.

Verse 4

4. O cit-y of glad-ness, now lift up your

voice. Pro - claim the good tid - ings

D.S.

that all may re - joice!

Text: Dan Schutte, b.1947, © 1981, Daniel L. Schutte and New Dawn Music
Tune: Dan Schutte, b.1947, © 1981, Daniel L. Schutte and New Dawn Music; acc. by Robert J. Batastini, b.1942

372 You Have Anointed Me

Text: Mike Balhoff, b.1946, Gary Daigle, b.1957, Darryl Ducote, b.1945
Tune: Mike Balhoff, b.1946, Gary Daigle, b.1957, Darryl Ducote, b.1945; acc. by Gary Daigle, b.1945
© 1981, Damean Music. Distributed by GIA Publications, Inc.

Here I Am, Lord 373

Verses

1. I, the Lord of sea and sky, I have heard my
2. I, the Lord of snow and rain, I have borne my
3. I, the Lord of wind and flame, I will tend the

peo - ple cry. All who dwell in dark and sin
peo - ple's pain. I have wept for love of them.
poor and lame. I will set a feast for them.

My hand will save. I who made the
They turn a - way. I will break their
My hand will save. Fin - est bread I

stars of night, I will make their dark - ness bright.
hearts of stone, Give them hearts for love a - lone.
will pro - vide Till their hearts be sat - is - fied.

Who will bear my light to them? Whom shall I send?
I will speak my word to them. Whom shall I send?
I will give my life to them. Whom shall I send?

Refrain

Here I am, Lord. Is it I, Lord? I have heard you

call - ing in the night. I will go, Lord, if you

lead me. I will hold your peo - ple in my heart.

Text: Isaiah 6; Dan Schutte. b.1947
Tune: Dan Schutte. b.1947; arr. by Michael Pope, SJ, John Weissrock
© 1981, Daniel L. Schutte and New Dawn Music

374 Go Make of All Disciples

1. "Go make of all dis - ci - ples:" We hear the call, O
2. "Go make of all dis - ci - ples:" Bap-tiz - ing in the
3. "Go make of all dis - ci - ples:" We at your feet would
4. "Go make of all dis - ci - ples:" We wel-come your com -

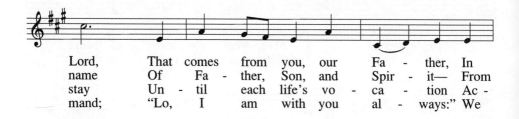

Lord, That comes from you, our Fa - ther, In
name Of Fa - ther, Son, and Spir - it— From
stay Un - til each life's vo - ca - tion Ac -
mand; "Lo, I am with you al - ways:" We

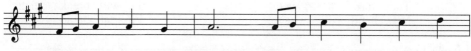

your e - ter - nal Word. In - spire our ways of
age to age the same. We call each new dis -
cents your ho - ly way. We cul - ti - vate the
take your guid - ing hand. The task looms large be -

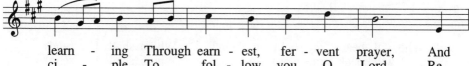

learn - ing Through earn - est, fer - vent prayer, And
ci - ple To fol - low you, O Lord, Re -
na - ture God plants in ev - 'ry heart, Re -
fore us— We fol - low with - out fear. In

let our dai - ly liv - ing Re - veal you ev - 'ry-where.
deem - ing soul and bod - y By wa - ter and the Word.
veal - ing in our wit - ness The Mas - ter Teach-er's art.
heav'n and earth your pow - er Shall bring God's king - dom here.

Text: Matthew 28:19-20; Leon M. Adkins, 1896-1986, alt., © 1955, 1964, Abingdon Press
Tune: ELLACOMBE, 7 6 7 6 D; *Gesangbuch der Herzogl,* Wirtemberg, 1784

The Summons 375

Text: John L. Bell, b.1949, © 1987, Iona Community, GIA Publications, Inc., agent
Tune: KELVINGROVE, 7 6 7 6 777 6; Scottish traditional; arr. by John L. Bell, b.1949, © 1987, Iona Community, GIA Publications, Inc., agent

376 Two Fishermen

1. Two fish-er-men, who lived a-long The Sea of Gal-i-
2. And as he walked a-long the shore 'Twas James and John he'd
3. O Si-mon Pe-ter, An-drew, James And John be-lov-ed
4. And you, good Chris-tians, one and all Who'd fol-low Je-sus'

lee, Stood by the shore to cast their nets In-
find, And these two sons of Zeb-e-dee Would
one, You heard Christ's call to speak good news Re-
way, Come leave be-hind what keeps you bound To

to an age-less sea. Now Je-sus watched them
leave their boats be-hind. Their work and all they
vealed to God's own Son. Su-san-na, Mar-y,
trap-pings of our day, And lis-ten as he

from a-far Then called them each by name; It
held so dear They left be-side their nets. Their
Mag-da-lene Who trav-eled with your Lord, You
calls your name To come and fol-low near, For

changed their lives, these sim-ple men; They'd nev-er be the same.
names they'd heard as Je-sus called; They came with-out re-gret.
min-is-tered to him with joy For he is God a-dored.
still he speaks in var-ied ways To those his call will hear.

Leave all things you have And come and fol-low

me, And come and fol-low me.

Text: Suzanne Toolan, SM, b.1927, © 1986, GIA Publications, Inc.
Tune: LEAVE ALL THINGS, CMD with refrain; Suzanne Toolan, SM, b.1927, © 1970, GIA Publications, Inc.

The Love of the Lord   377

1. All that I count - ed as gain
2. Rich - es and hon - ors will fade,
3. Sil - ver and gold have I none,
4. Faith is the wealth I pos - sess

now I con - sid - er as loss,
earth - ly de - light dis - ap - pear,
no land to count as my home, yet
Find - ing its source in my God:

emp - ty and worth - less to me in the
fade like the grass of the field in the
wealth be - yond meas - ure I own in the
faith in the prom - ise of Christ is my

1., 3. / *2., 4.*

light of the love of the Lord.
light of the love of the Lord.
light of the love of the Lord.
life and my love of the Lord.

What more could bring us hope than to know the pow'r of his

life? What more could bring us peace than to

share in his suf-f'ring and death? What more could be our

fi - nal wish than to live in the love of the Lord?

Text: Philippians 3:7-11; Michael Joncas, b.1951
Tune: Michael Joncas, b.1951
© 1988, GIA Publications, Inc.

378 Lord, When You Came / Pescador de Hombres

Verses

1. Lord, when you came to the sea - shore
2. Lord, you knew what my boat car - ried:
3. Lord, have you need of my la - bor,
4. Lord, send me where you would have me,
1. Tú has ve - ni - do_a la_o - ri - lla,
2. Tú sa - bes bien lo que ten - go,
3. Tú ne - ce - si - tas mis ma - nos,
4. Tú pes - ca - dor de_o - tros, ma - res,

You weren't seek - ing the wise or the wealth-y,
Nei - ther mon - ey nor weap-ons for fight - ing,
Hands for serv - ice, a heart made for lov - ing,
To a vil - lage, or heart of the cit - y;
no_has bus - ca - do ni_a sa - bios, ni_a ri - cos,
en mi bar - ca no_hay o - ro ni_es - pa - das,
mi can - san - cio que_a o - tros des - can - se,
an - sia_e - ter - na, al - mas que es - pe - ran.

But on - ly ask - ing that I might fol - low.
But nets for fish - ing, my dai - ly la - bor.
My arms for lift - ing the poor and bro - ken?
I will re-mem - ber that you are with me.
tan só - lo quie - res que yo te si - ga.
tan só - lo re - des y mi tra - ba - jo.
a - mor que quie - ra se-guir a - man - do.
A - mi - go bue - no, que_a-sí me lla - mas.

Refrain

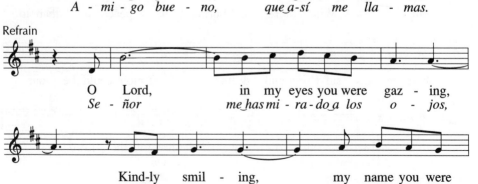

O Lord, in my eyes you were gaz - ing,
Se - ñor me_has mi - ra - do_a los o - jos,

Kind-ly smil - ing, my name you were
son - ri - en - do has di - cho mi

say - ing;   All I treas - ured,
nom - bre,   *en la a - re - na*

I have left on the sand there;   Close to
he de - ja - do mi bar - ca,   *jun - to a*

you,   I will find oth - er seas.
ti   *bus - ca - ré o - tro mar.*

Text: Pescador de Hombres, Cesáreo Gabaráin, © 1979, published by OCP Publications; trans. by Willard Francis Jabusch, b.1930, © 1982,
   administered by OCP Publications
Tune: Cesáreo Gabaráin, © 1979, published by OCP Publications; acc. by Diana Kodner, b.1957

Only This I Want   379

Refrain

On-ly this I want: but to know the Lord,

and to bear his cross   so to wear the crown he wore.

Verses

1. All but this is loss,   worth-less ref - use to me,
2. I will run the race;   I will fight the good fight,
3. Let your heart be glad,   al - ways glad in the Lord,

D.C.

for to gain the Lord   is to gain all I need.
so to win the prize   of the King-dom of my Lord.
so to shine like stars   in the dark-ness of the night.

Text: Philippians 3:7-16; 2:15, 18; Dan Schutte, b.1947
Tune: Dan Schutte, b.1947; arr. by Michael Pope, SJ
© 1981, Daniel L. Schutte and New Dawn Music

380 Now We Remain

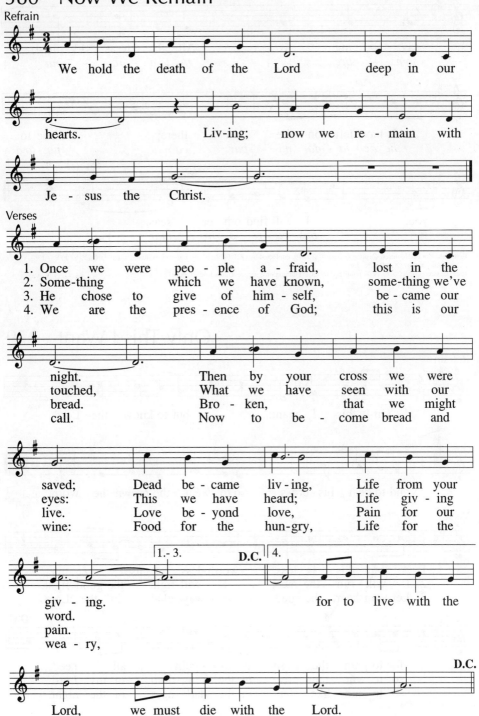

Refrain

We hold the death of the Lord deep in our hearts. Liv-ing; now we re - main with Je - sus the Christ.

Verses

1. Once we were peo - ple a - fraid, lost in the night. Then by your cross we were saved; Dead be - came liv-ing, Life from your giv - ing.

2. Some-thing which we have known, some-thing we've touched, What we have seen with our eyes: This we have heard; Life giv - ing word.

3. He chose to give of him - self, be - came our bread. Bro - ken, that we might live. Love be - yond love, Pain for our pain.

4. We are the pres - ence of God; this is our call. Now to be - come bread and wine: Food for the hun-gry, Life for the wea - ry,

D.C. 4. for to live with the Lord, we must die with the Lord.

D.C.

Text: Corinthians, 1 John, 2 Timothy; David Haas, b.1957
Tune: David Haas, b.1957
© 1983, GIA Publications, Inc.

We Have Been Told   381

Refrain

We have been told, we've seen his face, and heard his voice a - live in our hearts;

"Live in my love with all your heart,

as the Fa - ther has loved me, so I have loved you."

Verse 1

1. "I am the vine, you are the branch - es, and all who live in me will bear great fruit."

Verses 2, 3

2. "You are my friends, if you keep my com - mands, no long - er slaves, I call you friends."

3. "No great - er love is there than this: to lay down one's life, for a friend."

Text: David Haas, b.1957
Tune: David Haas, b.1957; vocal arr. by David Haas, b.1957, Marty Haugen, b.1950
© 1983, GIA Publications, Inc.

382 I Danced in the Morning

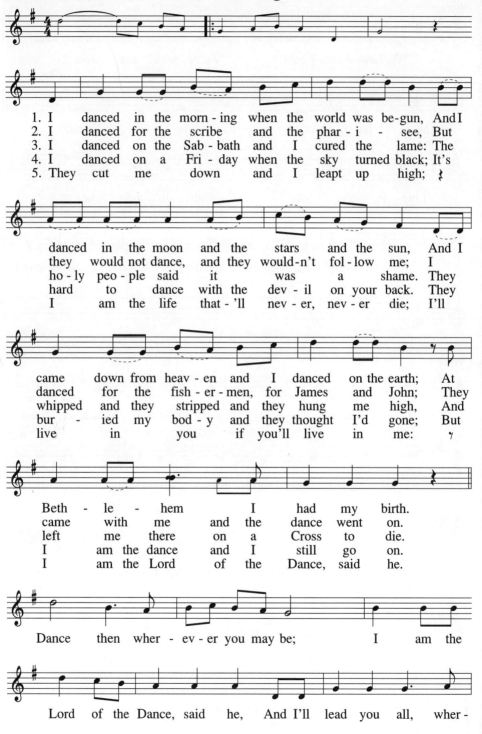

1. I danced in the morn-ing when the world was be-gun, And I
2. I danced for the scribe and the phar-i - see, But
3. I danced on the Sab-bath and I cured the lame: The
4. I danced on a Fri - day when the sky turned black; It's
5. They cut me down and I leapt up high; ♩

danced in the moon and the stars and the sun, And I
they would not dance, and they would-n't fol-low me; I
ho - ly peo - ple said it was a shame. They
hard to dance with the dev - il on your back. They
I am the life that - 'll nev - er, nev - er die; I'll

came down from heav - en and I danced on the earth; At
danced for the fish - er - men, for James and John; They
whipped and they stripped and they hung me high, And
bur - ied my bod - y and they thought I'd gone; But
live in you if you'll live in me:

Beth - le - hem I had my birth.
came with me and the dance went on.
left me there on a Cross to die.
I am the dance and I still go on.
I am the Lord of the Dance, said he.

Dance then wher - ev - er you may be; I am the

Lord of the Dance, said he, And I'll lead you all, wher -

ev - er you may be, And I'll lead you all in the Dance, said he.

Text: Sydney Carter, b.1915, © Stainer and Bell Ltd., London, England. Administered by Hope Publishing Co.
Tune: LORD OF THE DANCE, Irregular; adapted from a traditional Shaker melody; harm. by Sydney Carter, b.1915, © Stainer and Bell Ltd.,
London, England. Administered by Hope Publishing Co.

Great Is the Lord 383

Refrain

Great is the Lord, wor-thy of praise, tell all the na-tions

1.- 3. *To verses* 4.

God is King! Spread the news of God's love! love!

Verses

1. The Spir-it of the Lord is up - on me be - cause the
2. How beau-ti - ful up - on the moun - tains, the feet of
3. Give glo - ry to the Fa - ther, the Son and

Lord has a-noint-ed me. God has sent me to bring glad
those who bring glad tid - ings, an-nounc-ing peace, bear - ing
Ho - ly Spir - it blest, the God who is, who was, who

D.C.

tid - ings to the low - ly, to the low - ly.
good news that the Lord God is King!
will be, for ev - er, A - men.

Text: Isaiah 61:1 - 4; 52:7; Suzanne Toolan, SM, b.1927
Tune: Suzanne Toolan, SM, b.1927
© 1974, GIA Publications, Inc.

384 Take Up Your Cross

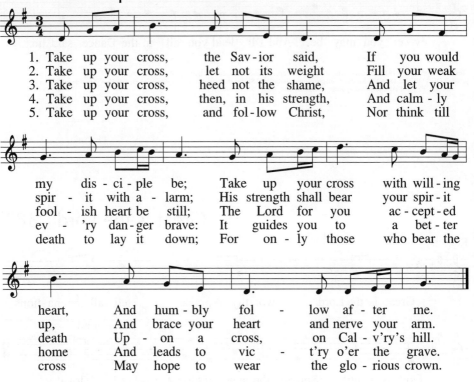

1. Take up your cross, the Sav-ior said, If you would
2. Take up your cross, let not its weight Fill your weak
3. Take up your cross, heed not the shame, And let your
4. Take up your cross, then, in his strength, And calm - ly
5. Take up your cross, and fol-low Christ, Nor think till

my dis - ci - ple be; Take up your cross with will - ing
spir - it with a - larm; His strength shall bear your spir - it
fool - ish heart be still; The Lord for you ac - cept - ed
ev - 'ry dan-ger brave: It guides you to a bet - ter
death to lay it down; For on - ly those who bear the

heart, And hum - bly fol - low af - ter me.
up, And brace your heart and nerve your arm.
death Up - on a cross, on Cal - v'ry's hill.
home And leads to vic - t'ry o'er the grave.
cross May hope to wear the glo - rious crown.

Text: Charles W. Everest, 1814-1877, alt.
Tune: O WALY WALY, LM; English; harm. by Martin West, b.1929, © 1983, Hope Publishing Co.

385 If You Believe and I Believe

If you be - lieve and I be - lieve And we to-geth - er

pray, The Ho - ly Spir - it must come down And

set God's peo - ple free, And set God's peo - ple

free, And set God's peo - ple free; The

Ho - ly Spir - it must come down And set God's peo - ple free.

Text: Zimbabwean traditional
Tune: Zimbabwean traditional; adapt. of English traditional; as taught by Tarasai; arr. by John L. Bell, b.1949, © 1991, Iona Community,
GIA Publications, Inc., agent

Go Down, Moses 386

1. When Is - rael was in E - gypt's land:
2. The Lord told Mo - ses what to do,
3. As Is - rael stood by the wa - ter side,
4. When they had reached the oth - er shore,
5. Oh, let us all from bond - age flee,

Let my peo - ple go:
Op - pressed so hard they
To lead the chil - dren of
At God's com - mand it
They sang the song of
And let us all in

could not stand,
Is - rael through,
did di - vide, Let my peo - ple go. Go down,
tri - umph o'er,
Christ be free,

Mo - ses, 'Way down in E - gypt land,

Tell ol' Phar - aoh, to let my peo - ple go.

Text: Exodus; African-American spiritual
Tune: African-American spiritual

387 The Harvest of Justice

Refrain: May we find rich - ness in the har - vest of jus -
1. Gath - er with pa - tience ⁊ for those who have noth -
2. For to have mer - cy ⁊ on those for - got -
3. For to have lit - tle is to be in a - bun -

tice which Christ Je - sus has rip-ened for
ing. Leave them your rich - es, and you will re -
ten, this is my true law, this is my com -
dance. To give what re - mains, to give all we

us. Bread for the jour - ney,
ceive. Make room for the poor ones,
mand: Clothe the na - ked,
have, is to walk with the poor ones,

bread for the hun - gry, all for the
make way for the stran - ger; for I am the
be home for the or - phan, be hope for the
and be - come the stran - ger, one with the

glo - ry and praise of God.
Lord, the Lord your God.
wid - ow, and wel - come the lost.
Lord, the Lord our God.

Text: Philippians 1:11, Leviticus 19:9, 23:22, Deuteronomy 24:19; David Haas, b.1957
Tune: David Haas, b.1957
© 1985, GIA Publications, Inc.

God, Whose Purpose Is to Kindle 388

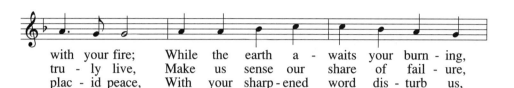

1. God, whose pur - pose is to kin - dle: Now ig - nite us
2. God, who in your ho - ly gos - pel Wills that all should
3. God, who still a sword de - liv - ers Rath - er than a

with your fire; While the earth a - waits your burn - ing,
tru - ly live, Make us sense our share of fail - ure,
plac - id peace, With your sharp - ened word dis - turb us,

With your pas - sion us in - spire. O - ver - come our
Our tran - quil - li - ty for - give. Teach us cour - age
From com - pla - cen - cy re - lease! Save us now from

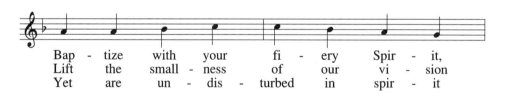

sin - ful calm - ness, Stir us with your sav - ing name;
as we strug - gle In all lib - er - at - ing strife;
sat - is - fac - tion, When we pri - vate - ly are free,

Bap - tize with your fi - ery Spir - it,
Lift the small - ness of our vi - sion
Yet are un - dis - turbed in spir - it

Crown our lives with tongues of flame.
By your own a - bun - dant life.
By our neigh - bor's mis - er - y.

Text: Luke 12:49; David E. Trueblood, b.1900, © 1967, David Elton Trueblood
Tune: HYMN TO JOY, 8 7 8 7 D; arr. from Ludwig van Beethoven, 1770-1827, by Edward Hodges, 1796-1867

389 We Are Called

1. Come! Live in the light! Shine with the
2. Come! O - pen your heart! Show your
3. Sing! Sing a new song! Sing of that

joy and the love of the Lord! We are called
mer - cy to all those in fear! We are called
great day when all will be one! God will reign,

to be light for the king - dom, to
to be hope for the hope - less so all
and we'll walk with each oth - er as

live in the free - dom of the cit - y of God!
ha - tred and blind - ness will be no more!
sis - ters and broth - ers u - nit - ed in love!

We are called to act with jus - tice, we are called to

love ten - der - ly, we are called to serve one an - oth - er;

to walk hum - bly with God!

Text: Micah 6:8; David Haas, b.1957
Tune: David Haas, b.1957
© 1988, GIA Publications, Inc.

We Shall Overcome 390

1. We shall o - ver - come, we shall o - ver - come,
2. We'll walk hand in hand, we'll walk hand in hand,
3. We shall live in peace, we shall live in peace,
4. We are not a - fraid, we are not a - fraid,

we shall o - ver - come some - day. Oh,
we'll walk hand in hand some - day. Oh,
we shall live in peace some - day. Oh,
we are not a - fraid to - day. Oh,

deep in my heart I do be - lieve
deep in my heart I do be - lieve
deep in my heart I do be - lieve
deep in my heart I do be - lieve

we shall o - ver - come some - day.
we shall o - ver - come some - day.
we shall o - ver - come some - day.
we shall o - ver - come some - day.

5. We shall stand together...
6. The truth will make us free...
7. The Lord will see us through...
8. We shall be like him...
9. The whole wide world around...

Text: adapt. by Zilphia Horton, Frank Hamilton, Guy Carawan, and Pete Seeger, © 1960, 1963, Ludlow Music.
Tune: adapt. by Zilphia Horton, Frank Hamilton, Guy Carawan, and Pete Seeger, © 1960, 1963, Ludlow Music;
   harm. by J. Jefferson Cleveland, b.1937, from *Songs of Zion*, harm. © 1981, by Abingdon Press

391 Let There Be Peace on Earth

Let there be peace on earth, and let it be - gin with me.

Let there be peace on earth, the peace that was meant to be. With

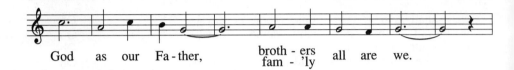

God as our Fa - ther, broth - ers all are we.
fam - 'ly

Let me walk with my broth-er in per-fect har-mo - ny.
us each oth - er

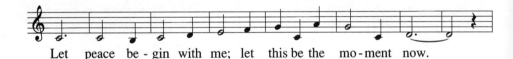

Let peace be - gin with me; let this be the mo - ment now.

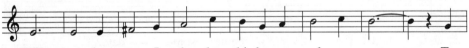

With ev - 'ry step I take, let this be my sol - emn vow; To

take each mo-ment, and live each mo-ment in peace e - ter - nal - ly!

Let there be peace on earth, and let it be - gin with me.

Text: Sy Miller, 1908-1941, Jill Jackson, © 1955, 1983, Jan-Lee Music
Tune: Sy Miller, 1908-1941, Jill Jackson © 1955, 1983, Jan-Lee Music; acc. by Diana Kodner, b.1957, © 1993 GIA Publications, Inc.
Used with permission

Make Me a Channel of Your Peace 392

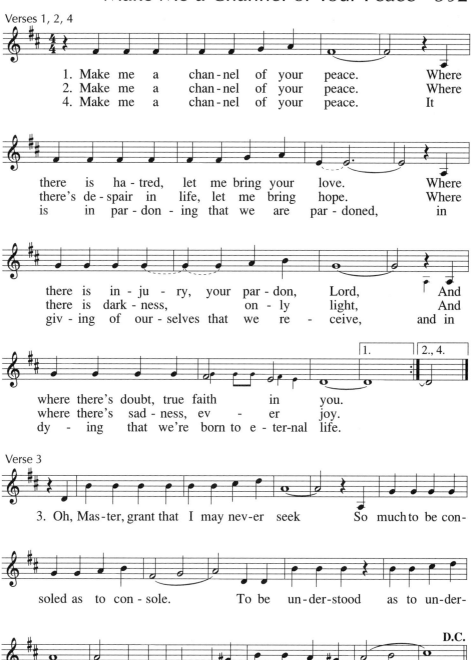

Verses 1, 2, 4

1. Make me a chan-nel of your peace. Where
2. Make me a chan-nel of your peace. Where
4. Make me a chan-nel of your peace. It

there is ha-tred, let me bring your love. Where
there's de-spair in life, let me bring hope. Where
is in par-don-ing that we are par-doned, in

there is in-ju-ry, your par-don, Lord, And
there is dark-ness, on-ly light, And
giv-ing of our-selves that we re-ceive, and in

where there's doubt, true faith in you.
where there's sad-ness, ev-er joy.
dy-ing that we're born to e-ter-nal life.

Verse 3

3. Oh, Mas-ter, grant that I may nev-er seek So much to be con-

soled as to con-sole. To be un-der-stood as to un-der-

stand. To be loved as to love with all my soul.

Text: *Prayer of St. Francis;* adapt. by Sebastian Temple, b.1928
Tune: Sebastian Temple, b.1928; acc. by Robert J. Batastini, b.1942
© 1967, OCP Publications
Dedicated to Mrs. Frances Tracy

393 Peace Is Flowing Like a River

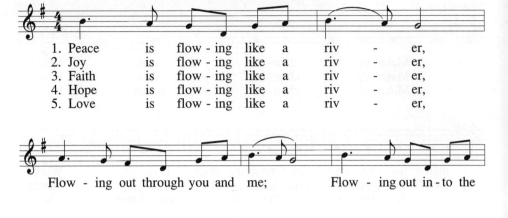

1. Peace is flow-ing like a riv - er,
2. Joy is flow-ing like a riv - er,
3. Faith is flow-ing like a riv - er,
4. Hope is flow-ing like a riv - er,
5. Love is flow-ing like a riv - er,

Flow - ing out through you and me; Flow - ing out in - to the

des - ert, Set - ting all the cap - tives free.

Text: Unknown
Tune: Unknown; acc. by Diana Kodner, b.1957, © 1993, GIA Publications, Inc.

394 Prayer of Peace

1. Peace be - fore us, peace be - hind us, peace
2. Love be - fore us, love be - hind us, love
3. Light be - fore us, light be - hind us, light
4. Christ be - fore us, Christ be - hind us, Christ
5. Al - le - lu - ia, al - le - lu - ia, al - le -
6. Peace be - fore us, peace be - hind us, peace

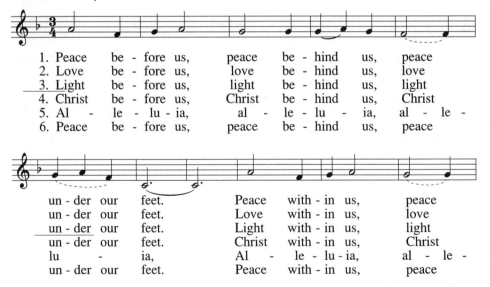

un - der our feet. Peace with - in us, peace
un - der our feet. Love with - in us, love
un - der our feet. Light with - in us, light
un - der our feet. Christ with - in us, Christ
lu - ia, Al - le - lu - ia, al - le -
un - der our feet. Peace with - in us, peace

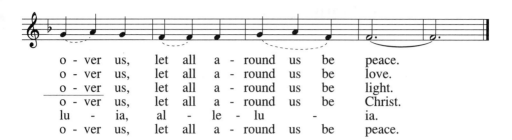

o - ver us, let all a - round us be peace.
o - ver us, let all a - round us be love.
o - ver us, let all a - round us be light.
o - ver us, let all a - round us be Christ.
lu - ia, al - le - lu - ia.
o - ver us, let all a - round us be peace.

Text: Based on a Navajo prayer; David Haas, b.1957
Tune: David Haas, b.1957
© 1987, GIA Publications, Inc.

In Christ There Is No East or West   395

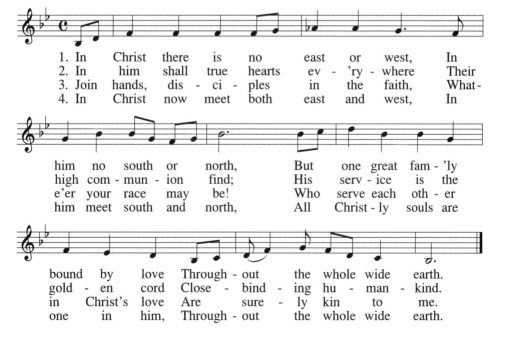

1. In Christ there is no east or west, In
2. In him shall true hearts ev - 'ry - where Their
3. Join hands, dis - ci - ples in the faith, What-
4. In Christ now meet both east and west, In

him no south or north, But one great fam - 'ly
high com - mun - ion find; His serv - ice is the
e'er your race may be! Who serve each oth - er
him meet south and north, All Christ - ly souls are

bound by love Through - out the whole wide earth.
gold - en cord Close - bind - ing hu - man - kind.
in Christ's love Are sure - ly kin to me.
one in him, Through - out the whole wide earth.

Text: Galatians 3:23; John Oxenham, 1852-1941
Tune: MC KEE, CM; African-American; adapt. by Harry T. Burleigh, 1866-1949

396 We Are Many Parts

Refrain

We are man-y parts, we are all one bod-y, and the gifts we have we are giv-en to share.

May the Spir-it of love make us one in-deed; one, the love that we share, one, our hope in de-spair, one, the cross that we bear.

Verses

1. God of all, we look to you, we would be your ser-vants true, let us be your love to all the world.
2. So my pain is pain for you, in your joy is my joy, too; all is brought to-geth-er in the Lord.
3. All you seek-ers, great and small, seek the great-est gift of all; if you love, then you will know the Lord.

D.C.

Text: 1 Corinthians 12, 13; Marty Haugen, b.1950
Tune: Marty Haugen, b.1950
© 1980, 1986, GIA Publications, Inc.

They'll Know We Are Christians   397

1. We are one in the Spir-it, we are one in the Lord, We are one in the Spir-it, we are one in the Lord, And we pray that all u-ni-ty may one day be re-stored:
2. We will walk with each oth-er, we will walk hand in hand, We will walk with each oth-er, we will walk hand in hand, And to-geth-er we'll spread the news that God is in our land:
3. We will work with each oth-er, we will work side by side, We will work with each oth-er, we will work side by side, And we'll guard hu-man's dig-ni-ty and save hu-man's pride:
4. All praise to the Fa-ther, from whom all things come, And all praise to Christ Je-sus, his on-ly Son, And all praise to the Spir-it, who makes us one:

And they'll know we are Chris-tians by our love, by our love, Yes, they'll know we are Chris-tians by our love.

Text: Peter Scholtes, b.1938
Tune: ST. BRENDAN'S, 7 6 7 6 8 6 with refrain; Peter Scholtes, b.1938
© 1966, F.E.L. Publications, assigned to The Lorenz Corp., 1991

398 Diverse in Culture, Nation, Race

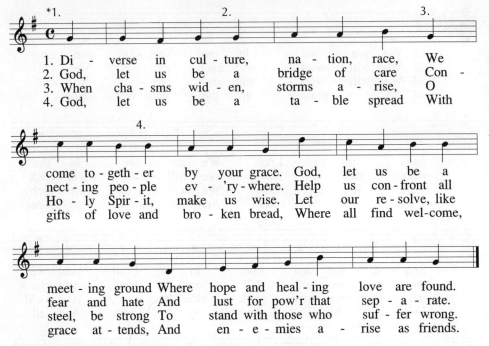

1. Di - verse in cul - ture, na - tion, race, We
2. God, let us be a bridge of care Con -
3. When cha - sms wid - en, storms a - rise, O
4. God, let us be a ta - ble spread With

come to - geth - er by your grace. God, let us be a
nect - ing peo - ple ev - 'ry - where. Help us con - front all
Ho - ly Spir - it, make us wise. Let our re - solve, like
gifts of love and bro - ken bread, Where all find wel - come,

meet - ing ground Where hope and heal - ing love are found.
fear and hate And lust for pow'r that sep - a - rate.
steel, be strong To stand with those who suf - fer wrong.
grace at - tends, And en - e - mies a - rise as friends.

May be sung as a two or four-voice canon.

Text: Ruth Duck, b.1947, © 1992, GIA Publications, Inc.
Tune: TALLIS' CANON, LM; Thomas Tallis, c.1510-1583

399 Jesus Christ, Yesterday, Today and for Ever

Ostinato Refrain

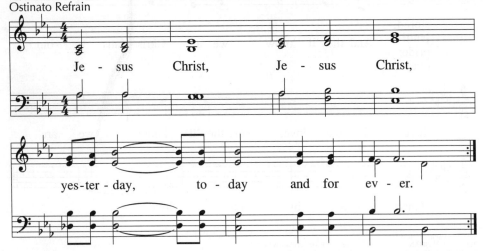

Je - sus Christ, Je - sus Christ,

yes - ter - day, to - day and for ev - er.

Text: Suzanne Toolan, SM, b.1927
Tune: Suzanne Toolan, SM, b.1927
© 1988, GIA Publications, Inc.

God Is Here! As We His People   400

1. God is here! As we his peo - ple, Meet to
2. Here are sym - bols to re - mind us Of our
3. Here our chil - dren find a wel - come In the
4. Lord of all, of church and king-dom, In an

of - fer praise and prayer, May we find in ful - ler
life - long need of grace; Here are ta - ble, font and
Shep - herd's flock and fold; Here, as bread and wine are
age of change and doubt, Keep us faith - ful to the

meas-ure What it is in Christ we share:
pul - pit, Here the cross has cen - tral place:
tak - en, Christ sus - tains us as of old:
gos - pel, Help us work your pur - pose out:

Here, as in the world a - round us, All our
Here in hon - es - ty of preach-ing, Here in
Here the ser - vants of the Ser - vant Seek in
Here, in this day's ded - i - ca - tion, All we

var - ied skills and arts Wait the com - ing
si - lence as in speech, Here in new - ness
wor - ship to ex - plore What it means in
have to give, re - ceive; We who can - not

of his Spir - it In - to o - pen minds and hearts.
and re - new - al God the Spir - it comes to each.
dai - ly liv - ing To be - lieve and to a - dore.
live with - out you, We a - dore you! We be - lieve!

Text: Fred Pratt Green, b.1903, © 1979, Hope Publishing Co.
Tune: ABBOT'S LEIGH, 8 7 8 7 D; Cyril V. Taylor, 1907-1991, © 1942, 1970, Hope Publishing Co.

401 All Are Welcome

1. Let us build a house where love can dwell And
2. Let us build a house where proph - ets speak, And
3. Let us build a house where love is found In
4. Let us build a house where hands will reach Be -
5. Let us build a house where all are named, Their

all can safe - ly live, A place where saints and
words are strong and true, Where all God's chil - dren
wa - ter, wine and wheat: A ban - quet hall on
yond the wood and stone To heal and strength-en,
songs and vi - sions heard And loved and treas - ured,

chil - dren tell How hearts learn to for -
dare to seek To dream God's reign a -
ho - ly ground, Where peace and jus - tice
serve and teach, And live the Word they've
taught and claimed As words with - in the

give. Built of hopes and dreams and vi - sions,
new. Here the cross shall stand as wit - ness
meet. Here the love of God, through Je - sus,
known. Here the out - cast and the stran - ger
Word. Built of tears and cries and laugh-ter,

Rock of faith and vault of grace; Here the
And as sym - bol of God's grace; Here as
Is re - vealed in time and space; As we
Bear the im - age of God's face; Let us
Prayers of faith and songs of grace, Let this

love of Christ shall end di - vi - sions:
one we claim the faith of Je - sus:
share in Christ the feast that frees us: All are wel - come,
bring an end to fear and dan - ger:
house pro - claim from floor to raft - er:

all are wel-come, all are wel-come in this place.

Text: Marty Haugen, b. 1950
Tune: TWO OAKS, 9 6 8 6 8 7 10 with refrain; Marty Haugen, b. 1950
© 1994, GIA Publications, Inc.

All People That on Earth Do Dwell   402

1. All	peo	- ple	that	on	earth	do	dwell,
2. Know	that	the	Lord	is	God	in	- deed;
3. O	en	- ter	then	his	gates	with	praise;
4. For	why?	the	Lord	our	God	is	good:
5. To	Fa	- ther,	Son,	and	Ho	- ly	Ghost,
* Praise	God,	from	whom	all	bless	- ings	flow;

Sing to the Lord with cheer - ful voice;
With - out our aid he did us make;
Ap - proach with joy his courts un - to;
His mer - cy is for ev - er sure;
The God whom heaven and earth a - dore,
Praise him, all crea - tures here be - low;

Him serve with mirth, his praise forth tell,
We are his folk, he does us feed,
Praise, laud, and bless his Name al - ways,
His truth at all times firm - ly stood,
From us and from the an - gel host
Praise him a - bove, you heav'n - ly host:

Come we be - fore him, and re - joice.
And for his sheep he does us take.
For it is seem - ly so to do.
And shall from age to age en - dure.
Be praise and glo - ry ev - er - more.
Praise Fa - ther, Son and Ho - ly Ghost.

May be sung alone or as an alternate to stanza 5.

Text: Psalm (99)100; William Kethe, d. c.1593; Doxology, Thomas Ken, 1637-1711
Tune: OLD HUNDREDTH, LM; Louis Bourgeois, c.1510-1561

403 Gather Us In

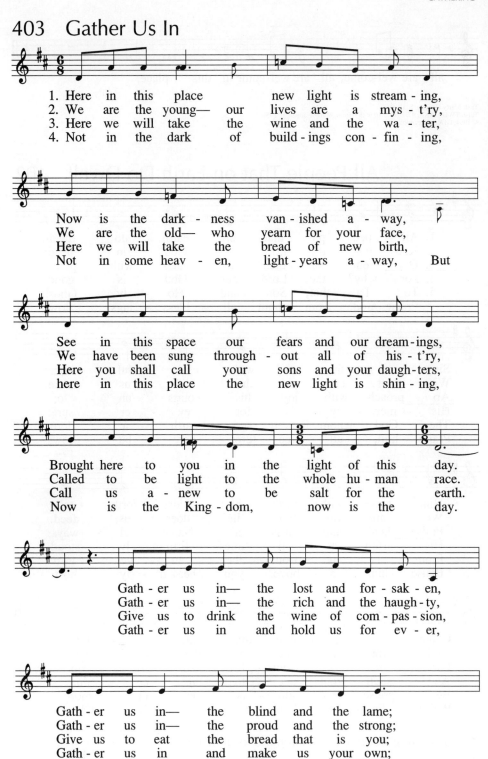

1. Here in this place new light is stream-ing,
2. We are the young— our lives are a mys-t'ry,
3. Here we will take the wine and the wa-ter,
4. Not in the dark of build-ings con-fin-ing,

Now is the dark-ness van-ished a - way,
We are the old— who yearn for your face,
Here we will take the bread of new birth,
Not in some heav - en, light-years a - way, But

See in this space our fears and our dream-ings,
We have been sung through-out all of his - t'ry,
Here you shall call your sons and your daugh-ters,
here in this place the new light is shin - ing,

Brought here to you in the light of this day.
Called to be light to the whole hu - man race.
Call us a - new to be salt for the earth.
Now is the King - dom, now is the day.

Gath - er us in— the lost and for-sak - en,
Gath - er us in— the rich and the haugh-ty,
Give us to drink the wine of com - pas - sion,
Gath - er us in and hold us for ev - er,

Gath - er us in— the blind and the lame;
Gath - er us in— the proud and the strong;
Give us to eat the bread that is you;
Gath - er us in and make us your own;

Call to us now, and we shall a - wak - en,
Give us a heart so meek and so low - ly,
Nour - ish us well, and teach us to fash - ion
Gath - er us in— all peo - ples to - geth - er,

We shall a - rise at the sound of our name.
Give us the cour-age to en - ter the song.
Lives that are ho - ly and hearts that are true.
Fire of love in our flesh and our bone.

Text: Marty Haugen, b.1950
Tune: GATHER US IN, Irregular; Marty Haugen, b.1950
© 1982, GIA Publications, Inc.

This Day God Gives Me   404

1. This day God gives me Strength of high heav - en,
2. This day God sends me Strength as my guar - dian,
3. God's way is my way, God's shield is 'round me,
4. Ris - ing I thank you, Might - y and strong One,

Sun and moon shin - ing, Flame in my hearth,
Might to up - hold me, Wis - dom as guide.
God's host de - fends me, Sav - ing from ill.
King of cre - a - tion, Giv - er of rest,

Flash-ing of light - ning, Wind in its swift - ness,
Your eyes are watch - ful, Your ears are lis - t'ning,
An - gels of heav - en, Drive from me al - ways
Firm - ly con - fess - ing God in three Per - sons,

Depths of the o - cean, Firm - ness of earth.
Your lips are speak - ing, Friend at my side.
All that would harm me, Stand by me still.
One - ness of God - head, Trin - i - ty blest.

Text: Ascribed to St. Patrick; James Quinn, SJ, b.1919, © 1969. Used by permission of Selah Publishing Co., Inc., Kingston, N.Y.
Tune: BUNESSAN, 5 5 5 4 D; Gaelic; acc. by Robert J. Batastini, b.1942, © 1999, GIA Publications, Inc.

405 God of Day and God of Darkness

1. God of day and God of darkness, Now we stand be - fore the night; As the shad - ows stretch and deep - en, Come and make our dark - ness bright. All cre - a - tion still is groan - ing For the dawn - ing of your might, When the Sun of peace and jus - tice Fills the earth with ra - diant light.

2. Still the na - tions curse the darkness, Still the rich op - press the poor; Still the earth is bruised and bro - ken By the ones who still want more. Come and wake us from our sleep - ing, So our hearts can - not ig - nore All your peo - ple lost and bro - ken, All your chil - dren at our door.

3. Show us Christ in one an - oth - er, Make us ser - vants strong and true; Give us all your love of jus - tice So we do what you would do. Let us call all peo - ple ho - ly, Let us pledge our lives a - new, Make us one with all the low - ly, Let us all be one in you.

4. You shall be the path that guides us, You the light that in us burns; Shin - ing deep with - in all peo - ple, Yours the love that we must learn, For our hearts shall wan - der rest - less 'Til they safe to you re - turn; Find - ing you in one an - oth - er, We shall all your face dis - cern.

5. Praise to you in day and darkness, You our source and you our end; Praise to you who love and nur - ture us As a fa - ther, moth - er, friend. Grant us all a peace - ful rest - ing, Let each mind and bod - y mend, So we rise re - freshed to - mor - row, Hearts re - newed to King - dom tend.

Text: Marty Haugen, b.1950, © 1985, 1994, GIA Publications, Inc.
Tune: BEACH SPRING, 8 7 8 7 D; *The Sacred Harp,* 1844; harm. by Marty Haugen, b.1950, © 1985, GIA Publications, Inc.

Day Is Done   406

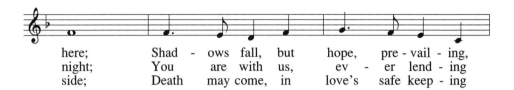

1. Day   is   done, but   love   un - fail - ing   Dwells   ev - er
2. Dark   de-scends, but light   un - end - ing   Shines   through our
3. Eyes   will close, but you   un - sleep-ing   Watch   by   our

here;   Shad - ows fall, but   hope,   pre - vail - ing,
night;   You   are with   us,   ev - er lend - ing
side;   Death may come, in love's safe keep - ing

Calms   ev - 'ry fear.   God, our Mak - er, none for - sak - ing,
New   strength to sight: One in love, your truth con - fess - ing,
Still   we   a - bide.   God of love, all e - vil quell-ing,

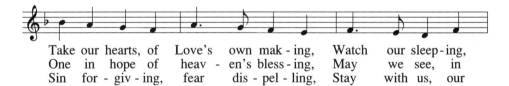

Take our hearts, of Love's own mak - ing, Watch   our sleep-ing,
One in hope of   heav - en's bless-ing, May   we see, in
Sin for - giv - ing, fear dis - pel - ling, Stay   with us, our

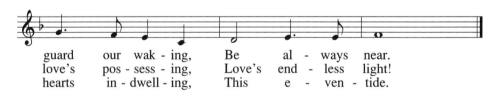

guard   our wak - ing, Be   al - ways near.
love's   pos - sess - ing, Love's end - less light!
hearts   in - dwell-ing, This e - ven - tide.

Text: James Quinn, SJ, b.1919, © 1969, Used by permission of Selah Publishing Co., Inc.
Tune: AR HYD Y NOS, 8 4 8 4 888 4; Welsh

407 Praise and Thanksgiving

1. Praise and thanks - giv - ing, Fa - ther, we of - fer,
2. Lord, bless the la - bor We bring to serve you,
3. Fa - ther, pro - vid - ing Food for your chil - dren,
4. Then will your bless - ing Reach ev - 'ry peo - ple,

For all things liv - ing You have made good.
That with our neigh - bor We may be fed.
Your wis - dom guid - ing Teach - es us share
Free - ly con - fess - ing Your gra - cious hand.

Har - vest of sown fields, Fruits of the or - chard,
Sow - ing or till - ing, We would work with you,
One with an - oth - er, So that re - joic - ing
Where you are reign - ing No one will hun - ger,

Hay from the mown fields, Blos - som and wood.
Har - vest - ing, mill - ing, For dai - ly bread.
With us, all oth - ers May know your care.
Your love sus - tain - ing Fruit - ful the land.

Text: Albert F. Bayly, 1901-1984, © 1988, Oxford University Press
Tune: BUNESSAN, 5 5 5 4 D; Gaelic; harm. by A. Gregory Murray, OSB, 1905-1992, © Downside Abbey

408 Mine Eyes Have Seen the Glory

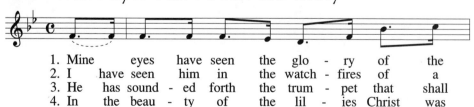

1. Mine eyes have seen the glo - ry of the
2. I have seen him in the watch - fires of a
3. He has sound - ed forth the trum - pet that shall
4. In the beau - ty of the lil - ies Christ was

com - ing of the Lord; He is tram - pling out the
hun - dred cir - cling camps; They have build - ed him an
nev - er call re - treat; He is sift - ing out all
born a - cross the sea, With a glo - ry in his

vin - tage where the grapes of wrath are stored; He hath
al - tar in the eve - ning dews and damps; I can
hu - man hearts be - fore his judg - ment seat; O be
bos - om that trans - fig - ures you and me; As he

loosed the fate - ful light - ning of his ter - ri - ble swift
read the right - eous sen - tence by the dim and flar - ing
swift, my soul, to an - swer him; be ju - bi - lant, my
died to make us ho - ly, let us die that all be

sword; His truth is march - ing on.
lamps; His day is march - ing on.
feet! Our God is march - ing on.
free! While God is march - ing on.

Glo - ry! Glo - ry! Hal - le - lu - jah! Glo - ry!

Glo - ry! Hal - le - lu - jah! Glo - ry! Glo - ry!

Hal - le - lu - jah! His truth is march - ing on.

Text: Julia W. Howe, 1819-1910
Tune: BATTLE HYMN OF THE REPUBLIC, 15 15 15 6 with refrain; attr. to William Steffe, d.1911

409 Soon and Very Soon

1. Soon and ver - y soon we are goin' to see the King,
2. No more cry - in' there we are goin' to see the King,
3. No more dy - in' there we are goin' to see the King,
4. Soon and ver - y soon we are goin' to see the King,

Soon and ver - y soon we are goin' to see the King,
No more cry - in' there we are goin' to see the King,
No more dy - in' there we are goin' to see the King,
Soon and ver - y soon we are goin' to see the King,

Soon and ver - y soon we are goin' to see the King,
No more cry - in' there we are goin' to see the King,
No more dy - in' there we are goin' to see the King, Hal - le -
Soon and ver - y soon we are goin' to see the King,

1., 2.

lu - jah, Hal - le - lu - jah, we're goin' to see the King!

3., 4.

Hal - le - lu - jah, Hal - le - lu -

jah, Hal - le - lu - jah, Hal - le - lu - jah.

Text: Andraé Crouch
Tune: Andraé Crouch
© 1976, Bud John Songs, Inc./Crouch Music/ASCAP

Shall We Gather at the River   410

1. Shall we gath - er at the riv - er, Where bright
2. On the mar - gin of the riv - er, Wash - ing
3. Ere we reach the shin - ing riv - er, Lay we
4. Soon we'll reach the shin - ing riv - er, Soon our

an - gel feet have trod; With its crys - tal tide for
up its sil - ver spray, We will walk and wor - ship
ev - 'ry bur - den down; Grace our spir - its will de-
pil - grim-age will cease, Soon our hap - py hearts will

ev - er Flow-ing by the throne of God?
ev - er, All the hap - py gold - en day.
liv - er, And pro - vide a robe and crown.
quiv - er With the mel - o - dy of peace.

Yes, we'll gath - er at the riv - er, The beau - ti - ful, the

beau - ti - ful riv - er; Gath - er with the saints at the

riv - er That flows by the throne of God.

Text: Robert Lowry, 1826-1899
Tune: HANSON PLACE, 8 7 8 7 with refrain, Robert Lowry, 1826-1899

411 Steal Away to Jesus

Refrain

Steal a-way, steal a-way, steal a-way to Je-sus!

Steal a-way, steal a-way home, I ain't got long to stay here.

Verses

1. My Lord, he calls me, He calls me by the thun-der; The
2. Green trees are bend-ing, Poor sin-ners stand a trem-bling; The
3. My Lord, he calls me, He calls me by the light-ning; The

D.C.

trum-pet sounds with-in my soul; I ain't got long to stay here.

Text: African-American spiritual
Tune: African-American spiritual

412 Jerusalem, My Happy Home

1. Je - ru - sa - lem, my hap - py home, When
2. Your saints are crowned with glo - ry great; They
3. There Da - vid stands with harp in hand As
4. Our La - dy sings Mag - nif - i - cat With
5. There Mag - da - lene has left her tears, And
6. Je - ru - sa - lem, Je - ru - sa - lem, God

shall I with you be? When shall my sor - rows
see God face to face; They tri - umph still, they
mas - ter of the choir: Ten thou - sand times that
tune sur - pass - ing sweet; And all the vir - gins
cheer - ful - ly does sing With bless - ed saints, whose
grant that I may see Your end - less joy, and

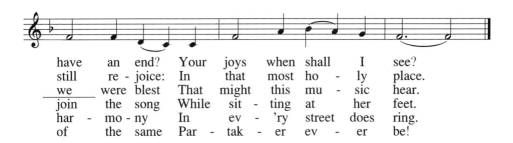

have	an	end?	Your	joys	when	shall	I	see?
still	re -	joice:	In	that	most	ho -	ly	place.
we	were	blest	That	might	this	mu -	sic	hear.
join	the	song	While	sit -	ting	at	her	feet.
har -	mo -	ny	In	ev -	'ry	street	does	ring.
of	the	same	Par -	tak -	er	ev -	er	be!

Text: Joseph Bromehead, 1747-1826, alt.
Tune: LAND OF REST, CM; American; harm. by Richard Proulx, b.1937, © 1975, GIA Publications, Inc.

'Tis Good, Lord, to Be Here 413

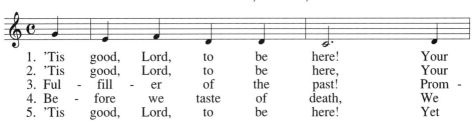

1. 'Tis	good,	Lord,	to	be	here!		Your
2. 'Tis	good,	Lord,	to	be	here,		Your
3. Ful -	fill -	er	of	the	past!		Prom -
4. Be -	fore	we	taste	of	death,		We
5. 'Tis	good,	Lord,	to	be	here!		Yet

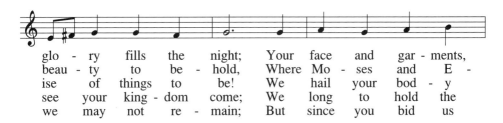

glo -	ry	fills	the	night;	Your	face	and	gar - ments,
beau -	ty	to	be -	hold,	Where	Mo -	ses	and	E -
ise	of	things	to	be!	We	hail	your	bod -	y
see	your	king -	dom	come;	We	long	to	hold	the
we	may	not	re -	main;	But	since	you	bid	us

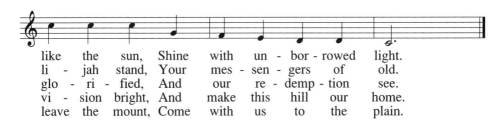

like	the	sun,	Shine	with	un -	bor - rowed	light.
li -	jah	stand,	Your	mes -	sen -	gers	of	old.
glo -	ri -	fied,	And	our	re -	demp - tion	see.
vi -	sion	bright,	And	make	this	hill	our	home.
leave	the	mount,	Come	with	us	to	the	plain.

Text: Luke 9:32-33; Joseph A. Robinson, 1858-1933, alt., © Esme. D. E. Bird
Tune: SWABIA, SM; Johann M. Speiss, 1715-1772; adapt. by William H. Havergal, 1793-1870

414 On This Day, O Beautiful Mother

Refrain

On this day, O beau-ti-ful Moth-er, On this day we give thee our love. Near thee, Ma-don-na, fond-ly we hov-er, Trust-ing thy gen-tle care to prove.

Verses

1. On this day we ask to share, Dear-est Moth-er, thy sweet care; Aid us ere our feet a-stray Wan-der from thy guid-ing way.
2. Queen of an-gels, deign to hear Thy dear chil-dren's hum-ble prayer; Young hearts gain, O Vir-gin pure, Je-sus' love for them as-sure.

D.C.

Text: Anonymous
Tune: BEAUTIFUL MOTHER, 77 77 with refrain; Louis Lambillotte, 1796-1855

415 Salve, Regina / Hail, Queen of Heaven

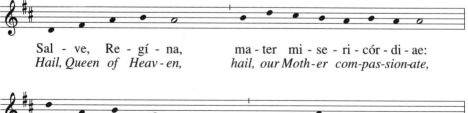

Sal - ve, Re - gí - na, ma - ter mi - se - ri - cór - di - ae:
Hail, Queen of Heav-en, hail, our Moth-er com-pas-sion-ate,

Vi - ta, dul - cé - do et spes no - stra sal - ve.
True life and com - fort and our hope, we greet you!

Ad te cla-má-mus, éx-su-les fí-li-i He-vae.
To you we ex-iles, chil-dren of Eve, raise our voic-es.

Ad te sus-pi-rá-mus, ge-mén-tes et flen-tes
We send up sighs to you, as mourn-ing and weep-ing,

in hac la-cri-má-rum val-le. E-ia er-go,
we pass through this vale of sor-row. Then turn to us,

ad-vo-cá-ta no-stra, il-los tu-os mi-se-ri-
O most gra-cious Wom-an, those eyes of yours, so full of

cór-des ó-cu-los ad nos con-vér-te.
love and ten-der-ness, so full of pit-y.

Et Je-sum, be-ne-dí-ctum fru-ctum ven-tris tu-i,
And grant us af-ter these, our days of lone-ly ex-ile,

no-bis post hoc ex-sí-li-um o-stén-de.
the sight of your blest Son and Lord, Christ Je-sus.

O cle-mens, O pi-a,
O gen-tle, O lov-ing,

O dul-cis Vir-go Ma-rí-a.
O ho-ly, sweet Vir-gin Mar-y.

Text: Latin, c.1080, tr. by John C. Selner, SS, b.1904, © 1954, GIA Publications, Inc.
Tune: SALVE REGINA, Irregular; Mode V; acc. by Gerard Farrell, OSB, b.1919, © 1986, GIA Publications, Inc.

416 Hail Mary: Gentle Woman

Hail Mar - y, full of grace, the
Lord is with you. Bless-ed are you a - mong
wo - men, and blest is the fruit of your womb, Je - sus.
Ho - ly Mar - y, Moth - er of God,
pray for us sin - ners now and at the hour of
death. A - men.

Refrain

Gen - tle wom - an, qui - et light, morn - ing
star, so strong and bright, gen - tle
Moth - er, peace - ful dove, teach us
wis - dom; teach us love.

Verse 1

1. You were cho - sen by the Fa - ther;

you were cho - sen for the Son.

You were cho - sen from all wom-en

and for wom-an, shin-ing one.

D.S.

Verse 2

2. Bless-ed are you a-mong wom-en,

blest in turn all wom-en, too.

Bless-ed they with peace-ful spir-its.

Bless-ed they with gen-tle hearts.

D.S.

417 Sing of Mary, Meek and Lowly

1. Sing of Mar-y meek and low-ly, Vir-gin-moth-er
2. Sing of Je-sus, son of Mar-y, In the home at
3. Glo-ry be to God the Fa-ther; Glo-ry be to

pure and mild, Sing of God's own Son most ho-ly,
Naz-a-reth. Toil and la-bor can-not wea-ry
God the Son; Glor-ry be to God the Spir-it;

Who be-came her lit-tle child. Fair-est child of
Love en-dur-ing un-to death. Con-stant was the
Glo-ry to the Three in One. From the heart of

fair-est moth-er, God the Lord who came to earth,
love he gave her, Though he went forth from her side,
bless-ed Mar-y, From all saints the song as-cends,

Word made flesh, our ver-y broth-er,
Forth to preach, and heal, and suf-fer,
And the church the strain re-ech-oes

Takes our na-ture by his birth.
Till on Cal-va-ry he died.
Un-to earth's re-mot-est ends.

Text: Roland F. Palmer, 1891-1985
Tune: PLEADING SAVIOR, 8 7 8 7 D; *Christian Lyre,* 1830; harm. by Richard Proulx, b.1937, © 1986, GIA Publications, Inc.

Sing We of the Blessed Mother 418

1. Sing we of the bless-ed Moth-er Who re-ceived the
2. Sing we, too, of Mar-y's sor-rows, Of the sword that
3. Sing a-gain the joys of Mar-y When she saw the
4. Sing the great-est joy of Mar-y When on earth her

an-gel's word, And o-be-dient to the sum-mons
pierced her through, When be-neath the cross of Je-sus
ris-en Lord, And in prayer with Christ's a-pos-tles,
work was done, And the Lord of all cre-a-tion

Bore in love the in-fant Lord; Sing we of the
She his weight of suf-f'ring knew, Looked up-on her
Wait-ed on his prom-ised word: From on high the
Brought her to his heav'n-ly home: Vir-gin Moth-er,

joys of Mar-y At whose breast that child was fed
Son and Sav-ior Reign-ing from the aw-ful tree,
blaz-ing glo-ry Of the Spir-it's pres-ence came,
Mar-y bless-ed, Raised on high and crowned with grace,

Who is Son of God e-ter-nal
Saw the price of our re-demp-tion
Heav'n-ly breath of God's own be-ing,
May your Son, the world's re-deem-er,

And the ev-er-last-ing Bread.
Paid to set the sin-ner free.
To-kened in the wind and flame.
Grant us all to see his face.

Text: George B. Timms, b.1910, © 1975, Oxford University Press
Tune: OMNE DIE, 8 7 8 7 D; *Trier Gesängbuch*, 1695

419 Hail, Holy Queen Enthroned Above

1. Hail, ho-ly Queen en-throned a-bove, O Ma-
2. The cause of joy to all be-low, O Ma-
3. O gen-tle, lov-ing, ho-ly one, O Ma-

ri - a. Hail, Queen of mer - cy and of love,
ri - a. The spring through which all grac - es flow,
ri - a. The God of light be - came your Son,

O Ma - ri - a. Tri - umph, all ye
O Ma - ri - a. An - gels, all your
O Ma - ri - a. Tri - umph, all ye

Cher - u - bim, Sing with us, ye Ser - a - phim,
prais - es bring, Earth and heav - en, with us sing,
Cher - u - bim, Sing with us, ye Ser - a - phim,

Heav'n and earth re - sound the hymn: Sal - ve,
All cre - a - tion ech - o - ing: Sal - ve,
Heav'n and earth re - sound the hymn: Sal - ve,

Sal - ve, Sal - ve, Re - gi - na.
Sal - ve, Sal - ve, Re - gi - na.
Sal - ve, Sal - ve, Re - gi - na.

Text: *Salve, Regina, mater misericordia;* c.1080; tr. *Roman Hymnal,* 1884; st. 2-3 adapt. by M. Owen Lee, CSB, b.1930
Tune: SALVE REGINA COELITUM, 8 4 8 4 777 4 5; *Choralmelodien zum Heiligen Gesänge,* 1808; harm. by Healey Willan, 1880-1968, © Willis Music Co.

O Sanctissima / O Most Virtuous   420

1. O san - ctís - si - ma, O pi - ís - si - ma,
2. Tu so - lá - ti - um Et re - fú - gi - um,
3. Ec - ce dé - bi - les, Per - quam flé - bi - les,
4. Vir - go ré - spi - ce, Ma - ter, ád - spi - ce,

1. O most vir - tu - ous And most pi - ous,
2. Our pro - tec - tion and Con - so - la - tion,
3. See us pow - er - less In our hope - less - ness:
4. Maid - en, look on us, Moth - er, care for us.

Dul - cis vir - go Ma - rí - a!
Vir - go ma - ter Ma - rí - a!
Sal - va nos, Ma - rí - a!
Au - di nos, Ma - rí - a!

Dear - est maid - en, sweet Mar - y,
Vir - gin moth - er, good Mar - y,
Aid us, save us, Mar - y!
Hear our pleas, O Mar - y!

Ma - ter a - má - ta, In - te - me - rá - ta,
Quid - quid op - tá - mus, Per te spe - rá - mus,
Tol - le lan - guó - res, Sa - na do - ló - res,
Tu me - di - cí - nam, Por - tas di - ví - nam;

Moth - er af - fec - tion - ate, Vir - gin in - vi - o - late,
What - e'er our souls de - sire, May you help us to ac - quire.
Wipe a - way the tears we shed, Heal us of our grief and dread.
Balm and our sur - e - ty, Gate - way to di - vin - i - ty,

O - ra, o - ra pro no - bis.
O - ra, o - ra pro no - bis.
O - ra, o - ra pro no - bis.
O - ra, o - ra pro no - bis.

In - ter - cede and pray for us, O Mar - y!
In - ter - cede and pray for us, O Mar - y!
In - ter - cede and pray for us, O Mar - y!
In - ter - cede and pray for us, O Mar - y!

Text: St. 1, *Stimmen der Völker in Liedern*, 1807; st. 2, *Arundel Hymnal*, 1902; tr. Neil Borgstrom, b.1953, © 1994, GIA Publications, Inc.
Tune: O DU FRÖLICHE, 55 7 55 7; Tattersall's *Improved Psalmody*, 1794

421 Immaculate Mary

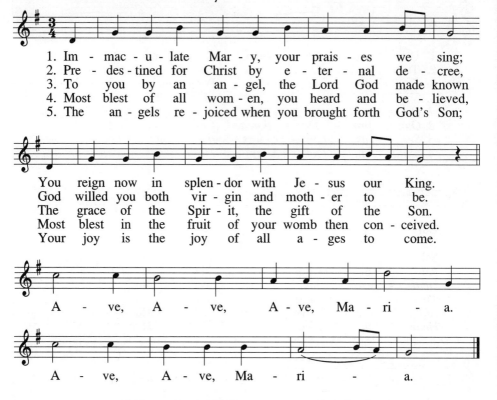

1. Im - mac - u - late Mar - y, your prais - es we sing;
2. Pre - des - tined for Christ by e - ter - nal de - cree,
3. To you by an an - gel, the Lord God made known
4. Most blest of all wom - en, you heard and be - lieved,
5. The an - gels re - joiced when you brought forth God's Son;

You reign now in splen - dor with Je - sus our King.
God willed you both vir - gin and moth - er to be.
The grace of the Spir - it, the gift of the Son.
Most blest in the fruit of your womb then con - ceived.
Your joy is the joy of all a - ges to come.

A - ve, A - ve, A - ve, Ma - ri - a.

A - ve, A - ve, Ma - ri - a.

6. Your child is the Savior, all hope lies in him:
   He gives us new life and redeems us from sin.

7. In glory for ever now close to your Son,
   All ages will praise you for all God has done.

Text: St. 1 Jeremiah Cummings, 1814-1866, alt.; St. 2-7, Brian Foley, b.1919, © 1971, Faber Music Ltd.
Tune: LOURDES HYMN, 11 11 with refrain; Grenoble, 1882

422 Ave Maria

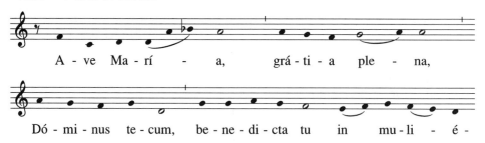

A - ve Ma - rí - a, grá - ti - a ple - na,

Dó - mi - nus te - cum, be - ne - di - cta tu in mu - li - é -

ri - bus, et be-ne-dí-ctus fru-ctus ven-tris tu - i, Je - sus.

San-cta Ma - rí - a, Ma-ter De - i, o - ra pro no - bis pec-ca -

tó - ri-bus, nunc et in ho - ra mor-tis no - strae. A-men.

Text: *Hail, Mary, full of grace,* Luke 1:29; Latin, 13th C.
Tune: AVE MARIA, Irregular; Mode I; acc. by Robert LeBlanc, b.1948, © 1986, GIA Publications, Inc.

Lift High the Cross 423

Lift high the cross, the love of Christ pro - claim till

all the world a - dore his sa - cred name.

1. Come,	Chris - tians,	fol - low	where	the Mas - ter	trod, our
2. Led	on	their way	by	this	tri - um-phant	sign, the
3. Each	new - born	fol - l'wer	of	the Cru - ci -	fied bears
4. O	Lord,	once lift - ed	on	the glo-rious	tree, your
5. So	shall	our song of	tri - umph ev - er	be: praise

D.C.

King	vic - to - rious,	Christ,	the	Son	of	God.
hosts	of	God	in	con - quering ranks com - bine.
on	the	brow	the	seal	of	him who died.
death	has	bought	us	life	e - ter - nal - ly.
to	the	Cru - ci -	fied	for	vic - to - ry!

Text: 1 Corinthians 1:18; George W. Kitchin, 1827-1912, and Michael R. Newbolt, 1874-1956, alt.
Tune: CRUCIFER, 10 10 with refrain; Sydney H. Nicholson, 1875-1947
© 1974, Hope Publishing Co.

424 For All the Saints

1. For all the saints who from their la - bors
2. You were their rock, their for - tress and their
3. O may your sol - diers, faith - ful, true and
4. O blest com - mun - ion, fam - i - ly di -
5. And when the strife is fierce, the war - fare
6. The gold - en eve - ning bright - ens in the

rest, All who by faith be - fore the world con -
might; You, Lord, their Cap - tain in the well - fought
bold, Fight as the saints who no - bly fought of
vine! We fee - bly strug - gle, they in glo - ry
long, Steals on the ear the dis - tant tri - umph
west; Soon, soon to faith - ful war - riors comes their

fessed, Your name, O Je - sus, be for ev - er blest.
fight; You in the dark - ness drear, their one true light.
old, And win with them, the vic - tor's crown of gold.
shine; Yet all are one with - in your great de - sign.
song, And hearts are brave a - gain, and arms are strong.
rest; Sweet is the calm of par - a - dise the blest.

Al - le - lu - ia! Al - le - lu - ia!

7. But then there breaks a yet more glorious day:
   The saints triumphant rise in bright array;
   The King of glory passes on his way.
   Alleluia! Alleluia!

8. From earth's wide bounds, from ocean's farthest coast,
   Through gates of pearl streams in the countless host,
   Singing to Father, Son, and Holy Ghost:
   Alleluia! Alleluia!

Text: William W. How, 1823-1897
Tune: SINE NOMINE, 10 10 10 with alleluias; Ralph Vaughan Williams, 1872-1958, © Oxford University Press

Ye Watchers and Ye Holy Ones 425

1. Ye watch - ers and ye ho - ly ones,
2. O high - er than the cher - u - bim,
3. Re - spond, ye souls in end - less rest,
4. O friends, in glad - ness let us sing,

Bright ser - aphs, cher - u - bim, and thrones,
More glo - rious than the ser - a - phim,
Ye pa - tri - archs and proph - ets blest,
Su - per - nal an - thems ech - o - ing,

[⌢]

Raise the glad strain,
Lead their prais - es,
Al - le - lu - ia,   Al - le - lu - ia!
Al - le - lu - ia,

Cry out, do - min - ions, prince - doms, powers,
O bear - er of the e - ter - nal Word,
Ye ho - ly Twelve, ye mar - tyrs strong,
To God the Fa - ther, God the Son,

Vir - tues, arch - an - gels, an - gels' choirs,
Most gra - cious, mag - ni - fy the Lord,
All saints tri - um - phant, raise in song,
And God the Spir - it, Three in One,

Al - le - lu - ia,   Al - le - lu - ia,   Al - le - lu - ia,

Al - le - lu - ia,   Al - le - lu - ia!

Text: Athelston Riley, 1858-1945, © Oxford University Press
Tune: LASST UNS ERFREUEN, LM with alleluias; *Geistliche Kirchengasänge,* Cologne, 1623; harm. by Ralph Vaughan Williams, 1872-1958,
  © Oxford University Press

426 Baptized in Water

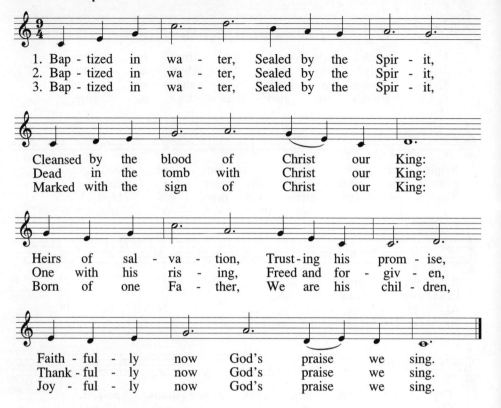

1. Bap - tized in wa - ter, Sealed by the Spir - it,
2. Bap - tized in wa - ter, Sealed by the Spir - it,
3. Bap - tized in wa - ter, Sealed by the Spir - it,

Cleansed by the blood of Christ our King:
Dead in the tomb with Christ our King:
Marked with the sign of Christ our King:

Heirs of sal - va - tion, Trust-ing his prom - ise,
One with his ris - ing, Freed and for - giv - en,
Born of one Fa - ther, We are his chil - dren,

Faith - ful - ly now God's praise we sing.
Thank - ful - ly now God's praise we sing.
Joy - ful - ly now God's praise we sing.

Text: Michael Saward, b.1932, © 1982, Hope Publishing Co.
Tune: BUNESSAN, 5 5 8 D; Gaelic melody; acc. by Robert J. Batastini, b.1942, © 1999, GIA Publications, Inc.

427 I Come with Joy

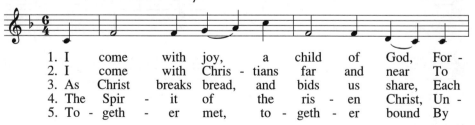

1. I come with joy, a child of God, For -
2. I come with Chris - tians far and near To
3. As Christ breaks bread, and bids us share, Each
4. The Spir - it of the ris - en Christ, Un -
5. To - geth - er met, to - geth - er bound By

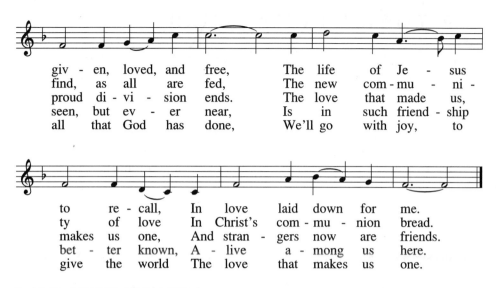

giv - en, loved, and free, The life of Je - sus
find, as all are fed, The new com - mu - ni -
proud di - vi - sion ends. The love that made us,
seen, but ev - er near, Is in such friend - ship
all that God has done, We'll go with joy, to

to re - call, In love laid down for me.
ty of love In Christ's com - mu - nion bread.
makes us one, And stran - gers now are friends.
bet - ter known, A - live a - mong us here.
give the world The love that makes us one.

Text: Brian Wren, b.1936, © 1971, 1995, Hope Publishing Co.
Tune: LAND OF REST, CM; American; harm. by Annabel M. Buchanan, 1888-1983, © 1938, 1966, J. Fisher and Bro.

O Breathe on Me, O Breath of God 428

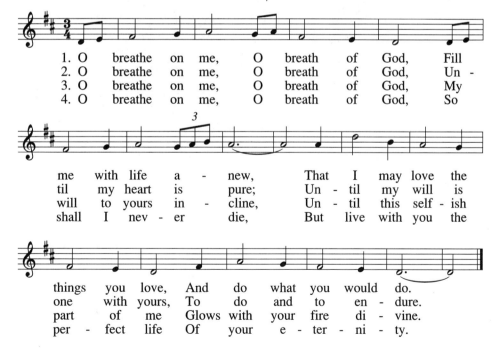

1. O breathe on me, O breath of God, Fill
2. O breathe on me, O breath of God, Un -
3. O breathe on me, O breath of God, My
4. O breathe on me, O breath of God, So

me with life a - new, That I may love the
til my heart is pure; Un - til my will is
will to yours in - cline, Un - til this self - ish
shall I nev - er die, But live with you the

things you love, And do what you would do.
one with yours, To do and to en - dure.
part of me Glows with your fire di - vine.
per - fect life Of your e - ter - ni - ty.

Text: Edwin Hatch, 1835-1889
Tune: ST. COLUMBA, CM; Gaelic; harm. by A. Gregory Murray, OSB, 1905-1992, © Downside Abbey

429 You Satisfy the Hungry Heart

Refrain

You sat-is-fy the hun-gry heart With gift of fin-est wheat;
Come give to us, O sav-ing Lord, The bread of life to eat.

Verses

1. As when the shep - herd calls his sheep, They
2. With joy - ful lips we sing to you Our
3. Is not the cup we bless and share The
4. The mys - t'ry of your pres - ence, Lord, No
5. You give your - self to us, O Lord; Then

know and heed his voice; So when you call your
praise and grat - i - tude, That you should count us
blood of Christ out - poured? Do not one cup, one
mor - tal tongue can tell: Whom all the world can -
self - less let us be, To serve each oth - er

D.C.

fam - 'ly, Lord, We fol - low and re - joice.
wor - thy, Lord, To share this heav'n - ly food.
loaf, de - clare Our one - ness in the Lord?
not con - tain Comes in our hearts to dwell.
in your name In truth and char - i - ty.

Text: Omer Westendorf, 1916-1998
Tune: BICENTENNIAL, CM, with refrain; Robert E. Kreutz, 1922-1996
© 1977, Archdiocese of Philadelphia

430 Let Us Break Bread Together

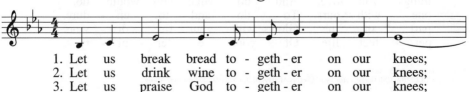

1. Let us break bread to - geth - er on our knees;
2. Let us drink wine to - geth - er on our knees;
3. Let us praise God to - geth - er on our knees;

Let us break bread to-geth-er on our knees;
Let us drink wine to-geth-er on our knees;
Let us praise God to-geth-er on our knees;

When I fall on my knees, With my face to the ris-ing

sun, O Lord, have mer-cy on me.

Text: American folk hymn
Tune: LET US BREAK BREAD, 10 10 6 8 7; American folk hymn; harm. by David Hurd, b.1950, © 1968, GIA Publications, Inc.

O Lord, I Am Not Worthy 431

1. O Lord, I am not wor-thy That
2. O come, all ye who la-bor In
3. O Je-sus, we a-dore thee, Our
4. O sac-ra-ment most ho-ly, O

thou should'st come to me, But speak the words of
sor-row and in pain; Come, eat this bread from
vic-tim and our priest, Whose pre-cious blood and
sac-ra-ment di-vine, All praise and all thanks-

com-fort; My spir-it healed shall be.
heav-en; Thy peace and strength re-gain.
bod-y Be-come our sa-cred feast.
giv-ing Be ev-'ry mo-ment thine.

Text: Vs. 1, anonymous; vss. 2-3, Irvin Udulutsch, © 1958, The Basilian Fathers; vs. 4, the *Raccolta*
Tune: NON DIGNUS, 7 6 7 6; "Burns" traditional melody

432 Shepherd of Souls, in Love, Come

1. Shep - herd of souls, in love, come, feed us,
2. Life - giv - ing vine, come, feed and nour - ish,
3. Sin - ful are we who kneel be - fore you,
4. Fol - low - ing you, O Lord, who led them,
5. Fa - ther, who fed the He - brew na - tion,
6. Help us, dear Lord, pre - pare a dwell - ing

Life - giv - ing bread for hun - gry hearts!
Strength - en each branch with life di - vine;
Wor - thy of you are you a - lone;
Mul - ti - tudes thronged the moun - tain - side;
Giv - ing them man - na from the sky,
Wor - thy of you who made us all;

To those re - fresh - ing wa - ters lead us
Ev - er in you, O may we flour - ish,
Yet in your name do we im - plore you,
Filled with com - pas - sion, Lord, you fed them,
Give now the bread of our sal - va - tion
Cleanse then our hearts, our guilt dis - pel - ling,

Where dwells that peace your grace im - parts.
Fruit - ful the branch - es on the vine.
Rich are the mer - cies you have shown.
Fed them with loaves you mul - ti - plied.
That we who eat shall nev - er die.
Pu - ri - fy us who heed your call.

May we, the way - ward in your fold,
Lord, may our souls be pu - ri - fied
Say but the word, O Lord di - vine,
Come, feed us now, O Lord, we pray;
We are your peo - ple, God, in need;
"Take this and eat" were words you said;

By your for - give - ness rest con - soled.
So that in Christ may we a - bide.
Then are our hearts made pure like thine.
Life - giv - ing bread give us this day.
May we on liv - ing bread now feed.
So do we gath - er for this bread.

Text: Omer Westendorf, 1916-1998, © 1964, World Library Publications, Inc.
Tune: ICH WILL DICH LIEBEN, 9 8 9 8 88; Georg Joseph, c. 1630-1668; arr. by Eugene E. Englert, © 1964, World Library Publications, Inc.

One Bread, One Body 433

Refrain

One bread, one bod-y, one Lord of all,

one cup of bless - ing which we bless. And

we, though man-y, through-out the earth,

we are one bod - y in this one Lord.

Verses

1. Gen - tile or Jew, ser - vant or free,
2. Man - y the gifts, man - y the works,
3. Grain for the fields, scat-tered and grown,

D.C.

wom - an or man no more.
one in the Lord of all.
gath-ered to one for all.

Text: 1 Corinthians 10:16; 17, 12:4, Galatians 3:28; the *Didache* 9; John Foley, SJ, b.1939
Tune: John Foley, SJ, b.1939
© 1978, John B. Foley, SJ, and New Dawn Music

434 I Myself Am the Bread of Life

Refrain

I my-self am the bread of life. You and I
are the bread of life, tak-en and blessed,
bro-ken and shared by Christ that the world might live.

Verses

1. This bread is spir-it, gift of the Mak-er's
2. Here is God's king-dom giv-en to us as
3. Lives bro-ken o-pen, sto-ries shared a-

love, and we who share it know that we can be
food. This is our bod-y, this is our
loud, be-come a ban-quet, a shel-ter for the

D.C.

one:
blood: a liv-ing sign of God in Christ.
world:

Text: Rory Cooney, b.1952
Tune: Rory Cooney, b.1952
© 1987, North American Liturgy Resources

435 Eat This Bread

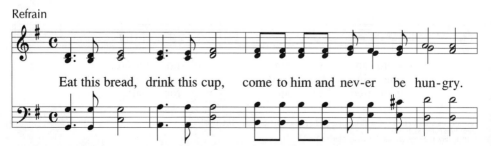

Refrain

Eat this bread, drink this cup, come to him and nev-er be hun-gry.

Eat this bread, drink this cup, trust in him and you will not thirst.

Text: John 6; adapt. by Robert J. Batastini, b.1942, and the Taizé Community
Tune: Jacques Berthier, 1923-1994
© 1984, Les Presses de Taizé, GIA Publications, Inc., agent

All Who Hunger 436

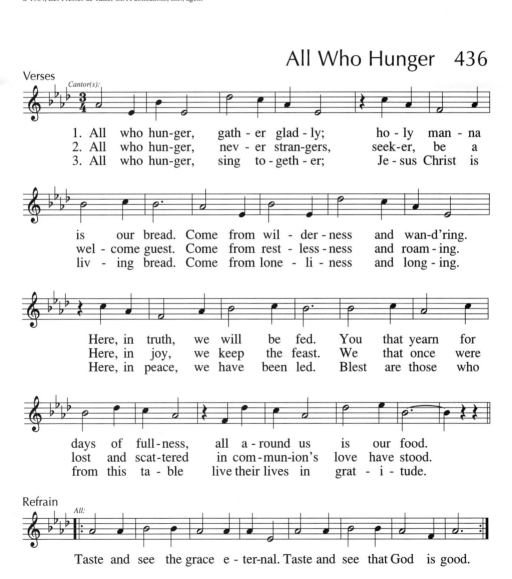

Verses

Cantor(s):

1. All who hun-ger, gath-er glad-ly; ho-ly man-na
2. All who hun-ger, nev-er stran-gers, seek-er, be a
3. All who hun-ger, sing to-geth-er; Je-sus Christ is

is our bread. Come from wil-der-ness and wan-d'ring.
wel-come guest. Come from rest-less-ness and roam-ing.
liv-ing bread. Come from lone-li-ness and long-ing.

Here, in truth, we will be fed. You that yearn for
Here, in joy, we keep the feast. We that once were
Here, in peace, we have been led. Blest are those who

days of full-ness, all a-round us is our food.
lost and scat-tered in com-mun-ion's love have stood.
from this ta-ble live their lives in grat-i-tude.

Refrain

All:

Taste and see the grace e-ter-nal. Taste and see that God is good.

Text: Sylvia G. Dunstan, 1955-1993, © 1991, GIA Publications, Inc.
Tune: Bob Moore, b. 1962, © 1993, GIA Publications, Inc.

437 Taste and See

Refrain

Taste and see, taste and see the good-ness of the Lord. O taste and see, taste and see the good-ness of the Lord, of the Lord.

Verses

1. I will bless the Lord at all times.
2. Glo - ri - fy the Lord with me.
3. Wor - ship the Lord, all you peo-ple.

Praise shall al - ways be on my lips;
To - geth-er let us all praise God's name.
You'll want for noth-ing if you ask.

my soul shall glo - ry in the Lord
I called the Lord who an - swered me;
Taste and see that the Lord is good;

D.C.

for God has been so good to me.
from all my troub-les I was set free.
in God we need put all our trust.

Text: Psalm 34; James E. Moore, Jr., b.1951
Tune: James E. Moore, Jr., b.1951
© 1983, GIA Publications, Inc.

Life-Giving Bread, Saving Cup 438

Refrain

Life-giv-ing bread, sav-ing cup, we of-fer in thanks-giv-ing, O God.

Life-giv-ing bread, sav-ing cup, we of-fer as a sign of our love.

Verses

1. For bread that is bro - ken, we give thanks. For
2. We thank you, O Fa - ther, for your name which
3. Cre - a - tor of all, we of - fer thanks. You
4. Re - mem - ber your Church which sings your praise. Per -

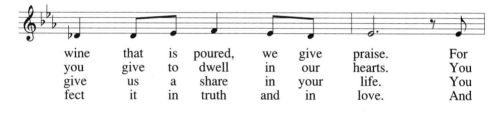

wine that is poured, we give praise. For
you give to dwell in our hearts. You
give us a share in your life. You
fect it in truth and in love. And

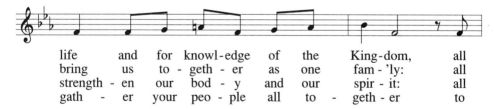

life and for knowl-edge of the King-dom, all
bring us to - geth - er as one fam - 'ly: all
strength - en our bod - y and our spir - it: all
gath - er your peo - ple all to - geth - er to

D.C.

praise to you un - til the end of time!
praise to you un - til the end of time!
praise to you un - til the end of time!
praise you un - til the end of time!

Text: Adapted from the *Didache*, 2nd C.; James J. Chepponis, b.1956
Tune: James J. Chepponis, b.1956
© 1987, GIA Publications, Inc.

439　Let Us Be Bread

Refrain

Let us be bread, blessed by the Lord, bro-ken and shared,

life for the world. Let us be wine, love free-ly poured.

Let us be one in the Lord.

Verse 1

1. I am the bread of life, bro-ken for all.

D.C.

Eat now and hun-ger no more.

Verse 2

2. You are my friends if you keep my com-mands,

D.C.

no long - er ser-vants but friends.

Verse 3

3. See how my peo-ple have noth-ing to eat.

D.C.

Give them the bread that is you.

Verse 4

4. As God has loved me so I have loved you.

Go and live on in my love.

Text: Thomas J. Porter, b.1958
Tune: Thomas J. Porter, b.1958
© 1990, GIA Publications, Inc.

Take Our Bread 440

Refrain

Take our bread, we ask you; take our hearts, we love you. Take our lives, O Fa-ther; we are yours we are yours.

Verse 1

1. Yours as we stand at the ta - ble you set; Yours as we eat the bread our hearts can't for - get. We are the sign of your life with us yet, We are yours, we are yours.

Verse 2

2. Your ho-ly peo-ple stand-ing washed in your blood, Spir-it filled yet hun-gry we a-wait your food. We are poor, but we've brought our-selves the best we could; We are yours, we are yours.

Text: Joe Wise, © 1966
Tune: Joe Wise, © 1966; acc. by Robert J. Batastini, b.1942, © 1987, GIA Publications, Inc.

441 Take and Eat

Refrain

Take and eat; take and eat: this is my bod - y giv - en up for you. Take and drink; take and drink: this is my blood giv - en up for you.

Verses

1. I am the Word that spoke and light was made;
2. I am the way that leads the ex - ile home;
3. I am the Lamb that takes a - way your sin;
4. I am the cor - ner - stone that God has laid;
5. I am the light that came in - to the world;
6. I am the first and last, the Liv - ing One;

I am the seed that died to be re - born;
I am the truth that sets the cap - tive free;
I am the gate that guards you night and day;
A cho - sen stone and pre - cious in his eyes;
I am the light that dark - ness can - not hide;
I am the Lord who died that you might live;

I am the bread that comes from heav'n a - bove;
I am the life that rais - es up the dead;
You are my flock: you know the shep - herd's voice;
You are God's dwell - ing place, on me you rest;
I am the morn - ing star that nev - er sets;
I am the bride - groom, this my wed - ding song;

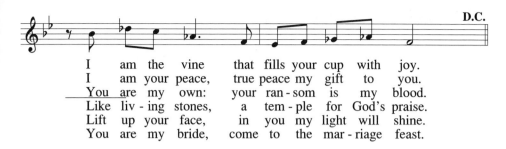

I am the vine that fills your cup with joy.
I am your peace, true peace my gift to you.
You are my own: your ran-som is my blood.
Like liv-ing stones, a tem-ple for God's praise.
Lift up your face, in you my light will shine.
You are my bride, come to the mar-riage feast.

Text: Verse text, James Quinn, SJ, b.1919, © 1989. Used by permission of Selah Publishing., Inc., Kingston, N.Y.; refrain text,
    Michael Joncas, b.1951, © 1989, GIA Publications, Inc.
Tune: Michael Joncas, b.1951, © 1989, GIA Publications, Inc.

Look Beyond 442

Refrain

Look be-yond the bread you eat; See your Sav-ior and your
Lord. Look be-yond the cup you drink;
To verses
See his love poured out as blood.

Final ending
See his life poured out as blood.

Verses

1. Give us a sign that we might be-lieve in
2. I am the bread which from the heav-ens
3. The bread I give you will be my ver-y

you. Mos-es had man-na from the sky.
came; Those who eat this bread will nev-er die.
flesh; My blood will tru-ly be your drink.

Text: Darryl Ducote, b.1945
Tune: Darryl Ducote, b.1945
© 1969, 1979, Damean Music. Distributed by GIA Publications, Inc.

443 Without Seeing You

Refrain

With-out see-ing you, we love you; with-out

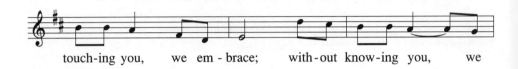

touch-ing you, we em-brace; with-out know-ing you, we

fol - low; with-out see-ing you, we be - lieve.

Verses

1. We re - turn to you deep with - in, leave the
2. The spar - row will find a home, near to
3. For - ev - er we sing to you of your
4. For you are our shep - herd, there is

past to the dust; turn to you with tears and
you, O God; how hap - py, we who
good - ness, O God; pro - claim - ing to
noth - ing that we need; in green pas - tures we will

D.C.

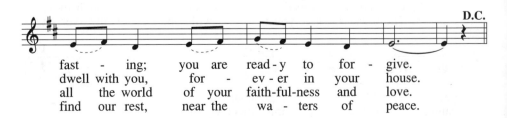

fast - ing; you are read-y to for - give.
dwell with you, for - ev - er in your house.
all the world of your faith-ful-ness and love.
find our rest, near the wa - ters of peace.

Alleluia! Sing to Jesus 444

1. Al - le - lu - ia! sing to Je - sus! His the
2. Al - le - lu - ia! not as or - phans Are we
3. Al - le - lu - ia! Bread of An - gels, Here on
4. Al - le - lu - ia! King e - ter - nal, You the

scep - ter, his the throne; Al - le - lu - ia!
left in sor - row now; Al - le - lu - ia!
earth our food, our stay! Al - le - lu - ia!
Lord of lords we own; Al - le - lu - ia!

his the tri - umph, His the vic - to - ry a - lone;
he is near us, Faith be - lieves, nor ques - tions how:
here the sin - ful Flee to you from day to day:
born of Mar - y, Earth your foot - stool, heav'n your throne:

Hark! the songs of peace - ful Zi - on Thun - der
Though the cloud from sight re - ceived him, When the
In - ter - ces - sor, friend of sin - ners, Earth's re -
You, with - in the veil, have en - tered, Robed in

like a might - y flood; Je - sus out of
for - ty days were o'er, Shall our hearts for -
deem - er, plead for me, Where the songs of
flesh, our great high priest; Here on earth both

ev - 'ry na - tion Has re - deemed us by his blood.
get his prom - ise, "I am with you ev - er - more"?
all the sin - less Sweep a - cross the crys - tal sea.
priest and vic - tim In the eu - cha - ris - tic feast.

Text: Revelation 5:9; William C. Dix, 1837-1898
Tune: HYFRYDOL, 8 7 8 7 D; Rowland H. Prichard, 1811-1887

445　We Come to Your Feast

Verses
Cantor or choir:

1. We place up - on your ta - ble　　a　gleam-ing cloth of
2. We place up - on your ta - ble　　a　hum - ble loaf of
3. We place up - on your ta - ble　　a　sim - ple cup of
4. We　ga - ther 'round your ta - ble,　　we　pause with-in our

white:　　　　　the weav-ing of our　sto - ries,
bread:　　　　　the gift of field and　hill - side,
wine:　　　　　the fruit of hu - man　la - bor,
quest,　　　　　we stand be - side our　neigh-bors,

the fab - ric of our lives;　　the dreams of those be -
the grain by which we're fed;　we come to taste the
the gift of sun and vine;　　we come to taste the
we name the stran - ger "guest."　The feast is spread be -

fore us,　　　　the an - cient hope - ful　cries,
pres - ence　　　of him on whom we　feed,
pres - ence　　　of him we claim as　Lord,
fore us;　　　　you bid us come and　dine:

the prom - ise of our fu - ture:　our need - ing and our
to strength-en and con - nect us,　to chal - lenge and cor -
his dy - ing and his liv - ing,　his lead - ing and his
in bless - ing we'll un - cov - er,　in shar - ing we'll dis -

nur - ture　　　lie here be - fore our　eyes.
rect us,　　　　to love in word and　deed.
giv - ing,　　　his love in cup out - poured.
cov - er　　　　your sub - stance and your　sign.

Refrain

We come to your feast, we come to your feast: the young and the old, the fright-ened, the bold, the great-est and the least. We come to your feast, we come to your feast with the fruit of our lands and the work of our hands, we come to your feast.

Text: Michael Joncas, b.1951
Tune: Michael Joncas, b.1951
© 1994, GIA Publications, Inc.

446 In the Breaking of the Bread / Cuando Partimos el Pan del Señor

Refrain

In the break - ing of the bread
Cuan-do par - ti - mos el pan del Se - ñor,

We have known him; we have been fed. Je -
lo co - no - ce - mos, nos da de co - mer. Je -

Je - sus the stran - ger, Je - sus the Lord,
sús des - co - no - ci - do, Je - sús, Se - ñor,

Be our com - pan - ion, be our hope.
nues - tro com-pa - ñe - ro, y fuen - te de fe.

Verses

1. Bread for the jour - ney, strength for our years,
1. *Pan pa - ra el via - je, Pan de la vi - da,*
2. Bread of the prom - ise, peo - ple of hope,
2. *Pan del pro - me - sa, Pan de es - pe - ran - za,*

Man - na of a - ges, of strug - gle and tears.
Pan de los si - glos de lu - cha y do - lor,
Wine of com - pas - sion, life for the world
Vi - no de vi - da, de su com - pa - sión,

Cup of sal - va - tion, fruit of the land,
y es - te vi - no, fru - to de la tie - rra ben-
Gath-ered at ta - ble, joined as his bod - y,
En es - ta me - sa un so - lo cuer - po

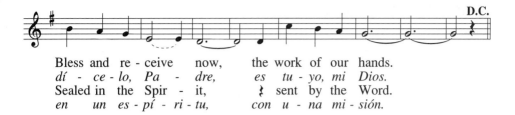

D.C.

Bless and re - ceive now, the work of our hands.
dí - ce - lo, Pa - dre, es tu - yo, mi Dios.
Sealed in the Spir - it, ⸕ sent by the Word.
en un es - pí - ri - tu, con u - na mi - sión.

Original Verses:

1. Once I was helpless, sad and confused; darkness surrounded me, courage removed.
   And then I saw him by my side. Carry my burden, open my eyes.

2. There is no sorrow, pain or woe; there is no suffering he did not know.
   He did not waver; he did not bend. He is the victor. He is my friend.

Text: Bob Hurd, b.1950, and Michael Downey, © 1984, 1987; Spanish text by Stephen Dean and Kathleen Orozco, © 1989, OCP Publications
Tune: Bob Hurd, b.1950, © 1984; acc. by Dominic MacAller, b.1959, © 1984, OCP Publications
Published by OCP Publications

Shepherd of Souls   447

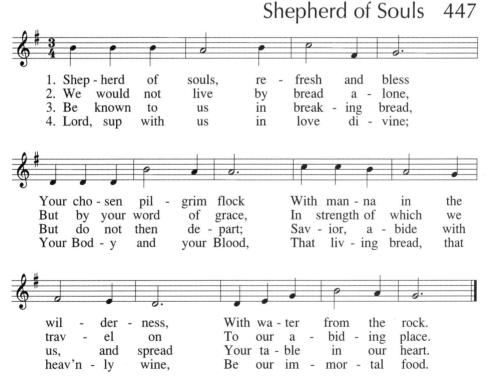

1. Shep - herd of souls, re - fresh and bless
2. We would not live by bread a - lone,
3. Be known to us in break - ing bread,
4. Lord, sup with us in love di - vine;

Your cho - sen pil - grim flock With man - na in the
But by your word of grace, In strength of which we
But do not then de - part; Sav - ior, a - bide with
Your Bod - y and your Blood, That liv - ing bread, that

wil - der - ness, With wa - ter from the rock.
trav - el on, To our a - bid - ing place.
us, and spread Your ta - ble in our heart.
heav'n - ly wine, Be our im - mor - tal food.

Text: James Montgomery, 1771-1854, alt.
Tune: ST. AGNES, CM; John B. Dykes, 1823-1876; harm. by Richard Proulx, b.1937, © 1986, GIA Publications, Inc.

448 Now in This Banquet

Refrain

Now in this ban-quet, Christ is our bread;
Advent: God of our jour-neys, day-break to night;
Lent: Lord, you can o-pen hearts that are stone;

Here shall all hun-gers be fed.
Lead us to jus-tice and light.
Live in our flesh and our bone;

Bread that is bro-ken, wine that is poured,
Grant us com-pas-sion, strength for the day,
Lead us to won-der, mys-t'ry and grace,

Love is the sign of our Lord.
Wis-dom to walk in your way.
One in your lov-ing em-brace.

Verses 1, 2

1. You who have touched us and graced us with love,
2. Let our hearts burn with the fire of your love;

D.C.

make us your peo-ple of good-ness and light.
o-pen our eyes to the glo-ry of God.

Verse 3

3. God who makes the blind to see, God who makes the

May be sung in canon.

Text: Marty Haugen, b.1950
Tune: Marty Haugen, b.1950
© 1986, GIA Publications, Inc.

449 I Am the Bread of Life / Yo Soy el Pan de Vida

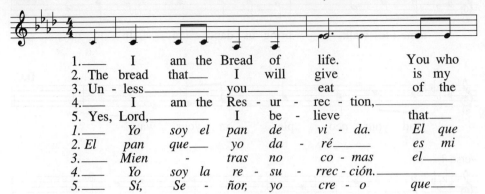

1.___ I am the Bread of life. You who
2. The bread that___ I will give is my
3. Un - less___ you___ eat of the
4.___ I am the Res - ur - rec - tion,___
5. Yes, Lord,___ I be - lieve that___

1.___ Yo soy el pan de vi - da. El que
2. El pan que___ yo da - ré___ es mi
3.___ Mien - tras no co - mas el___
4.___ Yo soy la re - su - rrec - ción.___
5.___ Sí, Se - ñor, yo cre - o que___

come to me shall not hun - ger;___ and who be -
flesh for the life of the world,___ and if you
flesh of the Son of Man___ and___
I___ am the life.___ If you be -
you___ are the Christ,___ the___

vie - ne a mí no ten - drá ham - bre.___ El que
cuer - po___ vi - da del mun - do,___ y el que
cuer - po del hi - jo del hom - bre,___ y___
Yo___ soy la vi - da.___ El que
tú e - res el Cris - to,___ El___

lieve in me shall not thirst.___ No one can come to
eat___ of this bread,___ you shall___ live for
drink___ of his blood,_ and drink___ of his
lieve___ in___ me,___ e - ven___ though you
Son___ of___ God,___ Who___ has___

cree en mí no ten - drá sed.___ Na - die___ vie - ne a
co - ma___ de mi car - ne___ ten - drá___ vi - da e -
be - bas___ de su san - gre, y be - bas___ de su
cree___ en___ mí,___ aun - que___ mu - rie -
Hi - jo de Dios,_ que vi - no al

me   un - less   the____   Fa - ther   beck - ons.
ev - er,____   you   shall____ live   for   ev - er.
blood,   you   shall   not have life   with - in   you.
die,____   you   shall____ live   for   ev - er.
come   in - to____   the____   world.____
mí____   mien - tras el Pa - dre   lla - me.
ter - na,____   ten - drá____   vi - da e - ter - na.
san - gre,   no   ten - drá____   vi - da   en   ti.
ra,____   ten - drá vi - da   e   -   ter - na.
mun - do____   pa   -   ra   sal   - var - nos.

And   I   will   raise   you   up,   and   I   will
Yo   le   re - su - ci - ta - ré,   Yo   le   re -

raise   you   up,   and   I   will   raise   you
su   -   ci - ta - ré,   Yo   le   re - su - ci - ta -

up   on   the   last   day.
ré   el   di   - a   de El.

Text: John 6; Suzanne Toolan, SM, b.1927
Tune: BREAD OF LIFE, Irregular with refrain; Suzanne Toolan, SM, b.1927
© 1966, 1970, 1986, 1993, GIA Publications, Inc.

450 Song of the Body of Christ / Canción del Cuerpo de Cristo

Refrain

We come to share our sto - ry, we
Ve - ni-mos a de - cir del mis - te - rio, y par -

come to break the bread, We come to know our
tir el pan de vi - da. Ve - ni-mos a sa - ber de

ris - ing from the dead.
nues - tra̱ e - ter - ni - dad.

Verses

1. We come as your peo - ple, we
2. We are called to heal the bro - ken, to be
3. Bread of life and cup of prom - ise, in this
4. You will lead and we shall fol - low, you will
5. We will live and sing: "A - lo - ha," "Al - le -
   (live and sing your prais - es,)

come as your own, u - nit - ed with each
hope for the poor, we are called to feed the
meal we all are one. In our dy - ing and our
be the breath of life; liv - ing wa - ter, we are
lu - ia" is our song. May we live in love and

D.C.

oth - er, love finds a home.
hun - gry at our door.
ris - ing, may your king - dom come.
thirst - ing for your light.
peace our whole life long.

Verses

1. Ve - ni - mos, co - mo   su pueb - lo   en es -
2. Nos   lla - ma pa - ra cu - rar   y
3. Pan de vi - da y co - pa de pro - me - sa,   so - mos
4. Nos guia - rás   y   te   se - gui - re - mos,   por - que
5. Vi - vi - re - mos can - tan - do "A - lo - ha."   "A - le -

pí - ri - tu de ver - dad.   U - ni - dos en su a-
ser su es - per - an - za.   So - mos su - yos pa - ra a - li - men-
u - no en es - ta co - mi - da.   Ven - drá su rei - no en
e - res la luz que bus - ca - mos.   En el di - a o en la
lu - ya" es nues - tra can - ción.   Por siem - pre vi - vi -

D.C.

mor, so - mos un cor - a - zón.
tar a los po - bres.
nues - tra trans - for - ma - ción.
no - che, bri - lla - rás.
re - mos en su paz.

Text: David Haas, b.1957, Spanish translation by Donna Peña, b.1955
Tune: NO KE ANO' AHI AHI, Irregular, Hawaiian traditional, arr. by David Haas, b.1957
© 1989, GIA Publications, Inc.

451 Pan de Vida

Refrain

* Pan de Vi - da, cuer-po del Se - ñor,

cup of bless - ing, blood of Christ the Lord.

At this ta - ble the last shall be first, ** po -

der es ser - vir, por-que Dios es a - mor.

Verses

1. We are the dwell-ing of God,
*** 2. Us - te - des me lla - man "Se - ñor," me in-
3. There is no Jew or Greek,

fra - gile and wound-ed and weak. We are the
cli - no a la - var - les los pies: Ha - gan lo
there is no slave or free: there is no

bod - y of Christ, called to be the com -
mis - mo, hu - mil - des, sir - vién - do - se
wom-an or man; on - ly heirs of the

D.C.

pas - sion of God.
u - nos a o - tros.
prom - ise of God.

* Bread of Life, body of the Lord,   **power is for service, because God is Love.
***You call me "Lord," and I bow to wash your feet:
you must do the same, humbly serving each other.

Text: John 13:1-15, Galatians 3:28-29; Bob Hurd, b.1950, and Pia Moriarty, © 1988, Bob Hurd and Pia Moriarty
Tune: Bob Hurd, b.1950, © 1988; acc. by Craig Kingsbury, b.1952, © 1988, OCP Publications; arr. © 1988, OCP Publications
Published by OCP Publications

At That First Eucharist 452

1. At that first Eu - cha - rist be - fore you died,
2. For all your church, O Lord, we in - ter - cede;
3. We pray for those who wan - der from the fold;

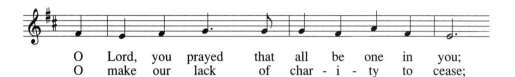

O Lord, you prayed that all be one in you;
O make our lack of char - i - ty to cease;
O bring them back, Good Shep - herd of the sheep,

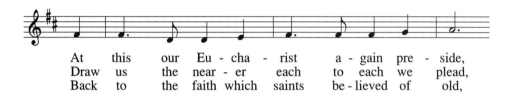

At this our Eu - cha - rist a - gain pre - side,
Draw us the near - er each to each we plead,
Back to the faith which saints be - lieved of old,

And in our hearts your law of love re - new.
By draw - ing all to you, O Prince of Peace.
Back to the Church which still that faith does keep.

Thus may we all one Bread, one Bod - y be;

Through this blest Sac - ra - ment of U - ni - ty.

Text: William H. Turton, 1859-1938, alt.
Tune: UNDE ET MEMORES, 10 10 10 10 with refrain; William H. Monk, 1823-1889, alt.

453 I Received the Living God

Refrain

I re - ceived the liv-ing God, and my heart is full of joy. I re-ceived the liv-ing God, and my heart is full of joy.

Verses

1. Je - sus said: "I am the Bread Knead - ed
2. Je - sus said: "I am the Vine, And my
3. Je - sus said: "I am the Truth; If you
4. Je - sus said: "I am the Life Far from

long to give you life; You who will par-take of
branch-es you shall be; Come and drink the sav - ing
fol - low close to me, You will know me in your
whom no thing can grow, But re - ceive this liv - ing

D.C.

me Need not ev - er fear to die."
cup, Till the King - dom you shall see."
heart, And my word shall make you free."
bread, And my Spir - it you shall know."

Text: Anonymous; verse 2, Alan J. Hommerding, b.1956, © 1994, World Library Publications, Inc.
Tune: LIVING GOD, 7 7 7 7 with refrain; Anonymous; harm. by Richard Proulx, b.1937, © 1986, GIA Publications, Inc.

454 May the Angels Lead You into Paradise

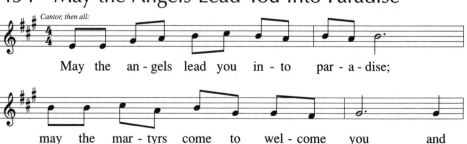

Cantor, then all:

May the an - gels lead you in - to par - a - dise;

may the mar - tyrs come to wel - come you and

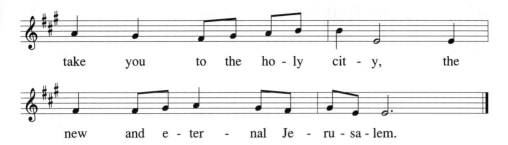

take you to the ho - ly cit - y, the

new and e - ter - nal Je - ru - sa - lem.

Text: *In paradisum; Rite of Funerals,* © 1970, ICEL
Tune: *Music for Rite of Funerals and Rite of Baptism for Children,* Howard Hughes, SM, © 1977, ICEL

Song of Farewell 455

1. Come to his/her aid, O saints of God;
2. May Christ, who called you, take you home,
3. Give him/her e - ter - nal rest, O Lord.
4. I know that my Re - deem - er lives;

Come, meet him/her, an - gels of the Lord.
And an - gels lead you to A - bra - ham.
May light un - end - ing shine on him/her.
The last day I shall rise a - gain.

Re - ceive his/her soul, O ho - ly ones;

Pre - sent him/her now to God, Most High.

Text: Based on Subvenite and Job 19:25-27; Dennis C. Smolarski, © 1981
Tune: OLD HUNDREDTH, LM; Louis Bourgeois, c.1510-1561, alt.

456 I Know That My Redeemer Lives

Text: *Rite of Funerals,* © 1970, ICEL
Music: *Music for Rite of Funerals and Rite of Baptism for Children,* Howard Hughes, SM, © 1977, ICEL

In Paradisum / May Choirs of Angels 457

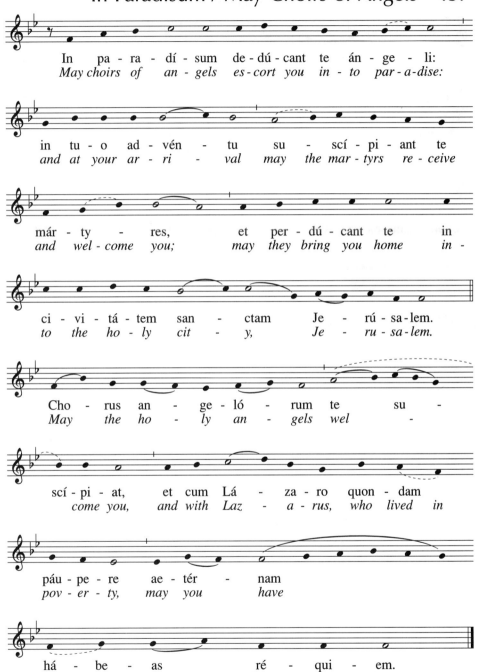

In pa - ra - dí - sum de - dú - cant te án - ge - li:
May choirs of an - gels es - cort you in - to par - a-dise:

in tu - o ad - vén - tu su - scí - pi - ant te
and at your ar - ri - val may the mar - tyrs re - ceive

már - ty - res, et per - dú - cant te in
and wel - come you; may they bring you home in -

ci - vi - tá - tem san - ctam Je - rú - sa - lem.
to the ho - ly cit - y, Je - ru - sa-lem.

Cho - rus an - ge - ló - rum te su -
May the ho - ly an - gels wel -

scí - pi - at, et cum Lá - za - ro quon - dam
come you, and with Laz - a - rus, who lived in

páu - pe - re ae - tér - nam
pov - er - ty, may you have

há - be - as ré - qui - em.
ev - er - last - ing rest.

Text: *In Paradisum*, tr. © 1986, GIA Publications, Inc.
Tune: Mode VII; acc. by Richard Proulx, b.1937, © 1986, GIA Publications, Inc.

458 May Saints and Angels Lead You On

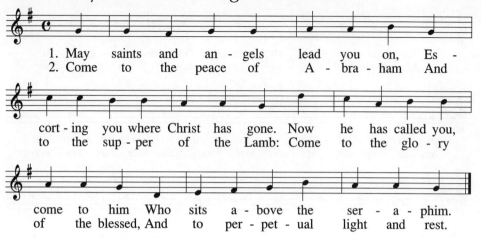

1. May saints and an - gels lead you on, Es -
2. Come to the peace of A - bra - ham And

cort - ing you where Christ has gone. Now he has called you,
to the sup - per of the Lamb: Come to the glo - ry

come to him Who sits a - bove the ser - a - phim.
of the blessed, And to per - pet - ual light and rest.

Text: *In Paradisum,* © 1985, ICEL
Tune: TALLIS' CANON, LM; Thomas Tallis, c.1505-1585

459 Love Is the Sunlight

1. Love is the sun - light Shaped of your splen - dor,
2. Love is the spa - cious Qui - et of shad - ows,
3. May we in glad - ness Grow in your sun - shine,

Love is the star bright Born of your hand,
Love is the gra - cious Shade of re - lease,
May we in sad - ness Rest in your shade,

Bless-ing of heav - en Gra - cious - ly giv - en,
Mist of the morn - ing, Mid - day a - dorn - ing,
Giv - ing and gain - ing, Ev - er re - main - ing,

Ra - diant with glo - ry From your com - mand.
Cool with the twi - light Breath of your peace.
One in the mar - riage Your love has made.

Text: Borghild Jacobson, © 1981, Concordia Publishing House
Tune: BUNESSAN, 5 5 5 4 D; Gaelic; harm. by A. Gregory Murray, OSB, 1905-1992, © Downside Abbey

Wherever You Go   460

1. Wher - ev - er you go   I shall go.

Wher - ev - er you live   so shall I   live.

Your peo - ple will   be   my peo - ple,   and

your God   will be   my God   too.

2. Wher - ev - er you die   I shall die

and there shall I   be bur - ied be - side   you.

We will be to - geth - er   for   ev - er,   and

our love   will be the gift   of   our   life.

Text: Ruth 1:16, 17; Gregory Norbet, b.1940
Tune: Gregory Norbet, b.1940; arr. by Mary David Callahan, b.1923
© 1972, 1980, The Benedictine Foundation of the State of Vermont, Inc.

461 When Love Is Found

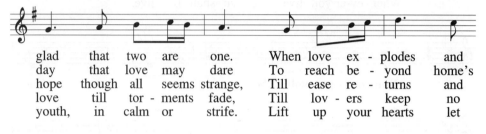

1. When love is found and hope comes home, Sing and be
2. When love has flow'red in trust and care, Build both each
3. When love is tried as loved - ones change, Hold still to
4. When love is torn and trust be - trayed, Pray strength to
5. Praise God for love, praise God for life, In age or

glad that two are one. When love ex - plodes and
day that love may dare To reach be - yond home's
hope though all seems strange, Till ease re - turns and
love till tor - ments fade, Till lov - ers keep no
youth, in calm or strife. Lift up your hearts let

fills the sky, Praise God and share our Mak - er's joy.
warmth and light, To serve and strive for truth and right.
love grows wise Through lis - t'ning ears and o - pened eyes.
score of wrong But hear through pain love's Eas - ter song.
love be fed Through death and life in bro - ken bread.

Text: Brian Wren, b.1936
Tune: O WALY WALY, LM; English; harm. by Martin West, b.1929
© 1983, Hope Publishing Co.

462 God, in the Planning

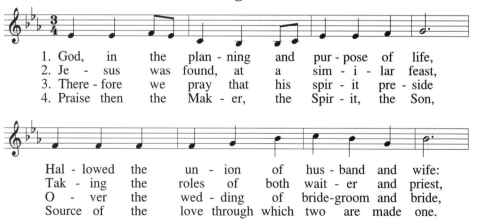

1. God, in the plan - ning and pur - pose of life,
2. Je - sus was found, at a sim - i - lar feast,
3. There - fore we pray that his spir - it pre - side
4. Praise then the Mak - er, the Spir - it, the Son,

Hal - lowed the un - ion of hus - band and wife:
Tak - ing the roles of both wait - er and priest,
O - ver the wed - ding of bride-groom and bride,
Source of the love through which two are made one.

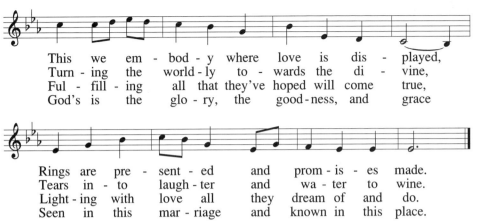

This we em-bod-y where love is dis-played,
Turn-ing the world-ly to-wards the di-vine,
Ful-fill-ing all that they've hoped will come true,
God's is the glo-ry, the good-ness, and grace

Rings are pre-sent-ed and prom-is-es made.
Tears in-to laugh-ter and wa-ter to wine.
Light-ing with love all they dream of and do.
Seen in this mar-riage and known in this place.

Text: John L. Bell, b.1949, © 1989, Iona Community, GIA Publication, Inc., agent
Tune: SLANE, 10 10 10 10; Irish traditional; harm. by Erik Routley, 1917-1982, © 1985, Hope Publishing Co.

Precious Lord, Take My Hand 463

1. Pre-cious Lord, take my hand, Lead me on, let me
2. When my way grows drear, Pre-cious Lord, lin-ger
3. When the dark-ness ap-pears And the night draws

stand, I am tired, I am weak, I am worn.
near, When my life is al-most gone,
near, And the day is past and gone,

Through the storm, through the night, Lead me on to the
Hear my cry, hear my call, Hold my hand lest I
At the riv-er I stand, Guide my feet, hold my

light, Take my hand, pre-cious Lord, lead me home.
fall. Take my hand, pre-cious Lord, lead me home.
hand. Take my hand, pre-cious Lord, lead me home.

Text: Thomas A. Dorsey, 1899-1993
Tune: PRECIOUS LORD, 66 9 D; George N. Allen; arr. by Kelly Dobbs Mickus, b.1966
© 1938, Unichappell Music, Inc.

464 Jesus, Heal Us

Refrain

Je - sus, heal us; Je - sus.

Je - sus, hear us now.

Verse 1

1. All who fear the Lord: Wait for God's mer - cy.

D.C.

All who love the Lord: Come, he will fill you.

Verse 2

2. All who fear the Lord: Fol - low the way.

D.C.

All who love the Lord: Hope in God's good - ness.

Verse 3

3. All who fear the Lord: Keep your hearts pre - pared.

D.C.

All who love the Lord: Be hum - bled in God's pres - ence.

Verse 4

4. All who trust the Lord: God will up -

hold you. Let us cling to our God; let us

D.C.

fall in the arms of the Lord!

Text: David Haas, b.1957
Tune: David Haas, b.1957
© 1988, GIA Publications, Inc.

Forgive Our Sins 465

1. "For - give our sins as we for - give," You
2. How can your par - don reach and bless The
3. In blaz - ing light your Cross re - veals The
4. Lord, cleanse the depths with - in our souls And

taught us, Lord, to pray, But you a - lone can
un - for - giv - ing heart That broods on wrongs and
truth we dim - ly knew: What triv - ial debts are
bid re - sent - ment cease. Then, bound to all in

grant us grace To live the words we say.
will not let Old bit - ter - ness de - part?
owed to us, How great our debt to you!
bonds of love, Our lives will spread your peace.

Text: Rosamund Herklots, b.1905, © Oxford University Press
Tune: DETROIT, CM; Supplement to *Kentucky Harmony*, 1820; harm. by Gerald H. Knight, 1908-1979, © The Royal School of Church Music

466 The Master Came to Bring Good News

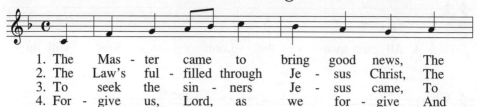

1. The Mas - ter came to bring good news, The
2. The Law's ful - filled through Je - sus Christ, The
3. To seek the sin - ners Je - sus came, To
4. For - give us, Lord, as we for - give And

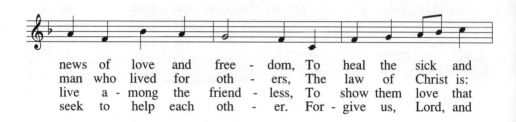

news of love and free - dom, To heal the sick and
man who lived for oth - ers, The law of Christ is:
live a - mong the friend - less, To show them love that
seek to help each oth - er. For - give us, Lord, and

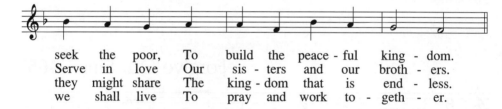

seek the poor, To build the peace - ful king - dom.
Serve in love Our sis - ters and our broth - ers.
they might share The king - dom that is end - less.
we shall live To pray and work to - geth - er.

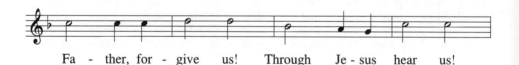

Fa - ther, for - give us! Through Je - sus hear us!

As we for - give one an - oth - er!

Text: Ralph Finn b.1941, © 1965, GIA Publications, Inc.
Tune: ICH GLAUB AN GOTT, 8 7 8 7 with refrain; *Mainz Gesangbuch*, 1870; harm. by Richard Proulx, b.1937, © 1986, GIA Publications, Inc.

Remember Your Love 467

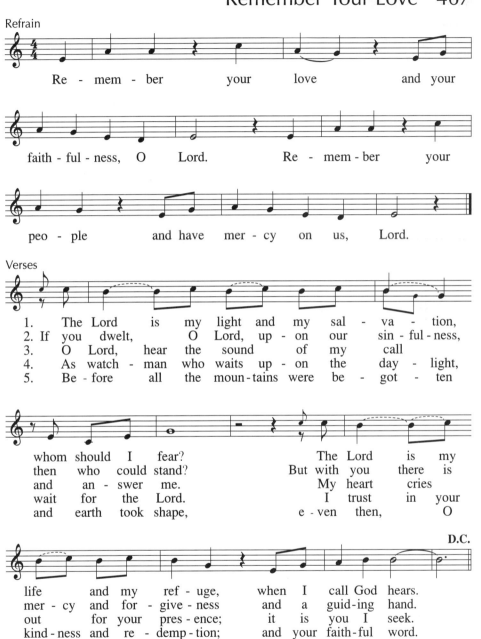

Refrain

Re - mem - ber your love and your faith - ful - ness, O Lord. Re - mem - ber your peo - ple and have mer - cy on us, Lord.

Verses

1. The Lord is my light and my sal - va - tion,
2. If you dwelt, O Lord, up - on our sin - ful - ness,
3. O Lord, hear the sound of my call
4. As watch - man who waits up - on the day - light,
5. Be - fore all the moun - tains were be - got - ten

whom should I fear? The Lord is my
then who could stand? But with you there is
and an - swer me. My heart cries
wait for the Lord. I trust in your
and earth took shape, e - ven then, O

D.C.

life and my ref - uge, when I call God hears.
mer - cy and for - give - ness and a guid - ing hand.
out for your pres - ence; it is you I seek.
kind - ness and re - demp - tion; and your faith - ful word.
Lord, you were our ref - uge through - out ev - 'ry age.

Text: Psalm 27; Mike Balhoff, b.1946
Tune: Darryl Ducote, b.1945, and Gary Daigle, b.1957
© 1978, Damean Music. Distributed by GIA Publications, Inc.

468　Healer of Our Every Ill

Refrain

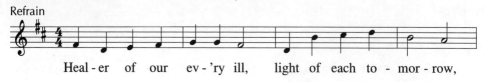

Heal - er of our ev - 'ry ill, light of each to - mor - row,

give us peace be - yond our fear, and hope be - yond our sor - row.

Verses

1. You who know our fears and sad - ness,
2. In the pain and joy be - hold - ing,
3. Give us strength to love each oth - er,
4. You who know each thought and feel - ing,

Grace us with your peace and glad - ness,
How your grace is still un - fold - ing,
Ev - 'ry sis - ter, ev - 'ry broth - er,
Teach us all your way of heal - ing,

D.C.

Spir - it of all com - fort: fill our hearts.
Give us all your vi - sion: God of love.
Spir - it of all kind - ness: be our guide.
Spir - it of com - pas - sion: fill each heart.

Text: Marty Haugen, b.1950
Tune: Marty Haugen, b.1950
© 1987, GIA Publications, Inc.

Ashes 469

1. We rise a-gain from ash - es, from the good we've failed to do. We rise a-gain from ash - es, to cre - ate our-selves a - new. If all our world is ash - es, then must our lives be true, An of - fer-ing of ash - es, an of - fer - ing to you.

2. We of - fer you our fail - ures, we of - fer you at - tempts, The gifts not ful - ly giv - en, the dreams not ful - ly dreamt. Give our stum - bl - ings di - rec - tion, give our vi - sions wid - er view, An of - fer-ing of ash - es, an of - fer - ing to you.

3. Then rise a - gain from ash - es, let heal - ing come to pain, Though spring has turned to win - ter, and sun - shine turned to rain. The rain we'll use for grow - ing, and cre - ate the world a - new From an of - fer-ing of ash - es, an of - fer - ing to you.

4. Thanks be to the Fa - ther, who made us like him - self. Thanks be to the Son, who saved us by his death. Thanks be to the Spir - it, who cre - ates the world a - new From an of - fer-ing of ash - es, an of - fer - ing to you.

Text: Tom Conry, b.1951
Tune: Tom Conry, b.1951; acc. by Michael Joncas, b.1951
© 1978, New Dawn Music

470 O Lord, with Wondrous Mystery

1. O Lord, with won-drous mys - ter - y You
2. You are the same, our Christ and Lord, Who

take our bread and wine, And make of these two
blessed the sup - per room; You are the God who

hum - ble things Your - self, our Lord di - vine.
died and rose Tri - um - phant from the tomb.

Our wheat and drink be - come our Light, Our
This bread bears your di - vin - i - ty, This

al - tar bears your awe-some might; O Lord, we thank you
cup con - tains in - fin - i - ty; The mys - t'ry fills our

for the gift That lies be - fore our sight.
souls with love, O Ho - ly Maj - es - ty.

Text: Michael Gannon, © 1955, World Library Publications, Inc.
Tune: ANDRIESSEN, 8 6 8 6 88 8 6; Hendrik F. Andriessen, 1892-1981, ©

471 O Sacrament Most Holy

1. O Je - sus, we a - dore you, Who in your love di - vine,
2. O Je - sus, we a - dore you, Our vic - tim and our priest,
3. O Je - sus, we a - dore you, Our Sav - ior and our King,
4. O Je - sus, we a - dore you; Come, live in us, we pray,
5. O come, all you who la - bor In sor - row and in pain;

Con - ceal your might - y God-head In forms of bread and wine.
Whose pre-cious blood and bod - y Be - come our sa - cred feast.
And with the saints and an - gels Our hum - ble hom - age bring.
That all our thoughts and ac - tions Be yours a - lone to - day.
Come, eat this bread from heav - en; Your peace and strength re - gain.

O sac - ra - ment most ho - ly, O sac - ra - ment di - vine,

All praise and all thanks-giv - ing Be ev - 'ry mo - ment thine!

Text: Irvin Udulutsch; refrain from the *Raccolta*
Tune: FULDA MELODY, 7 6 7 6 with refrain; Fulda *Gesangbuch;* arr. by Charles G. Frischmann, © 1976, World Library Publications, Inc.

My Country, 'Tis of Thee   472

1. My coun - try, 'tis of thee, Sweet land of lib - er - ty,
2. My na - tive coun - try, thee, Land of the no - ble, free;
3. Let mu - sic swell the breeze, And ring from all the trees
4. Our fa - thers' God, to thee, Au - thor of lib - er - ty,

Of thee I sing; Land where my fa - thers died, Land of the
Thy name I love; I love thy rocks and rills, Thy woods and
Sweet free-dom's song; Let mor - tal tongues a - wake; Let all that
To thee we sing; Long may our land be bright With free-dom's

pil - grim's pride, From ev - 'ry moun - tain - side Let free-dom ring!
tem - pled hills; My heart with rap - ture thrills, Like that a - bove.
breathe par - take; Let rocks their si - lence break, The sound pro - long.
ho - ly light; Pro - tect us by thy might, Great God, our King.

Text: Samuel F. Smith, 1808-1895
Tune: AMERICA, 66 4 666 4; *Thesaurus Musicus,* 1744

473　Star-Spangled Banner

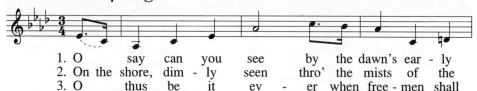

1. O　　　say　can　you　see　　by　the dawn's ear - ly
2. On the shore, dim - ly　seen　thro' the mists of　the
3. O　　thus　be　it　ev　-　er　when free - men shall

light, What　so proud - ly　we　hailed　at　the twi - light's last
deep, Where the foe's　haugh - ty　host　in dead si - lence re -
stand Be　-　tween　their loved homes　and the war's des - o -

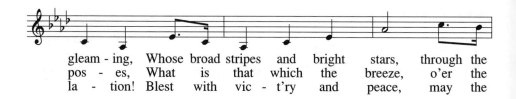

gleam - ing, Whose broad stripes　and　bright　stars,　through the
pos - es,　What　is　that　which　the　breeze,　o'er the
la - tion! Blest　with　vic - t'ry　and　peace,　may　the

per - il - ous　fight,　O'er　the　ram　-　parts we
tow - er - ing　steep,　As　it　fit　-　ful - ly
heav'n - res - cued　land　Praise the　Pow'r　that hath

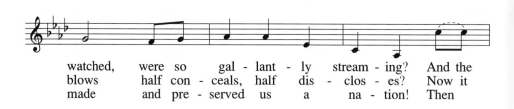

watched,　were so　gal - lant - ly　stream - ing? And the
blows　half con - ceals, half　dis - clos - es? Now it
made　and pre - served us　a　na - tion! Then

rock - ets'　red　glare,　the bombs　burst - ing　in
catch - es　the　gleam　of　the　morn - ing's first
con - quer　we　must,　when our　cause　it　is

air,   Gave   proof   through the   night   that our
beam,   In full   glo - ry   re - flect - ed   now
just,   And   this   be   our   mot - to,   "In

flag   was   still   there.   O   say   does   that
shined on   the   stream,   'Tis the   Star - Span - gled
God   is   our   trust."   And the   Star - Span - gled

Star - Span - gled Ban - ner   yet   wave   O'er the
Ban - ner   O   long   may   it   wave   O'er the
Ban - ner   in   tri - umph shall   wave   O'er the

land   of the   free   and the home   of the brave?
land   of the   free   and the home   of the brave!
land   of the   free   and the home   of the brave!

Text: Francis S. Key, 1779-1843
Tune: STAR SPANGLED BANNER; Irregular, John S. Smith, 1750-1836

474 America the Beautiful

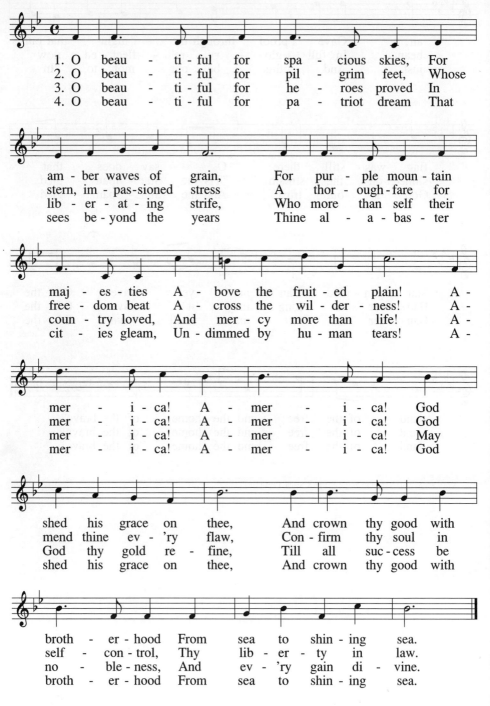

1. O beau - ti - ful for spa - cious skies, For
2. O beau - ti - ful for pil - grim feet, Whose
3. O beau - ti - ful for he - roes proved In
4. O beau - ti - ful for pa - triot dream That

am - ber waves of grain, For pur - ple moun - tain
stern, im - pas-sioned stress A thor - ough-fare for
lib - er - at - ing strife, Who more than self their
sees be - yond the years Thine al - a - bas - ter

maj - es - ties A - bove the fruit - ed plain! A -
free - dom beat A - cross the wil - der - ness! A -
coun - try loved, And mer - cy more than life! A -
cit - ies gleam, Un - dimmed by hu - man tears! A -

mer - i - ca! A - mer - i - ca! God
mer - i - ca! A - mer - i - ca! God
mer - i - ca! A - mer - i - ca! May
mer - i - ca! A - mer - i - ca! God

shed his grace on thee, And crown thy good with
mend thine ev - 'ry flaw, Con - firm thy soul in
God thy gold re - fine, Till all suc - cess be
shed his grace on thee, And crown thy good with

broth - er - hood From sea to shin - ing sea.
self - con - trol, Thy lib - er - ty in law.
no - ble - ness, And ev - 'ry gain di - vine.
broth - er - hood From sea to shin - ing sea.

Text: Katherine L. Bates, 1859-1929
Tune: MATERNA, CMD; Samuel A. Ward, 1848-1903

The God of All Eternity 475

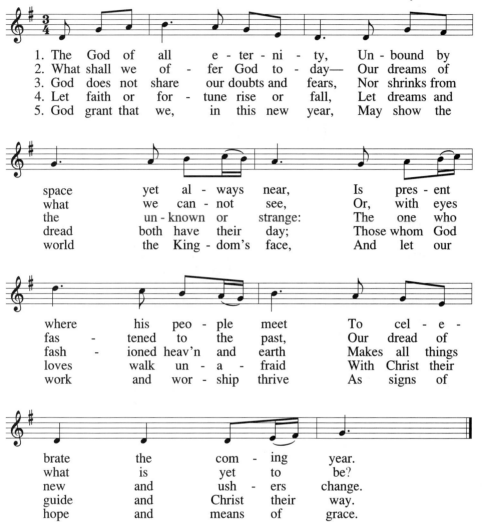

1. The God of all e - ter - ni - ty, Un - bound by
2. What shall we of - fer God to - day— Our dreams of
3. God does not share our doubts and fears, Nor shrinks from
4. Let faith or for - tune rise or fall, Let dreams and
5. God grant that we, in this new year, May show the

space yet al - ways near, Is pres - ent
what we can - not see, Or, with eyes
the un - known or strange: The one who
dread both have their day; Those whom God
world the King - dom's face, And let our

where his peo - ple meet To cel - e -
fas - tened to the past, Our dread of
fash - ioned heav'n and earth Makes all things
loves walk un - a - fraid With Christ their
work and wor - ship thrive As signs of

brate the com - ing year.
what is yet to be?
new and ush - ers change.
guide and Christ their way.
hope and means of grace.

Text: John L. Bell, b.1949, © 1989, Iona Community, GIA Publications, Inc., agent
Tune: O WALY WALY, 8 8 8 8; English traditional; arr. by John L. Bell, b.1949, © 1989, Iona Community, GIA Publications, Inc., agent

Advent/Christmas

476   In various ways and various places the churches have marked the days around the winter solstice (adapting when possible in the southern hemisphere when December and January surround the summer solstice). Christians have quite naturally kept from their former religions and traditions all manner of customs and rituals, giving these a home around the many-faceted celebration of the Word-made-flesh, the manifestation of God-with-us.

The present Roman calendar has a period of three to four weeks before December 25. This is called Advent and it is filled with beautiful scriptures, songs, prayers and gestures. These have no single focus but abound with images: of God's promise and human longing, of the beauty in both darkness and light, of the earth's sorrows and its fullness, of the goodness and mystery of time. The spirit of the church's Advent is in the silence and song that arise from constant attention to the human condition.

At Christmas this spirit blossoms in acclamation: the stories of nativity and epiphany, of Mary and of the Innocents, of Jesus baptized and of water become wine. Until well into January the songs and sights and smells of Christmas surround the church not with sentimental fantasies but with everyday faith in a gracious God. The festivals of the Christmas season bear their own reflection of what is proclaimed on every Sunday of the year and in every baptism: our lives are caught up now in Jesus who was born of the virgin Mary, who suffered, died and has been raised.

The lectionary of Advent/Christmas is the foundation of these winter days. These scriptures, read and pondered year after year, turn the Christian and the church toward that peace and glory we name but do not yet know.

FIRST SUNDAY OF ADVENT / A   477

READING I   *Isaiah 2:1-5 / 1*

This is what Isaiah, son of Amoz,
saw concerning Judah and Jerusalem.
  In days to come,
the mountain of the LORD's house
    shall be established as
      the highest mountain
    and raised above the hills.
All nations shall stream toward it;
  many peoples shall come and say:
"Come, let us climb the LORD's
  mountain,
  to the house of the God of Jacob,
that he may instruct us in his ways,
  and we may walk in his paths."

For from Zion shall go forth
  instruction,
  and the word of the LORD from
  Jerusalem.
He shall judge between the nations,
  and impose terms on many peoples.
They shall beat their swords into
  plowshares
  and their spears into pruning hooks;
one nation shall not raise the sword
  against another,
  nor shall they train for war again.
O house of Jacob, come,
  let us walk in the light of the Lord!

RESPONSORIAL PSALM   *Psalm 122:1-2, 3-4, 4-5, 6-7, 8-9*

Let us go re - joic - ing   to the house   of the   Lord.

I rejoiced because they said to me,
  "We will go up to the house of the
  LORD."
And now we have set foot
  within your gates, O Jerusalem. ℟.

Jerusalem, built as a city
  with compact unity.
To it the tribes go up,
  the tribes of the LORD. ℟.

According to the decree for Israel,
  to give thanks to the name of the
  LORD.

In it are set up judgment seats,
  seats for the house of David. ℟.

Pray for the peace of Jerusalem!
  May those who love you prosper!
May peace be within your walls,
  prosperity in your buildings. ℟.

Because of my brothers and friends
  I will say, "Peace be within you!"
Because of the house of the LORD, our
  God,
  I will pray for your good. ℟.

READING II   *Romans 13:11-14*

Brothers and sisters: You know the time; it is the hour now for you to awake from sleep. For our salvation is nearer now than when we first believed; the night is advanced, the day is at hand. Let us then throw off the works of darkness and put on the armor of light; let us conduct ourselves properly as in the day, not in orgies and drunkenness, not in promiscuity and lust, not in rivalry and jealousy. But put on the Lord Jesus Christ, and make no provision for the desires of the flesh.

GOSPEL   *Matthew 24:37-44*

Jesus said to his disciples: "As it was in the days of Noah, so it will be at the coming of the Son of Man. In those days before the flood, they were eating and drinking, marrying and giving in marriage, up to the day that Noah entered the ark. They did not know until the flood came and carried them all away. So will it be also at the coming of the Son of Man. Two men will be out in the field; one will be taken, and one will be left. Two women will be grinding at the mill; one will be taken, and one will be left. Therefore, stay awake! For you do not know on which day your Lord will come. Be sure of this: if the master of the house had known the hour of night when the thief was coming, he would have stayed awake and not let his house be broken into. So too, you also must be prepared, for at an hour you do not expect, the Son of Man will come."

478 FIRST SUNDAY OF ADVENT / B

READING I
Isaiah 63:16b-17, 19b; 64:2-7 / 2

You, Lord, are our father,
  our redeemer you are named forever.
Why do you let us wander, O Lord, from
    your ways,
    and harden our hearts so that we fear
      you not?
Return for the sake of your servants,
  the tribes of your heritage.
Oh, that you would rend the heavens and
    come down,
    with the mountains quaking before
      you,
while you wrought awesome deeds we
    could not hope for,
    such as they had not heard of from
      of old.
No ear has ever heard, no eye ever seen,
    any God but you
    doing such deeds for those who
      wait for him.

Would that you might meet us doing
    right,
    that we were mindful of you in our
      ways!
Behold, you are angry, and we are sinful;
  all of us have become like unclean
    people,
  all our good deeds are like polluted
    rags;
we have all withered like leaves,
  and our guilt carries us away like
    the wind.
There is none who calls upon your name,
  who rouses himself to cling to you;
for you have hidden your face from us
  and have delivered us up to our guilt.
Yet, O Lord, you are our father;
  we are the clay and you the potter:
  we are all the work of your hands.

RESPONSORIAL PSALM
Psalm 80:2-3, 15-16, 18-19

Lord,   make us   turn to   you;   let   us   see your

face   and   we   shall   be   saved.

O shepherd of Israel, hearken,
  from your throne upon the cherubim,
    shine forth.
Rouse your power,
  and come to save us. ℟.

Once again, O Lord of hosts,
  look down from heaven, and see;
take care of this vine,
  and protect what your right hand has
    planted,

the son of man whom you yourself
    made strong. ℟.

May your help be with the man of your
    right hand,
  with the son of man whom you
    yourself made strong.
Then we will no more withdraw from
    you;
  give us new life, and we will call
    upon your name. ℟.

READING II
1 Corinthians 1:3-9

Brothers and sisters: Grace to you and peace from God our Father and the Lord Jesus Christ.

I give thanks to my God always on your account for the grace of God bestowed on you in Christ Jesus, that in him you were enriched in every way, with all discourse and all knowledge, as the testimony to Christ was confirmed among you, so that you are not lacking in any spiritual gift as you wait for the revelation of our Lord Jesus Christ. He will keep you firm to the end, irreproachable on the day of our Lord Jesus Christ. God is faithful, and by him you were called to fellowship with his Son, Jesus Christ our Lord.

GOSPEL   *Mark 13:33-37*

Jesus said to his disciples: "Be watchful! Be alert! You do not know when the time will come. It is like a man traveling abroad. He leaves home and places his servants in charge, each with his own work, and orders the gatekeeper to be on the watch. Watch, therefore; you do not know when the lord of the house is coming, whether in the evening, or at midnight, or at cockcrow, or in the morning. May he not come suddenly and find you sleeping. What I say to you, I say to all: 'Watch!'"

FIRST SUNDAY OF ADVENT / C   479

READING I   *Jeremiah 33:14-16 / 3*

The days are coming, says the Lord,
    when I will fulfill the promise
    I made to the house of Israel and
        Judah.
In those days, in that time,
    I will raise up for David a just shoot;
he shall do what is right and just in
        the land.
In those days Judah shall be safe
    and Jerusalem shall dwell secure;
    this is what they shall call her:
    "The Lord our justice."

RESPONSORIAL PSALM   *Psalm 25:4-5, 8-9, 10, 14*

To you, O Lord, I lift my soul,
to you I lift my soul.

Your ways, O Lord, make known to me;
    teach me your paths,
guide me in your truth and teach me,
    for you are God my savior,
    and for you I wait all the day. ℞.

Good and upright is the Lord;
    thus he shows sinners the way.
He guides the humble to justice,
    and teaches the humble his way. ℞.

All the paths of the Lord are kindness
        and constancy
    toward those who keep his covenant
        and his decrees.
The friendship of the Lord is with those
        who fear him,
    and his covenant, for their
        instruction. ℞.

READING II   *1 Thessalonians 3:12—4:2*

Brothers and sisters: May the Lord make you increase and abound in love for one another and for all, just as we have for you, so as to strengthen your hearts, to be blameless in holiness before our God and Father at the coming of our Lord Jesus with all his holy ones. Amen.

Finally, brothers and sisters, we earnestly ask and exhort you in the Lord Jesus that, as you received from us how you should conduct yourselves to please God—and as you are conducting yourselves—you do so even more. For you know what instructions we gave you through the Lord Jesus.

GOSPEL
Luke 21:25-28, 34-36

Jesus said to his disciples: "There will be signs in the sun, the moon, and the stars, and on earth nations will be in dismay, perplexed by the roaring of the sea and the waves. People will die of fright in anticipation of what is coming upon the world, for the powers of the heavens will be shaken. And then they will see the Son of Man coming in a cloud with power and great glory. But when these signs begin to happen, stand erect and raise your heads because your redemption is at hand.

"Beware that your hearts do not become drowsy from carousing and drunkenness and the anxieties of daily life, and that day catch you by surprise like a trap. For that day will assault everyone who lives on the face of the earth. Be vigilant at all times and pray that you have the strength to escape the tribulations that are imminent and to stand before the Son of Man."

480   SECOND SUNDAY OF ADVENT / A

READING I
Isaiah 11:1-10 / 4

On that day, a shoot shall sprout from the
    stump of Jesse,
    and from his roots a bud shall
    blossom.
The spirit of the Lord shall rest upon him:
    a spirit of wisdom and of
    understanding,
a spirit of counsel and of strength,
    a spirit of knowledge and of fear of
    the Lord,
    and his delight shall be the fear of
    the Lord.
Not by appearance shall he judge,
    nor by hearsay shall he decide,
but he shall judge the poor with justice,
    and decide aright for the land's
    afflicted.
He shall strike the ruthless with the rod
    of his mouth,
    and with the breath of his lips he shall
    slay the wicked.
Justice shall be the band around his waist,
    and faithfulness a belt upon his hips.

Then the wolf shall be a guest of the
    lamb,
    and the leopard shall lie down with
    the kid;
the calf and the young lion shall browse
    together,
    with a little child to guide them.
The cow and the bear shall be neighbors,
    together their young shall rest;
    the lion shall eat hay like the ox.
The baby shall play by the cobra's den,
    and the child lay his hand on the
    adder's lair.
There shall be no harm or ruin on all my
    holy mountain;
    for the earth shall be filled with
    knowledge of the Lord,
    as water covers the sea.
On that day, the root of Jesse,
    set up as a signal for the nations,
the Gentiles shall seek out,
    for his dwelling shall be glorious.

RESPONSORIAL PSALM
Psalm 72:1-2, 7-8, 12-13, 17

Jus - tice shall flour - ish in his time, and

full - ness of peace for ev - er.

O God, with your judgment endow the king,
and with your justice, the king's son;
he shall govern your people with justice
and your afflicted ones with judgment. ℟.

Justice shall flower in his days,
and profound peace, till the moon be no more.
May he rule from sea to sea,
and from the River to the ends of the earth. ℟.

For he shall rescue the poor when he cries out,
and the afflicted when he has no one to help him.
He shall have pity for the lowly and the poor;
the lives of the poor he shall save. ℟.

May his name be blessed forever;
as long as the sun his name shall remain.
In him shall all the tribes of the earth be blessed;
all the nations shall proclaim his happiness. ℟.

READING II   *Romans 15:4-9*

Brothers and sisters: Whatever was written previously was written for our instruction, that by endurance and by the encouragement of the Scriptures we might have hope. May the God of endurance and encouragement grant you to think in harmony with one another, in keeping with Christ Jesus, that with one accord you may with one voice glorify the God and Father of our Lord Jesus Christ.

Welcome one another, then, as Christ welcomed you, for the glory of God. For I say that Christ became a minister of the circumcised to show God's truthfulness, to confirm the promises to the patriarchs, but so that the Gentiles might glorify God for his mercy. As it is written:

"Therefore, I will praise you among the Gentiles
and sing praises to your name."

GOSPEL   *Matthew 3:1-12*

John the Baptist appeared, preaching in the desert of Judea and saying, "Repent, for the kingdom of heaven is at hand!" It was of him that the prophet Isaiah had spoken when he said:

"A voice of one crying out in the desert,
'Prepare the way of the Lord,
make straight his paths.'"

John wore clothing made of camel's hair and had a leather belt around his waist. His food was locusts and wild honey. At that time Jerusalem, all Judea, and the whole region around the Jordan were going out to him and were being baptized by him in the Jordan River as they acknowledged their sins.

When he saw many of the Pharisees and Sadducees coming to his baptism, he said to them, "You brood of vipers! Who warned you to flee from the coming wrath? Produce good fruit as evidence of your repentance. And do not presume to say to yourselves, 'We have Abraham as our father.' For I tell you, God can raise up children to Abraham from these stones. Even now the ax lies at the root of the trees. Therefore every tree that does not bear good fruit will be cut down and thrown into the fire. I am baptizing you with water, for repentance, but the one who is coming after me is mightier than I. I am not worthy to carry his sandals. He will baptize you with the Holy Spirit and fire. His winnowing fan is in his hand. He will clear his threshing floor and gather his wheat into his barn, but the chaff he will burn with unquenchable fire."

481 SECOND SUNDAY OF ADVENT / B

READING I *Isaiah 40:1-5, 9-11 / 5*

Comfort, give comfort to my people,
  says your God.
Speak tenderly to Jerusalem, and proclaim
    to her
    that her service is at an end,
    her guilt is expiated;
indeed, she has received from the hand of
    the LORD
    double for all her sins.

A voice cries out:
In the desert prepare the way of the LORD!
  Make straight in the wasteland a
    highway for our God!
Every valley shall be filled in,
    every mountain and hill shall be made
      low;
the rugged land shall be made a plain,
    the rough country, a broad valley.
Then the glory of the LORD shall be
    revealed,

and all people shall see it together;
  for the mouth of the LORD has
    spoken.

Go up on to a high mountain,
  Zion, herald of glad tidings;
cry out at the top of your voice,
  Jerusalem, herald of good news!
Fear not to cry out
  and say to the cities of Judah:
  Here is your God!
Here comes with power
  the Lord GOD,
  who rules by his strong arm;
here is his reward with him,
  his recompense before him.
Like a shepherd he feeds his flock;
  in his arms he gathers the lambs,
carrying them in his bosom,
  and leading the ewes with care.

RESPONSORIAL PSALM *Psalm 85:9-10, 11-12, 13-14*

Lord, let us see your kind- ness, and grant us your sal - va - tion.

I will hear what God proclaims;
    the Lord—for he proclaims peace to
      his people.
Near indeed is his salvation to those who
      fear him,
    glory dwelling in our land. ℟.

Kindness and truth shall meet;
    justice and peace shall kiss.

Truth shall spring out of the earth,
    and justice shall look down from
      heaven. ℟.

The Lord himself will give his benefits;
    our land shall yield its increase.
Justice shall walk before him,
    and prepare the way of his steps. ℟.

READING II *2 Peter 3:8-14*

Do not ignore this one fact, beloved, that with the Lord one day is like a thousand years
and a thousand years like one day. The Lord does not delay his promise, as some regard
"delay," but he is patient with you, not wishing that any should perish but that all should
come to repentance. But the day of the Lord will come like a thief, and then the heavens will pass away with a mighty roar and the elements will be dissolved by fire, and the
earth and everything done on it will be found out.

Since everything is to be dissolved in this way, what sort of persons ought you to
be, conducting yourselves in holiness and devotion, waiting for and hastening the coming of the day of God, because of which the heavens will be dissolved in flames and the
elements melted by fire. But according to his promise we await new heavens and a new
earth in which righteousness dwells. Therefore, beloved, since you await these things,
be eager to be found without spot or blemish before him, at peace.

GOSPEL *Mark 1:1-8*

The beginning of the gospel of Jesus Christ the Son of God.
As it is written in Isaiah the prophet:

"Behold, I am sending my messenger ahead of you;
he will prepare your way.
A voice of one crying out in the desert:
'Prepare the way of the Lord,
make straight his paths.'"

John the Baptist appeared in the desert proclaiming a baptism of repentance for the forgiveness of sins. People of the whole Judean countryside and all the inhabitants of Jerusalem were going out to him and were being baptized by him in the Jordan River as they acknowledged their sins. John was clothed in camel's hair, with a leather belt around his waist. He fed on locusts and wild honey. And this is what he proclaimed: "One mightier than I is coming after me. I am not worthy to stoop and loosen the thongs of his sandals. I have baptized you with water; he will baptize you with the Holy Spirit."

SECOND SUNDAY OF ADVENT / C 482

READING I *Baruch 5:1-9 / 6*

Jerusalem, take off your robe of
mourning and misery;
put on the splendor of glory from
God forever:
wrapped in the cloak of justice from God,
bear on your head the mitre
that displays the glory of the eternal
name.
For God will show all the earth your
splendor:
you will be named by God forever
the peace of justice, the glory of
God's worship.

Up, Jerusalem! stand upon the heights;
look to the east and see your children
gathered from the east and the west
at the word of the Holy One,
rejoicing that they are remembered
by God.

Led away on foot by their enemies they
left you:
but God will bring them back to you
borne aloft in glory as on royal
thrones.
For God has commanded
that every lofty mountain be made
low,
and that the age-old depths and gorges
be filled to level ground,
that Israel may advance secure in
the glory of God.
The forests and every fragrant kind of
tree
have overshadowed Israel at God's
command;
for God is leading Israel in joy
by the light of his glory,
with his mercy and justice for
company.

RESPONSORIAL PSALM *Psalm 126:1-2, 2-3, 4-5, 6*

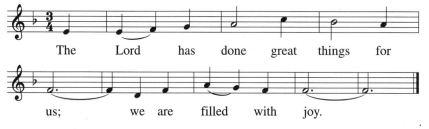

The Lord has done great things for us; we are filled with joy.

When the Lord brought back the captives
of Zion,
we were like men dreaming.

Then our mouth was filled with laughter,
and our tongue with rejoicing. ℟.

Then they said among the nations,
"The Lord has done great things for
them."
The Lord has done great things for us;
we are glad indeed. ℟.

Restore our fortunes, O Lord,
like the torrents in the southern
desert.
Those who sow in tears
shall reap rejoicing. ℟.

Although they go forth weeping,
carrying the seed to be sown,
they shall come back rejoicing,
carrying their sheaves. ℟.

READING II   *Philippians 1:4-6, 8-11*

Brothers and sisters: I pray always with joy in my every prayer for all of you, because of your partnership for the gospel from the first day until now. I am confident of this, that the one who began a good work in you will continue to complete it until the day of Christ Jesus. God is my witness, how I long for all of you with the affection of Christ Jesus. And this is my prayer: that your love may increase ever more and more in knowledge and every kind of perception, to discern what is of value, so that you may be pure and blameless for the day of Christ, filled with the fruit of righteousness that comes through Jesus Christ for the glory and praise of God.

GOSPEL   *Luke 3:1-6*

In the fifteenth year of the reign of Tiberius Caesar, when Pontius Pilate was governor of Judea, and Herod was tetrarch of Galilee, and his brother Philip tetrarch of the region of Ituraea and Trachonitis, and Lysanias was tetrarch of Abilene, during the high priesthood of Annas and Caiaphas, the word of God came to John the son of Zechariah in the desert. John went throughout the whole region of the Jordan, proclaiming a baptism of repentance for the forgiveness of sins, as it is written in the book of the words of the prophet Isaiah:
"A voice of one crying out in the desert:
'Prepare the way of the Lord,
make straight his paths.
Every valley shall be filled
and every mountain and hill shall be made low.
The winding roads shall be made straight,
and the rough ways made smooth,
and all flesh shall see the salvation of God.'"

---

483   THIRD SUNDAY OF ADVENT / A

READING I   *Isaiah 35:1-6a, 10 / 7*

The desert and the parched land will
exult;
the steppe will rejoice and bloom.
They will bloom with abundant flowers,
and rejoice with joyful song.
The glory of Lebanon will be given to
them,
the splendor of Carmel and Sharon;
they will see the glory of the Lord,
the splendor of our God.
Strengthen the hands that are feeble,
make firm the knees that are weak,
say to those whose hearts are frightened:
Be strong, fear not!
Here is your God,
he comes with vindication;
with divine recompense
he comes to save you.
Then will the eyes of the blind be
opened,
the ears of the deaf be cleared;
then will the lame leap like a stag,
then the tongue of the mute will sing.

Those whom the Lord has ransomed
will return
and enter Zion singing,
crowned with everlasting joy;
they will meet with joy and gladness,
sorrow and mourning will flee.

RESPONSORIAL PSALM

Psalm 146:6-7, 8-9, 9-10

Lord, come and save us.

The Lord God keeps faith forever,
  secures justice for the oppressed,
  gives food to the hungry.
The Lord sets captives free. ℟.

The Lord gives sight to the blind;
  the Lord raises up those who were
    bowed down.

The Lord loves the just;
  the Lord protects strangers. ℟.

The fatherless and the widow he sustains,
  but the way of the wicked he thwarts.
The Lord shall reign forever;
  your God, O Zion, through all
    generations. ℟.

READING II

James 5:7-10

Be patient, brothers and sisters, until the coming of the Lord. See how the farmer waits for the precious fruit of the earth, being patient with it until it receives the early and the late rains. You too must be patient. Make your hearts firm, because the coming of the Lord is at hand. Do not complain, brothers and sisters, about one another, that you may not be judged. Behold, the Judge is standing before the gates. Take as an example of hardship and patience, brothers and sisters, the prophets who spoke in the name of the Lord.

GOSPEL

Matthew 11:2-11

When John the Baptist heard in prison of the works of the Christ, he sent his disciples to Jesus with this question, "Are you the one who is to come, or should we look for another?" Jesus said to them in reply, "Go and tell John what you hear and see: the blind regain their sight, the lame walk, lepers are cleansed, the deaf hear, the dead are raised, and the poor have the good news proclaimed to them. And blessed is the one who takes no offense at me."

As they were going off, Jesus began to speak to the crowds about John, "What did you go out to the desert to see? A reed swayed by the wind? Then what did you go out to see? Someone dressed in fine clothing? Those who wear fine clothing are in royal palaces. Then why did you go out? To see a prophet? Yes, I tell you, and more than a prophet. This is the one about whom it is written:

  'Behold, I am sending my messenger ahead of you;
  he will prepare your way before you.'
Amen, I say to you, among those born of women there has been none greater than John the Baptist; yet the least in the kingdom of heaven is greater than he."

THIRD SUNDAY OF ADVENT / B

484

READING I

Isaiah 61:1-2a, 10-11 / 8

The spirit of the Lord GOD is upon me,
  because the LORD has anointed me;
he has sent me to bring glad tidings to
    the poor,
  to heal the brokenhearted,
to proclaim liberty to the captives
  and release to the prisoners,
to announce a year of favor from the
    LORD
  and a day of vindication by our God.

I rejoice heartily in the LORD,
  in my God is the joy of my soul;
for he has clothed me with a robe of
    salvation
  and wrapped me in a mantle of justice,
like a bridegroom adorned with a diadem,
  like a bride bedecked with her jewels.
As the earth brings forth its plants,
  and a garden makes its growth spring
    up,

so will the Lord GOD make justice and
praise
spring up before all the nations.

RESPONSORIAL PSALM *Luke 1:46-48, 49-50, 53-54*

My soul re - joic - es in my God,

my soul re - joic - es in my God.

My soul proclaims the greatness of the
Lord;
my spirit rejoices in God my Savior,
for he has looked upon his lowly servant.
From this day all generations will call me
blessed: ℟.

The Almighty has done great things for
me,
and holy is his Name.

He has mercy on those who fear him
in every generation. ℟.

He has filled the hungry with good
things,
and the rich he has sent away empty.
He has come to the help of his servant
Israel
for he has remembered his promise
of mercy. ℟.

READING II *1 Thessalonians 5:16-24*

Brothers and sisters: Rejoice always. Pray without ceasing. In all circumstances give
thanks, for this is the will of God for you in Christ Jesus. Do not quench the Spirit. Do
not despise prophetic utterances. Test everything; retain what is good. Refrain from
every kind of evil.

May the God of peace make you perfectly holy and may you entirely, spirit, soul,
and body, be preserved blameless for the coming of our Lord Jesus Christ. The one who
calls you is faithful, and he will also accomplish it.

GOSPEL *John 1:6-8, 19-28*

A man named John was sent from God. He came for testimony, to testify to the light, so
that all might believe through him. He was not the light, but came to testify to the light.

And this is the testimony of John. When the Jews from Jerusalem sent priests and
Levites to him to ask him, "Who are you?" he admitted and did not deny it, but admitted, "I am not the Christ." So they asked him, "What are you then? Are you Elijah?" And
he said, "I am not." "Are you the Prophet?" He answered, "No." So they said to him,
"Who are you, so we can give an answer to those who sent us? What do you have to say
for yourself?" He said:

"I am 'the voice of one crying out in the desert,
"make straight the way of the Lord,'"

as Isaiah the prophet said." Some Pharisees were also sent. They asked him, "Why then
do you baptize if you are not the Christ or Elijah or the Prophet?" John answered them,
"I baptize with water; but there is one among you whom you do not recognize, the one
who is coming after me, whose sandal strap I am not worthy to untie." This happened in
Bethany across the Jordan, where John was baptizing.

THIRD SUNDAY OF ADVENT / C

READING I

Zephaniah 3:14-18a / 9

Shout for joy, O daughter Zion!
Sing joyfully, O Israel!
Be glad and exult with all your heart,
O daughter Jerusalem!
The LORD has removed the judgment
against you
he has turned away your enemies;
the King of Israel, the LORD, is in your
midst,
you have no further misfortune to
fear.
On that day, it shall be said to Jerusalem:
Fear not, O Zion, be not discouraged!
The LORD, your God, is in your midst,
a mighty savior;
he will rejoice over you with gladness,
and renew you in his love,
he will sing joyfully because of you,
as one sings at festivals.

RESPONSORIAL PSALM

Isaiah 12:2-3, 4, 5-6

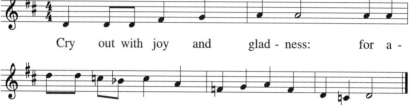

Cry out with joy and glad - ness: for a - mong you is the great and Ho - ly One of Is - ra - el.

God indeed is my savior;
I am confident and unafraid.
My strength and my courage is the LORD,
and he has been my savior.
With joy you will draw water
at the fountain of salvation. ℟.

Give thanks to the LORD, acclaim his
name;
among the nations make known his
deeds,
proclaim how exalted is his name. ℟.

Sing praise to the LORD for his glorious
achievement;
let this be known throughout all the
earth.
Shout with exultation, O city of Zion,
for great in your midst
is the Holy One of Israel! ℟.

READING II

Philippians 4:4-7

Brothers and sisters: Rejoice in the Lord always. I shall say it again: rejoice! Your kindness should be known to all. The Lord is near. Have no anxiety at all, but in everything, by prayer and petition, with thanksgiving, make your requests known to God. Then the peace of God that surpasses all understanding will guard your hearts and minds in Christ Jesus.

GOSPEL

Luke 3:10-18

The crowds asked John the Baptist, "What should we do?" He said to them in reply, "Whoever has two cloaks should share with the person who has none. And whoever has food should do likewise." Even tax collectors came to be baptized and they said to him, "Teacher, what should we do?" He answered them, "Stop collecting more than what is prescribed." Soldiers also asked him, "And what is it that we should do?" He told them, "Do not practice extortion, do not falsely accuse anyone, and be satisfied with your wages."

Now the people were filled with expectation, and all were asking in their hearts whether John might be the Christ. John answered them all, saying, "I am baptizing you with water, but one mightier than I is coming. I am not worthy to loosen the thongs of his sandals. He will baptize you with the Holy Spirit and fire. His winnowing fan is in his hand to clear his threshing floor and to gather the wheat into his barn, but the chaff he will burn with unquenchable fire." Exhorting them in many other ways, he preached good news to the people.

486 FOURTH SUNDAY OF ADVENT / A

READING I
Isaiah 7:10-14 / 10

The LORD spoke to Ahaz, saying: Ask for a sign from the LORD, your God; let it be deep as the netherworld, or high as the sky! But Ahaz answered, "I will not ask! I will not tempt the LORD!" Then Isaiah said: Listen, O house of David! Is it not enough for you to weary people, must you also weary my God? Therefore the Lord himself will give you this sign: the virgin shall conceive, and bear a son, and shall name him Emmanuel.

RESPONSORIAL PSALM
Psalm 24:1-2, 3-4, 5-6

Let the Lord en - ter; he is king of glo - ry.

The LORD's are the earth and its fullness;
  the world and those who dwell in it.
For he founded it upon the seas
  and established it upon the rivers. ℞.

Who can ascend the mountain of the
  LORD?
  or who may stand in his holy place?
One whose hands are sinless, whose heart

is clean,
  who desires not what is vain. ℞.

He shall receive a blessing from the
  LORD,
  a reward from God his savior.
Such is the race that seeks for him,
  that seeks the face of God of
  Jacob. ℞.

READING II
Romans 1:1-7

Paul, a slave of Christ Jesus, called to be an apostle and set apart for the gospel of God, which he promised previously through his prophets in the holy Scriptures, the gospel about his Son, descended from David according to the flesh, but established as Son of God in power according to the Spirit of holiness through resurrection from the dead, Jesus Christ our Lord. Through him we have received the grace of apostleship, to bring about the obedience of faith, for the sake of his name, among all the Gentiles, among whom are you also, who are called to belong to Jesus Christ; to all the beloved of God in Rome, called to be holy. Grace to you and peace from God our Father and the Lord Jesus Christ.

GOSPEL
Matthew 1:18-24

This is how the birth of Jesus Christ came about. When his mother Mary was betrothed to Joseph, but before they lived together, she was found with child through the Holy Spirit. Joseph her husband, since he was a righteous man, yet unwilling to expose her to shame, decided to divorce her quietly. Such was his intention when, behold, the angel of the Lord appeared to him in a dream and said, "Joseph, son of David, do not be afraid to take Mary your wife into your home. For it is through the Holy Spirit that this child has been conceived in her. She will bear a son and you are to name him Jesus, because he will save his people from their sins." All this took place to fulfill what the Lord had said through the prophet:
  "Behold, the virgin shall conceive and bear a son,
  and they shall name him Emmanuel,"

which means "God is with us." When Joseph awoke, he did as the angel of the Lord had commanded him and took his wife into his home.

FOURTH SUNDAY OF ADVENT / B 487

READING I
2 Samuel 7:1-5, 8b-12, 14a, 16 / 11

When King David was settled in his palace, and the LORD had given him rest from his enemies on every side, he said to Nathan the prophet, "Here I am living in a house of cedar, while the ark of God dwells in a tent!" Nathan answered the king, "Go, do whatever you have in mind, for the LORD is with you." But that night the LORD spoke to Nathan and said: "Go, tell my servant David, 'Thus says the LORD: Should you build me a house to dwell in?'

"It was I who took you from the pasture and from the care of the flock to be commander of my people Israel. I have been with you wherever you went, and I have destroyed all your enemies before you. And I will make you famous like the great ones of the earth. I will fix a place for my people Israel; I will plant them so that they may dwell in their place without further disturbance. Neither shall the wicked continue to afflict them as they did of old, since the time I first appointed judges over my people Israel. I will give you rest from all your enemies. The LORD also reveals to you that he will establish a house for you. And when your time comes and you rest with your ancestors, I will raise up your heir after you, sprung from your loins, and I will make his kingdom firm. I will be a father to him, and he shall be a son to me. Your house and your kingdom shall endure forever before me; your throne shall stand firm forever."

RESPONSORIAL PSALM
Psalm 89:2-3, 4-5, 27, 29

For ev-er I will sing the good-ness of the Lord.

The promises of the LORD I will sing
    forever;
      through all generations my mouth
        shall proclaim your faithfulness.
For you have said, "My kindness is
      established forever";
    in heaven you have confirmed your
      faithfulness. ℟.

"I have made a covenant with my chosen
    one,

I have sworn to David my servant:
    forever will I confirm your posterity
    and establish your throne for all
      generations." ℟.

"He shall say of me, 'You are my father,
    my God, the Rock, my savior.'
Forever I will maintain my kindness
    toward him,
    and my covenant with him stands
      firm." ℟.

READING II
Romans 16:25-27

Brothers and sisters: To him who can strengthen you, according to my gospel and the proclamation of Jesus Christ, according to the revelation of the mystery kept secret for long ages but now manifested through the prophetic writings and, according to the command of the eternal God, made known to all nations to bring about the obedience of faith, to the only wise God, through Jesus Christ be glory forever and ever. Amen.

GOSPEL
Luke 1:26-38

The angel Gabriel was sent from God to a town of Galilee called Nazareth, to a virgin betrothed to a man named Joseph, of the house of David, and the virgin's name was

Mary. And coming to her, he said, "Hail, full of grace! The Lord is with you." But she was greatly troubled at what was said and pondered what sort of greeting this might be. Then the angel said to her, "Do not be afraid, Mary, for you have found favor with God.

"Behold, you will conceive in your womb and bear a son, and you shall name him Jesus. He will be great and will be called Son of the Most High, and the Lord God will give him the throne of David his father, and he will rule over the house of Jacob forever, and of his kingdom there will be no end." But Mary said to the angel, "How can this be, since I have no relations with a man?" And the angel said to her in reply, "The Holy Spirit will come upon you, and the power of the Most High will overshadow you. Therefore the child to be born will be called holy, the Son of God. And behold, Elizabeth, your relative, has also conceived a son in her old age, and this is the sixth month for her who was called barren; for nothing will be impossible for God." Mary said, "Behold, I am the handmaid of the Lord. May it be done to me according to your word." Then the angel departed from her.

488 FOURTH SUNDAY OF ADVENT / C

READING I
Micah 5:1-4a / 12

Thus says the LORD:
You, Bethlehem-Ephrathah
    too small to be among the clans of
      Judah,
from you shall come forth for me
    one who is to be ruler in Israel;
whose origin is from of old,
    from ancient times.
Therefore the Lord will give them up,
      until the time
    when she who is to give birth has
      borne,

and the rest of his kindred shall return
    to the children of Israel.
He shall stand firm and shepherd his
      flock
    by the strength of the LORD,
    in the majestic name of the LORD,
      his God;
and they shall remain, for now his
      greatness
    shall reach to the ends of the earth;
    he shall be peace.

RESPONSORIAL PSALM
Psalm 80:2-3, 15-16, 18-19

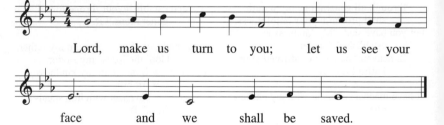

Lord, make us turn to you; let us see your face and we shall be saved.

O shepherd of Israel, hearken,
    from your throne upon the cherubim,
      shine forth.
Rouse your power,
    and come to save us. ℟.

Once again, O Lord of hosts,
    look down from heaven, and see;
take care of this vine,
    and protect what your right hand has
      planted

the son of man whom you yourself
    made strong. ℟.

May your help be with the man of your
    right hand,
    with the son of man whom you
      yourself made strong.
Then we will no more withdraw from
    you;
    give us new life, and we will call
      upon your name. ℟.

READING II
Hebrews 10:5-10

Brothers and sisters: When Christ came into the world, he said:
"Sacrifice and offering you did not desire,
but a body you prepared for me;
in holocausts and sin offerings you took no delight.
Then I said, 'As is written of me in the scroll,
behold, I come to do your will, O God.'"
First he says, "Sacrifices and offerings, holocausts and sin offerings, you neither desired nor delighted in." These are offered according to the law. Then he says, "Behold, I come to do your will." He takes away the first to establish the second. By this "will," we have been consecrated through the offering of the body of Jesus Christ once for all.

GOSPEL
Luke 1:39-45

Mary set out and traveled to the hill country in haste to a town of Judah, where she entered the house of Zechariah and greeted Elizabeth. When Elizabeth heard Mary's greeting, the infant leaped in her womb, and Elizabeth, filled with the Holy Spirit, cried out in a loud voice and said, "Blessed are you among women, and blessed is the fruit of your womb. And how does this happen to me, that the mother of my Lord should come to me? For at the moment the sound of your greeting reached my ears, the infant in my womb leaped for joy. Blessed are you who believed that what was spoken to you by the Lord would be fulfilled."

DECEMBER 25: CHRISTMAS—VIGIL / ABC
489

READING I
Isaiah 62:1-5 / 13

For Zion's sake I will not be silent,
for Jerusalem's sake I will not be
quiet,
until her vindication shines forth like
the dawn
and her victory like a burning torch.

Nations shall behold your vindication,
and all the kings your glory;
you shall be called by a new name
pronounced by the mouth of the
LORD.
You shall be a glorious crown in the
hand of the LORD,
a royal diadem held by your God.
No more shall people call you
"Forsaken,"
or your land "Desolate,"
but you shall be called "My Delight,"
and your land "Espoused."
For the LORD delights in you
and makes your land his spouse.
As a young man marries a virgin,
your Builder shall marry you;
and as a bridegroom rejoices in his bride
so shall your God rejoice in you.

RESPONSORIAL PSALM
Psalm 89:4-5, 16-17, 27, 29

For ev-er I will sing the good-ness of the Lord.

I have made a covenant with my chosen
one,
I have sworn to David my servant:
forever will I confirm your posterity
and establish your throne for all
generations. ℟.

Blessed the people who know the joyful
shout;
in the light of your countenance, O
LORD, they walk.
At your name they rejoice all the day,
and through your justice they are
exalted. ℟.

He shall say of me, "You are my father,
   my God, the rock, my savior."
Forever I will maintain my kindness
                    toward him,
             and my covenant with him stands
             firm. ℟.

READING II   *Acts 13:16-17, 22-25*

When Paul reached Antioch in Pisidia and entered the synagogue, he stood up, motioned with his hand, and said, "Fellow Israelites and you others who are God-fearing, listen. The God of this people Israel chose our ancestors and exalted the people during their sojourn in the land of Egypt. With uplifted arm he led them out of it. Then he removed Saul and raised up David as king; of him he testified, 'I have found David, son of Jesse, a man after my own heart; he will carry out my every wish.' From this man's descendants God, according to his promise, has brought to Israel a savior, Jesus. John heralded his coming by proclaiming a baptism of repentance to all the people of Israel; and as John was completing his course, he would say, 'What do you suppose that I am? I am not he. Behold, one is coming after me; I am not worthy to unfasten the sandals of his feet.'"

GOSPEL   *Matthew 1:1-25 or 1:18-25*
For short form read only the part in brackets.

The book of the genealogy of Jesus Christ, the son of David, the son of Abraham.

Abraham became the father of Isaac, Isaac the father of Jacob, Jacob the father of Judah and his brothers. Judah became the father of Perez and Zerah, whose mother was Tamar. Perez became the father of Hezron, Hezron the father of Ram, Ram the father of Amminadab. Amminadab became the father of Nahshon, Nahshon the father of Salmon, Salmon the father of Boaz, whose mother was Rahab. Boaz became the father of Obed, whose mother was Ruth. Obed became the father of Jesse, Jesse the father of David the king.

David became the father of Solomon, whose mother had been the wife of Uriah. Solomon became the father of Rehoboam, Rehoboam the father of Abijah, Abijah the father of Asaph. Asaph became the father of Jehoshaphat, Jehoshaphat the father of Joram, Joram the father of Uzziah. Uzziah became the father of Jotham, Jotham the father of Ahaz, Ahaz the father of Hezekiah. Hezekiah became the father of Manasseh, Manasseh the father of Amos, Amos the father of Josiah. Josiah became the father of Jechoniah and his brothers at the time of the Babylonian exile.

After the Babylonian exile, Jechoniah became the father of Shealtiel, Shealtiel the father of Zerubbabel, Zerubbabel the father of Abiud. Abiud became the father of Eliakim, Eliakim the father of Azor, Azor the father of Zadok. Zadok became the father of Achim, Achim the father of Eliud, Eliud the father of Eleazar. Eleazar became the father of Matthan, Matthan the father of Jacob, Jacob the father of Joseph, the husband of Mary. Of her was born Jesus who is called the Christ.

Thus the total number of generations from Abraham to David is fourteen generations; from David to the Babylonian exile, fourteen generations; from the Babylonian exile to the Christ, fourteen generations.

Now [this is how the birth of Jesus Christ came about. When his mother Mary was betrothed to Joseph, but before they lived together, she was found with child through the Holy Spirit. Joseph her husband, since he was a righteous man, yet unwilling to expose her to shame, decided to divorce her quietly. Such was his intention when, behold, the angel of the Lord appeared to him in a dream and said, "Joseph, son of David, do not be afraid to take Mary your wife into your home. For it is through the Holy Spirit that this child has been conceived in her. She will bear a son and you are to name him Jesus, because he will save his people from their sins." All this took place to fulfill what the Lord had said through the prophet:

"Behold, the virgin shall conceive and bear a son,
   and they shall name him Emmanuel,"

which means "God is with us." When Joseph awoke, he did as the angel of the Lord had commanded him and took his wife into his home. He had no relations with her until she bore a son, and he named him Jesus.]

DECEMBER 25: CHRISTMAS—MASS AT MIDNIGHT / ABC   490

READING I
Isaiah 9:1-6 / 14

The people who walked in darkness
    have seen a great light;
upon those who dwelt in the land of
    gloom
    a light has shone.
You have brought them abundant joy
    and great rejoicing,
as they rejoice before you as at the
    harvest,
    as people make merry when dividing
      spoils.
For the yoke that burdened them,
    the pole on their shoulder,
and the rod of their taskmaster
    you have smashed, as on the day of
      Midian.
For every boot that tramped in battle,

every cloak rolled in blood,
    will be burned as fuel for flames.
For a child is born to us, a son is given
    us;
    upon his shoulder dominion rests
They name him Wonder-Counselor,
    God-Hero,
    Father-Forever, Prince of Peace.
His dominion is vast
    and forever peaceful,
from David's throne, and over his
    kingdom,
    which he confirms and sustains
by judgment and justice,
    both now and forever.
The zeal of the LORD of hosts will do
    this!

RESPONSORIAL PSALM
Psalm 96:1-2, 2-3, 11-12, 13

To-day, to-day, to-day is born our Sav-ior, Christ the Lord.

Sing to the LORD a new song;
    sing to the LORD, all you lands.
Sing to the LORD; bless his name. ℟.

Announce his salvation, day after day.
    Tell his glory among the nations;
among all peoples, his wondrous
    deeds. ℟.

Let the heavens be glad and the earth
    rejoice;
    let the sea and what fills it resound;

let the plains be joyful and all that is
    in them!
Then shall all the trees of the forest
    exult. ℟.

They shall exult before the LORD, for he
    comes;
    for he comes to rule the earth.
He shall rule the world with justice
    and the peoples with his
      constancy. ℟.

READING II
Titus 2:11-14

Beloved: The grace of God has appeared, saving all and training us to reject godless ways and worldly desires and to live temperately, justly, and devoutly in this age, as we await the blessed hope, the appearance of the glory of our great God and savior Jesus Christ, who gave himself for us to deliver us from all lawlessness and to cleanse for himself a people as his own, eager to do what is good.

GOSPEL
Luke 2:1-14

In those days a decree went out from Caesar Augustus that the whole world should be enrolled. This was the first enrollment, when Quirinius was governor of Syria. So all went to be enrolled, each to his own town. And Joseph too went up from Galilee from the town of Nazareth to Judea, to the city of David that is called Bethlehem, because he was of the house and family of David, to be enrolled with Mary, his betrothed, who was with child. While they were there, the time came for her to have her child, and she gave birth to her firstborn son. She wrapped him in swaddling clothes and laid him in a manger, because there was no room for them in the inn.

Now there were shepherds in that region living in the fields and keeping the night watch over their flock. The angel of the Lord appeared to them and the glory of the Lord shone around them, and they were struck with great fear. The angel said to them, "Do not be afraid; for behold, I proclaim to you good news of great joy that will be for all the people. For today in the city of David a savior has been born for you who is Christ and Lord. And this will be a sign for you: you will find an infant wrapped in swaddling clothes and lying in a manger." And suddenly there was a multitude of the heavenly host with the angel, praising God and saying:

"Glory to God in the highest
and on earth peace to those on whom his favor rests."

---

491 DECEMBER 25: CHRISTMAS—MASS AT DAWN / ABC

READING I
Isaiah 62:11-12 / 15

See, the LORD proclaims
  to the ends of the earth:
say to daughter Zion,
  your savior comes!
Here is his reward with him,

his recompense before him.
They shall be called the holy people,
  the redeemed of the LORD,
and you shall be called "Frequented,"
  a city that is not forsaken.

RESPONSORIAL PSALM
Psalm 97:1, 6, 11-12

A light will shine on us this day: the Lord is born for us.

The LORD is king; let the earth rejoice;
  let the many islands be glad.
The heavens proclaim his justice,
  and all peoples see his glory. ℟.

Light dawns for the just;
  and gladness, for the upright of heart.
Be glad in the LORD, you just,
  and give thanks to his holy name. ℟.

READING II
Titus 3:4-7

Beloved:
  When the kindness and generous love
    of God our savior appeared,
  not because of any righteous deeds
    we had done
  but because of his mercy,
he saved us through the bath of
  rebirth

and renewal by the Holy Spirit,
whom he richly poured out on us
  through Jesus Christ our savior,
so that we might be justified by his
  grace
and become heirs in hope of
  eternal life.

GOSPEL
Luke 2:15-20

When the angels went away from them to heaven, the shepherds said to one another, "Let us go, then, to Bethlehem to see this thing that has taken place, which the Lord has made known to us." So they went in haste and found Mary and Joseph, and the infant lying in the manger. When they saw this, they made known the message that had been told them about this child. All who heard it were amazed by what had been told them by the shepherds. And Mary kept all these things, reflecting on them in her heart. Then the shepherds returned, glorifying and praising God for all they had heard and seen, just as it had been told to them.

DECEMBER 25: CHRISTMAS-MASS DURING THE DAY / ABC   492

READING I
Isaiah 52:7-10 / 16

How beautiful upon the mountains
  are the feet of him who brings glad
    tidings,
announcing peace, bearing good news,
  announcing salvation, and saying to
    Zion,
  "Your God is King!"

Hark! Your sentinels raise a cry,
  together they shout for joy,

for they see directly, before their eyes,
  the Lord restoring Zion.
Break out together in song,
  O ruins of Jerusalem!
For the LORD comforts his people,
  he redeems Jerusalem.
The LORD has bared his holy arm
  in the sight of all the nations;
all the ends of the earth will behold
  the salvation of our God.

RESPONSORIAL PSALM
Psalm 98:1, 2-3, 3-4, 5-6

All the ends of the earth have seen the sav - ing pow'r of God.

Sing to the LORD a new song,
  for he has done wondrous deeds;
his right hand has won victory for him,
  his holy arm. ℟.

The LORD has made his salvation known:
  in the sight of the nations he has
    revealed his justice.
He has remembered his kindness and his
    faithfulness
  toward the house of Israel. ℟.

All the ends of the earth have seen
  the salvation by our God.
Sing joyfully to the LORD, all you lands;
  break into song; sing praise. ℟.

Sing praise to the LORD with the harp,
  with the harp and melodious song.
With trumpets and the sound of the horn
  sing joyfully before the King, the
    LORD. ℟.

READING II
Hebrews 1:1-6

Brothers and sisters: In times past, God spoke in partial and various ways to our ancestors
through the prophets; in these last days, he has spoken to us through the Son, whom he
made heir of all things and through whom he created the universe,
  who is the refulgence of his glory,
    the very imprint of his being,
  and who sustains all things by his mighty word.
  When he had accomplished purification from sins,
  he took his seat at the right hand of the Majesty on high,
  as far superior to the angels
  as the name he has inherited is more excellent than theirs.

For to which of the angels did God ever say:
  "You are my son; this day I have begotten you"?
Or again:
  "I will be a father to him, and he shall be a son to me"?
And again, when he leads the firstborn into the world, he says:
  "Let all the angels of God worship him."

GOSPEL
John 1:1-18 or 1:1-5, 9-14

For short form read only the parts in brackets.

[In the beginning was the Word,
  and the Word was with God,
  and the Word was God.

He was in the beginning with God.
All things came to be through him,
   and without him nothing came to be.
What came to be through him was life,
   and this life was the light of the human race;
the light shines in the darkness,
   and the darkness has not overcome it.]
A man named John was sent from God. He came for testimony, to testify to the light, so that all might believe through him. He was not the light, but came to testify to the light. [The true light, which enlightens everyone, was coming into the world.
He was in the world,
   and the world came to be through him,
   but the world did not know him.
He came to what was his own,
   but his own people did not accept him.

But to those who did accept him he gave power to become children of God, to those who believe in his name, who were born not by natural generation nor by human choice nor by a man's decision but of God.
And the Word became flesh
   and made his dwelling among us,
   and we saw his glory,
   the glory as of the Father's only Son,
   full of grace and truth.]
John testified to him and cried out, saying, "This was he of whom I said, 'The one who is coming after me ranks ahead of me because he existed before me.'" From his fullness we have all received, grace in place of grace, because while the law was given through Moses, grace and truth came through Jesus Christ. No one has ever seen God. The only Son, God, who is at the Father's side, has revealed him.

493 SUNDAY IN THE OCTAVE OF CHRISTMAS-HOLY FAMILY / ABC

READING I *Sirach 3:2-7, 12-14 / 17*

God sets a father in honor over his
   children;
   a mother's authority he confirms
     over her sons.
Whoever honors his father atones for sins,
   and preserves himself from them.
When he prays, he is heard;
   he stores up riches who reveres his
     mother.
Whoever honors his father is gladdened
   by children,
and, when he prays, is heard.
Whoever reveres his father will live a

long life;
he who obeys his father brings
   comfort to his mother.
My son, take care of your father when
   he is old;
   grieve him not as long as he lives.
Even if his mind fail, be considerate of
   him;
   revile him not all the days of his life;
kindness to a father will not be forgotten,
   firmly planted against the debt of
     your sins
—a house raised in justice to you.

RESPONSORIAL PSALM *Psalm 128:1-2, 3, 4-5*

Bless-ed are those who fear the Lord and walk in his ways.

Blessed is everyone who fears the LORD,
   who walks in his ways!
For you shall eat the fruit of your

handiwork;
blessed shall you be, and favored. ℟.

Your wife shall be like a fruitful vine
 in the recesses of your home;
your children like olive plants
 around your table. ℟.

Behold, thus is the man blessed

who fears the LORD.
The LORD bless you from Zion:
 may you see the prosperity of
 Jerusalem
all the days of your life. ℟.

READING II
Colossians 3:12-21 or 3:12-17

For short form read only the part in brackets.

[Brothers and sisters: Put on, as God's chosen ones, holy and beloved, heartfelt compassion, kindness, humility, gentleness, and patience, bearing with one another and forgiving one another, if one has a grievance against another; as the Lord has forgiven you, so must you also do. And over all these put on love, that is, the bond of perfection. And let the peace of Christ control your hearts, the peace into which you were also called in one body. And be thankful. Let the word of Christ dwell in you richly, as in all wisdom you teach and admonish one another, singing psalms, hymns, and spiritual songs with gratitude in your hearts to God. And whatever you do, in word or in deed, do everything in the name of the Lord Jesus, giving thanks to God the Father through him.]

 Wives, be subordinate to your husbands, as is proper in the Lord. Husbands, love your wives, and avoid any bitterness toward them. Children, obey your parents in everything, for this is pleasing to the Lord. Fathers, do not provoke your children, so they may not become discouraged.

GOSPEL / A
Matthew 2:13-15, 19-23

When the magi had departed, behold, the angel of the Lord appeared to Joseph in a dream and said, "Rise, take the child and his mother, flee to Egypt, and stay there until I tell you. Herod is going to search for the child to destroy him." Joseph rose and took the child and his mother by night and departed for Egypt. He stayed there until the death of Herod, that what the Lord had said through the prophet might be fulfilled, "Out of Egypt I called my son."

 When Herod had died, behold, the angel of the Lord appeared in a dream to Joseph in Egypt and said, "Rise, take the child and his mother and go to the land of Israel, for those who sought the child's life are dead." He rose, took the child and his mother, and went to the land of Israel. But when he heard that Archelaus was ruling over Judea in place of his father Herod, he was afraid to go back there. And because he had been warned in a dream, he departed for the region of Galilee. He went and dwelt in a town called Nazareth, so that what had been spoken through the prophets might be fulfilled, "He shall be called a Nazorean."

GOSPEL / B
Luke 2:22-40 or 2:22, 39-40

For short form read only the parts in brackets.

[When the days were completed for their purification according to the law of Moses, they took him up to Jerusalem to present him to the Lord,] just as it is written in the law of the Lord, "Every male that opens the womb shall be consecrated to the Lord," and to offer the sacrifice of "a pair of turtledoves or two young pigeons," in accordance with the dictate in the law of the Lord.

 Now there was a man in Jerusalem whose name was Simeon. This man was righteous and devout, awaiting the consolation of Israel, and the Holy Spirit was upon him. It had been revealed to him by the Holy Spirit that he should not see death before he had seen the Christ of the Lord. He came in the Spirit into the temple; and when the parents brought in the child Jesus to perform the custom of the law in regard to him, he took him into his arms and blessed God, saying:

 "Now, Master, you may let your servant go
  in peace, according to your word,
 for my eyes have seen your salvation,

which you prepared in sight of all the peoples,
a light for revelation to the Gentiles,
and glory for your people Israel."

The child's father and mother were amazed at what was said about him; and Simeon blessed them and said to Mary his mother, "Behold, this child is destined for the fall and rise of many in Israel, and to be a sign that will be contradicted (and you yourself a sword will pierce) so that the thoughts of many hearts may be revealed." There was also a prophetess, Anna, the daughter of Phanuel, of the tribe of Asher. She was advanced in years, having lived seven years with her husband after her marriage, and then as a widow until she was eighty-four. She never left the temple, but worshiped night and day with fasting and prayer. And coming forward at that very time, she gave thanks to God and spoke about the child to all who were awaiting the redemption of Jerusalem.

[When they had fulfilled all the prescriptions of the law of the Lord, they returned to Galilee, to their own town of Nazareth. The child grew and became strong, filled with wisdom; and the favor of God was upon him.]

GOSPEL / C

Luke 2:41-52

Each year Jesus' parents went to Jerusalem for the feast of Passover, and when he was twelve years old, they went up according to festival custom. After they had completed its days, as they were returning, the boy Jesus remained behind in Jerusalem, but his parents did not know it. Thinking that he was in the caravan, they journeyed for a day and looked for him among their relatives and acquaintances, but not finding him, they returned to Jerusalem to look for him. After three days they found him in the temple, sitting in the midst of the teachers, listening to them and asking them questions, and all who heard him were astounded at his understanding and his answers. When his parents saw him, they were astonished, and his mother said to him, "Son, why have you done this to us? Your father and I have been looking for you with great anxiety." And he said to them, "Why were you looking for me? Did you not know that I must be in my Father's house?" But they did not understand what he said to them. He went down with them and came to Nazareth, and was obedient to them; and his mother kept all these things in her heart. And Jesus advanced in wisdom and age and favor before God and man.

494 IN YEAR B, THESE READINGS MAY BE USED

READING I

Genesis 15:1-6; 21:1-3

The word of the LORD came to Abram in a vision, saying:
"Fear not, Abram!
I am your shield;
I will make your reward very great."

But Abram said, "O Lord GOD, what good will your gifts be, if I keep on being childless and have as my heir the steward of my house, Eliezer?" Abram continued, "See, you have given me no offspring, and so one of my servants will be my heir." Then the word of the LORD came to him: "No, that one shall not be your heir; your own issue shall be your heir." The Lord took Abram outside and said, "Look up at the sky and count the stars, if you can. Just so," he added, "shall your descendants be." Abram put his faith in the LORD, who credited it to him as an act of righteousness.

The LORD took note of Sarah as he had said he would; he did for her as he had promised. Sarah became pregnant and bore Abraham a son in his old age, at the set time that God had stated. Abraham gave the name Isaac to this son of his whom Sarah bore him.

RESPONSORIAL PSALM

Psalm 105:1-2, 3-4, 6-7, 8-9

The Lord re-mem-bers his cov-e-nant for ev-er.

Give thanks to the LORD, invoke his
name;
make known among the nations his
deeds.
Sing to him, sing his praise,
proclaim all his wondrous deeds. ℟.

Glory in his holy name;
rejoice, O hearts that seek the LORD!
Look to the LORD in his strength;
constantly seek his face. ℟.

You descendants of Abraham, his
servants,
sons of Jacob, his chosen ones!
He, the LORD, is our God;
throughout the earth his judgments
prevail. ℟.

He remembers forever his covenant
which he made binding for a
thousand generations
which he entered into with Abraham
and by his oath to Isaac. ℟.

READING II   *Hebrews 11:8, 11-12, 17-19*

Brothers and sisters: By faith Abraham obeyed when he was called to go out to a place
that he was to receive as an inheritance; he went out, not knowing where he was to go.
By faith he received power to generate, even though he was past the normal age—and
Sarah herself was sterile—for he thought that the one who had made the promise was
trustworthy. So it was that there came forth from one man, himself as good as dead,
descendants as numerous as the stars in the sky and as countless as the sands on the
seashore.

By faith Abraham, when put to the test, offered up Isaac, and he who had received
the promises was ready to offer his only son, of whom it was said, "Through Isaac
descendants shall bear your name." He reasoned that God was able to raise even from
the dead, and he received Isaac back as a symbol.

IN YEAR C, THESE READINGS MAY BE USED   495

READING I   *1 Samuel 1:20-22, 24-28*

In those days Hannah conceived, and at the end of her term bore a son whom she called
Samuel, since she had asked the LORD for him. The next time her husband Elkanah was
going up with the rest of his household to offer the customary sacrifice to the LORD and
to fulfill his vows, Hannah did not go, explaining to her husband, "Once the child is
weaned, I will take him to appear before the LORD and to remain there forever; I will
offer him as a perpetual nazirite."

Once Samuel was weaned, Hannah brought him up with her, along with a three-
year-old bull, an ephah of flour, and a skin of wine, and presented him at the temple of
the LORD in Shiloh. After the boy's father had sacrificed the young bull, Hannah, his
mother, approached Eli and said: "Pardon, my lord! As you live, my lord, I am the
woman who stood near you here, praying to the LORD. I prayed for this child, and the
LORD granted my request. Now I, in turn, give him to the LORD; as long as he lives, he
shall be dedicated to the LORD." Hannah left Samuel there.

RESPONSORIAL PSALM   *Psalm 84:2-3, 5-6, 9-10*

Bless-ed are they who dwell in your house, O Lord.

How lovely is your dwelling place, O
LORD of hosts!
My soul yearns and pines for the
courts of the LORD.
My heart and my flesh cry out for the
living God. ℟.

Happy they who dwell in your house!
Continually they praise you.
Happy the men whose strength you are!
Their hearts are set upon the
pilgrimage. ℟.

O LORD of hosts, hear our prayer;
  hearken, O God of Jacob!
O God, behold our shield,

and look upon the face of your
  anointed. ℟.

READING II   *John 3:1-2, 21-24*

Beloved: See what love the Father has bestowed on us that we may be called the children of God. And so we are. The reason the world does not know us is that it did not know him. Beloved, we are God's children now; what we shall be has not yet been revealed. We do know that when it is revealed we shall be like him, for we shall see him as he is.

Beloved, if our hearts do not condemn us, we have confidence in God and receive from him whatever we ask, because we keep his commandments and do what pleases him. And his commandment is this: we should believe in the name of his Son, Jesus Christ, and love one another just as he commanded us. Those who keep his commandments remain in him, and he in them, and the way we know that he remains in us is from the Spirit he gave us.

496   JAN. 1: SOLEMNITY OF MARY, THE MOTHER OF GOD / ABC

READING I   *Numbers 6:22-27 / 18*

The LORD said to Moses: "Speak to Aaron and his sons and tell them: This is how you shall bless the Israelites. Say to them: The LORD bless you and keep you! The LORD let his face shine upon you, and be gracious to you! The LORD look upon you kindly and give you peace! So shall they invoke my name upon the Israelites, and I will bless them."

RESPONSORIAL PSALM   *Psalm 67:2-3, 5, 6, 8*

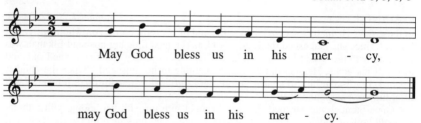

May God bless us in his mer - cy,
may God bless us in his mer - cy.

May God have pity on us and bless us;
  may he let his face shine upon us.
So may your way be known upon earth;
  among all nations, your salvation. ℟.

May the nations be glad and exult
  because you rule the peoples in equity;

the nations on the earth you guide. ℟.

May the peoples praise you, O God;
  may all the peoples praise you!
May God bless us,
  and may all the ends of the earth fear
  him! ℟.

READING II   *Galatians 4:4-7*

Brothers and sisters: When the fullness of time had come, God sent his Son, born of a woman, born under the law, to ransom those under the law, so that we might receive adoption as sons. As proof that you are sons, God sent the Spirit of his Son into our hearts, crying out, "Abba, Father!" So you are no longer a slave but a son, and if a son then also an heir, through God.

GOSPEL   *Luke 2:16-21*

The shepherds went in haste to Bethlehem and found Mary and Joseph, and the infant lying in the manger. When they saw this, they made known the message that had been told them about this child. All who heard it were amazed by what had been told them by the shepherds. And Mary kept all these things, reflecting on them in her heart. Then the shepherds returned, glorifying and praising God for all they had heard and seen, just as it had been told to them. When eight days were completed for his circumcision, he was named Jesus, the name given him by the angel before he was conceived in the womb.

THE EPIPHANY OF THE LORD / ABC 497

READING I
Isaiah 60:1-6 / 20

Rise up in splendor, Jerusalem! Your
  light has come,
   the glory of the Lord shines upon
     you.
See, darkness covers the earth,
   and thick clouds cover the peoples;
but upon you the LORD shines,
   and over you appears his glory.
Nations shall walk by your light,
   and kings by your shining radiance.
Raise your eyes and look about;
   they all gather and come to you:
your sons come from afar,
   and your daughters in the arms of
     their nurses.

Then you shall be radiant at what you see,
   your heart shall throb and overflow,
for the riches of the sea shall be emptied
     out before you,
   the wealth of nations shall be
     brought to you.
Caravans of camels shall fill you,
   dromedaries from Midian and Ephah;
all from Sheba shall come
   bearing gold and frankincense,
   and proclaiming the praises of the
     LORD.

RESPONSORIAL PSALM
Psalm 72:1-2, 7-8, 10-11, 12-13

Lord, ev-'ry na-tion on earth will a-dore you.

O God, with your judgment endow the
     king,
   and with your justice, the king's son;
he shall govern your people with justice
   and your afflicted ones with
     judgment. ℟.

Justice shall flower in his days,
   and profound peace, till the moon be
     no more.
May he rule from sea to sea,
   and from the River to the ends of the
     earth. ℟.

The kings of Tarshish and the Isles shall
     offer gifts;
   the kings of Arabia and Seba shall
     bring tribute.
All kings shall pay him homage,
   all nations shall serve him. ℟.

For he shall rescue the poor when he
     cries out,
   and the afflicted when he has no one
     to help him.
He shall have pity for the lowly and the
     poor;
   the lives of the poor he shall save. ℟.

READING II
Ephesians 3:2-3a, 5-6

Brothers and sisters: You have heard of the stewardship of God's grace that was given to me for your benefit, namely, that the mystery was made known to me by revelation. It was not made known to people in other generations as it has now been revealed to his holy apostles and prophets by the Spirit: that the Gentiles are coheirs, members of the same body, and copartners in the promise in Christ Jesus through the gospel.

GOSPEL
Matthew 2:1-12

When Jesus was born in Bethlehem of Judea, in the days of King Herod, behold, magi from the east arrived in Jerusalem, saying, "Where is the newborn king of the Jews? We saw his star at its rising and have come to do him homage." When King Herod heard

this, he was greatly troubled, and all Jerusalem with him. Assembling all the chief priests and the scribes of the people, he inquired of them where the Christ was to be born. They said to him, "In Bethlehem of Judea, for thus it has been written through the prophet:
> 'And you, Bethlehem, land of Judah,
>> are by no means least among the rulers of Judah;
> since from you shall come a ruler,
>> who is to shepherd my people Israel.'"

Then Herod called the magi secretly and ascertained from them the time of the star's appearance. He sent them to Bethlehem and said, "Go and search diligently for the child. When you have found him, bring me word, that I too may go and do him homage." After their audience with the king they set out. And behold, the star that they had seen at its rising preceded them, until it came and stopped over the place where the child was. They were overjoyed at seeing the star, and on entering the house they saw the child with Mary his mother. They prostrated themselves and did him homage. Then they opened their treasures and offered him gifts of gold, frankincense, and myrrh. And having been warned in a dream not to return to Herod, they departed for their country by another way.

498 BAPTISM OF THE LORD / ABC

READING I
Isaiah 42:1-4, 6-7 / 21

Thus says the LORD:
Here is my servant whom I uphold,
> my chosen one with whom I am
>> pleased,
upon whom I have put my spirit;
> he shall bring forth justice to the
>> nations,
not crying out, not shouting,
> not making his voice heard in the
>> street.
A bruised reed he shall not break,
> and a smoldering wick he shall not
>> quench,
until he establishes justice on the earth;

the coastlands will wait for his
> teaching.

I, the LORD, have called you for the
> victory of justice,
I have grasped you by the hand;
I formed you, and set you
> as a covenant of the people,
> a light for the nations,
to open the eyes of the blind,
> to bring out prisoners from
>> confinement,
> and from the dungeon, those who
>> live in darkness.

RESPONSORIAL PSALM
Psalm 29:1-2, 3-4, 3, 9-10

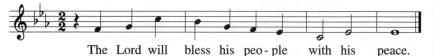

The Lord will bless his peo-ple with his peace.

Give to the LORD, you sons of God,
> give to the LORD glory and praise,
Give to the LORD the glory due his name;
> adore the LORD in holy attire. ℟.

The voice of the LORD is over the waters,
> the LORD, over vast waters.
The voice of the LORD is mighty;

the voice of the LORD is majestic. ℟.

The God of glory thunders,
> and in his temple all say, "Glory!"
The LORD is enthroned above the flood;
> the LORD is enthroned as king
> forever. ℟.

READING II
Acts 10:34-38

Peter proceeded to speak to those gathered in the house of Cornelius, saying: "In truth, I see that God shows no partiality. Rather, in every nation whoever fears him and acts uprightly is acceptable to him. You know the word that he sent to the Israelites as he proclaimed peace through Jesus Christ, who is Lord of all, what has happened all over Judea, beginning in Galilee after the baptism that John preached, how God anointed Jesus of Nazareth with the Holy Spirit and power. He went about doing good and healing all those oppressed by the devil, for God was with him."

GOSPEL / A   *Matthew 3:13-17*

Jesus came from Galilee to John at the Jordan to be baptized by him. John tried to prevent him, saying, "I need to be baptized by you, and yet you are coming to me?" Jesus said to him in reply, "Allow it now, for thus it is fitting for us to fulfill all righteousness." Then he allowed him. After Jesus was baptized, he came up from the water and behold, the heavens were opened for him, and he saw the Spirit of God descending like a dove and coming upon him. And a voice came from the heavens, saying, "This is my beloved Son, with whom I am well pleased."

GOSPEL / B   *Mark 1:7-11*

This is what he proclaimed:
"One mightier than I is coming after me. I am not worthy to stoop and loosen the thongs of his sandals. I have baptized you with water; he will baptize you with the Holy Spirit."
It happened in those days that Jesus came from Nazareth of Galilee and was baptized in the Jordan by John. On coming up out of the water he saw the heavens being torn open and the Spirit, like a dove, descending upon him. And a voice came from the heavens, "You are my beloved Son; with you I am well pleased."

GOSPEL / C   *Luke 3:15-16, 21-22*

The people were filled with expectation, and all were asking in their hearts whether John might be the Christ. John answered them all, saying, "I am baptizing you with water, but one mightier than I is coming. I am not worthy to loosen the thongs of his sandals. He will baptize you with the Holy Spirit and fire."
After all the people had been baptized and Jesus also had been baptized and was praying, heaven was opened and the Holy Spirit descended upon him in bodily form like a dove. And a voice came from heaven, "You are my beloved Son; with you I am well pleased."

IN YEAR B, THESE READINGS MAY BE USED   499

READING I   *Isaiah 55:1-11*

Thus says the LORD:
All you who are thirsty,
   come to the water!
You who have no money,
   come, receive grain and eat;
come, without paying and without cost,
   drink wine and milk!
Why spend your money for what is not
   bread,
   your wages for what fails to satisfy?
Heed me, and you shall eat well,
   you shall delight in rich fare.
Come to me heedfully,
   listen, that you may have life.
I will renew with you the everlasting
   covenant,
   the benefits assured to David.

As I made him a witness to the peoples,
   a leader and commander of nations,
so shall you summon a nation you knew
   not,
   and nations that knew you not shall
   run to you,
because of the LORD, your God
   the Holy One of Israel, who has
   glorified you.

Seek the LORD while he may be found,
   call him while he is near.
Let the scoundrel forsake his way,
   and the wicked man his thoughts;
let him turn to the LORD for mercy;
   to our God, who is generous in
   forgiving.

For my thoughts are not your thoughts,
    nor are your ways my ways, says
        the Lord.
As high as the heavens are above the
      earth
    so high are my ways above your
      ways
    and my thoughts above your
      thoughts.

For just as from the heavens

the rain and snow come down
and do not return there
    till they have watered the earth,
    making it fertile and fruitful,
giving seed to the one who sows
    and bread to the one who eats,
so shall my word be
    that goes forth from my mouth;
my word shall not return to me void,
    but shall do my will,
    achieving the end for which I sent it.

RESPONSORIAL PSALM   *Isaiah 12:2-3, 4bcd, 5-6*

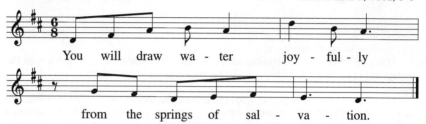

God indeed is my savior;
    I am confident and unafraid.
My strength and my courage is the Lord,
    and he has been my savior.
With joy you will draw water
    at the fountain of salvation. ℟.

Give thanks to the Lord, acclaim his
    name;
    among the nations make known his

deeds,
proclaim how exalted is his name. ℟.

Sing praise to the Lord for his glorious
    achievement;
    let this be known throughout all the
      earth.
Shout with exultation, O city of Zion,
    for great in your midst
    is the Holy One of Israel! ℟.

READING II   *1 John 5:1-9*

Beloved: Everyone who believes that Jesus is the Christ is begotten by God, and everyone who loves the Father loves also the one begotten by him. In this way we know that we love the children of God when we love God and obey his commandments. For the love of God is this, that we keep his commandments. And his commandments are not burdensome, for whoever is begotten by God conquers the world. And the victory that conquers the world is our faith. Who indeed is the victor over the world but the one who believes that Jesus is the Son of God? This is the one who came through water and blood, Jesus Christ, not by water alone, but by water and blood. The Spirit is the one who testifies, and the Spirit is truth. So there are three that testify, the Spirit, the water, and the blood, and the three are of one accord. If we accept human testimony, the testimony of God is surely greater. Now the testimony of God is this, that he has testified on behalf of his Son.

500   IN YEAR C, THESE READINGS MAY BE USED

READING I   *Isaiah 40:1-5, 9-11*

Comfort, give comfort to my people,
    says your God.
Speak tenderly to Jerusalem, and proclaim
      to her
    that her service is at an end,

    her guilt is expiated;
indeed, she has received from the hand of
      the Lord
    double for all her sins.

A voice cries out:
In the desert prepare the way of the LORD!
Make straight in the wasteland a
highway for our God!
Every valley shall be filled in,
every mountain and hill shall be made
low;
the rugged land shall be made a plain,
the rough country, a broad valley.
Then the glory of the LORD shall be
revealed,
and all people shall see it together;
for the mouth of the LORD has
spoken.

Go up onto a high mountain,

Zion, herald of glad tidings;
cry out at the top of your voice,
Jerusalem, herald of good news!
Fear not to cry out
and say to the cities of Judah:
Here is your God!
Here comes with power
the Lord GOD,
who rules by a strong arm;
here is his reward with him,
his recompense before him.
Like a shepherd he feeds his flock;
in his arms he gathers the lambs,
carrying them in his bosom,
and leading the ewes with care.

RESPONSORIAL PSALM

Psalm 104:1b-2, 3-4, 24-25, 27-28, 29-30

O bless the Lord, my soul, O bless the Lord.

O LORD, my God, you are great indeed!
you are clothed with majesty and
glory,
robed in light as with a cloak.
You have spread out the heavens like
a tent-cloth. ℟.

You have constructed your palace upon
the waters.
You make the clouds your chariot;
you travel on the wings of the wind.
You make the winds your messengers,
and flaming fire your ministers. ℟.

How manifold are your works, O LORD!
In wisdom you have wrought them all—
the earth is full of your creatures;

the sea also, great and wide,
in which are schools without number
of living things both small and
great. ℟.

They look to you to give them food in
due time.
When you give it to them, they
gather it;
when you open your hand, they are filled
with good things. ℟.

If you take away their breath, they perish
and return to the dust.
When you send forth your spirit, they
are created,
and you renew the face of the earth. ℟.

READING II

Titus 2:11-14; 3:4-7

Beloved: The grace of God has appeared, saving all and training us to reject godless
ways and worldly desires and to live temperately, justly, and devoutly in this age, as we
await the blessed hope, the appearance of the glory of our great God and savior Jesus
Christ, who gave himself for us to deliver us from all lawlessness and to cleanse for himself a people as his own, eager to do what is good.
When the kindness and generous love
of God our savior appeared,
not because of any righteous deeds we had done
but because of his mercy,
He saved us through the bath of rebirth
and renewal by the Holy Spirit,
whom he richly poured out on us
through Jesus Christ our savior,
so that we might be justified by his grace
and become heirs in hope of eternal life.

Lent/Easter

501   On a Wednesday in February or early March the church enters into prayer
and fasting and almsgiving, attending with great seriousness to its calling.
Forty days later on a Thursday evening, that season of Lent ends. From
Holy Thursday night until Easter Sunday afternoon, the church keeps the
Paschal Triduum, the "Easter Three Days." Good Friday and Holy Saturday
find Christians fasting, keeping vigil, remembering the passion, death and
resurrection of the Lord until, at the great Vigil liturgy, the church celebrates this paschal mystery in baptism, confirmation and eucharist. Then,
for the fifty days of Eastertime the church again sings the alleluia and
rejoices to bring God's peace to the world.

The origins of Lent are bound up with the final stages in the initiation
of those seeking to be baptized. After months or years of learning gradually
the Christian way of life, the catechumens were called to spend the last
weeks before baptism in fasting and prayer. The whole church stayed by
the catechumens in these days. The lenten season was also kept intensely
by those doing penance for their sins. Today both catechumens and
penitents keep Lent with the whole church. Lent's scriptures, prayers and
rites give clarity and strength to the life-long struggle against evil. That
struggle is waged with many forms of prayer and fasting and practices of
charity.

The origins of the fifty days of Eastertime are even more ancient. This
is the springtime rejoicing of people who know their dependence on fields
and flocks. It is the rejoicing of Israel remembering the exodus from slavery
to freedom. It became the rejoicing of the church in the resurrection of
Jesus and the presence of that risen life in the newly baptized. The Eastertime lectionary is filled with a lively peace and the quiet exuberance of
those who believe that evil is not finally triumphant. When the fifty days
conclude at Pentecost the church knows again how disturbing, how restless,
how strong is the Spirit given by Christ.

FIRST SUNDAY OF LENT / A 502

READING I
Genesis 2:7-9; 3:1-7 / 22

The LORD God formed man out of the clay of the ground and blew into his nostrils the breath of life, and so man became a living being.

Then the LORD God planted a garden in Eden, in the east, and placed there the man whom he had formed. Out of the ground the LORD God made various trees grow that were delightful to look at and good for food, with the tree of life in the middle of the garden and the tree of the knowledge of good and evil.

Now the serpent was the most cunning of all the animals that the LORD God had made. The serpent asked the woman, "Did God really tell you not to eat from any of the trees in the garden?" The woman answered the serpent: "We may eat of the fruit of the trees in the garden; it is only about the fruit of the tree in the middle of the garden that God said, 'You shall not eat it or even touch it, lest you die.'" But the serpent said to the woman: "You certainly will not die! No, God knows well that the moment you eat of it your eyes will be opened and you will be like gods who know what is good and what is evil." The woman saw that the tree was good for food, pleasing to the eyes, and desirable for gaining wisdom. So she took some of its fruit and ate it; and she also gave some to her husband, who was with her, and he ate it. Then the eyes of both of them were opened, and they realized that they were naked; so they sewed fig leaves together and made loincloths for themselves.

RESPONSORIAL PSALM
Psalm 51:3-4, 5-6, 12-13, 14, 17

Be mer-ci-ful, O Lord, for we have sinned.

Have mercy on me, O God, in your
    goodness;
  in the greatness of your compassion
    wipe out my offense.
Thoroughly wash me from my guilt
  and of my sin cleanse me. ℟.

For I acknowledge my offense,
  and my sin is before me always:
"Against you only have I sinned,
  and done what is evil in your
    sight." ℟.

A clean heart create for me, O God,
  and a steadfast spirit renew within
  me.
Cast me not out from your presence,
  and your Holy Spirit take not from
  me. ℟.

Give me back the joy of your salvation,
  and a willing spirit sustain in me.
O Lord, open my lips,
  and my mouth shall proclaim your
  praise. ℟.

READING II
Romans 5:12-19 or 5:12, 17-19

For short form read only the parts in brackets.

[Brothers and sisters: Through one man sin entered the world, and through sin, death, and thus death came to all men, inasmuch as all sinned—] for up to the time of the law, sin was in the world, though sin is not accounted when there is no law. But death reigned from Adam to Moses, even over those who did not sin after the pattern of the trespass of Adam, who is the type of the one who was to come.

But the gift is not like the transgression. For if by the transgression of the one, the many died, how much more did the grace of God and the gracious gift of the one man Jesus Christ overflow for the many. And the gift is not like the result of the one who sinned. For after one sin there was the judgment that brought condemnation; but the gift, after many transgressions, brought acquittal. [For if, by the transgression of the one, death came to reign through that one, how much more will those who receive the abundance of grace and of the gift of justification come to reign in life through the one Jesus Christ. In conclusion, just as through one transgression condemnation came upon all, so, through one righteous act, acquittal and life came to all. For just as through the disobedience of the one man the many were made sinners, so, through the obedience of the one, the many will be made righteous.]

GOSPEL
Matthew 4:1-11

At that time Jesus was led by the Spirit into the desert to be tempted by the devil. He fasted for forty days and forty nights, and afterwards he was hungry. The tempter approached and said to him, "If you are the Son of God, command that these stones become loaves of bread."
He said in reply, "It is written:
'One does not live on bread alone,
but on every word that comes forth
from the mouth of God.'"

Then the devil took him to the holy city, and made him stand on the parapet of the temple, and said to him, "If you are the Son of God, throw yourself down. For it is written:
'He will command his angels concerning you'
and 'with their hands they will support you,
lest you dash your foot against a stone.'"
Jesus answered him, "Again it is written, 'You shall not put the Lord, your God, to the test.'" Then the devil took him up to a very high mountain, and showed him all the kingdoms of the world in their magnificence, and he said to him, "All these I shall give to you, if you will prostrate yourself and worship me." At this, Jesus said to him, "Get away, Satan! It is written:
'The Lord, your God, shall you worship
and him alone shall you serve.'"
Then the devil left him and, behold, angels came and ministered to him.

RITE OF ELECTION

At the beginning of Lent, it is the responsibility of the bishop to call those who are judged ready to prepare for the sacraments of initiation at Easter. The bishop is to consult first with the pastors, catechists and others. The rite may take place at the cathedral. If the rite takes place in the parish church, the bishop may designate the pastor to act in his place.

This rite is also called the "Enrollment of Names." Each candidate now gives his/her name, or writes it down. When all have been enrolled, the bishop says: "You have been chosen to be initiated into the sacred mysteries at the Easter Vigil." He then speaks to them and to their sponsors about their lenten preparation for baptism.

The faithful join in prayers of intercession for the elect, as the catechumens are now called. If the eucharist is to be celebrated, the elect are first dismissed.

503 FIRST SUNDAY OF LENT / B

READING I
Genesis 9:8-15 / 23

God said to Noah and to his sons with him: "See, I am now establishing my covenant with you and your descendants after you and with every living creature that was with you: all the birds, and the various tame and wild animals that were with you and came out of the ark. I will establish my covenant with you, that never again shall all bodily creatures be destroyed by the waters of a flood; there shall not be another flood to devastate the earth."
God added: "This is the sign that I am giving for all ages to come, of the covenant

between me and you and every living creature with you: I set my bow in the clouds to serve as a sign of the covenant between me and the earth.

When I bring clouds over the earth, and the bow appears in the clouds, I will recall the covenant I have made between me and you and all living beings, so that the waters shall never again become a flood to destroy all mortal beings."

RESPONSORIAL PSALM
Psalm 25:4-5, 6-7, 8-9

Your ways, O Lord, are love and truth to those who keep your cov - e - nant.

Your ways, O LORD, make known to me;
  teach me your paths,
Guide me in your truth and teach me,
  for you are God my savior. ℟.

Remember that your compassion, O LORD,
  and your love are from of old.

In your kindness remember me,
  because of your goodness, O
  LORD. ℟.

Good and upright is the LORD,
  thus he shows sinners the way.
He guides the humble to justice,
  and he teaches the humble his way. ℟.

READING II
1 Peter 3:18-22

Beloved: Christ suffered for sins once, the righteous for the sake of the unrighteous, that he might lead you to God. Put to death in the flesh, he was brought to life in the Spirit. In it he also went to preach to the spirits in prison, who had once been disobedient while God patiently waited in the days of Noah during the building of the ark, in which a few persons, eight in all, were saved through water. This prefigured baptism, which saves you now. It is not a removal of dirt from the body but an appeal to God for a clear conscience, through the resurrection of Jesus Christ, who has gone into heaven and is at the right hand of God, with angels, authorities, and powers subject to him.

GOSPEL
Mark 1:12-15

The Spirit drove Jesus out into the desert, and he remained in the desert for forty days, tempted by Satan. He was among wild beasts, and the angels ministered to him.

After John had been arrested, Jesus came to Galilee proclaiming the gospel of God: "This is the time of fulfillment. The kingdom of God is at hand. Repent, and believe in the gospel."

RITE OF ELECTION
See no. 502

FIRST SUNDAY OF LENT / C
504

READING I
Deuteronomy 26:4-10 / 24

Moses spoke to the people, saying: "The priest shall receive the basket from you and shall set it in front of the altar of the LORD, your God. Then you shall declare before the

Lord, your God, 'My father was a wandering Aramean who went down to Egypt with a small household and lived there as an alien. But there he became a nation great, strong, and numerous. When the Egyptians maltreated and oppressed us, imposing hard labor upon us, we cried to the LORD, the God of our fathers, and he heard our cry and saw our affliction, our toil, and our oppression. He brought us out of Egypt with his strong hand and outstretched arm, with terrifying power, with signs and wonders; and bringing us into this country, he gave us this land flowing with milk and honey. Therefore, I have now brought you the firstfruits of the products of the soil which you, O LORD, have given me.' And having set them before the Lord, your God, you shall bow down in his presence."

RESPONSORIAL PSALM

Psalm 91:1-2, 10-11, 12-13, 14-15

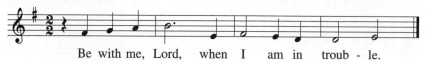

Be with me, Lord, when I am in troub - le.

You who dwell in the shelter of the Most High,
who abide in the shadow of the Almighty,
say to the LORD, "My refuge and fortress,
my God in whom I trust." ℟.

No evil shall befall you,
nor shall affliction come near your tent,
for to his angels he has given command about you,
that they guard you in all your ways. ℟.

Upon their hands they shall bear you up,
lest you dash your foot against a stone.
You shall tread upon the asp and the viper;
you shall trample down the lion and the dragon. ℟.

Because he clings to me, I will deliver him;
I will set him on high because he acknowledges my name.
He shall call upon me, and I will answer him;
I will be with him in distress;
I will deliver him and glorify him. ℟.

READING II

Romans 10:8-13

Brothers and sisters: What does Scripture say?
"The word is near you,
in your mouth and in your heart"
(that is, the word of faith that we preach), for, if you confess with your mouth that Jesus is Lord and believe in your heart that God raised him from the dead, you will be saved. For one believes with the heart and so is justified, and one confesses with the mouth and so is saved. For the Scripture says, "No one who believes in him will be put to shame." For there is no distinction between Jew and Greek; the same Lord is Lord of all, enriching all who call upon him. For "everyone who calls on the name of the Lord will be saved."

GOSPEL

Luke 4:1-13

Filled with the Holy Spirit, Jesus returned from the Jordan and was led by the Spirit into the desert for forty days, to be tempted by the devil. He ate nothing during those days, and when they were over he was hungry. The devil said to him, "If you are the Son of God, command this stone to become bread." Jesus answered him, "It is written, 'One does not live on bread alone.'" Then he took him up and showed him all the kingdoms of the world in a single instant. The devil said to him, "I shall give to you all this power and glory; for it has been handed over to me, and I may give it to whomever I wish. All this will be yours, if you worship me." Jesus said to him in reply, "It is written:
'You shall worship the Lord, your God,
and him alone shall you serve.'"
Then he led him to Jerusalem, made him stand on the parapet of the temple, and said to him, "If you are the Son of God, throw yourself down from here, for it is written:

'He will command his angels concerning you, to guard you,'
and:
'With their hands they will support you,
lest you dash your foot against a stone.'"
Jesus said to him in reply, "It also says, 'You shall not put the Lord, your God, to the
test.'" When the devil had finished every temptation, he departed from him for a time.

RITE OF ELECTION

See no. 502

SECOND SUNDAY OF LENT / A 505

READING I *Genesis 12:1-4a / 25*

The LORD said to Abram: "Go forth from the land of your kinsfolk and from your
father's house to a land that I will show you.

"I will make of you a great nation,
and I will bless you;
I will make your name great,
so that you will be a blessing.
I will bless those who bless you
and curse those who curse you.
All the communities of the earth
shall find blessing in you."

Abram went as the LORD directed him.

RESPONSORIAL PSALM *Psalm 33:4-5, 18-19, 20, 22*

Lord, let your mer-cy be on us, as we place our trust in you.

Upright is the word of the LORD,
and all his works are trustworthy.
He loves justice and right;
of the kindness of the LORD the earth
is full. ℟.

See, the eyes of the LORD are upon those
who fear him,
upon those who hope for his

kindness,
to deliver them from death
and preserve them in spite of
famine. ℟.

Our soul waits for the LORD,
who is our help and our shield.
May your kindness, O LORD, be upon us
who have put our hope in you. ℟.

READING II *2 Timothy 1:8b-10*

Beloved: Bear your share of hardship for the gospel with the strength that comes from
God.

He saved us and called us to a holy life, not according to our works but according
to his own design and the grace bestowed on us in Christ Jesus before time began, but
now made manifest through the appearance of our savior Christ Jesus, who destroyed
death and brought life and immortality to light through the gospel.

GOSPEL *Matthew 17:1-9*

Jesus took Peter, James, and John his brother, and led them up a high mountain by
themselves. And he was transfigured before them; his face shone like the sun and his

clothes became white as light. And behold, Moses and Elijah appeared to them, conversing with him. Then Peter said to Jesus in reply, "Lord, it is good that we are here. If you wish, I will make three tents here, one for you, one for Moses, and one for Elijah." While he was still speaking, behold, a bright cloud cast a shadow over them, then from the cloud came a voice that said, "This is my beloved Son, with whom I am well pleased; listen to him." When the disciples heard this, they fell prostrate and were very much afraid. But Jesus came and touched them, saying, "Rise, and do not be afraid." And when the disciples raised their eyes, they saw no one else but Jesus alone.

As they were coming down from the mountain, Jesus charged them, "Do not tell the vision to anyone until the Son of Man has been raised from the dead."

506 SECOND SUNDAY OF LENT / B

READING I
Genesis 22:1-2, 9a, 10-13, 15-18 / 26

God put Abraham to the test. He called to him, "Abraham!" "Here I am!" he replied. Then God said: "Take your son Isaac, your only one, whom you love, and go to the land of Moriah. There you shall offer him up as a holocaust on a height that I will point out to you."

When they came to the place of which God had told him, Abraham built an altar there and arranged the wood on it. Then he reached out and took the knife to slaughter his son. But the LORD's messenger called to him from heaven, "Abraham, Abraham!" "Here I am!" he answered. "Do not lay your hand on the boy," said the messenger. "Do not do the least thing to him. I know now how devoted you are to God, since you did not withhold from me your own beloved son." As Abraham looked about, he spied a ram caught by its horns in the thicket. So he went and took the ram and offered it up as a holocaust in place of his son.

Again the LORD's messenger called to Abraham from heaven and said: "I swear by myself, declares the LORD, that because you acted as you did in not withholding from me your beloved son, I will bless you abundantly and make your descendants as countless as the stars of the sky and the sands of the seashore; your descendants shall take possession of the gates of their enemies, and in your descendants all the nations of the earth shall find blessing—all this because you obeyed my command."

RESPONSORIAL PSALM
Psalm 116:10, 15, 16-17, 18-19

I will walk be-fore the Lord, in the land of the liv - ing.

I believed, even when I said,
"I am greatly afflicted."
Precious in the eyes of the LORD
is the death of his faithful ones. ℟.

O LORD, I am your servant;
I am your servant, the son of your
handmaid;
you have loosed my bonds.

To you will I offer sacrifice of
thanksgiving,
and I will call upon the name of the
LORD. ℟.

My vows to the LORD I will pay
in the presence of all his people,
in the courts of the house of the LORD,
in your midst, O Jerusalem. ℟.

READING II
Romans 8:31b-34

Brothers and sisters: If God is for us, who can be against us? He who did not spare his own Son but handed him over for us all, how will he not also give us everything else along with him? Who will bring a charge against God's chosen ones? It is God who acquits us, who will condemn? Christ Jesus it is who died - or, rather, was raised - who also is at the right hand of God, who indeed intercedes for us.

GOSPEL   *Mark 9:2-10*

Jesus took Peter, James, and John and led them up a high mountain apart by themselves. And he was transfigured before them, and his clothes became dazzling white, such as no fuller on earth could bleach them. Then Elijah appeared to them along with Moses, and they were conversing with Jesus. Then Peter said to Jesus in reply, "Rabbi, it is good that we are here! Let us make three tents: one for you, one for Moses, and one for Elijah." He hardly knew what to say, they were so terrified. Then a cloud came, casting a shadow over them; from the cloud came a voice, "This is my beloved Son. Listen to him." Suddenly, looking around, they no longer saw anyone but Jesus alone with them.

As they were coming down from the mountain, he charged them not to relate what they had seen to anyone, except when the Son of Man had risen from the dead. So they kept the matter to themselves, questioning what rising from the dead meant.

SECOND SUNDAY OF LENT / C   507

READING I   *Genesis 15:5-12, 17-18 / 27*

The Lord God took Abram outside and said, "Look up at the sky and count the stars, if you can. Just so," he added, "shall your descendants be." Abram put his faith in the LORD, who credited it to him as an act of righteousness.

He then said to him, "I am the LORD who brought you from Ur of the Chaldeans to give you this land as a possession." "O Lord GOD," he asked, "how am I to know that I shall possess it?" He answered him, "Bring me a three-year-old heifer, a three-year-old she-goat, a three-year-old ram, a turtledove, and a young pigeon." Abram brought him all these, split them in two, and placed each half opposite the other; but the birds he did not cut up. Birds of prey swooped down on the carcasses, but Abram stayed with them. As the sun was about to set, a trance fell upon Abram, and a deep, terrifying darkness enveloped him.

When the sun had set and it was dark, there appeared a smoking fire pot and a flaming torch, which passed between those pieces. It was on that occasion that the LORD made a covenant with Abram, saying: "To your descendants I give this land, from the Wadi of Egypt to the Great River, the Euphrates."

RESPONSORIAL PSALM   *Psalm 27:1, 7-8, 8-9, 13-14*

The Lord is my light and my sal - va - tion.

The LORD is my light and my salvation;
 whom should I fear?
The LORD is my life's refuge;
 of whom should I be afraid? ℟.

Hear, O LORD, the sound of my call;
 have pity on me, and answer me.
Of you my heart speaks; you my glance
 seeks. ℟.

Your presence, O LORD, I seek.
 Hide not your face from me;
do not in anger repel your servant.
 You are my helper: cast me not
  off. ℟.

I believe that I shall see the bounty of the
 LORD
 in the land of the living.
Wait for the LORD with courage;
 be stouthearted, and wait for the
  LORD. ℟.

READING II *Philippians 3:17—4:1 or 3:20—4:1*

For short form read only the parts in brackets.

Join with others in being imitators of me, [brothers and sisters,] and observe those who thus conduct themselves according to the model you have in us. For many, as I have often told you and now tell you even in tears, conduct themselves as enemies of the cross of Christ. Their end is destruction. Their God is their stomach; their glory is in their "shame." Their minds are occupied with earthly things. But [our citizenship is in heaven, and from it we also await a savior, the Lord Jesus Christ. He will change our lowly body to conform with his glorified body by the power that enables him also to bring all things into subjection to himself.

Therefore, my brothers and sisters, whom I love and long for, my joy and crown, in this way stand firm in the Lord, beloved.]

GOSPEL *Luke 9:28b-36*

Jesus took Peter, John, and James and went up the mountain to pray. While he was praying his face changed in appearance and his clothing became dazzling white. And behold, two men were conversing with him, Moses and Elijah, who appeared in glory and spoke of his exodus that he was going to accomplish in Jerusalem. Peter and his companions had been overcome by sleep, but becoming fully awake, they saw his glory and the two men standing with him. As they were about to part from him, Peter said to Jesus, "Master, it is good that we are here; let us make three tents, one for you, one for Moses, and one for Elijah." But he did not know what he was saying. While he was still speaking, a cloud came and cast a shadow over them, and they became frightened when they entered the cloud. Then from the cloud came a voice that said, "This is my chosen Son; listen to him." After the voice had spoken, Jesus was found alone. They fell silent and did not at that time tell anyone what they had seen.

---

508 THIRD SUNDAY OF LENT / A

READING I *Exodus 17:3-7 / 28*

In those days, in their thirst for water, the people grumbled against Moses, saying, "Why did you ever make us leave Egypt? Was it just to have us die here of thirst with our children and our livestock?" So Moses cried out to the LORD, "What shall I do with this people? A little more and they will stone me!" The LORD answered Moses, "Go over there in front of the people, along with some of the elders of Israel, holding in your hand, as you go, the staff with which you struck the river. I will be standing there in front of you on the rock in Horeb. Strike the rock, and the water will flow from it for the people to drink." This Moses did, in the presence of the elders of Israel. The place was called Massah and Meribah, because the Israelites quarreled there and tested the LORD, saying, "Is the LORD in our midst or not?"

RESPONSORIAL PSALM *Psalm 95:1-2, 6-7, 8-9*

If to - day you hear his voice,

hard - en not your hearts.

Come, let us sing joyfully to the LORD;
   let us acclaim the Rock of our
      salvation.
Let us come into his presence with
   thanksgiving;
   let us joyfully sing psalms to him. ℟.

Come, let us bow down in worship;
   let us kneel before the LORD who
      made us.
For he is our God,

and we are the people he shepherds,
   the flock he guides. ℟.

Oh, that today you would hear his
   voice:
   "Harden not your hearts as at
      Meribah,
as in the day of Massah in the desert,
   where your fathers tempted me;
they tested me though they had seen my
   works." ℟.

READING II
Romans 5:1-2, 5-8

Brothers and sisters: Since we have been justified by faith, we have peace with God through our Lord Jesus Christ, through whom we have gained access by faith to this grace in which we stand, and we boast in hope of the glory of God.

And hope does not disappoint, because the love of God has been poured out into our hearts through the Holy Spirit who has been given to us. For Christ, while we were still helpless, died at the appointed time for the ungodly. Indeed, only with difficulty does one die for a just person, though perhaps for a good person one might even find courage to die. But God proves his love for us in that while we were still sinners Christ died for us.

GOSPEL
John 4:5-42 or 4:5-15, 19b-26, 39a, 40-42

For short form read only the parts in brackets.

[Jesus came to a town of Samaria called Sychar, near the plot of land that Jacob had given to his son Joseph. Jacob's well was there. Jesus, tired from his journey, sat down there at the well. It was about noon.

A woman of Samaria came to draw water. Jesus said to her, "Give me a drink." His disciples had gone into the town to buy food. The Samaritan woman said to him, "How can you, a Jew, ask me, a Samaritan woman, for a drink?" (For Jews use nothing in common with Samaritans.) Jesus answered and said to her, "If you knew the gift of God and who is saying to you, 'Give me a drink,' you would have asked him and he would have given you living water." The woman said to him, "Sir, you do not even have a bucket and the cistern is deep; where then can you get this living water? Are you greater than our father Jacob, who gave us this cistern and drank from it himself with his children and his flocks?" Jesus answered and said to her, "Everyone who drinks this water will be thirsty again; but whoever drinks the water I shall give will never thirst; the water I shall give will become in him a spring of water welling up to eternal life." The woman said to him, "Sir, give me this water, so that I may not be thirsty or have to keep coming here to draw water."]

Jesus said to her, "Go call your husband and come back." The woman answered and said to him, "I do not have a husband." Jesus answered her, "You are right in saying, 'I do not have a husband.' For you have had five husbands, and the one you have now is not your husband. What you have said is true." The woman said to him, "Sir, [I can see that you are a prophet. Our ancestors worshiped on this mountain; but you people say that the place to worship is in Jerusalem." Jesus said to her, "Believe me, woman, the hour is coming when you will worship the Father neither on this mountain nor in Jerusalem. You people worship what you do not understand; we worship what we understand, because salvation is from the Jews. But the hour is coming, and is now here, when true worshipers will worship the Father in Spirit and truth; and indeed the Father seeks such people to worship him. God is Spirit, and those who worship him must worship in Spirit and truth." The woman said to him, "I know that the Messiah is coming, the one called the Christ; when he comes, he will tell us everything." Jesus said to her, "I am he, the one speaking with you."]

At that moment his disciples returned, and were amazed that he was talking with a woman, but still no one said, "What are you looking for?" or "Why are you talking with her?" The woman left her water jar and went into the town and said to the people, "Come see a man who told me everything I have done. Could he possibly be the Christ?" They went out of the town and came to him. Meanwhile, the disciples urged him, "Rabbi, eat." But he said to them, "I have food to eat of which you do not know." So the disciples said to one another, "Could someone have brought him something to eat?" Jesus said to them, "My food is to do the will of the one who sent me and to finish his work. Do you not say, 'In four months the harvest will be here'? I tell you, look up and see the fields ripe for the harvest. The reaper is already receiving payment and gathering crops for eternal life, so that the sower and reaper can rejoice together. For here the saying is verified that 'One sows and another reaps.' I sent you to reap what you have not worked for; others have done the work, and you are sharing the fruits of their work."

[Many of the Samaritans of that town began to believe in him] because of the word of the woman who testified, "He told me everything I have done." [When the Samaritans came to him, they invited him to stay with them; and he stayed there two days. Many more began to believe in him because of his word, and they said to the woman, "We no longer believe because of your word; for we have heard for ourselves, and we know that this is truly the savior of the world."]

FIRST SCRUTINY

During Lent, the elect (those catechumens who have been called to prepare for baptism at Easter) are called to come before the community for exorcisms and prayers. This takes place after the liturgy of the word on the Third, Fourth, and Fifth Sundays of Lent. These rites are intended to purify the hearts and minds of the elect, to strengthen them against temptation, to help them progress in the love of God.

The presider asks the assembly to pray in silence for the elect, then to join in intercessions for them. The presider lays hands on each of the elect and prays that the elect be delivered from the power of evil and become witnesses to the gospel. A song or psalm may be sung, then the elect are dismissed as usual and the faithful continue with the liturgy of the eucharist.

509 THIRD SUNDAY OF LENT / B

READING I *Exodus 20:1-17 or 20:1-3, 7-8, 12-17 / 29*
For short form read only the parts in brackets.

[In those days, God delivered all these commandments: "I, the LORD, am your God, who brought you out of the land of Egypt, that place of slavery. You shall not have other gods besides me.] You shall not carve idols for yourselves in the shape of anything in the sky above or on the earth below or in the waters beneath the earth; you shall not bow down before them or worship them. For I, the LORD, your God, am a jealous God, inflicting punishment for their fathers' wickedness on the children of those who hate me, down to the third and fourth generation; but bestowing mercy down to the thousandth generation on the children of those who love me and keep my commandments.

["You shall not take the name of the LORD, your God, in vain. For the LORD will not leave unpunished the one who takes his name in vain.

"Remember to keep holy the sabbath day.] Six days you may labor and do all your work, but the seventh day is the sabbath of the LORD, your God. No work may be done then either by you, or your son or daughter, or your male or female slave, or your beast, or by the alien who lives with you. In six days the Lord made the heavens and the earth, the sea and all that is in them; but on the seventh day he rested. That is why the LORD has blessed the sabbath day and made it holy.

["Honor your father and your mother, that you may have a long life in the land which the LORD, your God, is giving you.

"You shall not kill.
"You shall not commit adultery.
"You shall not steal.
"You shall not bear false witness against your neighbor.
"You shall not covet your neighbor's house. You shall not covet your neighbor's wife, nor his male or female slave, nor his ox or ass, nor anything else that belongs to him."]

RESPONSORIAL PSALM
Psalm 19:8, 9, 10, 11

Lord, you have the words of ev - er - last - ing life.

The law of the LORD is perfect,
    refreshing the soul;
the decree of the LORD is trustworthy,
    giving wisdom to the simple. ℟.

The precepts of the LORD are right,
    rejoicing the heart;
the command of the LORD is clear,
    enlightening the eye. ℟.

The fear of the LORD is pure,
    enduring forever;
the ordinances of the LORD are true,
    all of them just. ℟.

They are more precious than gold,
    than a heap of purest gold;
sweeter also than syrup
    or honey from the comb. ℟.

READING II
1 Corinthians 1:22-25

Brothers and sisters: Jews demand signs and Greeks look for wisdom, but we proclaim Christ crucified, a stumbling block to Jews and foolishness to Gentiles, but to those who are called, Jews and Greeks alike, Christ the power of God and the wisdom of God. For the foolishness of God is wiser than human wisdom, and the weakness of God is stronger than human strength.

GOSPEL
John 2:13-25

Since the Passover of the Jews was near, Jesus went up to Jerusalem. He found in the temple area those who sold oxen, sheep, and doves, as well as the money changers seated there. He made a whip out of cords and drove them all out of the temple area, with the sheep and oxen, and spilled the coins of the money changers and overturned their tables, and to those who sold doves he said, "Take these out of here, and stop making my Father's house a marketplace." His disciples recalled the words of Scripture, "Zeal for your house will consume me." At this the Jews answered and said to him, "What sign can you show us for doing this?" Jesus answered and said to them, "Destroy this temple and in three days I will raise it up." The Jews said, "This temple has been under construction for forty-six years, and you will raise it up in three days?" But he was speaking about the temple of his body. Therefore, when he was raised from the dead, his disciples remembered that he had said this, and they came to believe the Scripture and the word Jesus had spoken.

While he was in Jerusalem for the feast of Passover, many began to believe in his name when they saw the signs he was doing. But Jesus would not trust himself to them because he knew them all, and did not need anyone to testify about human nature. He himself understood it well.

FIRST SCRUTINY

See no. 508

510 THIRD SUNDAY OF LENT / C

READING I   *Exodus 3:1-8a, 13-15 / 30*

Moses was tending the flock of his father-in-law Jethro, the priest of Midian. Leading the flock across the desert, he came to Horeb, the mountain of God. There an angel of the LORD appeared to Moses in fire flaming out of a bush. As he looked on, he was surprised to see that the bush, though on fire, was not consumed. So Moses decided, "I must go over to look at this remarkable sight, and see why the bush is not burned."

When the LORD saw him coming over to look at it more closely, God called out to him from the bush, "Moses! Moses!" He answered, "Here I am." God said, "Come no nearer! Remove the sandals from your feet, for the place where you stand is holy ground. I am the God of your fathers," he continued, "the God of Abraham, the God of Isaac, the God of Jacob." Moses hid his face, for he was afraid to look at God. But the LORD said, "I have witnessed the affliction of my people in Egypt and have heard their cry of complaint against their slave drivers, so I know well what they are suffering. Therefore I have come down to rescue them from the hands of the Egyptians and lead them out of that land into a good and spacious land, a land flowing with milk and honey."

Moses said to God, "But when I go to the Israelites and say to them, 'The God of your fathers has sent me to you,' if they ask me, 'What is his name?' what am I to tell them?" God replied, "I am who am." Then he added, "This is what you shall tell the Israelites: I AM sent me to you." God spoke further to Moses, "Thus shall you say to the Israelites: The LORD, the God of your fathers, the God of Abraham, the God of Isaac, the God of Jacob, has sent me to you.

"This is my name forever;
        thus am I to be remembered through all generations."

RESPONSORIAL PSALM   *Psalm 103:1-2, 3-4, 6-7, 8, 11*

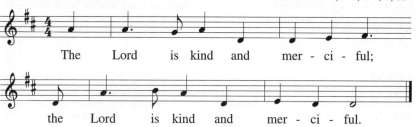

The Lord is kind and mer - ci - ful;
the Lord is kind and mer - ci - ful.

Bless the LORD, O my soul;
    and all my being, bless his holy
        name.
Bless the LORD, O my soul,
    and forget not all his benefits. ℟.

He pardons all your iniquities,
    heals all your ills.
He redeems your life from destruction,
    crowns you with kindness and
        compassion. ℟.

The LORD secures justice
    and the rights of all the oppressed.
He has made known his ways to Moses,
    and his deeds to the children of
        Israel. ℟.

Merciful and gracious is the LORD,
    slow to anger and abounding in
        kindness.
For as the heavens are high above the earth,
    so surpassing is his kindness toward
        those who fear him. ℟.

READING II   *1 Corinthians 10:1-6, 10-12*

I do not want you to be unaware, brothers and sisters, that our ancestors were all under the cloud and all passed through the sea, and all of them were baptized into Moses in the cloud and in the sea. All ate the same spiritual food, and all drank the same spiritual drink, for they drank from a spiritual rock that followed them, and the rock was the

Christ. Yet God was not pleased with most of them, for they were struck down in the desert.

These things happened as examples for us, so that we might not desire evil things, as they did. Do not grumble as some of them did, and suffered death by the destroyer. These things happened to them as an example, and they have been written down as a warning to us, upon whom the end of the ages has come. Therefore, whoever thinks he is standing secure should take care not to fall.

GOSPEL   *Luke 13:1-9*

Some people told Jesus about the Galileans whose blood Pilate had mingled with the blood of their sacrifices. Jesus said to them in reply, "Do you think that because these Galileans suffered in this way they were greater sinners than all other Galileans? By no means! But I tell you, if you do not repent, you will all perish as they did! Or those eighteen people who were killed when the tower at Siloam fell on them—do you think they were more guilty than everyone else who lived in Jerusalem? By no means! But I tell you, if you do not repent, you will all perish as they did!"

And he told them this parable: "There once was a person who had a fig tree planted in his orchard, and when he came in search of fruit on it but found none, he said to the gardener, 'For three years now I have come in search of fruit on this fig tree but have found none. So cut it down. Why should it exhaust the soil?' He said to him in reply, 'Sir, leave it for this year also, and I shall cultivate the ground around it and fertilize it; it may bear fruit in the future. If not you can cut it down.'"

FIRST SCRUTINY
See no. 508

FOURTH SUNDAY OF LENT / A   511

READING I   *1 Samuel 16:1b, 6-7, 10-13a / 31*

The LORD said to Samuel: "Fill your horn with oil, and be on your way. I am sending you to Jesse of Bethlehem, for I have chosen my king from among his sons."

As Jesse and his sons came to the sacrifice, Samuel looked at Eliab and thought, "Surely the Lord's anointed is here before him." But the LORD said to Samuel: "Do not judge from his appearance or from his lofty stature, because I have rejected him. Not as man sees does God see, because man sees the appearance but the LORD looks into the heart." In the same way Jesse presented seven sons before Samuel, but Samuel said to Jesse, "The LORD has not chosen any one of these." Then Samuel asked Jesse, "Are these all the sons you have?" Jesse replied, "There is still the youngest, who is tending the sheep." Samuel said to Jesse, "Send for him; we will not begin the sacrificial banquet until he arrives here." Jesse sent and had the young man brought to them. He was ruddy, a youth handsome to behold and making a splendid appearance. The LORD said, "There—anoint him, for this is the one!" Then Samuel, with the horn of oil in hand, anointed David in the presence of his brothers; and from that day on, the spirit of the LORD rushed upon David.

RESPONSORIAL PSALM   *Psalm 23:1-3a, 3b-4, 5, 6*

The Lord is my shep-herd; there is noth - ing I shall want.

The LORD is my shepherd; I shall not want.
In verdant pastures he gives me repose;
beside restful waters he leads me;
he refreshes my soul. ℟.

He guides me in right paths
   for his name's sake.
Even though I walk in the dark valley
   I fear no evil; for you are at my side
with your rod and your staff
   that give me courage. ℞.

You spread the table before me

in the sight of my foes;
   you anoint my head with oil;
   my cup overflows. ℞.

Only goodness and kindness follow me
   all the days of my life;
and I shall dwell in the house of the LORD
   for years to come. ℞.

READING II *Ephesians 5:8-14*

Brothers and sisters: You were once darkness, but now you are light in the Lord. Live as children of light, for light produces every kind of goodness and righteousness and truth. Try to learn what is pleasing to the Lord. Take no part in the fruitless works of darkness; rather expose them, for it is shameful even to mention the things done by them in secret; but everything exposed by the light becomes visible, for everything that becomes visible is light. Therefore, it says:
   "Awake, O sleeper,
   and arise from the dead,
   and Christ will give you light."

GOSPEL *John 9:1-41 or 9:1, 6-9, 13-17, 34-38*

For short form read only the parts in brackets.

[As Jesus passed by he saw a man blind from birth.]
His disciples asked him, "Rabbi, who sinned, this man or his parents, that he was born blind?" Jesus answered, "Neither he nor his parents sinned; it is so that the works of God might be made visible through him. We have to do the works of the one who sent me while it is day. Night is coming when no one can work. While I am in the world, I am the light of the world." When he had said this, [he spat on the ground and made clay with the saliva, and smeared the clay on his eyes, and said to him, "Go wash in the Pool of Siloam" (which means Sent). So he went and washed, and came back able to see.

His neighbors and those who had seen him earlier as a beggar said, "Isn't this the one who used to sit and beg?" Some said, "It is, " but others said, "No, he just looks like him." He said, "I am."] So they said to him, "How were your eyes opened?" He replied, "The man called Jesus made clay and anointed my eyes and told me, 'Go to Siloam and wash.' So I went there and washed and was able to see." And they said to him, "Where is he?" He said, "I don't know."

[They brought the one who was once blind to the Pharisees. Now Jesus had made clay and opened his eyes on a sabbath. So then the Pharisees also asked him how he was able to see. He said to them, "He put clay on my eyes, and I washed, and now I can see." So some of the Pharisees said, "This man is not from God, because he does not keep the sabbath." But others said, "How can a sinful man do such signs?" And there was a division among them. So they said to the blind man again, "What do you have to say about him, since he opened your eyes?" He said, "He is a prophet."]

Now the Jews did not believe that he had been blind and gained his sight until they summoned the parents of the one who had gained his sight. They asked them, "Is this your son, who you say was born blind? How does he now see?" His parents answered and said, "We know that this is our son and that he was born blind. We do not know how he sees now, nor do we know who opened his eyes. Ask him, he is of age; he can speak for himself." His parents said this because they were afraid of the Jews, for the Jews had already agreed that if anyone acknowledged him as the Christ, he would be expelled from the synagogue. For this reason his parents said, "He is of age; question him."

So a second time they called the man who had been blind and said to him, "Give God the praise! We know that this man is a sinner." He replied, "If he is a sinner, I do not know. One thing I do know is that I was blind and now I see." So they said to him, "What did he do to you? How did he open your eyes?" He answered them, "I told you already and you did not listen. Why do you want to hear it again? Do you want to become his disciples, too?" They ridiculed him and said, "You are that man's disciple; we are disciples of Moses! We know that God spoke to Moses, but we do not know where this one is from." The man answered and said to them, "This is what is so amazing, that you do not know where he is from, yet he opened my eyes. We know that God does not listen to sinners, but if one is devout and does his will, he listens to him. It is unheard of that anyone ever opened the eyes of a person born blind. If this man were not from God, he would not be able to do anything." [They answered and said to him, "You were born totally in sin, and are you trying to teach us?" Then they threw him out.

When Jesus heard that they had thrown him out, he found him and said, "Do you believe in the Son of Man?" He answered and said, "Who is he, sir, that I may believe in him?" Jesus said to him, "You have seen him, the one speaking with you is he." He said, "I do believe, Lord," and he worshiped him.] Then Jesus said, "I came into this world for judgment, so that those who do not see might see, and those who do see might become blind."

Some of the Pharisees who were with him heard this and said to him, "Surely we are not also blind, are we?" Jesus said to them, "If you were blind, you would have no sin; but now you are saying, 'We see,' so your sin remains.

SECOND SCRUTINY

During Lent, the elect (those catechumens who have been called to prepare for baptism at Easter) are called to come before the community for exorcisms and prayers. This takes place after the liturgy of the word on the Third, Fourth, and Fifth Sundays of Lent. These rites are intended to purify the hearts and minds of the elect, to strengthen them against temptation, to help them progress in the love of God.

The presider asks the assembly to pray in silence for the elect, then to join in inter-cessions for them. The presider lays hands on each of the elect and prays that the elect be delivered from the power of evil and become witnesses to the gospel. A song or psalm may be sung, then the elect are dismissed as usual and the faithful continue with the liturgy of the eucharist.

FOURTH SUNDAY OF LENT / B   512

READING I   *2 Chronicles 36:14-16, 19-23 / 32*

In those days, all the princes of Judah, the priests, and the people added infidelity to infidelity, practicing all the abominations of the nations and polluting the LORD's temple which he had consecrated in Jerusalem.

Early and often did the LORD, the God of their fathers, send his messengers to them, for he had compassion on his people and his dwelling place. But they mocked the messengers of God, despised his warnings, and scoffed at his prophets, until the anger of the LORD against his people was so inflamed that there was no remedy. Their enemies burnt the house of God, tore down the walls of Jerusalem, set all its palaces afire, and destroyed all its precious objects. Those who escaped the sword were carried captive to Babylon, where they became servants of the king of the Chaldeans and his sons until the kingdom of the Persians came to power. All this was to fulfill the word of the Lord spoken by Jeremiah: "Until the land has retrieved its lost sabbaths, during all the time it lies waste it shall have rest while seventy years are fulfilled."

In the first year of Cyrus, king of Persia, in order to fulfill the word of the LORD spoken by Jeremiah, the LORD inspired King Cyrus of Persia to issue this proclamation throughout his kingdom, both by word of mouth and in writing: "Thus says Cyrus, king of Persia: All the kingdoms of the earth the LORD, the God of heaven, has given to me, and he has also charged me to build him a house in Jerusalem, which is in Judah. Whoever, therefore, among you belongs to any part of his people, let him go up, and may his God be with him!"

RESPONSORIAL PSALM   *Psalm 137:1-2, 3, 4-5, 6*

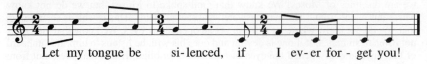

Let my tongue be si-lenced, if I ev-er for - get you!

By the streams of Babylon
    we sat and wept
when we remembered Zion.
    On the aspens of that land
we hung up our harps. ℟.

For there our captors asked of us
    the lyrics of our songs,
and our despoilers urged us to be joyous:
    "Sing for us the songs of Zion!" ℟.

How could we sing a song of the LORD
    in a foreign land?
If I forget you, Jerusalem,
    may my right hand be forgotten! ℟.

May my tongue cleave to my palate
    if I remember you not,
if I place not Jerusalem
    ahead of my joy. ℟.

READING II   *Ephesians 2:4-10*

Brothers and sisters: God, who is rich in mercy, because of the great love he had for us, even when we were dead in our transgressions, brought us to life with Christ (by grace you have been saved), raised us up with him, and seated us with him in the heavens in Christ Jesus, that in the ages to come he might show the immeasurable riches of his grace in his kindness to us in Christ Jesus. For by grace you have been saved through faith, and this is not from you; it is the gift of God; it is not from works, so no one may boast. For we are his handiwork, created in Christ Jesus for the good works that God has prepared in advance, that we should live in them.

GOSPEL   *John 3:14-21*

Jesus said to Nicodemus: "Just as Moses lifted up the serpent in the desert, so must the Son of Man be lifted up, so that everyone who believes in him may have eternal life."

For God so loved the world that he gave his only Son, so that everyone who believes in him might not perish but might have eternal life. For God did not send his Son into the world to condemn the world, but that the world might be saved through him. Whoever believes in him will not be condemned, but whoever does not believe has already been condemned, because he has not believed in the name of the only Son of God. And this is the verdict, that the light came into the world, but people preferred darkness to light, because their works were evil. For everyone who does wicked things hates the light and does not come toward the light, so that his works might not be exposed. But whoever lives the truth comes to the light, so that his works may be clearly seen as done in God.

SECOND SCRUTINY

See no. 511

---

513   FOURTH SUNDAY OF LENT / C

READING I   *Joshua 5:9a, 10-12 / 33*

The LORD said to Joshua, "Today I have removed the reproach of Egypt from you."

While the Israelites were encamped at Gilgal on the plains of Jericho, they celebrated the Passover on the evening of the fourteenth of the month. On the day after the Passover, they ate of the produce of the land in the form of unleavened cakes and parched grain. On that same day after the Passover, on which they ate of the produce of the land, the manna ceased. No longer was there manna for the Israelites, who that year ate of the yield of the land of Canaan.

RESPONSORIAL PSALM

Psalm 34:2-3, 4-5, 6-7

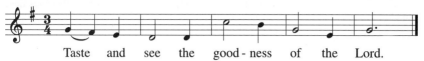

Taste and see the good - ness of the Lord.

I will bless the LORD at all times;
  his praise shall be ever in my mouth.
Let my soul glory in the LORD;
  the lowly will hear me and be glad. ℟.

Glorify the LORD with me,
  let us together extol his name.
I sought the LORD, and he answered me
  and delivered me from all my fears. ℟.

Look to him that you may be radiant
  with joy,
  and your faces may not blush with
  shame.
When the poor one called out, the LORD
  heard,
  and from all his distress he saved
  him. ℟.

READING II

2 Corinthians 5:17-21

Brothers and sisters: Whoever is in Christ is a new creation: the old things have passed away; behold, new things have come. And all this is from God, who has reconciled us to himself through Christ and given us the ministry of reconciliation, namely, God was reconciling the world to himself in Christ, not counting their trespasses against them and entrusting to us the message of reconciliation. So we are ambassadors for Christ, as if God were appealing through us. We implore you on behalf of Christ, be reconciled to God. For our sake he made him to be sin who did not know sin, so that we might become the righteousness of God in him.

GOSPEL

Luke 15:1-3, 11-32

Tax collectors and sinners were all drawing near to listen to Jesus, but the Pharisees and scribes began to complain, saying, "This man welcomes sinners and eats with them." So to them Jesus addressed this parable: "A man had two sons, and the younger son said to his father, 'Father give me the share of your estate that should come to me.' So the father divided the property between them. After a few days, the younger son collected all his belongings and set off to a distant country where he squandered his inheritance on a life of dissipation. When he had freely spent everything, a severe famine struck that country, and he found himself in dire need. So he hired himself out to one of the local citizens who sent him to his farm to tend the swine. And he longed to eat his fill of the pods on which the swine fed, but nobody gave him any. Coming to his senses he thought, 'How many of my father's hired workers have more than enough food to eat, but here am I, dying from hunger. I shall get up and go to my father and I shall say to him, "Father, I have sinned against heaven and against you. I no longer deserve to be called your son; treat me as you would treat one of your hired workers."' So he got up and went back to his father. While he was still a long way off, his father caught sight of him, and was filled with compassion. He ran to his son, embraced him and kissed him. His son said to him, 'Father, I have sinned against heaven and against you; I no longer deserve to be called your son.' But his father ordered his servants, 'Quickly bring the finest robe and put it on him; put a ring on his finger and sandals on his feet. Take the fattened calf and slaughter it. Then let us celebrate with a feast, because this son of mine was dead, and has come to life again; he was lost, and has been found.' Then the celebration began. Now the older son had been out in the field and, on his way back, as he neared the house, he heard the sound of music and dancing. He called one of the servants and asked what this might mean. The servant said to him, 'Your brother has returned and your father has slaughtered the fattened calf because he has him back safe and sound.' He became angry, and when he refused to enter the house, his father came out and pleaded with him. He said to his father in reply, 'Look, all these years I served you and not once did I disobey your orders; yet you never gave me even a young goat to feast on with my friends. But when your son returns who swallowed up your property with prostitutes, for him you slaughter the fattened calf.' He said to him, 'My son, you are here with me always; everything I have is yours. But now we must celebrate and rejoice, because your brother was dead and has come to life again; he was lost and has been found.'"

SECOND SCRUTINY

See no. 511

514 FIFTH SUNDAY OF LENT / A

READING I
Ezekiel 37:12-14 / 34

Thus says the Lord GOD: O my people, I will open your graves and have you rise from them, and bring you back to the land of Israel. Then you shall know that I am the LORD, when I open your graves and have you rise from them, O my people! I will put my spirit in you that you may live, and I will settle you upon your land; thus you shall know that I am the LORD. I have promised, and I will do it, says the LORD.

RESPONSORIAL PSALM
Psalm 130:1-2, 3-4, 5-6, 7-8

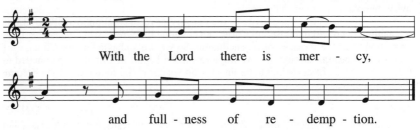

With the Lord there is mer - cy, and full - ness of re - demp - tion.

Out of the depths I cry to you, O LORD;
  LORD, hear my voice!
Let your ears be attentive
  to my voice in supplication. ℟.

If you, O LORD, mark iniquities,
  LORD, who can stand?
But with you is forgiveness,
  that you may be revered. ℟.

I trust in the LORD;
  my soul trusts in his word.
More than sentinels wait for the dawn,
  let Israel wait for the LORD. ℟.

For with the LORD is kindness
  and with him is plenteous
    redemption;
and he will redeem Israel
  from all their iniquities. ℟.

READING II
Romans 8:8-11

Brothers and sisters: Those who are in the flesh cannot please God. But you are not in the flesh; on the contrary, you are in the spirit, if only the Spirit of God dwells in you. Whoever does not have the Spirit of Christ does not belong to him. But if Christ is in you, although the body is dead because of sin, the spirit is alive because of righteousness. If the Spirit of the one who raised Jesus from the dead dwells in you, the one who raised Christ from the dead will give life to your mortal bodies also, through his Spirit dwelling in you.

GOSPEL
John 11:1-45 or 11:3-7, 17, 20-27, 33b-45

For short form read only the parts in brackets.

Now a man was ill, Lazarus from Bethany, the village of Mary and her sister Martha. Mary was the one who had anointed the Lord with perfumed oil and dried his feet with her hair; it was her brother Lazarus who was ill. So [the sisters sent word to Jesus saying, "Master, the one you love is ill." When Jesus heard this he said, "This illness is not to end in death, but is for the glory of God, that the Son of God may be glorified through it." Now Jesus loved Martha and her sister and Lazarus. So when he heard that he was ill, he remained for two days in the place where he was. Then after this he said to his disciples, "Let us go back to Judea."] The disciples said to him, "Rabbi, the Jews were just trying to stone you, and you want to go back there?" Jesus answered, "Are there not twelve hours in a day? If one walks during the day, he does not stumble, because he sees the light of this world. But if one walks at night, he stumbles, because the light is not in him." He said this, and then told them, "Our friend Lazarus is asleep, but I am going to awaken him." So the disciples said to him, "Master, if he is asleep, he will be saved." But Jesus was talking about his death, while they thought that he meant ordinary sleep. So then Jesus said to them clearly, "Lazarus has died. And I am glad for you that I was not there, that you may believe. Let us go to him." So Thomas, called Didymus, said to his fellow disciples, "Let us also go to die with him."

[When Jesus arrived, he found that Lazarus had already been in the tomb for four days.] Now Bethany was near Jerusalem, only about two miles away. And many of the Jews had come to Martha and Mary to comfort them about their brother. [When Martha heard that Jesus was coming, she went to meet him; but Mary sat at home. Martha said to Jesus, "Lord, if you had been here, my brother would not have died. But even now I know that whatever you ask of God, God will give you." Jesus said to her, "Your brother will rise." Martha said to him, "I know he will rise, in the resurrection on the last day." Jesus told her, "I am the resurrection and the life; whoever believes in me, even if he dies, will live, and everyone who lives and believes in me will never die. Do you believe this?" She said to him, "Yes, Lord. I have come to believe that you are the Christ, the Son of God, the one who is coming into the world."]

When she had said this, she went and called her sister Mary secretly, saying, "The teacher is here and is asking for you." As soon as she heard this, she rose quickly and went to him. For Jesus had not yet come into the village, but was still where Martha had met him. So when the Jews who were with her in the house comforting her saw Mary get up quickly and go out, they followed her, presuming that she was going to the tomb to weep there. When Mary came to where Jesus was and saw him, she fell at his feet and said to him, "Lord, if you had been here, my brother would not have died." When Jesus saw her weeping and the Jews who had come with her weeping, [he became perturbed and deeply troubled, and said, "Where have you laid him?" They said to him, "Sir, come and see." And Jesus wept. So the Jews said, "See how he loved him." But some of them said, "Could not the one who opened the eyes of the blind man have done something so that this man would not have died?"

So Jesus, perturbed again, came to the tomb. It was a cave, and a stone lay across it. Jesus said, "Take away the stone." Martha, the dead man's sister, said to him, "Lord, by now there will be a stench; he has been dead for four days." Jesus said to her, "Did I not tell you that if you believe you will see the glory of God?" So they took away the stone. And Jesus raised his eyes and said, "Father, I thank you for hearing me. I know that you always hear me; but because of the crowd here I have said this, that they may believe that you sent me." And when he had said this, he cried out in a loud voice, "Lazarus, come out!" The dead man came out, tied hand and foot with burial bands, and his face was wrapped in a cloth. So Jesus said to them, "Untie him and let him go."

Now many of the Jews who had come to Mary and seen what he had done began to believe in him.]

THIRD SCRUTINY

During Lent, the elect (those catechumens who have been called to prepare for baptism at Easter) are called to come before the community for exorcisms and prayers. This takes place after the liturgy of the word on the Third, Fourth, and Fifth Sundays of Lent. These rites are intended to purify the hearts and minds of the elect, to strengthen them against temptation, to help them progress in the love of God.

The presider asks the assembly to pray in silence for the elect, then to join in inter-cessions for them. The presider lays hands on each of the elect and prays that the elect be delivered from the power of evil and become witnesses to the gospel. A song or psalm may be sung, then the elect are dismissed as usual and the faithful continue with the liturgy of the eucharist.

515 FIFTH SUNDAY OF LENT / B

READING I
Jeremiah 31:31-34 / 35

The days are coming, says the LORD, when I will make a new covenant with the house of Israel and the house of Judah. It will not be like the covenant I made with their fathers the day I took them by the hand to lead them forth from the land of Egypt; for they broke my covenant, and I had to show myself their master, says the LORD. But this is the covenant that I will make with the house of Israel after those days, says the LORD. I will place my law within them and write it upon their hearts; I will be their God, and they shall be my people. No longer will they have need to teach their friends and relatives how to know the LORD. All, from least to greatest, shall know me, says the LORD, for I will forgive their evildoing and remember their sin no more.

RESPONSORIAL PSALM
Psalm 51:3-4, 12-13, 14-15

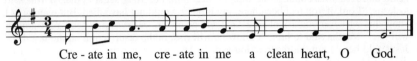

Cre - ate in me, cre - ate in me a clean heart, O God.

Have mercy on me, O God, in your
    goodness;
    in the greatness of your compassion
      wipe out my offense.
Thoroughly wash me from my guilt
    and of my sin cleanse me. ℟.

A clean heart create for me, O God,
    and a steadfast spirit renew within

me.
Cast me not out from your presence,
    and your Holy Spirit take not from
    me. ℟.

Give me back the joy of your salvation,
    and a willing spirit sustain in me.
I will teach transgressors your ways,
    and sinners shall return to you. ℟.

READING II
Hebrews 5:7-9

In the days when Christ Jesus was in the flesh, he offered prayers and supplications with loud cries and tears to the one who was able to save him from death, and he was heard because of his reverence. Son though he was, he learned obedience from what he suffered; and when he was made perfect, he became the source of eternal salvation for all who obey him.

GOSPEL
John 12:20-33

Some Greeks who had come to worship at the Passover Feast came to Philip, who was from Bethsaida in Galilee, and asked him, "Sir, we would like to see Jesus." Philip went and told Andrew; then Andrew and Philip went and told Jesus. Jesus answered them, "The hour has come for the Son of Man to be glorified. Amen, amen, I say to you, unless a grain of wheat falls to the ground and dies, it remains just a grain of wheat; but if it dies, it produces much fruit. Whoever loves his life loses it, and whoever hates his life in this world will preserve it for eternal life. Whoever serves me must follow me, and where I am, there also will my servant be. The Father will honor whoever serves me.

"I am troubled now. Yet what should I say? 'Father, save me from this hour'? But it was for this purpose that I came to this hour. Father, glorify your name." Then a voice came from heaven, "I have glorified it and will glorify it again." The crowd there heard it and said it was thunder; but others said, "An angel has spoken to him." Jesus answered and said, "This voice did not come for my sake but for yours. Now is the time of judgment on this world; now the ruler of this world will be driven out. And when I am lifted up from the earth, I will draw everyone to myself." He said this indicating the kind of death he would die.

THIRD SCRUTINY
See no. 514

FIFTH SUNDAY OF LENT / C 516

READING I
Isaiah 43:16-21 / 36

Thus says the LORD,
  who opens a way in the sea
  and a path in the mighty waters,
who leads out chariots and horsemen,
  a powerful army,
till they lie prostrate together, never to
    rise,
  snuffed out and quenched like a wick.
Remember not the events of the past,
  the things of long ago consider not;
see, I am doing something new!

Now it springs forth, do you not
  perceive it?
In the desert I make a way,
  in the wasteland, rivers.
Wild beasts honor me,
  jackals and ostriches,
for I put water in the desert
  and rivers in the wasteland
for my chosen people to drink,
the people whom I formed for myself,
  that they might announce my praise.

RESPONSORIAL PSALM
Psalm 126:1-2, 2-3, 4-5, 6

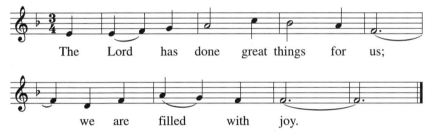

The Lord has done great things for us;
we are filled with joy.

When the LORD brought back the captives
  of Zion,
  we were like men dreaming.
Then our mouth was filled with laughter,
  and our tongue with rejoicing. ℟.

Then they said among the nations,
  "The LORD has done great things for
    them."
The LORD has done great things for us;
  we are glad indeed. ℟.

Restore our fortunes, O LORD,
  like the torrents in the southern
    desert.
Those that sow in tears
  shall reap rejoicing. ℟.

Although they go forth weeping,
  carrying the seed to be sown,
They shall come back rejoicing,
  carrying their sheaves. ℟.

READING II
Philippians 3:8-14

Brothers and sisters: I consider everything as a loss because of the supreme good of knowing Christ Jesus my Lord. For his sake I have accepted the loss of all things and I consider them so much rubbish, that I may gain Christ and be found in him, not having any righteousness of my own based on the law but that which comes through faith in Christ, the righteousness from God, depending on faith to know him and the power of his resurrection and the sharing of his sufferings by being conformed to his death, if somehow I may attain the resurrection from the dead.

It is not that I have already taken hold of it or have already attained perfect maturity, but I continue my pursuit in hope that I may possess it, since I have indeed been taken possession of by Christ Jesus. Brothers and sisters, I for my part do not consider myself to have taken possession. Just one thing: forgetting what lies behind but straining forward to what lies ahead, I continue my pursuit toward the goal, the prize of God's upward calling, in Christ Jesus.

GOSPEL   *John 8:1-11*

Jesus went to the Mount of Olives. But early in the morning he arrived again in the temple area, and all the people started coming to him, and he sat down and taught them. Then the scribes and the Pharisees brought a woman who had been caught in adultery and made her stand in the middle. They said to him, "Teacher, this woman was caught in the very act of committing adultery. Now in the law, Moses commanded us to stone such women. So what do you say?" They said this to test him, so that they could have some charge to bring against him. Jesus bent down and began to write on the ground with his finger. But when they continued asking him, he straightened up and said to them, "Let the one among you who is without sin be the first to throw a stone at her." Again he bent down and wrote on the ground. And in response, they went away one by one, beginning with the elders. So he was left alone with the woman before him. Then Jesus straightened up and said to her, "Woman, where are they? Has no one condemned you?" She replied, "No one, sir." Then Jesus said, "Neither do I condemn you. Go, and from now on do not sin any more."

THIRD SCRUTINY
See no. 514

517 PASSION SUNDAY (PALM SUNDAY)

Passion or Palm Sunday is the last Sunday in Lent. Its closeness to the end of Lent has given this liturgy two distinct features: the procession with palms and the gospel reading of the Lord's passion. The blessing and carrying of palms celebrates Jesus' entrance into Jerusalem to accomplish his paschal mystery. The reading of the passion comes as a conclusion to all the gospel readings of the lenten Sundays: these scriptures yearly prepare catechumens and the faithful to approach the celebration of Christ's death and resurrection. That celebration takes place most especially in the sacraments of initiation at the Easter Vigil.

COMMEMORATION OF THE LORD'S ENTRANCE INTO JERUSALEM

This rite may be very simple or may involve the entire assembly in a procession with the blessing of palms and the gospel reading of Jesus' entrance into Jerusalem. Depending on the local church, then, some of the following hymns, psalms and readings will be used.

518 OPENING ANTIPHON
The following or another appropriate acclamation may be sung.

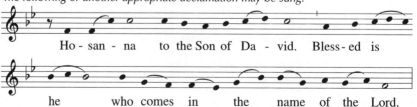

Ho - san - na to the Son of Da - vid. Bless- ed is he who comes in the name of the Lord.

O King of Is - ra - el.   Ho- san -na   in the high-est.

Music: Mode VII; adapt. by Richard Proulx, © 1986, GIA Publications, Inc.

BLESSING OF BRANCHES   519

All hold branches as these are blessed. The branches may be of palm or from a tree that is native to the area. The green or flowering branches signify the victory of life.

GOSPEL / A   *Matthew 21:1-11 / 37*

When Jesus and the disciples drew near Jerusalem and came to Bethphage on the Mount of Olives, Jesus sent two disciples, saying to them, "Go into the village opposite you, and immediately you will find an ass tethered, and a colt with her. Untie them and bring them here to me. And if anyone should say anything to you, reply, 'The master has need of them.' Then he will send them at once." This happened so that what had been spoken through the prophet might be fulfilled:
  "Say to daughter Zion,
  'Behold, your king comes to you,
  meek and riding on an ass,
  and on a colt, the foal of a beast of burden.'"
The disicples went and did as Jesus had ordered them. They brought the ass and the colt and laid their cloaks over them, and he sat upon them. The very large crowd spread their cloaks on the road, while others cut branches from the trees and strewed them on the road. The crowds preceding him and those following kept crying out and saying:
  "Hosanna to the Son of David;
  blessed is he who comes in the name of the Lord;
  hosanna in the highest."
And when he entered Jerusalem the whole city was shaken and asked, "Who is this?" And the crowds replied, "This is Jesus the prophet, from Nazareth in Galilee."

GOSPEL / B   *Mark 11:1-10*

When Jesus and his disciples drew near to Jerusalem, to Bethphage and Bethany at the Mount of Olives, he sent two of his disciples and said to them, "Go into the village opposite you, and immediately on entering it, you will find a colt tethered on which no one has ever sat. Untie it and bring it here. If anyone should say to you, 'Why are you doing this?' reply, 'The Master has need of it and will send it back here at once.'" So they went off and found a colt tethered at a gate outside on the street, and they untied it. Some of the bystanders said to them, "What are you doing, untying the colt?" They answered them just as Jesus had told them to, and they permitted them to do it. So they brought the colt to Jesus and put their cloaks over it. And he sat on it. Many people spread their cloaks on the road, and others spread leafy branches that they had cut from the fields. Those preceding him as well as those following kept crying out:
  "Hosanna!
  Blessed is he who comes in the name of the Lord!
  Blessed is the kingdom of our father David that is to come!
  Hosanna in the highest!"

Or:

GOSPEL / B   *John 12:12-16*

When the great crowd that had come to the feast heard that Jesus was coming to Jerusalem, they took palm branches and went out to meet him, and cried out:
  "Hosanna!
  "Blessed is he who comes in the name of the Lord,
  the king of Israel."
Jesus found an ass and sat upon it, as is written:

"Fear no more, O daughter Zion;
see, your king comes, seated upon an ass's colt."
His disciples did not understand this at first, but when Jesus had been glorified they remembered that these things were written about him and that they had done this for him.

GOSPEL / C

Luke 19:28-40

Jesus proceeded on his journey up to Jerusalem. As he drew near to Bethphage and Bethany at the place called the Mount of Olives, he sent two of his disciples. He said, "Go into the village opposite you, and as you enter it you will find a colt tethered on which no one has ever sat. Untie it and bring it here. And if anyone should ask you, 'Why are you untying it?' you will answer, 'The Master has need of it.'" So those who had been sent went off and found everything just as he had told them. And as they were untying the colt, its owners said to them, "Why are you untying this colt?" They answered, "The Master has need of it." So they brought it to Jesus, threw their cloaks over the colt, and helped Jesus to mount. As he rode along, the people were spreading their cloaks on the road; and now as he was approaching the slope of the Mount of Olives, the whole multitude of his disciples began to praise God aloud with joy for all the mighty deeds they had seen. They proclaimed:
"Blessed is the king who comes
in the name of the Lord.
Peace in heaven
and glory in the highest."
Some of the Pharisees in the crowd said to him, "Teacher, rebuke your disciples." He said in reply, "I tell you, if they keep silent, the stones will cry out!"

520   PROCESSION

All join in the procession or at least in the song. Such a movement of people expresses the experience of Lent: the church has been called to move on, to go ever further toward the paschal mystery of death and resurrection. Hymn no. 244, or another appropriate song is sung.

The commemoration of the Lord's entrance into Jerusalem, whether this is done in a simple or solemn manner, concludes with the opening prayer of the Mass.

521   LITURGY OF THE WORD / ABC

READING I

Isaiah 50:4-7 / 38

The Lord GOD has given me
a well-trained tongue,
that I might know how to speak to the weary
a word that will rouse them.
Morning after morning
he opens my ear that I may hear;
and I have not rebelled,
have not turned back.
I gave my back to those who beat me,
my cheeks to those who plucked my beard;
my face I did not shield
from buffets and spitting.

The Lord GOD is my help,
therefore I am not disgraced;
I have set my face like flint,
knowing that I shall not be put to shame.

RESPONSORIAL PSALM

Psalm 22:8-9, 17-18, 19-20, 23-24

My God, my God, why have you a - ban - doned me?

All who see me scoff at me;
    they mock me with parted lips, they
      wag their heads:
"He relied on the LORD; let him deliver
      him,
    let him rescue him, if he loves
      him." ℟.

Indeed, many dogs surround me,
    a pack of evildoers closes in upon
      me;
They have pierced my hands and my feet;
    I can count all my bones. ℟.

They divide my garments among them,
    and for my vesture they cast lots.
But you, O LORD, be not far from me;
    O my help, hasten to aid me. ℟.

I will proclaim your name to my
      brethren;
    in the midst of the assembly I will
      praise you:
"You who fear the LORD, praise him;
    all you descendants of Jacob, give
      glory to him;
revere him, all you descendants of
      Israel!" ℟.

READING II
Philippians 2:6-11

Christ Jesus, though he was in the form
    of God,
    did not regard equality with God
      something to be grasped.
Rather, he emptied himself,
    taking the form of a slave,
    coming in human likeness;
    and found human in appearance,
    he humbled himself,
    becoming obedient to the point of
      death,

    even death on a cross.
Because of this, God greatly exalted him
    and bestowed on him the name
    which is above every name,
    that at the name of Jesus
    every knee should bend,
    of those in heaven and on earth and
      under the earth,
    and every tongue confess that
    Jesus Christ is Lord,
    to the glory of God the Father.

GOSPEL / A
Matthew 26:14—27:66 or 27:11-54   **522**

The symbols of the following passion narrative represent:
    + *Christ;*   *N narrator;*   *V voice;*   *C crowd.*

N The Passion of our Lord Jesus Christ according to Matthew.

For short form read only the part in brackets.

N One of the Twelve, who was called Judas Iscariot, went to the chief priests and said,

V "What are you willing to give me if I hand him over to you?"

N They paid him thirty pieces of silver, and from that time on he looked for an opportunity to hand him over.

On the first day of the Feast of Unleavened Bread, the disciples approached Jesus and said,

V "Where do you want us to prepare for you to eat the Passover?"

N He said,

+ "Go into the city to a certain man and tell him, 'The teacher says, "My appointed time draws near; in your house I shall celebrate the Passover with my disciples."'"

N The disciples then did as Jesus had ordered, and prepared the Passover. When it was evening, he reclined at table with the Twelve. And while they were eating, he said,

+ "Amen, I say to you, one of you will betray me."

N Deeply distressed at this, they began to say to him one after another,

V "Surely it is not I, Lord?"

N He said in reply,

+ "He who has dipped his hand into the dish with me is the one who will betray me. The Son of Man indeed goes, as it is written of him, but woe to that man by whom the Son of Man is betrayed. It would be better for that man if he had never been born."

N Then Judas, his betrayer, said in reply,

V "Surely it is not I, Rabbi?"

N He answered,

+ "You have said so."

N While they were eating, Jesus took bread, said the blessing, broke it, and giving it to his disciples said,

+ "Take and eat; this is my body."

N Then he took a cup, gave thanks, and gave it to them, saying,

+ "Drink from it, all of you, for this is my blood of the covenant, which will be shed on behalf of many for the forgiveness of sins. I tell you, from now on I shall not drink this fruit of the vine until the day when I drink it with you new in the kingdom of my Father."

N Then, after singing a hymn, they went out to the Mount of Olives.

Then Jesus said to them,

+ "This night all of you will have your faith in me shaken, for it is written: *'I will strike the shepherd, and the sheep of the flock will be dispersed;'* but after I have been raised up, I shall go before you to Galilee."

N Peter said to him in reply,

V "Though all may have their faith in you shaken, mine will never be."

N Jesus said to him,

+ "Amen, I say to you, this very night before the cock crows, you will deny me three times."

N Peter said to him,

V "Even though I should have to die with you, I will not deny you."

N And all the disciples spoke likewise.

Then Jesus came with them to a place called Gethsemane, and he said to his disciples,

+ "Sit here while I go over there and pray."

N He took along Peter and the two sons of Zebedee, and began to feel sorrow and distress. Then he said to them,

+ "My soul is sorrowful even to death. Remain here and keep watch with me."

N He advanced a little and fell prostrate in prayer, saying,

+ "My Father, if it is possible, let this cup pass from me; yet, not as I will, but as you will."

N When he returned to his disciples he found them asleep. He said to Peter,

+ "So you could not keep watch with me for one hour? Watch and pray that you may not undergo the test. The spirit is willing, but the flesh is weak."

N Withdrawing a second time, he prayed again,

+ "My Father, if it is not possible that this cup pass without my drinking it, your will be done!"

N Then he returned once more and found them asleep, for they could not keep their eyes open. He left them and withdrew again and prayed a third time, saying the same thing again. Then he returned to his disciples and said to them,

+ "Are you still sleeping and taking your rest? Behold, the hour is at hand when the Son of Man is to be handed over to sinners. Get up, let us go. Look, my betrayer is at hand."

N While he was still speaking, Judas, one of the Twelve, arrived, accompanied by a large crowd, with swords and clubs, who had come from the chief priests and the elders of the people. His betrayer had arranged a sign with them, saying,

V "The man I shall kiss is the one; arrest him."

N Immediately he went over to Jesus and said,

V "Hail, Rabbi!"

N and he kissed him. Jesus answered him,

+ "Friend, do what you have come for."

N Then stepping forward they laid hands on Jesus and arrested him. And behold, one of those who accompanied Jesus put his hand to his sword, drew it, and struck the high priest's servant, cutting off his ear. Then Jesus said to him,

+ "Put your sword back into its sheath, for all who take the sword will perish by the sword. Do you think that I cannot call upon my Father and he will not provide me at this moment with more than twelve legions of angels? But then how would the Scriptures be fulfilled which say that it must come to pass in this way?"

N At that hour Jesus said to the crowds,

+ "Have you come out as against a robber, with swords and clubs to seize me? Day after day I sat teaching in the temple area, yet you did not arrest me. But all this has come to pass that the writings of the prophets may be fulfilled."

N Then all the disciples left him and fled.

Those who had arrested Jesus led him away to Caiaphas the high priest, where the scribes and the elders were assembled. Peter was following him at a distance as far as the high priest's courtyard, and going inside he sat down with the servants to see the outcome.

The chief priests and the entire Sanhedrin kept trying to obtain false testimony against Jesus in order to put him to death, but they found none, though many false witnesses came forward. Finally two came forward who stated,

C "This man said, 'I can destroy the temple of God and within three days rebuild it.'"

N The high priest rose and addressed him,

V "Have you no answer? What are these men testifying against you?"

N But Jesus was silent. Then the high priest said to him,

V "I order you to tell us under oath before the living God whether you are the Christ, the Son of God."

N Jesus said to him in reply,

+ "You have said so. But I tell you: From now on you will see 'the Son of Man seated at the right hand of the Power' and 'coming on the clouds of heaven.'"

N Then the high priest tore his robes and said,

V "He has blasphemed! What further need have we of witnesses? You have now heard the blasphemy; what is your opinion?"

N They said in reply,

C "He deserves to die!"

N Then they spat in his face and struck him, while some slapped him, saying,

C "Prophesy for us, Christ: who is it that struck you?"

N Now Peter was sitting outside in the courtyard. One of the maids came over to him and said,

C "You too were with Jesus the Galilean."

N But he denied it in front of everyone, saying,

V "I do not know what you are talking about!"

N As he went out to the gate, another girl saw him and said to those who were there,

C "This man was with Jesus the Nazorean."

N Again he denied it with an oath,

V "I do not know the man!"

N A little later the bystanders came over and said to Peter,

C "Surely you too are one of them; even your speech gives you away."

N At that he began to curse and to swear,

V "I do not know the man."

N And immediately a cock crowed. Then Peter remembered the word that Jesus had spoken: "Before the cock crows you will deny me three times." He went out and began to weep bitterly.

When it was morning, all the chief priests and the elders of the people took counsel against Jesus to put him to death. They bound him, led him away, and handed him over to Pilate, the governor.

Then Judas, his betrayer, seeing that Jesus had been condemned, deeply regretted what he had done. He returned the thirty pieces of silver to the chief priests and elders, saying,

V "I have sinned in betraying innocent blood."

N They said,

C "What is that to us? Look to it yourself."

N Flinging the money into the temple, he departed and went off and hanged himself. The chief priests gathered up the money, but said,

C "It is not lawful to deposit this in the temple treasury, for it is the price of blood."

N After consultation, they used it to buy the potter's field as a burial place for foreigners. That is why that field even today is called the Field of Blood. Then was fulfilled what had been said through Jeremiah the prophet, *And they took the thirty pieces of silver, the value of a man with a price on his head, a price set by some of the Israelites, and they paid it out for the potter's field just as the Lord had commanded me."*

Now [Jesus stood before the governor, and he questioned him,

V "Are you the king of the Jews?"

N Jesus said,

+ "You say so."

N And when he was accused by the chief priests and elders, he made no answer. Then Pilate said to him,

V "Do you not hear how many things they are testifying against you?"

N But he did not answer him one word, so that the governor was greatly amazed.

Now on the occasion of the feast the governor was accustomed to release to the crowd one prisoner whom they wished. And at that time they had a notorious prisoner called Barabbas. So when they had assembled, Pilate said to them,

V "Which one do you want me to release to you, Barabbas, or Jesus called Christ?"

N For he knew that it was out of envy that

they had handed him over. While he was still seated on the bench, his wife sent him a message, "Have nothing to do with that righteous man. I suffered much in a dream today because of him."

The chief priests and the elders persuaded the crowds to ask for Barabbas but to destroy Jesus. The governor said to them in reply,

V "Which of the two do you want me to release to you?"

N They answered,

C "Barabbas!"

N Pilate said to them,

V "Then what shall I do with Jesus called Christ?"

N They all said,

C "Let him be crucified!"

N But he said,

V "Why? What evil has he done?"

N They only shouted the louder,

C "Let him be crucified!"

N When Pilate saw that he was not succeeding at all, but that a riot was breaking out instead, he took water and washed his hands in the sight of the crowd, saying,

V "I am innocent of this man's blood. Look to it yourselves."

N And the whole people said in reply,

C "His blood be upon us and upon our children."

N Then he released Barabbas to them, but after he had Jesus scourged, he handed him over to be crucified.

Then the soldiers of the governor took Jesus inside the praetorium and gathered the whole cohort around him. They stripped off his clothes and threw a scarlet military cloak about him. Weaving a crown out of thorns, they placed it on his head, and a reed in his right hand. And kneeling before him, they mocked him, saying,

C "Hail, King of the Jews!"

N They spat upon him and took the reed and kept striking him on the head. And when they had mocked him, they stripped him of the cloak, dressed him in his own clothes, and led him off to crucify him.

As they were going out, they met a Cyrenian named Simon; this man they pressed into service to carry his cross.

And when they came to a place called Golgotha—which means Place of the Skull—, they gave Jesus wine to drink mixed with gall. But when he had tasted it, he refused to drink. After they had crucified him, they divided his garments by casting lots; then they sat down and kept watch over him there. And they placed over his head the written charge against him: This is Jesus, the King of the Jews. Two revolutionaries were crucified with him, one on his right and the other on his left. Those passing by reviled him, shaking their heads and saying,

C "You who would destroy the temple and rebuild it in three days, save yourself, if you are the Son of God, and come down from the cross!"

N Likewise the chief priests with the scribes and elders mocked him and said,

C "He saved others; he cannot save himself. So he is the king of Israel! Let him come down from the cross now, and we will believe in him. He trusted in God; let him deliver him now if he wants him. For he said, 'I am the Son of God.'"

N The revolutionaries who were crucified with him also kept abusing him in the same way.

From noon onward, darkness came over the whole land until three in the afternoon. And about three o'clock Jesus cried out in a loud voice,

+ *"Eli, Eli, lema vabachthani?"*

N which means,

+ "My God, my God, why have you forsaken me?"

N Some of the bystanders who heard it said,

C "This one is calling for Elijah."

N Immediately one of them ran to get a sponge; he soaked it in wine, and putting it on a reed, gave it to him to drink. But the rest said,

C "Wait, let us see if Elijah comes to save him."

N But Jesus cried out again in a loud voice, and gave up his spirit.

Here all kneel and pause for a short time.

N And behold, the veil of the sanctuary was torn in two from top to bottom. The earth quaked, rocks were split, tombs were opened, and the bodies of many saints who had fallen asleep were raised. And coming forth from their tombs after his resurrection, they entered the holy city and appeared to many. The centurion and the men with him who were keeping watch over Jesus feared greatly when they saw the earthquake and all that was happening, and they said,

C "Truly, this was the Son of God!"]

N There were many women there, looking on from a distance, who had followed Jesus from Galilee, ministering to him. Among them were Mary Magdalene and Mary the mother of James and Joseph, and the mother of the sons of Zebedee.

When it was evening, there came a rich man from Arimathea named Joseph, who was himself a disciple of Jesus. He went to Pilate and asked for the body of Jesus; then Pilate ordered it to be handed over. Taking the body, Joseph wrapped it in clean linen and laid it in his new tomb that he had hewn in the rock. Then he rolled a huge stone across the entrance to the tomb and departed. But Mary Magdalene and the other Mary remained sitting there, facing the tomb. The next day, the one following the day of preparation, the chief priests and the Pharisees gathered before Pilate and said,

C "Sir, we remember that this impostor while still alive said, 'After three days I will be raised up.' Give orders, then, that the grave be secured until the third day, lest his disciples come and steal him and say to the people, 'He has been raised from the dead.' This last imposture would be worse than the first."

N Pilate said to them,

V "The guard is yours; go, secure it as best you can."

N So they went and secured the tomb by fixing a seal to the stone and setting the guard.

GOSPEL / B

Mark 14:1—15:47 or 15:1-39 523

The symbols of the following passion narrative represent:

+ *Christ;*   N *narrator;*   V *voice;*   C *crowd.*

N The Passion of our Lord Jesus Christ according to Mark.

For short form read only the part in brackets.

N The Passover and the Feast of Unleavened Bread were to take place in two days' time. So the chief priests and the scribes were seeking a way to arrest him by treachery and put him to death. They said,

V "Not during the festival, for fear that there may be a riot among the people."

N When he was in Bethany reclining at table in the house of Simon the leper, a woman came with an alabaster jar of perfumed oil, costly genuine spikenard. She broke the alabaster jar and poured it on his head. There were some who were indignant.

V "Why has there been this waste of perfumed oil? It could have been sold for more than three hundred days' wages and the money given to the poor."

N They were infuriated with her. Jesus said,

+ "Let her alone. Why do you make trouble for her? She has done a good thing for me. The poor you will always have with you, and whenever you wish you can do good to them, but you will not always have me. She has done what she could. She has antici-pated anointing my body for burial. Amen, I say to you, wherever the gospel is proclaimed to the whole world, what she has done will be told in memory of her."

N Then Judas Iscariot, one of the Twelve, went off to the chief priests to hand him over to them. When they heard him they were pleased and promised to pay him money. Then he looked for an opportunity to hand him over.

On the first day of the Feast of Unleavened Bread, when they sacrificed the Passover lamb, his disciples said to him,

V "Where do you want us to go and prepare for you to eat the Passover?"

N He sent two of his disciples and said to them,

+ "Go into the city and a man will meet you, carrying a jar of water. Follow him. Wherever he enters, say to the master of the house, 'The Teacher says, "Where is my guest room where I may eat the Passover with my disciples?"' Then he will show you a large upper room furnished and ready. Make the preparations for us there."

N The disciples then went off, entered the city, and found it just as he had told them; and they prepared the Passover.

When it was evening, he came with the Twelve. And as they reclined at table and were eating, Jesus said,

+ "Amen, I say to you, one of you will betray me, one who is eating with me."

N They began to be distressed and to say to him, one by one,

V "Surely it is not I?"

N He said to them,

+ "One of the Twelve, the one who dips with me into the dish. For the Son of Man indeed goes, as it is written of him, but woe to that man by whom the Son of Man is betrayed. It would be better for that man if he had never been born."

N While they were eating, he took bread, said the blessing, broke it, and gave it to them, and said,

+ "Take it; this is my body."

N Then he took a cup, gave thanks, and gave it to them, and they all drank from it. He said to them,

+ "This is my blood of the covenant, which will be shed for many. Amen, I say to you, I shall not drink again the fruit of the vine until the day when I drink it new in the kingdom of God."

N Then, after singing a hymn, they went out to the Mount of Olives.

Then Jesus said to them,

+ "All of you will have your faith shaken, for it is written: *'I will strike the shepherd, and the sheep will be dispersed.'* But after I have been raised up, I shall go before you to Galilee."

N Peter said to him,

V "Even though all should have their faith shaken, mine will not be."

N Then Jesus said to him,

+ "Amen, I say to you, this very night before the cock crows twice you will deny me three times."

N But he vehemently replied,

V "Even though I should have to die with you, I will not deny you."

N And they all spoke similarly. Then they came to a place named Gethsemane, and he said to his disciples,

+ "Sit here while I pray."

N He took with him Peter, James, and John, and began to be troubled and distressed. Then he said to them,

+ "My soul is sorrowful even to death. Remain here and keep watch."

N He advanced a little and fell to the ground and prayed that if it were possible the hour might pass by him; he said,

+ "Abba, Father, all things are possible to you. Take this cup away from me, but not what I will but what you will."

N When he returned he found them asleep. He said to Peter,

+ "Simon, are you asleep? Could you not keep watch for one hour? Watch and pray that you may not undergo the test. The spirit is willing but the flesh is weak."

N Withdrawing again, he prayed, saying the same thing. Then he returned once more and found them asleep, for they could not keep their eyes open and did not know what to answer him. He returned a third time and said to them,

+ "Are you still sleeping and taking your rest? It is enough. The hour has come. Behold, the Son of Man is to be handed over to sinners. Get up, let us go. See, my betrayer is at hand."

N Then, while he was still speaking, Judas, one of the Twelve, arrived, accompanied by a crowd with swords and clubs who had come from the chief priests, the scribes, and the elders. His betrayer had arranged a signal with them, saying,

V "The man I shall kiss is the one; arrest him and lead him away securely."

N He came and immediately went over to him and said,

V "Rabbi."

N And he kissed him. At this they laid hands on him and arrested him. One of the bystanders drew his sword, struck the high priest's servant, and cut off his ear. Jesus said to them in reply,

+ "Have you come out as against a robber, with swords and clubs, to seize me? Day after day I was with you teaching in the temple area, yet you did not arrest me; but that the Scriptures may be fulfilled."

N And they all left him and fled. Now a young man followed him wearing nothing but a linen cloth about his body. They seized him, but he left the cloth behind and ran off naked.

They led Jesus away to the high priest, and all the chief priests and the elders and the scribes came together. Peter followed him at a distance into the high priest's courtyard and was seated with the guards, warming himself at the fire. The chief priests and the entire Sanhedrin kept trying to obtain testimony against Jesus in order to put him to death, but they found none. Many gave false witness against him, but their testimony did not agree. Some took the stand and testified falsely against him, alleging,

C "We heard him say, 'I will destroy this temple made with hands and within three days I will build another not made with hands.'"

N Even so their testimony did not agree. The high priest rose before the assembly and questioned Jesus, saying,

V "Have you no answer? What are these men testifying against you?"

N But he was silent and answered nothing. Again the high priest asked him and said to him,

V "Are you the Christ, the son of the Blessed One?"

N Then Jesus answered,

+ "I am; and 'you will see the Son of Man seated at the right hand of the Power and coming with the clouds of heaven.'"

N At that the high priest tore his garments and said,

V "What further need have we of witnesses? You have heard the blasphemy. What do you think?"

N They all condemned him as deserving to die. Some began to spit on him. They blindfolded him and struck him and said to him,

C "Prophesy!"

N And the guards greeted him with blows. While Peter was below in the courtyard, one of the high priest's maids came along. Seeing Peter warming himself, she looked intently at him and said,

C "You too were with the Nazorean, Jesus."

N But he denied it saying,

V "I neither know nor understand what you are talking about."

N So he went out into the outer court. Then the cock crowed. The maid saw him and began again to say to the bystanders,

C "This man is one of them."

N Once again he denied it. A little later the bystanders said to Peter once more,

C "Surely you are one of them; for you too are a Galilean."

N He began to curse and to swear,

V "I do not know this man about whom you are talking."

N And immediately a cock crowed a second time. Then Peter remembered the word that Jesus had said to him, "Before the cock crows twice you will deny me three times." He broke down and wept.

[As soon as morning came, the chief priests with the elders and the scribes, that is, the whole Sanhedrin held a council. They bound Jesus, led him away, and handed him over to Pilate. Pilate questioned him,

V "Are you the king of the Jews?"

N He said to him in reply,

+ "You say so."

N The chief priests accused him of many things. Again Pilate questioned him,

V "Have you no answer? See how many things they accuse you of."

N Jesus gave him no further answer, so that Pilate was amazed.

Now on the occasion of the feast he used to release to them one prisoner whom they requested. A man called Barabbas was then in prison along with the rebels who had committed murder in a rebellion. The crowd came forward and began to ask him to do for them as he was accustomed. Pilate answered,

V "Do you want me to release to you the king of the Jews?"

N For he knew that it was out of envy that the chief priests had handed him over. But the chief priests stirred up the crowd to have him release Barabbas for them instead. Pilate again said to them in reply,

V "Then what do you want me to do with the man you call the king of the Jews?"

N They shouted again,

C "Crucify him."

N Pilate said to them,

V "Why? What evil has he done?"

N They only shouted the louder,

C "Crucify him."

N So Pilate, wishing to satisfy the crowd, released Barabbas to them and, after he had Jesus scourged, handed him over to be crucified.

The soldiers led him away inside the palace, that is, the praetorium, and assembled the whole cohort. They clothed him in purple and, weaving a crown of thorns, placed it on him. They began to salute him with,

C "Hail, King of the Jews!"

N and kept striking his head with a reed and spitting upon him. They knelt before him in homage. And when they had mocked him, they stripped him of the purple cloak, dressed him in his own clothes, and led him out to crucify him.

They pressed into service a passer-by, Simon, a Cyrenian, who was coming in from the country, the father of Alexander and Rufus, to carry his cross.

They brought him to the place of Golgotha (which is translated Place of the Skull). They gave him wine drugged with myrrh, but he did not take it. Then they crucified him and divided his garments by casting lots for them to see what each should take. It was nine o'clock in the morning when they crucified him. The inscription of the charge against him read, "The King of the Jews." With him they crucified two revolutionaries, one on his right and one on his left. Those passing by reviled him, shaking their heads and saying,

C "Aha! You who would destroy the temple and rebuild it in three days, save yourself by coming down from the cross."

N Likewise the chief priests, with the scribes, mocked him among themselves and said,

C "He saved others; he cannot save himself. Let the Christ, the King of Israel, come down now from the cross that we may see and believe."

N Those who were crucified with him also kept abusing him.

At noon darkness came over the whole land until three in the afternoon. And at three o'clock Jesus cried out in a loud voice,

+ "Eloi, Eloi, lema sabachthani?"

N which is translated,

+ "My God, my God, why have you forsaken me?"

N Some of the bystanders who heard it said,

C "Look, he is calling Elijah."

N One of them ran, soaked a sponge with wine, put it on a reed and gave it to him to drink saying,

V "Wait, let us see if Elijah comes to take him down."

N Jesus gave a loud cry and breathed his last.

Here all kneel and pause for a short time.

N The veil of the sanctuary was torn in two from top to bottom. When the centurion who stood facing him saw how he breathed his last he said,

V "Truly this man was the Son of God!"]

N There were also women looking on from a distance. Among them were Mary Magdalene, Mary the mother of the younger James and of Joses, and Salome. These women had followed him when he was in Galilee and ministered to him. There were also many other women who had come up with him to Jerusalem.

When it was already evening, since it was the day of preparation, the day before the sabbath, Joseph of Arimathea, a distinguished member of the council, who was himself awaiting the kingdom of God, came and courageously went to Pilate and asked for the body of Jesus. Pilate was amazed that he was already dead. He summoned the centurion and asked him if Jesus had already died. And when he learned of it from the centurion, he gave the body to Joseph. Having bought a linen cloth, he took him down, wrapped him in the linen cloth, and laid him in a tomb that had been hewn out of the rock. Then he rolled a stone against the entrance to the tomb. Mary Magdalene and Mary the mother of Joses watched where he was laid.

524 **GOSPEL / C**   *Luke 22:14—23:56 or 23:1-49*

The symbols of the following passion narrative represent:
   + Christ;   *N narrator;*   *V voice;*   *C crowd.*

N The Passion of our Lord Jesus Christ according to Luke.

For short form read only the part in brackets.

N When the hour came, Jesus took his place at table with the apostles. He said to them,

+ "I have eagerly desired to eat this Passover with you before I suffer, for, I tell you, I shall not eat it again until there is fulfillment in the kingdom of God."

N Then he took a cup, gave thanks, and said,

+ "Take this and share it among yourselves; for I tell you that from this time on I shall not drink of the fruit of the vine until the kingdom of God comes."

N Then he took the bread, said the blessing, broke it, and gave it to them, saying,

+ "This is my body, which will be given for you; do this in memory of me."

N And likewise the cup after they had eaten, saying,

+ "This cup is the new covenant in my blood, which will be shed for you.

"And yet behold, the hand of the one who is to betray me is with me on the table; for the Son of Man indeed goes as it has been determined; but woe to that man by whom he is betrayed."

N And they began to debate among themselves who among them would do such a deed.

Then an argument broke out among them about which of them should be regarded as the greatest. He said to them,

+ "The kings of the Gentiles lord it over them and those in authority over them are addressed as 'Benefactors'; but among you it shall not be so. Rather, let the greatest among you be as the youngest, and the leader as the servant. For who is greater: the one seated at table or the one who serves? Is it not the one seated at table? I am among you as the one who serves. It is you who have stood by me in my trials; and I confer a kingdom on you, just as my Father has conferred one on me, that you may eat and drink at my table in my kingdom; and you will sit on thrones judging the twelve tribes of Israel.

"Simon, Simon, behold Satan has demanded to sift all of you like wheat, but I have prayed that your own faith may not fail; and once you have turned back, you must strengthen your brothers."

N He said to him,

V "Lord, I am prepared to go to prison and to die with you."

N But he replied,

+ "I tell you, Peter, before the cock crows this day, you will deny three times that you know me."

N He said to them,

+ "When I sent you forth without a money bag or a sack or sandals, were you in need of anything?"

C "No, nothing,"

N they replied. He said to them,

+ "But now one who has a money bag should take it, and likewise a sack, and one who does not have a sword should sell his cloak and buy one. For I tell you that this Scripture must be fulfilled in me, namely, 'He was counted among the wicked;' and indeed what is written about me is coming to fulfillment."

N Then they said,

V "Lord, look, there are two swords here."

N But he replied,

+ "It is enough!"

N Then going out, he went, as was his custom, to the Mount of Olives, and the disciples followed him. When he arrived at the place he said to them,

+ "Pray that you may not undergo the test."

N After withdrawing about a stone's throw from them and kneeling, he prayed, saying,

+ "Father, if you are willing, take this cup away from me; still, not my will but yours be done."

N And to strengthen him an angel from heaven appeared to him. He was in such agony and he prayed so fervently that his sweat became like drops of blood falling on the ground. When he rose from prayer and returned to his disciples, he found them sleeping from grief. He said to them,

+ "Why are you sleeping? Get up and pray that you may not undergo the test."

N While he was still speaking, a crowd approached and in front was one of the Twelve, a man named Judas. He went up to Jesus to kiss him. Jesus said to him,

+ "Judas, are you betraying the Son of Man with a kiss?"

N His disciples realized what was about to happen, and they asked,

V "Lord, shall we strike with a sword?"

N And one of them struck the high priest's servant and cut off his right ear. But Jesus said in reply,

+ "Stop, no more of this!"

N Then he touched the servant's ear and healed him. And Jesus said to the chief priests and temple guards and elders who had come for him,

+ "Have you come out as against a robber, with swords and clubs? Day after day I was with you in the temple area, and you did not seize me; but this is your hour, the time for the power of darkness."

N After arresting him they led him away and took him into the house of the high priest; Peter was following at a distance. They lit a fire in the middle of the courtyard and sat around it, and Peter sat down with them. When a maid saw him seated in the light, she looked intently at him and said,

C "This man too was with him."

N But he denied it saying,

V "Woman, I do not know him."

N A short while later someone else saw him and said,

C "You too are one of them";

N but Peter answered,

V "My friend, I am not."

N About an hour later, still another insisted,

C "Assuredly, this man too was with him, for he also is a Galilean."

N But Peter said,

V "My friend, I do not know what you are talking about."

N Just as he was saying this, the cock crowed, and the Lord turned and looked at Peter; and Peter remembered the word of the Lord, how he had said to him, "Before the cock crows today, you will deny me three times." He went out and began to weep bitterly. The men who held Jesus in custody were ridiculing and beating him. They blindfolded him and questioned him, saying,

C "Prophesy! Who is it that struck you?"

N And they reviled him in saying many other things against him.

When day came the council of elders of the people met, both chief priests and scribes, and they brought him before their Sanhedrin. They said,

C "If you are the Christ, tell us,"

N but he replied to them,

+ "If I tell you, you will not believe, and if I question, you will not respond. But from this time on the Son of Man will be seated at the right hand of the power of God."

N They all asked,

C "Are you then the Son of God?"

N He replied to them,

+ "You say that I am."

N Then they said,

C "What further need have we for testimony? We have heard it from his own mouth."

N [Then the whole assembly of them arose and brought him before Pilate. They brought charges against him, saying,

C "We found this man misleading our people; he opposes the payment of taxes to Caesar and maintains that he is the Christ, a king."

N Pilate asked him,

V "Are you the king of the Jews?"

N He said to him in reply,

+ "You say so."

N Pilate then addressed the chief priests and the crowds,

V "I find this man not guilty."

N But they were adamant and said,

C "He is inciting the people with his teaching throughout all Judea, from Galilee where he began even to here."

N On hearing this Pilate asked if the man was a Galilean; and upon learning that he was under Herod's jurisdiction, he sent him to Herod who was in Jerusalem at that time. Herod was very glad to see Jesus; he had been wanting to see him for a long time, for he had heard about him and had been hoping to see him perform some sign. He questioned him at length, but he gave him no answer. The chief priests and scribes, meanwhile, stood by accusing him harshly. Herod and his soldiers treated him contemptuously and mocked him, and after clothing him in resplendent garb, he sent him back to Pilate. Herod and Pilate became friends that very day, even though they had been enemies formerly. Pilate then summoned the chief priests, the rulers, and the people and said to them,

V "You brought this man to me and accused him of inciting the people to revolt. I have conducted my investigation in your presence and have not found this man guilty of the charges you have brought against him, nor did Herod, for he sent him back to us. So no capital crime has been committed by him. Therefore I shall have him flogged and then release him."

N But all together they shouted out,

C "Away with this man! Release Barabbas to us."

N (Now Barabbas had been imprisoned for a rebellion that had taken place in the city and for murder.) Again Pilate addressed them, still wishing to release Jesus, but they continued their shouting,

C "Crucify him! Crucify him!"

N Pilate addressed them a third time,

V "What evil has this man done? I found him guilty of no capital crime. Therefore I shall have him flogged and then release him."

N With loud shouts, however, they persisted in calling for his crucifixion, and their voices prevailed. The verdict of Pilate was that their demand should be granted. So he released the man who had been imprisoned for rebellion and murder, for whom they asked, and he handed Jesus over to them to deal with as they wished.

As they led him away they took hold of a certain Simon, a Cyrenian, who was coming in from the country; and after laying the cross on him, they made him carry it behind Jesus. A large crowd of people followed Jesus, including many women who mourned and lamented him. Jesus turned to them and said,

+ "Daughters of Jerusalem, do not weep for me; weep instead for yourselves and for your children for indeed, the days are coming when people will say, 'Blessed are the barren, the wombs that never bore and the breasts that never nursed.' At that time people will say to the mountains, 'Fall upon us!' and to the hills, 'Cover us!' for if these things are done when the wood is green what will happen when it is dry?"

N Now two others, both criminals, were led away with him to be executed.

When they came to the place called the Skull, they crucified him and the criminals there, one on his right, the other on his left. Then Jesus said,

+ "Father, forgive them, they know not what they do."

N They divided his garments by casting lots. The people stood by and watched; the rulers, meanwhile, sneered at him and said,

C "He saved others, let him save himself if he is the chosen one, the Christ of God."

N Even the soldiers jeered at him. As they approached to offer him wine they called out,

C "If you are King of the Jews, save yourself."

N Above him there was an inscription that read, "This is the King of the Jews."

Now one of the criminals hanging there reviled Jesus, saying,

V "Are you not the Christ? Save yourself and us."

N The other, however, rebuking him, said in reply,

V "Have you no fear of God, for you are subject to the same condemnation? And indeed, we have been condemned justly, for the sentence we received corresponds to our crimes, but this man has done nothing criminal."

N Then he said,

V "Jesus, remember me when you come into your kingdom."

N He replied to him,

+ "Amen, I say to you, today you will be with me in Paradise."

N It was now about noon and darkness came over the whole land until three in the afternoon because of an eclipse of the sun. Then the veil of the temple was torn down the middle. Jesus cried out in a loud voice,

+ "Father, into your hands I commend my spirit";

N and when he had said this he breathed his last.

Here all kneel and pause for a short time.

N The centurion who witnessed what had happened glorified God and said,

V "This man was innocent beyond doubt."

N When all the people who had gathered for this spectacle saw what had happened, they returned home beating their breasts; but all his acquaintances stood at a distance, including the women who had followed him from Galilee and saw these events.]

Now there was a virtuous and righteous man named Joseph who, though he was a member of the council, had not consented to their plan of action. He came from the Jewish town of Arimathea and was awaiting the kingdom of God. He went to Pilate and asked for the body of Jesus. After he had taken the body down, he wrapped it in a linen cloth and laid him in a rock-hewn tomb in which no one had yet been buried. It was the day of preparation, and the sabbath was about to begin. The women who had come from Galilee with him followed behind, and when they had seen the tomb and the way in which his body was laid in it, they returned and prepared spices and perfumed oils. Then they rested on the sabbath according to the commandment.

Easter Triduum

525 "The Easter Triduum of the passion and resurrection of Christ is...the culmination of the entire liturgical year. What Sunday is to the week, the solemnity of Easter is to the liturgical year" (General Norms for the Liturgical Year, #18).

Lent ends quietly on Thursday afternoon. The church enters the Triduum ("three days"). On Thursday night the church begins a time of prayer and fasting, a time of keeping watch, that lasts into the great Vigil between Saturday and Sunday. The church emphasizes that the fasting of Good Friday and, if possible, of Holy Saturday are integral to the keeping of these days and the preparation for the sacraments of initiation celebrated at the Vigil. On Thursday night and on Friday afternoon or evening the church gathers to pray and to remember the many facets of the single mystery.

---

526 **HOLY THURSDAY: EVENING MASS OF THE LORD'S SUPPER**

On Thursday night Lent has ended and the church, at this Mass of the Lord's Supper, enters into the Easter Triduum. From the very first moment the all-embracing experience of these three days is proclaimed: "We should glory in the cross of our Lord Jesus Christ. For he is our salvation, our life, and our resurrection. Through him we are saved and made free." This is the whole of the great Triduum. On Thursday night, the liturgy draws us toward this through the scriptures, through the mandatum or washing of the feet which is the direct expression of our service to one another and the world, through the eucharistic banquet itself.

LITURGY OF THE WORD / ABC

READING I   *Exodus 12:1-8, 11-14 / 39*

The LORD said to Moses and Aaron in the land of Egypt, "This month shall stand at the head of your calendar; you shall reckon it the first month of the year. Tell the whole community of Israel: On the tenth of this month every one of your families must procure for itself a lamb, one apiece for each household. If a family is too small for a whole lamb, it shall join the nearest household in procuring one and shall share in the lamb in proportion to the number of persons who partake of it. The lamb must be a year-old male and without blemish. You may take it from either the sheep or the goats. You shall keep it until the fourteenth day of this month, and then, with the whole assembly of Israel present, it shall be slaughtered during the evening twilight. They shall take some of its blood and apply it to the two doorposts and the lintel of every house in which they partake of the lamb. That same night they shall eat its roasted flesh with unleavened bread and bitter herbs.

"This is how you are to eat it: with your loins girt, sandals on your feet and your staff in hand, you shall eat like those who are in flight. It is the Passover of the LORD. For on this same night I will go through Egypt, striking down every firstborn of the land, both man and beast, and executing judgment on all the gods of Egypt—I, the LORD! But the blood will mark the houses where you are. Seeing the blood, I will pass over you; thus, when I strike the land of Egypt, no destructive blow will come upon you.

"This day shall be a memorial feast for you, which all your generations shall celebrate with pilgrimage to the LORD, as a perpetual institution."

RESPONSORIAL PSALM
Psalm 116:12-13, 15-16bc, 17-18

Our bless-ing cup is a com-mun-ion with the blood of Christ.

How shall I make a return to the LORD
for all the good he has done for me?
The cup of salvation I will take up,
and I will call upon the name of the
LORD. ℟.

Precious in the eyes of the LORD
is the death of his faithful ones.
I am your servant, the son of your
handmaid;
you have loosed my bonds. ℟.

To you will I offer sacrifice of
thanksgiving,
and I will call upon the name of the
LORD.
My vows to the LORD I will pay
in the presence of all his people. ℟.

READING II
I Corinthians 11:23-26

Brothers and sisters: I received from the Lord what I also handed on to you, that the Lord Jesus, on the night he was handed over, took bread, and, after he had given thanks, broke it and said, "This is my body that is for you. Do this in remembrance of me." In the same way also the cup, after supper, saying, "This cup is the new covenant in my blood. Do this, as often as you drink it, in remembrance of me." For as often as you eat this bread and drink the cup, you proclaim the death of the Lord until he comes.

GOSPEL
John 13:1-15

Before the feast of Passover, Jesus knew that his hour had come to pass from this world to the Father. He loved his own in the world and he loved them to the end. The devil had already induced Judas, son of Simon the Iscariot, to hand him over. So, during supper, fully aware that the Father had put everything into his power and that he had come from God and was returning to God, he rose from supper and took off his outer garments. He took a towel and tied it around his waist. Then he poured water into a basin and began to wash the disciples' feet and dry them with the towel around his waist. He came to Simon Peter, who said to him, "Master, are you going to wash my feet?" Jesus answered and said to him, "What I am doing, you do not understand now, but you will understand later." Peter said to him, "You will never wash my feet." Jesus answered him, "Unless I wash you, you will have no inheritance with me." Simon Peter said to him, "Master, then not only my feet, but my hands and head as well." Jesus said to him, "Whoever has bathed has no need except to have his feet washed, for he is clean all over; so you are clean, but not all." For he knew who would betray him; for this reason, he said, "Not all of you are clean."

So when he had washed their feet and put his garments back on and reclined at table again, he said to them, "Do you realize what I have done for you? You call me 'teacher' and 'master,' and rightly so, for indeed I am. If I, therefore, the master and teacher, have washed your feet, you ought to wash one another's feet. I have given you a model to follow, so that as I have done for you, you should also do."

527 WASHING OF FEET

The homily is followed by the washing of feet, the mandatum (from the Latin word for "command": "A new commandment I give to you..."). This is a simple gesture of humble service: the presider and others wash the feet of various members of the assembly. Such a gesture, with the song which accompanies it, speaks directly of the way of life Christians seek. Appropriate songs are nos. 247, 248, and 351.

The Mass continues with the general intercessions.

528 TRANSFER OF THE HOLY EUCHARIST

When the communion rite is concluded, the eucharistic bread that remains is solemnly carried from the altar. The following, or another appropriate selection, accompanies the procession.

1. Weave a song with - in the si - lence That these mys - ter-
2. Mar - y bore him, sin-less Vir - gin, When to this our
3. While re - clin - ing that last eve - ning Tak - ing sup - per
4. See the won - der of this mo -ment! Watch with awe what
1. Pan - ge lín - gua glo - ri - ó - si, Cor - po - ris my-
2. No - bis da - tus, no - bis na - tus Ex in - tá - cta
3. In su - pré - mae no - cte coe - nae, Re - cum-bens cum
4. Ver - bum ca - ro, pa-nem ve - rum Ver - bo car-nem

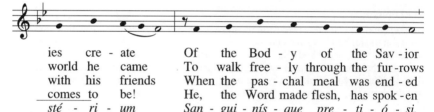

ies cre - ate Of the Bod - y of the Sav -ior
world he came To walk free - ly through the fur -rows
with his friends When the pas - chal meal was end - ed
comes to be! He, the Word made flesh, has spok -en
sté - ri - um San - gui - nís - que pre - ti - ó - si,
Vír - gi - ne, Et in mún - do con - ver - sá - tus,
frá - tri - bus, Ob - ser - vá - ta le - ge ple - ne
éf - fi - cit: Fit - que san - guis Chri - sti me -rum,

Who was tor-tured for our sake And the Blood that left his
Scat - ter -ing his Fa-ther's grain Till he end - ed his brief
With the rites the Law de - mands He gave them as bread his
And the bread and wine per - ceived Are now tru - ly his own
Quem in mún - di pré - ti - um Fru-ctus ven - tris ge - ne-
Spar - so vér - bi sé - mi - ne, Su - i mo - ras in - co-
Ci - bis in le - gá - li - bus, Ci - bum tur - bae du - o-
Et si sen - sus dé - fi - cit, Ad fir - mán-dum cor sin-

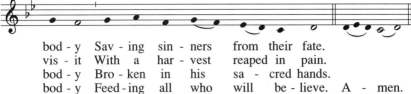

bod - y	Sav - ing	sin - ners	from their fate.	
vis - it	With a	har - vest	reaped in pain.	
bod - y	Bro - ken	in his	sa - cred hands.	
bod - y	Feed - ing	all who	will be - lieve.	A - men.
ró - si	*Rex ef* -	*fú - dit*	*gén - ti - um.*	
lá - tus	*Mi - ro*	*clau - sit*	*ór - di - ne.*	
dé - nae	*Se dat*	*su - is*	*má - ni - bus.*	
cé - rum	*So - la*	*fi - des*	*súf - fi - cit.*	A - men.

5. Humbly we bow down before him
   And in awe we do proclaim
   This his presence on our altar
   Glorified beyond all pain.
   What our senses cannot master
   By our faith we now acclaim.

5. *Tantum ergo Sacraméntum*
   Venerémur cérnui:
   Et antíquum documéntum
   Novo cedat rítui;
   Praestet fides suppleméntum
   Sénsuum deféctui.

6. Honor, praise and thanks be given
   To the Father and the Son.
   Sing with joy in their own Spirit
   Who alone can make us one,
   And from heaven now with power
   Gently to our hearts has come. Amen.

6. *Genitóri, Genitóque*
   Laus et jubilátio,
   Salus, honor, virtus quoque
   Sit et benedíctio:
   Procedénti ab utróque
   Compar sit laudátio. Amen.

Text: *Pange lingua,* Thomas Aquinas, 1227-1274; tr. by Ralph Wright, OSB, b.1938, © 1989, GIA Publications, Inc.
Tune: PANGE LINGUA, 8 7 8 7 8 7: Mode III; acc. by Eugene Lapierre, © 1964, GIA Publications, Inc.

The liturgy has no concluding rite, no dismissal. Rather, the church continues to watch and pray throughout the Triduum.

GOOD FRIDAY / ABC   529

In Good Friday's liturgy of the word and veneration of the cross there is great solemnity: a pondering of the "mystery of our faith," the passion, death and resurrection of our Lord Jesus Christ. Fasting and praying during these days, the catechumens and the baptized assemble on Good Friday in the afternoon or evening for a time of prayer together. This begins a time of silence.

LITURGY OF THE WORD

READING I   *Isaiah 52:13—53:12 / 40*

See, my servant shall prosper,
  he shall be raised high and greatly
    exalted.
Even as many were amazed at him—
  so marred was his look beyond
    human semblance
  and his appearance beyond that of
    the sons of man—
so shall he startle many nations,

because of him kings shall stand
    speechless;
for those who have not been told shall see,
  those who have not heard shall
    ponder it.
Who would believe what we have heard?
  To whom has the arm of the LORD
    been revealed?
He grew up like a sapling before him,

like a shoot from the parched earth;
there was in him no stately bearing to
make us look at him,
nor appearance that would attract us
to him.
He was spurned and avoided by people,
a man of suffering, accustomed to
infirmity,
one of those from whom people hide
their faces,
spurned, and we held him in no esteem.
Yet it was our infirmities that he bore,
our sufferings that he endured,
while we thought of him as stricken,
as one smitten by God and afflicted.
But he was pierced for our offenses,
crushed for our sins;
upon him was the chastisement that
makes us whole,
by his stripes we were healed.
We had all gone astray like sheep,
each following his own way;
but the LORD laid upon him
the guilt of us all.

Though he was harshly treated, he
submitted
and opened not his mouth;
like a lamb led to the slaughter
or a sheep before the shearers,
he was silent and opened not his mouth.
Oppressed and condemned, he was taken
away,

and who would have thought any
more of his destiny?
When he was cut off from the land of the
living,
and smitten for the sin of his people,
a grave was assigned him among the
wicked
and a burial place with evildoers,
though he had done no wrong
nor spoken any falsehood.
But the LORD was pleased
to crush him in infirmity.

If he gives his life as an offering for sin,
he shall see his descendants in a
long life,
and the will of the LORD shall be
accomplished through him.

Because of his affliction
he shall see the light
in fullness of days;
through his suffering, my servant shall
justify many,
and their guilt he shall bear.
Therefore I will give him his portion
among the great,
and he shall divide the spoils with
the mighty,
because he surrendered himself to death
and was counted among the wicked;
and he shall take away the sins of many,
and win pardon for their offenses.

RESPONSORIAL PSALM

Psalm 31:2, 6, 12-13, 15-16, 17, 25

Fa - ther, in - to your hands, I com- mend my spir-it.

In you, O LORD, I take refuge;
let me never be put to shame.
In your justice rescue me.
Into your hands I commend my
spirit;
you will redeem me, O LORD, O faithful
God. ℟.

For all my foes I am an object of
reproach,
a laughingstock to my neighbors,
and a dread to my friends;
they who see me abroad flee from me.
I am forgotten like the

unremembered dead;
I am like a dish that is broken. ℟.

But my trust is in you, O LORD;
I say, "You are my God.
In your hands is my destiny; rescue me
from the clutches of my enemies and
my persecutors." ℟.

Let your face shine upon your servant;
save me in your kindness.
Take courage and be stouthearted,
all you who hope in the LORD. ℟.

READING II

Hebrews 4:14-16; 5:7-9

Brothers and sisters: Since we have a great high priest who has passed through the heavens, Jesus, the Son of God, let us hold fast to our confession. For we do not have a high priest who is unable to sympathize with our weaknesses, but one who has similarly been tested in every way, yet without sin. So let us confidently approach the throne of grace to receive mercy and to find grace for timely help.

In the days when Christ was in the flesh, he offered prayers and supplications with loud cries and tears to the one who was able to save him from death, and he was heard because of his reverence. Son though he was, he learned obedience from what he suffered; and when he was made perfect, he became the source of eternal salvation for all who obey him.

GOSPEL

John 18:1—19:42

The symbols of the following passion narrative represent:
   + *Christ;*   N *narrator;*   V *voice;*   C *crowd.*

N The Passion of our Lord Jesus Christ according to John.

For short form read only the part in brackets.

N Jesus went out with his disciples across the Kidron valley to where there was a garden, into which he and his disciples entered. Judas his betrayer also knew the place, because Jesus had often met there with his disciples. So Judas got a band of soldiers and guards from the chief priests and the Pharisees and went there with lanterns, torches, and weapons. Jesus, knowing everything that was going to happen to him, went out and said to them,

+ "Whom are you looking for?"

N They answered him,

C "Jesus the Nazorean."

N He said to them,

+ "I AM."

N Judas his betrayer was also with them. When he said to them, "I AM," they turned away and fell to the ground. So he again asked them,

+ "Whom are you looking for?"

N They said,

C "Jesus the Nazorean."

N Jesus answered,

+ "I told you that I AM. So if you are looking for me, let these men go."

N This was to fulfill what he had said, "I have not lost any of those you gave me."

Then Simon Peter, who had a sword, drew it, struck the high priest's slave, and cut off his right ear. The slave's name was Malchus. Jesus said to Peter,

+ "Put your sword into its scabbard. Shall I not drink the cup that the Father gave me?"

N So the band of soldiers, the tribune, and the Jewish guards seized Jesus, bound him, and brought him to Annas first. He was the father-in-law of Caiaphas, who was high priest that year. It was Caiaphas who had counseled the Jews that it was better that one man should die rather than the people.

Simon Peter and another disciple followed Jesus. Now the other disciple was known to the high priest, and he entered the courtyard of the high priest with Jesus. But Peter stood at the gate outside. So the other disciple, the acquaintance of the high priest, went out and spoke to the gatekeeper and brought Peter in. Then the maid who was the gatekeeper said to Peter,

C "You are not one of this man's disciples, are you?"

N He said,

V "I am not."

N Now the slaves and the guards were standing around a charcoal fire that they had made, because it was cold, and were warming themselves. Peter was also standing there keeping warm.

The high priest questioned Jesus about his disciples and about his doctrine. Jesus answered him,

+ "I have spoken publicly to the world. I have always taught in a synagogue or in the temple area where all the Jews gather, and in secret I have said nothing. Why ask me? Ask those who heard me what I said to them. They know what I said."

N When he had said this, one of the temple guards standing there struck Jesus and said,

V "Is this the way you answer the high priest?"

N Jesus answered him,

+ "If I have spoken wrongly, testify to the

N Then Annas sent him bound to Caiaphas the high priest.

Now Simon Peter was standing there keeping warm. And they said to him,

C "You are not one of his disciples, are you?"

N He denied it and said,

V "I am not."

N One of the slaves of the high priest, a relative of the one whose ear Peter had cut off, said,

C "Didn't I see you in the garden with him?"

N Again Peter denied it. And immediately the cock crowed.

Then they brought Jesus from Caiaphas to the praetorium. It was morning. And they themselves did not enter the praetorium, in order not to be defiled so that they could eat the Passover. So Pilate came out to them and said,

V "What charge do you bring against this man?"

N They answered and said to him,

C "If he were not a criminal, we would not have handed him over to you."

N At this, Pilate said to them,

V "Take him yourselves, and judge him according to your law."

N The Jews answered him,

C "We do not have the right to execute anyone,"

N in order that the word of Jesus might be fulfilled that he said indicating the kind of death he would die.

So Pilate went back into the praetorium and summoned Jesus and said to him,

V "Are you the King of the Jews?"

N Jesus answered,

+ "Do you say this on your own or have others told you about me?"

N Pilate answered,

V "I am not a Jew, am I? Your own nation and the chief priests handed you over to me. What have you done?"

N Jesus answered,

+ "My kingdom does not belong to this world. If my kingdom did belong to this world, my attendants would be fighting to keep me from being handed over to the Jews. But as it is, my kingdom is not here."

N So Pilate said to him,

V "Then you are a king?"

N Jesus answered,

+ "You say I am a king. For this I was born and for this I came into the world, to testify to the truth. Everyone who belongs to the truth listens to my voice."

N Pilate said to him,

V "What is truth?"

N When he had said this, he again went out to the Jews and said to them,

V "I find no guilt in him. But you have a custom that I release one prisoner to you at Passover. Do you want me to release to you the King of the Jews?"

N They cried out again,

C "Not this one but Barabbas!"

N Now Barabbas was a revolutionary. Then Pilate took Jesus and had him scourged. And the soldiers wove a crown out of thorns and placed it on his head, and clothed him in a purple cloak, and they came to him and said,

C "Hail, King of the Jews!"

N And they struck him repeatedly. Once more Pilate went out and said to them,

V "Look, I am bringing him out to you, so that you may know that I find no guilt in him."

N So Jesus came out, wearing the crown of thorns and the purple cloak. And Pilate said to them,

V "Behold, the man!"

N When the chief priests and the guards saw him they cried out,

C "Crucify him, crucify him!"

N Pilate said to them,

V "Take him yourselves and crucify him. I find no guilt in him."

N The Jews answered,

C "We have a law, and according to that law he ought to die, because he made himself the Son of God."

N Now when Pilate heard this statement, he became even more afraid, and went back into the praetorium and said to Jesus,

V "Where are you from?"

N Jesus did not answer him. So Pilate said to him,

V "Do you not speak to me? Do you not know that I have power to release you and I have power to crucify you?"

N Jesus answered him,

+ "You would have no power over me if it had not been given to you from above. For this reason the one who handed me over to you has the greater sin."

N Consequently, Pilate tried to release him; but the Jews cried out,

C "If you release him, you are not a Friend of Caesar. Everyone who makes himself a king opposes Caesar."

N When Pilate heard these words he brought Jesus out and seated him on the judge's bench in the place called Stone Pavement, in Hebrew, Gabbatha. It was preparation day for Passover, and it was about noon. And he said to the Jews,

V "Behold, your king!"

N They cried out,

C "Take him away, take him away! Crucify him!"

N Pilate said to them,

V "Shall I crucify your king?"

N The chief priests answered,

C "We have no king but Caesar."

N Then he handed him over to them to be crucified.

So they took Jesus, and, carrying the cross himself, he went out to what is called the Place of the Skull, in Hebrew, Golgotha. There they crucified him, and with him two others, one on either side, with Jesus in the middle. Pilate also had an inscription written and put on the cross. It read, "Jesus the Nazorean, the King of the Jews." Now many of the Jews read this inscription, because the place where Jesus was crucified was near the city; and it was written in Hebrew, Latin, and Greek. So the chief priests of the Jews said to Pilate,

C "Do not write 'The King of the Jews,' but that he said, 'I am the King of the Jews'."

N Pilate answered,

V "What I have written, I have written."

N When the soldiers had crucified Jesus, they took his clothes and divided them into four shares, a share for each soldier. They also took his tunic, but the tunic was seamless, woven in one piece from the top down. So they said to one another,

C "Let's not tear it, but cast lots for it to see whose it will be,"

N in order that the passage of Scripture might be fulfilled that says: *They divided my garments among them, and for my vesture they cast lots.*

This is what the soldiers did. Standing by the cross of Jesus were his mother and his mother's sister, Mary the wife of Clopas, and Mary of Magdala. When Jesus saw his mother and the disciple there whom he loved he said to his mother,

+ "Woman, behold, your son."

N Then he said to the disciple,

+ "Behold, your mother."

N And from that hour the disciple took her into his home.

After this, aware that everything was now finished, in order that the Scripture might be fulfilled, Jesus said,

+ "I thirst."

N There was a vessel filled with common wine. So they put a sponge soaked in wine on a sprig of hyssop and put it up to his mouth. When Jesus had taken the wine, he said,

+ "It is finished."

N And bowing his head, he handed over the spirit.

Here all kneel and pause for a short time.

N Now since it was preparation day, in order that the bodies might not remain on the cross on the sabbath, for the sabbath day of that week was a solemn one, the Jews asked Pilate that their legs be broken and that they be taken down. So the soldiers came and broke the legs of the first and then of the other one who was crucified with Jesus. But when they came to Jesus and saw that he was already dead, they did not break his legs, but one soldier thrust his lance into his side, and immediately blood and water flowed out. An eyewitness has testified, and his testimony is true; he knows that he is speaking the truth, so that you also may come to believe. For this happened so that the Scripture passage might be fulfilled: *Not a bone of it will be broken.* And again another passage says: *They will look upon him whom they have pierced.*

After this, Joseph of Arimathea, secretly a disciple of Jesus for fear of the Jews, asked Pilate if he could remove the body of Jesus. And Pilate permitted it. So he came and took his body. Nicodemus, the one who had first come to him at night, also came bringing a mixture of myrrh and aloes weighing about one hundred pounds. They took the body of Jesus and bound it with burial cloths along with the spices, according to the Jewish burial custom. Now in the place where he had been crucified there was a garden, and in the garden a new tomb, in which no one had yet been buried. So they laid Jesus there because of the Jewish preparation day; for the tomb was close by.

GENERAL INTERCESSIONS

*As at Sunday liturgy, the word service concludes with prayers of intercession. Today
these prayers take a more solemn form as the church lifts up to God its own needs and
those of the world.*

530 VENERATION OF THE CROSS

*An ancient liturgical text reads: "See here the true and most revered Tree. Hasten to kiss
it and to cry out with faith: You are our help, most revered Cross." For many centuries
the church has solemnly venerated the relic or image of the cross on Good Friday. It is
not present as a picture of suffering only but as a symbol of Christ's passover, where
"dying he destroyed our death and rising restored our life." It is the glorious, the life-giv-
ing cross that the faithful venerate with song, prayer, kneeling and a kiss.*

As the cross is shown to the assembly, the following is sung.

Priest

This   is the wood of the cross,   on which hung the Sav-ior of the world.

All

Come,   let us   wor - ship.

*As the assembly comes forward to venerate the cross, appropriate chants and hymns
may be sung, e.g., nos. 249, 250, and 251.*

531 HOLY COMMUNION

*This liturgy concludes with a simple communion rite. All recite the Lord's Prayer and
receive holy communion. There is no concluding rite or dismissal for the church continues to be at prayer throughout the Triduum.*

532 HOLY SATURDAY

The church continues to fast and pray and to make ready for this night's
great Vigil. Saturday is a day of great quiet and reflection. Catechumens,
sponsors and some of the faithful may assemble during the day for prayer,
the recitation of the Creed, and for the rite of Ephpheta (opening of ears
and mouth).

533 EASTER VIGIL

The long preparation of the catechumens, the lenten disciplines and fast
of the faithful, the vigiling and fasting and prayer that have gone on since
Thursday night—all culminate in the great liturgy of this night. On this
night the church assembles to spend much time listening to scriptures,
praying psalms, acclaiming the death and resurrection of the Lord. Only
then are the catechumens called forward and prayed over, challenged to
renounce evil and affirm their faith in God, led to the font and baptized in
the blessed water. The newly baptized are then anointed with chrism and
the entire assembly joins in intercession and finally in the eucharist.

INTRODUCTORY RITE

BLESSING OF THE FIRE AND LIGHTING OF THE PASCHAL CANDLE
The night vigil begins with the kindling of new fire and the lighting of the assembly's paschal candle.

PROCESSION
The ministers and assembly go in procession to the place where the scriptures will be read. The following is sung during the procession.

Deacon or Priest: All:

Christ   our   light.   Thanks   be   to   God.

EASTER PROCLAMATION: THE EXSULTET
In this ancient text the church gives thanks and praise to God for all that is recalled this night: Adam's fall, the deliverance from Egypt, the passover of Christ, the wedding of earth and heaven, our reconciliation.

LITURGY OF THE WORD

At the Vigil, the liturgy of the word is an extended time of readings, silence and the chanting of psalms. On this night when the faithful know the death and resurrection of the Lord in baptism and eucharist, the church needs first to hear these scriptures which are the foundation of our life together: the creation story, Abraham and Isaac, the dividing of the sea, the poetry of Isaiah and Baruch and Ezekiel, the proclamation of Paul to the Romans and the gospel account of Jesus' resurrection.

READING I
Genesis 1:1—2:2 or 1:1, 26-31a / 41   534

For short form read only the parts in brackets.

[In the beginning, when God created the heavens and the earth,] the earth was a formless wasteland, and darkness covered the abyss, while a mighty wind swept over the waters.

Then God said, "Let there be light," and there was light. God saw how good the light was. God then separated the light from the darkness. God called the light "day," and the darkness he called "night." Thus evening came, and morning followed—the first day.

Then God said, "Let there be a dome in the middle of the waters, to separate one body of water from the other." And so it happened: God made the dome, and it separated the water above the dome from the water below it. God called the dome "the sky." Evening came, and morning followed—the second day.

Then God said, "Let the water under the sky be gathered into a single basin, so that the dry land may appear." And so it happened: the water under the sky was gathered into its basin, and the dry land appeared. God called the dry land "the earth," and the basin of the water he called "the sea." God saw how good it was. Then God said, "Let the earth bring forth vegetation: every kind of plant that bears seed and every kind of fruit tree on earth that bears fruit with its seed in it." And so it happened: the earth brought forth every kind of plant that bears seed and every kind of fruit tree on earth that bears fruit with its seed in it. God saw how good it was. Evening came, and morning followed—the third day.

Then God said: "Let there be lights in the dome of the sky, to separate day from night. Let them mark the fixed times, the days and the years, and serve as luminaries in the dome of the sky, to shed light upon the earth." And so it happened: God made the two great lights, the greater one to govern the day, and the lesser one to govern the night;

and he made the stars. God set them in the dome of the sky, to shed light upon the earth, to govern the day and the night, and to separate the light from the darkness. God saw how good it was. Evening came, and morning followed—the fourth day.

Then God said, "Let the water teem with an abundance of living creatures, and on the earth let birds fly beneath the dome of the sky." And so it happened: God created the great sea monsters and all kinds of swimming creatures with which the water teems, and all kinds of winged birds. God saw how good it was, and God blessed them, saying, "Be fertile, multiply, and fill the water of the seas; and let the birds multiply on the earth." Evening came, and morning followed—the fifth day.

Then God said, "Let the earth bring forth all kinds of living creatures: cattle, creeping things, and wild animals of all kinds." And so it happened: God made all kinds of wild animals, all kinds of cattle, and all kinds of creeping things of the earth. God saw how good it was. Then [God said: "Let us make man in our image, after our likeness. Let them have dominion over the fish of the sea, the birds of the air, and the cattle, and over all the wild animals and all the creatures that crawl on the ground."

God created man in his image;
in the image of God he created him;
male and female he created them.

God blessed them, saying: "Be fertile and multiply; fill the earth and subdue it. Have dominion over the fish of the sea, the birds of the air, and all the living things that move on the earth." God also said: "See, I give you every seed-bearing plant all over the earth and every tree that has seed-bearing fruit on it to be your food; and to all the animals of the land, all the birds of the air, and all the living creatures that crawl on the ground, I give all the green plants for food." And so it happened. God looked at everything he had made, and he found it very good.] Evening came, and morning followed—the sixth day.

Thus the heavens and the earth and all their array were completed. Since on the seventh day God was finished with the work he had been doing, he rested on the seventh day from all the work he had undertaken.

RESPONSORIAL PSALM

1. Psalm 104:1-2, 5-6, 10, 12, 13-14, 24, 35

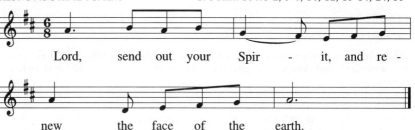

Lord, send out your Spir - it, and re - new the face of the earth.

Bless the LORD, O my soul!
  O LORD, my God, you are great
    indeed!
You are clothed with majesty and
    glory,
  robed in light as with a cloak. ℟.

You fixed the earth upon its foundation,
  not to be moved forever;
with the ocean, as with a garment, you
    covered it;
  above the mountains the waters
    stood. ℟.

You send forth springs into the
    watercourses
  that wind among the mountains.
Beside them the birds of heaven dwell;
  from among the branches they send
    forth their song. ℟.

You water the mountains from your
    palace;
  the earth is replete with the fruit of
    your works.
You raise grass for the cattle,
  and vegetation for man's use,
producing bread from the earth. ℟.

How manifold are your works, O LORD!
  In wisdom you have wrought them
    all —

the earth is full of your creatures.
  Bless the LORD, O my soul! ℞.

Or:

RESPONSORIAL PSALM   *2. Psalm 33:4-5, 6-7, 12-13, 20, 22*

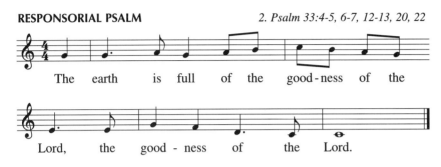

The earth is full of the good-ness of the Lord, the good-ness of the Lord.

Upright is the word of the LORD,
  and all his works are trustworthy.
He loves justice and right;
  of the kindness of the LORD the earth
    is full. ℞.

By the word of the LORD the heavens
    were made;
  by the breath of his mouth all their
    host.
He gathers the waters of the sea as in a
    flask;
  in cellars he confines the deep. ℞.

Blessed the nation whose God is the
    LORD,
  the people he has chosen for his
    own inheritance.
From heaven the LORD looks down;
  he sees all mankind. ℞.

Our soul waits for the LORD,
  who is our help and our shield.
May your kindness, O LORD, be upon us
  who have put our hope in you. ℞.

READING II   *Genesis 22:1-18 or 22:1-2, 9a, 10-13, 15-18*   535

For short form read only the parts in brackets.

[God put Abraham to the test. He called to him, "Abraham!" "Here I am," he replied. Then God said: "Take your son Isaac, your only one, whom you love, and go to the land of Moriah. There you shall offer him up as a holocaust on a height that I will point out to you."]

Early the next morning Abraham saddled his donkey, took with him his son Isaac and two of his servants as well, and with the wood that he had cut for the holocaust, set out for the place of which God had told him.

On the third day Abraham got sight of the place from afar. Then he said to his servants: "Both of you stay here with the donkey, while the boy and I go on over yonder. We will worship and then come back to you." Thereupon Abraham took the wood for the holocaust and laid it on his son Isaac's shoulders, while he himself carried the fire and the knife. As the two walked on together, Isaac spoke to his father Abraham: "Father!" Isaac said. "Yes, son," he replied. Isaac continued, "Here are the fire and the wood, but where is the sheep for the holocaust?" "Son," Abraham answered, "God himself will provide the sheep for the holocaust." Then the two continued going forward.

[When they came to the place of which God had told him, Abraham built an altar there and arranged the wood on it.] Next he tied up his son Isaac, and put him on top of the wood on the altar. [Then he reached out and took the knife to slaughter his son. But the LORD's messenger called to him from heaven, "Abraham, Abraham!" "Here I am," he answered. "Do not lay your hand on the boy," said the messenger. "Do not do the least thing to him. I know now how devoted you are to God, since you did not withhold from me your own beloved son." As Abraham looked about, he spied a ram caught by its horns in the thicket. So he went and took the ram and offered it up as a holocaust in place of his son.] Abraham named the site Yahweh-yireh; hence people now say, "On the mountain the LORD will see."

[Again the LORD's messenger called to Abraham from heaven and said: "I swear by myself, declares the LORD, that because you acted as you did in not withholding from me your beloved son, I will bless you abundantly and make your descendants as count-less as the stars of the sky and the sands of the seashore; your descendants shall take pos-session of the gates of their enemies, and in your descendants all the nations of the earth shall find blessing—all this because you obeyed my command."]

RESPONSORIAL PSALM

Psalm 16:5, 8, 9-10, 11

You are my in - her - i - tance, O Lord.

O LORD, my allotted portion and my cup,
    you it is who hold fast my lot.
I set the LORD ever before me;
    with him at my right hand I shall not
    be disturbed. ℟.

Therefore my heart is glad and my soul
    rejoices,
    my body, too, abides in confidence;

because you will not abandon my soul to
    the netherworld,
    nor will you suffer your faithful one
    to undergo corruption. ℟.

You will show me the path to life,
    fullness of joys in your presence,
    the delights at your right hand forever. ℟.

536 READING III

Exodus 14:15—15:1

The LORD said to Moses, "Why are you crying out to me? Tell the Israelites to go forward. And you, lift up your staff and, with hand outstretched over the sea, split the sea in two, that the Israelites may pass through it on dry land. But I will make the Egyp-tians so obstinate that they will go in after them. Then I will receive glory through Pharaoh and all his army, his chariots and charioteers. The Egyptians shall know that I am the LORD, when I receive glory through Pharaoh and his chariots and charioteers."

The angel of God, who had been leading Israel's camp, now moved and went around behind them. The column of cloud also, leaving the front, took up its place behind them, so that it came between the camp of the Egyptians and that of Israel. But the cloud now became dark, and thus the night passed without the rival camps coming any closer together all night long. Then Moses stretched out his hand over the sea, and the LORD swept the sea with a strong east wind throughout the night and so turned it into dry land. When the water was thus divided, the Israelites marched into the midst of the sea on dry land, with the water like a wall to their right and to their left.

The Egyptians followed in pursuit; all Pharaoh's horses and chariots and charioteers went after them right into the midst of the sea. In the night watch just before dawn the LORD cast through the column of the fiery cloud upon the Egyptian force a glance that threw it into a panic; and he so clogged their chariot wheels that they could hardly dri-ve. With that the Egyptians sounded the retreat before Israel, because the LORD was fighting for them against the Egyptians.

Then the LORD told Moses, "Stretch out your hand over the sea, that the water may flow back upon the Egyptians, upon their chariots and their charioteers." So Moses stretched out his hand over the sea, and at dawn the sea flowed back to its normal depth. The Egyptians were fleeing head on toward the sea, when the LORD hurled them into its midst. As the water flowed back, it covered the chariots and the charioteers of Pharaoh's whole army which had followed the Israelites into the sea. Not a single one of them escaped. But the Israelites had marched on dry land through the midst of the sea, with the water like a wall to their right and to their left. Thus the LORD saved Israel on that day from the power of the Egyptians. When Israel saw the Egyptians lying dead on the seashore and beheld the great power that the LORD had shown against the Egyptians, they feared the LORD and believed in him and in his servant Moses.

    Then Moses and the Israelites sang this song to the LORD:
        I will sing to the LORD, for he is gloriously triumphant;
           horse and chariot he has cast into the sea.

RESPONSORIAL PSALM

Exodus 15:1-2, 3-4, 5-6, 17-18

Let us sing to the Lord; he has cov-ered him-self in glo - ry.

I will sing to the LORD, for he is
    gloriously triumphant;
    horse and chariot he has cast into the
      sea.
My strength and my courage is the LORD,
    and he has been my savior.
He is my God, I praise him;
    the God of my father, I extol him. ℟.

The LORD is a warrior,
    LORD is his name!
Pharaoh's chariots and army he hurled
    into the sea;
    the elite of his officers were
      submerged in the Red Sea. ℟.

The flood waters covered them,
    they sank into the depths like a stone.
Your right hand, O LORD, magnificent in
    power,
    your right hand, O LORD, has
    shattered the enemy. ℟.

You brought in the people you redeemed
    and planted them on the mountain
      of your inheritance—
the place where you made your seat, O
    LORD,
    the sanctuary, Lord, which your
    hands established.
The LORD shall reign forever and ever. ℟.

READING IV

Isaiah 54:5-14   **537**

The One who has become your husband
    is your Maker;
    his name is the LORD of hosts;
your redeemer is the Holy One of Israel,
    called God of all the earth.
The LORD calls you back,
    like a wife forsaken and grieved in
      spirit,
    a wife married in youth and then
      cast off,
    says your God.
For a brief moment I abandoned you,
    but with great tenderness I will take
      you back.
In an outburst of wrath, for a moment
    I hid my face from you;
but with enduring love I take pity on you,
    says the LORD, your redeemer.
This is for me like the days of Noah,
    when I swore that the waters of Noah
    should never again deluge the earth;
so I have sworn not to be angry with you,

    or to rebuke you.
Though the mountains leave their place
    and the hills be shaken,
my love shall never leave you
    nor my covenant of peace be shaken,
    says the LORD, who has mercy on
      you.
O afflicted one, storm-battered and
    unconsoled,
    I lay your pavements in carnelians,
    and your foundations in sapphires;
I will make your battlements of rubies,
    your gates of carbuncles,
    and all your walls of precious stones.
All your children shall be taught by the
    LORD,
    and great shall be the peace of your
    children.
In justice shall you be established,
    far from the fear of oppression,
    where destruction cannot come near
    you.

RESPONSORIAL PSALM   *Psalm 30:2, 4, 5-6, 11-12, 13*

I will praise you, Lord, for you have res-cued me.

I will extol you, O LORD, for you drew me
        clear
    and did not let my enemies rejoice
        over me.
O LORD, you brought me up from the
        netherworld;
    you preserved me from among those
        going down into the pit. ℟.

Sing praise to the LORD, you his faithful
        ones,
    and give thanks to his holy name.

For his anger lasts but a moment;
        a lifetime, his good will.
At nightfall, weeping enters in,
    but with the dawn, rejoicing. ℟.

Hear, O LORD, and have pity on me;
    O LORD, be my helper.
You changed my mourning into
        dancing;
    O LORD, my God, forever will I
        give you thanks. ℟.

538 **READING V**   *Isaiah 55:1-11*

Thus says the LORD:
All you who are thirsty,
    come to the water!
You who have no money,
    come, receive grain and eat;
come, without paying and without cost,
    drink wine and milk!
Why spend your money for what is not
        bread,
    your wages for what fails to satisfy?
Heed me, and you shall eat well,
    you shall delight in rich fare.
Come to me heedfully,
    listen, that you may have life.
I will renew with you the everlasting
        covenant,
    the benefits assured to David.
As I made him a witness to the peoples,
    a leader and commander of nations,
so shall you summon a nation you knew
        not,
    and nations that knew you not shall
        run to you,
because of the LORD, your God,
    the Holy One of Israel, who has
        glorified you.

Seek the LORD while he may be found,

call him while he is near.
Let the scoundrel forsake his way,
    and the wicked man his thoughts;
let him turn to the LORD for mercy;
    to our God, who is generous in
        forgiving.
For my thoughts are not your thoughts,
    nor are your ways my ways, says the
        LORD.
As high as the heavens are above the
        earth,
    so high are my ways above your
        ways
    and my thoughts above your
        thoughts.

For just as from the heavens
    the rain and snow come down
and do not return there
    till they have watered the earth,
        making it fertile and fruitful,
giving seed to the one who sows
    and bread to the one who eats,
so shall my word be
    that goes forth from my mouth;
my word shall not return to me void,
    but shall do my will,
    achieving the end for which I sent it.

RESPONSORIAL PSALM   *Isaiah 12:2-3, 4bcd, 5-6*

You will draw wa - ter   joy - ful - ly

from the springs of sal - va - tion.

God indeed is my savior;
    I am confident and unafraid.
My strength and my courage is the LORD,
    and he has been my savior.
With joy you will draw water
    at the fountain of salvation. ℟.

Give thanks to the Lord, acclaim his
    name;
    among the nations make known his

deeds,
    proclaim how exalted is his name. ℟.

Sing praise to the LORD for his glorious
    achievement;
    let this be known throughout all the
    earth.
Shout with exultation, O city of Zion,
    for great in your midst
is the Holy One of Israel! ℟.

READING VI

Baruch 3:9-15, 32—4:4   539

Hear, O Israel, the commandments of
    life:
    listen, and know prudence!
How is it, Israel,
    that you are in the land of your foes,
    grown old in a foreign land,
defiled with the dead,
    accounted with those destined for
    the netherworld?
You have forsaken the fountain of
    wisdom!
    Had you walked in the way of God,
    you would have dwelt in enduring
    peace.
Learn where prudence is,
    where strength, where understanding;
that you may know also
    where are length of days, and life,
    where light of the eyes, and peace.
Who has found the place of wisdom,
    who has entered into her treasuries?

The One who knows all things knows
    her;
    he has probed her by his
    knowledge—
the One who established the earth for
    all time,
    and filled it with four-footed beasts;

he who dismisses the light, and it
    departs,
    calls it, and it obeys him trembling;
before whom the stars at their posts
    shine and rejoice;
when he calls them, they answer, "Here
    we are!"
    shining with joy for their Maker.
Such is our God;
    no other is be compared to him:
he has traced out the whole way of
    understanding,
    and has given her to Jacob, his
    servant,
    to Israel, his beloved son.

Since then she has appeared on earth,
    and moved among people.
She is the book of the precepts of God,
    the law that endures forever;
all who cling to her will live,
    but those will die who forsake her.
Turn, O Jacob, and receive her:
    walk by her light toward splendor.
Give not your glory to another,
    your privileges to an alien race.
Blessed are we, O Israel;
    for what pleases God is known to
    us!

RESPONSORIAL PSALM

Psalm 19:8, 9, 10, 11

Lord, you have the words of ev - er-last-ing life.

The law of the LORD is perfect,
    refreshing the soul;

the decree of the LORD is trustworthy,
    giving wisdom to the simple. ℟.

The precepts of the LORD are right,
rejoicing the heart;
the command of the LORD is clear,
enlightening the eye. ℞.

The fear of the LORD is pure,
enduring forever;

the ordinances of the LORD are true,
all of them just. ℞.

They are more precious than gold,
than a heap of purest gold;
sweeter also than syrup
or honey from the comb. ℞.

540 READING VII
Ezekiel 36:16-17a, 18-28

The word of the LORD came to me, saying: Son of man, when the house of Israel lived in their land, they defiled it by their conduct and deeds. Therefore I poured out my fury upon them because of the blood that they poured out on the ground, and because they defiled it with idols. I scattered them among the nations, dispersing them over foreign lands; according to their conduct and deeds I judged them. But when they came among the nations wherever they came, they served to profane my holy name, because it was said of them: "These are the people of the LORD, yet they had to leave their land." So I have relented because of my holy name which the house of Israel profaned among the nations where they came. Therefore say to the house of Israel: Thus says the Lord GOD: Not for your sakes do I act, house of Israel, but for the sake of my holy name, which you profaned among the nations to which you came. I will prove the holiness of my great name, profaned among the nations, in whose midst you have profaned it. Thus the nations shall know that I am the LORD, says the Lord GOD, when in their sight I prove my holiness through you. For I will take you away from among the nations, gather you from all the foreign lands, and bring you back to your own land. I will sprinkle clean water upon you to cleanse you from all your impurities, and from all your idols I will cleanse you. I will give you a new heart and place a new spirit within you, taking from your bodies your stony hearts and giving you natural hearts. I will put my spirit within you and make you live by my statutes, careful to observe my decrees. You shall live in the land I gave your fathers; you shall be my people, and I will be your God.

RESPONSORIAL PSALM

1. When baptism is celebrated   *Psalm 42:3, 5; 43:3, 4*

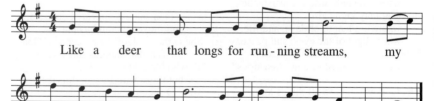

Like a deer that longs for run-ning streams, my soul longs for you, my God; my soul longs for you, my God.

Athirst is my soul for God, the living
God.
When shall I go and behold the
face of God? ℞.

I went with the throng
and led them in procession to the
house of God,
amid loud cries of joy and thanksgiving,
with the multitude keeping
festival. ℞.

Send forth your light and your fidelity;
they shall lead me on
and bring me to your holy mountain,
to your dwelling-place. ℞.

Then will I go in to the altar of God,
the God of my gladness and joy;
then will I give you thanks upon the harp,
O God, my God! ℞.

2. When baptism is not celebrated

Isaiah 12:2-3, 4bcd, 5-6

You will draw wa - ter joy - ful - ly

from the springs of sal - va - tion.

God indeed is my savior;
  I am confident and unafraid.
My strength and my courage is the LORD,
  and he has been my savior.
With joy you will draw water
  at the fountain of salvation. ℟.

Give thanks to the LORD, acclaim his
  name;
  among the nations make known his
deeds,
proclaim how exalted is his name. ℟.

Sing praise to the LORD for his glorious
  achievement;
  let this be known throughout all the
  earth.
Shout with exultation, O city of Zion,
  for great in your midst
is the Holy One of Israel! ℟.

3. When baptism is not celebrated

Psalm 51:12-13, 14-15, 18-19

Cre - ate in me, cre - ate in me a clean heart, O God.

A clean heart create for me, O God,
  and a steadfast spirit renew within
  me.
Cast me not out from your presence,
  and your Holy Spirit take not from
  me. ℟.

Give me back the joy of your salvation,
  and a willing spirit sustain in me.

I will teach transgressors your ways,
  and sinners shall return to you. ℟.

For you are not pleased with sacrifices;
  should I offer a holocaust, you
  would not accept it.
My sacrifice, O God, is a contrite spirit;
  a heart contrite and humbled, O God,
  you will not spurn. ℟.

GLORIA

PRAYER

EPISTLE

Romans 6:3-11 541

Brothers and sisters: Are you unaware that we who were baptized into Christ Jesus were baptized into his death? We were indeed buried with him through baptism into death, so that, just as Christ was raised from the dead by the glory of the Father, we too might live in newness of life.

For if we have grown into union with him through a death like his, we shall also be united with him in the resurrection. We know that our old self was crucified with him, so that our sinful body might be done away with, that we might no longer be in slavery to sin. For a dead person has been absolved from sin. If, then, we have died with Christ, we believe that we shall also live with him. We know that Christ, raised from the dead, dies no more; death no longer has power over him. As to his death, he died to sin once and for all; as to his life, he lives for God. Consequently, you too must think of yourselves as being dead to sin and living for God in Christ Jesus.

RESPONSORIAL PSALM *Psalm 118:1-2, 16-17, 22-23*

Al - le-lu - ia, al - le - lu - ia, al - le - lu - ia!

Give thanks to the LORD, for he is good,
for his mercy endures forever.
Let the house of Israel say,
"His mercy endures forever." ℟.

The right hand of the LORD has struck
with power;
the right hand of the LORD is exalted.

I shall not die, but live,
and declare the works of the
LORD. ℟.

The stone which the builders rejected
has become the cornerstone.
By the LORD has this been done;
it is wonderful in our eyes. ℟.

GOSPEL / A *Matthew 28:1-10*

After the sabbath, as the first day of the week was dawning, Mary Magdalene and the other Mary came to see the tomb. And behold, there was a great earthquake; for an angel of the Lord descended from heaven, approached, rolled back the stone, and sat upon it. His appearance was like lightning and his clothing was white as snow. The guards were shaken with fear of him and became like dead men. Then the angel said to the women in reply, "Do not be afraid! I know that you are seeking Jesus the crucified. He is not here, for he has been raised just as he said. Come and see the place where he lay. Then go quickly and tell his disciples, 'He has been raised from the dead, and he is going before you to Galilee; there you will see him.' Behold, I have told you." Then they went away quickly from the tomb, fearful yet overjoyed, and ran to announce this to his disciples. And behold, Jesus met them on their way and greeted them. They approached, embraced his feet, and did him homage. Then Jesus said to them, "Do not be afraid. Go tell my brothers to go to Galilee, and there they will see me."

GOSPEL / B *Mark 16:1-7*

When the sabbath was over, Mary Magdalene, Mary, the mother of James, and Salome bought spices so that they might go and anoint him. Very early when the sun had risen, on the first day of the week, they came to the tomb. They were saying to one another, "Who will roll back the stone for us from the entrance to the tomb?" When they looked up, they saw that the stone had been rolled back; it was very large. On entering the tomb they saw a young man sitting on the right side, clothed in a white robe, and they were utterly amazed. He said to them, "Do not be amazed! You seek Jesus of Nazareth, the crucified. He has been raised; he is not here. Behold the place where they laid him. But go and tell his disciples and Peter, 'He is going before you to Galilee; there you will see him, as he told you.'"

GOSPEL / C *Luke 24:1-12*

At daybreak on the first day of the week the women who had come from Galilee with Jesus took the spices they had prepared and went to the tomb. They found the stone rolled away from the tomb; but when they entered, they did not find the body of the Lord Jesus. While they were puzzling over this, behold, two men in dazzling garments appeared to them. They were terrified and bowed their faces to the ground. They said to them, "Why do you seek the living one among the dead? He is not here, but he has been raised. Remember what he said to you while he was still in Galilee, that the Son of Man must be handed over to sinners and be crucified, and rise on the third day." And they remembered his words. Then they returned from the tomb and announced all these things to the eleven and to all the others. The women were Mary Magdalene, Joanna, and Mary the mother of James; the others who accompanied them also told this to the apostles, but their story seemed like nonsense and they did not believe them. But Peter got up and ran to the tomb, bent down, and saw the burial cloths alone; then he went home amazed at what had happened.

LITURGY OF BAPTISM

After the homily the catechumens are called forward. The assembly chants the litany of the saints, invoking the holy women and men of all centuries. Patron saints of the church and of the catechumens and the faithful may be included in the litany.

Holy Mary, Mother of	God,	pray	for us.
Saint	Mich - ael,	pray	for us.
Holy angels of	God,	pray	for us.
Saint John the	Bap - tist,	pray	for us.
Saint	Jo - seph,	pray	for us.
Saint Peter and Saint	Paul,	pray	for us.
Saint	An - drew,	pray	for us.
Saint	John,	pray	for us.
Saint Mary	Mag - dalene,	pray	for us.
Saint	Ste - phen,	pray	for us.
Saint Ig -	na - tius,	pray	for us.
Saint	Law - rence,	pray	for us.
Saint Perpetua and Saint Fe -	lic - ity,	pray	for us.
Saint	Ag - nes,	pray	for us.
Saint	Gre - gory,	pray	for us.
Saint Au -	gus - tine,	pray	for us.
Saint Atha -	na - sius,	pray	for us.
Saint	Ba - sil,	pray	for us.
Saint	Mar - tin,	pray	for us.
Saint	Ben - edict,	pray	for us.
Saint Francis and Saint	Dom - inic,	pray	for us.
Saint Francis	Xa - vier,	pray	for us.
Saint John Vi -	an - ney,	pray	for us.
Saint	Cath - erine,	pray	for us.
Saint Te -	re - sa,	pray	for us.
All holy men and	wo - men,	pray	for us.

Cantor:
Assembly:

Lord, be mer - ci - ful, Lord, save your peo - ple.
From all e - vil, Lord, save your peo - ple.
From ev - 'ry sin, Lord, save your peo - ple.
From ev - er - last-ing death, Lord, save your peo - ple.

Cantor:
Assembly:

By your com - ing as man, Lord, save your peo - ple.
By your death and ris - ing to new life, Lord, save your peo - ple.
By your gift of the Ho-ly Spir - it, Lord, save your peo - ple.

Cantor:
Assembly:

Be merciful to us sin - ers. Lord, hear our prayer.
Give new life to these
 chosen ones by the grace of bap-tism. Lord, hear our prayer.
Jesus, Son of the liv-ing God. Lord, hear our prayer.

Cantor:
Assembly:

Christ, hear us. Christ, hear us.

Cantor:
Assembly:

Lord Je - sus, hear our prayer. Lord Je - sus, hear our prayer.

Text: *Litany of the Saints, Roman Missal*
Music: *Litany of the Saints, Roman Missal*

---

543 **BLESSING OF WATER**

The presider gives thanks and praise to God over the waters of baptism. This acclamation is sung by all.

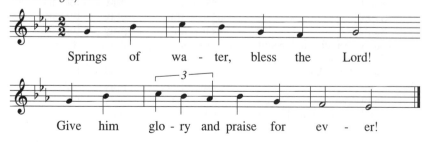

Springs of wa - ter, bless the Lord!

Give him glo - ry and praise for ev - er!

Text: Refrain trans. © 1973, ICEL
Music: Marty Haugen, © 1994, GIA Publications, Inc.

RENUNCIATION OF SIN AND PROFESSION OF FAITH 544

Each candidate for baptism is asked to reject sin and the ways of evil and to testify to faith in Father, Son and Holy Spirit. All join to affirm this faith.

THE BAPTISMS 545

One by one the candidates are led into the waters, or they bend over the font, and water is poured over them as the presider says: "N., I baptize you in the name of the Father, and of the Son, and of the Holy Spirit." After each baptism, the assembly sings an acclamation.

You have put on Christ, in him you have been bap - tized.

Al - le - lu - ia, al - le - lu - ia.

Music: Howard Hughes, SM, © 1977, ICEL

Each of the newly baptized is then clothed in a baptismal garment.

RECEPTION INTO FULL COMMUNION 546

Those who have been previously baptized are now called forward to profess their faith and to be received into the full communion of the Roman Catholic Church.

CONFIRMATION 547

Infants who have been baptized are anointed with chrism. Children and adults are usually confirmed: the presider prays and lays hands on them, then anoints each of the newly baptized with chrism saying: "N., be sealed with the Gift of the Holy Spirit."

RENEWAL OF BAPTISMAL PROMISES 548

All of the faithful repeat and affirm the rejection of sin made at baptism and profess faith in the Father, Son and Holy Spirit. The assembly is sprinkled with the baptismal water. The newly baptized then take their places in the assembly and, for the first time, join in the prayer of the faithful, the prayers of intercession.

LITURGY OF THE EUCHARIST 549

The gifts and table are prepared and the eucharist is celebrated in the usual way.

CONCLUDING RITE 550

The dismissal is sung with "alleluia", and all respond.

Deacon or Priest:
Go in the peace of Christ, al-le-lu - ia, al-le - lu - ia.

Assembly:
Thanks be to God, al-le-lu - ia, al-le - lu - ia.

551 EASTER SUNDAY / ABC

READING I
Acts 10:34a, 37-43 / 42

Peter proceeded to speak and said: "You know what has happened all over Judea, beginning in Galilee after the baptism that John preached, how God anointed Jesus of Nazareth with the Holy Spirit and power. He went about doing good and healing all those oppressed by the devil, for God was with him. We are witnesses of all that he did both in the country of the Jews and in Jerusalem. They put him to death by hanging him on a tree. This man God raised on the third day and granted that he be visible, not to all the people, but to us, the witnesses chosen by God in advance, who ate and drank with him after he rose from the dead. He commissioned us to preach to the people and testify that he is the one appointed by God as judge of the living and the dead. To him all the prophets bear witness, that everyone who believes in him will receive forgiveness of sins through his name.

RESPONSORIAL PSALM
Psalm 118:1-2, 16-17, 22-23

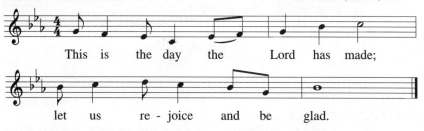

This is the day the Lord has made; let us re-joice and be glad.

Give thanks to the LORD, for he is good,
    for his mercy endures forever.
Let the house of Israel say,
    "His mercy endures forever." ℟.

"The right hand of the LORD has struck
    with power;
    the right hand of the LORD is exalted.

I shall not die, but live,
    and declare the works of the LORD. ℟.

The stone which the builders rejected
    has become the cornerstone.
By the LORD has this been done;
    it is wonderful in our eyes. ℟.

READING II
Colossians 3:1-4

Brothers and sisters: If then you were raised with Christ, seek what is above, where Christ is seated at the right hand of God. Think of what is above, not of what is on earth. For you have died, and your life is hidden with Christ in God. When Christ your life appears, then you too will appear with him in glory.

Or:

READING II
1 Corinthians 5:6b-8

Brothers and sisters: Do you not know that a little yeast leavens all the dough? Clear out the old yeast, so that you may become a fresh batch of dough, inasmuch as you are unleavened. For our paschal lamb, Christ, has been sacrificed. Therefore, let us celebrate the feast, not with the old yeast, the yeast of malice and wickedness, but with the unleavened bread of sincerity and truth.

SEQUENCE

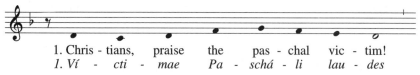

1. Chris - tians, praise the pas - chal vic - tim!
1. Ví - cti - mae Pa - schá - li lau - des

Of - fer thank - ful sac - ri - fice!
im - mó - lent Chri - sti - á - ni.

2. Christ the Lamb has saved the sheep,
3. Death and life fought bit - ter - ly
2. *A - gnus ré - de - mit ó - ves:*
3. *Mors et vi - ta du - él - lo*

Christ the just one paid the price,
For this won - drous vic - to - ry;
Chri - stus ín - no - cens Pá - tri
con - fli - xé - re mi - rán - do:

Rec - on - cil - ing sin - ners to the Fa - ther.
The Lord of life who died reigns glo - ri - fied!
re - con - ci - li - á - vit pec - ca - tó - res.
dux vi - tae mór - tu - us re - gnat vi - vus.

4. O Mar - y, come and say what you
6. Bright an - gels tes - ti - fied, Shroud and
4. *Dic no - bis Ma - rí - a, quid vi -*
6. *An - gé - li - cos te - stes, su - dá -*

saw at break of day. 5. "The emp - ty tomb
grave clothes side by side! 7. "Yes, Christ my hope
dí - sti in vi - a? 5. Se - púl - crum Chri -
ri - um, et ve - stes. 7. Sur - ré - xit Chri -

of my liv - ing Lord! I saw Christ Je -
rose glo - ri - ous - ly. He goes be - fore
sti vi - vén - tis, et gló - ri - am
stus spes me - a: prae - cé - det su -

sus ris - en and a - dored!"
you in - to Gal - i - lee."
vi - di re - sur - gén - tis.
os in Ga - li - láe - am.

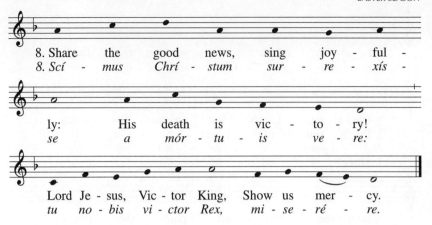

8. Share the good news, sing joy - ful -
8. *Sci - mus Chri - stum sur - re - xis -*

ly: His death is vic - to - ry!
se a mór - tu - is ve - re:

Lord Je - sus, Vic - tor King, Show us mer - cy.
tu no - bis vi - ctor Rex, mi - se - ré - re.

Text: Sequence for Easter, ascr. to Wipo of Burgundy, d.1048; tr. by Peter J. Scagnelli, b.1949, © 1983
Music: Mode I; acc. by Richard Proulx, b.1937, © 1975, GIA Publications, Inc.

GOSPEL
John 20:1-9

On the first day of the week, Mary of Magdala came to the tomb early in the morning, while it was still dark, and saw the stone removed from the tomb. So she ran and went to Simon Peter and to the other disciple whom Jesus loved, and told them, "They have taken the Lord from the tomb, and we don't know where they put him." So Peter and the other disciple went out and came to the tomb. They both ran, but the other disciple ran faster than Peter and arrived at the tomb first; he bent down and saw the burial cloths there, but did not go in. When Simon Peter arrived after him, he went into the tomb and saw the burial cloths there, and the cloth that had covered his head, not with the burial cloths but rolled up in a separate place. Then the other disciple also went in, the one who had arrived at the tomb first, and he saw and believed. For they did not yet understand the Scripture that he had to rise from the dead.

552 SECOND SUNDAY OF EASTER / ABC

READING I / A
Acts 2:42-47 / 43

They devoted themselves to the teaching of the apostles and to the communal life, to the breaking of bread and to the prayers. Awe came upon everyone, and many wonders and signs were done through the apostles. All who believed were together and had all things in common; they would sell their property and possessions and divide them among all according to each one's need. Every day they devoted themselves to meeting together in the temple area and to breaking bread in their homes. They ate their meals with exultation and sincerity of heart, praising God and enjoying favor with all the people. And every day the Lord added to their number those who were being saved.

READING I / B
Acts 4:32-35 / 44

The community of believers was of one heart and mind, and no one claimed that any of his possessions was his own, but they had everything in common. With great power the apostles bore witness to the resurrection of the Lord Jesus, and great favor was accorded them all. There was no needy person among them, for those who owned property or houses would sell them, bring the proceeds of the sale, and put them at the feet of the apostles, and they were distributed to each according to need.

READING I / C
Acts 5:12-16 / 45

Many signs and wonders were done among the people at the hands of the apostles. They were all together in Solomon's portico. None of the others dared to join them, but the people esteemed them. Yet more than ever, believers in the Lord, great numbers of men and women, were added to them. Thus they even carried the sick out into the streets and laid them on cots and mats so that when Peter came by, at least his shadow might fall on one or another of them. A large number of people from the towns in the vicinity of Jerusalem also gathered, bringing the sick and those disturbed by unclean spirits, and they were all cured.

RESPONSORIAL PSALM
Psalm 118:2-4, 13-15, 22-24

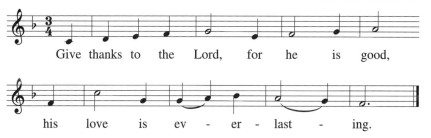

Give thanks to the Lord, for he is good, his love is ev - er - last - ing.

Let the house of Israel say,
"His mercy endures forever."
Let the house of Aaron say,
"His mercy endures forever."
Let those who fear the LORD say,
"His mercy endures forever." ℟.

I was hard pressed and was falling,
but the LORD helped me.
My strength and my courage is the LORD,
and he has been my savior.
The joyful shout of victory
in the tents of the just. ℟.

The stone which the builders rejected
has become the cornerstone.
By the LORD has this been done;
it is wonderful in our eyes.
This is the day the LORD has made;
let us be glad and rejoice in it. ℟.

READING II / A
1 Peter 1:3-9

Blessed be the God and Father of our Lord Jesus Christ, who in his great mercy gave us a new birth to a living hope through the resurrection of Jesus Christ from the dead, to an inheritance that is imperishable, undefiled, and unfading, kept in heaven for you who by the power of God are safeguarded through faith, to a salvation that is ready to be revealed in the final time. In this you rejoice, although now for a little while you may have to suffer through various trials, so that the genuineness of your faith, more precious than gold that is perishable even though tested by fire, may prove to be for praise, glory, and honor at the revelation of Jesus Christ. Although you have not seen him you love him; even though you do not see him now yet believe in him, you rejoice with an indescribable and glorious joy, as you attain the goal of your faith, the salvation of your souls.

READING II / B
1 John 5:1-6

Beloved: Everyone who believes that Jesus is the Christ is begotten by God, and everyone who loves the Father loves also the one begotten by him. In this way we know that we love the children of God when we love God and obey his commandments. For the love of God is this, that we keep his commandments. And his commandments are not burdensome, for whoever is begotten by God conquers the world. And the victory that conquers the world is our faith. Who indeed is the victor over the world but the one who believes that Jesus is the Son of God?

This is the one who came through water and blood, Jesus Christ, not by water alone, but by water and blood. The Spirit is the one that testifies, and the Spirit is truth.

READING II / C   *Revelation 1:9-11a, 12-13, 17-19*

I, John, your brother, who share with you the distress, the kingdom, and the endurance we have in Jesus, found myself on the island called Patmos because I proclaimed God's word and gave testimony to Jesus. I was caught up in spirit on the Lord's day and heard behind me a voice as loud as a trumpet, which said, "Write on a scroll what you see." Then I turned to see whose voice it was that spoke to me, and when I turned, I saw seven gold lampstands and in the midst of the lampstands one like a son of man, wearing an ankle-length robe, with a gold sash around his chest.

When I caught sight of him, I fell down at his feet as though dead. He touched me with his right hand and said, "Do not be afraid. I am the first and the last, the one who lives. Once I was dead, but now I am alive forever and ever. I hold the keys to death and the netherworld. Write down, therefore, what you have seen, and what is happening, and what will happen afterwards."

GOSPEL   *John 20:19-31*

On the evening of that first day of the week, when the doors were locked, where the disciples were, for fear of the Jews, Jesus came and stood in their midst and said to them, "Peace be with you." When he had said this, he showed them his hands and his side. The disciples rejoiced when they saw the Lord. Jesus said to them again, "Peace be with you. As the Father has sent me, so I send you." And when he had said this, he breathed on them and said to them, "Receive the Holy Spirit. Whose sins you forgive are forgiven them, and whose sins you retain are retained."

Thomas, called Didymus, one of the Twelve, was not with them when Jesus came. So the other disciples said to him, "We have seen the Lord." But he said to them, "Unless I see the mark of the nails in his hands and put my finger into the nailmarks and put my hand into his side, I will not believe."

Now a week later his disciples were again inside and Thomas was with them. Jesus came, although the doors were locked, and stood in their midst and said, "Peace be with you." Then he said to Thomas, "Put your finger here and see my hands, and bring your hand and put it into my side, and do not be unbelieving, but believe." Thomas answered and said to him, "My Lord and my God!" Jesus said to him, "Have you come to believe because you have seen me? Blessed are those who have not seen and have believed."

Now, Jesus did many other signs in the presence of his disciples that are not written in this book. But these are written that you may come to believe that Jesus is the Christ, the Son of God, and that through this belief you may have life in his name.

---

553   THIRD SUNDAY OF EASTER / A

READING I   *Acts 2:14, 22-33 / 46*

Then Peter stood up with the Eleven, raised his voice, and proclaimed: "You who are Jews, indeed all of you staying in Jerusalem. Let this be known to you, and listen to my words. You who are Israelites, hear these words. Jesus the Nazarene was a man commended to you by God with mighty deeds, wonders, and signs, which God worked through him in your midst, as you yourselves know. This man, delivered up by the set plan and foreknowledge of God, you killed, using lawless men to crucify him. But God raised him up, releasing him from the throes of death, because it was impossible for him to be held by it. For David says of him:

'I saw the Lord ever before me,
with him at my right hand I shall not be disturbed.
Therefore my heart has been glad and my tongue has exulted;
my flesh, too, will dwell in hope,

because you will not abandon my soul to the netherworld,
    nor will you suffer your holy one to see corruption.
You have made known to me the paths of life;
    you will fill me with joy in your presence.'
"My brothers, one can confidently say to you about the patriarch David that he died and
was buried, and his tomb is in our midst to this day. But since he was a prophet and knew
that God had sworn an oath to him that he would set one of his descendants upon his
throne, he foresaw and spoke of the resurrection of the Christ, that neither was he abandoned to the netherworld nor did his flesh see corruption. God raised this Jesus; of this
we are all witnesses. Exalted at the right hand of God, he received the promise of the
Holy Spirit from the Father and poured him forth, as you see and hear."

RESPONSORIAL PSALM

Psalm 16:1-2, 5, 7-8, 9-10, 11

Lord,   you will   show us   the   path   of   life.

Keep me, O God, for in you I take refuge;
    I say to the LORD, "My LORD are
        you."
O LORD, my allotted portion and my cup,
    you it is who hold fast my lot. ℟.

I bless the LORD who counsels me;
    even in the night my heart exhorts
        me.
I set the LORD ever before me;
    with him at my right hand I shall
        not be disturbed. ℟.

Therefore my heart is glad and my soul
        rejoices,
    my body, too, abides in confidence;
because you will not abandon my soul to
        the netherworld,
    nor will you suffer your faithful one
        to undergo corruption. ℟.

You will show me the path to life,
    abounding joy in your presence,
the delights at your right hand forever. ℟.

READING II

1 Peter 1:17-21

Beloved: If you invoke as Father him who judges impartially according to each one's
works, conduct yourselves with reverence during the time of your sojourning, realizing
that you were ransomed from your futile conduct, handed on by your ancestors, not with
perishable things like silver or gold but with the precious blood of Christ as of a spot-
less unblemished lamb. He was known before the foundation of the world but revealed
in the final time for you, who through him believe in God who raised him from the dead
and gave him glory, so that your faith and hope are in God.

GOSPEL

Luke 24:13-35

That very day, the first day of the week, two of Jesus' disciples were going to a village
seven miles from Jerusalem called Emmaus, and they were conversing about all the
things that had occurred. And it happened that while they were conversing and debating,
Jesus himself drew near and walked with them, but their eyes were prevented from rec-
ognizing him. He asked them, "What are you discussing as you walk along?" They
stopped, looking downcast. One of them, named Cleopas, said to him in reply, "Are you
the only visitor to Jerusalem who does not know of the things that have taken place there
in these days?" And he replied to them, "What sort of things?" They said to him, "The
things that happened to Jesus the Nazorean, who was a prophet mighty in deed and word
before God and all the people, how our chief priests and rulers both handed him over to
a sentence of death and crucified him. But we were hoping that he would be the one to
redeem Israel; and besides all this, it is now the third day since this took place. Some
women from our group, however, have astounded us: they were at the tomb early in the

morning and did not find his body; they came back and reported that they had indeed seen a vision of angels who announced that he was alive. Then some of those with us went to the tomb and found things just as the women had described, but him they did not see." And he said to them, "Oh, how foolish you are! How slow of heart to believe all that the prophets spoke! Was it not necessary that the Christ should suffer these things and enter into his glory?" Then beginning with Moses and all the prophets, he interpreted to them what referred to him in all the Scriptures. As they approached the village to which they were going, he gave the impression that he was going on farther. But they urged him, "Stay with us, for it is nearly evening and the day is almost over." So he went in to stay with them. And it happened that, while he was with them at table, he took bread, said the blessing, broke it, and gave it to them. With that their eyes were opened and they recognized him, but he vanished from their sight. Then they said to each other, "Were not our hearts burning within us while he spoke to us on the way and opened the Scriptures to us?" So they set out at once and returned to Jerusalem where they found gathered together the eleven and those with them who were saying, "The Lord has truly been raised and has appeared to Simon!" Then the two recounted what had taken place on the way and how he was made known to them in the breaking of bread.

554 THIRD SUNDAY OF EASTER / B

READING I
Acts 3:13-15, 17-19 / 47

Peter said to the people: "The God of Abraham, the God of Isaac, and the God of Jacob, the God of our fathers, has glorified his servant Jesus, whom you handed over and denied in Pilate's presence when he had decided to release him. You denied the Holy and Righteous One and asked that a murderer be released to you. The author of life you put to death, but God raised him from the dead; of this we are witnesses. Now I know, brothers, that you acted out of ignorance, just as your leaders did; but God has thus brought to fulfillment what he had announced beforehand through the mouth of all the prophets, that his Christ would suffer. Repent, therefore, and be converted, that your sins may be wiped away."

RESPONSORIAL PSALM
Psalm 4:2, 4, 7-8, 9

Lord, let your face shine on us.

When I call, answer me, O my just God,
  you who relieve me when I am in
    distress;
have pity on me, and hear my prayer! ℟.

Know that the LORD does wonders for
    his faithful one;
  the LORD will hear me when I call
    upon him. ℟.

O LORD, let the light of your
    countenance shine upon us!
  You put gladness into my heart. ℟.

As soon as I lie down, I fall peacefully
    asleep,
  for you alone, O LORD,
bring security to my dwelling. ℟.

READING II
1 John 2:1-5a

My children, I am writing this to you so that you may not commit sin. But if anyone does sin, we have an Advocate with the Father, Jesus Christ the righteous one. He is expiation for our sins, and not for our sins only but for those of the whole world. The way we may be sure that we know him is to keep his commandments. Those who say, "I know him," but do not keep his commandments are liars, and the truth is not in them. But whoever keeps his word, the love of God is truly perfected in him.

GOSPEL

Luke 24:35-48

The two disciples recounted what had taken place on the way, and how Jesus was made known to them in the breaking of bread.

While they were still speaking about this, he stood in their midst and said to them, "Peace be with you." But they were startled and terrified and thought that they were seeing a ghost. Then he said to them, "Why are you troubled? And why do questions arise in your hearts? Look at my hands and my feet, that it is I myself. Touch me and see, because a ghost does not have flesh and bones as you can see I have." And as he said this, he showed them his hands and his feet. While they were still incredulous for joy and were amazed, he asked them, "Have you anything here to eat?" They gave him a piece of baked fish; he took it and ate it in front of them.

He said to them, "These are my words that I spoke to you while I was still with you, that everything written about me in the law of Moses and in the prophets and psalms must be fulfilled." Then he opened their minds to understand the Scriptures. And he said to them, "Thus it is written that the Christ would suffer and rise from the dead on the third day and that repentance, for the forgiveness of sins, would be preached in his name to all the nations, beginning from Jerusalem. You are witnesses of these things."

THIRD SUNDAY OF EASTER / C
555

READING I

Acts 5:27-32, 40b-41 / 48

When the captain and the court officers had brought the apostles in and made them stand before the Sanhedrin, the high priest questioned them, "We gave you strict orders, did we not, to stop teaching in that name? Yet you have filled Jerusalem with your teaching and want to bring this man's blood upon us." But Peter and the apostles said in reply, "We must obey God rather than men. The God of our ancestors raised Jesus, though you had him killed by hanging him on a tree. God exalted him at his right hand as leader and savior to grant Israel repentance and forgiveness of sins. We are witnesses of these things, as is the Holy Spirit whom God has given to those who obey him."

The Sanhedrin ordered the apostles to stop speaking in the name of Jesus, and dismissed them. So they left the presence of the Sanhedrin, rejoicing that they had been found worthy to suffer dishonor for the sake of the name.

RESPONSORIAL PSALM

Psalm 30:2, 4, 5-6, 11-12, 13

I will praise you, Lord, for you have res-cued me.

I will extol you, O LORD, for you drew
  me clear
  and did not let my enemies rejoice
    over me.
O LORD, you brought me up from the
  netherworld;
  you preserved me from among those
    going down into the pit. ℟.

Sing praise to the LORD, you his faithful
  ones,

and give thanks to his holy name.
For his anger lasts but a moment;
  a lifetime, his good will.
At nightfall, weeping enters in,
  but with the dawn, rejoicing. ℟.

Hear, O LORD, and have pity on me;
  O LORD, be my helper.
You changed my mourning into
  dancing;
  O LORD, my God, forever will I give
    you thanks. ℟.

READING II   *Revelation 5:11-14*

I, John, looked and heard the voices of many angels who surrounded the throne and the living creatures and the elders. They were countless in number, and they cried out in a loud voice:

"Worthy is the Lamb that was slain

to receive power and riches, wisdom and strength,

honor and glory and blessing."

Then I heard every creature in heaven and on earth and under the earth and in the sea, everything in the universe, cry out:

"To the one who sits on the throne and to the Lamb

be blessing and honor, glory and might,

forever and ever."

The four living creatures answered, "Amen," and the elders fell down and worshiped.

GOSPEL   *John 21:1-19 or 21:1-14*

For short form read only the part in brackets.

[At that time, Jesus revealed himself again to his disciples at the Sea of Tiberias. He revealed himself in this way. Together were Simon Peter, Thomas called Didymus, Nathanael from Cana in Galilee, Zebedee's sons, and two others of his disciples. Simon Peter said to them, "I am going fishing." They said to him, "We also will come with you." So they went out and got into the boat, but that night they caught nothing. When it was already dawn, Jesus was standing on the shore; but the disciples did not realize that it was Jesus. Jesus said to them, "Children, have you caught anything to eat?" They answered him, "No." So he said to them, "Cast the net over the right side of the boat and you will find something." So they cast it, and were not able to pull it in because of the number of fish. So the disciple whom Jesus loved said to Peter, "It is the Lord." When Simon Peter heard that it was the Lord, he tucked in his garment, for he was lightly clad, and jumped into the sea. The other disciples came in the boat, for they were not far from shore, only about a hundred yards, dragging the net with the fish. When they climbed out on shore, they saw a charcoal fire with fish on it and bread. Jesus said to them, "Bring some of the fish you just caught." So Simon Peter went over and dragged the net ashore full of one hundred fifty-three large fish. Even though there were so many, the net was not torn. Jesus said to them, "Come, have breakfast." And none of the disciples dared to ask him, "Who are you?" because they realized it was the Lord. Jesus came over and took the bread and gave it to them, and in like manner the fish. This was now the third time Jesus was revealed to his disciples after being raised from the dead.]

When they had finished breakfast, Jesus said to Simon Peter, "Simon, son of John, do you love me more than these?" Simon Peter answered him, "Yes, Lord, you know that I love you." Jesus said to him, "Feed my lambs." He then said to Simon Peter a second time, "Simon, son of John, do you love me?" Simon Peter answered him, "Yes, Lord, you know that I love you." Jesus said to him, "Tend my sheep." Jesus said to him the third time, "Simon, son of John, do you love me?" Peter was distressed that Jesus had said to him a third time, "Do you love me?" and he said to him, "Lord, you know everything; you know that I love you." Jesus said to him, "Feed my sheep. Amen, amen, I say to you, when you were younger, you used to dress yourself and go where you wanted; but when you grow old, you will stretch out your hands, and someone else will dress you and lead you where you do not want to go." He said this signifying by what kind of death he would glorify God. And when he had said this, he said to him, "Follow me."

---

556   FOURTH SUNDAY OF EASTER / A

READING I   *Acts 2:14a, 36-41 / 49*

Then Peter stood up with the Eleven, raised his voice, and proclaimed: "Let the whole house of Israel know for certain that God has made both Lord and Christ, this Jesus whom you crucified."

Now when they heard this, they were cut to the heart, and they asked Peter and the other apostles, "What are we to do, my brothers?" Peter said to them, "Repent and be baptized, every one of you, in the name of Jesus Christ for the forgiveness of your sins; and you will receive the gift of the Holy Spirit. For the promise is made to you and to your children and to all those far off, whomever the Lord our God will call." He testified with many other arguments, and was exhorting them, "Save yourselves from this corrupt generation." Those who accepted his message were baptized, and about three thousand persons were added that day.

RESPONSORIAL PSALM
Psalm 23:1-3a, 3b-4, 5, 6

The Lord is my shep-herd; there is noth - ing I shall want.

The LORD is my shepherd; I shall not want.
In verdant pastures he gives me repose;
beside restful waters he leads me;
he refreshes my soul. ℟.

He guides me in right paths
for his name's sake.
Even though I walk in the dark valley
I fear no evil; for you are at my side;
with your rod and your staff

that give me courage. ℟.

You spread the table before me
in the sight of my foes;
you anoint my head with oil;
my cup overflows. ℟.

Only goodness and kindness follow me
all the days of my life;
and I shall dwell in the house of the LORD
for years to come. ℟.

READING II
1 Peter 2:20b-25

Beloved: If you are patient when you suffer for doing what is good, this is a grace before God. For to this you have been called, because Christ also suffered for you, leaving you an example that you should follow in his footsteps.
"He committed no sin,
and no deceit was found in his mouth."
When he was insulted, he returned no insult; when he suffered, he did not threaten; instead, he handed himself over to the one who judges justly. He himself bore our sins in his body upon the cross, so that, free from sin, we might live for righteousness. By his wounds you have been healed. For you had gone astray like sheep, but you have now returned to the shepherd and guardian of your souls.

GOSPEL
John 10:1-10

Jesus said: "Amen, amen, I say to you, whoever does not enter a sheepfold through the gate but climbs over elsewhere is a thief and a robber. But whoever enters through the gate is the shepherd of the sheep. The gatekeeper opens it for him, and the sheep hear his voice, as the shepherd calls his own sheep by name and leads them out. When he has driven out all his own, he walks ahead of them, and the sheep follow him, because they recognize his voice. But they will not follow a stranger; they will run away from him, because they do not recognize the voice of strangers." Although Jesus used this figure of speech, the Pharisees did not realize what he was trying to tell them.

So Jesus said again, "Amen, amen, I say to you, I am the gate for the sheep. All who came before me are thieves and robbers, but the sheep did not listen to them. I am the gate. Whoever enters through me will be saved, and will come in and go out and find pasture. A thief comes only to steal and slaughter and destroy; I came so that they might have life and have it more abundantly."

557 FOURTH SUNDAY OF EASTER / B

READING I *Acts 4:8-12 / 50*

Peter, filled with the Holy Spirit, said: "Leaders of the people and elders: If we are being examined today about a good deed done to a cripple, namely, by what means he was saved, then all of you and all the people of Israel should know that it was in the name of Jesus Christ the Nazorean whom you crucified, whom God raised from the dead; in his name this man stands before you healed. He is 'the stone rejected by you, the builders, which has become the cornerstone.' There is no salvation through anyone else, nor is there any other name under heaven given to the human race by which we are to be saved."

RESPONSORIAL PSALM  *Psalm 118:1, 8-9, 21-23, 26, 28, 29*

The stone re-ject-ed by the build-ers has be-come the cor-ner-stone.

Give thanks to the LORD, for he is good,
    for his mercy endures forever.
It is better to take refuge in the LORD
    than to trust in man.
It is better to take refuge in the LORD
    than to trust in princes. ℟.

I will give thanks to you, for you have
    answered me
and have been my savior.
The stone which the builders rejected
    has become the cornerstone.
By the LORD has this been done;
    it is wonderful in our eyes. ℟.

Blessed is he who comes in the name of
    the LORD;
    we bless you from the house of the
    LORD.
I will give thanks to you, for you have
    answered me
and have been my savior.
Give thanks to the LORD, for he is good;
    for his kindness endures forever. ℟.

READING II *1 John 3:1-2*

Beloved: See what love the Father has bestowed on us that we may be called the children of God. Yet so we are. The reason the world does not know us is that it did not know him. Beloved, we are God's children now; what we shall be has not yet been revealed. We do know that when it is revealed we shall be like him, for we shall see him as he is.

GOSPEL *John 10:11-18*

Jesus said: "I am the good shepherd. A good shepherd lays down his life for the sheep. A hired man, who is not a shepherd and whose sheep are not his own, sees a wolf coming and leaves the sheep and runs away, and the wolf catches and scatters them. This is because he works for pay and has no concern for the sheep. I am the good shepherd, and I know mine and mine know me, just as the Father knows me and I know the Father; and I will lay down my life for the sheep. I have other sheep that do not belong to this fold. These also I must lead, and they will hear my voice, and there will be one flock, one shepherd. This is why the Father loves me, because I lay down my life in order to take it up again. No one takes it from me, but I lay it down on my own. I have power to lay it down, and power to take it up again. This command I have received from my Father."

FOURTH SUNDAY OF EASTER / C   558

READING I   *Acts 13:14, 43-52 / 51*

Paul and Barnabas continued on from Perga and reached Antioch in Pisidia. On the sabbath they entered the synagogue and took their seats. Many Jews and worshipers who were converts to Judaism followed Paul and Barnabas, who spoke to them and urged them to remain faithful to the grace of God.

On the following sabbath almost the whole city gathered to hear the word of the Lord. When the Jews saw the crowds, they were filled with jealousy and with violent abuse contradicted what Paul said. Both Paul and Barnabas spoke out boldly and said, "It was necessary that the word of God be spoken to you first, but since you reject it and condemn yourselves as unworthy of eternal life, we now turn to the Gentiles. For so the Lord has commanded us, 'I have made you a light to the Gentiles, that you may be an instrument of salvation to the ends of the earth.'"

The Gentiles were delighted when they heard this and glorified the word of the Lord. All who were destined for eternal life came to believe, and the word of the Lord continued to spread through the whole region. The Jews, however, incited the women of prominence who were worshipers and the leading men of the city, stirred up a persecution against Paul and Barnabas, and expelled them from their territory. So they shook the dust from their feet in protest against them, and went to Iconium. The disciples were filled with joy and the Holy Spirit.

RESPONSORIAL PSALM   *Psalm 100:1-2, 3, 5*

We are his peo-ple, the sheep of his flock.

Sing joyfully to the LORD, all you lands;
 serve the LORD with gladness;
come before him with joyful song. ℟.

Know that the LORD is God;
 he made us, his we are;

his people, the flock he tends. ℟.

The LORD is good:
 his kindness endures forever,
and his faithfulness, to all generations. ℟.

READING II   *Revelation 7:9, 14b-17*

I, John, had a vision of a great multitude, which no one could count, from every nation, race, people, and tongue. They stood before the throne and before the Lamb, wearing white robes and holding palm branches in their hands.

Then one of the elders said to me, "These are the ones who have survived the time of great distress; they have washed their robes and made them white in the blood of the Lamb.

"For this reason they stand before God's throne
 and worship him day and night in his temple.
The one who sits on the throne will shelter them.
They will not hunger or thirst anymore,
 nor will the sun or any heat strike them.

For the Lamb who is in the center of the throne
will shepherd them
and lead them to springs of life-giving water,
and God will wipe away every tear from their eyes."

GOSPEL   *John 10:27-30*

Jesus said: "My sheep hear my voice; I know them, and they follow me. I give them eternal life, and they shall never perish. No one can take them out of my hand. My Father, who has given them to me, is greater than all, and no one can take them out of the Father's hand. The Father and I are one."

559   FIFTH SUNDAY OF EASTER / A

READING I   *Acts 6:1-7 / 52*

As the number of disciples continued to grow, the Hellenists complained against the Hebrews because their widows were being neglected in the daily distribution. So the Twelve called together the community of the disciples and said, "It is not right for us to neglect the word of God to serve at table. Brothers, select from among you seven reputable men, filled with the Spirit and wisdom, whom we shall appoint to this task, whereas we shall devote ourselves to prayer and to the ministry of the word." The proposal was acceptable to the whole community, so they chose Stephen, a man filled with faith and the Holy Spirit, also Philip, Prochorus, Nicanor, Timon, Parmenas, and Nicholas of Antioch, a convert to Judaism. They presented these men to the apostles who prayed and laid hands on them. The word of God continued to spread, and the number of the disciples in Jerusalem increased greatly; even a large group of priests were becoming obedient to the faith.

RESPONSORIAL PSALM   *Psalm 33:1-2, 4-5, 18-19*

Lord, let your mer-cy be on us, as we place our trust in you.

Exult, you just, in the LORD;
    praise from the upright is fitting.
Give thanks to the LORD on the harp;
    with the ten-stringed lyre chant his
    praises. ℟.

Upright is the word of the LORD,
    and all his works are trustworthy.
He loves justice and right;

of the kindness of the LORD the earth
    is full. ℟.

See, the eyes of the LORD are upon those
    who fear him,
upon those who hope for his
    kindness,
to deliver them from death
    and preserve them in spite of
    famine. ℟.

READING II   *1 Peter 2:4-9*

Beloved: Come to him, a living stone, rejected by human beings but chosen and precious in the sight of God, and, like living stones, let yourselves be built into a spiritual house to be a holy priesthood to offer spiritual sacrifices acceptable to God through Jesus Christ. For it says in Scripture:
    "Behold, I am laying a stone in Zion,
    a cornerstone, chosen and precious,
    and whoever believes in it shall not be put to shame."
Therefore, its value is for you who have faith, but for those without faith:
    "The stone that the builders rejected

has become the cornerstone,"
and
"A stone that will make people stumble,
and a rock that will make them fall."
They stumble by disobeying the word, as is their destiny.

You are "a chosen race, a royal priesthood, a holy nation, a people of his own, so that you may announce the praises" of him who called you out of darkness into his wonderful light.

GOSPEL   *John 14:1-12*

Jesus said to his disciples: "Do not let your hearts be troubled. You have faith in God; have faith also in me. In my Father's house there are many dwelling places. If there were not, would I have told you that I am going to prepare a place for you? And if I go and prepare a place for you, I will come back again and take you to myself, so that where I am you also may be. Where I am going you know the way." Thomas said to him, "Master, we do not know where you are going; how can we know the way?" Jesus said to him, "I am the way and the truth and the life. No one comes to the Father except through me. If you know me, then you will also know my Father. From now on you do know him and have seen him." Philip said to him, "Master, show us the Father, and that will be enough for us." Jesus said to him, "Have I been with you for so long a time and you still do not know me, Philip? Whoever has seen me has seen the Father. How can you say, 'Show us the Father'? Do you not believe that I am in the Father and the Father is in me? The words that I speak to you I do not speak on my own. The Father who dwells in me is doing his works. Believe me that I am in the Father and the Father is in me, or else, believe because of the works themselves. Amen, amen, I say to you, whoever believes in me will do the works that I do, and will do greater ones than these, because I am going to the Father."

FIFTH SUNDAY OF EASTER / B   560

READING I   *Acts 9:26-31 / 53*

When Saul arrived in Jerusalem he tried to join the disciples, but they were all afraid of him, not believing that he was a disciple. Then Barnabas took charge of him and brought him to the apostles, and he reported to them how he had seen the Lord, and that he had spoken to him, and how in Damascus he had spoken out boldly in the name of Jesus. He moved about freely with them in Jerusalem, and spoke out boldly in the name of the Lord. He also spoke and debated with the Hellenists, but they tried to kill him. And when the brothers learned of this, they took him down to Caesarea and sent him on his way to Tarsus. The church throughout all Judea, Galilee, and Samaria was at peace. It was being built up and walked in the fear of the Lord, and with the consolation of the Holy Spirit it grew in numbers.

RESPONSORIAL PSALM   *Psalm 22:26-27, 28, 30, 31-32*

I will praise you, Lord, in the as - sem - bly of your peo - ple.

I will fulfill my vows before those who
fear the LORD.
The lowly shall eat their fill;
they who seek the LORD shall praise him:
"May your hearts live forever!" ℟.

All the ends of the earth
shall remember and turn to the LORD;
all the families of the nations
shall bow down before him. ℟.

To him alone shall bow down

all who sleep in the earth;
before him shall bend
all who go down into the dust. ℟.

And to him my soul shall live;
my descendants shall serve him.
Let the coming generation be told of the
LORD
that they may proclaim to a people
yet to be born
the justice he has shown. ℟.

READING II
1 John 3:18-24

Children, let us love not in word or speech but in deed and truth. Now this is how we shall know that we belong to the truth and reassure our hearts before him in whatever our hearts condemn, for God is greater than our hearts and knows everything. Beloved, if our hearts do not condemn us, we have confidence in God and receive from him whatever we ask, because we keep his commandments and do what pleases him. And his commandment is this: we should believe in the name of his Son, Jesus Christ, and love one another just as he commanded us. Those who keep his commandments remain in him, and he in them, and the way we know that he remains in us is from the Spirit he gave us.

GOSPEL
John 15:1-8

Jesus said to his disciples: "I am the true vine, and my Father is the vine grower. He takes away every branch in me that does not bear fruit, and every one that does he prunes so that it bears more fruit. You are already pruned because of the word that I spoke to you. Remain in me, as I remain in you. Just as a branch cannot bear fruit on its own unless it remains on the vine, so neither can you unless you remain in me. I am the vine, you are the branches. Whoever remains in me and I in him will bear much fruit, because without me you can do nothing. Anyone who does not remain in me will be thrown out like a branch and wither; people will gather them and throw them into a fire and they will be burned. If you remain in me and my words remain in you, ask for whatever you want and it will be done for you. By this is my Father glorified, that you bear much fruit and become my disciples."

561 FIFTH SUNDAY OF EASTER / C

READING I
Acts 14:21-27 / 54

After Paul and Barnabas had proclaimed the good news to that city and made a considerable number of disciples, they returned to Lystra and to Iconium and to Antioch. They strengthened the spirits of the disciples and exhorted them to persevere in the faith, saying, "It is necessary for us to undergo many hardships to enter the kingdom of God." They appointed elders for them in each church and, with prayer and fasting, commended them to the Lord in whom they had put their faith. Then they traveled through Pisidia and reached Pamphylia. After proclaiming the word at Perga they went down to Attalia. From there they sailed to Antioch, where they had been commended to the grace of God for the work they had now accomplished. And when they arrived, they called the church together and reported what God had done with them and how he had opened the door of faith to the Gentiles.

RESPONSORIAL PSALM   *Psalm 145:8-9, 10-11, 12-13*

I will praise your name for ev - er,

my king and my God.

The LORD is gracious and merciful,
  slow to anger and of great kindness.
The LORD is good to all
  and compassionate toward all his
    works. ℟.

Let all your works give you thanks, O
  LORD,
  and let your faithful ones bless you.
Let them discourse of the glory of your

kingdom
and speak of your might. ℟.

Let them make known your might to the
  children of Adam,
  and the glorious splendor of your
    kingdom.
Your kingdom is a kingdom for all ages,
  and your dominion endures through
    all generations. ℟.

READING II   *Revelation 21:1-5a*

Then I, John, saw a new heaven and a new earth. The former heaven and the former earth had passed away, and the sea was no more. I also saw the holy city, a new Jerusalem, coming down out of heaven from God, prepared as a bride adorned for her husband. I heard a loud voice from the throne saying, "Behold, God's dwelling is with the human race. He will dwell with them and they will be his people and God himself will always be with them as their God. He will wipe every tear from their eyes, and there shall be no more death or mourning, wailing or pain, for the old order has passed away."

The One who sat on the throne said, "Behold, I make all things new."

GOSPEL   *John 13:31-33a, 34-35*

When Judas had left them, Jesus said, "Now is the Son of Man glorified, and God is glorified in him. If God is glorified in him, God will also glorify him in himself, and God will glorify him at once. My children, I will be with you only a little while longer. I give you a new commandment: love one another. As I have loved you, so you also should love one another. This is how all will know that you are my disciples, if you have love for one another."

SIXTH SUNDAY OF EASTER / A   562

READING I   *Acts 8:5-8, 14-17 / 55*

Philip went down to the city of Samaria and proclaimed the Christ to them. With one accord, the crowds paid attention to what was said by Philip when they heard it and saw the signs he was doing. For unclean spirits, crying out in a loud voice, came out of many possessed people, and many paralyzed or crippled people were cured. There was great joy in that city.

Now when the apostles in Jerusalem heard that Samaria had accepted the word of God, they sent them Peter and John, who went down and prayed for them, that they might receive the Holy Spirit, for it had not yet fallen upon any of them; they had only been baptized in the name of the Lord Jesus. Then they laid hands on them and they received the Holy Spirit.

RESPONSORIAL PSALM *Psalm 66:1-3, 4-5, 6-7, 16, 20*

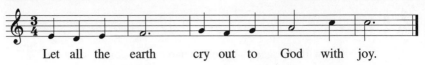

Let all the earth cry out to God with joy.

Shout joyfully to God, all the earth,
    sing praise to the glory of his name;
proclaim his glorious praise.
      Say to God, "How tremendous are
        your deeds! ℞.

Let all on earth worship and sing praise
    to you,
    sing praise to your name!"
Come and see the works of God,
    his tremendous deeds among the
    children of Adam. ℞.

He has changed the sea into dry land;
    through the river they passed on foot;
therefore let us rejoice in him.
    He rules by his might forever. ℞.

Hear now, all you who fear God, while
    I declare
    what he has done for me.
Blessed be God who refused me not
    my prayer or his kindness! ℞.

READING II *1 Peter 3:15-18*

Beloved: Sanctify Christ as Lord in your hearts. Always be ready to give an explanation to anyone who asks you for a reason for your hope, but do it with gentleness and reverence, keeping your conscience clear, so that, when you are maligned, those who defame your good conduct in Christ may themselves be put to shame. For it is better to suffer for doing good, if that be the will of God, than for doing evil. For Christ also suffered for sins once, the righteous for the sake of the unrighteous, that he might lead you to God. Put to death in the flesh, he was brought to life in the Spirit.

GOSPEL *John 14:15-21*

Jesus said to his disciples: "If you love me, you will keep my commandments. And I will ask the Father, and he will give you another Advocate to be with you always, the Spirit of truth, whom the world cannot accept, because it neither sees nor knows him. But you know him, because he remains with you, and will be in you. I will not leave you orphans; I will come to you. In a little while the world will no longer see me, but you will see me, because I live and you will live. On that day you will realize that I am in my Father and you are in me and I in you. Whoever has my commandments and observes them is the one who loves me. And whoever loves me will be loved by my Father, and I will love him and reveal myself to him."

563   SIXTH SUNDAY OF EASTER / B

READING I *Acts 10:25-26, 34-35, 44-48 / 56*

When Peter entered, Cornelius met him and, falling at his feet, paid him homage. Peter, however, raised him up, saying, "Get up. I myself am also a human being."

Then Peter proceeded to speak and said, "In truth, I see that God shows no partiality. Rather, in every nation whoever fears him and acts uprightly is acceptable to him."

While Peter was still speaking these things, the Holy Spirit fell upon all who were listening to the word. The circumcised believers who had accompanied Peter were astounded that the gift of the Holy Spirit should have been poured out on the Gentiles also, for they could hear them speaking in tongues and glorifying God. Then Peter responded, "Can anyone withhold the water for baptizing these people, who have received the Holy Spirit even as we have?" He ordered them to be baptized in the name of Jesus Christ.

RESPONSORIAL PSALM

Psalm 98:1, 2-3, 3-4

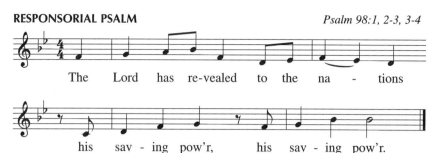

The Lord has re-vealed to the na - tions his sav - ing pow'r, his sav - ing pow'r.

Sing to the LORD a new song,
for he has done wondrous deeds;
His right hand has won victory for him,
his holy arm. ℟.

The LORD has made his salvation known:
in the sight of the nations he has
revealed his justice.

He has remembered his kindness and his
faithfulness
toward the house of Israel. ℟.

All the ends of the earth have seen
the salvation by our God.
Sing joyfully to the LORD, all you lands;
break into song; sing praise. ℟.

READING II

1 John 4:7-10

Beloved, let us love one another, because love is of God; everyone who loves is begotten by God and knows God. Whoever is without love does not know God, for God is love. In this way the love of God was revealed to us: God sent his only Son into the world so that we might have life through him. In this is love: not that we have loved God, but that he loved us and sent his Son as expiation for our sins.

GOSPEL

John 15:9-17

Jesus said to his disciples: "As the Father loves me, so I also love you. Remain in my love. If you keep my commandments, you will remain in my love, just as I have kept my Father's commandments and remain in his love.

"I have told you this so that my joy may be in you and your joy might be complete. This is my commandment: love one another as I love you. No one has greater love than this, to lay down one's life for one's friends. You are my friends if you do what I command you. I no longer call you slaves, because a slave does not know what his master is doing. I have called you friends, because I have told you everything I have heard from my Father. It was not you who chose me, but I who chose you and appointed you to go and bear fruit that will remain, so that whatever you ask the Father in my name he may give you. This I command you: love one another."

SIXTH SUNDAY OF EASTER / C

564

READING I

Acts 15:1-2, 22-29 / 57

Some who had come down from Judea were instructing the brothers, "Unless you are circumcised according to the Mosaic practice, you cannot be saved." Because there arose no little dissension and debate by Paul and Barnabas with them, it was decided that Paul, Barnabas, and some of the others should go up to Jerusalem to the apostles and elders about this question.

The apostles and elders, in agreement with the whole church, decided to choose representatives and to send them to Antioch with Paul and Barnabas. The ones chosen were Judas, who was called Barsabbas, and Silas, leaders among the brothers. This is the letter delivered by them:

"The apostles and the elders, your brothers, to the brothers in Antioch, Syria, and Cilicia of Gentile origin: greetings. Since we have heard that some of our number who went out without any mandate from us have upset you with their teachings and disturbed your peace of mind, we have with one accord decided to choose representatives and to send them to you along with our beloved Barnabas and Paul, who have dedicated their lives to the name of our Lord Jesus Christ. So we are sending Judas and Silas who will also convey this same message by word of mouth: 'It is the decision of the Holy Spirit and of us not to place on you any burden beyond these necessities, namely, to abstain from meat sacrificed to idols, from blood, from meats of strangled animals, and from unlawful marriage. If you keep free of these, you will be doing what is right. Farewell.'"

RESPONSORIAL PSALM

Psalm 67:2-3, 5, 6, 8

O God, O God, let all the na-tions praise you!

May God have pity on us and bless us;
    may he let his face shine upon us.
So may your way be known upon earth;
    among all nations, your salvation. ℟.

May the nations be glad and exult
    because you rule the peoples in
      equity;

the nations on the earth you guide. ℟.

May the peoples praise you, O God;
    may all the peoples praise you!
May God bless us,
    and may all the ends of the earth
      fear him! ℟.

READING II

Revelation 21:10-14, 22-23

The angel took me in spirit to a great, high mountain and showed me the holy city Jerusalem coming down out of heaven from God. It gleamed with the splendor of God. Its radiance was like that of a precious stone, like jasper, clear as crystal. It had a massive, high wall, with twelve gates where twelve angels were stationed and on which names were inscribed, the names of the twelve tribes of the Israelites. There were three gates facing east, three north, three south, and three west. The wall of the city had twelve courses of stones as its foundation, on which were inscribed the twelve names of the twelve apostles of the Lamb.

I saw no temple in the city for its temple is the Lord God almighty and the Lamb. The city had no need of sun or moon to shine on it, for the glory of God gave it light, and its lamp was the Lamb.

GOSPEL

John 14:23-29

Jesus said to his disciples: "Whoever loves me will keep my word, and my Father will love him, and we will come to him and make our dwelling with him. Whoever does not love me does not keep my words; yet the word you hear is not mine but that of the Father who sent me.

"I have told you this while I am with you. The Advocate, the Holy Spirit, whom the Father will send in my name, will teach you everything and remind you of all that I told you. Peace I leave with you; my peace I give to you. Not as the world gives do I give it to you. Do not let your hearts be troubled or afraid. You heard me tell you, 'I am going away and I will come back to you.' If you loved me, you would rejoice that I am going to the Father; for the Father is greater than I. And now I have told you this before it happens, so that when it happens you may believe."

THE ASCENSION OF THE LORD / ABC

READING I

Acts 1:1-11 / 58

In the first book, Theophilus, I dealt with all that Jesus did and taught until the day he was taken up, after giving instructions through the Holy Spirit to the apostles whom he had chosen. He presented himself alive to them by many proofs after he had suffered, appearing to them during forty days and speaking about the kingdom of God. While meeting with them, he enjoined them not to depart from Jerusalem, but to wait for "the promise of the Father about which you have heard me speak; for John baptized with water, but in a few days you will be baptized with the Holy Spirit."

When they had gathered together they asked him, "Lord, are you at this time going to restore the kingdom to Israel?" He answered them, "It is not for you to know the times or seasons that the Father has established by his own authority. But you will receive power when the Holy Spirit comes upon you, and you will be my witnesses in Jerusalem, throughout Judea and Samaria, and to the ends of the earth." When he had said this, as they were looking on, he was lifted up, and a cloud took him from their sight. While they were looking intently at the sky as he was going, suddenly two men dressed in white garments stood beside them. They said, "Men of Galilee, why are you standing there looking at the sky? This Jesus who has been taken up from you into heaven will return in the same way as you have seen him going into heaven."

RESPONSORIAL PSALM

Psalm 47:2-3, 6-7, 8-9

God mounts his throne to shouts of joy: a blare of trum-pets for the Lord.

All you peoples, clap your hands,
  shout to God with cries of gladness,
For the LORD, the Most High, the
    awesome,
  is the great king over all the earth. ℟.

God mounts his throne amid shouts of
    joy;
  the LORD, amid trumpet blasts.

Sing praise to God, sing praise;
  sing praise to our king, sing praise. ℟.

For king of all the earth is God;
  sing hymns of praise.
God reigns over the nations,
  God sits upon his holy throne. ℟.

READING II

Ephesians 1:17-23

Brothers and sisters: May the God of our Lord Jesus Christ, the Father of glory, give you a Spirit of wisdom and revelation resulting in knowledge of him. May the eyes of your hearts be enlightened, that you may know what is the hope that belongs to his call, what are the riches of glory in his inheritance among the holy ones, and what is the surpassing greatness of his power for us who believe, in accord with the exercise of his great might, which he worked in Christ, raising him from the dead and seating him at his right hand in the heavens, far above every principality, authority, power, and dominion, and every name that is named not only in this age but also in the one to come. And he put all things beneath his feet and gave him as head over all things to the church, which is his body, the fullness of the one who fills all things in every way.

Or:

READING II / B   *Ephesians 4:1-13 or 4:1-7, 11-13*
For short form read only the parts in brackets.

[Brothers and sisters, I, a prisoner for the Lord, urge you to live in a manner worthy of the call you have received, with all humility and gentleness, with patience, bearing with one another through love, striving to preserve the unity of the spirit through the bond of peace: one body and one Spirit, as you were also called to the one hope of your call; one Lord, one faith, one baptism; one God and Father of all, who is over all and through all and in all.

But grace was given to each of us according to the measure of Christ's gift.]
Therefore, it says:
"He ascended on high and took prisoners captive;
he gave gifts to men."
What does "he ascended" mean except that he also descended into the lower regions of the earth? The one who descended is also the one who ascended far above all the heavens, that he might fill all things.

[And he gave some as apostles, others as prophets, others as evangelists, others as pastors and teachers, to equip the holy ones for the work of ministry, for building up the body of Christ, until we all attain to the unity of faith and knowledge of the Son of God, to mature manhood, to the extent of the full stature of Christ.]

Or:

READING II / C   *Hebrews 9:24-28; 10:19-23*
Christ did not enter into a sanctuary made by hands, a copy of the true one, but heaven itself, that he might now appear before God on our behalf. Not that he might offer himself repeatedly, as the high priest enters each year into the sanctuary with blood that is not his own; if that were so, he would have had to suffer repeatedly from the foundation of the world. But now once for all he has appeared at the end of the ages to take away sin by his sacrifice. Just as it is appointed that men and women die once, and after this the judgment, so also Christ, offered once to take away the sins of many, will appear a second time, not to take away sin but to bring salvation to those who eagerly await him.

Therefore, brothers and sisters, since through the blood of Jesus we have confidence of entrance into the sanctuary by the new and living way he opened for us through the veil, that is, his flesh, and since we have "a great priest over the house of God," let us approach with a sincere heart and in absolute trust, with our hearts sprinkled clean from an evil conscience and our bodies washed in pure water. Let us hold unwaveringly to our confession that gives us hope, for he who made the promise is trustworthy.

GOSPEL / A   *Matthew 28:16-20*
The eleven disciples went to Galilee, to the mountain to which Jesus had ordered them. When they saw him, they worshiped, but they doubted. Then Jesus approached and said to them, "All power in heaven and on earth has been given to me. Go, therefore, and make disciples of all nations, baptizing them in the name of the Father, and of the Son, and of the Holy Spirit, teaching them to observe all that I have commanded you. And behold, I am with you always, until the end of the age."

GOSPEL / B   *Mark 16:15-20*
Jesus said to his disciples: "Go into the whole world and proclaim the gospel to every creature. Whoever believes and is baptized will be saved; whoever does not believe will be condemned. These signs will accompany those who believe: in my name they will drive out demons, they will speak new languages. They will pick up serpents with their

hands, and if they drink any deadly thing, it will not harm them. They will lay hands on the sick, and they will recover."

So then the Lord Jesus, after he spoke to them, was taken up into heaven and took his seat at the right hand of God. But they went forth and preached everywhere, while the Lord worked with them and confirmed the word through accompanying signs.

GOSPEL / C
Luke 24:46-53

Jesus said to his disciples: "Thus it is written that the Christ would suffer and rise from the dead on the third day and that repentance, for the forgiveness of sins, would be preached in his name to all the nations, beginning from Jerusalem. You are witnesses of these things. And behold I am sending the promise of my Father upon you; but stay in the city until you are clothed with power from on high."

Then he led them out as far as Bethany, raised his hands, and blessed them. As he blessed them he parted from them and was taken up to heaven. They did him homage and then returned to Jerusalem with great joy, and they were continually in the temple praising God.

SEVENTH SUNDAY OF EASTER / A   566

READING I
Acts 1:12-14 / 59

After Jesus had been taken up to heaven the apostles returned to Jerusalem from the mount called Olivet, which is near Jerusalem, a sabbath day's journey away.

When they entered the city they went to the upper room where they were staying, Peter and John and James and Andrew, Philip and Thomas, Bartholomew and Matthew, James son of Alphaeus, Simon the Zealot, and Judas son of James. All these devoted themselves with one accord to prayer, together with some women, and Mary the mother of Jesus, and his brothers.

RESPONSORIAL PSALM
Psalm 27:1, 4, 7-8

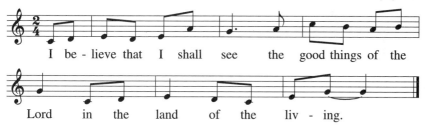

I be-lieve that I shall see the good things of the Lord in the land of the liv-ing.

The LORD is my light and my salvation;
  whom should I fear?
The LORD is my life's refuge;
  of whom should I be afraid? ℟.

One thing I ask of the LORD; this I seek:
  To dwell in the house of the LORD
all the days of my life,

That I may gaze on the loveliness of
  the LORD
and contemplate his temple. ℟.

Hear, O Lord, the sound of my call;
  have pity on me, and answer me.
Of you my heart speaks; you my glance
  seeks. ℟.

READING II
1 Peter 4:13-16

Beloved: Rejoice to the extent that you share in the sufferings of Christ, so that when his glory is revealed you may also rejoice exultantly. If you are insulted for the name of Christ, blessed are you, for the Spirit of glory and of God rests upon you. But let no one among you be made to suffer as a murderer, a thief, an evildoer, or as an intriguer. But whoever is made to suffer as a Christian should not be ashamed but glorify God because of the name.

GOSPEL   *John 17:1-11a*

Jesus raised his eyes to heaven and said, "Father, the hour has come. Give glory to your son, so that your son may glorify you, just as you gave him authority over all people, so that your son may give eternal life to all you gave him. Now this is eternal life, that they should know you, the only true God, and the one whom you sent, Jesus Christ. I glorified you on earth by accomplishing the work that you gave me to do. Now glorify me, Father, with you, with the glory that I had with you before the world began.

"I revealed your name to those whom you gave me out of the world. They belonged to you, and you gave them to me, and they have kept your word. Now they know that everything you gave me is from you, because the words you gave to me I have given to them, and they accepted them and truly understood that I came from you, and they have believed that you sent me. I pray for them. I do not pray for the world but for the ones you have given me, because they are yours, and everything of mine is yours and everything of yours is mine, and I have been glorified in them. And now I will no longer be in the world, but they are in the world, while I am coming to you."

567 SEVENTH SUNDAY OF EASTER / B

READING I   *Acts 1:15-17, 20a, 20c-26 / 60*

Peter stood up in the midst of the brothers (there was a group of about one hundred and twenty persons in the one place). He said, "My brothers, the Scripture had to be fulfilled which the Holy Spirit spoke beforehand through the mouth of David, concerning Judas, who was the guide for those who arrested Jesus. He was numbered among us and was allotted a share in this ministry. "For it is written in the Book of Psalms:

'May another take his office.'

"Therefore, it is necessary that one of the men who accompanied us the whole time the Lord Jesus came and went among us, beginning from the baptism of John until the day on which he was taken up from us, become with us a witness to his resurrection." So they proposed two, Judas called Barsabbas, who was also known as Justus, and Matthias. Then they prayed, "You, Lord, who know the hearts of all, show which one of these two you have chosen to take the place in this apostolic ministry from which Judas turned away to go to his own place." Then they gave lots to them, and the lot fell upon Matthias, and he was counted with the eleven apostles.

RESPONSORIAL PSALM   *Psalm 103:1-2, 11-12, 19-20*

The Lord has set his throne in heav - en.

Bless the LORD, O my soul;
    and all my being, bless his holy
        name.
Bless the LORD, O my soul,
    and forget not all his benefits. ℟.

For as the heavens are high above the
        earth,
    ⁿurpassing is his kindness toward
    ⁿ who fear him.

As far as the east is from the west,
    so far has he put our transgressions
        from us. ℟.

The LORD has established his throne in
        heaven,
    and his kingdom rules over all.
Bless the LORD, all you his angels,
    you mighty in strength, who do his
        bidding. ℟.

READING II   *1 John 4:11-16*

Beloved, if God so loved us, we also must love one another. No one has ever seen God. Yet, if we love one another, God remains in us, and his love is brought to perfection in us.

This is how we know that we remain in him and he in us, that he has given us of his Spirit. Moreover, we have seen and testify that the Father sent his Son as savior of the world. Whoever acknowledges that Jesus is the Son of God, God remains in him and he in God. We have come to know and to believe in the love God has for us.

God is love, and whoever remains in love remains in God and God in him.

GOSPEL   *John 17:11b-19*

Lifting up his eyes to heaven, Jesus prayed saying: "Holy Father, keep them in your name that you have given me, so that they may be one just as we are one. When I was with them I protected them in your name that you gave me, and I guarded them, and none of them was lost except the son of destruction, in order that the Scripture might be fulfilled. But now I am coming to you. I speak this in the world so that they may share my joy completely. I gave them your word, and the world hated them, because they do not belong to the world any more than I belong to the world. I do not ask that you take them out of the world but that you keep them from the evil one. They do not belong to the world any more than I belong to the world. Consecrate them in the truth. Your word is truth. As you sent me into the world, so I sent them into the world. And I consecrate myself for them, so that they also may be consecrated in truth."

SEVENTH SUNDAY OF EASTER / C   568

READING I   *Acts 7:55-60 / 61*

Stephen, filled with the Holy Spirit, looked up intently to heaven and saw the glory of God and Jesus standing at the right hand of God, and Stephen said, "Behold, I see the heavens opened and the Son of Man standing at the right hand of God." But they cried out in a loud voice, covered their ears, and rushed upon him together. They threw him out of the city, and began to stone him. The witnesses laid down their cloaks at the feet of a young man named Saul. As they were stoning Stephen, he called out, "Lord Jesus, receive my spirit." Then he fell to his knees and cried out in a loud voice, "Lord, do not hold this sin against them;" and when he said this, he fell asleep.

RESPONSORIAL PSALM   *Psalm 97:1-2, 6-7, 9*

The Lord is king, the Lord most high o-ver all the earth.

The LORD is king; let the earth rejoice;
    let the many islands be glad.
Justice and judgment are the foundation
    of his throne. ℟.

You, O LORD, are the Most High over
    all the earth,
    exalted far above all gods. ℟.

The heavens proclaim his justice,
    and all peoples see his glory.
All gods are prostrate before him. ℟.

READING II *Revelation 22:12-14, 16-17, 20*

I, John, heard a voice saying to me: "Behold, I am coming soon. I bring with me the recompense I will give to each according to his deeds. I am the Alpha and the Omega, the first and the last, the beginning and the end."

Blessed are they who wash their robes so as to have the right to the tree of life and enter the city through its gates.

"I, Jesus, sent my angel to give you this testimony for the churches. I am the root and offspring of David, the bright morning star."

The Spirit and the bride say, "Come." Let the hearer say, "Come." Let the one who thirsts come forward, and the one who wants it receive the gift of life-giving water.

The one who gives this testimony says, "Yes, I am coming soon." Amen! Come, Lord Jesus!

GOSPEL *John 17:20-26*

Lifting up his eyes to heaven, Jesus prayed saying: "Holy Father, I pray not only for them, but also for those who will believe in me through their word, so that they may all be one, as you, Father, are in me and I in you, that they also may be in us, that the world may believe that you sent me. And I have given them the glory you gave me, so that they may be one, as we are one, I in them and you in me, that they may be brought to perfection as one, that the world may know that you sent me, and that you loved them even as you loved me. Father, they are your gift to me. I wish that where I am they also may be with me, that they may see my glory that you gave me, because you loved me before the foundation of the world. Righteous Father, the world also does not know you, but I know you, and they know that you sent me. I made known to them your name and I will make it known, that the love with which you loved me may be in them and I in them."

569 PENTECOST / VIGIL / ABC

READING I *Genesis 11:1-9 / 62*

The whole world spoke the same language, using the same words. While the people were migrating in the east, they came upon a valley in the land of Shinar and settled there. They said to one another, "Come, let us mold bricks and harden them with fire." They used bricks for stone, and bitumen for mortar. Then they said, "Come, let us build ourselves a city and a tower with its top in the sky, and so make a name for ourselves; otherwise we shall be scattered all over the earth."

The LORD came down to see the city and the tower that the people had built. Then the LORD said: "If now, while they are one people, all speaking the same language, they have started to do this, nothing will later stop them from doing whatever they presume to do. Let us then go down there and confuse their language, so that one will not understand what another says." Thus the LORD scattered them from there all over the earth, and they stopped building the city. That is why it was called Babel, because there the LORD confused the speech of all the world. It was from that place that he scattered them all over the earth.

Or:

READING I *Exodus 19:3-8a, 16-20b*

Moses went up the mountain to God. Then the LORD called to him and said, "Thus shall you say to the house of Jacob; tell the Israelites: You have seen for yourselves how I treated the Egyptians and how I bore you up on eagle wings and brought you here to myself. Therefore, if you hearken to my voice and keep my covenant, you shall be my special possession, dearer to me than all other people, though all the earth is mine. You shall be to me a kingdom of priests, a holy nation. That is what you must tell the Israelites." So Moses went and summoned the elders of the people. When he set before them all that the LORD had ordered him to tell them, the people all answered together, "Everything the LORD has said, we will do."

On the morning of the third day there were peals of thunder and lightning, and a heavy cloud over the mountain, and a very loud trumpet blast, so that all the people in the camp trembled. But Moses led the people out of the camp to meet God, and they stationed themselves at the foot of the mountain. Mount Sinai was all wrapped in smoke, for the LORD came down upon it in fire. The smoke rose from it as though from a furnace, and the whole mountain trembled violently. The trumpet blast grew louder and louder, while Moses was speaking, and God answering him with thunder.

When the LORD came down to the top of Mount Sinai, he summoned Moses to the top of the mountain.

Or:

READING I   *Ezekiel 37:1-14*
The hand of the LORD came upon me, and he led me out in the spirit of the LORD and set me in the center of the plain, which was now filled with bones. He made me walk among the bones in every direction so that I saw how many they were on the surface of the plain. How dry they were! He asked me: Son of man, can these bones come to life? I answered, "Lord GOD, you alone know that." Then he said to me: Prophesy over these bones, and say to them: Dry bones, hear the word of the LORD! Thus says the Lord GOD to these bones: See! I will bring spirit into you, that you may come to life. I will put sinews upon you, make flesh grow over you, cover you with skin, and put spirit in you so that you may come to life and know that I am the LORD. I, Ezekiel, prophesied as I had been told, and even as I was prophesying I heard a noise; it was a rattling as the bones came together, bone joining bone. I saw the sinews and the flesh come upon them, and the skin cover them, but there was no spirit in them. Then the LORD said to me: Prophesy to the spirit, prophesy, son of man, and say to the spirit: Thus says the Lord GOD: From the four winds come, O spirit, and breathe into these slain that they may come to life. I prophesied as he told me, and the spirit came into them; they came alive and stood upright, a vast army. Then he said to me: Son of man, these bones are the whole house of Israel. They have been saying, "Our bones are dried up, our hope is lost, and we are cut off." Therefore, prophesy and say to them: Thus says the Lord GOD: O my people, I will open your graves and have you rise from them, and bring you back to the land of Israel. Then you shall know that I am the LORD, when I open your graves and have you rise from them, O my people! I will put my spirit in you that you may live, and I will settle you upon your land; thus you shall know that I am the LORD. I have promised, and I will do it, says the LORD.

Or:

READING I   *Joel 3:1-5*
Thus says the Lord: I will pour out my spirit upon all flesh. Your sons and daughters shall prophesy, your old men shall dream dreams, your young men shall see visions; even upon the servants and the handmaids, in those days, I will pour out my spirit. And I will work wonders in the heavens and on the earth, blood, fire, and columns of smoke; the sun will be turned to darkness, and the moon to blood, at the coming of the day of the LORD, the great and terrible day. Then everyone shall be rescued who calls on the name of the LORD; for on Mount Zion there shall be a remnant, as the LORD has said, and in Jerusalem survivors whom the LORD shall call.

RESPONSORIAL PSALM   *Psalm 104:1-2, 24, 35, 27-28, 29, 30*

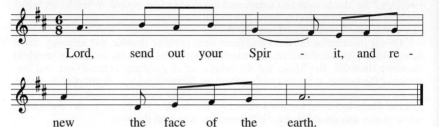

Lord, send out your Spir - it, and re -
new the face of the earth.

Bless the LORD, O my soul!
    O LORD, my God, you are great
        indeed!
You are clothed with majesty and glory,
    robed in light as with a cloak. ℟.

How manifold are your works, O LORD!
    In wisdom you have wrought them
        all—
the earth is full of your creatures;
    bless the LORD, O my soul!
        Alleluia. ℟.

Creatures all look to you
    to give them food in due time.
When you give it to them, they gather it;
    when you open your hand, they are
        filled with good things. ℟.

If you take away their breath, they
        perish
    and return to their dust.
When you send forth your spirit, they
        are created,
    and you renew the face of the
        earth. ℟.

READING II   *Romans 8:22-27*

Brothers and sisters: We know that all creation is groaning in labor pains even until now; and not only that, but we ourselves, who have the firstfruits of the Spirit, we also groan within ourselves as we wait for adoption, the redemption of our bodies. For in hope we were saved. Now hope that sees is not hope. For who hopes for what one sees? But if we hope for what we do not see, we wait with endurance.

In the same way, the Spirit too comes to the aid of our weakness; for we do not know how to pray as we ought, but the Spirit himself intercedes with inexpressible groanings. And the one who searches hearts knows what is the intention of the Spirit, because he intercedes for the holy ones according to God's will.

GOSPEL   *John 7:37-39*

On the last and greatest day of the feast, Jesus stood up and exclaimed, "Let anyone who thirsts come to me and drink. As Scripture says:
    'Rivers of living water will flow from within him' who believes in me."
He said this in reference to the Spirit that those who came to believe in him were to receive. There was, of course, no Spirit yet, because Jesus had not yet been glorified.

570   PENTECOST SUNDAY / ABC

READING I   *Acts 2:1-11 / 63*

When the time for Pentecost was fulfilled, they were all in one place together. And suddenly there came from the sky a noise like a strong driving wind, and it filled the entire house in which they were. Then there appeared to them tongues as of fire, which parted and came to rest on each one of them. And they were all filled with the Holy Spirit and began to speak in different tongues, as the Spirit enabled them to proclaim.

Now there were devout Jews from every nation under heaven staying in Jerusalem. At this sound, they gathered in a large crowd, but they were confused because each one heard them speaking in his own language. They were astounded, and in amazement they asked, "Are not all these people who are speaking Galileans? Then how does each of us hear them in his native language? We are Parthians, Medes, and Elamites, inhabitants of Mesopotamia, Judea and Cappadocia, Pontus and Asia, Phrygia and Pamphylia, Egypt and the districts of Libya near Cyrene, as well as travelers from Rome, both Jews and converts to Judaism, Cretans and Arabs, yet we hear them speaking in our own tongues of the mighty acts of God."

RESPONSORIAL PSALM *Psalm 104:1, 24, 29-30, 31, 34*

Lord, send out your Spir - it, and re - new the face of the earth.

Bless the LORD, O my soul!
  O LORD, my God, you are great
    indeed!
How manifold are your works, O Lord!
  the earth is full of your creatures. ℟.

May the glory of the LORD endure
    forever;
  may the LORD be glad in his works!

Pleasing to him be my theme;
  I will be glad in the LORD. ℟.

If you take away their breath, they perish
  and return to their dust.
When you send forth your spirit, they are
    created,
  and you renew the face of the
    earth. ℟.

READING II / ABC *1 Corinthians 12:3b-7, 12-13*

Brothers and sisters: No one can say, "Jesus is Lord," except by the Holy Spirit. There are different kinds of spiritual gifts but the same Spirit; there are different forms of service but the same Lord; there are different workings but the same God who produces all of them in everyone. To each individual the manifestation of the Spirit is given for some benefit.

As a body is one though it has many parts, and all the parts of the body, though many, are one body, so also Christ. For in one Spirit we were all baptized into one body, whether Jews or Greeks, slaves or free persons, and we were all given to drink of one Spirit.

Or:

READING II / B *Galatians 5:16-25*

Brothers and sisters, live by the Spirit and you will certainly not gratify the desire of the flesh. For the flesh has desires against the Spirit, and the Spirit against the flesh; these are opposed to each other, so that you may not do what you want. But if you are guided by the Spirit, you are not under the law. Now the works of the flesh are obvious: immorality, impurity, lust, idolatry, sorcery, hatreds, rivalry, jealousy, outbursts of fury, acts of selfishness, dissensions, factions, occasions of envy, drinking bouts, orgies, and the like. I warn you, as I warned you before, that those who do such things will not inherit the kingdom of God. In contrast, the fruit of the Spirit is love, joy, peace, patience, kindness, generosity, faithfulness, gentleness, self-control. Against such there is no law. Now those who belong to Christ Jesus have crucified their flesh with its passions and desires. If we live in the Spirit, let us also follow the Spirit.

Or:

READING II / C
Romans 8:8-17

Brothers and sisters: Those who are in the flesh cannot please God. But you are not in the flesh; on the contrary, you are in the spirit, if only the Spirit of God dwells in you. Whoever does not have the Spirit of Christ does not belong to him. But if Christ is in you, although the body is dead because of sin, the spirit is alive because of righteousness. If the Spirit of the one who raised Jesus from the dead dwells in you, the one who raised Christ from the dead will give life to your mortal bodies also, through his Spirit that dwells in you. Consequently, brothers and sisters, we are not debtors to the flesh, to live according to the flesh. For if you live according to the flesh, you will die, but if by the Spirit you put to death the deeds of the body, you will live.

For those who are led by the Spirit of God are sons of God. For you did not receive a spirit of slavery to fall back into fear, but you received a Spirit of adoption, through whom we cry, "Abba, Father!" The Spirit himself bears witness with our spirit that we are children of God, and if children, then heirs, heirs of God and joint heirs with Christ, if only we suffer with him so that we may also be glorified with him.

SEQUENCE

1. Ho - ly Spir - it, Lord Di - vine, Come, from heights of
2. Come, O Fa - ther of the poor, Come, whose treas - ured

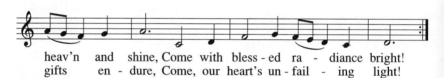

heav'n and shine, Come with bless - ed ra - diance bright!
gifts en - dure, Come, our heart's un - fail - ing light!

3. Of con - sol - ers, wis - est, best, And our soul's most
4. In our la - bor rest most sweet, Pleas - ant cool - ness

wel - come guest, Sweet re - fresh - ment, sweet re - pose.
in the heat, Con - so - la - tion in our woes.

5. Light most bless - ed, shine with grace In our heart's most
6. Left with - out your pres - ence here, Life it - self would

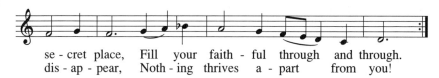

se - cret place,   Fill   your   faith - ful   through   and through.
dis - ap - pear,   Noth - ing   thrives   a - part   from   you!

7. Cleanse our   soil - ed   hearts of   sin,   Ar - id   souls   re -
8. Bend   the   stub - born heart and   will,   Melt the   fro - zen,

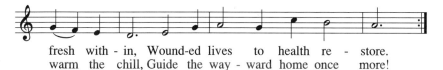

fresh   with - in,   Wound-ed lives   to   health   re - store.
warm   the   chill, Guide   the way - ward   home once   more!

9. On   the   faith - ful who   are   true   And   pro - fess   their
10. Give   us   vir - tue's sure   re - ward,   Give   us   your   sal -

faith in   you,   In   your sev'n - fold gift de - scend!
va - tion, Lord,   Give   us   joys   that nev - er   end!

Text: Sequence for Pentecost, 13th. C.; tr. by Peter J. Scagnelli; b.1949, © 1983
Tune: Mode I; acc. Adriaan Engels, b.1906, © Interkerkelijke Stichting voor het Kerklied Den Haag

GOSPEL / ABC   *John 20:19-23*

On the evening of that first day of the week, when the doors were locked, where the disciples were, for fear of the Jews, Jesus came and stood in their midst and said to them, "Peace be with you." When he had said this, he showed them his hands and his side. The disciples rejoiced when they saw the Lord. Jesus said to them again, "Peace be with you. As the Father has sent me, so I send you." And when he had said this, he breathed on them and said to them, "Receive the Holy Spirit. Whose sins you forgive are forgiven them, and whose sins you retain are retained."

Or:

GOSPEL / B   *John 15:26-27; 16:12-15*

Jesus said to his disciples: "When the Advocate comes whom I will send you from the Father, the Spirit of truth that proceeds from the Father, he will testify to me. And you also testify, because you have been with me from the beginning.

"I have much more to tell you, but you cannot bear it now. But when he comes, the Spirit of truth, he will guide you to all truth. He will not speak on his own, but he will speak what he hears, and will declare to you the things that are coming. He will glorify me, because he will take from what is mine and declare it to you. Everything that the Father has is mine; for this reason I told you that he will take from what is mine and declare it to you."

Or:

GOSPEL / C   *John 14:15-16, 23b-26*

Jesus said to his disciples: "If you love me, you will keep my commandments. And I will ask the Father, and he will give you another Advocate to be with you always. "Whoever loves me will keep my word, and my Father will love him, and we will come to him and make our dwelling with him. Those who do not love me do not keep my words; yet the word you hear is not mine but that of the Father who sent me. "I have told you this while I am with you. The Advocate, the Holy Spirit whom the Father will send in my name, will teach you everything and remind you of all that I told you."

Ordinary Time

When the church assembles, there is always time to read from the scriptures.
This is the book the church carries: the Law and the prophets, the books
of wisdom and psalms, the letters and writings of Paul and of the other
apostles, the gospels themselves. In various places and times the readings
from scripture have been arranged so that the various Sundays have their
assigned texts. This book of assigned scriptures is the lectionary. In the present Roman lectionary the scriptures are marked for reading through a
cycle of three years.

Most of each year is called "Ordinary Time" or "Sundays of the Year."
These are the weeks between the Christmas season and Lent, and the long
period between Pentecost (the conclusion of the Easter season) and
Advent (usually the first Sunday in December). On the Sundays of
Ordinary Time, the lectionary has us read in order through the letters of
the New Testament and the gospels. In the first year of the cycle, the
gospel of Matthew is read from beginning to end; in the second year,
Mark; in the third, Luke. Likewise, each Sunday finds the church picking
up the reading of one of the letters of the New Testament roughly where
the previous week's reading concluded. At present, the first reading at
Sunday Mass in Ordinary Time is chosen from the Hebrew Scriptures;
these texts show the richness and the continuity of faith.

Sunday by Sunday, year after year, the church reads through its book
in the weeks of Ordinary Time. Each Christian, each local church, each
generation listens and so finds its own life in God's word.

The Church assembles around the scriptures and around the Lord's
table on Sunday. This day is called by Christians the Lord's Day. Whether
the church is in Ordinary Time or in the seasons of Advent/Christmas or
Lent/Easter, the Lord's Day is kept holy; it is the original feast day. The
rhythm of the weekdays and the Sunday is the basic rhythm of life in
Christian churches. The practices with which a church keeps the Lord's
Day vary, but always and everywhere Christians assemble on this day so
that the church may listen to God's word. Through the days of the week,
the Sunday's scriptures are to be for reflection and nourishment as they are
repeated and pondered in the households of the assembly.

572 SUNDAY AFTER PENTECOST—TRINITY SUNDAY / A

READING I
Exodus 34:4b-6, 8-9 / 164

Early in the morning Moses went up Mount Sinai as the LORD had commanded him, taking along the two stone tablets.

Having come down in a cloud, the LORD stood with Moses there and proclaimed his name, "LORD." Thus the LORD passed before him and cried out, "The LORD, the LORD, a merciful and gracious God, slow to anger and rich in kindness and fidelity." Moses at once bowed down to the ground in worship. Then he said, "If I find favor with you, O Lord, do come along in our company. This is indeed a stiff-necked people; yet pardon our wickedness and sins, and receive us as your own."

RESPONSORIAL PSALM
Daniel 3:52, 53, 54, 55

Glo - ry and praise for ev - er- more.

Blessed are you, O Lord, the God of our
  fathers,
    praiseworthy and exalted above all
    forever;
and blessed is your holy and glorious
    name,
    praiseworthy and exalted above all
    for all ages. ℟.

Blessed are you in the temple of your
    holy glory,
    praiseworthy and glorious above all
    forever. ℟.

Blessed are you on the throne of your
    kingdom,
    praiseworthy and exalted above all
    forever. ℟.

Blessed are you who look into the
    depths
    from your throne upon the cherubim,
    praiseworthy and exalted above all
    forever. ℟.

READING II
2 Corinthians 13:11-13

Brothers and sisters, rejoice. Mend your ways, encourage one another, agree with one another, live in peace, and the God of love and peace will be with you. Greet one another with a holy kiss. All the holy ones greet you.

The grace of the Lord Jesus Christ and the love of God and the fellowship of the Holy Spirit be with all of you.

GOSPEL
John 3:16-18

God so loved the world that he gave his only Son, so that everyone who believes in him might not perish but might have eternal life. For God did not send his Son into the world to condemn the world, but that the world might be saved through him. Whoever believes in him will not be condemned, but whoever does not believe has already been condemned, because he has not believed in the name of the only Son of God.

SUNDAY AFTER PENTECOST—TRINITY SUNDAY / B   573

READING I   *Deuteronomy 4:32-34, 39-40 / 165*

Moses said to the people: "Ask now of the days of old, before your time, ever since God created man upon the earth; ask from one end of the sky to the other: Did anything so great ever happen before? Was it ever heard of? Did a people ever hear the voice of God speaking from the midst of fire, as you did, and live? Or did any god venture to go and take a nation for himself from the midst of another nation, by testings, by signs and wonders, by war, with strong hand and outstretched arm, and by great terrors, all of which the LORD, your God, did for you in Egypt before your very eyes? This is why you must now know, and fix in your heart, that the LORD is God in the heavens above and on earth below, and that there is no other. You must keep his statutes and commandments that I enjoin on you today, that you and your children after you may prosper, and that you may have long life on the land which the LORD, your God, is giving you forever."

RESPONSORIAL PSALM   *Psalm 33:4-5, 6, 9, 18-19, 20, 22*

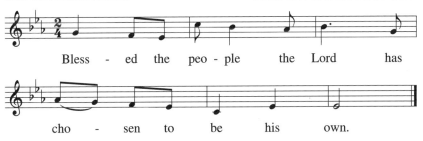

Bless - ed the peo - ple the Lord has cho - sen to be his own.

Upright is the word of the LORD,
and all his works are trustworthy.
He loves justice and right;
of the kindness of the Lord the earth
is full. ℟.

By the word of the Lord the heavens
were made;
by the breath of his mouth all their
host.
For he spoke, and it was made;
he commanded, and it stood forth. ℟.

See, the eyes of the Lord are upon those
who fear him,
upon those who hope for his
kindness,
to deliver them from death
and preserve them in spite of
famine. ℟.

Our soul waits for the Lord,
who is our help and our shield.
May your kindness, O Lord, be upon us
who have put our hope in you. ℟.

READING II   *Romans 8:14-17*

Brothers and sisters: those who are led by the Spirit of God are sons of God. For you did not receive a spirit of slavery to fall back into fear, but you received a Spirit of adoption, through whom we cry, "Abba, Father!" The Spirit himself bears witness with our spirit that we are children of God, and if children, then heirs, heirs of God and joint heirs with Christ, if only we suffer with him so that we may also be glorified with him.

GOSPEL   *Matthew 28:16-20*

The eleven disciples went to Galilee, to the mountain to which Jesus had ordered them. When they all saw him, they worshiped, but they doubted. Then Jesus approached and said to them, "All power in heaven and on earth has been given to me. Go, therefore, and make disciples of all nations, baptizing them in the name of the Father, and of the Son, and of the Holy Spirit, teaching them to observe all that I have commanded you. And behold, I am with you always, until the end of the age."

574 SUNDAY AFTER PENTECOST—TRINITY SUNDAY / C

READING I   *Proverbs 8:22-31 / 166*

Thus says the wisdom of God:
"The LORD possessed me, the beginning
    of his ways,
      the forerunner of his prodigies of
        long ago;
from of old I was poured forth,
    at the first, before the earth.
When there were no depths I was brought
    forth,
      when there were no fountains or
        springs of water;
before the mountains were settled into
    place,
      before the hills, I was brought forth;
while as yet the earth and fields were not
    made,
      nor the first clods of the world.

"When the Lord established the heavens
    I was there,
      when he marked out the vault over
        the face of the deep;
when he made firm the skies above,
    when he fixed fast the foundations
      of the earth;
when he set for the sea its limit,
    so that the waters should not
      transgress his command;
then was I beside him as his craftsman,
    and I was his delight day by day,
playing before him all the while,
    playing on the surface of his earth;
    and I found delight in the human
      race."

RESPONSORIAL PSALM   *Psalm 8:4-5, 6-7, 8-9*

O Lord, our God, how won-der-ful your name in

all the earth!

When I behold your heavens, the work
    of your fingers,
      the moon and the stars which you
        set in place—
what is man that you should be mindful
    of him,
      or the son of man that you should
        care for him? ℟.

You have made him little less than the
    angels,

and crowned him with glory and
    honor.
You have given him rule over the works
    of your hands,
      putting all things under his feet. ℟.

All sheep and oxen,
    yes, and the beasts of the field,
the birds of the air, the fishes of the sea,
    and whatever swims the paths of
      the seas. ℟.

READING II   *Romans 5:1-5*

Brothers and sisters: Therefore, since we have been justified by faith, we have peace with God through our Lord Jesus Christ, through whom we have gained access by faith to this grace in which we stand, and we boast in hope of the glory of God. Not only that, but we even boast of our afflictions, knowing that affliction produces endurance, and endurance, proven character, and proven character, hope, and hope does not disappoint, because the love of God has been poured out into our hearts through the Holy Spirit that has been given to us.

GOSPEL *John 16:12-15*

Jesus said to his disciples: "I have much more to tell you, but you cannot bear it now. But when he comes, the Spirit of truth, he will guide you to all truth. He will not speak on his own, but he will speak what he hears, and will declare to you the things that are coming. He will glorify me, because he will take from what is mine and declare it to you. Everything that the Father has is mine; for this reason I told you that he will take from what is mine and declare it to you."

BODY AND BLOOD OF CHRIST / A 575

READING I *Deuteronomy 8:2-3, 14b-16a / 167*

Moses said to the people: "Remember how for forty years now the LORD, your God, has directed all your journeying in the desert, so as to test you by affliction and find out whether or not it was your intention to keep his commandments. He therefore let you be afflicted with hunger, and then fed you with manna, a food unknown to you and your fathers, in order to show you that not by bread alone does one live, but by every word that comes forth from the mouth of the LORD.

"Do not forget the LORD, your God, who brought you out of the land of Egypt, that place of slavery; who guided you through the vast and terrible desert with its saraph serpents and scorpions, its parched and waterless ground; who brought forth water for you from the flinty rock and fed you in the desert with manna, a food unknown to your fathers."

RESPONSORIAL PSALM *Psalm 147:12-13, 14-15, 19-20*

O praise the Lord, Je - ru - sa - lem.

Glorify the LORD, O Jerusalem;
  praise your God, O Zion.
For he has strengthened the bars of your
    gates;
  he has blessed your children within
    you. ℟.

He has granted peace in your borders;
  with the best of wheat he fills you.

He sends forth his command to the earth;
  swiftly runs his word! ℟.

He has proclaimed his word to Jacob,
  his statutes and his ordinances to
    Israel.
He has not done thus for any other
    nation;
  his ordinances he has not made
    known to them. Alleluia. ℟.

READING II *1 Corinthians 10:16-17*

Brothers and sisters: The cup of blessing that we bless, is it not a participation in the blood of Christ? The bread that we break, is it not a participation in the body of Christ? Because the loaf of bread is one, we, though many, are one body, for we all partake of the one loaf.

GOSPEL *John 6:51-58*

Jesus said to the Jewish crowds: "I am the living bread that came down from heaven; whoever eats this bread will live forever; and the bread that I will give is my flesh for the life of the world."

The Jews quarreled among themselves, saying, "How can this man give us his flesh to eat?" Jesus said to them, "Amen, amen, I say to you, unless you eat the flesh of the

Son of Man and drink his blood, you do not have life within you. Whoever eats my flesh and drinks my blood has eternal life, and I will raise him on the last day. For my flesh is true food, and my blood is true drink. Whoever eats my flesh and drinks my blood remains in me and I in him. Just as the living Father sent me and I have life because of the Father, so also the one who feeds on me will have life because of me. This is the bread that came down from heaven. Unlike your ancestors who ate and still died, whoever eats this bread will live forever."

576 BODY AND BLOOD OF CHRIST / B

READING I *Exodus 24:3-8 / 168*

When Moses came to the people and related all the words and ordinances of the LORD, they all answered with one voice, "We will do everything that the LORD has told us." Moses then wrote down all the words of the LORD and, rising early the next day, he erected at the foot of the mountain an altar and twelve pillars for the twelve tribes of Israel. Then, having sent certain young men of the Israelites to offer holocausts and sacrifice young bulls as peace offerings to the LORD, Moses took half of the blood and put it in large bowls; the other half he splashed on the altar. Taking the book of the covenant, he read it aloud to the people, who answered, "All that the LORD has said, we will heed and do." Then he took the blood and sprinkled it on the people, saying, "This is the blood of the covenant that the LORD has made with you in accordance with all these words of his."

RESPONSORIAL PSALM *Psalm 116:12-13, 15-16, 17-18*

I will take the cup of sal - va - tion, and call on the name of the Lord.

How shall I make a return to the LORD
    for all the good he has done for me?
The cup of salvation I will take up,
    and I will call upon the name of the
    LORD. ℟.

Precious in the eyes of the LORD
    is the death of his faithful ones.
I am your servant, the son of your
handmaid;
you have loosed my bonds. ℟.

To you will I offer sacrifice of
    thanksgiving,
and I will call upon the name of the
    LORD.
My vows to the LORD I will pay
    in the presence of all his people. ℟.

READING II *Hebrews 9:11-15*

Brothers and sisters: When Christ came as high priest of the good things that have come to be, passing through the greater and more perfect tabernacle not made by hands, that is, not belonging to this creation, he entered once for all into the sanctuary, not with the blood of goats and calves but with his own blood, thus obtaining eternal redemption. For if the blood of goats and bulls and the sprinkling of a heifer's ashes can sanctify those who are defiled so that their flesh is cleansed, how much more will the blood of Christ, who through the eternal Spirit offered himself unblemished to God, cleanse our consciences from dead works to worship the living God.

For this reason he is mediator of a new covenant: since a death has taken place for deliverance from transgressions under the first covenant, those who are called may receive the promised eternal inheritance.

GOSPEL   *Mark 14:12-16, 22-26*

On the first day of the Feast of Unleavened Bread, when they sacrificed the Passover lamb, Jesus' disciples said to him, "Where do you want us to go and prepare for you to eat the Passover?" He sent two of his disciples and said to them, "Go into the city and a man will meet you, carrying a jar of water. Follow him. Wherever he enters, say to the master of the house, 'The Teacher says, "Where is my guest room where I may eat the Passover with my disciples?"' Then he will show you a large upper room furnished and ready. Make the preparations for us there." The disciples then went off, entered the city, and found it just as he had told them; and they prepared the Passover.

While they were eating, he took bread, said the blessing, broke it, gave it to them, and said, "Take it; this is my body." Then he took a cup, gave thanks, and gave it to them, and they all drank from it. He said to them, "This is my blood of the covenant, which will be shed for many. Amen, I say to you, I shall not drink again the fruit of the vine until the day when I drink it new in the kingdom of God." Then, after singing a hymn, they went out to the Mount of Olives.

BODY AND BLOOD OF CHRIST / C   577

READING I   *Genesis 14:18-20 / 169*

In those days, Melchizedek, king of Salem, brought out bread and wine, and being a priest of God Most High, he blessed Abram with these words:
"Blessed be Abram by God Most High,
   the creator of heaven and earth;
and blessed be God Most High,
   who delivered your foes into your hand."
Then Abram gave him a tenth of everything.

RESPONSORIAL PSALM   *Psalm 110:1, 2, 3, 4*

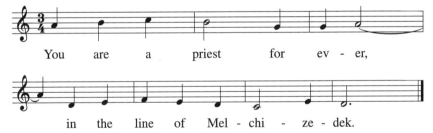

You are a priest for ev - er,

in the line of Mel - chi - ze - dek.

The LORD said to my Lord: "Sit at my
   right hand
till I make your enemies your
   footstool." ℞.

The scepter of your power the LORD will
   stretch forth from Zion:
"Rule in the midst of your
   enemies." ℞.

"Yours is princely power in the day of
   your birth, in holy splendor;
before the daystar, like the dew, I
   have begotten you." ℞.

The LORD has sworn, and he will not
   repent:
"You are a priest forever,
   according to the order of
      Melchizedek." ℞.

READING II   *1 Corinthians 11:23-26*

Brothers and sisters: I received from the Lord what I also handed on to you, that the Lord Jesus, on the night he was handed over, took bread, and, after he had given thanks, broke it and said, "This is my body that is for you. Do this in remembrance of me." In the same way also the cup, after supper, saying, "This cup is the new covenant in my blood. Do this, as often as you drink it, in remembrance of me." For as often as you eat this bread and drink the cup, you proclaim the death of the Lord until he comes.

GOSPEL   *Luke 9:11b-17*

Jesus spoke to the crowds about the kingdom of God, and he healed those who needed to be cured. As the day was drawing to a close, the Twelve approached him and said, "Dismiss the crowd so that they can go to the surrounding villages and farms and find lodging and provisions; for we are in a deserted place here." He said to them, "Give them some food yourselves." They replied, "Five loaves and two fish are all we have, unless we ourselves go and buy food for all these people." Now the men there numbered about five thousand. Then he said to his disciples, "Have them sit down in groups of about fifty." They did so and made them all sit down. Then taking the five loaves and the two fish, and looking up to heaven, he said the blessing over them, broke them, and gave them to the disciples to set before the crowd. They all ate and were satisfied. And when the leftover fragments were picked up, they filled twelve wicker baskets.

---

578   SACRED HEART / A

READING I   *Deuteronomy 7:6-11 / 170*

Moses said to the people: "You are a people sacred to the LORD, your God; he has chosen you from all the nations on the face of the earth to be a people peculiarly his own. It was not because you are the largest of all nations that the LORD set his heart on you and chose you, for you are really the smallest of all nations. It was because the LORD loved you and because of his fidelity to the oath he had sworn to your fathers, that he brought you out with his strong hand from the place of slavery, and ransomed you from the hand of Pharaoh, king of Egypt. Understand, then, that the LORD, your God, is God indeed, the faithful God who keeps his merciful covenant down to the thousandth generation toward those who love him and keep his commandments, but who repays with destruction a person who hates him; he does not dally with such a one, but makes them personally pay for it. You shall therefore carefully observe the commandments, the statutes and the decrees that I enjoin on you today."

RESPONSORIAL PSALM   *Psalm 103:1-2, 3-4, 6-7, 8, 10*

The Lord's kind - ness   is ev-er - last - ing   to those who fear him.

Bless the LORD, O my soul;
    all my being, bless his holy name.
Bless the LORD, O my soul;
    and forget not all his benefits. ℟.

He pardons all your iniquities,
    heals all your ills.
He redeems your life from destruction,
    crowns you with kindness and
      compassion. ℟.

Merciful and gracious is the Lord,
    slow to anger and abounding in
      kindness.
Not according to our sins does he deal
    with us,
    nor does he requite us according to
      our crimes. ℟.

READING II
1 John 4:7-16

Beloved, let us love one another, because love is of God; everyone who loves is begotten by God and knows God. Whoever is without love does not know God, for God is love. In this way the love of God was revealed to us: God sent his only Son into the world so that we might have life through him. In this is love: not that we have loved God, but that he loved us and sent his Son as expiation for our sins. Beloved, if God so loved us, we also must love one another. No one has ever seen God. Yet, if we love one another, God remains in us, and his love is brought to perfection in us.

This is how we know that we remain in him and he in us, that he has given us of his Spirit. Moreover, we have seen and testify that the Father sent his Son as savior of the world. Whoever acknowledges that Jesus is the Son of God, God remains in him and he in God. We have come to know and to believe in the love God has for us.

God is love, and whoever remains in love remains in God and God in him.

GOSPEL
Matthew 11:25-30

At that time Jesus exclaimed: "I give praise to you, Father, Lord of heaven and earth, for although you have hidden these things from the wise and the learned you have revealed them to little ones. Yes, Father, such has been your gracious will. All things have been handed over to me by my Father. No one knows the Son except the Father, and no one knows the Father except the Son and anyone to whom the Son wishes to reveal him."

"Come to me, all you who labor and are burdened, and I will give you rest. Take my yoke upon you and learn from me, for I am meek and humble of heart; and you will find rest for yourselves. For my yoke is easy, and my burden light."

SACRED HEART / B   579

READING I
Hosea 11:1, 3-4, 8c-9 / 171

Thus says the LORD:
When Israel was a child I loved him,
    out of Egypt I called my son.
Yet it was I who taught Ephraim to walk,
    who took them in my arms;
I drew them with human cords,
    with bands of love;
I fostered them like one
    who raises an infant to his cheeks;
Yet, though I stooped to feed my child,

they did not know that I was their
    healer.

My heart is overwhelmed,
    my pity is stirred.
I will not give vent to my blazing anger,
    I will not destroy Ephraim again;
For I am God and not a man,
    the Holy One present among you;
I will not let the flames consume you.

RESPONSORIAL PSALM
Isaiah 12:2-3, 4bcd, 5-6

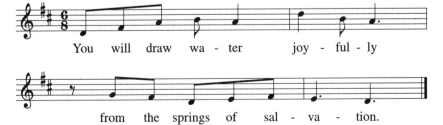

You will draw wa - ter joy - ful - ly from the springs of sal - va - tion.

God indeed is my savior;
    I am confident and unafraid.
My strength and my courage is the LORD,

and he has been my savior.
With joy you will draw water
    at the fountain of salvation. ℟.

Give thanks to the LORD, acclaim his
    name;
  among the nations make known his
    deeds,
  proclaim how exalted is his name. ℟.

Sing praise to the LORD for his glorious
    achievement;
  let this be known throughout all the
    earth.
Shout with exultation, O city of Zion,
  for great in your midst
  is the Holy One of Israel! ℟.

READING II   *Ephesians 3:8-12, 14-19*

Brothers and sisters: To me, the very least of all the holy ones, this grace was given, to preach to the Gentiles the inscrutable riches of Christ, and to bring to light for all what is the plan of the mystery hidden from ages past in God who created all things, so that the manifold wisdom of God might now be made known through the church to the principalities and authorities in the heavens. This was according to the eternal purpose that he accomplished in Christ Jesus our Lord, in whom we have boldness of speech and confidence of access through faith in him.

For this reason I kneel before the Father, from whom every family in heaven and on earth is named, that he may grant you in accord with the riches of his glory to be strengthened with power through his Spirit in the inner self, and that Christ may dwell in your hearts through faith; that you, rooted and grounded in love, may have strength to comprehend with all the holy ones what is the breadth and length and height and depth, and to know the love of Christ which surpasses knowledge, so that you may be filled with all the fullness of God.

GOSPEL   *John 19:31-37*

Since it was preparation day, in order that the bodies might not remain on the cross on the sabbath, for the sabbath day of that week was a solemn one, the Jews asked Pilate that their legs be broken and they be taken down. So the soldiers came and broke the legs of the first and then of the other one who was crucified with Jesus. But when they came to Jesus and saw that he was already dead, they did not break his legs, but one soldier thrust his lance into his side, and immediately blood and water flowed out. An eyewitness has testified, and his testimony is true; he knows that he is speaking the truth, so that you also may come to believe. For this happened so that the Scripture passage might be fulfilled:

  'Not a bone of it will be broken.'
And again another passage says:
  'They will look upon him whom they have pierced.'

580   SACRED HEART / C

READING I   *Ezekiel 34:11-16 / 172*

Thus says the Lord GOD: I myself will look after and tend my sheep. As a shepherd tends his flock when he finds himself among his scattered sheep, so will I tend my sheep. I will rescue them from every place where they were scattered when it was cloudy and dark. I will lead them out from among the peoples and gather them from the foreign lands; I will bring them back to their own country and pasture them upon the mountains of Israel in the land's ravines and all its inhabited places. In good pastures will I pasture them, and on the mountain heights of Israel shall be their grazing ground. There they shall lie down on good grazing ground, and in rich pastures shall they be pastured on the mountains of Israel. I myself will pasture my sheep; I myself will give them rest, says the Lord GOD. The lost I will seek out, the strayed I will bring back, the injured I will bind up, the sick I will heal, but the sleek and the strong I will destroy, shepherding them rightly.

RESPONSORIAL PSALM *Psalm 23:1-3a, 3b-4, 5, 6*

The Lord is my shep-herd; there is noth-ing I shall want.

The LORD is my shepherd; I shall not
    want.
  In verdant pastures he gives me
    repose;
beside restful waters he leads me;
  he refreshes my soul. ℟.

He guides me in right paths
  for his name's sake.
Even though I walk in the dark valley
  I fear no evil; for you are at my side
with your rod and your staff

that give me courage. ℟.

You spread the table before me
  in the sight of my foes;
you anoint my head with oil;
  my cup overflows. ℟.

Only goodness and kindness follow me
  all the days of my life;
and I shall dwell in the house of the LORD
  for years to come. ℟.

READING II *Romans 5:5b-11*

Brothers and sisters: The love of God has been poured out into our hearts through the Holy Spirit that has been given to us. For Christ, while we were still helpless, died at the appointed time for the ungodly. Indeed, only with difficulty does one die for a just person, though perhaps for a good person one might even find courage to die. But God proves his love for us in that while we were still sinners Christ died for us. How much more then, since we are now justified by his blood, will we be saved through him from the wrath. Indeed, if, while we were enemies, we were reconciled to God through the death of his Son, how much more, once reconciled, will we be saved by his life. Not only that, but we also boast of God through our Lord Jesus Christ, through whom we have now received reconciliation.

GOSPEL *Luke 15:3-7*

Jesus addressed this parable to the Pharisees and scribes: "What man among you having a hundred sheep and losing one of them would not leave the ninety-nine in the desert and go after the lost one until he finds it? And when he does find it, he sets it on his shoulders with great joy and, upon his arrival home, he calls together his friends and neighbors and says to them, 'Rejoice with me because I have found my lost sheep.' I tell you, in just the same way there will be more joy in heaven over one sinner who repents than over ninety-nine righteous people who have no need of repentance."

SECOND SUNDAY IN ORDINARY TIME / A   581

READING I *Isaiah 49:3, 5-6 / 64*

The LORD said to me: You are my
    servant,
  Israel, through whom I show my
    glory.
Now the LORD has spoken
  who formed me as his servant from
    the womb,
  that Jacob may be brought back to
    him
  and Israel gathered to him;

and I am made glorious in the sight
  of the LORD,
  and my God is now my strength!
It is too little, the LORD says, for you to
  be my servant,
  to raise up the tribes of Jacob,
  and restore the survivors of Israel;
I will make you a light to the nations,
  that my salvation may reach to the
    ends of the earth.

RESPONSORIAL PSALM   *Psalm 40:2, 4, 7-8, 8-9, 10*

Here am I, Lord; here am I, Lord; I come to do your will.

I have waited, waited for the LORD,
and he stooped toward me and heard
my cry.
And he put a new song into my mouth,
a hymn to our God. ℟.

Sacrifice or offering you wished not,
but ears open to obedience you gave
me.
Holocausts or sin-offerings you sought
not;
then said I, "Behold I come." ℟.

"In the written scroll it is prescribed for
me,
to do your will, O my God, is my
delight,
And your law is within my heart!" ℟.

I announced your justice in the vast
assembly;
I did not restrain my lips, as you,
O LORD, know. ℟.

READING II   *1 Corinthians 1:1-3*

Paul, called to be an apostle of Christ Jesus by the will of God, and Sosthenes our brother, to the church of God that is in Corinth, to you who have been sanctified in Christ Jesus, called to be holy, with all those everywhere who call upon the name of our Lord Jesus Christ, their Lord and ours. Grace to you and peace from God our Father and the Lord Jesus Christ.

GOSPEL   *John 1:29-34*

John the Baptist saw Jesus coming toward him and said, "Behold, the Lamb of God, who takes away the sin of the world. He is the one of whom I said, 'A man is coming after me who ranks ahead of me because he existed before me.' I did not know him, but the reason why I came baptizing with water was that he might be made known to Israel." John testified further, saying, "I saw the Spirit come down like a dove from heaven and remain upon him. I did not know him, but the one who sent me to baptize with water told me, 'On whomever you see the Spirit come down and remain, he is the one who will baptize with the Holy Spirit.' Now I have seen and testified that he is the Son of God."

582   **SECOND SUNDAY IN ORDINARY TIME / B**

READING I   *1 Samuel 3:3b-10, 19 / 65*

Samuel was sleeping in the temple of the LORD where the ark of God was. The LORD called to Samuel, who answered, "Here I am." Samuel ran to Eli and said, "Here I am. You called me." "I did not call you," Eli said. "Go back to sleep." So he went back to sleep. Again the LORD called Samuel, who rose and went to Eli. "Here I am," he said. "You called me." But Eli answered, "I did not call you, my son. Go back to sleep."

At that time Samuel was not familiar with the LORD, because the LORD had not revealed anything to him as yet. The LORD called Samuel again, for the third time.

Getting up and going to Eli, he said, "Here I am. You called me." Then Eli understood that the LORD was calling the youth. So he said to Samuel, "Go to sleep, and if you are called, reply, 'Speak, LORD, for your servant is listening.'" When Samuel went to sleep in his place, the LORD came and revealed his presence, calling out as before, "Samuel, Samuel!" Samuel answered, "Speak, for your servant is listening."

Samuel grew up, and the LORD was with him, not permitting any word of his to be without effect.

RESPONSORIAL PSALM
Psalm 40:2, 4, 7-8, 8-9, 10

Here am I, Lord; here am I, Lord; I come to do your will.

I have waited, waited for the LORD,
    and he stooped toward me and heard
        my cry.
And he put a new song into my mouth,
    a hymn to our God. ℟.

Sacrifice or offering you wished not,
    but ears open to obedience you gave
        me.
Holocausts or sin-offerings you sought
    not;
    then said I, "Behold I come." ℟.

"In the written scroll it is prescribed for
    me,
    to do your will, O my God, is my
        delight,
and your law is within my heart!" ℟.

I announced your justice in the vast
    assembly;
    I did not restrain my lips, as you,
        O LORD, know. ℟.

READING II
1 Corinthians 6:13c-15a, 17-20

Brothers and sisters: The body is not for immorality, but for the Lord, and the Lord is for the body; God raised the Lord and will also raise us by his power.

Do you not know that your bodies are members of Christ? But whoever is joined to the Lord becomes one Spirit with him. Avoid immorality. Every other sin a person commits is outside the body, but the immoral person sins against his own body. Do you not know that your body is a temple of the Holy Spirit within you, whom you have from God, and that you are not your own? For you have been purchased at a price. Therefore glorify God in your body.

GOSPEL
John 1:35-42

John was standing with two of his disciples, and as he watched Jesus walk by, he said, "Behold, the Lamb of God." The two disciples heard what he said and followed Jesus. Jesus turned and saw them following him and said to them, "What are you looking for?" They said to him, "Rabbi" (which translated means Teacher), "where are you staying?" He said to them, "Come, and you will see." So they went and saw where Jesus was staying, and they stayed with him that day. It was about four in the afternoon. Andrew, the brother of Simon Peter, was one of the two who heard John and followed Jesus. He first found his own brother Simon and told him, "We have found the Messiah" (which is translated Christ). Then he brought him to Jesus. Jesus looked at him and said, "You are Simon the son of John; you will be called Cephas" (which is translated Peter).

583 SECOND SUNDAY IN ORDINARY TIME / C

READING I   *Isaiah 62:1-5 / 66*

For Zion's sake I will not be silent,
    for Jerusalem's sake I will not be
      quiet,
until her vindication shines forth like
      the dawn
    and her victory like a burning torch.

Nations shall behold your vindication,
    and all the kings your glory;
you shall be called by a new name
    pronounced by the mouth of the
      LORD.
You shall be a glorious crown in the

hand of the LORD,
    a royal diadem held by your God.
No more shall people call you
    "Forsaken,"
    or your land "Desolate,"
but you shall be called "My Delight,"
    and your land "Espoused."
For the LORD delights in you
    and makes your land his spouse.
As a young man marries a virgin,
    your Builder shall marry you;
and as a bridegroom rejoices in his bride
    so shall your God rejoice in you.

RESPONSORIAL PSALM   *Psalm 96:1-2, 2-3, 7-8, 9-10*

Pro-claim his mar-vel-ous deeds to all the na - tions.

Sing to the LORD a new song;
    sing to the LORD, all you lands.
Sing to the LORD; bless his name. ℟.

Announce his salvation, day after day.
    Tell his glory among the nations;
among all peoples, his wondrous deeds. ℟.

Give to the LORD, you families of nations,

give to the LORD glory and praise;
give to the LORD the glory due his
    name! ℟.

Worship the LORD in holy attire.
    Tremble before him, all the earth;
say among the nations: The LORD is king.
He governs the peoples with
    equity. ℟.

READING II   *1 Corinthians 12:4-11*

Brothers and sisters: There are different kinds of spiritual gifts but the same Spirit; there
are different forms of service but the same Lord; there are different workings but the
same God who produces all of them in everyone. To each individual the manifestation
of the Spirit is given for some benefit. To one is given through the Spirit the expression
of wisdom; to another, the expression of knowledge according to the same Spirit; to
another, faith by the same Spirit; to another, gifts of healing by the one Spirit; to another, mighty deeds; to another, prophecy; to another, discernment of spirits; to another,
varieties of tongues; to another, interpretation of tongues. But one and the same Spirit
produces all of these, distributing them individually to each person as he wishes.

GOSPEL   *John 2:1-11*

There was a wedding at Cana in Galilee, and the mother of Jesus was there. Jesus and
his disciples were also invited to the wedding. When the wine ran short, the mother of
Jesus said to him, "They have no wine." And Jesus said to her, "Woman, how does your
concern affect me? My hour has not yet come." His mother said to the servers, "Do
whatever he tells you." Now there were six stone water jars there for Jewish ceremoni-
al washings, each holding twenty to thirty gallons. Jesus told them, "Fill the jars with
water." So they filled them to the brim. Then he told them, "Draw some out now and
take it to the headwaiter." So they took it. And when the headwaiter tasted the water that

had become wine, without knowing where it came from (although the servers who had drawn the water knew), the headwaiter called the bridegroom and said to him, "Everyone serves good wine first, and then when people have drunk freely, an inferior one; but you have kept the good wine until now." Jesus did this as the beginning of his signs at Cana in Galilee and so revealed his glory, and his disciples began to believe in him.

THIRD SUNDAY IN ORDINARY TIME / A 584

READING I *Isaiah 8:23—9:3 / 67*

First the Lord degraded the land of Zebulun and the land of Naphtali; but in the end he has glorified the seaward road, the land west of the Jordan, the District of the Gentiles.

Anguish has taken wing, dispelled is darkness:
 for there is no gloom where but now there was distress.

The people who walked in darkness
 have seen a great light;
 upon those who dwelt in the land of gloom a light has shone.
You have brought them abundant joy
 and great rejoicing,
 as they rejoice before you as at the harvest,
 as people make merry when dividing spoils.
For the yoke that burdened them,
 the pole on their shoulder,
 and the rod of their taskmaster
 you have smashed, as on the day of Midian.

RESPONSORIAL PSALM *Psalm 27:1, 4, 13-14*

The Lord is my light and my sal - va - tion.

The LORD is my light and my salvation;
 whom should I fear?
The LORD is my life's refuge;
 of whom should I be afraid? ℟.

One thing I ask of the LORD;
 this I seek:
to dwell in the house of the LORD
 all the days of my life,
that I may gaze on the loveliness of the

LORD
and contemplate his temple. ℟.

I believe that I shall see the bounty of the
 LORD
 in the land of the living.
Wait for the LORD with courage;
 be stouthearted, and wait for the
 LORD. ℟.

READING II *1 Corinthians 1:10-13, 17*

I urge you, brothers and sisters, in the name of our Lord Jesus Christ, that all of you agree in what you say, and that there be no divisions among you, but that you be united in the same mind and in the same purpose. For it has been reported to me about you, my brothers and sisters, by Chloe's people, that there are rivalries among you. I mean that each of you is saying, "I belong to Paul," or "I belong to Apollos," or "I belong to Cephas," or "I belong to Christ." Is Christ divided? Was Paul crucified for you? Or were you baptized in the name of Paul? For Christ did not send me to baptize but to preach the gospel, and not with the wisdom of human eloquence, so that the cross of Christ might not be emptied of its meaning.

GOSPEL   *Matthew 4:12-23 or 4:12-17*

For short form read only the part in brackets.

[When Jesus heard that John had been arrested, he withdrew to Galilee. He left Nazareth and went to live in Capernaum by the sea, in the region of Zebulun and Naphtali, that what had been said through Isaiah the prophet might be fulfilled:

"Land of Zebulun and land of Naphtali,
     the way to the sea, beyond the Jordan,
     Galilee of the Gentiles,
     the people who sit in darkness have seen a great light,
     on those dwelling in a land overshadowed by death
          light has arisen."

From that time on, Jesus began to preach and say, "Repent, for the kingdom of heaven is at hand."]

As he was walking by the Sea of Galilee, he saw two brothers, Simon who is called Peter, and his brother Andrew, casting a net into the sea; they were fishermen. He said to them, "Come after me, and I will make you fishers of men." At once they left their nets and followed him. He walked along from there and saw two other brothers, James, the son of Zebedee, and his brother John. They were in a boat, with their father Zebedee, mending their nets. He called them, and immediately they left their boat and their father and followed him. He went around all of Galilee, teaching in their synagogues, proclaiming the gospel of the kingdom, and curing every disease and illness among the people.

---

585 **THIRD SUNDAY IN ORDINARY TIME / B**

READING I   *Jonah 3:1-5, 10 / 68*

The word of the LORD came to Jonah, saying: "Set out for the great city of Nineveh, and announce to it the message that I will tell you." So Jonah made ready and went to Nineveh, according to the LORD's bidding. Now Nineveh was an enormously large city; it took three days to go through it. Jonah began his journey through the city, and had gone but a single day's walk announcing, "Forty days more and Nineveh shall be destroyed," when the people of Nineveh believed God; they proclaimed a fast and all of them, great and small, put on sackcloth.

When God saw by their actions how they turned from their evil way, he repented of the evil that he had threatened to do to them; he did not carry it out.

RESPONSORIAL PSALM   *Psalm 25:4-5, 6-7, 8-9*

Teach me your ways, O Lord, teach me your ways.

Your ways, O LORD, make known to me;
     teach me your paths,
Guide me in your truth and teach me,
     for you are God my savior. ℟.

Remember that your compassion, O
     LORD,
     and your love are from of old.

In your kindness remember me,
     because of your goodness, O
     LORD. ℟.

Good and upright is the LORD;
     thus he shows sinners the way.
He guides the humble to justice
     and teaches the humble his way. ℟.

READING II
1 Corinthians 7:29-31

I tell you, brothers and sisters, the time is running out. From now on, let those having wives act as not having them, those weeping as not weeping, those rejoicing as not rejoicing, those buying as not owning, those using the world as not using it fully. For the world in its present form is passing away.

GOSPEL
Mark 1:14-20

After John had been arrested, Jesus came to Galilee proclaiming the gospel of God: "This is the time of fulfillment. The kingdom of God is at hand. Repent, and believe in the gospel."

As he passed by the Sea of Galilee, he saw Simon and his brother Andrew casting their nets into the sea; they were fishermen. Jesus said to them, "Come after me, and I will make you fishers of men." Then they abandoned their nets and followed him. He walked along a little farther and saw James, the son of Zebedee, and his brother John. They too were in a boat mending their nets. Then he called them. So they left their father Zebedee in the boat along with the hired men and followed him.

THIRD SUNDAY IN ORDINARY TIME / C
586

READING I
Nehemiah 8:2-4a, 5-6, 8-10 / 69

Ezra the priest brought the law before the assembly, which consisted of men, women, and those children old enough to understand. Standing at one end of the open place that was before the Water Gate, he read out of the book from daybreak till midday, in the presence of the men, the women, and those children old enough to understand; and all the people listened attentively to the book of the law. Ezra the scribe stood on a wooden platform that had been made for the occasion. He opened the scroll so that all the people might see it (for he was standing higher up than any of the people); and, as he opened it, all the people rose. Ezra blessed the LORD, the great God, and all the people, their hands raised high, answered, "Amen, amen!" Then they bowed down and prostrated themselves before the LORD, their faces to the ground. Ezra read plainly from the book of the law of God, interpreting it so that all could understand what was read. Then Nehemiah, that is, His Excellency, and Ezra the priest-scribe and the Levites who were instructing the people said to all the people: "Today is holy to the LORD your God. Do not be sad, and do not weep"— for all the people were weeping as they heard the words of the law. He said further: "Go, eat rich foods and drink sweet drinks, and allot portions to those who had nothing prepared; for today is holy to our LORD. Do not be saddened this day, for rejoicing in the LORD must be your strength!"

RESPONSORIAL PSALM
Psalm 19:8, 9, 10, 15

Your words, O Lord, are Spir-it and life.

The law of the LORD is perfect,
　　refreshing the soul;
the decree of the LORD is trustworthy,
　　giving wisdom to the simple. ℟.

The precepts of the LORD are right,
　　rejoicing the heart;
the command of the LORD is clear,
　　enlightening the eye. ℟.

The fear of the Lord is pure,
　　enduring forever;
the ordinances of the Lord are true,
　　all of them just. ℟.

Let the words of my mouth and the
　　thought of my heart
　　find favor before you,
O Lord, my rock and my redeemer. ℟.

READING II

1 Corinthians 12:12-30 or 12:12-14, 27

For short form read only the parts in brackets.

[Brothers and sisters: As a body is one though it has many parts, and all the parts of the body, though many, are one body, so also Christ. For in one Spirit we were all baptized into one body, whether Jews or Greeks, slaves or free persons, and we were all given to drink of one Spirit.

Now the body is not a single part, but many.] If a foot should say, "Because I am not a hand I do not belong to the body," it does not for this reason belong any less to the body. Or if an ear should say, "Because I am not an eye I do not belong to the body," it does not for this reason belong any less to the body. If the whole body were an eye, where would the hearing be? If the whole body were hearing, where would the sense of smell be? But as it is, God placed the parts, each one of them, in the body as he intended. If they were all one part, where would the body be? But as it is, there are many parts, yet one body. The eye cannot say to the hand, "I do not need you," nor again the head to the feet, "I do not need you." Indeed, the parts of the body that seem to be weaker are all the more necessary, and those parts of the body that we consider less honorable we surround with greater honor, and our less presentable parts are treated with greater propriety, whereas our more presentable parts do not need this. But God has so constructed the body as to give greater honor to a part that is without it, so that there may be no division in the body, but that the parts may have the same concern for one another. If one part suffers, all the parts suffer with it; if one part is honored, all the parts share its joy.

Now [you are Christ's body, and individually parts of it.] Some people God has designated in the church to be, first, apostles; second, prophets; third, teachers; then, mighty deeds; then gifts of healing, assistance, administration, and varieties of tongues. Are all apostles? Are all prophets? Are all teachers? Do all work mighty deeds? Do all have gifts of healing? Do all speak in tongues? Do all interpret?

GOSPEL

Luke 1:1-4; 4:14-21

Since many have undertaken to compile a narrative of the events that have been fulfilled among us, just as those who were eyewitnesses from the beginning and ministers of the word have handed them down to us, I too have decided, after investigating everything accurately anew, to write it down in an orderly sequence for you, most excellent Theophilus, so that you may realize the certainty of the teachings you have received.

Jesus returned to Galilee in the power of the Spirit, and news of him spread throughout the whole region. He taught in their synagogues and was praised by all.

He came to Nazareth, where he had grown up, and went according to his custom into the synagogue on the sabbath day. He stood up to read and was handed a scroll of the prophet Isaiah. He unrolled the scroll and found the passage where it was written:
"The Spirit of the Lord is upon me,
    because he has anointed me
    to bring glad tidings to the poor.
He has sent me to proclaim liberty to captives
    and recovery of sight to the blind,
    to let the oppressed go free,
    and to proclaim a year acceptable to the Lord."
Rolling up the scroll, he handed it back to the attendant and sat down, and the eyes of all in the synagogue looked intently at him. He said to them, "Today this Scripture passage is fulfilled in your hearing."

FOURTH SUNDAY IN ORDINARY TIME / A

READING I

Zephaniah 2:3; 3:12-13 / 70

Seek the LORD, all you humble of the
earth,
who have observed his law;
seek justice, seek humility;
perhaps you may be sheltered
on the day of the LORD's anger.

But I will leave as a remnant in your
midst
a people humble and lowly,

who shall take refuge in the name of the
LORD:
the remnant of Israel.
They shall do no wrong
and speak no lies;
nor shall there be found in their mouths
a deceitful tongue;
they shall pasture and couch their flocks
with none to disturb them.

RESPONSORIAL PSALM

Psalm 146:6-7, 8-9, 9-10

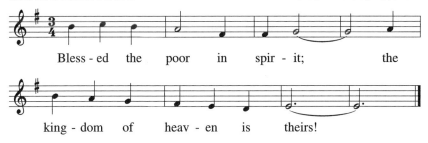

Bless - ed the poor in spir - it; the king - dom of heav - en is theirs!

The LORD keeps faith forever,
secures justice for the oppressed,
gives food to the hungry.
The LORD sets captives free. ℟.

The LORD gives sight to the blind;
the LORD raises up those who were
bowed down.
The LORD loves the just;
the LORD protects strangers. ℟.

The fatherless and the widow the LORD
sustains,
but the way of the wicked he thwarts.
The LORD shall reign forever;
your God, O Zion, through all
generations.
Alleluia. ℟.

READING II

1 Corinthians 1:26-31

Consider your own calling, brothers and sisters. Not many of you were wise by human
standards, not many were powerful, not many were of noble birth. Rather, God chose
the foolish of the world to shame the wise, and God chose the weak of the world to
shame the strong, and God chose the lowly and despised of the world, those who count
for nothing, to reduce to nothing those who are something, so that no human being might
boast before God. It is due to him that you are in Christ Jesus, who became for us wisdom from God, as well as righteousness, sanctification, and redemption, so that, as it is
written, "Whoever boasts, should boast in the Lord."

GOSPEL

Matthew 5:1-12a

When Jesus saw the crowds, he went up the mountain, and after he had sat down, his
disciples came to him. He began to teach them, saying:
"Blessed are the poor in spirit,
for theirs is the kingdom of heaven.
Blessed are they who mourn,
for they will be comforted.

Blessed are the meek,
> for they will inherit the land.
Blessed are they who hunger and thirst for righteousness,
> for they will be satisfied.
Blessed are the merciful,
> for they will be shown mercy.
Blessed are the clean of heart,
> for they will see God.
Blessed are the peacemakers,
> for they will be called children of God.
Blessed are they who are persecuted for the sake of
> righteousness,
> for theirs is the kingdom of heaven.
Blessed are you when they insult you and persecute you and utter every kind of evil against you falsely because of me. Rejoice and be glad, for your reward will be great in heaven."

588 FOURTH SUNDAY IN ORDINARY TIME / B

READING I   *Deuteronomy 18:15-20 / 71*

Moses spoke to all the people, saying: "A prophet like me will the LORD, your God, raise up for you from among your own kin; to him you shall listen. This is exactly what you requested of the LORD, your God, at Horeb on the day of the assembly, when you said, 'Let us not again hear the voice of the LORD, our God, nor see this great fire any more, lest we die.' And the LORD said to me, 'This was well said. I will raise up for them a prophet like you from among their kin, and will put my words into his mouth; he shall tell them all that I command him.'" Whoever will not listen to my words which he speaks in my name, I myself will make him answer for it. But if a prophet presumes to speak in my name an oracle that I have not commanded him to speak, or speaks in the name of other gods, he shall die."

RESPONSORIAL PSALM   *Psalm 95:1-2, 6-7, 7-9*

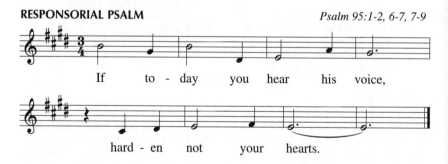

If to - day you hear his voice, hard - en not your hearts.

Come, let us sing joyfully to the LORD;
> let us acclaim the rock of our
> salvation.
Let us come into his presence with
> thanksgiving;
> let us joyfully sing psalms to him. ℟.

Come, let us bow down in worship;
> let us kneel before the LORD who
> made us.
For he is our God,

and we are the people he shepherds,
> the flock he guides. ℟.

Oh, that today you would hear his voice:
> "Harden not your hearts as at
> Meribah,
as in the day of Massah in the desert,
> where your fathers tempted me;
they tested me though they had seen my
> works." ℟.

READING II
1 Corinthians 7:32-35

Brothers and sisters: I should like you to be free of anxieties. An unmarried man is anxious about the things of the Lord, how he may please the Lord. But a married man is anxious about the things of the world, how he may please his wife, and he is divided. An unmarried woman or a virgin is anxious about the things of the Lord, so that she may be holy in both body and spirit. A married woman, on the other hand, is anxious about the things of the world, how she may please her husband. I am telling you this for your own benefit, not to impose a restraint upon you, but for the sake of propriety and adherence to the Lord without distraction.

GOSPEL
Mark 1:21-28

Then they came to Capernaum, and on the sabbath Jesus entered the synagogue and taught. The people were astonished at his teaching, for he taught them as one having authority and not as the scribes. In their synagogue was a man with an unclean spirit; he cried out, "What have you to do with us, Jesus of Nazareth? Have you come to destroy us? I know who you are—the Holy One of God!" Jesus rebuked him and said, "Quiet! Come out of him!" The unclean spirit convulsed him and with a loud cry came out of him. All were amazed and asked one another, "What is this? A new teaching with authority. He commands even the unclean spirits and they obey him." His fame spread everywhere throughout the whole region of Galilee.

FOURTH SUNDAY IN ORDINARY TIME / C   589

READING I
Jeremiah 1:4-5, 17-19 / 72

The word of the LORD came to me, saying:
Before I formed you in the womb I
knew you,
before you were born I dedicated
you,
a prophet to the nations I
appointed you.

But do you gird your loins;
stand up and tell them
all that I command you.
Be not crushed on their account,
as though I would leave you

crushed before them;
for it is I this day
who have made you a fortified
city,
a pillar of iron, a wall of brass,
against the whole land:
against Judah's kings and princes,
against its priests and people.
They will fight against you but not
prevail over you,
for I am with you to deliver you,
says the LORD.

RESPONSORIAL PSALM
Psalm 71:1-2, 3-4, 5-6, 15, 17

I will sing of your sal - va - tion.

In you, O LORD, I take refuge;
let me never be put to shame.
In your justice rescue me, and deliver me;
incline your ear to me, and save
me. ℟.

Be my rock of refuge,
a stronghold to give me safety,
for you are my rock and my fortress.
O my God, rescue me from the hand
of the wicked. ℟.

For you are my hope, O Lord;
  my trust, O God, from my youth.
On you I depend from birth;
  from my mother's womb you are my
  strength. ℟.

My mouth shall declare your justice,
  day by day your salvation.
O God, you have taught me from my
  youth,
and till the present I proclaim your
  wondrous deeds. ℟.

READING II
1 Corinthians 12:31—13:13 or 13:4-13

For short form read only the parts in brackets.

[Brothers and sisters:] Strive eagerly for the greatest spiritual gifts. But I shall show you a still more excellent way.

If I speak in human and angelic tongues, but do not have love, I am a resounding gong or a clashing cymbal. And if I have the gift of prophecy, and comprehend all mysteries and all knowledge; if I have all faith so as to move mountains, but do not have love, I am nothing. If I give away everything I own, and if I hand my body over so that I may boast, but do not have love, I gain nothing.

[Love is patient, love is kind. It is not jealous, it is not pompous, it is not inflated, it is not rude, it does not seek its own interests, it is not quick-tempered, it does not brood over injury, it does not rejoice over wrongdoing but rejoices with the truth. It bears all things, believes all things, hopes all things, endures all things. Love never fails. If there are prophecies, they will be brought to nothing; if tongues, they will cease; if knowledge, it will be brought to nothing. For we know partially and we prophesy partially, but when the perfect comes, the partial will pass away. When I was a child, I used to talk as a child, think as a child, reason as a child; when I became a man, I put aside childish things. At present we see indistinctly, as in a mirror, but then face to face. At present I know partially; then I shall know fully, as I am fully known. So faith, hope, love remain, these three; but the greatest of these is love.]

GOSPEL
Luke 4:21-30

Jesus began speaking in the synagogue, saying: "Today this Scripture passage is fulfilled in your hearing." And all spoke highly of him and were amazed at the gracious words that came from his mouth. They also asked, "Isn't this the son of Joseph?" He said to them, "Surely you will quote me this proverb, 'Physician, cure yourself,' and say, 'Do here in your native place the things that we heard were done in Capernaum.'" And he said, "Amen, I say to you, no prophet is accepted in his own native place. Indeed, I tell you, there were many widows in Israel in the days of Elijah when the sky was closed for three and a half years and a severe famine spread over the entire land. It was to none of these that Elijah was sent, but only to a widow in Zarephath in the land of Sidon. Again, there were many lepers in Israel during the time of Elisha the prophet; yet not one of them was cleansed, but only Naaman the Syrian." When the people in the synagogue heard this, they were all filled with fury. They rose up, drove him out of the town, and led him to the brow of the hill on which their town had been built, to hurl him down headlong. But Jesus passed through the midst of them and went away.

590 FIFTH SUNDAY IN ORDINARY TIME / A

READING I
Isaiah 58:7-10 / 73

Thus says the Lord:
  Share your bread with the hungry,
    shelter the oppressed and the homeless;
  clothe the naked when you see them,

and do not turn your back on your own.
Then your light shall break forth like the dawn,
and your wound shall quickly be healed;
your vindication shall go before you,
and the glory of the LORD shall be your rear guard.
Then you shall call, and the LORD will answer,
you shall cry for help, and he will say: Here I am!
If you remove from your midst
oppression, false accusation and malicious speech;
if you bestow your bread on the hungry
and satisfy the afflicted;
then light shall rise for you in the darkness,
and the gloom shall become for you like midday.

RESPONSORIAL PSALM

Psalm 112:4-5, 6-7, 8-9

The just man is a light in dark-ness to the up - right.

Light shines through the darkness for the
upright;
he is gracious and merciful and just.
Well for the man who is gracious and
lends,
who conducts his affairs with
justice. ℟.

He shall never be moved;
the just one shall be in everlasting
remembrance.
An evil report he shall not fear;
his heart is firm, trusting in the
LORD. ℟.

His heart is steadfast; he shall not fear.
Lavishly he gives to the poor;
His justice shall endure forever;
his horn shall be exalted in glory. ℟.

READING II

1 Corinthians 2:1-5

When I came to you, brothers and sisters, proclaiming the mystery of God, I did not
come with sublimity of words or of wisdom. For I resolved to know nothing while I was
with you except Jesus Christ, and him crucified. I came to you in weakness and fear and
much trembling, and my message and my proclamation were not with persuasive words
of wisdom, but with a demonstration of Spirit and power, so that your faith might rest
not on human wisdom but on the power of God.

GOSPEL

Matthew 5:13-16

Jesus said to his disciples: "You are the salt of the earth. But if salt loses its taste, with
what can it be seasoned? It is no longer good for anything but to be thrown out and tram-
pled underfoot. You are the light of the world. A city set on a mountain cannot be hidden. Nor do they light a lamp and then put it under a bushel basket; it is set on a lamp
stand, where it gives light to all in the house. Just so, your light must shine before others, that they may see your good deeds and glorify your heavenly Father."

591 FIFTH SUNDAY IN ORDINARY TIME / B

READING I
Job 7:1-4, 6-7 / 74

Job spoke, saying:
Is not man's life on earth a drudgery?
    Are not his days those of hirelings?
He is a slave who longs for the shade,
    a hireling who waits for his wages.
So I have been assigned months of
        misery,
    and troubled nights have been
        allotted to me.

If in bed I say, "When shall I arise?"
    then the night drags on;
I am filled with restlessness until the
        dawn.
My days are swifter than a weaver's
        shuttle;
    they come to an end without hope.
Remember that my life is like the wind;
    I shall not see happiness again.

RESPONSORIAL PSALM
Psalm 147:1-2, 3-4, 5-6

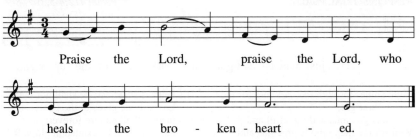

Praise the Lord, praise the Lord, who heals the bro - ken - heart - ed.

Praise the LORD, for he is good;
    sing praise to our God, for he is
        gracious;
it is fitting to praise him.
    The LORD rebuilds Jerusalem;
the dispersed of Israel he gathers. ℟.

He heals the brokenhearted

and binds up their wounds.
He tells the number of the stars;
    he calls each by name. ℟.

Great is our Lord and mighty in power;
    to his wisdom there is no limit.
The LORD sustains the lowly;
    the wicked he casts to the ground. ℟.

READING II
1 Corinthians 9:16-19, 22-23

Brothers and sisters: If I preach the gospel, this is no reason for me to boast, for an obligation has been imposed on me, and woe to me if I do not preach it! If I do so willingly, I have a recompense, but if unwillingly, then I have been entrusted with a stewardship. What then is my recompense? That, when I preach, I offer the gospel free of charge so as not to make full use of my right in the gospel. Although I am free in regard to all, I have made myself a slave to all so as to win over as many as possible. To the weak I became weak, to win over the weak. I have become all things to all, to save at least some. All this I do for the sake of the gospel, so that I too may have a share in it.

GOSPEL
Mark 1:29-39

On leaving the synagogue Jesus entered the house of Simon and Andrew with James and John. Simon's mother-in-law lay sick with a fever. They immediately told him about her. He approached, grasped her hand, and helped her up. Then the fever left her and she waited on them.
    When it was evening, after sunset, they brought to him all who were ill or possessed by demons. The whole town was gathered at the door. He cured many who were sick with various diseases, and he drove out many demons, not permitting them to speak because they knew him.

Rising very early before dawn, he left and went off to a deserted place, where he prayed. Simon and those who were with him pursued him and on finding him said, "Everyone is looking for you." He told them, "Let us go on to the nearby villages that I may preach there also. For this purpose have I come." So he went into their synagogues, preaching and driving out demons throughout the whole of Galilee.

FIFTH SUNDAY IN ORDINARY TIME / C   592

READING I   *Isaiah 6:1-2a, 3-8 / 75*

In the year King Uzziah died, I saw the Lord seated on a high and lofty throne, with the train of his garment filling the temple. Seraphim were stationed above.

They cried one to the other, "Holy, holy, holy is the LORD of hosts! All the earth is filled with his glory!" At the sound of that cry, the frame of the door shook and the house was filled with smoke.

Then I said, "Woe is me, I am doomed! For I am a man of unclean lips, living among a people of unclean lips; yet my eyes have seen the King, the LORD of hosts!" Then one of the seraphim flew to me, holding an ember that he had taken with tongs from the altar.

He touched my mouth with it, and said, "See, now that this has touched your lips, your wickedness is removed, your sin purged."

Then I heard the voice of the Lord saying, "Whom shall I send? Who will go for us?" "Here I am," I said; "send me!"

RESPONSORIAL PSALM   *Psalm 138:1-2, 2-3, 4-5, 7-8*

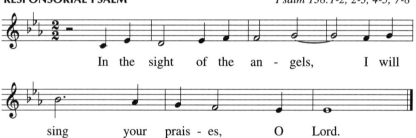

In the sight of the an - gels, I will sing your prais - es, O Lord.

I will give thanks to you, O LORD, with
    all my heart,
      for you have heard the words of my
        mouth;
in the presence of the angels I will sing
    your praise;
    I will worship at your holy temple
and give thanks to your name. ℟.

Because of your kindness and your truth;
    for you have made great above all
      things
your name and your promise.
    When I called, you answered me;
you built up strength within me. ℟.

All the kings of the earth shall give
    thanks to you, O LORD,
      when they hear the words of your
        mouth;
and they shall sing of the ways of the
    LORD:
    "Great is the glory of the LORD." ℟.

Your right hand saves me.
    The LORD will complete what he
      has done for me;
your kindness, O LORD, endures forever;
    forsake not the work of your
      hands. ℟.

READING II
1 Corinthians 15:1-11 or 15:3-8, 11

For short form read only the parts in brackets.

I am reminding you, [brothers and sisters,] of the gospel I preached to you, which you indeed received and in which you also stand. Through it you are also being saved, if you hold fast to the word I preached to you, unless you believed in vain. For [I handed on to you as of first importance what I also received: that Christ died for our sins in accordance with the Scriptures; that he was buried; that he was raised on the third day in accordance with the Scriptures; that he appeared to Cephas, then to the Twelve. After that, he appeared to more than five hundred brothers at once, most of whom are still living, though some have fallen asleep. After that he appeared to James, then to all the apostles. Last of all, as to one born abnormally, he appeared to me.] For I am the least of the apostles, not fit to be called an apostle, because I persecuted the church of God. But by the grace of God I am what I am, and his grace to me has not been ineffective. Indeed, I have toiled harder than all of them; not I, however, but the grace of God that is with me. [Therefore, whether it be I or they, so we preach and so you believed.]

GOSPEL
Luke 5:1-11

While the crowd was pressing in on Jesus and listening to the word of God, he was standing by the Lake of Gennesaret. He saw two boats there alongside the lake; the fishermen had disembarked and were washing their nets. Getting into one of the boats, the one belonging to Simon, he asked him to put out a short distance from the shore. Then he sat down and taught the crowds from the boat. After he had finished speaking, he said to Simon, "Put out into deep water and lower your nets for a catch." Simon said in reply, "Master, we have worked hard all night and have caught nothing, but at your command I will lower the nets." When they had done this, they caught a great number of fish and their nets were tearing. They signaled to their partners in the other boat to come to help them. They came and filled both boats so that the boats were in danger of sinking. When Simon Peter saw this, he fell at the knees of Jesus and said, "Depart from me, Lord, for I am a sinful man." For astonishment at the catch of fish they had made seized him and all those with him, and likewise James and John, the sons of Zebedee, who were partners of Simon. Jesus said to Simon, "Do not be afraid; from now on you will be catching men." When they brought their boats to the shore, they left everything and followed him.

---

593 SIXTH SUNDAY IN ORDINARY TIME / A

READING I
Sirach 15:15-20 / 76

If you choose you can keep the
    commandments, they will save
     you;
    if you trust in God, you too shall
     live;
he has set before you fire and water;
    to whichever you choose, stretch
     forth your hand.
Before man are life and death, good and
    evil,

whichever he chooses shall be given
    him.
Immense is the wisdom of the Lord;
    he is mighty in power, and all-seeing.
The eyes of God are on those who fear
    him;
    he understands man's every deed.
No one does he command to act unjustly,
    to none does he give license to sin.

RESPONSORIAL PSALM

Psalm 119:1-2, 4-5, 17-18, 33-34

Bless - ed are they who fol - low the law of the Lord!

Blessed are they whose way is
  blameless,
 who walk in the law of the LORD.
Blessed are they who observe his
  decrees,
 who seek him with all their heart. ℟.

You have commanded that your precepts
  be diligently kept.
Oh, that I might be firm in the ways
 of keeping your statutes! ℟.

Be good to your servant, that I may live
  and keep your words.
Open my eyes, that I may consider
 the wonders of your law. ℟.

Instruct me, O LORD, in the way of
  your statutes,
 that I may exactly observe them.
Give me discernment, that I may observe
  your law
 and keep it with all my heart. ℟.

READING II

1 Corinthians 2:6-10

Brothers and sisters: We speak a wisdom to those who are mature, not a wisdom of this age, nor of the rulers of this age who are passing away. Rather, we speak God's wisdom, mysterious, hidden, which God predetermined before the ages for our glory, and which none of the rulers of this age knew; for, if they had known it, they would not have crucified the Lord of glory. But as it is written:
  "What eye has not seen, and ear has not heard,
    and what has not entered the human heart,
    what God has prepared for those who love him,"
this God has revealed to us through the Spirit.

For the Spirit scrutinizes everything, even the depths of God.

GOSPEL

Matthew 5:17-37 or 5:20-22a, 27-28, 33-34a, 37

For short form read only the parts in brackets.

[Jesus said to his disciples:] "Do not think that I have come to abolish the law or the prophets. I have come not to abolish but to fulfill. Amen, I say to you, until heaven and earth pass away, not the smallest letter or the smallest part of a letter will pass from the law, until all things have taken place. Therefore, whoever breaks one of the least of these commandments and teaches others to do so will be called least in the kingdom of heaven. But whoever obeys and teaches these commandments will be called greatest in the kingdom of heaven. [I tell you, unless your righteousness surpasses that of the scribes and Pharisees, you will not enter the kingdom of heaven.

"You have heard that it was said to your ancestors 'You shall not kill; and whoever kills will be liable to judgment.' But I say to you, whoever is angry with brother will be liable to judgment;] and whoever says to brother, 'Raqa,' will be answerable to the Sanhedrin; and whoever says, 'You fool,' will be liable to fiery Gehenna. Therefore, if you bring your gift to the altar, and there recall that your brother has anything against you, leave your gift there at the altar, go first and be reconciled with your brother, and then come and offer your gift. Settle with your opponent quickly while on the way to court. Otherwise your opponent will hand you over to the judge, and the judge will hand you over to the guard, and you will be thrown into prison. Amen, I say to you, you will not be released until you have paid the last penny.

["You have heard that it was said, 'You shall not commit adultery.' But I say to you, everyone who looks at a woman with lust has already committed adultery with her in his heart.] If your right eye causes you to sin, tear it out and throw it away. It is better for you to lose one of your members than to have your whole body thrown into Gehenna. And if your right hand causes you to sin, cut it off and throw it away. It is better for you to lose one of your members than to have your whole body go into Gehenna.

"It was also said, 'Whoever divorces his wife must give her a bill of divorce.' But I say to you, whoever divorces his wife (unless the marriage is unlawful) causes her to commit adultery, and whoever marries a divorced woman commits adultery.

["Again you have heard that it was said to your ancestors, 'Do not take a false oath, but make good to the Lord all that you vow.' But I say to you, do not swear at all;] not by heaven, for it is God's throne; nor by the earth, for it is his footstool; nor by Jerusalem, for it is the city of the great King. Do not swear by your head, for you cannot make a single hair white or black. [Let your 'Yes' mean 'Yes,' and your 'No' mean 'No.' Anything more is from the evil one."]

594   SIXTH SUNDAY IN ORDINARY TIME / B

READING I
Leviticus 13:1-2, 44-46 / 77

The Lord said to Moses and Aaron, "If someone has on his skin a scab or pustule or blotch which appears to be the sore of leprosy, he shall be brought to Aaron, the priest, or to one of the priests among his descendants. If the man is leprous and unclean, the priest shall declare him unclean by reason of the sore on his head.

"The one who bears the sore of leprosy shall keep his garments rent and his head bare, and shall muffle his beard; he shall cry out, 'Unclean, unclean!' As long as the sore is on him he shall declare himself unclean, since he is in fact unclean. He shall dwell apart, making his abode outside the camp."

RESPONSORIAL PSALM
Psalm 32:1-2, 5, 11

I turn to you, O Lord, in time of trouble, and you fill me with the joy of sal-va-tion.

Blessed is he whose fault is taken away,
    whose sin is covered.
Blessed the man to whom the LORD
    imputes not guilt,
    in whose spirit there is no guile. ℟.

Then I acknowledged my sin to you,

my guilt I covered not.
I said, "I confess my faults to the LORD,"
    and you took away the guilt of my
    sin. ℟.

Be glad in the LORD and rejoice, you just;
    exult, all you upright of heart. ℟.

READING II
1 Corinthians 10:31—11:1

Brothers and sisters, Whether you eat or drink, or whatever you do, do everything for the glory of God. Avoid giving offense, whether to the Jews or Greeks or the church of God, just as I try to please everyone in every way, not seeking my own benefit but that of the many, that they may be saved. Be imitators of me, as I am of Christ.

GOSPEL *Mark 1:40-45*

A leper came to Jesus and kneeling down begged him and said, "If you wish, you can make me clean." Moved with pity, he stretched out his hand, touched him, and said to him, "I do will it. Be made clean." The leprosy left him immediately, and he was made clean. Then, warning him sternly, he dismissed him at once.

He said to him, "See that you tell no one anything, but go, show yourself to the priest and offer for your cleansing what Moses prescribed; that will be proof for them."

The man went away and began to publicize the whole matter. He spread the report abroad so that it was impossible for Jesus to enter a town openly. He remained outside in deserted places, and people kept coming to him from everywhere.

SIXTH SUNDAY IN ORDINARY TIME / C 595

READING I *Jeremiah 17:5-8 / 78*

Thus says the LORD:
    Cursed is the one who trusts in
        human beings,
      who seeks his strength in flesh,
      whose heart turns away from the
        LORD.
    He is like a barren bush in the desert
      that enjoys no change of season,
    but stands in a lava waste,
      a salt and empty earth.
    Blessed is the one who trusts in the

      LORD.
      whose hope is the LORD.
    He is like a tree planted beside the
      waters
      that stretches out its roots to the
        stream:
    it fears not the heat when it comes;
      its leaves stay green;
    in the year of drought it shows no
      distress,
    but still bears fruit.

RESPONSORIAL PSALM *Psalm 1:1-2, 3, 4, 6*

Bless-ed are they, bless-ed are they who hope in the Lord.

Blessed the man who follows not
    the counsel of the wicked,
nor walks in the way of sinners,
    nor sits in the company of the
      insolent,
but delights in the law of the LORD
    and meditates on his law day and
      night. ℟.

He is like a tree
    planted near running water,

that yields its fruit in due season,
    and whose leaves never fade.
Whatever he does, prospers. ℟.

Not so the wicked, not so;
    they are like chaff which the wind
      drives away.
For the LORD watches over the way of
    the just,
    but the way of the wicked
      vanishes. ℟.

READING II *1 Corinthians 15:12, 16-20*

Brothers and sisters: If Christ is preached as raised from the dead, how can some among you say there is no resurrection of the dead? If the dead are not raised, neither has Christ been raised, and if Christ has not been raised, your faith is vain; you are still in your sins. Then those who have fallen asleep in Christ have perished. If for this life only we have hoped in Christ, we are the most pitiable people of all.

But now Christ has been raised from the dead, the firstfruits of those who have fallen asleep.

GOSPEL   *Luke 6:17, 20-26*

Jesus came down with the Twelve and stood on a stretch of level ground with a great crowd of his disciples and a large number of the people from all Judea and Jerusalem and the coastal region of Tyre and Sidon. And raising his eyes toward his disciples he said:

"Blessed are you who are poor,
    for the kingdom of God is yours.
Blessed are you who are now hungry,
    for you will be satisfied.
Blessed are you who are now weeping,
    for you will laugh.
Blessed are you when people hate you,
    and when they exclude and insult you,
    and denounce your name as evil
    on account of the Son of Man.

Rejoice and leap for joy on that day! Behold, your reward will be great in heaven. For their ancestors treated the prophets in the same way.

But woe to you who are rich,
    for you have received your consolation.
Woe to you who are filled now,
    for you will be hungry.
Woe to you who laugh now,
    for you will grieve and weep.
Woe to you when all speak well of you,
    for their ancestors treated the false
        prophets in this way."

---

596   SEVENTH SUNDAY IN ORDINARY TIME / A

READING I   *Leviticus 19:1-2, 17-18 / 79*

The LORD said to Moses, "Speak to the whole Israelite community and tell them: Be holy, for I, the LORD, your God, am holy.

"You shall not bear hatred for your brother or sister in your heart. Though you may have to reprove your fellow citizen, do not incur sin because of him. Take no revenge and cherish no grudge against any of your people. You shall love your neighbor as yourself. I am the LORD."

RESPONSORIAL PSALM   *Psalm 103:1-2, 3-4, 8, 10, 12-13*

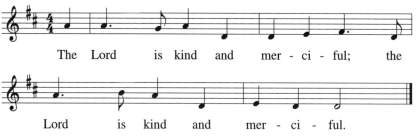

The Lord is kind and mer - ci - ful; the

Lord is kind and mer - ci - ful.

Bless the LORD, O my soul;
    and all my being, bless his holy
    name.

Bless the LORD, O my soul,
    and forget not all his benefits. ℟.

He pardons all your iniquities,
  heals all your ills.
He redeems your life from destruction,
  crowns you with kindness and
    compassion. ℟.

Merciful and gracious is the LORD,
  slow to anger and abounding in
    kindness.
Not according to our sins does he deal
    with us,
  nor does he requite us according to
    our crimes. ℟.

As far as the east is from the west,
  so far has he put our transgressions
    from us.
As a father has compassion on his
    children,
  so the LORD has compassion on
    those who fear him. ℟.

READING II   *1 Corinthians 3:16-23*

Brothers and sisters: Do you not know that you are the temple of God, and that the Spirit of God dwells in you? If anyone destroys God's temple, God will destroy that person; for the temple of God, which you are, is holy.

Let no one deceive himself. If any one among you considers himself wise in this age, let him become a fool, so as to become wise. For the wisdom of this world is foolishness in the eyes of God, for it is written:
"God catches the wise in their own ruses,"
and again:
"The Lord knows the thoughts of the wise,
  that they are vain."

So let no one boast about human beings, for everything belongs to you, Paul or Apollos or Cephas, or the world or life or death, or the present or the future: all belong to you, and you to Christ, and Christ to God.

GOSPEL   *Matthew 5:38-48*

Jesus said to his disciples: "You have heard that it was said, 'An eye for an eye and a tooth for a tooth.' But I say to you, offer no resistance to one who is evil. When someone strikes you on your right cheek, turn the other one as well. If anyone wants to go to law with you over your tunic, hand over your cloak as well. Should anyone press you into service for one mile, go for two miles. Give to the one who asks of you, and do not turn your back on one who wants to borrow.

"You have heard that it was said, 'You shall love your neighbor and hate your enemy.' But I say to you, love your enemies and pray for those who persecute you, that you may be children of your heavenly Father, for he makes his sun rise on the bad and the good, and causes rain to fall on the just and the unjust. For if you love those who love you, what recompense will you have? Do not the tax collectors do the same? And if you greet your brothers only, what is unusual about that? Do not the pagans do the same? So be perfect, just as your heavenly Father is perfect."

SEVENTH SUNDAY IN ORDINARY TIME / B   597

READING I   *Isaiah 43:18-19, 21-22, 24b-25 / 80*

Thus says the LORD:
Remember not the events of the past,
  the things of long ago consider not;

see, I am doing something new!
  Now it springs forth, do you not
    perceive it?

In the desert I make a way,
in the wasteland, rivers.
The people I formed for myself,
that they might announce my praise.
Yet you did not call upon me, O Jacob,
for you grew weary of me, O Israel.

You burdened me with your sins,
and wearied me with your crimes.
It is I, I, who wipe out,
for my own sake, your offenses;
your sins I remember no more.

RESPONSORIAL PSALM

Psalm 41:2-3, 4-5, 13-14

Lord, heal my soul, for I have sinned a - gainst you.

Blessed is the one who has regard for the
lowly and the poor;
in the day of misfortune the LORD
will deliver him.
The LORD will keep and preserve him;
and make him blessed on earth,
and not give him over to the will of his
enemies. ℟.

The LORD will help him on his sickbed,
he will take away all his ailment

when he is ill.
Once I said, "O LORD, have pity on me;
heal me, though I have sinned against
you." ℟.

But because of my integrity you sustain
me
and let me stand before you forever.
Blessed be the LORD, the God of Israel,
from all eternity. Amen. Amen. ℟.

READING II

2 Corinthians 1:18-22

Brothers and sisters: As God is faithful, our word to you is not "yes" and "no." For the Son of God, Jesus Christ, who was proclaimed to you by us, Silvanus and Timothy and me, was not "yes" and "no," but "yes" has been in him. For however many are the promises of God, their Yes is in him; therefore, the Amen from us also goes through him to God for glory. But the one who gives us security with you in Christ and who anointed us is God; he has also put his seal upon us and given the Spirit in our hearts as a first installment.

GOSPEL

Mark 2:1-12

When Jesus returned to Capernaum after some days, it became known that he was at home. Many gathered together so that there was no longer room for them, not even around the door, and he preached the word to them. They came bringing to him a paralytic carried by four men. Unable to get near Jesus because of the crowd, they opened up the roof above him. After they had broken through, they let down the mat on which the paralytic was lying. When Jesus saw their faith, he said to the paralytic, "Child, your sins are forgiven." Now some of the scribes were sitting there asking themselves, "Why does this man speak that way? He is blaspheming. Who but God alone can forgive sins?" Jesus immediately knew in his mind what they were thinking to themselves, so he said, "Why are you thinking such things in your hearts? Which is easier, to say to the paralytic, 'Your sins are forgiven,' or to say, 'Rise, pick up your mat and walk?' But that you may know that the Son of Man has authority to forgive sins on earth" —he said to the paralytic, "I say to you, rise, pick up your mat, and go home." He rose, picked up his mat at once, and went away in the sight of everyone. They were all astounded and glorified God, saying, "We have never seen anything like this."

SEVENTH SUNDAY IN ORDINARY TIME / C 598

READING I *1 Samuel 26:2, 7-9, 12-13, 22-23 / 81*

In those days, Saul went down to the desert of Ziph with three thousand picked men of Israel, to search for David in the desert of Ziph. So David and Abishai went among Saul's soldiers by night and found Saul lying asleep within the barricade, with his spear thrust into the ground at his head and Abner and his men sleeping around him.

Abishai whispered to David: "God has delivered your enemy into your grasp this day. Let me nail him to the ground with one thrust of the spear; I will not need a second thrust!" But David said to Abishai, "Do not harm him, for who can lay hands on the LORD's anointed and remain unpunished?" So David took the spear and the water jug from their place at Saul's head, and they got away without anyone's seeing or knowing or awakening. All remained asleep, because the LORD had put them into a deep slumber.

Going across to an opposite slope, David stood on a remote hilltop at a great distance from Abner, son of Ner, and the troops. He said: "Here is the king's spear. Let an attendant come over to get it. The LORD will reward each man for his justice and faithfulness. Today, though the LORD delivered you into my grasp, I would not harm the LORD's anointed."

RESPONSORIAL PSALM *Psalm 103:1-2, 3-4, 8, 10, 12-13*

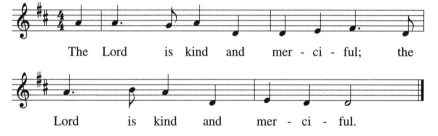

The Lord is kind and mer - ci - ful; the
Lord is kind and mer - ci - ful.

Bless the LORD, O my soul;
and all my being, bless his holy
name.
Bless the LORD, O my soul,
and forget not all his benefits. ℟.

He pardons all your iniquities,
heals all your ills.
He redeems your life from destruction,
crowns you with kindness and
compassion. ℟.

Merciful and gracious is the LORD,
slow to anger and abounding in
kindness.
Not according to our sins does he deal
with us,
nor does he requite us according to
our crimes. ℟.

As far as the east is from the west,
so far has he put our transgressions
from us.
As a father has compassion on his
children,
so the LORD has compassion on those
who fear him. ℟.

READING II *1 Corinthians 15:45-49*

Brothers and sisters: It is written, "The first man, Adam, became a living being," the last Adam a life-giving spirit. But the spiritual was not first; rather the natural and then the spiritual. The first man was from the earth, earthly; the second man, from heaven. As was the earthly one, so also are the earthly, and as is the heavenly one, so also are the heavenly. Just as we have borne the image of the earthly one, we shall also bear the image of the heavenly one.

GOSPEL

Luke 6:27-38

Jesus said to his disciples: "To you who hear I say, love your enemies, do good to those who hate you, bless those who curse you, pray for those who mistreat you. To the person who strikes you on one cheek, offer the other one as well, and from the person who takes your cloak, do not withhold even your tunic. Give to everyone who asks of you, and from the one who takes what is yours do not demand it back. Do to others as you would have them do to you. For if you love those who love you, what credit is that to you? Even sinners love those who love them. And if you do good to those who do good to you, what credit is that to you? Even sinners do the same. If you lend money to those from whom you expect repayment, what credit is that to you? Even sinners lend to sinners, and get back the same amount. But rather, love your enemies and do good to them, and lend expecting nothing back; then your reward will be great and you will be children of the Most High, for he himself is kind to the ungrateful and the wicked. Be merciful, just as your Father is merciful.

"Stop judging and you will not be judged. Stop condemning and you will not be condemned. Forgive and you will be forgiven. Give, and gifts will be given to you; a good measure, packed together, shaken down, and overflowing, will be poured into your lap. For the measure with which you measure will in return be measured out to you."

599 EIGHTH SUNDAY IN ORDINARY TIME / A

READING I

Isaiah 49:14-15 / 82

Zion said, "The Lord has forsaken me;
   my Lord has forgotten me."
Can a mother forget her infant,
   be without tenderness for the child

of her womb?
Even should she forget,
   I will never forget you.

RESPONSORIAL PSALM

Psalm 62:2-3, 6-7, 8-9

Rest in God a-lone, rest in God a-lone, my soul.

Only in God is my soul at rest;
   from him comes my salvation.
He only is my rock and my salvation,
   my stronghold; I shall not be
    disturbed at all. ℟.

Only in God be at rest, my soul,
   for from him comes my hope.
He only is my rock and my salvation,

my stronghold; I shall not be
   disturbed. ℟.

With God is my safety and my glory,
   he is the rock of my strength; my
    refuge is in God.
Trust in him at all times, O my people!
   Pour out your hearts before him. ℟.

READING II

1 Corinthians 4:1-5

Brothers and sisters: Thus should one regard us: as servants of Christ and stewards of the mysteries of God. Now it is of course required of stewards that they be found trustworthy. It does not concern me in the least that I be judged by you or any human tribunal; I do not even pass judgment on myself; I am not conscious of anything against me, but I do not thereby stand acquitted; the one who judges me is the Lord. Therefore do not make any judgment before the appointed time, until the Lord comes, for he will bring to light what is hidden in darkness and will manifest the motives of our hearts, and then everyone will receive praise from God.

GOSPEL
Matthew 6:24-34

Jesus said to his disciples: "No one can serve two masters. He will either hate one and love the other, or be devoted to one and despise the other. You cannot serve God and mammon.

"Therefore I tell you, do not worry about your life, what you will eat or drink, or about your body, what you will wear. Is not life more than food and the body more than clothing? Look at the birds in the sky; they do not sow or reap, they gather nothing into barns, yet your heavenly Father feeds them. Are not you more important than they? Can any of you by worrying add a single moment to your life-span? Why are you anxious about clothes? Learn from the way the wild flowers grow. They do not work or spin. But I tell you that not even Solomon in all his splendor was clothed like one of them. If God so clothes the grass of the field, which grows today and is thrown into the oven tomorrow, will he not much more provide for you, O you of little faith? So do not worry and say, 'What are we to eat?' or 'What are we to drink?' or 'What are we to wear?' All these things the pagans seek. Your heavenly Father knows that you need them all. But seek first the kingdom of God and his righteousness, and all these things will be given you besides. Do not worry about tomorrow; tomorrow will take care of itself. Sufficient for a day is its own evil."

EIGHTH SUNDAY IN ORDINARY TIME / B
600

READING I
Hosea 2:16b, 17b, 21-22 / 83

Thus says the Lord:
I will lead her into the desert
  and speak to her heart.
She shall respond there as in the days of
    her youth,
    when she came up from the land of
    Egypt.

I will espouse you to me forever:
  I will espouse you in right and in
    justice,
  in love and in mercy;
I will espouse you in fidelity,
  and you shall know the Lord.

RESPONSORIAL PSALM
Psalm 103:1-2, 3-4, 8, 10, 12-13

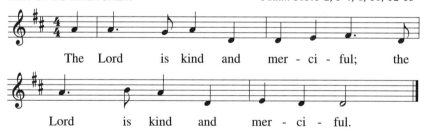

The Lord is kind and merciful; the
Lord is kind and merciful.

Bless the Lord, O my soul;
  and all my being, bless his holy
    name.
Bless the Lord, O my soul,
  and forget not all his benefits. ℟.

He pardons all your iniquities,
  heals all your ills.
He redeems your life from destruction,
  crowns you with kindness and
    compassion. ℟.

Merciful and gracious is the Lord,
  slow to anger and abounding in
    kindness.
Not according to our sins does he deal
  with us,
  nor does he requite us according to
    our crimes. ℟.

As far as the east is from the west,
  so far has he put our transgressions
    from us.
As a father has compassion on his
    children,
  so the Lord has compassion on those
    who fear him. ℟.

READING II
2 Corinthians 3:1b-6

Brothers and sisters: Do we need, as some do, letters of recommendation to you or from you? You are our letter, written on our hearts, known and read by all, shown to be a letter of Christ ministered by us, written not in ink but by the Spirit of the living God, not on tablets of stone but on tablets that are hearts of flesh.

Such confidence we have through Christ toward God. Not that of ourselves we are qualified to take credit for anything as coming from us; rather, our qualification comes from God, who has indeed qualified us as ministers of a new covenant, not of letter but of spirit; for the letter brings death, but the Spirit gives life.

GOSPEL
Mark 2:18-22

The disciples of John and of the Pharisees were accustomed to fast. People came to him and objected, "Why do the disciples of John and the disciples of the Pharisees fast, but your disciples do not fast?" Jesus answered them, "Can the wedding guests fast while the bridegroom is with them? As long as they have the bridegroom with them they cannot fast. But the days will come when the bridegroom is taken away from them, and then they will fast on that day. No one sews a piece of unshrunken cloth on an old cloak. If he does, its fullness pulls away, the new from the old, and the tear gets worse. Likewise, no one pours new wine into old wineskins. Otherwise, the wine will burst the skins, and both the wine and the skins are ruined. Rather, new wine is poured into fresh wineskins."

---

601 EIGHTH SUNDAY IN ORDINARY TIME / C

READING I
Sirach 27:4-7 / 84

When a sieve is shaken, the husks
    appear;
    so do one's faults when one speaks.
As the test of what the potter molds is in
    the furnace,
    so in tribulation is the test of the just.

The fruit of a tree shows the care it has
    had;
    so too does one's speech disclose the
    bent of one's mind.
Praise no one before he speaks,
    for it is then that people are tested.

RESPONSORIAL PSALM
Psalm 92:2-3, 13-14, 15-16

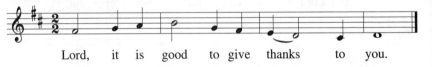

Lord, it is good to give thanks to you.

It is good to give thanks to the Lord,
    to sing praise to your name, Most
    High,
To proclaim your kindness at dawn
    and your faithfulness throughout the
    night. ℟.

The just one shall flourish like the palm
    tree,
    like a cedar of Lebanon shall he grow.

They that are planted in the house of the
    Lord
    shall flourish in the courts of our
    God. ℟.

They shall bear fruit even in old age;
    vigorous and sturdy shall they be,
Declaring how just is the Lord,
    my rock, in whom there is no
    wrong. ℟.

READING II
1 Corinthians 15:54-58

Brothers and sisters: When this which is corruptible clothes itself with incorruptibility and this which is mortal clothes itself with immortality, then the word that is written shall come about:

"Death is swallowed up in victory.
Where, O death, is your victory?
Where, O death, is your sting?"

The sting of death is sin, and the power of sin is the law. But thanks be to God who gives us the victory through our Lord Jesus Christ.

Therefore, my beloved brothers and sisters, be firm, steadfast, always fully devoted to the work of the Lord, knowing that in the Lord your labor is not in vain.

GOSPEL
Luke 6:39-45

Jesus told his disciples a parable, "Can a blind person guide a blind person? Will not both fall into a pit? No disciple is superior to the teacher; but when fully trained, every disciple will be like his teacher. Why do you notice the splinter in your brother's eye, but do not perceive the wooden beam in your own? How can you say to your brother, 'Brother, let me remove that splinter in your eye,' when you do not even notice the wooden beam in your own eye? You hypocrite! Remove the wooden beam from your eye first; then you will see clearly to remove the splinter in your brother's eye.

"A good tree does not bear rotten fruit, nor does a rotten tree bear good fruit. For every tree is known by its own fruit. For people do not pick figs from thornbushes, nor do they gather grapes from brambles. A good person out of the store of goodness in his heart produces good, but an evil person out of a store of evil produces evil; for from the fullness of the heart the mouth speaks."

NINTH SUNDAY IN ORDINARY TIME / A   602

READING I
Deuteronomy 11:18, 26-28, 32 / 85

Moses told the people, "Take these words of mine into your heart and soul. Bind them at your wrist as a sign, and let them be a pendant on your forehead.

"I set before you here, this day, a blessing and a curse: a blessing for obeying the commandments of the Lord, your God, which I enjoin on you today; a curse if you do not obey the commandments of the Lord, your God, but turn aside from the way I ordain for you today, to follow other gods, whom you have not known. Be careful to observe all the statutes and decrees that I set before you today."

RESPONSORIAL PSALM
Psalm 31:2-3, 3-4, 17, 25

Lord, be my rock of safe - ty.

In you, O Lord, I take refuge;
   let me never be put to shame.
In your justice rescue me,
   incline your ear to me,
make haste to deliver me! ℟.

Be my rock of refuge,
   a stronghold to give me safety.

You are my rock and my fortress;
   for your name's sake you will lead
     and guide me. ℟.

Let your face shine upon your servant;
   save me in your kindness.
Take courage and be stouthearted,
   all you who hope in the Lord. ℟.

READING II   *Romans 3:21-25, 28*

Brothers and sisters, Now the righteousness of God has been manifested apart from the law, though testified to by the law and the prophets, the righteousness of God through faith in Jesus Christ for all who believe. For there is no distinction; all have sinned and are deprived of the glory of God. They are justified freely by his grace through the redemption in Christ Jesus, whom God set forth as an expiation, through faith, by his blood. For we consider that a person is justified by faith apart from works of the law.

GOSPEL   *Matthew 7:21-27*

Jesus said to his disciples: "Not everyone who says to me, 'Lord, Lord,' will enter the kingdom of heaven, but only the one who does the will of my Father in heaven. Many will say to me on that day, 'Lord, Lord, did we not prophesy in your name? Did we not drive out demons in your name? Did we not do mighty deeds in your name?' Then I will declare to them solemnly, 'I never knew you. Depart from me, you evildoers.' "Everyone who listens to these words of mine and acts on them will be like a wise man who built his house on rock. The rain fell, the floods came, and the winds blew and buffeted the house. But it did not collapse; it had been set solidly on rock. And everyone who listens to these words of mine but does not act on them will be like a fool who built his house on sand. The rain fell, the floods came, and the winds blew and buffeted the house. And it collapsed and was completely ruined."

603 NINTH SUNDAY IN ORDINARY TIME / B

READING I   *Deuteronomy 5:12-15 / 86*

Thus says the Lord: "Take care to keep holy the sabbath day as the Lord, your God, commanded you. Six days you may labor and do all your work; but the seventh day is the sabbath of the Lord, your God. No work may be done then, whether by you, or your son or daughter, or your male or female slave, or your ox or ass or any of your beasts, or the alien who lives with you. Your male and female slave should rest as you do. For remember that you too were once a slave in Egypt, and the Lord, your God, brought you from there with his strong hand and outstretched arm. That is why the Lord, your God, has commanded you to observe the sabbath day."

RESPONSORIAL PSALM   *Psalm 81:3-4, 5-6, 6-8, 10-11*

Sing with joy to God!   Sing to God our help!

Take up a melody, and sound the timbrel,
   the pleasant harp and the lyre.
Blow the trumpet at the new moon,
   at the full moon, on our solemn
     feast. ℟.

For it is a statute in Israel,
   an ordinance of the God of Jacob,
who made it a decree for Joseph
   when he came forth from the land of
     Egypt. ℟.

An unfamiliar speech I hear:

"I relieved his shoulder of the
   burden;
his hands were freed from the basket.
   In distress you called, and I rescued
     you." ℟.

"There shall be no strange god among
   you
   nor shall you worship any alien god.
I, the Lord, am your God
   who led you forth from the land of
     Egypt." ℟.

READING II
2 Corinthians 4:6-11

Brothers and sisters: God who said, "Let light shine out of darkness," has shone in our hearts to bring to light the knowledge of the glory of God on the face of Jesus Christ. But we hold this treasure in earthen vessels, that the surpassing power may be of God and not from us. We are afflicted in every way, but not constrained; perplexed, but not driven to despair; persecuted, but not abandoned; struck down, but not destroyed; always carrying about in the body the dying of Jesus, so that the life of Jesus may also be manifested in our body. For we who live are constantly being given up to death for the sake of Jesus, so that the life of Jesus may be manifested in our mortal flesh.

GOSPEL
Mark 2:23—3:6 or 2:23-28

For short form read only the part in brackets.

[As Jesus was passing through a field of grain on the sabbath, his disciples began to make a path while picking the heads of grain. At this the Pharisees said to him, "Look, why are they doing what is unlawful on the sabbath?" He said to them, "Have you never read what David did when he was in need and he and his companions were hungry? How he went into the house of God when Abiathar was high priest and ate the bread of offering that only the priests could lawfully eat, and shared it with his companions?" Then he said to them, "The sabbath was made for man, not man for the sabbath. That is why the Son of Man is lord even of the sabbath."]

Again he entered the synagogue. There was a man there who had a withered hand. They watched him closely to see if he would cure him on the sabbath so that they might accuse him. He said to the man with the withered hand, "Come up here before us." Then he said to them, "Is it lawful to do good on the sabbath rather than to do evil, to save life rather than to destroy it?" But they remained silent. Looking around at them with anger and grieved at their hardness of heart, he said to the man, "Stretch out your hand." He stretched it out and his hand was restored. The Pharisees went out and immediately took counsel with the Herodians against him to put him to death.

NINTH SUNDAY IN ORDINARY TIME / C
604

READING I
1 Kings 8:41-43 / 87

In those days, Solomon prayed in the temple, saying, "To the foreigner, who is not of your people Israel, but comes from a distant land to honor you (since they will learn of your great name and your mighty hand and your outstretched arm) when he comes and prays toward this temple, listen from your heavenly dwelling. Do all that foreigner asks of you, that all the peoples of the earth may know your name, may fear you as do your people Israel, and may acknowledge that this temple which I have built is dedicated to your honor."

RESPONSORIAL PSALM
Psalm 117:1, 2

Go out to all the world and tell the Good News.

Praise the Lord, all you nations; glorify him, all you peoples! ℟.

For steadfast is his kindness toward us, and the fidelity of the Lord endures forever. ℟.

READING II *Galatians 1:1-2, 6-10*

Paul, an apostle not from human beings nor through a human being but through Jesus Christ and God the Father who raised him from the dead, and all the brothers who are with me, to the churches of Galatia.

I am amazed that you are so quickly forsaking the one who called you by the grace of Christ for a different gospel (not that there is another). But there are some who are disturbing you and wish to pervert the gospel of Christ. But even if we or an angel from heaven should preach to you a gospel other than the one that we preached to you, let that one be accursed! As we have said before, and now I say again, if anyone preaches to you a gospel other than what you have received, let that one be accursed!

Am I now currying favor with humans or with God? Or am I seeking to please people? If I were still trying to please people, I would not be a slave of Christ.

GOSPEL *Luke 7:1-10*

When Jesus had finished all his words to the people, he entered Capernaum. A centurion there had a slave who was ill and about to die, and he was valuable to him. When he heard about Jesus, he sent elders of the Jews to him, asking him to come and save the life of his slave. They approached Jesus and strongly urged him to come, saying, "He deserves to have you do this for him, for he loves our nation and built the synagogue for us." And Jesus went with them, but when he was only a short distance from the house, the centurion sent friends to tell him, "Lord, do not trouble yourself, for I am not worthy to have you enter under my roof. Therefore, I did not consider myself worthy to come to you; but say the word and let my servant be healed. For I too am a person subject to authority, with soldiers subject to me. And I say to one, 'Go,' and he goes; and to another, 'Come here,' and he comes; and to my slave, 'Do this,' and he does it." When Jesus heard this he was amazed at him and, turning, said to the crowd following him, "I tell you, not even in Israel have I found such faith." When the messengers returned to the house, they found the slave in good health.

605 **TENTH SUNDAY IN ORDINARY TIME / A**

READING I *Hosea 6:3-6 / 88*

In their affliction, people will say:
"Let us know, let us strive to know the
  Lord;
    as certain as the dawn is his coming,
    and his judgment shines forth like
      the light of day!
He will come to us like the rain,
  like spring rain that waters the earth."
What can I do with you, Ephraim?
  What can I do with you, Judah?

Your piety is like a morning cloud,
  like the dew that early passes away.
For this reason I smote them through the
    prophets,
  I slew them by the words of my
    mouth;
for it is love that I desire, not sacrifice,
  and knowledge of God rather than
    holocausts.

RESPONSORIAL PSALM *Psalm 50:1, 8, 12-13, 14-15*

To the up-right I will show the sav-ing pow'r of God.

God the Lord has spoken and summoned
    the earth,
  from the rising of the sun to its
    setting.

"Not for your sacrifices do I rebuke you,
  for your holocausts are before me
    always." ℟.

"If I were hungry, I would not tell you,
   for mine are the world and its
      fullness.
Do I eat the flesh of strong bulls,
   or is the blood of goats my drink?" ℟.

"Offer to God praise as your sacrifice
   and fulfill your vows to the Most
      High;
then call upon me in time of distress;
   I will rescue you, and you shall
      glorify me." ℟.

READING II
Romans 4:18-25

Brothers and sisters: Abraham believed, hoping against hope, that he would become "the father of many nations," according to what was said, "Thus shall your descendants be." He did not weaken in faith when he considered his own body as already dead (for he was almost a hundred years old) and the dead womb of Sarah. He did not doubt God's promise in unbelief; rather, he was strengthened by faith and gave glory to God and was fully convinced that what he had promised he was also able to do. That is why "it was credited to him as righteousness." But it was not for him alone that it was written that "it was credited to him;" it was also for us, to whom it will be credited, who believe in the one who raised Jesus our Lord from the dead, who was handed over for our transgressions and was raised for our justification.

GOSPEL
Matthew 9:9-13

As Jesus passed on from there, he saw a man named Matthew sitting at the customs post. He said to him, "Follow me." And he got up and followed him. While he was at table in his house, many tax collectors and sinners came and sat with Jesus and his disciples. The Pharisees saw this and said to his disciples, "Why does your teacher eat with tax collectors and sinners?" He heard this and said, "Those who are well do not need a physician, but the sick do. Go and learn the meaning of the words, 'I desire mercy, not sacrifice.' I did not come to call the righteous but sinners."

TENTH SUNDAY IN ORDINARY TIME / B
606

READING I
Genesis 3:9-15 / 89

After the man, Adam, had eaten of the tree, the Lord God called to the man and asked him, "Where are you?" He answered, "I heard you in the garden; but I was afraid, because I was naked, so I hid myself." Then he asked, "Who told you that you were naked? You have eaten, then, from the tree of which I had forbidden you to eat!" The man replied, "The woman whom you put here with me— she gave me fruit from the tree, and so I ate it." The Lord God then asked the woman, "Why did you do such a thing?" The woman answered, "The serpent tricked me into it, so I ate it."

Then the Lord God said to the serpent:
   "Because you have done this, you shall be banned from
      all the animals
      and from all the wild creatures;
   on your belly shall you crawl,
      and dirt shall you eat
      all the days of your life.
   I will put enmity between you and the woman,
      and between your offspring and hers;
   he will strike at your head,
      while you strike at his heel."

RESPONSORIAL PSALM

Psalm 130:1-2, 3-4, 5-6, 7-8

With the Lord there is mer - cy, and full - ness of re - demp - tion.

Out of the depths I cry to you, O Lord;
  Lord, hear my voice!
Let your ears be attentive
  to my voice in supplication. ℟.

If you, O Lord, mark iniquities,
  Lord, who can stand?
But with you is forgiveness,
  that you may be revered. ℟.

I trust in the Lord;
  my soul trusts in his word.
More than sentinels wait for the dawn,
  let Israel wait for the Lord. ℟.

For with the Lord is kindness
  and with him is plenteous redemption;
and he will redeem Israel
  from all their iniquities. ℟.

READING II

2 Corinthians 4:13—5:1

Brothers and sisters: Since we have the same spirit of faith, according to what is written, "I believed, therefore I spoke," we too believe and therefore we speak, knowing that the one who raised the Lord Jesus will raise us also with Jesus and place us with you in his presence. Everything indeed is for you, so that the grace bestowed in abundance on more and more people may cause the thanksgiving to overflow for the glory of God. Therefore, we are not discouraged; rather, although our outer self is wasting away, our inner self is being renewed day by day. For this momentary light affliction is producing for us an eternal weight of glory beyond all comparison, as we look not to what is seen but to what is unseen; for what is seen is transitory, but what is unseen is eternal. For we know that if our earthly dwelling, a tent, should be destroyed, we have a building from God, a dwelling not made with hands, eternal in heaven.

GOSPEL

Mark 3:20-35

Jesus came home with his disciples. Again the crowd gathered, making it impossible for them even to eat. When his relatives heard of this they set out to seize him, for they said, "He is out of his mind." The scribes who had come from Jerusalem said, "He is possessed by Beelzebul," and "By the prince of demons he drives out demons."
  Summoning them, he began to speak to them in parables, "How can Satan drive out Satan? If a kingdom is divided against itself, that kingdom cannot stand. And if a house is divided against itself, that house will not be able to stand. And if Satan has risen up against himself and is divided, he cannot stand; that is the end of him. But no one can enter a strong man's house to plunder his property unless he first ties up the strong man. Then he can plunder the house. Amen, I say to you, all sins and all blasphemies that people utter will be forgiven them. But whoever blasphemes against the Holy Spirit will never have forgiveness, but is guilty of an everlasting sin." For they had said, "He has an unclean spirit." His mother and his brothers arrived. Standing outside they sent word to him and called him. A crowd seated around him told him, "Your mother and your brothers and your sisters are outside asking for you." But he said to them in reply, "Who are my mother and my brothers?" And looking around at those seated in the circle he said, "Here are my mother and my brothers. For whoever does the will of God is my brother and sister and mother."

TENNTH SUNDAY IN ORDINARY TIME / C

READING I
1 Kings 17:17-24 / 90

Elijah went to Zarephath of Sidon to the house of a widow. The son of the mistress of the house fell sick, and his sickness grew more severe until he stopped breathing. So she said to Elijah, "Why have you done this to me, O man of God? Have you come to me to call attention to my guilt and to kill my son?" Elijah said to her, "Give me your son." Taking him from her lap, he carried the son to the upper room where he was staying, and put him on his bed. Elijah called out to the Lord: "O Lord, my God, will you afflict even the widow with whom I am staying by killing her son?" Then he stretched himself out upon the child three times and called out to the Lord: "O Lord, my God, let the life breath return to the body of this child." The Lord heard the prayer of Elijah; the life breath returned to the child's body and he revived. Taking the child, Elijah brought him down into the house from the upper room and gave him to his mother. Elijah said to her, "See! Your son is alive." The woman replied to Elijah, "Now indeed I know that you are a man of God. The word of the Lord comes truly from your mouth."

RESPONSORIAL PSALM
Psalm 30:2, 4, 5-6, 11, 12, 13

I will praise you, Lord, for you have res-cued me.

I will extol you, O Lord, for you drew
　　me clear
　　and did not let my enemies rejoice
　　　over me.
O Lord, you brought me up from the
　　nether world;
　　you preserved me from among those
　　going down into the pit. ℟.

Sing praise to the Lord, you his faithful
　　ones,
　　and give thanks to his holy name.
For his anger lasts but a moment;
　　a lifetime, his good will.
At nightfall, weeping enters in,
　　but with the dawn, rejoicing. ℟.

Hear, O Lord, and have pity on me;
　　O Lord, be my helper.
You changed my mourning into dancing;
　　O Lord, my God, forever will I give
　　you thanks. ℟.

READING II
Galatians 1:11-19

I want you to know, brothers and sisters, that the gospel preached by me is not of human origin. For I did not receive it from a human being, nor was I taught it, but it came through a revelation of Jesus Christ.

For you heard of my former way of life in Judaism, how I persecuted the church of God beyond measure and tried to destroy it, and progressed in Judaism beyond many of my contemporaries among my race, since I was even more a zealot for my ancestral traditions. But when God, who from my mother's womb had set me apart and called me through his grace, was pleased to reveal his Son to me, so that I might proclaim him to the Gentiles, I did not immediately consult flesh and blood, nor did I go up to Jerusalem to those who were apostles before me; rather, I went into Arabia and then returned to Damascus.

Then after three years I went up to Jerusalem to confer with Cephas and remained with him for fifteen days. But I did not see any other of the apostles, only James the brother of the Lord.

GOSPEL *Luke 7:11-17*

Jesus journeyed to a city called Nain, and his disciples and a large crowd accompanied him. As he drew near to the gate of the city, a man who had died was being carried out, the only son of his mother, and she was a widow. A large crowd from the city was with her. When the Lord saw her, he was moved with pity for her and said to her, "Do not weep." He stepped forward and touched the coffin; at this the bearers halted, and he said, "Young man, I tell you, arise!" The dead man sat up and began to speak, and Jesus gave him to his mother. Fear seized them all, and they glorified God, exclaiming, "A great prophet has arisen in our midst," and "God has visited his people." This report about him spread through the whole of Judea and in all the surrounding region.

608 ELEVENTH SUNDAY IN ORDINARY TIME / A

READING I *Exodus 19:2-6a / 91*

In those days, the Israelites came to the desert of Sinai and pitched camp. While Israel was encamped here in front of the mountain, Moses went up the mountain to God. Then the Lord called to him and said, "Thus shall you say to the house of Jacob; tell the Israelites: You have seen for yourselves how I treated the Egyptians and how I bore you up on eagle wings and brought you here to myself. Therefore, if you hearken to my voice and keep my covenant, you shall be my special possession, dearer to me than all other people, though all the earth is mine. You shall be to me a kingdom of priests, a holy nation."

RESPONSORIAL PSALM *Psalm 100:1-2, 3, 5*

We are his peo-ple, the sheep of his flock.

Sing joyfully to the Lord, all you lands;
　　serve the Lord with gladness;
　　come before him with joyful song. ℟.

Know that the Lord is God;
　　he made us, his we are;

his people, the flock he tends. ℟.

The Lord is good:
　　his kindness endures forever,
　　and his faithfulness to all
　　　generations. ℟.

READING II *Romans 5:6-11*

Brothers and sisters: Christ, while we were still helpless, yet died at the appointed time for the ungodly. Indeed, only with difficulty does one die for a just person, though perhaps for a good person one might even find courage to die. But God proves his love for us in that while we were still sinners Christ died for us. How much more then, since we are now justified by his blood, will we be saved through him from the wrath. Indeed, if, while we were enemies, we were reconciled to God through the death of his Son, how much more, once reconciled, will we be saved by his life. Not only that, but we also boast of God through our Lord Jesus Christ, through whom we have now received reconciliation.

GOSPEL *Matthew 9:36—10:8*

At the sight of the crowds, Jesus' heart was moved with pity for them because they were troubled and abandoned, like sheep without a shepherd. Then he said to his disciples, "The harvest is abundant but the laborers are few; so ask the master of the harvest to send out laborers for his harvest."

Then he summoned his twelve disciples and gave them authority over unclean spirits to drive them out and to cure every disease and every illness. The names of the twelve apostles are these: first, Simon called Peter, and his brother Andrew; James, the son of Zebedee, and his brother John; Philip and Bartholomew, Thomas and Matthew the tax collector; James, the son of Alphaeus, and Thaddeus; Simon from Cana, and Judas Iscariot who betrayed him.

Jesus sent out these twelve after instructing them thus, "Do not go into pagan territory or enter a Samaritan town. Go rather to the lost sheep of the house of Israel. As you go, make this proclamation: 'The kingdom of heaven is at hand.' Cure the sick, raise the dead, cleanse lepers, drive out demons. Without cost you have received; without cost you are to give."

ELEVENTH SUNDAY IN ORDINARY TIME / B   609

READING I

Ezekiel 17:22-24 / 92

Thus says the Lord GOD:
  I, too, will take from the crest of the
    cedar,
    from its topmost branches tear
      off a tender shoot,
  and plant it on a high and lofty
    mountain;
    on the mountain heights of Israel
      I will plant it.
  It shall put forth branches and bear
    fruit,
    and become a majestic cedar.
  Birds of every kind shall dwell

beneath it,
    every winged thing in the shade
      of its boughs.
And all the trees of the field shall
    know
    that I, the Lord,
  bring low the high tree,
    lift high the lowly tree,
  wither up the green tree,
    and make the withered tree
      bloom.
As I, the Lord, have spoken, so will I do.

RESPONSORIAL PSALM

Psalm 92:2-3, 13-14, 15-16

Lord, it is good to give thanks to you.

It is good to give thanks to the Lord,
  to sing praise to your name, Most
    High,
To proclaim your kindness at dawn
  and your faithfulness throughout the
    night. ℟.

The just one shall flourish like the palm
    tree,
  like a cedar of Lebanon shall he grow.

They that are planted in the house of the
    Lord
  shall flourish in the courts of our
    God. ℟.

They shall bear fruit even in old age;
  vigorous and sturdy shall they be,
Declaring how just is the Lord,
  my rock, in whom there is no
    wrong. ℟.

READING II

2 Corinthians 5:6-10

Brothers and sisters: We are always courageous, although we know that while we are at home in the body we are away from the Lord, for we walk by faith, not by sight. Yet we are courageous, and we would rather leave the body and go home to the Lord. Therefore, we aspire to please him, whether we are at home or away. For we must all appear before the judgment seat of Christ, so that each may receive recompense, according to what he did in the body, whether good or evil.

GOSPEL   *Mark 4:26-34*

Jesus said to the crowds: "This is how it is with the kingdom of God; it is as if a man were to scatter seed on the land and would sleep and rise night and day and through it all the seed would sprout and grow, he knows not how. Of its own accord the land yields fruit, first the blade, then the ear, then the full grain in the ear. And when the grain is ripe, he wields the sickle at once, for the harvest has come."

He said, "To what shall we compare the kingdom of God, or what parable can we use for it? It is like a mustard seed that, when it is sown in the ground, is the smallest of all the seeds on the earth. But once it is sown, it springs up and becomes the largest of plants and puts forth large branches, so that the birds of the sky can dwell in its shade." With many such parables he spoke the word to them as they were able to understand it. Without parables he did not speak to them, but to his own disciples he explained everything in private.

610 ELEVENTH SUNDAY IN ORDINARY TIME / C

READING I   *2 Samuel 12:7-10, 13 / 93*

Nathan said to David: "Thus says the Lord God of Israel: 'I anointed you king of Israel. I rescued you from the hand of Saul. I gave you your lord's house and your lord's wives for your own. I gave you the house of Israel and of Judah. And if this were not enough, I could count up for you still more. Why have you spurned the Lord and done evil in his sight? You have cut down Uriah the Hittite with the sword; you took his wife as your own, and him you killed with the sword of the Ammonites. Now, therefore, the sword shall never depart from your house, because you have despised me and have taken the wife of Uriah to be your wife.' Then David said to Nathan, "I have sinned against the Lord." Nathan answered David: "The Lord on his part has forgiven your sin: you shall not die."

RESPONSORIAL PSALM   *Psalm 32:1-2, 5, 7, 11*

Lord, for - give the wrong I have done.

Blessed is the one whose fault is taken
    away,
  whose sin is covered.
Blessed the man to whom the Lord
    imputes not guilt,
  in whose spirit there is no guile. ℟.

I acknowledged my sin to you,
  my guilt I covered not.
I said, "I confess my faults to the Lord,"
  and you took away the guilt of my
    sin. ℟.

You are my shelter; from distress you
    will preserve me;
  with glad cries of freedom you will
    ring me round. ℟.

Be glad in the Lord and rejoice, you
    just;
  exult, all you upright of heart. ℟.

READING II   *Galatians 2:16, 19-21*

Brothers and sisters: We who know that a person is not justified by works of the law but through faith in Jesus Christ, even we have believed in Christ Jesus that we may be justified by faith in Christ and not by works of the law, because by works of the law no one will be justified. For through the law I died to the law, that I might live for God. I have been crucified with Christ; yet I live, no longer I, but Christ lives in me; insofar as I now live in the flesh, I live by faith in the Son of God who has loved me and given himself up for me. I do not nullify the grace of God; for if justification comes through the law, then Christ died for nothing.

GOSPEL
Luke 7:36—8:3 or 7:36-50

For short form read only the part in brackets.

[A Pharisee invited Jesus to dine with him, and he entered the Pharisee's house and reclined at table. Now there was a sinful woman in the city who learned that he was at table in the house of the Pharisee. Bringing an alabaster flask of ointment, she stood behind him at his feet weeping and began to bathe his feet with her tears. Then she wiped them with her hair, kissed them, and anointed them with the ointment. When the Pharisee who had invited him saw this he said to himself, "If this man were a prophet, he would know who and what sort of woman this is who is touching him, that she is a sinner." Jesus said to him in reply, "Simon, I have something to say to you." "Tell me, teacher," he said. "Two people were in debt to a certain creditor; one owed five hundred days' wages and the other owed fifty. Since they were unable to repay the debt, he forgave it for both. Which of them will love him more?" Simon said in reply, "The one, I suppose, whose larger debt was forgiven." He said to him, "You have judged rightly."

Then he turned to the woman and said to Simon, "Do you see this woman? When I entered your house, you did not give me water for my feet, but she has bathed them with her tears and wiped them with her hair. You did not give me a kiss, but she has not ceased kissing my feet since the time I entered. You did not anoint my head with oil, but she anointed my feet with ointment. So I tell you, her many sins have been forgiven because she has shown great love. But the one to whom little is forgiven, loves little." He said to her, "Your sins are forgiven." The others at table said to themselves, "Who is this who even forgives sins?" But he said to the woman, "Your faith has saved you; go in peace."]

Afterward he journeyed from one town and village to another, preaching and proclaiming the good news of the kingdom of God. Accompanying him were the Twelve and some women who had been cured of evil spirits and infirmities, Mary, called Magdalene, from whom seven demons had gone out, Joanna, the wife of Herod's steward Chuza, Susanna, and many others who provided for them out of their resources.

TWELFTH SUNDAY IN ORDINARY TIME / A
611

READING I
Jeremiah 20:10-13 / 94

Jeremiah said:
"I hear the whisperings of many:
  'Terror on every side!
  Denounce! let us denounce him!'
All those who were my friends
  are on the watch for any misstep
    of mine.
'Perhaps he will be trapped; then we
    can prevail,
  and take our vengeance on him.'
But the LORD is with me, like a
    mighty champion:
  my persecutors will stumble,
    they will not triumph.
In their failure they will be put to

utter shame,
  to lasting, unforgettable
    confusion.
O LORD of hosts, you who test the
    just,
  who probe mind and heart,
let me witness the vengeance you
    take on them,
  for to you I have entrusted my
    cause.
Sing to the LORD,
  praise the LORD,
for he has rescued the life of the poor
  from the power of the wicked!"

RESPONSORIAL PSALM *Psalm 69:8-10, 14, 17, 33-35*

Lord, in your great love, an - swer me.

For your sake I bear insult,
and shame covers my face.
I have become an outcast to my brothers,
a stranger to my children,
because zeal for your house consumes
me,
and the insults of those who
blaspheme you fall upon me. ℟.

I pray to you, O Lord,
for the time of your favor, O God!
In your great kindness answer me
with your constant help.
Answer me, O Lord, for bounteous is

your kindness;
in your great mercy turn toward
me. ℟.

"See, you lowly ones, and be glad;
you who seek God, may your hearts
revive!
For the Lord hears the poor,
and his own who are in bonds he
spurns not.
Let the heavens and the earth praise him,
the seas and whatever moves in
them!" ℟.

READING II *Romans 5:12-15*

Brothers and sisters: Through one man sin entered the world, and through sin, death, and thus death came to all men, inasmuch as all sinned—for up to the time of the law, sin was in the world, though sin is not accounted when there is no law. But death reigned from Adam to Moses, even over those who did not sin after the pattern of the trespass of Adam, who is the type of the one who was to come.

But the gift is not like the transgression. For if by the transgression of the one the many died, how much more did the grace of God and the gracious gift of the one man Jesus Christ overflow for the many.

GOSPEL *Matthew 10:26-33*

Jesus said to the Twelve: "Fear no one. Nothing is concealed that will not be revealed, nor secret that will not be known. What I say to you in the darkness, speak in the light; what you hear whispered, proclaim on the housetops. And do not be afraid of those who kill the body but cannot kill the soul; rather, be afraid of the one who can destroy both soul and body in Gehenna. Are not two sparrows sold for a small coin? Yet not one of them falls to the ground without your Father's knowledge. Even all the hairs of your head are counted. So do not be afraid; you are worth more than many sparrows. Everyone who acknowledges me before others I will acknowledge before my heavenly Father. But whoever denies me before others, I will deny before my heavenly Father."

612 TWELFTH SUNDAY IN ORDINARY TIME / B

READING I *Job 38:1, 8-11 / 95*

The Lord addressed Job out of the storm
and said:
Who shut within doors the sea,
when it burst forth from the womb;
when I made the clouds its garment
and thick darkness its swaddling
bands?

When I set limits for it
and fastened the bar of its door,
and said: Thus far shall you come but
no farther,
and here shall your proud waves be
stilled!

RESPONSORIAL PSALM *Psalm 107:23-24, 25-26, 28-29, 30-31*

Give thanks to the Lord, his love is ev-er-last - ing.

They who sailed the sea in ships,
  trading on the deep waters,
these saw the works of the Lord
  and his wonders in the abyss. ℟.

His command raised up a storm wind
  which tossed its waves on high.
They mounted up to heaven; they sank
    to the depths;
  their hearts melted away in their
    plight. ℟.

They cried to the Lord in their distress;

from their straits he rescued them,
He hushed the storm to a gentle breeze,
  and the billows of the sea were
    stilled. ℟.

They rejoiced that they were calmed,
  and he brought them to their desired
    haven.
Let them give thanks to the Lord for his
    kindness
  and his wondrous deeds to the
    children of men. ℟.

READING II *2 Corinthians 5:14-17*
Brothers and sisters: The love of Christ impels us, once we have come to the conviction that one died for all; therefore, all have died. He indeed died for all, so that those who live might no longer live for themselves but for him who for their sake died and was raised.

Consequently, from now on we regard no one according to the flesh; even if we once knew Christ according to the flesh, yet now we know him so no longer. So whoever is in Christ is a new creation: the old things have passed away; behold, new things have come.

GOSPEL *Mark 4:35-41*
On that day, as evening drew on, Jesus said to his disciples: "Let us cross to the other side." Leaving the crowd, they took Jesus with them in the boat just as he was. And other boats were with him. A violent squall came up and waves were breaking over the boat, so that it was already filling up. Jesus was in the stern, asleep on a cushion. They woke him and said to him, "Teacher, do you not care that we are perishing?" He woke up, rebuked the wind, and said to the sea, "Quiet! Be still!" The wind ceased and there was great calm. Then he asked them, "Why are you terrified? Do you not yet have faith?" They were filled with great awe and said to one another, "Who then is this whom even wind and sea obey?"

TWELFTH SUNDAY IN ORDINARY TIME / C 613

READING I *Zechariah 12:10-11; 13:1 / 96*
Thus says the Lord: I will pour out on the house of David and on the inhabitants of Jerusalem a spirit of grace and petition; and they shall look on him whom they have pierced, and they shall mourn for him as one mourns for an only son, and they shall grieve over him as one grieves over a firstborn.

On that day the mourning in Jerusalem shall be as great as the mourning of Hadadrimmon in the plain of Megiddo.

On that day there shall be open to the house of David and to the inhabitants of Jerusalem, a fountain to purify from sin and uncleanness.

RESPONSORIAL PSALM *Psalm 63:2, 3-4, 5-6, 8-9*

My soul is thirst-ing for you, O Lord, thirst-ing for you my God.

O God, you are my God whom I seek;
    for you my flesh pines and my soul
        thirsts
    like the earth, parched, lifeless and
        without water. ℟.

Thus have I gazed toward you in the
        sanctuary
    to see your power and your glory,
for your kindness is a greater good than
        life;
    my lips shall glorify you. ℟.

Thus will I bless you while I live;
    lifting up my hands, I will call upon
        your name.
As with the riches of a banquet shall my
        soul be satisfied,
and with exultant lips my mouth
        shall praise you. ℟.

You are my help,
    and in the shadow of your wings I
        shout for joy.
My soul clings fast to you;
    your right hand upholds me. ℟.

READING II *Galatians 3:26-29*

Brothers and sisters: Through faith you are all children of God in Christ Jesus. For all of you who were baptized into Christ have clothed yourselves with Christ. There is neither Jew nor Greek, there is neither slave nor free person, there is not male and female; for you are all one in Christ Jesus. And if you belong to Christ, then you are Abraham's descendant, heirs according to the promise.

GOSPEL *Luke 9:18-24*

Once when Jesus was praying in solitude, and the disciples were with him, he asked them, "Who do the crowds say that I am?" They said in reply, "John the Baptist; others, Elijah; still others, 'One of the ancient prophets has arisen.'" Then he said to them, "But who do you say that I am?" Peter said in reply, "The Christ of God." He rebuked them and directed them not to tell this to anyone.

He said, "The Son of Man must suffer greatly and be rejected by the elders, the chief priests, and the scribes, and be killed and on the third day be raised."

Then he said to all, "If anyone wishes to come after me, he must deny himself and take up his cross daily and follow me. For whoever wishes to save his life will lose it, but whoever loses his life for my sake will save it."

614 THIRTEENTH SUNDAY IN ORDINARY TIME / A

READING I *2 Kings 4:8-11, 14-16a / 97*

One day Elisha came to Shunem, where there was a woman of influence, who urged him to dine with her. Afterward, whenever he passed by, he used to stop there to dine. So she said to her husband, "I know that Elisha is a holy man of God. Since he visits us often, let us arrange a little room on the roof and furnish it for him with a bed, table, chair, and lamp, so that when he comes to us he can stay there." Sometime later Elisha arrived and stayed in the room overnight.

Later Elisha asked, "Can something be done for her?" His servant Gehazi answered, "Yes! She has no son, and her husband is getting on in years." Elisha said, "Call her." When the woman had been called and stood at the door, Elisha promised, "This time next year you will be fondling a baby son."

RESPONSORIAL PSALM *Psalm 89:2-3, 16-17, 18-19*

For ev-er I will sing the good-ness of the Lord.

The promises of the Lord I will sing
     forever,
   through all generations my mouth
     shall proclaim your faithfulness.
For you have said, "My kindness is
     established forever;"
   in heaven you have confirmed your
     faithfulness. ℞.

Blessed the people who know the joyful
     shout;
   in the light of your countenance, O
     Lord, they walk.
At your name they rejoice all the day,
   and through your justice they are
     exalted. ℞.

You are the splendor of their strength,
   and by your favor our horn is
     exalted.
For to the Lord belongs our shield,
   and to the Holy One of Israel, our
     king. ℞.

READING II *Romans 6:3-4, 8-11*

Brothers and sisters: Are you unaware that we who were baptized into Christ Jesus were baptized into his death? We were indeed buried with him through baptism into death, so that, just as Christ was raised from the dead by the glory of the Father, we too might live in newness of life.

If, then, we have died with Christ, we believe that we shall also live with him. We know that Christ, raised from the dead, dies no more; death no longer has power over him. As to his death, he died to sin once and for all; as to his life, he lives for God. Consequently, you too must think of yourselves as dead to sin and living for God in Christ Jesus.

GOSPEL *Matthew 10:37-42*

Jesus said to his apostles: "Whoever loves father or mother more than me is not worthy of me, and whoever loves son or daughter more than me is not worthy of me; and whoever does not take up his cross and follow after me is not worthy of me. Whoever finds his life will lose it, and whoever loses his life for my sake will find it. Whoever receives you receives me, and whoever receives me receives the one who sent me. Whoever receives a prophet because he is a prophet will receive a prophet's reward, and whoever receives a righteous man because he is a righteous man will receive a righteous man's reward. And whoever gives only a cup of cold water to one of these little ones to drink because the little one is a disciple—amen, I say to you, he will surely not lose his reward."

615 THIRTEENTH SUNDAY IN ORDINARY TIME / B

READING I   *Wisdom 1:13-15; 2:23-24 / 98*

God did not make death,
    nor does he rejoice in the destruction
        of the living.
For he fashioned all things that they
    might have being;
    and the creatures of the world are
        wholesome,
and there is not a destructive drug among
    them
    nor any domain of the netherworld

on earth,
    for justice is undying.
For God formed man to be imperishable;
    the image of his own nature he made
        him.
But by the envy of the devil, death
    entered the world,
    and they who belong to his company
        experience it.

RESPONSORIAL PSALM   *Psalm 30:2, 4, 5-6, 11, 12, 13*

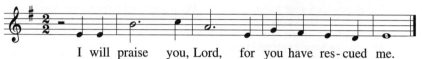

I will praise you, Lord, for you have res-cued me.

I will extol you, O Lord, for you drew
    me clear
    and did not let my enemies rejoice
        over me.
O Lord, you brought me up from the
    netherworld;
    you preserved me from among those
        going down into the pit. ℟.

Sing praise to the Lord, you his faithful
    ones,

and give thanks to his holy name.
For his anger lasts but a moment;
    a lifetime, his good will.
At nightfall, weeping enters in,
    but with the dawn, rejoicing. ℟.

Hear, O Lord, and have pity on me;
    O Lord, be my helper.
You changed my mourning into dancing;
    O Lord, my God, forever will I give
        you thanks. ℟.

READING II   *2 Corinthians 8:7, 9, 13-15*

Brothers and sisters: As you excel in every respect, in faith, discourse, knowledge, all earnestness, and in the love we have for you, may you excel in this gracious act also.

For you know the gracious act of our Lord Jesus Christ, that though he was rich, for your sake he became poor, so that by his poverty you might become rich. Not that others should have relief while you are burdened, but that as a matter of equality your abundance at the present time should supply their needs, so that their abundance may also supply your needs, that there may be equality. As it is written:
    "Whoever had much did not have more,
        and whoever had little did not have less."

GOSPEL   *Mark 5:21-43 or 5:21-24, 35b-43*

For short form read only the parts in brackets.

[When Jesus had crossed again in the boat to the other side, a large crowd gathered around him, and he stayed close to the sea. One of the synagogue officials, named Jairus, came forward. Seeing him he fell at his feet and pleaded earnestly with him, saying, "My daughter is at the point of death. Please, come lay your hands on her that she may get well and live." He went off with him, and a large crowd followed him and pressed upon him.]

    There was a woman afflicted with hemorrhages for twelve years. She had suffered greatly at the hands of many doctors and had spent all that she had. Yet she was not helped but only grew worse. She had heard about Jesus and came up behind him in the crowd and touched his cloak. She said, "If I but touch his clothes, I shall be cured." Immediately her flow of blood dried up. She felt in her body that she was healed of her affliction. Jesus, aware at once that power had gone out from him, turned around in the crowd and asked, "Who has touched my clothes?" But his disciples said to Jesus, "You see how the crowd is pressing upon you, and yet you ask, 'Who touched me?'" And he looked around to see who had done it. The woman, realizing what had happened to her, approached in fear and trembling. She fell down before Jesus and told him the whole truth. He said to her, "Daughter, your faith has saved you. Go in peace and be cured of your affliction."

[While he was still speaking, people from the synagogue official's house arrived and said, "Your daughter has died; why trouble the teacher any longer?" Disregarding the message that was reported, Jesus said to the synagogue official, "Do not be afraid; just have faith." He did not allow anyone to accompany him inside except Peter, James, and John, the brother of James. When they arrived at the house of the synagogue official, he caught sight of a commotion, people weeping and wailing loudly. So he went in and said to them, "Why this commotion and weeping? The child is not dead but asleep." And they ridiculed him. Then he put them all out. He took along the child's father and mother and those who were with him and entered the room where the child was. He took the child by the hand and said to her, "Talitha koum," which means, "Little girl, I say to you, arise!" The girl, a child of twelve, arose immediately and walked around. At that they were utterly astounded. He gave strict orders that no one should know this and said that she should be given something to eat.]

THIRTEENTH SUNDAY IN ORDINARY TIME / C   616

READING I
Kings 19:16b, 19-21 / 99

The Lord said to Elijah: "You shall anoint Elisha, son of Shaphat of Abel-Meholah, as prophet to succeed you."

Elijah set out and came upon Elisha, son of Shaphat, as he was plowing with twelve yoke of oxen; he was following the twelfth. Elijah went over to him and threw his cloak over him. Elisha left the oxen, ran after Elijah, and said, "Please, let me kiss my father and mother goodbye, and I will follow you." Elijah answered, "Go back! Have I done anything to you?" Elisha left him and, taking the yoke of oxen, slaughtered them; he used the plowing equipment for fuel to boil their flesh, and gave it to his people to eat. Then Elisha left and followed Elijah as his attendant.

RESPONSORIAL PSALM
Psalm 16:1-2, 5, 7-8, 9-10, 11

You are my in - her - i - tance, O Lord.

Keep me, O God, for in you I take refuge;
  I say to the Lord, "My Lord are you.
O Lord, my allotted portion and my cup,
  you it is who hold fast my lot." ℞.

I bless the Lord who counsels me;
  even in the night my heart exhorts me.
I set the Lord ever before me;
  with him at my right hand I shall not be disturbed. ℞.

Therefore my heart is glad and my soul rejoices,
  my body, too, abides in confidence
because you will not abandon my soul to the netherworld,
  nor will you suffer your faithful one to undergo corruption. ℞.

You will show me the path to life,
  fullness of joys in your presence,
  the delights at your right hand forever. ℞.

READING II
Galatians 5:1, 13-18

Brothers and sisters: For freedom Christ set us free; so stand firm and do not submit again to the yoke of slavery.

For you were called for freedom, brothers and sisters. But do not use this freedom as an opportunity for the flesh; rather, serve one another through love. For the whole law is fulfilled in one statement, namely, "You shall love your neighbor as yourself." But if you go on biting and devouring one another, beware that you are not consumed by one another.

I say, then: live by the Spirit and you will certainly not gratify the desire of the flesh. For the flesh has desires against the Spirit, and the Spirit against the flesh; these are opposed to each other, so that you may not do what you want. But if you are guided by the Spirit, you are not under the law.

GOSPEL
Luke 9:51-62

When the days for Jesus' being taken up were fulfilled, he resolutely determined to journey to Jerusalem, and he sent messengers ahead of him. On the way they entered a Samaritan village to prepare for his reception there, but they would not welcome him because the destination of his journey was Jerusalem. When the disciples James and John saw this they asked, "Lord, do you want us to call down fire from heaven to consume them?" Jesus turned and rebuked them, and they journeyed to another village.

As they were proceeding on their journey someone said to him, "I will follow you wherever you go." Jesus answered him, "Foxes have dens and birds of the sky have nests, but the Son of Man has nowhere to rest his head."

And to another he said, "Follow me." But he replied, "Lord, let me go first and bury my father." But he answered him, "Let the dead bury their dead. But you, go and proclaim the kingdom of God." And another said, "I will follow you, Lord, but first let me say farewell to my family at home." To him Jesus said, "No one who sets a hand to the plow and looks to what was left behind is fit for the kingdom of God."

---

617 FOURTEENTH SUNDAY IN ORDINARY TIME / A

READING I
Zechariah 9:9-10 / 100

Thus says the LORD:
Rejoice heartily, O daughter Zion,
  shout for joy, O daughter Jerusalem!
See, your king shall come to you;
  a just savior is he,
meek, and riding on an ass,
  on a colt, the foal of an ass.
He shall banish the chariot from Ephraim,

and the horse from Jerusalem;
the warrior's bow shall be banished,
  and he shall proclaim peace to the
    nations.
His dominion shall be from sea to sea,
  and from the River to the ends of
    the earth.

RESPONSORIAL PSALM
Psalm 145:1-2, 8-9, 10-11, 13-14

I will praise your name for ev - er,

my king and my God.

I will extol you, O my God and King,
    and I will bless your name forever
    and ever.
Every day will I bless you,
    and I will praise your name forever
    and ever. ℟.

The Lord is gracious and merciful,
    slow to anger and of great kindness.
The Lord is good to all
    and compassionate toward all his
    works. ℟.

Let all your works give you thanks, O
    Lord,
    and let your faithful ones bless you.
Let them discourse of the glory of your
    kingdom
    and speak of your might. ℟.

The Lord is faithful in all his words
    and holy in all his works.
The Lord lifts up all who are falling
    and raises up all who are bowed
    down. ℟.

READING II
Romans 8:9, 11-13

Brothers and sisters: You are not in the flesh; on the contrary, you are in the spirit, if only the Spirit of God dwells in you. Whoever does not have the Spirit of Christ does not belong to him. If the Spirit of the one who raised Jesus from the dead dwells in you, the one who raised Christ from the dead will give life to your mortal bodies also, through his Spirit that dwells in you. Consequently, brothers and sisters, we are not debtors to the flesh, to live according to the flesh. For if you live according to the flesh, you will die, but if by the Spirit you put to death the deeds of the body, you will live.

GOSPEL
Matthew 11:25-30

At that time Jesus exclaimed: "I give praise to you, Father, Lord of heaven and earth, for although you have hidden these things from the wise and the learned you have revealed them to little ones. Yes, Father, such has been your gracious will. All things have been handed over to me by my Father. No one knows the Son except the Father, and no one knows the Father except the Son and anyone to whom the Son wishes to reveal him."

"Come to me, all you who labor and are burdened, and I will give you rest. Take my yoke upon you and learn from me, for I am meek and humble of heart; and you will find rest for yourselves. For my yoke is easy, and my burden light."

FOURTEENTH SUNDAY IN ORDINARY TIME / B   618

READING I
Ezekiel 2:2-5 / 101

As the LORD spoke to me, the spirit entered into me and set me on my feet, and I heard the one who was speaking say to me: Son of man, I am sending you to the Israelites, rebels who have rebelled against me; they and their ancestors have revolted against me to this very day. Hard of face and obstinate of heart are they to whom I am sending you. But you shall say to them: Thus says the LORD God! And whether they heed or resist— for they are a rebellious house—they shall know that a prophet has been among them.

RESPONSORIAL PSALM
Psalm 123:1-2, 2, 3-4

Our eyes are fixed on the Lord, plead-ing for his mer-cy.

To you I lift up my eyes
    who are enthroned in heaven —
As the eyes of servants
    are on the hands of their masters. ℟.

As the eyes of a maid
    are on the hands of her mistress,
So are our eyes on the Lord, our God,
    till he have pity on us. ℟.

Have pity on us, O Lord, have pity on us,
    for we are more than sated with
        contempt;

our souls are more than sated
    with the mockery of the arrogant,
    with the contempt of the proud. ℟.

READING II

2 Corinthians 12:7-10

Brothers and sisters: That I, Paul, might not become too elated, because of the abundance of the revelations, a thorn in the flesh was given to me, an angel of Satan, to beat me, to keep me from being too elated. Three times I begged the Lord about this, that it might leave me, but he said to me, "My grace is sufficient for you, for power is made perfect in weakness." I will rather boast most gladly of my weaknesses, in order that the power of Christ may dwell with me. Therefore, I am content with weaknesses, insults, hardships, persecutions, and constraints, for the sake of Christ; for when I am weak, then I am strong.

GOSPEL

Mark 6:1-6

Jesus departed from there and came to his native place, accompanied by his disciples. When the sabbath came he began to teach in the synagogue, and many who heard him were astonished. They said, "Where did this man get all this? What kind of wisdom has been given him? What mighty deeds are wrought by his hands! Is he not the carpenter, the son of Mary, and the brother of James and Joses and Judas and Simon? And are not his sisters here with us?" And they took offense at him. Jesus said to them, "A prophet is not without honor except in his native place and among his own kin and in his own house." So he was not able to perform any mighty deed there, apart from curing a few sick people by laying his hands on them. He was amazed at their lack of faith.

619   FOURTEENTH SUNDAY IN ORDINARY TIME / C

READING I

Isaiah 66:10-14c / 102

Thus says the LORD:
Rejoice with Jerusalem and be glad
    because of her,
    all you who love her;
exult, exult with her,
    all you who were mourning over her!
Oh, that you may suck fully
    of the milk of her comfort,
that you may nurse with delight
    at her abundant breasts!
For thus says the LORD:
Lo, I will spread prosperity over
    Jerusalem like a river,
    and the wealth of the nations like an
        overflowing torrent.

As nurslings, you shall be carried in her
    arms,
    and fondled in her lap;
as a mother comforts her child,
    so will I comfort you;
    in Jerusalem you shall find your
        comfort.

When you see this, your heart shall
    rejoice
    and your bodies flourish like the
        grass;
the LORD's power shall be known to
    his servants.

RESPONSORIAL PSALM

Psalm 66:1-3, 4-5, 6-7, 16, 20

Let all the earth cry out to God with joy.

Shout joyfully to God, all the earth,
    sing praise to the glory of his name;
    proclaim his glorious praise.

Say to God, "How tremendous are your
    deeds!" ℟.

"Let all on earth worship and sing praise
    to you,
    sing praise to your name!"
Come and see the works of God,
    his tremendous deeds among the
    children of Adam. ℟.

He has changed the sea into dry land;
    through the river they passed on foot;

therefore let us rejoice in him.
He rules by his might forever. ℟.

Hear now, all you who fear God,
    while I declare what he has done for
    me.
Blessed be God who refused me not
    my prayer or his kindness! ℟.

READING II   *Galatians 6:14-18*

Brothers and sisters: May I never boast except in the cross of our Lord Jesus Christ, through which the world has been crucified to me, and I to the world. For neither does circumcision mean anything, nor does uncircumcision, but only a new creation. Peace and mercy be to all who follow this rule and to the Israel of God.

From now on, let no one make troubles for me; for I bear the marks of Jesus on my body.

The grace of our Lord Jesus Christ be with your spirit, brothers and sisters. Amen.

GOSPEL   *Luke 10:1-12, 17-20 or 10:1-9*

For short form read only the part in brackets.

[At that time the Lord appointed seventy-two others whom he sent ahead of him in pairs to every town and place he intended to visit. He said to them, "The harvest is abundant but the laborers are few; so ask the master of the harvest to send out laborers for his harvest. Go on your way; behold, I am sending you like lambs among wolves. Carry no money bag, no sack, no sandals; and greet no one along the way. Into whatever house you enter, first say, 'Peace to this household.' If a peaceful person lives there, your peace will rest on him; but if not, it will return to you. Stay in the same house and eat and drink what is offered to you, for the laborer deserves his payment. Do not move about from one house to another. Whatever town you enter and they welcome you, eat what is set before you, cure the sick in it and say to them, 'The kingdom of God is at hand for you.'] Whatever town you enter and they do not receive you, go out into the streets and say, 'The dust of your town that clings to our feet, even that we shake off against you.' Yet know this: the kingdom of God is at hand. I tell you, it will be more tolerable for Sodom on that day than for that town."

The seventy-two returned rejoicing, and said, "Lord, even the demons are subject to us because of your name." Jesus said, "I have observed Satan fall like lightning from the sky. Behold, I have given you the power to 'tread upon serpents' and scorpions and upon the full force of the enemy and nothing will harm you. Nevertheless, do not rejoice because the spirits are subject to you, but rejoice because your names are written in heaven."

FIFTEENTH SUNDAY IN ORDINARY TIME / A   620

READING I   *Isaiah 55:10-11 / 103*

Thus says the LORD:
Just as from the heavens
    the rain and snow come down
and do not return there
    till they have watered the earth,
    making it fertile and fruitful,
giving seed to the one who sows

and bread to the one who eats,
so shall my word be
    that goes forth from my mouth;
my word shall not return to me void,
    but shall do my will,
    achieving the end for which I sent
    it.

RESPONSORIAL PSALM   *Psalm 65:10, 11, 12-13, 14*

The seed that falls on good ground will yield a fruit - ful har - vest.

You have visited the land and watered it;
  greatly have you enriched it.
God's watercourses are filled;
  you have prepared the grain. ℟.

Thus have you prepared the land:
  drenching its furrows,
  breaking up its clods,
softening it with showers,
  blessing its yield. ℟.

You have crowned the year with your
    bounty,
  and your paths overflow with a rich
    harvest;
the untilled meadows overflow with it,
  and rejoicing clothes the hills. ℟.

The fields are garmented with flocks
  and the valleys blanketed with grain.
  They shout and sing for joy. ℟.

READING II   *Romans 8:18-23*

Brothers and sisters: I consider that the sufferings of this present time are as nothing compared with the glory to be revealed for us. For creation awaits with eager expectation the revelation of the children of God; for creation was made subject to futility, not of its own accord but because of the one who subjected it, in hope that creation itself would be set free from slavery to corruption and share in the glorious freedom of the children of God. We know that all creation is groaning in labor pains even until now; and not only that, but we ourselves, who have the firstfruits of the Spirit, we also groan within ourselves as we wait for adoption, the redemption of our bodies.

GOSPEL   *Matthew 13:1-23 or 13:1-9*

For short form read only the part in brackets.

[On that day, Jesus went out of the house and sat down by the sea. Such large crowds gathered around him that he got into a boat and sat down, and the whole crowd stood along the shore. And he spoke to them at length in parables, saying: "A sower went out to sow. And as he sowed, some seed fell on the path, and birds came and ate it up. Some fell on rocky ground, where it had little soil. It sprang up at once because the soil was not deep, and when the sun rose it was scorched, and it withered for lack of roots. Some seed fell among thorns, and the thorns grew up and choked it. But some seed fell on rich soil, and produced fruit, a hundred or sixty or thirtyfold. Whoever has ears ought to hear."]
    The disciples approached him and said, "Why do you speak to them in parables?" He said to them in reply, "Because knowledge of the mysteries of the kingdom of heaven has been granted to you, but to them it has not been granted. To anyone who has, more will be given and he will grow rich; from anyone who has not, even what he has will be taken away. This is why I speak to them in parables, because 'they look but do not see and hear but do not listen or understand.' Isaiah's prophecy is fulfilled in them, which says:
    'You shall indeed hear but not understand,
        you shall indeed look but never see.
    Gross is the heart of this people,
        they will hardly hear with their ears,
        they have closed their eyes,
        lest they see with their eyes

and hear with their ears
and understand with their hearts and be converted,
and I heal them.'

"But blessed are your eyes, because they see, and your ears, because they hear. Amen, I say to you, many prophets and righteous people longed to see what you see but did not see it, and to hear what you hear but did not hear it.

"Hear then the parable of the sower. The seed sown on the path is the one who hears the word of the kingdom without understanding it, and the evil one comes and steals away what was sown in his heart. The seed sown on rocky ground is the one who hears the word and receives it at once with joy. But he has no root and lasts only for a time. When some tribulation or persecution comes because of the word, he immediately falls away. The seed sown among thorns is the one who hears the word, but then worldly anxiety and the lure of riches choke the word and it bears no fruit. But the seed sown on rich soil is the one who hears the word and understands it, who indeed bears fruit and yields a hundred or sixty or thirtyfold."

FIFTEENTH SUNDAY IN ORDINARY TIME / B 621

READING I
Amos 7:12-15 / 104

Amaziah, priest of Bethel, said to Amos, "Off with you, visionary, flee to the land of Judah! There earn your bread by prophesying, but never again prophesy in Bethel; for it is the king's sanctuary and a royal temple." Amos answered Amaziah, "I was no prophet, nor have I belonged to a company of prophets; I was a shepherd and a dresser of sycamores. The LORD took me from following the flock, and said to me, Go, prophesy to my people Israel."

RESPONSORIAL PSALM
Psalm 85:9-10, 11-12, 13-14

Lord, let us see your kind-ness, and grant us your sal - va - tion.

I will hear what God proclaims;
    the Lord—for he proclaims peace.
Near indeed is his salvation to those who
    fear him,
    glory dwelling in our land. ℟.

Kindness and truth shall meet;
    justice and peace shall kiss.

Truth shall spring out of the earth,
    and justice shall look down from
    heaven. ℟.

The Lord himself will give his benefits;
    our land shall yield its increase.
Justice shall walk before him,
    and prepare the way of his steps. ℟.

READING II
Ephesians 1:3-14 or 1:3-10
For short form read only the part in brackets.

[Blessed be the God and Father of our Lord Jesus Christ, who has blessed us in Christ with every spiritual blessing in the heavens, as he chose us in him, before the foundation of the world, to be holy and without blemish before him. In love he destined us for adoption to himself through Jesus Christ, in accord with the favor of his will, for the praise of the glory of his grace that he granted us in the beloved. In him we have redemption by his blood, the forgiveness of transgressions, in accord with the riches of his grace that he lavished upon us. In all wisdom and insight, he has made known to us the mystery of his will in accord with his favor that he set forth in him as a plan for the fullness of times, to sum up all things in Christ, in heaven and on earth.]

In him we were also chosen, destined in accord with the purpose of the One who accomplishes all things according to the intention of his will, so that we might exist for the praise of his glory, we who first hoped in Christ. In him you also, who have heard the word of truth, the gospel of your salvation, and have believed in him, were sealed with the promised holy Spirit, which is the first installment of our inheritance toward redemption as God's possession, to the praise of his glory.

GOSPEL *Mark 6:7-13*

Jesus summoned the Twelve and began to send them out two by two and gave them authority over unclean spirits. He instructed them to take nothing for the journey but a walking stick—no food, no sack, no money in their belts. They were, however, to wear sandals but not a second tunic. He said to them, "Wherever you enter a house, stay there until you leave. Whatever place does not welcome you or listen to you, leave there and shake the dust off your feet in testimony against them." So they went off and preached repentance. The Twelve drove out many demons, and they anointed with oil many who were sick and cured them.

622 FIFTEENTH SUNDAY IN ORDINARY TIME / C

READING I *Deuteronomy 30:10-14 / 105*

Moses said to the people: "If only you would heed the voice of the LORD, your God, and keep his commandments and statutes that are written in this book of the law, when you return to the LORD, your God, with all your heart and all your soul.

"For this command that I enjoin on you today is not too mysterious and remote for you. It is not up in the sky, that you should say, 'Who will go up in the sky to get it for us and tell us of it, that we may carry it out?' Nor is it across the sea, that you should say, 'Who will cross the sea to get it for us and tell us of it, that we may carry it out?' No, it is something very near to you, already in your mouths and in your hearts; you have only to carry it out."

RESPONSORIAL PSALM *Psalm 69:14, 17, 30-31, 33-34, 36, 37*

Turn to the Lord in your need, and you will live.

I pray to you, O Lord,
    for the time of your favor, O God!
In your great kindness answer me
    with your constant help.
Answer me, O Lord, for bounteous is
    your kindness:
    in your great mercy turn toward me. ℟.

I am afflicted and in pain;
    let your saving help, O God, protect
    me.
I will praise the name of God in song,
    and I will glorify him with
    thanksgiving. ℟.

"See, you lowly ones, and be glad;
    you who seek God, may your hearts
    revive!
For the Lord hears the poor,
    and his own who are in bonds he
    spurns not." ℟.

For God will save Zion
    and rebuild the cities of Judah.
The descendants of his servants shall
    inherit it,
    and those who love his name shall
    inhabit it. ℟.

Or:

RESPONSORIAL PSALM *Psalm 19:8, 9, 10, 11*

Your words, O Lord, are Spir - it and life.

The law of the Lord is perfect,
refreshing the soul;
the decree of the Lord is trustworthy,
giving wisdom to the simple. ℟.

The precepts of the Lord are right,
rejoicing the heart;
the command of the Lord is clear,
enlightening the eye. ℟.

The fear of the Lord is pure,
enduring forever;
the ordinances of the Lord are true,
all of them just. ℟.

They are more precious than gold,
than a heap of purest gold;
sweeter also than syrup
or honey from the comb. ℟.

READING II *Colossians 1:15-20*

Christ Jesus is the image of the invisible God,
the firstborn of all creation.
For in him were created all things in heaven and on earth,
the visible and the invisible,
whether thrones or dominions or principalities or powers;
all things were created through him and for him.
He is before all things,
and in him all things hold together.
He is the head of the body, the church.

He is the beginning, the firstborn from the dead,
that in all things he himself might be preeminent.
For in him all the fullness was pleased to dwell,
and through him to reconcile all things for him,
making peace by the blood of his cross
through him, whether those on earth or those in heaven.

GOSPEL *Luke 10:25-37*

There was a scholar of the law who stood up to test him and said, "Teacher, what must I do to inherit eternal life?" Jesus said to him, "What is written in the law? How do you read it?" He said in reply, 'You shall love the Lord, your God, with all your heart, with all your being, with all your strength, and with all your mind, and your neighbor as yourself.'" He replied to him, "You have answered correctly; do this and you will live."

But because he wished to justify himself, he said to Jesus, "And who is my neighbor?" Jesus replied, "A man fell victim to robbers as he went down from Jerusalem to Jericho. They stripped and beat him and went off leaving him half-dead. A priest happened to be going down that road, but when he saw him, he passed by on the opposite side. Likewise a Levite came to the place, and when he saw him, he passed by on the opposite side. But a Samaritan traveler who came upon him was moved with compassion at the sight. He approached the victim, poured oil and wine over his wounds and bandaged them. Then he lifted him up on his own animal, took him to an inn, and cared for him. The next day he took out two silver coins and gave them to the innkeeper with the instruction, 'Take care of him. If you spend more than what I have given you, I shall repay you on my way back.' Which of these three, in your opinion, was neighbor to the robbers' victim?" He answered, "The one who treated him with mercy." Jesus said to him, "Go and do likewise."

623 SIXTEENTH SUNDAY IN ORDINARY TIME / A

READING I
Wisdom 12:13, 16-19 / 106

There is no god besides you who have the care of all,
  that you need show you have not unjustly condemned.
For your might is the source of justice;
  your mastery over all things makes you lenient to all.
For you show your might when the perfection of your power is disbelieved;
  and in those who know you, you rebuke temerity.
But though you are master of might, you judge with clemency,
  and with much lenience you govern us;
  for power, whenever you will, attends you.
And you taught your people, by these deeds,
  that those who are just must be kind;
and you gave your children good ground for hope
  that you would permit repentance for their sins.

RESPONSORIAL PSALM
Psalm 86:5-6, 9-10, 15-16

Lord, you are good and for - giv - ing.

You, O Lord, are good and forgiving,
  abounding in kindness to all who
    call upon you.
Hearken, O Lord, to my prayer
  and attend to the sound of my
    pleading. ℟.

All the nations you have made shall come
  and worship you, O Lord,
  and glorify your name.

For you are great, and you do wondrous
    deeds;
  you alone are God. ℟.

You, O Lord, are a God merciful and
    gracious,
  slow to anger, abounding in kindness
    and fidelity.
Turn toward me, and have pity on me;
  give your strength to your servant. ℟.

READING II
Romans 8:26-27

Brothers and sisters: The Spirit comes to the aid of our weakness; for we do not know how to pray as we ought, but the Spirit himself intercedes with inexpressible groanings. And the one who searches hearts knows what is the intention of the Spirit, because he intercedes for the holy ones according to God's will.

GOSPEL
Matthew 13:24-43 or 13:24-30

For short form read only the part in brackets.

[Jesus proposed another parable to the crowds, saying: "The kingdom of heaven may be likened to a man who sowed good seed in his field. While everyone was asleep his enemy came and sowed weeds all through the wheat, and then went off. When the crop grew and bore fruit, the weeds appeared as well. The slaves of the householder came to him and said, 'Master, did you not sow good seed in your field? Where have the weeds come from?' He answered, 'An enemy has done this.' His slaves said to him, 'Do you want us to go and pull them up?' He replied, 'No, if you pull up the weeds you might uproot the wheat along with them. Let them grow together until harvest; then at harvest time I will say to the harvesters, "First collect the weeds and tie them in bundles for burning; but gather the wheat into my barn."'"]
  He proposed another parable to them. "The kingdom of heaven is like a mustard

seed that a person took and sowed in a field. It is the smallest of all the seeds, yet when full-grown it is the largest of plants. It becomes a large bush, and the 'birds of the sky come and dwell in its branches.'"

He spoke to them another parable. "The kingdom of heaven is like yeast that a woman took and mixed with three measures of wheat flour until the whole batch was leavened."

All these things Jesus spoke to the crowds in parables. He spoke to them only in parables, to fulfill what had been said through the prophet:

"I will open my mouth in parables,
I will announce what has lain hidden from the foundation
of the world."

Then, dismissing the crowds, he went into the house. His disciples approached him and said, "Explain to us the parable of the weeds in the field." He said in reply, "He who sows good seed is the Son of Man, the field is the world, the good seed the children of the kingdom. The weeds are the children of the evil one, and the enemy who sows them is the devil. The harvest is the end of the age, and the harvesters are angels. Just as weeds are collected and burned up with fire, so will it be at the end of the age. The Son of Man will send his angels, and they will collect out of his kingdom all who cause others to sin and all evildoers. They will throw them into the fiery furnace, where there will be wailing and grinding of teeth. Then the righteous will shine like the sun in the kingdom of their Father. Whoever has ears ought to hear."

SIXTEENTH SUNDAY IN ORDINARY TIME / B   624

READING I   *Jeremiah 23:1-6 / 107*

Woe to the shepherds who mislead and scatter the flock of my pasture, says the LORD. Therefore, thus says the LORD, the God of Israel, against the shepherds who shepherd my people: You have scattered my sheep and driven them away. You have not cared for them, but I will take care to punish your evil deeds. I myself will gather the remnant of my flock from all the lands to which I have driven them and bring them back to their meadow; there they shall increase and multiply. I will appoint shepherds for them who will shepherd them so that they need no longer fear and tremble; and none shall be missing, says the LORD.

Behold, the days are coming, says the LORD,
when I will raise up a righteous shoot to David;
as king he shall reign and govern wisely,
he shall do what is just and right in the land.
In his days Judah shall be saved,
Israel shall dwell in security.
This is the name they give him:
"The LORD our justice."

RESPONSORIAL PSALM   *Psalm 23:1-3, 3-4, 5, 6*

The Lord is my shep-herd; there is noth-ing I shall want.

The Lord is my shepherd; I shall not
    want.
In verdant pastures he gives me
    repose;
beside restful waters he leads me;
    he refreshes my soul. ℟.

He guides me in right paths
    for his name's sake.
Even though I walk in the dark valley
    I fear no evil; for you are at my side
with your rod and your staff
    that give me courage. ℟.

You spread the table before me
   in the sight of my foes;
you anoint my head with oil;
   my cup overflows. ℟.
	Only goodness and kindness follow me
	   all the days of my life;
	and I shall dwell in the house of the Lord
	   for years to come. ℟.

READING II   *Ephesians 2:13-18*

Brothers and sisters: In Christ Jesus you who once were far off have become near by the blood of Christ.

For he is our peace, he who made both one and broke down the dividing wall of enmity, through his flesh, abolishing the law with its commandments and legal claims, that he might create in himself one new person in place of the two, thus establishing peace, and might reconcile both with God, in one body, through the cross, putting that enmity to death by it. He came and preached peace to you who were far off and peace to those who were near, for through him we both have access in one Spirit to the Father.

GOSPEL   *Mark 6:30-34*

The apostles gathered together with Jesus and reported all they had done and taught. He said to them, "Come away by yourselves to a deserted place and rest a while." People were coming and going in great numbers, and they had no opportunity even to eat. So they went off in the boat by themselves to a deserted place. People saw them leaving and many came to know about it. They hastened there on foot from all the towns and arrived at the place before them.

When he disembarked and saw the vast crowd, his heart was moved with pity for them, for they were like sheep without a shepherd; and he began to teach them many things.

625   SIXTEENTH SUNDAY IN ORDINARY TIME / C

READING I   *Genesis 18:1-10a / 108*

The LORD appeared to Abraham by the terebinth of Mamre, as he sat in the entrance of his tent, while the day was growing hot. Looking up, Abraham saw three men standing nearby. When he saw them, he ran from the entrance of the tent to greet them; and bowing to the ground, he said: "Sir, if I may ask you this favor, please do not go on past your servant. Let some water be brought, that you may bathe your feet, and then rest yourselves under the tree. Now that you have come this close to your servant, let me bring you a little food, that you may refresh yourselves; and afterward you may go on your way." The men replied, "Very well, do as you have said."

Abraham hastened into the tent and told Sarah, "Quick, three measures of fine flour! Knead it and make rolls." He ran to the herd, picked out a tender, choice steer, and gave it to a servant, who quickly prepared it. Then Abraham got some curds and milk, as well as the steer that had been prepared, and set these before the three men; and he waited on them under the tree while they ate.

They asked Abraham, "Where is your wife Sarah?" He replied, "There in the tent." One of them said, "I will surely return to you about this time next year, and Sarah will then have a son."

RESPONSORIAL PSALM   *Psalm 15:2-3, 3-4, 5*

He who does jus-tice will live in the pres-ence of the Lord.

One who walks blamelessly and does
    justice;
who thinks the truth in his heart
and slanders not with his tongue. ℟.

Who harms not his fellow man,
    nor takes up a reproach against his
    neighbor;
by whom the reprobate is despised,

while he honors those who fear the
    Lord. ℟.

Who lends not his money at usury
    and accepts no bribe against the
    innocent.
One who does these things
    shall never be disturbed. ℟.

READING II
Colossians 1:24-28

Brothers and sisters: Now I rejoice in my sufferings for your sake, and in my flesh I am filling up what is lacking in the afflictions of Christ on behalf of his body, which is the church, of which I am a minister in accordance with God's stewardship given to me to bring to completion for you the word of God, the mystery hidden from ages and from generations past. But now it has been manifested to his holy ones, to whom God chose to make known the riches of the glory of this mystery among the Gentiles; it is Christ in you, the hope for glory. It is he whom we proclaim, admonishing everyone and teaching everyone with all wisdom, that we may present everyone perfect in Christ.

GOSPEL
Luke 10:38-42

Jesus entered a village where a woman whose name was Martha welcomed him. She had a sister named Mary who sat beside the Lord at his feet listening to him speak. Martha, burdened with much serving, came to him and said, "Lord, do you not care that my sister has left me by myself to do the serving? Tell her to help me." The Lord said to her in reply, "Martha, Martha, you are anxious and worried about many things. There is need of only one thing. Mary has chosen the better part and it will not be taken from her."

SEVENTEENTH SUNDAY IN ORDINARY TIME / A
626

READING I
1 Kings 3:5, 7-12 / 109

The LORD appeared to Solomon in a dream at night. God said, "Ask something of me and I will give it to you." Solomon answered: "O LORD, my God, you have made me, your servant, king to succeed my father David; but I am a mere youth, not knowing at all how to act. I serve you in the midst of the people whom you have chosen, a people so vast that it cannot be numbered or counted. Give your servant, therefore, an understanding heart to judge your people and to distinguish right from wrong. For who is able to govern this vast people of yours?"

   The LORD was pleased that Solomon made this request. So God said to him: "Because you have asked for this— not for a long life for yourself, nor for riches, nor for the life of your enemies, but for understanding so that you may know what is right— I do as you requested. I give you a heart so wise and understanding that there has never been anyone like you up to now, and after you there will come no one to equal you."

RESPONSORIAL PSALM
Psalm 119:57, 72, 76-77, 127-128, 129-130

Lord,   I   love   your com - mands.

I have said, O Lord, that my part
    is to keep your words.
The law of your mouth is to me more

precious
than thousands of gold and silver
    pieces. ℟.

Let your kindness comfort me
  according to your promise to your
    servants.
Let your compassion come to me that I
    may live,
  for your law is my delight. ℟.

For I love your commands

more than gold, however fine.
For in all your precepts I go forward;
  every false way I hate. ℟.

Wonderful are your decrees;
  therefore I observe them.
The revelation of your words sheds light,
  giving understanding to the simple. ℟.

READING II
Romans 8:28-30

Brothers and sisters: We know that all things work for good for those who love God, who are called according to his purpose. For those he foreknew he also predestined to be conformed to the image of his Son, so that he might be the firstborn among many brothers and sisters. And those he predestined he also called; and those he called he also justified; and those he justified he also glorified.

GOSPEL
Matthew 13:44-52 or 13:44-46

For short form read only the part in brackets.

[Jesus said to his disciples: "The kingdom of heaven is like a treasure buried in a field, which a person finds and hides again, and out of joy goes and sells all that he has and buys that field. Again, the kingdom of heaven is like a merchant searching for fine pearls. When he finds a pearl of great price, he goes and sells all that he has and buys it.] Again, the kingdom of heaven is like a net thrown into the sea, which collects fish of every kind. When it is full they haul it ashore and sit down to put what is good into buckets. What is bad they throw away. Thus it will be at the end of the age. The angels will go out and separate the wicked from the righteous and throw them into the fiery furnace, where there will be wailing and grinding of teeth.

"Do you understand all these things?" They answered, "Yes." And he replied, "Then every scribe who has been instructed in the kingdom of heaven is like the head of a household who brings from his storeroom both the new and the old."

627 SEVENTEENTH SUNDAY IN ORDINARY TIME / B

READING I
2 Kings 4:42-44 / 110

A man came from Baal-shalishah bringing to Elisha, the man of God, twenty barley loaves made from the firstfruits, and fresh grain in the ear. Elisha said, "Give it to the people to eat." But his servant objected, "How can I set this before a hundred people?" Elisha insisted, "Give it to the people to eat. For thus says the LORD, 'They shall eat and there shall be some left over.'" And when they had eaten, there was some left over, as the LORD had said.

RESPONSORIAL PSALM
Psalm 145:10-11, 15-16, 17-18

The hand of the Lord   feeds us; he an - swers all our needs.

Let all your works give you thanks, O
    Lord,
  and let your faithful ones bless you.
Let them discourse of the glory of your
    kingdom
  and speak of your might. ℟.

The eyes of all look hopefully to you,
  and you give them their food in due
    season;
you open your hand
  and satisfy the desire of every living
    thing. ℟.

The Lord is just in all his ways
and holy in all his works.

The Lord is near to all who call upon him,
to all who call upon him in truth. ℟.

READING II   *Ephesians 4:1-6*

Brothers and sisters: I, a prisoner for the Lord, urge you to live in a manner worthy of
the call you have received, with all humility and gentleness, with patience, bearing with
one another through love, striving to preserve the unity of the spirit through the bond of
peace: one body and one Spirit, as you were also called to the one hope of your call; one
Lord, one faith, one baptism; one God and Father of all, who is over all and through all
and in all.

GOSPEL   *John 6:1-15*

Jesus went across the Sea of Galilee. A large crowd followed him, because they saw the
signs he was performing on the sick. Jesus went up on the mountain, and there he sat
down with his disciples. The Jewish feast of Passover was near. When Jesus raised his
eyes and saw that a large crowd was coming to him, he said to Philip, "Where can we
buy enough food for them to eat?" He said this to test him, because he himself knew
what he was going to do. Philip answered him, "Two hundred days' wages worth of food
would not be enough for each of them to have a little." One of his disciples, Andrew, the
brother of Simon Peter, said to him, "There is a boy here who has five barley loaves and
two fish; but what good are these for so many?" Jesus said, "Have the people recline."
Now there was a great deal of grass in that place. So the men reclined, about five thousand
in number. Then Jesus took the loaves, gave thanks, and distributed them to those who
were reclining, and also as much of the fish as they wanted. When they had had their
fill, he said to his disciples, "Gather the fragments left over, so that nothing will be
wasted." So they collected them, and filled twelve wicker baskets with fragments from
the five barley loaves that had been more than they could eat. When the people saw the
sign he had done, they said, "This is truly the Prophet, the one who is to come into the
world." Since Jesus knew that they were going to come and carry him off to make him
king, he withdrew again to the mountain alone.

SEVENTEENTH SUNDAY IN ORDINARY TIME / C   628

READING I   *Genesis 18:20-32 / 111*

In those days, the LORD said: "The outcry against Sodom and Gomorrah is so great, and
their sin so grave, that I must go down and see whether or not their actions fully correspond
to the cry against them that comes to me. I mean to find out."

While Abraham's visitors walked on farther toward Sodom, the LORD remained
standing before Abraham. Then Abraham drew nearer and said: "Will you sweep away
the innocent with the guilty? Suppose there were fifty innocent people in the city; would
you wipe out the place, rather than spare it for the sake of the fifty innocent people within
it? Far be it from you to do such a thing, to make the innocent die with the guilty so that
the innocent and the guilty would be treated alike! Should not the judge of all the world
act with justice?" The LORD replied, "If I find fifty innocent people in the city of Sodom,
I will spare the whole place for their sake." Abraham spoke up again: "See how I am
presuming to speak to my Lord, though I am but dust and ashes! What if there are five
less than fifty innocent people? Will you destroy the whole city because of those five?"
He answered, "I will not destroy it, if I find forty-five there." But Abraham persisted,
saying "What if only forty are found there?" He replied, "I will forbear doing it for the
sake of the forty." Then Abraham said, "Let not my Lord grow impatient if I go on. What
if only thirty are found there?" He replied, "I will forbear doing it if I can find but thirty
there." Still Abraham went on, "Since I have thus dared to speak to my Lord, what if
there are no more than twenty?" The LORD answered, "I will not destroy it, for the sake
of the twenty." But he still persisted: "Please, let not my Lord grow angry if I speak up
this last time. What if there are at least ten there?" He replied, "For the sake of those ten,
I will not destroy it."

RESPONSORIAL PSALM

Psalm 138:1-2, 2-3, 6-7, 7-8

Lord, on the day I called for help, you an- swered me.

I will give thanks to you, O Lord, with
  all my heart,
  for you have heard the words of my
    mouth;
  in the presence of the angels I will
    sing your praise;
I will worship at your holy temple
  and give thanks to your name. ℟.

Because of your kindness and your truth;
  for you have made great above all
    things
  your name and your promise.
When I called you answered me;
  you built up strength within me. ℟.

The Lord is exalted, yet the lowly he
  sees,
  and the proud he knows from afar.
Though I walk amid distress, you
  preserve me;
  against the anger of my enemies you
    raise your hand. ℟.

Your right hand saves me.
  The Lord will complete what he has
    done for me;
your kindness, O Lord, endures forever;
  forsake not the work of your
    hands. ℟.

READING II

Colossians 2:12-14

Brothers and sisters: You were buried with him in baptism, in which you were also raised with him through faith in the power of God, who raised him from the dead. And even when you were dead in transgressions and the uncircumcision of your flesh, he brought you to life along with him, having forgiven us all our transgressions; obliterating the bond against us, with its legal claims, which was opposed to us, he also removed it from our midst, nailing it to the cross.

GOSPEL

Luke 11:1-13

Jesus was praying in a certain place, and when he had finished, one of his disciples said to him, "Lord, teach us to pray just as John taught his disciples." He said to them, "When you pray, say:
  "Father, hallowed be your name,
    your kingdom come.
    Give us each day our daily bread
    and forgive us our sins
    for we ourselves forgive everyone in debt to us,
    and do not subject us to the final test."

And he said to them, "Suppose one of you has a friend to whom he goes at midnight and says, 'Friend, lend me three loaves of bread, for a friend of mine has arrived at my house from a journey and I have nothing to offer him,' and he says in reply from within, 'Do not bother me; the door has already been locked and my children and I are already in bed. I cannot get up to give you anything.' I tell you, if he does not get up to give the visitor the loaves because of their friendship, he will get up to give him whatever he needs because of his persistence.

  "And I tell you, ask and you will receive; seek and you will find; knock and the door will be opened to you. For everyone who asks, receives; and the one who seeks, finds; and to the one who knocks, the door will be opened. What father among you would hand his son a snake when he asks for a fish? Or hand him a scorpion when he asks for an egg? If you then, who are wicked, know how to give good gifts to your children, how much more will the Father in heaven give the Holy Spirit to those who ask him?"

EIGHTEENTH SUNDAY IN ORDINARY TIME / A 629

READING I

Isaiah 55:1-3 / 112

Thus says the LORD:
All you who are thirsty,
    come to the water!
You who have no money,
    come, receive grain and eat;
Come, without paying and without cost,
    drink wine and milk!
Why spend your money for what is not
    bread;

your wages for what fails to satisfy?
Heed me, and you shall eat well,
    you shall delight in rich fare.
Come to me heedfully,
    listen, that you may have life.
I will renew with you the everlasting
    covenant,
    the benefits assured to David.

RESPONSORIAL PSALM

Psalm 145:8-9, 15-16, 17-18

The hand of the Lord feeds us; he an-swers all our needs.

The Lord is gracious and merciful,
    slow to anger and of great kindness.
The Lord is good to all
    and compassionate toward all his
      works. ℟.

The Lord is just in all his ways
    and holy in all his works.
The Lord is near to all who call upon
    him,
    to all who call upon him in truth. ℟.

The eyes of all look hopefully to you,
    and you give them their food in due
      season;
you open your hand
    and satisfy the desire of every living
      thing. ℟.

READING II

Romans 8:35, 37-39

Brothers and sisters: What will separate us from the love of Christ? Will anguish, or distress, or persecution, or famine, or nakedness, or peril, or the sword? No, in all these things we conquer overwhelmingly through him who loved us. For I am convinced that neither death, nor life, nor angels, nor principalities, nor present things, nor future things, nor powers, nor height, nor depth, nor any other creature will be able to separate us from the love of God in Christ Jesus our Lord.

GOSPEL

Matthew 14:13-21

When Jesus heard of the death of John the Baptist, he withdrew in a boat to a deserted place by himself. The crowds heard of this and followed him on foot from their towns. When he disembarked and saw the vast crowd, his heart was moved with pity for them, and he cured their sick. When it was evening, the disciples approached him and said, "This is a deserted place and it is already late; dismiss the crowds so that they can go to the villages and buy food for themselves." Jesus said to them, "There is no need for them to go away; give them some food yourselves." But they said to him, "Five loaves and two fish are all we have here." Then he said, "Bring them here to me," and he ordered the crowds to sit down on the grass. Taking the five loaves and the two fish, and looking up to heaven, he said the blessing, broke the loaves, and gave them to the disciples, who in turn gave them to the crowds. They all ate and were satisfied, and they picked up the fragments left over— twelve wicker baskets full. Those who ate were about five thousand men, not counting women and children.

630 EIGHTEENTH SUNDAY IN ORDINARY TIME / B

READING I   *Exodus 16:2-4, 12-15 / 113*

The whole Israelite community grumbled against Moses and Aaron. The Israelites said to them, "Would that we had died at the LORD's hand in the land of Egypt, as we sat by our fleshpots and ate our fill of bread! But you had to lead us into this desert to make the whole community die of famine!"

Then the LORD said to Moses, "I will now rain down bread from heaven for you. Each day the people are to go out and gather their daily portion; thus will I test them, to see whether they follow my instructions or not.

"I have heard the grumbling of the Israelites. Tell them: In the evening twilight you shall eat flesh, and in the morning you shall have your fill of bread, so that you may know that I, the LORD am your God."

In the evening quail came up and covered the camp. In the morning a dew lay all about the camp, and when the dew evaporated, there on the surface of the desert were fine flakes like hoarfrost on the ground. On seeing it, the Israelites asked one another, "What is this?" for they did not know what it was. But Moses told them, "This is the bread that the LORD has given you to eat."

RESPONSORIAL PSALM   *Psalm 78:3-4, 23-24, 25, 54*

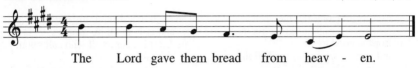

The Lord gave them bread from heav - en.

What we have heard and know,
   and what our fathers have declared
      to us,
We will declare to the generation to come
   the glorious deeds of the Lord and
      his strength
and the wonders that he wrought. ℟.

He commanded the skies above

and opened the doors of heaven;
he rained manna upon them for food
   and gave them heavenly bread. ℟.

Man ate the bread of angels,
   food he sent them in abundance.
And he brought them to his holy land,
   to the mountains his right hand had
      won. ℟.

READING II   *Ephesians 4:17, 20-24*

Brothers and sisters: I declare and testify in the Lord that you must no longer live as the Gentiles do, in the futility of their minds; that is not how you learned Christ, assuming that you have heard of him and were taught in him, as truth is in Jesus, that you should put away the old self of your former way of life, corrupted through deceitful desires, and be renewed in the spirit of your minds, and put on the new self, created in God's way in righteousness and holiness of truth.

GOSPEL   *John 6:24-35*

When the crowd saw that neither Jesus nor his disciples were there, they themselves got into boats and came to Capernaum looking for Jesus. And when they found him across the sea they said to him, "Rabbi, when did you get here?" Jesus answered them and said, "Amen, amen, I say to you, you are looking for me not because you saw signs but because you ate the loaves and were filled. Do not work for food that perishes but for the food that endures for eternal life, which the Son of Man will give you. For on him the Father, God, has set his seal." So they said to him, "What can we do to accomplish the works of God?" Jesus answered and said to them, "This is the work of God, that you believe in the one he sent." So they said to him, "What sign can you do, that we may see and believe in you? What can you do? Our ancestors ate manna in the desert, as it is written:

'He gave them bread from heaven to eat.'"

So Jesus said to them, "Amen, amen, I say to you, it was not Moses who gave the bread from heaven; my Father gives you the true bread from heaven. For the bread of God is that which comes down from heaven and gives life to the world."

So they said to him, "Sir, give us this bread always." Jesus said to them, "I am the bread of life; whoever comes to me will never hunger, and whoever believes in me will never thirst."

EIGHTEENTH SUNDAY IN ORDINARY TIME / C 631

READING I *Ecclesiastes 1:2; 2:21-23 / 114*

Vanity of vanities, says Qoheleth,
    vanity of vanities! All things are vanity!

Here is one who has labored with wisdom and knowledge and skill, and yet to another who has not labored over it, he must leave property. This also is vanity and a great misfortune. For what profit comes to man from all the toil and anxiety of heart with which he has labored under the sun? All his days sorrow and grief are his occupation; even at night his mind is not at rest. This also is vanity.

RESPONSORIAL PSALM *Psalm 90:3-4, 5-6, 12-13, 14, 17*

If to - day you hear his voice,

hard - en not your hearts.

You turn man back to dust,
saying, "Return, O children of men."
For a thousand years in your sight
are as yesterday, now that it is past,
or as a watch of the night. ℟.

You make an end of them in their sleep;
the next morning they are like the
    changing grass,
which at dawn springs up anew,
but by evening wilts and fades. ℟.

Teach us to number our days aright,
that we may gain wisdom of heart.
Return, O Lord! How long?
Have pity on your servants! ℟.

Fill us at daybreak with your kindness,
that we may shout for joy and gladness
    all our days.
And may the gracious care of the Lord
    our God be ours;
prosper the work of our hands for us!
Prosper the work of our hands! ℟.

READING II *Colossians 3:1-5, 9-11*

Brothers and sisters: If you were raised with Christ, seek what is above, where Christ is seated at the right hand of God. Think of what is above, not of what is on earth. For you have died, and your life is hidden with Christ in God. When Christ your life appears, then you too will appear with him in glory.

Put to death, then, the parts of you that are earthly: immorality, impurity, passion, evil desire, and the greed that is idolatry. Stop lying to one another, since you have taken off the old self with its practices and have put on the new self, which is being renewed, for knowledge, in the image of its creator. Here there is not Greek and Jew, circumcision and uncircumcision, barbarian, Scythian, slave, free; but Christ is all and in all.

GOSPEL *Luke 12:13-21*

Someone in the crowd said to Jesus, "Teacher, tell my brother to share the inheritance with me." He replied to him, "Friend, who appointed me as your judge and arbitrator?" Then he said to the crowd, "Take care to guard against all greed, for though one may be rich, one's life does not consist of possessions."

Then he told them a parable. "There was a rich man whose land produced a bountiful harvest. He asked himself, 'What shall I do, for I do not have space to store my harvest?' And he said, 'This is what I shall do: I shall tear down my barns and build larger ones. There I shall store all my grain and other goods and I shall say to myself, "Now as for you, you have so many good things stored up for many years, rest, eat, drink, be merry!"' But God said to him, 'You fool, this night your life will be demanded of you; and the things you have prepared, to whom will they belong?' Thus will it be for all who store up treasure for themselves but are not rich in what matters to God."

632 NINETEENTH SUNDAY IN ORDINARY TIME / A

READING I *1 Kings 19:9a, 11-13a / 115*

At the mountain of God, Horeb, Elijah came to a cave where he took shelter. Then the LORD said to him, "Go outside and stand on the mountain before the LORD; the LORD will be passing by." A strong and heavy wind was rending the mountains and crushing rocks before the LORD— but the LORD was not in the wind. After the wind there was an earthquake— but the LORD was not in the earthquake. After the earthquake there was fire— but the LORD was not in the fire. After the fire there was a tiny whispering sound. When he heard this, Elijah hid his face in his cloak and went and stood at the entrance of the cave.

RESPONSORIAL PSALM *Psalm 85:9, 10, 11-12, 13-14*

Lord, let us see your kind- ness, and grant us your sal - va - tion.

I will hear what God proclaims;
   the Lord — for he proclaims peace.
Near indeed is his salvation to those who
      fear him,
   glory dwelling in our land. ℟.

Kindness and truth shall meet;
   justice and peace shall kiss.

Truth shall spring out of the earth,
   and justice shall look down from
      heaven. ℟.

The Lord himself will give his benefits;
   our land shall yield its increase.
Justice shall walk before him,
   and prepare the way of his steps. ℟.

READING II *Romans 9:1-5*

Brothers and sisters: I speak the truth in Christ, I do not lie; my conscience joins with the Holy Spirit in bearing me witness that I have great sorrow and constant anguish in my heart. For I could wish that I myself were accursed and cut off from Christ for the sake of my own people, my kindred according to the flesh. They are Israelites; theirs the adoption, the glory, the covenants, the giving of the law, the worship, and the promises; theirs the patriarchs, and from them, according to the flesh, is the Christ, who is over all, God blessed forever. Amen.

GOSPEL *Matthew 14:22-33*

After he had fed the people, Jesus made the disciples get into a boat and precede him to the other side, while he dismissed the crowds. After doing so, he went up on the mountain by himself to pray. When it was evening he was there alone. Meanwhile the boat, already a few miles offshore, was being tossed about by the waves, for the wind was against it. During the fourth watch of the night, he came toward them walking on the sea. When the disciples saw him walking on the sea they were terrified. "It is a ghost," they said, and they cried out in fear. At once Jesus spoke to them, "Take courage, it is I; do not be afraid." Peter said to him in reply, "Lord, if it is you, command me to come to you on the water." He said, "Come." Peter got out of the boat and began to walk on the water toward Jesus. But when he saw how strong the wind was he became frightened; and, beginning to sink, he cried out, "Lord, save me!" Immediately Jesus stretched out his hand and caught Peter, and said to him, "O you of little faith, why did you doubt?" After they got into the boat, the wind died down. Those who were in the boat did him homage, saying, "Truly, you are the Son of God."

NINETEENTH SUNDAY IN ORDINARY TIME / B   633

READING I
1 Kings 19:4-8 / 116

Elijah went a day's journey into the desert, until he came to a broom tree and sat beneath it. He prayed for death, saying: "This is enough, O LORD! Take my life, for I am no better than my fathers." He lay down and fell asleep under the broom tree, but then an angel touched him and ordered him to get up and eat. Elijah looked and there at his head was a hearth cake and a jug of water. After he ate and drank, he lay down again, but the angel of the LORD came back a second time, touched him, and ordered, "Get up and eat, else the journey will be too long for you!" He got up, ate, and drank; then strengthened by that food, he walked forty days and forty nights to the mountain of God, Horeb.

RESPONSORIAL PSALM
Psalm 34:2-3, 4-5, 6-7, 8-9

Taste and see the good - ness of the Lord.

I will bless the Lord at all times;
  his praise shall be ever in my mouth.
Let my soul glory in the Lord;
  the lowly will hear me and be glad. ℟.

Glorify the Lord with me,
  let us together extol his name.
I sought the Lord, and he answered me
  and delivered me from all my
    fears. ℟.

Look to him that you may be radiant
  with joy.

And your faces may not blush with
  shame.
When the afflicted man called out, the
  Lord heard,
And from all his distress he saved
  him. ℟.

The angel of the Lord encamps
  around those who fear him and
    delivers them.
Taste and see how good the Lord is;
  blessed the man who takes refuge in
    him. ℟.

READING II
Ephesians 4:30—5:2

Brothers and sisters: Do not grieve the Holy Spirit of God, with which you were sealed for the day of redemption. All bitterness, fury, anger, shouting, and reviling must be removed from you, along with all malice. And be kind to one another, compassionate, forgiving one another as God has forgiven you in Christ.

So be imitators of God, as beloved children, and live in love, as Christ loved us and handed himself over for us as a sacrificial offering to God for a fragrant aroma.

GOSPEL   *John 6:41-51*

The Jews murmured about Jesus because he said, "I am the bread that came down from heaven," and they said, "Is this not Jesus, the son of Joseph? Do we not know his father and mother? Then how can he say, 'I have come down from heaven'?" Jesus answered and said to them, "Stop murmuring among yourselves. No one can come to me unless the Father who sent me draw him, and I will raise him on the last day. It is written in the prophets:

'They shall all be taught by God.'

Everyone who listens to my Father and learns from him comes to me. Not that anyone has seen the Father except the one who is from God; he has seen the Father. Amen, amen, I say to you, whoever believes has eternal life. I am the bread of life. Your ancestors ate the manna in the desert, but they died; this is the bread that comes down from heaven so that one may eat it and not die. I am the living bread that came down from heaven; whoever eats this bread will live forever; and the bread that I will give is my flesh for the life of the world."

---

634   NINETEENTH SUNDAY IN ORDINARY TIME / C

READING I   *Wisdom 18:6-9 / 117*

The night of the passover was known beforehand to our fathers,
    that, with sure knowledge of the oaths in which they put their faith,
    they might have courage.
Your people awaited the salvation of the just
    and the destruction of their foes.
For when you punished our adversaries,
    in this you glorified us whom you had summoned.
For in secret the holy children of the good were offering sacrifice
    and putting into effect with one accord the divine institution.

RESPONSORIAL PSALM   *Psalm 33:1, 12, 18-19, 20, 22*

Bless-ed the peo-ple the Lord has cho - sen to be his own.

Exult, you just, in the Lord;
    praise from the upright is fitting.
Blessed the nation whose God is the
    Lord,
    the people he has chosen for his own
      inheritance. ℟.

See, the eyes of the Lord are upon those
    who fear him,
    upon those who hope for his

kindness,
to deliver them from death
    and preserve them in spite of
    famine. ℟.

Our soul waits for the Lord,
    who is our help and our shield.
May your kindness, O Lord, be upon us
    who have put our hope in you. ℟.

READING II   *Hebrews 11:1-2, 8-19 or 11:1-2, 8-12*

For short form read only the part in brackets.

[Brothers and sisters: Faith is the realization of what is hoped for and evidence of things not seen. Because of it the ancients were well attested.

By faith Abraham obeyed when he was called to go out to a place that he was to receive as an inheritance; he went out, not knowing where he was to go. By faith he sojourned in the promised land as in a foreign country, dwelling in tents with Isaac and

Jacob, heirs of the same promise; for he was looking forward to the city with foundations, whose architect and maker is God. By faith he received power to generate, even though he was past the normal age —and Sarah herself was sterile— for he thought that the one who had made the promise was trustworthy. So it was that there came forth from one man, himself as good as dead, descendants as numerous as the stars in the sky and as countless as the sands on the seashore.]

All these died in faith. They did not receive what had been promised but saw it and greeted it from afar and acknowledged themselves to be strangers and aliens on earth, for those who speak thus show that they are seeking a homeland. If they had been thinking of the land from which they had come, they would have had opportunity to return. But now they desire a better homeland, a heavenly one. Therefore, God is not ashamed to be called their God, for he has prepared a city for them.

By faith Abraham, when put to the test, offered up Isaac, and he who had received the promises was ready to offer his only son, of whom it was said, "Through Isaac descendants shall bear your name." He reasoned that God was able to raise even from the dead, and he received Isaac back as a symbol.

GOSPEL
Luke 12:32-48 or 12:35-40

For short form read only the parts in brackets.

[Jesus said to his disciples:] "Do not be afraid any longer, little flock, for your Father is pleased to give you the kingdom. Sell your belongings and give alms. Provide money bags for yourselves that do not wear out, an inexhaustible treasure in heaven that no thief can reach nor moth destroy. For where your treasure is, there also will your heart be.

["Gird your loins and light your lamps and be like servants who await their master's return from a wedding, ready to open immediately when he comes and knocks. Blessed are those servants whom the master finds vigilant on his arrival. Amen, I say to you, he will gird himself, have them recline at table, and proceed to wait on them. And should he come in the second or third watch and find them prepared in this way, blessed are those servants. Be sure of this: if the master of the house had known the hour when the thief was coming, he would not have let his house be broken into. You also must be prepared, for at an hour you do not expect, the Son of Man will come."]

Then Peter said, "Lord, is this parable meant for us or for everyone?" And the Lord replied, "Who, then, is the faithful and prudent steward whom the master will put in charge of his servants to distribute the food allowance at the proper time? Blessed is that servant whom his master on arrival finds doing so. Truly, I say to you, the master will put the servant in charge of all his property. But if that servant says to himself, 'My master is delayed in coming,' and begins to beat the menservants and the maidservants, to eat and drink and get drunk, then that servant's master will come on an unexpected day and at an unknown hour and will punish the servant severely and assign him a place with the unfaithful. That servant who knew his master's will but did not make preparations nor act in accord with his will shall be beaten severely; and the servant who was ignorant of his master's will but acted in a way deserving of a severe beating shall be beaten only lightly. Much will be required of the person entrusted with much, and still more will be demanded of the person entrusted with more."

TWENTIETH SUNDAY IN ORDINARY TIME / A
635

READING I
Isaiah 56:1, 6-7 / 118

Thus says the Lord:
Observe what is right, do what is just;
    for my salvation is about to come,
    my justice, about to be revealed.

The foreigners who join themselves to

the Lord,
    ministering to him,
loving the name of the Lord,
    and becoming his servants—
all who keep the sabbath free from
    profanation

and hold to my covenant,
them I will bring to my holy mountain
and make joyful in my house of
prayer;

their burnt offerings and sacrifices
will be acceptable on my altar,
for my house shall be called
a house of prayer for all peoples.

RESPONSORIAL PSALM
Psalm 67:2-3, 5, 6, 8

O God, O God, let all the na-tions praise you!

May God have pity on us and bless us;
may he let his face shine upon us.
So may your way be known upon earth;
among all nations, your salvation. ℟.

May the peoples praise you, O God;
may all the peoples praise you!
May God bless us,
and may all the ends of the earth
fear him! ℟.

May the nations be glad and exult
because you rule the peoples in equity;
the nations on the earth you guide. ℟.

READING II
Romans 11:13-15, 29-32

Brothers and sisters: I am speaking to you Gentiles. Inasmuch as I am the apostle to the Gentiles, I glory in my ministry in order to make my race jealous and thus save some of them. For if their rejection is the reconciliation of the world, what will their acceptance be but life from the dead?

For the gifts and the call of God are irrevocable. Just as you once disobeyed God but have now received mercy because of their disobedience, so they have now disobeyed in order that, by virtue of the mercy shown to you, they too may now receive mercy. For God delivered all to disobedience, that he might have mercy upon all.

GOSPEL
Matthew 15:21-28

At that time, Jesus withdrew to the region of Tyre and Sidon. And behold, a Canaanite woman of that district came and called out, "Have pity on me, Lord, Son of David! My daughter is tormented by a demon." But Jesus did not say a word in answer to her. Jesus' disciples came and asked him, "Send her away, for she keeps calling out after us." He said in reply, "I was sent only to the lost sheep of the house of Israel." But the woman came and did Jesus homage, saying, "Lord, help me." He said in reply, "It is not right to take the food of the children and throw it to the dogs." She said, "Please, Lord, for even the dogs eat the scraps that fall from the table of their masters." Then Jesus said to her in reply, "O woman, great is your faith! Let it be done for you as you wish." And the woman's daughter was healed from that hour.

636 TWENTIETH SUNDAY IN ORDINARY TIME / B

READING I
Proverbs 9:1-6 / 119

Wisdom has built her house,
she has set up her seven columns;
she has dressed her meat, mixed her wine,
yes, she has spread her table.
She has sent out her maidens; she calls
from the heights out over the city:
"Let whoever is simple turn in here;

To the one who lacks understanding,
she says,
Come, eat of my food,
and drink of the wine I have mixed!
Forsake foolishness that you may live;
advance in the way of
understanding."

RESPONSORIAL PSALM *Psalm 34:2-3, 4-5, 6-7*

Taste and see the good-ness of the Lord.

I will bless the Lord at all times;
    his praise shall be ever in my mouth.
Let my soul glory in the Lord;
    the lowly will hear me and be glad. ℟.

Glorify the Lord with me,
    let us together extol his name.
I sought the Lord, and he answered me
    and delivered me from all my fears. ℟.

READING II *Ephesians 5:15-20*

Brothers and sisters: Watch carefully how you live, not as foolish persons but as wise, making the most of the opportunity, because the days are evil. Therefore, do not continue in ignorance, but try to understand what is the will of the Lord. And do not get drunk on wine, in which lies debauchery, but be filled with the Spirit, addressing one another in psalms and hymns and spiritual songs, singing and playing to the Lord in your hearts, giving thanks always and for everything in the name of our Lord Jesus Christ to God the Father.

GOSPEL *John 6:51-58*

Jesus said to the crowds: "I am the living bread that came down from heaven; whoever eats this bread will live forever; and the bread that I will give is my flesh for the life of the world."

The Jews quarreled among themselves, saying, "How can this man give us his flesh to eat?" Jesus said to them, "Amen, amen, I say to you, unless you eat the flesh of the Son of Man and drink his blood, you do not have life within you. Whoever eats my flesh and drinks my blood has eternal life, and I will raise him on the last day. For my flesh is true food, and my blood is true drink. Whoever eats my flesh and drinks my blood remains in me and I in him. Just as the living Father sent me and I have life because of the Father, so also the one who feeds on me will have life because of me. This is the bread that came down from heaven. Unlike your ancestors who ate and still died, whoever eats this bread will live forever."

TWENTIETH SUNDAY IN ORDINARY TIME / C 637

READING I *Jeremiah 38:4-6, 8-10 / 120*

In those days, the princes said to the king: "Jeremiah ought to be put to death; he is demoralizing the soldiers who are left in this city, and all the people, by speaking such things to them; he is not interested in the welfare of our people, but in their ruin." King Zedekiah answered: "He is in your power"; for the king could do nothing with them. And so they took Jeremiah and threw him into the cistern of Prince Malchiah, which was in the quarters of the guard, letting him down with ropes. There was no water in the cistern, only mud, and Jeremiah sank into the mud.

Ebed-melech, a court official, went there from the palace and said to him: "My lord king, these men have been at fault in all they have done to the prophet Jeremiah, casting him into the cistern. He will die of famine on the spot, for there is no more food in the city." Then the king ordered Ebed-melech the Cushite to take three men along with him, and draw the prophet Jeremiah out of the cistern before he should die.

RESPONSORIAL PSALM *Psalm 40:2, 3, 4, 18*

Lord, come to my aid,

Lord, come to my aid!

I have waited, waited for the Lord,
and he stooped toward me. ℟.

The Lord heard my cry.
He drew me out of the pit of destruction,
out of the mud of the swamp;
he set my feet upon a crag;
he made firm my steps. ℟.

And he put a new song into my mouth,
a hymn to our God.
Many shall look on in awe
and trust in the Lord. ℟.

Though I am afflicted and poor,
yet the Lord thinks of me.
You are my help and my deliverer;
O my God, hold not back! ℟.

READING II *Hebrews 12:1-4*

Brothers and sisters: Since we are surrounded by so great a cloud of witnesses, let us rid ourselves of every burden and sin that clings to us and persevere in running the race that lies before us while keeping our eyes fixed on Jesus, the leader and perfecter of faith. For the sake of the joy that lay before him he endured the cross, despising its shame, and has taken his seat at the right of the throne of God. Consider how he endured such opposition from sinners, in order that you may not grow weary and lose heart. In your struggle against sin you have not yet resisted to the point of shedding blood.

GOSPEL *Luke 12:49-53*

Jesus said to his disciples: "I have come to set the earth on fire, and how I wish it were already blazing! There is a baptism with which I must be baptized, and how great is my anguish until it is accomplished! Do you think that I have come to establish peace on the earth? No, I tell you, but rather division. From now on a household of five will be divided, three against two and two against three; a father will be divided against his son and a son against his father, a mother against her daughter and a daughter against her mother, a mother-in-law against her daughter-in-law and a daughter-in-law against her mother-in-law."

638 **TWENTY-FIRST SUNDAY IN ORDINARY TIME / A**

READING I *Isaiah 22:19-23 / 121*

Thus says the Lord to Shebna, master of the palace:
"I will thrust you from your office
and pull you down from your station.
On that day I will summon my servant
Eliakim, son of Hilkiah;
I will clothe him with your robe,
and gird him with your sash,
and give over to him your authority.

He shall be a father to the inhabitants of
Jerusalem,
and to the House of Judah.
I will place the key of the House of
David on Eliakim's shoulder;
when he opens, no one shall shut,
when he shuts, no one shall open.
I will fix him like a peg in a sure spot,
to be a place of honor for his family."

RESPONSORIAL PSALM

Psalm 138:1-2, 2-3, 6, 8

Lord, your love is e - ter - nal; do not for-sake the work of your hands.

I will give thanks to you, O Lord, with
all my heart,
for you have heard the words of my
mouth;
in the presence of the angels I will sing
your praise;
I will worship at your holy temple. ℟.

I will give thanks to your name,
because of your kindness and your
truth:
when I called, you answered me;
you built up strength within me. ℟.

The Lord is exalted, yet the lowly he
sees,
and the proud he knows from afar.
Your kindness, O Lord, endures forever;
forsake not the work of your
hands. ℟.

READING II

Romans 11:33-36

Oh, the depth of the riches and wisdom and knowledge of God! How inscrutable are his judgments and how unsearchable his ways!

'For who has known the mind of the Lord
or who has been his counselor?
Or who has given the Lord anything
that he may be repaid?'

For from him and through him and for him are all things. To him be glory forever. Amen.

GOSPEL

Matthew 16:13-20

Jesus went into the region of Caesarea Philippi and he asked his disciples, "Who do people say that the Son of Man is?" They replied, "Some say John the Baptist, others Elijah, still others Jeremiah or one of the prophets." He said to them, "But who do you say that I am?" Simon Peter said in reply, "You are the Christ, the Son of the living God." Jesus said to him in reply, "Blessed are you, Simon son of Jonah. For flesh and blood has not revealed this to you, but my heavenly Father. And so I say to you, you are Peter, and upon this rock I will build my church, and the gates of the netherworld shall not prevail against it. I will give you the keys to the kingdom of heaven. Whatever you bind on earth shall be bound in heaven; and whatever you loose on earth shall be loosed in heaven." Then he strictly ordered his disciples to tell no one that he was the Christ.

TWENTY-FIRST SUNDAY IN ORDINARY TIME / B 639

READING I

Joshua 24:1-2a, 15-17, 18b / 122

Joshua gathered together all the tribes of Israel at Shechem, summoning their elders, their leaders, their judges, and their officers. When they stood in ranks before God, Joshua addressed all the people: "If it does not please you to serve the LORD, decide today whom you will serve, the gods your fathers served beyond the River or the gods of the Amorites in whose country you are now dwelling. As for me and my household, we will serve the LORD."

But the people answered, "Far be it from us to forsake the LORD for the service of other gods. For it was the LORD, our God, who brought us and our fathers up out of the land of Egypt, out of a state of slavery. He performed those great miracles before our very eyes and protected us along our entire journey and among the peoples through whom we passed. Therefore we also will serve the LORD, for he is our God."

RESPONSORIAL PSALM   *Psalm 34:2-3, 16-17, 18-19, 20-21*

Taste and see the good-ness of the Lord.

I will bless the Lord at all times;
  his praise shall be ever in my mouth.
Let my soul glory in the Lord;
  the lowly will hear me and be glad. ℞.

The Lord has eyes for the just,
  and ears for their cry.
The Lord confronts the evildoers,
  to destroy remembrance of them
  from the earth. ℞.

When the just cry out, the Lord hears

them,
  and from all their distress he rescues
  them.
The Lord is close to the brokenhearted;
  and those who are crushed in spirit
  he saves. ℞.

Many are the troubles of the just one,
  but out of them all the Lord delivers
  him;
he watches over all his bones;
  not one of them shall be broken. ℞.

READING II   *Ephesians 5:21-32 or 5:2a, 25-32*

For long form, omit the phrase in double brackets; for short form read only the parts in brackets.

[Brothers and sisters:] [[Live in love, as Christ loved us.]] Be subordinate to one another out of reverence for Christ. Wives should be subordinate to their husbands as to the Lord. For the husband is head of his wife just as Christ is head of the church, he himself the savior of the body. As the church is subordinate to Christ, so wives should be subordinate to their husbands in everything. [Husbands, love your wives, even as Christ loved the church and handed himself over for her to sanctify her, cleansing her by the bath of water with the word, that he might present to himself the church in splendor, without spot or wrinkle or any such thing, that she might be holy and without blemish. So also husbands should love their wives as their own bodies. He who loves his wife loves himself. For no one hates his own flesh but rather nourishes and cherishes it, even as Christ does the church, because we are members of his body.
  'For this reason a man shall leave his father and his mother
      and be joined to his wife,
    and the two shall become one flesh.'
This is a great mystery, but I speak in reference to Christ and the church.]

GOSPEL   *John 6:60-69*

Many of Jesus' disciples who were listening said, "This saying is hard; who can accept it?" Since Jesus knew that his disciples were murmuring about this, he said to them, "Does this shock you? What if you were to see the Son of Man ascending to where he was before? It is the spirit that gives life, while the flesh is of no avail. The words I have spoken to you are Spirit and life. But there are some of you who do not believe." Jesus knew from the beginning the ones who would not believe and the one who would betray him. And he said, "For this reason I have told you that no one can come to me unless it is granted him by my Father."

As a result of this, many of his disciples returned to their former way of life and no longer accompanied him. Jesus then said to the Twelve, "Do you also want to leave?" Simon Peter answered him, "Master, to whom shall we go? You have the words of eternal life. We have come to believe and are convinced that you are the Holy One of God."

TWENTY-FIRST SUNDAY IN ORDINARY TIME / C   640

READING I   *Isaiah 66:18-21 / 123*

Thus says the LORD: I know their works and their thoughts, and I come to gather nations of every language; they shall come and see my glory. I will set a sign among them; from them I will send fugitives to the nations: to Tarshish, Put and Lud, Mosoch, Tubal and Javan, to the distant coastlands that have never heard of my fame, or seen my glory; and they shall proclaim my glory among the nations. They shall bring all your brothers and sisters from all the nations as an offering to the LORD, on horses and in chariots, in carts, upon mules and dromedaries, to Jerusalem, my holy mountain, says the LORD, just as the Israelites bring their offering to the house of the LORD in clean vessels. Some of these I will take as priests and Levites, says the LORD.

RESPONSORIAL PSALM   *Psalm 117:1-2*

Go out to all the world and tell the Good News.

Praise the Lord, all you nations; glorify him, all you peoples! ℟.

For steadfast is his kindness toward us, and the fidelity of the Lord endures forever. ℟.

READING II   *Hebrews 12:5-7, 11-13*

Brothers and sisters, You have forgotten the exhortation addressed to you as children:
"My son, do not disdain the discipline of the Lord
    or lose heart when reproved by him;
for whom the Lord loves, he disciplines;
    he scourges every son he acknowledges."
Endure your trials as "discipline"; God treats you as sons. For what "son" is there whom his father does not discipline? At the time, all discipline seems a cause not for joy but for pain, yet later it brings the peaceful fruit of righteousness to those who are trained by it.

So strengthen your drooping hands and your weak knees. Make straight paths for your feet, that what is lame may not be disjointed but healed.

GOSPEL   *Luke 13:22-30*

Jesus passed through towns and villages, teaching as he went and making his way to Jerusalem. Someone asked him, "Lord, will only a few people be saved?" He answered them, "Strive to enter through the narrow gate, for many, I tell you, will attempt to enter but will not be strong enough. After the master of the house has arisen and locked the door, then will you stand outside knocking and saying, 'Lord, open the door for us.' He will say to you in reply, 'I do not know where you are from.' And you will say, 'We ate and drank in your company and you taught in our streets.' Then he will say to you, 'I do not know where you are from. Depart from me, all you evildoers!' And there will be wailing and grinding of teeth when you see Abraham, Isaac, and Jacob and all the prophets in the kingdom of God and you yourselves cast out. And people will come from the east and the west and from the north and the south and will recline at table in the kingdom of God. For behold, some are last who will be first, and some are first who will be last."

641   TWENTY-SECOND SUNDAY IN ORDINARY TIME / A

READING I
Jeremiah 20:7-9 / 124

You duped me, O LORD, and I let myself
   be duped;
     you were too strong for me, and you
      triumphed.
All the day I am an object of laughter;
   everyone mocks me.

Whenever I speak, I must cry out,
   violence and outrage is my message;
the word of the LORD has brought me

derision and reproach all the day.

I say to myself, I will not mention him,
   I will speak in his name no more.
But then it becomes like fire burning in
   my heart,
   imprisoned in my bones;
I grow weary holding it in, I cannot
   endure it.

RESPONSORIAL PSALM
Psalm 63:2, 3-4, 5-6, 8-9

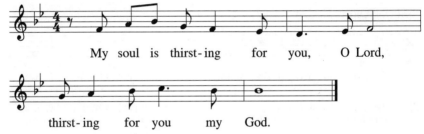

My soul is thirst-ing for you, O Lord, thirst-ing for you my God.

O God, you are my God whom I seek;
   for you my flesh pines and my soul
     thirsts
like the earth, parched, lifeless and
   without water. ℟.

Thus have I gazed toward you in the
   sanctuary
   to see your power and your glory,
for your kindness is a greater good than
   life;
   my lips shall glorify you. ℟.

Thus will I bless you while I live;
   lifting up my hands, I will call upon
     your name.
As with the riches of a banquet shall my
   soul be satisfied,
   and with exultant lips my mouth
     shall praise you. ℟.

You are my help,
   and in the shadow of your wings I
     shout for joy.
My soul clings fast to you;
   your right hand upholds me. ℟.

READING II
Romans 12:1-2

I urge you, brothers and sisters, by the mercies of God, to offer your bodies as a living sacrifice, holy and pleasing to God, your spiritual worship. Do not conform yourselves to this age but be transformed by the renewal of your mind, that you may discern what is the will of God, what is good and pleasing and perfect.

GOSPEL
Matthew 16:21-27

Jesus began to show his disciples that he must go to Jerusalem and suffer greatly from the elders, the chief priests, and the scribes, and be killed and on the third day be raised.

Then Peter took Jesus aside and began to rebuke him, "God forbid, Lord! No such thing shall ever happen to you." He turned and said to Peter, "Get behind me, Satan! You are an obstacle to me. You are thinking not as God does, but as human beings do."

Then Jesus said to his disciples, "Whoever wishes to come after me must deny himself, take up his cross, and follow me. For whoever wishes to save his life will lose it, but whoever loses his life for my sake will find it. What profit would there be for one to gain the whole world and forfeit his life? Or what can one give in exchange for his life? For the Son of Man will come with his angels in his Father's glory, and then he will repay all according to his conduct."

TWENTY-SECOND SUNDAY IN ORDINARY TIME / B   642

READING I   *Deuteronomy 4:1-2, 6-8 / 125*

Moses said to the people: "Now, Israel, hear the statutes and decrees which I am teaching you to observe, that you may live, and may enter in and take possession of the land which the LORD, the God of your fathers, is giving you. In your observance of the commandments of the LORD, your God, which I enjoin upon you, you shall not add to what I command you nor subtract from it. Observe them carefully, for thus will you give evidence of your wisdom and intelligence to the nations, who will hear of all these statutes and say, 'This great nation is truly a wise and intelligent people.' For what great nation is there that has gods so close to it as the LORD, our God, is to us whenever we call upon him? Or what great nation has statutes and decrees that are as just as this whole law which I am setting before you today?"

RESPONSORIAL PSALM   *Psalm 15:2-3, 3-4, 4-5*

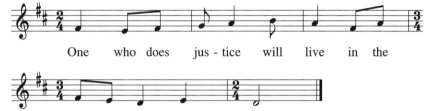

One who does jus-tice will live in the pres-ence of the Lord.

Whoever walks blamelessly and does justice;
    who thinks the truth in his heart
and slanders not with his tongue. ℟.

Who harms not his fellow man,
    nor takes up a reproach against his neighbor;
by whom the reprobate is despised,
    while he honors those who fear the Lord. ℟.

Who lends not his money at usury
    and accepts no bribe against the innocent.
Whoever does these things
    shall never be disturbed. ℟.

READING II   *James 1:17-18, 21b-22, 27*

Dearest brothers and sisters: All good giving and every perfect gift is from above, coming down from the Father of lights, with whom there is no alteration or shadow caused by change. He willed to give us birth by the word of truth that we may be a kind of firstfruits of his creatures.

Humbly welcome the word that has been planted in you and is able to save your souls. Be doers of the word and not hearers only, deluding yourselves.

Religion that is pure and undefiled before God and the Father is this: to care for orphans and widows in their affliction and to keep oneself unstained by the world.

GOSPEL   *Mark 7:1-8, 14-15, 21-23*

When the Pharisees with some scribes who had come from Jerusalem gathered around Jesus, they observed that some of his disciples ate their meals with unclean, that is, unwashed, hands. (For the Pharisees and, in fact, all Jews, do not eat without carefully washing their hands, keeping the tradition of the elders. And on coming from the marketplace they do not eat without purifying themselves. And there are many other things that they have traditionally observed, the purification of cups and jugs and kettles [and beds].) So the Pharisees and scribes questioned him, "Why do your disciples not follow the tradition of the elders but instead eat a meal with unclean hands?" He responded, "Well did Isaiah prophesy about you hypocrites, as it is written:

'This people honors me with their lips,
> but their hearts are far from me;
in vain do they worship me,
> teaching as doctrines human precepts.'

You disregard God's commandment but cling to human tradition."

He summoned the crowd again and said to them, "Hear me, all of you, and understand. Nothing that enters one from outside can defile that person; but the things that come out from within are what defile.

"From within people, from their hearts, come evil thoughts, unchastity, theft, murder, adultery, greed, malice, deceit, licentiousness, envy, blasphemy, arrogance, folly. All these evils come from within and they defile."

643   TWENTY-SECOND SUNDAY IN ORDINARY TIME / C

READING I   *Sirach 3:17-18, 20, 28-29 / 126*

My child, conduct your affairs with
> humility,
>> and you will be loved more than a
>> giver of gifts.
Humble yourself the more, the greater
> you are,
>> and you will find favor with God.
What is too sublime for you, seek not,
into things beyond your strength
> search not.
The mind of a sage appreciates proverbs,
> and an attentive ear is the joy of the
> wise.
Water quenches a flaming fire,
> and alms atone for sins.

RESPONSORIAL PSALM   *Psalm 68:4-5, 6-7, 10-11*

God, in your good-ness, you have made a home for the poor.

The just rejoice and exult before God;
> they are glad and rejoice.
Sing to God, chant praise to his name;
> whose name is the Lord. ℟.

The father of orphans and the defender
> of widows
> is God in his holy dwelling.
God gives a home to the forsaken;
> he leads forth prisoners to
> prosperity. ℟.

A bountiful rain you showered down, O
    God, upon your inheritance;
    you restored the land when it
      languished;

your flock settled in it;
    in your goodness, O God, you
      provided it for the needy. ℟.

READING II
Hebrews 12:18-19, 22-24a

Brothers and sisters: You have not approached that which could be touched and a blazing fire and gloomy darkness and storm and a trumpet blast and a voice speaking words such that those who heard begged that no message be further addressed to them. No, you have approached Mount Zion and the city of the living God, the heavenly Jerusalem, and countless angels in festal gathering, and the assembly of the firstborn enrolled in heaven, and God the judge of all, and the spirits of the just made perfect, and Jesus, the mediator of a new covenant, and the sprinkled blood that speaks more eloquently than that of Abel.

GOSPEL
Luke 14:1, 7-14

On a sabbath Jesus went to dine at the home of one of the leading Pharisees, and the people there were observing him carefully.

He told a parable to those who had been invited, noticing how they were choosing the places of honor at the table. "When you are invited by someone to a wedding banquet, do not recline at table in the place of honor. A more distinguished guest than you may have been invited by him, and the host who invited both of you may approach you and say, 'Give your place to this man,' and then you would proceed with embarrassment to take the lowest place. Rather, when you are invited, go and take the lowest place so that when the host comes to you he may say, 'My friend, move up to a higher position.' Then you will enjoy the esteem of your companions at the table. For everyone who exalts himself will be humbled, but the one who humbles himself will be exalted." Then he said to the host who invited him, "When you hold a lunch or a dinner, do not invite your friends or your brothers or your relatives or your wealthy neighbors, in case they may invite you back and you have repayment. Rather, when you hold a banquet, invite the poor, the crippled, the lame, the blind; blessed indeed will you be because of their inability to repay you. For you will be repaid at the resurrection of the righteous."

TWENTY-THIRD SUNDAY IN ORDINARY TIME / A
644

READING I
Ezekiel 33:7-9 / 127

Thus says the LORD: You, son of man, I have appointed watchman for the house of Israel; when you hear me say anything, you shall warn them for me. If I tell the wicked, "O wicked one, you shall surely die," and you do not speak out to dissuade the wicked from his way, the wicked shall die for his guilt, but I will hold you responsible for his death. But if you warn the wicked, trying to turn him from his way, and he refuses to turn from his way, he shall die for his guilt, but you shall save yourself.

RESPONSORIAL PSALM
Psalm 95:1-2, 6-7, 8-9

If to-day you hear his voice,

hard-en not your hearts.

Come, let us sing joyfully to the Lord;
  let us acclaim the rock of our
    salvation.
Let us come into his presence with
    thanksgiving;
  let us joyfully sing psalms to him. ℟.

Come, let us bow down in worship;
  let us kneel before the Lord who
    made us.
For he is our God,
  and we are the people he shepherds,
    the flock he guides. ℟.

Oh, that today you would hear his voice:
  "Harden not your hearts as at
    Meribah,
as in the day of Massah in the desert,
  Where your fathers tempted me;
they tested me though they had seen my
    works." ℟.

READING II   Romans 13:8-10

Brothers and sisters: Owe nothing to anyone, except to love one another; for the one who loves another has fulfilled the law. The commandments, "You shall not commit adultery; you shall not kill; you shall not steal; you shall not covet," and whatever other commandment there may be, are summed up in this saying, namely, "You shall love your neighbor as yourself." Love does no evil to the neighbor; hence, love is the fulfillment of the law.

GOSPEL   Matthew 18:15-20

Jesus said to his disciples: "If your brother sins against you, go and tell him his fault between you and him alone. If he listens to you, you have won over your brother. If he does not listen, take one or two others along with you, so that 'every fact may be established on the testimony of two or three witnesses.' If he refuses to listen to them, tell the church. If he refuses to listen even to the church, then treat him as you would a Gentile or a tax collector. Amen, I say to you, whatever you bind on earth shall be bound in heaven, and whatever you loose on earth shall be loosed in heaven. Again, amen, I say to you, if two of you agree on earth about anything for which they are to pray, it shall be granted to them by my heavenly Father. For where two or three are gathered together in my name, there am I in the midst of them."

645 TWENTY-THIRD SUNDAY IN ORDINARY TIME / B

READING I   Isaiah 35:4-7a / 128

Thus says the LORD:
  Say to those whose hearts are frightened:
    Be strong, fear not!
  Here is your God,
    he comes with vindication;
  with divine recompense
    he comes to save you.
  Then will the eyes of the blind be opened,
    the ears of the deaf be cleared;
  then will the lame leap like a stag,
    then the tongue of the mute will sing.
  Streams will burst forth in the desert,
    and rivers in the steppe.
  The burning sands will become pools,
    and the thirsty ground, springs of water.

RESPONSORIAL PSALM   *Psalm 146:7, 8-9, 9-10*

Praise the Lord, my soul! Praise the Lord!

The God of Jacob keeps faith forever,
  secures justice for the oppressed,
  gives food to the hungry.
The Lord sets captives free. ℟.

The Lord gives sight to the blind;
  the Lord raises up those who were
    bowed down.
The Lord loves the just;

the Lord protects strangers. ℟.

The fatherless and the widow the Lord
  sustains,
but the way of the wicked he thwarts.
The Lord shall reign forever;
  your God, O Zion, through all
    generations. Alleluia. ℟.

READING II   *James 2:1-5*

My brothers and sisters, show no partiality as you adhere to the faith in our glorious Lord Jesus Christ. For if a man with gold rings and fine clothes comes into your assembly, and a poor person in shabby clothes also comes in, and you pay attention to the one wearing the fine clothes and say, "Sit here, please," while you say to the poor one, "Stand there," or "Sit at my feet," have you not made distinctions among yourselves and become judges with evil designs?

Listen, my beloved brothers and sisters. Did not God choose those who are poor in the world to be rich in faith and heirs of the kingdom that he promised to those who love him?

GOSPEL   *Mark 7:31-37*

Again Jesus left the district of Tyre and went by way of Sidon to the Sea of Galilee, into the district of the Decapolis. And people brought to him a deaf man who had a speech impediment and begged him to lay his hand on him. He took him off by himself away from the crowd. He put his finger into the man's ears and, spitting, touched his tongue; then he looked up to heaven and groaned, and said to him, "*Ephphatha!*" (that is, "Be opened!") And immediately the man's ears were opened, his speech impediment was removed, and he spoke plainly. He ordered them not to tell anyone. But the more he ordered them not to, the more they proclaimed it. They were exceedingly astonished and they said, "He has done all things well. He makes the deaf hear and the mute speak."

TWENTY-THIRD SUNDAY IN ORDINARY TIME / C   646

READING I   *Wisdom 9:13-18b / 129*

Who can know God's counsel,
  or who can conceive what the LORD
    intends?
For the deliberations of mortals are timid,
  and unsure are our plans.
For the corruptible body burdens the soul
  and the earthen shelter weighs down
    the mind
    that has many concerns.
And scarce do we guess the things on
  earth,

and what is within our grasp we
  find with difficulty;
but when things are in heaven, who
  can search them out?
Or who ever knew your counsel, except
  you had given wisdom
  and sent your holy spirit from on
    high?
And thus were the paths of those on
  earth made straight.

RESPONSORIAL PSALM   *Psalm 90:3-4, 5-6, 12-13, 14-17*

In ev-'ry age, O Lord, you have been our ref - uge.

You turn man back to dust,
    saying, "Return, O children of men."
For a thousand years in your sight
    are as yesterday, now that it is past,
    or as a watch of the night. ℟.

You make an end of them in their sleep;
    the next morning they are like the
        changing grass,
Which at dawn springs up anew,
    but by evening wilts and fades. ℟.

Teach us to number our days aright,
    that we may gain wisdom of heart.
Return, O Lord! How long?
    Have pity on your servants! ℟.

Fill us at daybreak with your kindness,
    that we may shout for joy and
        gladness all our days.
And may the gracious care of the Lord
    our God be ours;
    prosper the work of our hands for us!
Prosper the work of our hands! ℟.

READING II   *Philemon 9-10, 12-17*

I, Paul, an old man, and now also a prisoner for Christ Jesus, urge you on behalf of my child Onesimus, whose father I have become in my imprisonment; I am sending him, that is, my own heart, back to you. I should have liked to retain him for myself, so that he might serve me on your behalf in my imprisonment for the gospel, but I did not want to do anything without your consent, so that the good you do might not be forced but voluntary. Perhaps this is why he was away from you for a while, that you might have him back forever, no longer as a slave but more than a slave, a brother, beloved especially to me, but even more so to you, as a man and in the Lord. So if you regard me as a partner, welcome him as you would me.

GOSPEL   *Luke 14:25-33*

Great crowds were traveling with Jesus, and he turned and addressed them, "If anyone comes to me without hating his father and mother, wife and children, brothers and sisters, and even his own life, he cannot be my disciple. Whoever does not carry his own cross and come after me cannot be my disciple. Which of you wishing to construct a tower does not first sit down and calculate the cost to see if there is enough for its completion? Otherwise, after laying the foundation and finding himself unable to finish the work the onlookers should laugh at him and say, 'This one began to build but did not have the resources to finish.' Or what king marching into battle would not first sit down and decide whether with ten thousand troops he can successfully oppose another king advancing upon him with twenty thousand troops? But if not, while he is still far away, he will send a delegation to ask for peace terms. In the same way, anyone of you who does not renounce all his possessions cannot be my disciple."

647 TWENTY-FOURTH SUNDAY IN ORDINARY TIME / A

READING I   *Sirach 27:30—28:9 / 130*

Wrath and anger are hateful things,
    yet the sinner hugs them tight.
The vengeful will suffer the LORD's
        vengeance,
    for he remembers their sins in detail.

Forgive your neighbor's injustice;
    then when you pray, your own sins
        will be forgiven.
Could anyone nourish anger against
    another

and expect healing from the LORD?
Could anyone refuse mercy to another
like himself,
can he seek pardon for his own sins?
If one who is but flesh cherishes wrath,
who will forgive his sins?
Remember your last days, set enmity

aside;
remember death and decay, and cease
from sin!
Think of the commandments, hate not
your neighbor;
remember the Most High's covenant,
and overlook faults.

RESPONSORIAL PSALM
Psalm 103:1-2, 3-4, 9-10, 11-12

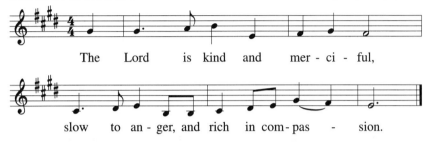

The Lord is kind and mer - ci - ful,
slow to an - ger, and rich in com - pas - sion.

Bless the Lord, O my soul;
and all my being, bless his holy name.
Bless the Lord, O my soul,
and forget not all his benefits. ℟.

He pardons all your iniquities,
heals all your ills.
redeems your life from destruction,
he crowns you with kindness and
compassion. ℟.

He will not always chide,
nor does he keep his wrath forever.

Not according to our sins does he deal
with us,
nor does he requite us according to
our crimes. ℟.

For as the heavens are high above the
earth,
so surpassing is his kindness toward
those who fear him.
As far as the east is from the west,
so far has he put our transgressions
from us. ℟.

READING II
Romans 14:7-9

Brothers and sisters: None of us lives for oneself, and no one dies for oneself. For if we live, we live for the Lord, and if we die, we die for the Lord; so then, whether we live or die, we are the Lord's. For this is why Christ died and came to life, that he might be Lord of both the dead and the living.

GOSPEL
Matthew 18:21-35

Peter approached Jesus and asked him, "Lord, if my brother sins against me, how often must I forgive? As many as seven times?" Jesus answered, "I say to you, not seven times but seventy-seven times. That is why the kingdom of heaven may be likened to a king who decided to settle accounts with his servants. When he began the accounting, a debtor was brought before him who owed him a huge amount. Since he had no way of paying it back, his master ordered him to be sold, along with his wife, his children, and all his property, in payment of the debt. At that, the servant fell down, did him homage, and said, 'Be patient with me, and I will pay you back in full.' Moved with compassion the master of that servant let him go and forgave him the loan. When that servant had left, he found one of his fellow servants who owed him a much smaller amount. He seized him and started to choke him, demanding, 'Pay back what you owe.' Falling to his knees, his fellow servant begged him, 'Be patient with me, and I will pay you back.' But he refused. Instead, he had the fellow servant put in prison until he paid back the debt. Now when his fellow servants saw what had happened, they were deeply disturbed, and went to their master and reported the whole affair. His master summoned him and said to him, 'You wicked servant! I forgave you your entire debt because you begged me to. Should you not have had pity on your fellow servant, as I had pity on you?' Then in anger his master handed him over to the torturers until he should pay back the whole debt. So will my heavenly Father do to you, unless each of you forgives your brother from your heart."

648   TWENTY-FOURTH SUNDAY IN ORDINARY TIME / B

READING I
Isaiah 50:5-9a / 131

The Lord GOD opens my ear that I
    may hear;
and I have not rebelled,
    have not turned back.
I gave my back to those who beat me,
    my cheeks to those who plucked my
      beard;
my face I did not shield
    from buffets and spitting.

The Lord GOD is my help,

therefore I am not disgraced;
I have set my face like flint,
    knowing that I shall not be put to
      shame.
He is near who upholds my right;
    if anyone wishes to oppose me,
    let us appear together.
Who disputes my right?
    Let that man confront me.
See, the Lord GOD is my help;
    who will prove me wrong?

RESPONSORIAL PSALM
Psalm 116:1-2, 3-4, 5-6, 8-9

I will walk be-fore the Lord,   in the land of the liv - ing.

I love the Lord because he has heard
    my voice in supplication,
because he has inclined his ear to me
    the day I called. ℟.

The cords of death encompassed me;
    the snares of the netherworld seized
      upon me;
I fell into distress and sorrow,
and I called upon the name of the Lord,
    "O Lord, save my life!" ℟.

Gracious is the Lord and just;
    yes, our God is merciful.
The Lord keeps the little ones;
    I was brought low, and he saved
      me. ℟.

For he has freed my soul from death,
    my eyes from tears, my feet from
      stumbling.
I shall walk before the Lord
    in the land of the living. ℟.

READING II
James 2:14-18

What good is it, my brothers and sisters, if someone says he has faith but does not have works? Can that faith save him? If a brother or sister has nothing to wear and has no food for the day, and one of you says to them, "Go in peace, keep warm, and eat well," but you do not give them the necessities of the body, what good is it? So also faith of itself, if it does not have works, is dead. Indeed someone might say, "You have faith and I have works." Demonstrate your faith to me without works, and I will demonstrate my faith to you from my works.

GOSPEL
Mark 8:27-35

Jesus and his disciples set out for the villages of Caesarea Philippi. Along the way he asked his disciples, "Who do people say that I am?" They said in reply, "John the

Baptist, others Elijah, still others one of the prophets." And he asked them, "But who do you say that I am?" Peter said to him in reply, "You are the Christ." Then he warned them not to tell anyone about him.

He began to teach them that the Son of Man must suffer greatly and be rejected by the elders, the chief priests, and the scribes, and be killed, and rise after three days. He spoke this openly. Then Peter took him aside and began to rebuke him. At this he turned around and, looking at his disciples, rebuked Peter and said, "Get behind me, Satan. You are thinking not as God does, but as human beings do."

He summoned the crowd with his disciples and said to them, "Whoever wishes to come after me must deny himself, take up his cross, and follow me. For whoever wishes to save his life will lose it, but whoever loses his life for my sake and that of the gospel will save it."

TWENTY-FOURTH SUNDAY IN ORDINARY TIME / C   649

READING I   *Exodus 32:7-11, 13-14 / 132*

The LORD said to Moses, "Go down at once to your people, whom you brought out of the land of Egypt, for they have become depraved. They have soon turned aside from the way I pointed out to them, making for themselves a molten calf and worshiping it, sacrificing to it and crying out, 'This is your God, O Israel, who brought you out of the land of Egypt!' I see how stiff-necked this people is," continued the LORD to Moses. "Let me alone, then, that my wrath may blaze up against them to consume them. Then I will make of you a great nation."

But Moses implored the LORD, his God, saying, "Why, O LORD, should your wrath blaze up against your own people, whom you brought out of the land of Egypt with such great power and with so strong a hand? Remember your servants Abraham, Isaac, and Israel, and how you swore to them by your own self, saying, 'I will make your descendants as numerous as the stars in the sky; and all this land that I promised, I will give your descendants as their perpetual heritage.'" So the LORD relented in the punishment he had threatened to inflict on his people.

RESPONSORIAL PSALM   *Psalm 51:3-4, 12-13, 17, 19*

I will rise and go to my fa - ther.

Have mercy on me, O God, in your goodness;
   in the greatness of your compassion wipe out my offense.
Thoroughly wash me from my guilt and of my sin cleanse me. ℟.

A clean heart create for me, O God, and a steadfast spirit renew within me.

Cast me not out from your presence, and your holy spirit take not from me. ℟.

O Lord, open my lips, and my mouth shall proclaim your praise.
My sacrifice, O God, is a contrite spirit; a heart contrite and humbled, O God, you will not spurn. ℟.

READING II   *1 Timothy 1:12-17*

Beloved: I am grateful to him who has strengthened me, Christ Jesus our Lord, because he considered me trustworthy in appointing me to the ministry. I was once a blasphemer and a persecutor and arrogant, but I have been mercifully treated because I acted out of ignorance in my unbelief. Indeed, the grace of our Lord has been abundant, along with the faith and love that are in Christ Jesus. This saying is trustworthy and deserves full acceptance: Christ Jesus came into the world to save sinners. Of these I am the foremost. But for that reason I was mercifully treated, so that in me, as the foremost, Christ Jesus might display all his patience as an example for those who would come to believe in him for everlasting life. To the king of ages, incorruptible, invisible, the only God, honor and glory forever and ever. Amen.

GOSPEL *Luke 15:1-32 or 15:1-10*

For short form read only the part in brackets.

[Tax collectors and sinners were all drawing near to listen to Jesus, but the Pharisees and scribes began to complain, saying, "This man welcomes sinners and eats with them." So to them he addressed this parable. "What man among you having a hundred sheep and losing one of them would not leave the ninety-nine in the desert and go after the lost one until he finds it? And when he does find it, he sets it on his shoulders with great joy and, upon his arrival home, he calls together his friends and neighbors and says to them, 'Rejoice with me because I have found my lost sheep.' I tell you, in just the same way there will be more joy in heaven over one sinner who repents than over ninety-nine righteous people who have no need of repentance.

"Or what woman having ten coins and losing one would not light a lamp and sweep the house, searching carefully until she finds it? And when she does find it, she calls together her friends and neighbors and says to them, 'Rejoice with me because I have found the coin that I lost.' In just the same way, I tell you, there will be rejoicing among the angels of God over one sinner who repents."]

Then he said, "A man had two sons, and the younger son said to his father, 'Father give me the share of your estate that should come to me.' So the father divided the property between them. After a few days, the younger son collected all his belongings and set off to a distant country where he squandered his inheritance on a life of dissipation. When he had freely spent everything, a severe famine struck that country, and he found himself in dire need. So he hired himself out to one of the local citizens who sent him to his farm to tend the swine. And he longed to eat his fill of the pods on which the swine fed, but nobody gave him any. Coming to his senses he thought, 'How many of my father's hired workers have more than enough food to eat, but here am I, dying from hunger. I shall get up and go to my father and I shall say to him, "Father, I have sinned against heaven and against you. I no longer deserve to be called your son; treat me as you would treat one of your hired workers."' So he got up and went back to his father. While he was still a long way off, his father caught sight of him, and was filled with compassion. He ran to his son, embraced him and kissed him. His son said to him, 'Father, I have sinned against heaven and against you; I no longer deserve to be called your son.' But his father ordered his servants, 'Quickly bring the finest robe and put it on him; put a ring on his finger and sandals on his feet. Take the fattened calf and slaughter it. Then let us celebrate with a feast, because this son of mine was dead, and has come to life again; he was lost, and has been found.' Then the celebration began. Now the older son had been out in the field and, on his way back, as he neared the house, he heard the sound of music and dancing. He called one of the servants and asked what this might mean. The servant said to him, 'Your brother has returned and your father has slaughtered the fattened calf because he has him back safe and sound.' He became angry, and when he refused to enter the house, his father came out and pleaded with him. He said to his father in reply, 'Look, all these years I served you and not once did I disobey your orders; yet you never gave me even a young goat to feast on with my friends. But when your son returns, who swallowed up your property with prostitutes, for him you slaughter the fattened calf.' He said to him, 'My son, you are here with me always; everything I have is yours. But now we must celebrate and rejoice, because your brother was dead and has come to life again; he was lost and has been found.'"

TWENTY-FIFTH SUNDAY IN ORDINARY TIME / A

READING I
Isaiah 55:6-9 / 133

Seek the LORD while he may be found,
    call him while he is near.
Let the scoundrel forsake his way,
    and the wicked his thoughts;
let him turn to the LORD for mercy;
    to our God, who is generous in
        forgiving.
For my thoughts are not your thoughts,
    nor are your ways my ways, says
        the LORD.
As high as the heavens are above the
    earth,
    so high are my ways above your
        ways
    and my thoughts above your
        thoughts.

RESPONSORIAL PSALM
Psalm 145:2-3, 8-9, 17-18

The Lord is near to all who call on him.

Every day will I bless you,
    and I will praise your name forever
        and ever.
Great is the Lord and highly to be
        praised;
    his greatness is unsearchable. ℟.

The Lord is gracious and merciful,
    slow to anger and of great kindness.

The Lord is good to all
    and compassionate toward all his
        works. ℟.

The Lord is just in all his ways
    and holy in all his works.
The Lord is near to all who call upon
        him,
    to all who call upon him in truth. ℟.

READING II
Philippians 1:20c-24, 27a

Brothers and sisters: Christ will be magnified in my body, whether by life or by death.
For to me life is Christ, and death is gain. If I go on living in the flesh, that means fruitful
labor for me. And I do not know which I shall choose. I am caught between the two. I
long to depart this life and be with Christ, for that is far better. Yet that I remain in the
flesh is more necessary for your benefit.

    Only, conduct yourselves in a way worthy of the gospel of Christ.

GOSPEL
Matthew 20:1-16a

Jesus told his disciples this parable: "The kingdom of heaven is like a landowner who
went out at dawn to hire laborers for his vineyard. After agreeing with them for the usual
daily wage, he sent them into his vineyard. Going out about nine o'clock, the landowner saw others standing idle in the marketplace, and he said to them, 'You too go into my
vineyard, and I will give you what is just.' So they went off. And he went out again
around noon, and around three o'clock, and did likewise. Going out about five o'clock,
the landowner found others standing around, and said to them, 'Why do you stand here
idle all day?' They answered, 'Because no one has hired us.' He said to them, 'You too
go into my vineyard.' When it was evening the owner of the vineyard said to his fore-
man, 'Summon the laborers and give them their pay, beginning with the last and ending
with the first.' When those who had started about five o'clock came, each received the
usual daily wage. So when the first came, they thought that they would receive more,
but each of them also got the usual wage. And on receiving it they grumbled against the
landowner, saying, 'These last ones worked only one hour, and you have made them
equal to us, who bore the day's burden and the heat.' He said to one of them in reply,

'My friend, I am not cheating you. Did you not agree with me for the usual daily wage? Take what is yours and go. What if I wish to give this last one the same as you? Or am I not free to do as I wish with my own money? Are you envious because I am generous?' Thus, the last will be first, and the first will be last."

651 TWENTY-FIFTH SUNDAY IN ORDINARY TIME / B

READING I *Wisdom 2:12, 17-20 / 134*

The wicked say:
> Let us beset the just one, because he is obnoxious to us;
>> he sets himself against our doings,
> reproaches us for transgressions of the law
>> and charges us with violations of our training.
> Let us see whether his words be true;
>> let us find out what will happen to him.
> For if the just one be the son of God, God will defend him
>> and deliver him from the hand of his foes.
> With revilement and torture let us put the just one to the test
>> that we may have proof of his gentleness
>> and try his patience.
> Let us condemn him to a shameful death;
>> for according to his own words, God will take care of him.

RESPONSORIAL PSALM *Psalm 54:3-4, 5, 6-8*

The Lord up-holds my life.

O God, by your name save me,
and by your might defend my cause.
O God, hear my prayer;
hearken to the words of my mouth. ℟.

For the haughty men have risen up
against me,
the ruthless seek my life;

they set not God before their eyes. ℟.

Behold, God is my helper;
the Lord sustains my life.
Freely will I offer you sacrifice;
I will praise your name, O Lord, for
its goodness. ℟.

READING II *James 3:16—4:3*

Beloved: Where jealousy and selfish ambition exist, there is disorder and every foul practice. But the wisdom from above is first of all pure, then peaceable, gentle, compliant, full of mercy and good fruits, without inconstancy or insincerity. And the fruit of righteousness is sown in peace for those who cultivate peace.

Where do the wars and where do the conflicts among you come from? Is it not from your passions that make war within your members? You covet but do not possess. You kill and envy but you cannot obtain; you fight and wage war. You do not possess because you do not ask. You ask but do not receive, because you ask wrongly, to spend it on your passions.

GOSPEL *Mark 9:30-37*

Jesus and his disciples left from there and began a journey through Galilee, but he did not wish anyone to know about it. He was teaching his disciples and telling them, "The Son of Man is to be handed over to men and they will kill him, and three days after his death the Son of Man will rise." But they did not understand the saying, and they were afraid to question him.

They came to Capernaum and, once inside the house, he began to ask them, "What were you arguing about on the way?" But they remained silent. They had been discussing among themselves on the way who was the greatest. Then he sat down, called the Twelve, and said to them, "If anyone wishes to be first, he shall be the last of all and the servant of all." Taking a child, he placed it in the their midst, and putting his arms around it, he said to them, "Whoever receives one child such as this in my name, receives me; and whoever receives me, receives not me but the One who sent me."

TWENTY-FIFTH SUNDAY IN ORDINARY TIME / C 652

READING I *Amos 8:4-7 / 135*

Hear this, you who trample upon the
     needy
   and destroy the poor of the land!
"When will the new moon be over," you
     ask,
   "that we may sell our grain,
   and the sabbath, that we may display
     the wheat?
We will diminish the ephah,

add to the shekel,
   and fix our scales for cheating!
We will buy the lowly for silver,
   and the poor for a pair of sandals;
   even the refuse of the wheat we will
     sell!"
The Lord has sworn by the pride of
     Jacob:
   Never will I forget a thing they have
     done!

RESPONSORIAL PSALM *Psalm 113:1-2, 4-6, 7-8*

Praise the Lord, praise the Lord who lifts up the poor.

Praise, you servants of the Lord,
   praise the name of the Lord.
Blessed be the name of the Lord
   both now and forever. ℟.

High above all nations is the Lord;
   above the heavens is his glory.
Who is like the Lord, our God, who is
   enthroned on high

and looks upon the heavens and the
   earth below? ℟.

He raises up the lowly from the dust;
   from the dunghill he lifts up the
   poor
to seat them with princes,
   with the princes of his own
   people. ℟.

READING II *1 Timothy 2:1-8*

Beloved: First of all, I ask that supplications, prayers, petitions, and thanksgivings be offered for everyone, for kings and for all in authority, that we may lead a quiet and tranquil life in all devotion and dignity. This is good and pleasing to God our savior, who wills everyone to be saved and to come to knowledge of the truth.

'For there is one God.
There is also one mediator between God and men,
     the man Christ Jesus,
   who gave himself as ransom for all.'

This was the testimony at the proper time. For this I was appointed preacher and apostle (I am speaking the truth, I am not lying), teacher of the Gentiles in faith and truth.

It is my wish, then, that in every place the men should pray, lifting up holy hands, without anger or argument.

GOSPEL *Luke 16:1-13 or 16:10-13*

For short form read only the parts in brackets.

[Jesus said to his disciples,] "A rich man had a steward who was reported to him for squandering his property. He summoned him and said, 'What is this I hear about you? Prepare a full account of your stewardship, because you can no longer be my steward.' The steward said to himself, 'What shall I do, now that my master is taking the position of steward away from me? I am not strong enough to dig and I am ashamed to beg. I know what I shall do so that, when I am removed from the stewardship, they may welcome me into their homes.' He called in his master's debtors one by one. To the first he said, 'How much do you owe my master?' He replied, 'One hundred measures of olive oil.' He said to him, 'Here is your promissory note. Sit down and quickly write one for fifty.' Then to another the steward said, 'And you, how much do you owe?' He replied, 'One hundred kors of wheat.' The steward said to him, 'Here is your promissory note; write one for eighty.' And the master commended that dishonest steward for acting prudently. "For the children of this world are more prudent in dealing with their own generation than are the children of light. I tell you, make friends for yourselves with dishonest wealth, so that when it fails, you will be welcomed into eternal dwellings. [The person who is trustworthy in very small matters is also trustworthy in great ones; and the person who is dishonest in very small matters is also dishonest in great ones. If, therefore, you are not trustworthy with dishonest wealth, who will trust you with true wealth? If you are not trustworthy with what belongs to another, who will give you what is yours? No servant can serve two masters. He will either hate one and love the other, or be devoted to one and despise the other. You cannot serve both God and mammon."]

---

653 TWENTY-SIXTH SUNDAY IN ORDINARY TIME / A

READING I *Ezekiel 18:25-28 / 136*

Thus says the LORD: You say, "The LORD's way is not fair!" Hear now, house of Israel: Is it my way that is unfair, or rather, are not your ways unfair? When someone virtuous turns away from virtue to commit iniquity, and dies, it is because of the iniquity he committed that he must die. But if he turns from the wickedness he has committed, and does what is right and just, he shall preserve his life; since he has turned away from all the sins that he has committed, he shall surely live, he shall not die.

RESPONSORIAL PSALM *Psalm 25:4-5, 6-7, 8-9*

Re - mem - ber your mer-cies, O Lord.

Your ways, O LORD, make known to me;
    teach me your paths,
guide me in your truth and teach me,
    for you are God my savior. ℟.

Remember that your compassion, O
    LORD,
    and your love are from of old.
The sins of my youth and my frailties

remember not;
in your kindness remember me,
because of your goodness, O
    LORD. ℟.

Good and upright is the LORD;
    thus he shows sinners the way.
He guides the humble to justice,
    and teaches the humble his way. ℟.

READING II   *Philippians 2:1-11 or 2:1-5*

For short form read only the part in brackets.

[Brothers and sisters: If there is any encouragement in Christ, any solace in love, any participation in the Spirit, any compassion and mercy, complete my joy by being of the same mind, with the same love, united in heart, thinking one thing. Do nothing out of selfishness or out of vainglory; rather, humbly regard others as more important than yourselves, each looking out not for his own interests, but also for those of others. Have in you the same attitude that is also in Christ Jesus,]

> Who, though he was in the form of God,
>> did not regard equality with God
>> something to be grasped.
> Rather, he emptied himself,
>> taking the form of a slave,
>> coming in human likeness;
>> and found human in appearance,
>> he humbled himself,
>> becoming obedient to the point of death,
> even death on a cross.
> Because of this, God greatly exalted him
>> and bestowed on him the name
>> which is above every name,
>> that at the name of Jesus
>> every knee should bend,
>> of those in heaven and on earth and under the earth,
>> and every tongue confess that
>> Jesus Christ is Lord,
>> to the glory of God the Father.

GOSPEL   *Matthew 21:28-32*

Jesus said to the chief priests and elders of the people: "What is your opinion? A man had two sons. He came to the first and said, 'Son, go out and work in the vineyard today.' He said in reply, 'I will not,' but afterwards changed his mind and went. The man came to the other son and gave the same order. He said in reply, 'Yes, sir,' but did not go. Which of the two did his father's will?" They answered, "The first." Jesus said to them, "Amen, I say to you, tax collectors and prostitutes are entering the kingdom of God before you. When John came to you in the way of righteousness, you did not believe him; but tax collectors and prostitutes did. Yet even when you saw that, you did not later change your minds and believe him."

TWENTY-SIXTH SUNDAY IN ORDINARY TIME / B   654

READING I   *Numbers 11:25-29 / 137*

The LORD came down in the cloud and spoke to Moses. Taking some of the spirit that was on Moses, the Lord bestowed it on the seventy elders; and as the spirit came to rest on them, they prophesied.

Now two men, one named Eldad and the other Medad, were not in the gathering but had been left in the camp. They too had been on the list, but had not gone out to the tent; yet the spirit came to rest on them also, and they prophesied in the camp. So, when a young man quickly told Moses, "Eldad and Medad are prophesying in the camp," Joshua, son of Nun, who from his youth had been Moses' aide, said, "Moses, my lord, stop them." But Moses answered him, "Are you jealous for my sake? Would that all the people of the LORD were prophets! Would that the LORD might bestow his spirit on them all!"

RESPONSORIAL PSALM *Psalm 19:8, 10, 12-13, 14*

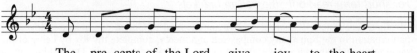

The pre-cepts of the Lord give joy to the heart.

The law of the LORD is perfect,
  refreshing the soul;
the decree of the LORD is trustworthy,
  giving wisdom to the simple. ℟.

The fear of the LORD is pure,
  enduring forever;
the ordinances of the LORD are true,
  all of them just. ℟.

Though your servant is careful of them,

very diligent in keeping them,
yet who can detect failings?
  Cleanse me from my unknown
    faults! ℟.

From wanton sin especially, restrain your
    servant;
  let it not rule over me.
Then shall I be blameless and innocent
  of serious sin. ℟.

READING II *James 5:1-6*

Come now, you rich, weep and wail over your impending miseries. Your wealth has rotted away, your clothes have become moth-eaten, your gold and silver have corroded, and that corrosion will be a testimony against you; it will devour your flesh like a fire. You have stored up treasure for the last days. Behold, the wages you withheld from the workers who harvested your fields are crying aloud; and the cries of the harvesters have reached the ears of the Lord of hosts. You have lived on earth in luxury and pleasure; you have fattened your hearts for the day of slaughter. You have condemned; you have murdered the righteous one; he offers you no resistance.

GOSPEL *Mark 9:38-43, 45, 47-48*

At that time, John said to Jesus, "Teacher, we saw someone driving out demons in your name, and we tried to prevent him because he does not follow us." Jesus replied, "Do not prevent him. There is no one who performs a mighty deed in my name who can at the same time speak ill of me. For whoever is not against us is for us. Anyone who gives you a cup of water to drink because you belong to Christ, amen, I say to you, will surely not lose his reward.

"Whoever causes one of these little ones who believe in me to sin, it would be better for him if a great millstone were put around his neck and he were thrown into the sea. If your hand causes you to sin, cut it off. It is better for you to enter into life maimed than with two hands to go into Gehenna, into the unquenchable fire. And if your foot causes you to sin, cut if off. It is better for you to enter into life crippled than with two feet to be thrown into Gehenna. And if your eye causes you to sin, pluck it out. Better for you to enter into the kingdom of God with one eye than with two eyes to be thrown into Gehenna, where 'their worm does not die, and the fire is not quenched.'"

---

655 **TWENTY-SIXTH SUNDAY IN ORDINARY TIME / C**

READING I *Amos 6:1a, 4-7 / 138*

Thus says the Lord the God of hosts:
Woe to the complacent in Zion!
Lying upon beds of ivory,
  stretched comfortably on their
    couches,

they eat lambs taken from the flock,
  and calves from the stall!
Improvising to the music of the harp,
  like David, they devise their own
    accompaniment.

They drink wine from bowls
and anoint themselves with the best
oils;
yet they are not made ill by the
collapse of Joseph!

Therefore, now they shall be the first to
go into exile,
and their wanton revelry shall be
done away with.

RESPONSORIAL PSALM

Psalm 146:7, 8-9, 9-10

Praise the Lord, my soul! Praise the Lord!

Blessed is he who keeps faith forever,
secures justice for the oppressed,
gives food to the hungry.
The LORD sets captives free. ℟.

The LORD gives sight to the blind.
The LORD raises up those who were
bowed down;

the LORD loves the just.
The LORD protects strangers. ℟.

The fatherless and the widow he sustains,
but the way of the wicked he thwarts.
The LORD shall reign forever;
your God, O Zion, through all
generations. Alleluia. ℟.

READING II

1 Timothy 6:11-16

But you, man of God, pursue righteousness, devotion, faith, love, patience, and gentleness. Compete well for the faith. Lay hold of eternal life, to which you were called when you made the noble confession in the presence of many witnesses. I charge you before God, who gives life to all things, and before Christ Jesus, who gave testimony under Pontius Pilate for the noble confession, to keep the commandment without stain or reproach until the appearance of our Lord Jesus Christ that the blessed and only ruler will make manifest at the proper time, the King of kings and Lord of lords, who alone has immortality, who dwells in unapproachable light, and whom no human being has seen or can see. To him be honor and eternal power. Amen.

GOSPEL

Luke 16:19-31

Jesus said to the Pharisees: "There was a rich man who dressed in purple garments and fine linen and dined sumptuously each day. And lying at his door was a poor man named Lazarus, covered with sores, who would gladly have eaten his fill of the scraps that fell from the rich man's table. Dogs even used to come and lick his sores. When the poor man died, he was carried away by angels to the bosom of Abraham. The rich man also died and was buried, and from the netherworld, where he was in torment, he raised his eyes and saw Abraham far off and Lazarus at his side. And he cried out, 'Father Abraham, have pity on me. Send Lazarus to dip the tip of his finger in water and cool my tongue, for I am suffering torment in these flames.' Abraham replied, 'My child, remember that you received what was good during your lifetime while Lazarus likewise received what was bad; but now he is comforted here, whereas you are tormented. Moreover, between us and you a great chasm is established to prevent anyone from crossing who might wish to go from our side to yours or from your side to ours.' He said, 'Then I beg you, father, send him to my father's house, for I have five brothers, so that he may warn them, lest they too come to this place of torment.' But Abraham replied, 'They have Moses and the prophets. Let them listen to them.' He said, 'Oh no, father Abraham, but if someone from the dead goes to them, they will repent.' Then Abraham said, 'If they will not listen to Moses and the prophets, neither will they be persuaded if someone should rise from the dead.'"

TWENTY-SEVENTH SUNDAY IN ORDINARY TIME / A

READING I *Isaiah 5:1-7 / 139*

Let me now sing of my friend,
  my friend's song concerning his
    vineyard.
My friend had a vineyard
  on a fertile hillside;
he spaded it, cleared it of stones,
  and planted the choicest vines;
within it he built a watchtower,
  and hewed out a wine press.
Then he looked for the crop of grapes,
  but what it yielded was wild grapes.

Now, inhabitants of Jerusalem and people
    of Judah,
  judge between me and my vineyard:
What more was there to do for my
    vineyard
  that I had not done?
Why, when I looked for the crop of grapes,

did it bring forth wild grapes?
Now, I will let you know
  what I mean to do with my vineyard:
take away its hedge, give it to grazing,
  break through its wall, let it be
    trampled!
Yes, I will make it a ruin:
  it shall not be pruned or hoed,
  but overgrown with thorns and
    briers;
I will command the clouds
  not to send rain upon it.
The vineyard of the LORD of hosts is the
    house of Israel,
  and the people of Judah are his
    cherished plant;
he looked for judgment, but see,
    bloodshed!
  for justice, but hark, the outcry!

RESPONSORIAL PSALM *Psalm 80:9, 12, 13-14, 15-16, 19-20*

The vine-yard of the Lord   is the house of Is-ra-el.

A vine from Egypt you transplanted;
  you drove away the nations and
    planted it.
It put forth its foliage to the Sea,
  its shoots as far as the River. ℟.

Why have you broken down its walls,
  so that every passer-by plucks its
    fruit,
The boar from the forest lays it waste,
  and the beasts of the field feed upon
    it? ℟.

Once again, O LORD of hosts,

look down from heaven, and see;
take care of this vine,
  and protect what your right hand has
    planted
  the son of man whom you yourself
    made strong. ℟.

Then we will no more withdraw from
    you;
  give us new life, and we will call
    upon your name.
O LORD, God of hosts, restore us;
  if your face shine upon us, then we
    shall be saved. ℟.

READING II *Philippians 4:6-9*

Brothers and sisters: Have no anxiety at all, but in everything, by prayer and petition,
with thanksgiving, make your requests known to God. Then the peace of God that
surpasses all understanding will guard your hearts and minds in Christ Jesus.

  Finally, brothers and sisters, whatever is true, whatever is honorable, whatever is
just, whatever is pure, whatever is lovely, whatever is gracious, if there is any excellence
and if there is anything worthy of praise, think about these things. Keep on doing what
you have learned and received and heard and seen in me. Then the God of peace will be
with you.

GOSPEL *Matthew 21:33-43*

Jesus said to the chief priests and the elders of the people: "Hear another parable. There was a landowner who planted a vineyard, put a hedge around it, dug a wine press in it, and built a tower. Then he leased it to tenants and went on a journey. When vintage time drew near, he sent his servants to the tenants to obtain his produce. But the tenants seized the servants and one they beat, another they killed, and a third they stoned. Again he sent other servants, more numerous than the first ones, but they treated them in the same way. Finally, he sent his son to them, thinking, 'They will respect my son.' But when the tenants saw the son, they said to one another, 'This is the heir. Come, let us kill him and acquire his inheritance.' They seized him, threw him out of the vineyard, and killed him. What will the owner of the vineyard do to those tenants when he comes?" They answered him, "He will put those wretched men to a wretched death and lease his vineyard to other tenants who will give him the produce at the proper times." Jesus said to them, "Did you never read in the Scriptures:

'The stone that the builders rejected
    has become the cornerstone;
by the Lord has this been done,
    and it is wonderful in our eyes?'

Therefore, I say to you, the kingdom of God will be taken away from you and given to a people that will produce its fruit."

TWENTY-SEVENTH SUNDAY IN ORDINARY TIME / B   657

READING I *Genesis 2:18-24 / 140*

The LORD God said: "It is not good for the man to be alone. I will make a suitable partner for him." So the LORD God formed out of the ground various wild animals and various birds of the air, and he brought them to the man to see what he would call them; whatever the man called each of them would be its name. The man gave names to all the cattle, all the birds of the air, and all wild animals; but none proved to be the suitable partner for the man.

So the LORD God cast a deep sleep on the man, and while he was asleep, he took out one of his ribs and closed up its place with flesh. The LORD God then built up into a woman the rib that he had taken from the man. When he brought her to the man, the man said:

"This one, at last, is bone of my bones
    and flesh of my flesh;
this one shall be called 'woman,'
    for out of 'her man' this one has been taken."

That is why a man leaves his father and mother and clings to his wife, and the two of them become one flesh.

RESPONSORIAL PSALM *Psalm 128:1-2, 3, 4-5, 6*

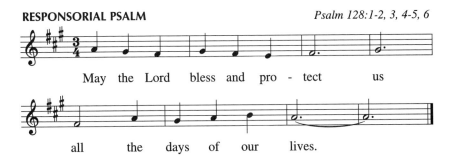

May the Lord bless and pro - tect us all the days of our lives.

Blessed are you who fear the LORD,
who walk in his ways!
For you shall eat the fruit of your
handiwork;
blessed shall you be, and favored. ℟.

Your wife shall be like a fruitful vine
in the recesses of your home;
your children like olive plants
around your table. ℟.

Behold, thus is the man blessed
who fears the LORD.
The LORD bless you from Zion:
may you see the prosperity of
Jerusalem
all the days of your life. ℟.

May you see your children's children.
Peace be upon Israel! ℟.

READING II   *Hebrews 2:9-11*

Brothers and sisters: He "for a little while" was made "lower than the angels," that by the grace of God he might taste death for everyone.

For it was fitting that he, for whom and through whom all things exist, in bringing many children to glory, should make the leader to their salvation perfect through suffering. He who consecrates and those who are being consecrated all have one origin. Therefore, he is not ashamed to call them "brothers."

GOSPEL   *Mark 10:2-16 or 10:2-12*

For short form read only the part in brackets.

[The Pharisees approached Jesus and asked, "Is it lawful for a husband to divorce his wife?" They were testing him. He said to them in reply, "What did Moses command you?" They replied, "Moses permitted a husband to write a bill of divorce and dismiss her." But Jesus told them, "Because of the hardness of your hearts he wrote you this commandment. But from the beginning of creation, 'God made them male and female. For this reason a man shall leave his father and mother and be joined to his wife, and the two shall become one flesh.' So they are no longer two but one flesh. Therefore what God has joined together, no human being must separate." In the house the disciples again questioned Jesus about this. He said to them, "Whoever divorces his wife and marries another commits adultery against her; and if she divorces her husband and marries another, she commits adultery."]

And people were bringing children to him that he might touch them, but the disciples rebuked them. When Jesus saw this he became indignant and said to them, "Let the children come to me; do not prevent them, for the kingdom of God belongs to such as these. Amen, I say to you, whoever does not accept the kingdom of God like a child will not enter it." Then he embraced them and blessed them, placing his hands on them.

658   TWENTY-SEVENTH SUNDAY IN ORDINARY TIME / C

READING I   *Habakkuk 1:2-3; 2:2-4 / 141*

How long, O LORD? I cry for help
but you do not listen!
I cry out to you, "Violence!"
but you do not intervene.
Why do you let me see ruin;
why must I look at misery?
Destruction and violence are before me;
there is strife, and clamorous discord.
Then the LORD answered me and said:
Write down the vision clearly upon

the tablets,
so that one can read it readily.
For the vision still has its time,
presses on to fulfillment, and will
not disappoint;
if it delays, wait for it,
it will surely come, it will not be late.
The rash one has no integrity;
but the just one, because of his faith,
shall live.

RESPONSORIAL PSALM
Psalm 95:1-2, 6-7, 8-9

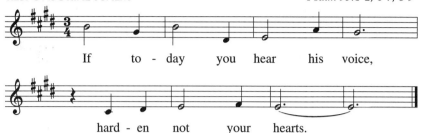

If to - day you hear his voice,
hard - en not your hearts.

Come, let us sing joyfully to the LORD;
let us acclaim the Rock of our
salvation.
Let us come into his presence with
thanksgiving;
let us joyfully sing psalms to him. ℟.

Come, let us bow down in worship;
let us kneel before the LORD who
made us.
For he is our God,

and we are the people he shepherds,
the flock he guides. ℟.

Oh, that today you would hear his voice:
"Harden not your hearts as at
Meribah,
as in the day of Massah in the desert,
Where your fathers tempted me;
they tested me though they had seen
my works." ℟.

READING II
2 Timothy 1:6-8, 13-14

Beloved: I remind you to stir into flame the gift of God that you have through the imposition of my hands. For God did not give us a spirit of cowardice but rather of power and love and self-control. So do not be ashamed of your testimony to our Lord, nor of me, a prisoner for his sake; but bear your share of hardship for the gospel with the strength that comes from God.

Take as your norm the sound words that you heard from me, in the faith and love that are in Christ Jesus. Guard this rich trust with the help of the Holy Spirit that dwells within us.

GOSPEL
Luke 17:5-10

The apostles said to the Lord, "Increase our faith." The Lord replied, "If you have faith the size of a mustard seed, you would say to this mulberry tree, 'Be uprooted and planted in the sea,' and it would obey you.

"Who among you would say to your servant who has just come in from plowing or tending sheep in the field, 'Come here immediately and take your place at table'? Would he not rather say to him, 'Prepare something for me to eat. Put on your apron and wait on me while I eat and drink. You may eat and drink when I am finished'? Is he grateful to that servant because he did what was commanded? So should it be with you. When you have done all you have been commanded, say, 'We are unprofitable servants; we have done what we were obliged to do.'"

TWENTY-EIGHTH SUNDAY IN ORDINARY TIME / A
659

READING I
Isaiah 25:6-10a / 142

On this mountain the LORD of hosts
will provide for all peoples
a feast of rich food and choice wines,
juicy, rich food and pure, choice

wines.
On this mountain he will destroy
the veil that veils all peoples,
the web that is woven over all nations;

he will destroy death forever.
The Lord GOD will wipe away
  the tears from every face;
the reproach of his people he will
  remove
from the whole earth; for the LORD
  has spoken.
On that day it will be said:

"Behold our God, to whom we looked to
  save us!
This is the LORD for whom we
  looked;
let us rejoice and be glad that he has
  saved us!"
For the hand of the LORD will rest on
  this mountain.

RESPONSORIAL PSALM

Psalm 23:1-3a, 3b-4, 5, 6

I shall live in the house of the Lord all the days of my life.

The LORD is my shepherd; I shall not
  want.
  In verdant pastures he gives me
    repose;
beside restful waters he leads me;
  he refreshes my soul. ℟.

He guides me in right paths
  for his name's sake.
Even though I walk in the dark valley
  I fear no evil; for you are at my side
with your rod and your staff

that give me courage. ℟.

You spread the table before me
  in the sight of my foes;
you anoint my head with oil;
  my cup overflows. ℟.

Only goodness and kindness follow me
  all the days of my life;
and I shall dwell in the house of the
  LORD
  for years to come. ℟.

READING II

Philippians 4:12-14, 19-20

Brothers and sisters: I know how to live in humble circumstances; I know also how to live with abundance. In every circumstance and in all things I have learned the secret of being well fed and of going hungry, of living in abundance and of being in need. I can do all things in him who strengthens me. Still, it was kind of you to share in my distress.

My God will fully supply whatever you need, in accord with his glorious riches in Christ Jesus. To our God and Father, glory forever and ever. Amen.

GOSPEL

Matthew 22:1-14 or 22:1-10

For short form read only the part in brackets.

[Jesus again in reply spoke to the chief priests and elders of the people in parables, saying, "The kingdom of heaven may be likened to a king who gave a wedding feast for his son. He dispatched his servants to summon the invited guests to the feast, but they refused to come. A second time he sent other servants, saying, 'Tell those invited: "Behold, I have prepared my banquet, my calves and fattened cattle are killed, and everything is ready; come to the feast."' Some ignored the invitation and went away, one to his farm, another to his business. The rest laid hold of his servants, mistreated them, and killed them. The king was enraged and sent his troops, destroyed those murderers, and burned their city. Then he said to his servants, 'The feast is ready, but those who were invited were not worthy to come. Go out, therefore, into the main roads and invite to the feast whomever you find.' The servants went out into the streets and gathered all they found, bad and good alike, and the hall was filled with guests.] But when the king came in to meet the guests, he saw a man there not dressed in a wedding garment. The king said to him, 'My friend, how is it that you came in here without a wedding garment?' But he was reduced to silence. Then the king said to his attendants, 'Bind his hands and feet, and cast him into the darkness outside, where there will be wailing and grinding of teeth.' Many are invited, but few are chosen."

TWENTY-EIGHTH SUNDAY IN ORDINARY TIME / B   660

READING I   *Wisdom 7:7-11 / 143*

I prayed, and prudence was given me;
    I pleaded, and the spirit of wisdom came to me.
I preferred her to scepter and throne,
and deemed riches nothing in comparison with her,
    nor did I liken any priceless gem to her;
because all gold, in view of her, is a little sand,
    and before her, silver is to be accounted mire.
Beyond health and comeliness I loved her,
and I chose to have her rather than the light,
    because the splendor of her never yields to sleep.
Yet all good things together came to me in her company,
    and countless riches at her hands.

RESPONSORIAL PSALM   *Psalm 90:12-13, 14-15, 16-17*

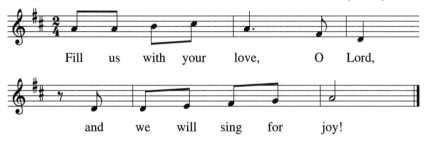

Fill us with your love, O Lord, and we will sing for joy!

Teach us to number our days aright,
    that we may gain wisdom of heart.
Return, O LORD! How long?
    Have pity on your servants! ℟.

Fill us at daybreak with your kindness,
    that we may shout for joy and
      gladness all our days.
Make us glad, for the days when you
      afflicted us,
    for the years when we saw evil. ℟.

Let your work be seen by your servants
    and your glory by their children;
and may the gracious care of the Lord
    our God be ours;
    prosper the work of our hands for us!
    Prosper the work of our hands! ℟.

READING II   *Hebrews 4:12-13*

Brothers and sisters: Indeed the word of God is living and effective, sharper than any two-edged sword, penetrating even between soul and spirit, joints and marrow, and able to discern reflections and thoughts of the heart. No creature is concealed from him, but everything is naked and exposed to the eyes of him to whom we must render an account.

GOSPEL *Mark 10:17-30 or 10:17-27*

For short form read only the part in brackets.

[As Jesus was setting out on a journey, a man ran up, knelt down before him, and asked him, "Good teacher, what must I do to inherit eternal life?" Jesus answered him, "Why do you call me good? No one is good but God alone. You know the commandments: 'You shall not kill; you shall not commit adultery; you shall not steal; you shall not bear false witness; you shall not defraud; honor your father and your mother.'" He replied and said to him, "Teacher, all of these I have observed from my youth." Jesus, looking at him, loved him and said to him, "You are lacking in one thing. Go, sell what you have, and give to the poor and you will have treasure in heaven; then come, follow me." At that statement his face fell, and he went away sad, for he had many possessions.

Jesus looked around and said to his disciples, "How hard it is for those who have wealth to enter the kingdom of God!" The disciples were amazed at his words. So Jesus again said to them in reply, "Children, how hard it is to enter the kingdom of God! It is easier for a camel to pass through the eye of a needle than for one who is rich to enter the kingdom of God." They were exceedingly astonished and said among themselves, "Then who can be saved?" Jesus looked at them and said, "For human beings it is impossible, but not for God. All things are possible for God."] Peter began to say to him, "We have given up everything and followed you." Jesus said, "Amen, I say to you, there is no one who has given up house or brothers or sisters or mother or father or children or lands for my sake and for the sake of the gospel who will not receive a hundred times more now in this present age: houses and brothers and sisters and mothers and children and lands, with persecutions, and eternal life in the age to come."

---

661 TWENTY-EIGHTH SUNDAY IN ORDINARY TIME / C

READING I *2 Kings 5:14-17 / 144*

Naaman went down and plunged into the Jordan seven times at the word of Elisha, the man of God. His flesh became again like the flesh of a little child, and he was clean of his leprosy.

Naaman returned with his whole retinue to the man of God. On his arrival he stood before Elisha and said, "Now I know that there is no God in all the earth, except in Israel. Please accept a gift from your servant."

Elisha replied, "As the LORD lives whom I serve, I will not take it;" and despite Naaman's urging, he still refused. Naaman said: "If you will not accept, please let me, your servant, have two mule-loads of earth, for I will no longer offer holocaust or sacrifice to any other god except to the LORD."

RESPONSORIAL PSALM *Psalm 98:1, 2-3, 3-4*

The Lord has re-vealed to the na - tions his sav - ing pow'r, his sav - ing pow'r.

Sing to the LORD a new song,
for he has done wondrous deeds;
his right hand has won victory for him,
his holy arm. ℟.

The LORD has made his salvation known:
in the sight of the nations he has
revealed his justice.

He has remembered his kindness and his
faithfulness
toward the house of Israel. ℟.

All the ends of the earth have seen
the salvation by our God.
Sing joyfully to the LORD, all you lands:
break into song; sing praise. ℟.

READING II
2 Timothy 2:8-13

Beloved: Remember Jesus Christ, raised from the dead, a descendant of David: such is
my gospel, for which I am suffering, even to the point of chains, like a criminal. But the
word of God is not chained. Therefore, I bear with everything for the sake of those who
are chosen, so that they too may obtain the salvation that is in Christ Jesus, together with
eternal glory. This saying is trustworthy:
If we have died with him
we shall also live with him;
if we persevere
we shall also reign with him.
But if we deny him
he will deny us.
If we are unfaithful
he remains faithful,
for he cannot deny himself.

GOSPEL
Luke 17:11-19

As Jesus continued his journey to Jerusalem, he traveled through Samaria and Galilee.
As he was entering a village, ten lepers met him. They stood at a distance from him and
raised their voices, saying, "Jesus, Master! Have pity on us!" And when he saw them,
he said, "Go show yourselves to the priests." As they were going they were cleansed.
And one of them, realizing he had been healed, returned, glorifying God in a loud voice;
and he fell at the feet of Jesus and thanked him. He was a Samaritan. Jesus said in reply,
"Ten were cleansed, were they not? Where are the other nine? Has none but this foreigner
returned to give thanks to God?" Then he said to him, "Stand up and go; your faith has
saved you."

TWENTY-NINTH SUNDAY IN ORDINARY TIME / A 662

READING I
Isaiah 45:1, 4-6 / 145

Thus says the LORD to his anointed,
Cyrus,
whose right hand I grasp,
subduing nations before him,
and making kings run in his service,
opening doors before him
and leaving the gates unbarred:
For the sake of Jacob, my servant,
of Israel, my chosen one,
I have called you by your name,
giving you a title, though you knew

me not.
I am the LORD and there is no other,
there is no God besides me.
It is I who arm you, though you know
me not,
so that toward the rising and the
setting of the sun
people may know that there is none
besides me.
I am the LORD, there is no other.

RESPONSORIAL PSALM   *Psalm 96:1, 3, 4-5, 7-8, 9-10*

Give the Lord glo - ry and hon - or.

Sing to the LORD a new song;
  sing to the LORD, all you lands.
Tell his glory among the nations;
  among all peoples, his wondrous
  deeds. ℟.

For great is the LORD and highly to be
  praised;
  awesome is he, beyond all gods.
For all the gods of the nations are things
  of nought,
  but the LORD made the heavens. ℟.

Give to the LORD, you families of
  nations,
  give to the LORD glory and praise;
  give to the LORD the glory due his
  name!
Bring gifts, and enter his courts. ℟.

Worship the LORD, in holy attire;
  tremble before him, all the earth;
say among the nations: The LORD is king,
  he governs the peoples with
  equity. ℟.

READING II   *1 Thessalonians 1:1-5b*
Paul, Silvanus, and Timothy to the church of the Thessalonians in God the Father and the Lord Jesus Christ: grace to you and peace. We give thanks to God always for all of you, remembering you in our prayers, unceasingly calling to mind your work of faith and labor of love and endurance in hope of our Lord Jesus Christ, before our God and Father, knowing, brothers and sisters loved by God, how you were chosen. For our gospel did not come to you in word alone, but also in power and in the Holy Spirit and with much conviction.

GOSPEL   *Matthew 22:15-21*
The Pharisees went off and plotted how they might entrap Jesus in speech. They sent their disciples to him, with the Herodians, saying, "Teacher, we know that you are a truthful man and that you teach the way of God in accordance with the truth. And you are not concerned with anyone's opinion, for you do not regard a person's status. Tell us, then, what is your opinion: Is it lawful to pay the census tax to Caesar or not?" Knowing their malice, Jesus said, "Why are you testing me, you hypocrites? Show me the coin that pays the census tax." Then they handed him the Roman coin. He said to them, "Whose image is this and whose inscription?" They replied, "Caesar's." At that he said to them, "Then repay to Caesar what belongs to Caesar and to God what belongs to God."

663 TWENTY-NINTH SUNDAY IN ORDINARY TIME / B

READING I   *Isaiah 53:10-11 / 146*
The LORD was pleased
  to crush him in infirmity.

If he gives his life as an offering for sin,
  he shall see his descendants in a
  long life,
  and the will of the LORD shall be
  accomplished through him.

Because of his affliction
  he shall see the light in fullness
  of days;
through his suffering, my servant shall
  justify many,
  and their guilt he shall bear.

RESPONSORIAL PSALM *Psalm 33:4-5, 18-19, 20, 22*

Lord, let your mer-cy be on us, as we place our trust in you.

Upright is the word of the LORD,
and all his works are trustworthy.
He loves justice and right;
of the kindness of the LORD the
earth is full. ℟.

See, the eyes of the LORD are upon those
who fear him,
upon those who hope for his

kindness,
to deliver them from death
and preserve them in spite of
famine. ℟.

Our soul waits for the LORD,
who is our help and our shield.
May your kindness, O LORD, be upon us
who have put our hope in you. ℟.

READING II *Hebrews 4:14-16*

Brothers and sisters: Since we have a great high priest who has passed through the heavens, Jesus, the Son of God, let us hold fast to our confession. For we do not have a high priest who is unable to sympathize with our weaknesses, but one who has similarly been tested in every way, yet without sin. So let us confidently approach the throne of grace to receive mercy and to find grace for timely help.

GOSPEL *Mark 10:35-45 or 10:42-45*

For short form read only the part in brackets.

James and John, the sons of Zebedee, came to Jesus and said to him, "Teacher, we want you to do for us whatever we ask of you." He replied, "What do you wish me to do for you?" They answered him, "Grant that in your glory we may sit one at your right and the other at your left." Jesus said to them, "You do not know what you are asking. Can you drink the cup that I drink or be baptized with the baptism with which I am baptized?" They said to him, "We can." Jesus said to them, "The cup that I drink, you will drink, and with the baptism with which I am baptized, you will be baptized; but to sit at my right or at my left is not mine to give but is for those for whom it has been prepared." When the ten heard this, they became indignant at James and John. [Jesus summoned them and said to them, "You know that those who are recognized as rulers over the Gentiles lord it over them, and their great ones make their authority over them felt. But it shall not be so among you. Rather, whoever wishes to be great among you will be your servant; whoever wishes to be first among you will be the slave of all. For the Son of Man did not come to be served but to serve and to give his life as a ransom for many."]

TWENTY-NINTH SUNDAY IN ORDINARY TIME / C 664

READING I *Exodus 17:8-13 / 147*

In those days, Amalek came and waged war against Israel. Moses, therefore, said to Joshua, "Pick out certain men, and tomorrow go out and engage Amalek in battle. I will be standing on top of the hill with the staff of God in my hand." So Joshua did as Moses told him: he engaged Amalek in battle after Moses had climbed to the top of the hill with Aaron and Hur. As long as Moses kept his hands raised up, Israel had the better of the fight, but when he let his hands rest, Amalek had the better of the fight. Moses' hands, however, grew tired; so they put a rock in place for him to sit on. Meanwhile Aaron and Hur supported his hands, one on one side and one on the other, so that his hands remained steady till sunset. And Joshua mowed down Amalek and his people with the edge of the sword.

RESPONSORIAL PSALM   *Psalm 121:1-2, 3-4, 5-6, 7-8*

Our help is from the Lord, who made heav-en   and earth.

I lift up my eyes toward the mountains;
    whence shall help come to me?
My help is from the LORD,
    who made heaven and earth. ℟.

May he not suffer your foot to slip;
    may he slumber not who guards you:
indeed he neither slumbers nor sleeps,
    the guardian of Israel. ℟.

The LORD is your guardian; the LORD is

your shade;
    he is beside you at your right hand.
The sun shall not harm you by day,
    nor the moon by night. ℟.

The LORD will guard you from all evil;
    he will guard your life.
The LORD will guard your coming and
    your going,
both now and forever. ℟.

READING II   *2 Timothy 3:14—4:2*

Beloved: Remain faithful to what you have learned and believed, because you know from whom you learned it, and that from infancy you have known the sacred Scriptures, which are capable of giving you wisdom for salvation through faith in Christ Jesus. All Scripture is inspired by God and is useful for teaching, for refutation, for correction, and for training in righteousness, so that one who belongs to God may be competent, equipped for every good work.
    I charge you in the presence of God and of Christ Jesus, who will judge the living and the dead, and by his appearing and his kingly power: proclaim the word; be persistent whether it is convenient or inconvenient; convince, reprimand, encourage through all patience and teaching.

GOSPEL   *Luke 18:1-8*

Jesus told his disciples a parable about the necessity for them to pray always without becoming weary. He said, "There was a judge in a certain town who neither feared God nor respected any human being. And a widow in that town used to come to him and say, 'Render a just decision for me against my adversary.' For a long time the judge was unwilling, but eventually he thought, 'While it is true that I neither fear God nor respect any human being, because this widow keeps bothering me I shall deliver a just decision for her lest she finally come and strike me.'" The Lord said, "Pay attention to what the dishonest judge says. Will not God then secure the rights of his chosen ones who call out to him day and night? Will he be slow to answer them? I tell you, he will see to it that justice is done for them speedily. But when the Son of Man comes, will he find faith on earth?"

---

665   **THIRTIETH SUNDAY IN ORDINARY TIME / A**

READING I   *Exodus 22:20-26 / 148*

Thus says the Lord: "You shall not molest or oppress an alien, for you were once aliens yourselves in the land of Egypt. You shall not wrong any widow or orphan. If ever you wrong them and they cry out to me, I will surely hear their cry. My wrath will flare up, and I will kill you with the sword; then your own wives will be widows, and your children orphans.

"If you lend money to one of your poor neighbors among my people, you shall not act like an extortioner toward him by demanding interest from him. If you take your neighbor's cloak as a pledge, you shall return it to him before sunset; for this cloak of his is the only covering he has for his body. What else has he to sleep in? If he cries out to me, I will hear him; for I am compassionate."

RESPONSORIAL PSALM
Psalm 18:2-3, 3-4, 47, 51

I love you, Lord, my strength, my strength.

I love you, O LORD, my strength,
O LORD, my rock, my fortress, my
deliverer.
My God, my rock of refuge,
my shield, the horn of my salvation,
my stronghold!
Praised be the LORD, I exclaim,
and I am safe from my enemies. ℟.

The LORD lives and blessed be my rock!
Extolled be God my savior.
You who gave great victories to your
king
and showed kindness to your
anointed. ℟.

READING II
1 Thessalonians 1:5c-10

Brothers and sisters: You know what sort of people we were among you for your sake. And you became imitators of us and of the Lord, receiving the word in great affliction, with joy from the Holy Spirit, so that you became a model for all the believers in Macedonia and in Achaia. For from you the word of the Lord has sounded forth not only in Macedonia and in Achaia, but in every place your faith in God has gone forth, so that we have no need to say anything. For they themselves openly declare about us what sort of reception we had among you, and how you turned to God from idols to serve the living and true God and to await his Son from heaven, whom he raised from the dead, Jesus, who delivers us from the coming wrath.

GOSPEL
Matthew 22:34-40

When the Pharisees heard that Jesus had silenced the Sadducees, they gathered together, and one of them, a scholar of the law, tested him by asking, "Teacher, which commandment in the law is the greatest?" He said to him, "You shall love the Lord, your God, with all your heart, with all your soul, and with all your mind. This is the greatest and the first commandment. The second is like it: You shall love your neighbor as yourself. The whole law and the prophets depend on these two commandments."

THIRTIETH SUNDAY IN ORDINARY TIME / B
666

READING I
Jeremiah 31:7-9 / 149

Thus says the LORD:
Shout with joy for Jacob,
exult at the head of the nations;
proclaim your praise and say:
The LORD has delivered his people,
the remnant of Israel.
Behold, I will bring them back
from the land of the north;

I will gather them from the ends of the
world,
with the blind and the lame in their
midst,
the mothers and those with child;
they shall return as an immense
throng.

They departed in tears,
but I will console them and guide
them;
I will lead them to brooks of water,
on a level road, so that none shall
stumble.
For I am a father to Israel,
Ephraim is my first-born.

RESPONSORIAL PSALM
Psalm 126:1-2, 2-3, 4-5, 6

The Lord has done great things for us; we are filled with joy.

When the LORD brought back the
captives of Zion,
we were like men dreaming.
Then our mouth was filled with laughter,
and our tongue with rejoicing. ℟.

Then they said among the nations,
"The LORD has done great things for
them."
The LORD has done great things for us;
we are glad indeed. ℟.

Restore our fortunes, O LORD,
like the torrents in the southern
desert.
Those that sow in tears
shall reap rejoicing. ℟.

Although they go forth weeping,
carrying the seed to be sown,
they shall come back rejoicing,
carrying their sheaves. ℟.

READING II
Hebrews 5:1-6

Brothers and sisters: Every high priest is taken from among men and made their representative before God, to offer gifts and sacrifices for sins. He is able to deal patiently with the ignorant and erring, for he himself is beset by weakness and so, for this reason, must make sin offerings for himself as well as for the people. No one takes this honor upon himself but only when called by God, just as Aaron was. In the same way, it was not Christ who glorified himself in becoming high priest, but rather the one who said to him:
"You are my son:
this day I have begotten you";
just as he says in another place:
"You are a priest forever
according to the order of Melchizedek."

GOSPEL
Mark 10:46-52

As Jesus was leaving Jericho with his disciples and a sizable crowd, Bartimaeus, a blind man, the son of Timaeus, sat by the roadside begging. On hearing that it was Jesus of Nazareth, he began to cry out and say, "Jesus, son of David, have pity on me." And many rebuked him, telling him to be silent. But he kept calling out all the more, "Son of David, have pity on me." Jesus stopped and said, "Call him." So they called the blind man, saying to him, "Take courage; get up, Jesus is calling you." He threw aside his cloak, sprang up, and came to Jesus. Jesus said to him in reply, "What do you want me to do for you?" The blind man replied to him, "Master, I want to see." Jesus told him, "Go your way; your faith has saved you." Immediately he received his sight and followed him on the way.

THIRTIETH SUNDAY IN ORDINARY TIME / C

READING I
Sirach 35:12-14, 16-18 / 150

The LORD is a God of justice,
who knows no favorites.
Though not unduly partial toward the
weak,
yet he hears the cry of the oppressed.
The Lord is not deaf to the wail of the
orphan,
nor to the widow when she pours out
her complaint.
The one who serves God willingly is
heard;
his petition reaches the heavens.
The prayer of the lowly pierces the
clouds;
it does not rest till it reaches its goal,
nor will it withdraw till the Most High
responds,
judges justly and affirms the right,
and the Lord will not delay.

RESPONSORIAL PSALM
Psalm 34:2-3, 17-18, 19, 23

The Lord hears the cry of the poor.

I will bless the LORD at all times;
his praise shall be ever in my mouth.
Let my soul glory in the Lord;
the lowly will hear me and be glad. ℟.

The LORD confronts the evildoers,
to destroy remembrance of them
from the earth.
When the just cry out, the Lord hears
them,
and from all their distress he rescues
them. ℟.

The LORD is close to the brokenhearted;
and those who are crushed in spirit
he saves.
The LORD redeems the lives of his
servants;
no one incurs guilt who takes refuge
in him. ℟.

READING II
2 Timothy 4:6-8, 16-18

Beloved: I am already being poured out like a libation, and the time of my departure is at hand. I have competed well; I have finished the race; I have kept the faith. From now on the crown of righteousness awaits me, which the Lord, the just judge, will award to me on that day, and not only to me, but to all who have longed for his appearance.

At my first defense no one appeared on my behalf, but everyone deserted me. May it not be held against them! But the Lord stood by me and gave me strength, so that through me the proclamation might be completed and all the Gentiles might hear it. And I was rescued from the lion's mouth. The Lord will rescue me from every evil threat and will bring me safe to his heavenly kingdom. To him be glory forever and ever. Amen.

GOSPEL
Luke 18:9-14

Jesus addressed this parable to those who were convinced of their own righteousness and despised everyone else. "Two people went up to the temple area to pray; one was a Pharisee and the other was a tax collector. The Pharisee took up his position and spoke this prayer to himself, 'O God, I thank you that I am not like the rest of humanity—greedy, dishonest, adulterous—or even like this tax collector. I fast twice a week, and I pay tithes on my whole income.' But the tax collector stood off at a distance and would not even raise his eyes to heaven but beat his breast and prayed, 'O God, be merciful to me a sinner.' I tell you, the latter went home justified, not the former; for whoever exalts himself will be humbled, and the one who humbles himself will be exalted."

668 **THIRTY-FIRST SUNDAY IN ORDINARY TIME / A**

READING I *Malachi 1:14b-2:2b, 8-10 / 151*

A great King am I, says the LORD of
hosts,
    and my name will be feared among
    the nations.
And now, O priests, this commandment
    is for you:
    If you do not listen,
if you do not lay it to heart,
    to give glory to my name, says the
    LORD of hosts,
I will send a curse upon you
    and of your blessing I will make a
    curse.
You have turned aside from the way,
and have caused many to falter by
    your instruction;
you have made void the covenant of
    Levi,
    says the LORD of hosts.
I, therefore, have made you contemptible
    and base before all the people,
since you do not keep my ways,
    but show partiality in your decisions.
Have we not all the one father?
    Has not the one God created us?
Why then do we break faith with one
    another,
    violating the covenant of our fathers?

RESPONSORIAL PSALM *Psalm 131:1, 2, 3*

In you, O Lord, I have found my peace.

O LORD, my heart is not proud,
    nor are my eyes haughty;
I busy not myself with great things,
    nor with things too sublime for me. ℟.

Nay rather, I have stilled and quieted

my soul like a weaned child.
Like a weaned child on its mother's lap,
    so is my soul within me. ℟.

O Israel, hope in the LORD,
    both now and forever. ℟.

READING II *1 Thessalonians 2:7b-9, 13*

Brothers and sisters: We were gentle among you, as a nursing mother cares for her children. With such affection for you, we were determined to share with you not only the gospel of God, but our very selves as well, so dearly beloved had you become to us. You recall, brothers and sisters, our toil and drudgery. Working night and day in order not to burden any of you, we proclaimed to you the gospel of God.

And for this reason we too give thanks to God unceasingly, that, in receiving the word of God from hearing us, you received not a human word but, as it truly is, the word of God, which is now at work in you who believe.

GOSPEL *Matthew 23:1-12*

Jesus spoke to the crowds and to his disciples, saying, "The scribes and the Pharisees have taken their seat on the chair of Moses. Therefore, do and observe all things whatsoever they tell you, but do not follow their example. For they preach but they do not practice. They tie up heavy burdens hard to carry and lay them on people's shoulders, but they will not lift a finger to move them. All their works are performed to be seen. They widen their phylacteries and lengthen their tassels. They love places of honor at banquets, seats of honor in synagogues, greetings in marketplaces, and the salutation 'Rabbi.' As for you, do not be called 'Rabbi.' You have but one teacher, and you are all brothers. Call no one on earth your father; you have but one Father in heaven. Do not be called 'Master'; you have but one master, the Christ. The greatest among you must be your servant. Whoever exalts himself will be humbled; but whoever humbles himself will be exalted."

THIRTY-FIRST SUNDAY IN ORDINARY TIME / B

READING I *Deuteronomy 6:2-6 / 152*

Moses spoke to the people, saying: "Fear the LORD, your God, and keep, throughout the days of your lives, all his statutes and commandments which I enjoin on you, and thus have long life. Hear then, Israel, and be careful to observe them, that you may grow and prosper the more, in keeping with the promise of the LORD, the God of your fathers, to give you a land flowing with milk and honey.

"Hear, O Israel! The LORD is our God, the LORD alone! Therefore, you shall love the LORD, your God, with all your heart, and with all your soul, and with all your strength. Take to heart these words which I enjoin on you today."

RESPONSORIAL PSALM *Psalm 18:2-3, 3-4, 47, 51*

I love you, Lord, my strength, my strength.

I love you, O LORD, my strength,
  O LORD, my rock, my fortress, my
    deliverer.
My God, my rock of refuge,
  my shield, the horn of my salvation,
    my stronghold!
Praised be the LORD, I exclaim,
  and I am safe from my enemies. ℟.

The LORD lives! And blessed be my rock!
  Extolled be God my savior,
you who gave great victories to your king
  and showed kindness to your
    anointed. ℟.

READING II *Hebrews 7:23-28*

Brothers and sisters: The levitical priests were many because they were prevented by death from remaining in office, but Jesus, because he remains forever, has a priesthood that does not pass away. Therefore, he is always able to save those who approach God through him, since he lives forever to make intercession for them.

It was fitting that we should have such a high priest: holy, innocent, undefiled, separated from sinners, higher than the heavens. He has no need, as did the high priests, to offer sacrifice day after day, first for his own sins and then for those of the people; he did that once for all when he offered himself. For the law appoints men subject to weakness to be high priests, but the word of the oath, which was taken after the law, appoints a son, who has been made perfect forever.

GOSPEL *Mark 12:28b-34*

One of the scribes came to Jesus and asked him, "Which is the first of all the commandments?" Jesus replied, "The first is this: 'Hear, O Israel! The Lord our God is Lord alone! You shall love the Lord your God with all your heart, with all your soul, with all your mind, and with all your strength.' The second is this: 'You shall love your neighbor as yourself.' There is no other commandment greater than these." The scribe said to him, "Well said, teacher. You are right in saying, 'He is One and there is no other than he.' And 'to love him with all your heart, with all your understanding, with all your strength, and to love your neighbor as yourself' is worth more than all burnt offerings and sacrifices." And when Jesus saw that he answered with understanding, he said to him, "You are not far from the kingdom of God." And no one dared to ask him any more questions.

670   THIRTY-FIRST SUNDAY IN ORDINARY TIME / C

READING I   *Wisdom 11:22—12:2 / 153*

Before the LORD the whole universe is as a grain
      from a balance
    or a drop of morning dew come down upon the earth.
But you have mercy on all, because you can do all things;
    and you overlook people's sins that they may repent.
For you love all things that are
    and loathe nothing that you have made;
    for what you hated, you would not have fashioned.
And how could a thing remain, unless you willed it;
    or be preserved, had it not been called forth by you?
But you spare all things, because they are yours,
    O LORD and lover of souls,
    for your imperishable spirit is in all things!
Therefore you rebuke offenders little by little,
    warn them and remind them of the sins
      they are committing,
    that they may abandon their wickedness
      and believe in you, O LORD!

RESPONSORIAL PSALM   *Psalm 145:1-2, 8-9, 10-11, 13, 14*

I will extol you, O my God and King,
    and I will bless your name forever
      and ever.
Every day will I bless you,
    and I will praise your name forever
      and ever. ℟.

Let all your works give you thanks, O
    LORD,
    and let your faithful ones bless you.
Let them discourse of the glory of your
    kingdom
    and speak of your might. ℟.

The LORD is gracious and merciful,
    slow to anger and of great kindness.
The LORD is good to all
    and compassionate toward all his
      works. ℟.

The LORD is faithful in all his words
    and holy in all his works.
The LORD lifts up all who are falling
    and raises up all who are bowed
      down. ℟.

READING II   *2 Thessalonians 1:11—2:2*

Brothers and sisters: We always pray for you, that our God may make you worthy of his calling and powerfully bring to fulfillment every good purpose and every effort of faith, that the name of our Lord Jesus may be glorified in you, and you in him, in accord with the grace of our God and Lord Jesus Christ.

We ask you, brothers and sisters, with regard to the coming of our Lord Jesus Christ and our assembling with him, not to be shaken out of your minds suddenly, or to be alarmed either by a "spirit," or by an oral statement, or by a letter allegedly from us to the effect that the day of the Lord is at hand.

GOSPEL
Luke 19:1-10

At that time, Jesus came to Jericho and intended to pass through the town. Now a man there named Zacchaeus, who was a chief tax collector and also a wealthy man, was seeking to see who Jesus was; but he could not see him because of the crowd, for he was short in stature. So he ran ahead and climbed a sycamore tree in order to see Jesus, who was about to pass that way. When he reached the place, Jesus looked up and said, "Zacchaeus, come down quickly, for today I must stay at your house." And he came down quickly and received him with joy. When they all saw this, they began to grumble, saying, "He has gone to stay at the house of a sinner." But Zacchaeus stood there and said to the Lord, "Behold, half of my possessions, Lord, I shall give to the poor, and if I have extorted anything from anyone I shall repay it four times over." And Jesus said to him, "Today salvation has come to this house because this man too is a descendant of Abraham. For the Son of Man has come to seek and to save what was lost."

THIRTY-SECOND SUNDAY IN ORDINARY TIME / A   671

READING I
Wisdom 6:12-16 / 154

Resplendent and unfading is wisdom,
  and she is readily perceived by those
    who love her,
  and found by those who seek her.
She hastens to make herself known in
    anticipation of their desire;
  whoever watches for her at dawn
    shall not be disappointed,
  for he shall find her sitting by his
    gate.

For taking thought of wisdom is the
    perfection of prudence,
  and whoever for her sake keeps vigil
    shall quickly be free from care;
because she makes her own rounds,
    seeking those worthy of her,
  and graciously appears to them in
    the ways,
  and meets them with all solicitude.

RESPONSORIAL PSALM
Psalm 63:2, 3-4, 5-6, 7-8

My soul is thirst-ing for you, O Lord,

thirst-ing for you my God.

O God, you are my God whom I seek;
  for you my flesh pines and my soul
    thirsts
  like the earth, parched, lifeless and
    without water. ℟.

Thus have I gazed toward you in the
    sanctuary
  to see your power and your glory,
for your kindness is a greater good than
    life;
  my lips shall glorify you. ℟.

Thus will I bless you while I live;
   lifting up my hands, I will call upon
     your name.
As with the riches of a banquet shall my
   soul be satisfied,
   and with exultant lips my mouth
     shall praise you. ℟.

I will remember you upon my couch,
   and through the night-watches I will
     meditate on you:
you are my help,
   and in the shadow of your wings I
     shout for joy. ℟.

READING II
1 Thessalonians 4:13-18 or 4:13-14

For short form read only the part in brackets.

[We do not want you to be unaware, brothers and sisters, about those who have fallen asleep, so that you may not grieve like the rest, who have no hope. For if we believe that Jesus died and rose, so too will God, through Jesus, bring with him those who have fallen asleep.] Indeed, we tell you this, on the word of the Lord, that we who are alive, who are left until the coming of the Lord, will surely not precede those who have fallen asleep. For the Lord himself, with a word of command, with the voice of an archangel and with the trumpet of God, will come down from heaven, and the dead in Christ will rise first. Then we who are alive, who are left, will be caught up together with them in the clouds to meet the Lord in the air. Thus we shall always be with the Lord. Therefore, console one another with these words.

GOSPEL
Matthew 25:1-13

Jesus told his disciples this parable: "The kingdom of heaven will be like ten virgins who took their lamps and went out to meet the bridegroom. Five of them were foolish and five were wise. The foolish ones, when taking their lamps, brought no oil with them, but the wise brought flasks of oil with their lamps. Since the bridegroom was long delayed, they all became drowsy and fell asleep. At midnight, there was a cry, 'Behold, the bridegroom! Come out to meet him!' Then all those virgins got up and trimmed their lamps. The foolish ones said to the wise, 'Give us some of your oil, for our lamps are going out.' But the wise ones replied, 'No, for there may not be enough for us and you. Go instead to the merchants and buy some for yourselves.' While they went off to buy it, the bridegroom came and those who were ready went into the wedding feast with him. Then the door was locked. Afterwards the other virgins came and said, 'Lord, Lord, open the door for us!' But he said in reply, 'Amen, I say to you, I do not know you.' Therefore, stay awake, for you know neither the day nor the hour."

672 THIRTY-SECOND SUNDAY IN ORDINARY TIME / B

READING I
1 Kings 17:10-16 / 155

In those days, Elijah the prophet went to Zarephath. As he arrived at the entrance of the city, a widow was gathering sticks there; he called out to her, "Please bring me a small cupful of water to drink." She left to get it, and he called out after her, "Please bring along a bit of bread." She answered, "As the LORD, your God, lives, I have nothing baked; there is only a handful of flour in my jar and a little oil in my jug. Just now I was collecting a couple of sticks, to go in and prepare something for myself and my son; when we have eaten it, we shall die." Elijah said to her, "Do not be afraid. Go and do as you propose. But first make me a little cake and bring it to me. Then you can prepare something for yourself and your son. For the LORD, the God of Israel, says, 'The jar of flour shall not go empty, nor the jug of oil run dry, until the day when the LORD sends rain upon the earth.'" She left and did as Elijah had said. She was able to eat for a year, and he and her son as well; the jar of flour did not go empty, nor the jug of oil run dry, as the LORD had foretold through Elijah.

RESPONSORIAL PSALM

Psalm 146:7, 8-9, 9-10

Praise the Lord, my soul! Praise the Lord!

The LORD keeps faith forever,
    secures justice for the oppressed,
    gives food to the hungry.
The LORD sets captives free. ℟.

The LORD gives sight to the blind;
    the LORD raises up those who were
    bowed down.

The LORD loves the just;
    the LORD protects strangers. ℟.

The fatherless and the widow he sustains,
    but the way of the wicked he thwarts.
The LORD shall reign forever;
    your God, O Zion, through all
    generations. Alleluia. ℟.

READING II

Hebrews 9:24-28

Christ did not enter into a sanctuary made by hands, a copy of the true one, but heaven itself, that he might now appear before God on our behalf. Not that he might offer himself repeatedly, as the high priest enters each year into the sanctuary with blood that is not his own; if that were so, he would have had to suffer repeatedly from the foundation of the world. But now once for all he has appeared at the end of the ages to take away sin by his sacrifice. Just as it is appointed that human beings die once, and after this the judgment, so also Christ, offered once to take away the sins of many, will appear a second time, not to take away sin but to bring salvation to those who eagerly await him.

GOSPEL

Mark 12:38-44 or 12:41-44

For short form read only the part in brackets.

In the course of his teaching Jesus said to the crowds, "Beware of the scribes, who like to go around in long robes and accept greetings in the marketplaces, seats of honor in synagogues, and places of honor at banquets. They devour the houses of widows and, as a pretext recite lengthy prayers. They will receive a very severe condemnation."

[He sat down opposite the treasury and observed how the crowd put money into the treasury. Many rich people put in large sums. A poor widow also came and put in two small coins worth a few cents. Calling his disciples to himself, he said to them, "Amen, I say to you, this poor widow put in more than all the other contributors to the treasury. For they have all contributed from their surplus wealth, but she, from her poverty, has contributed all she had, her whole livelihood."]

THIRTY-SECOND SUNDAY IN ORDINARY TIME / C   673

READING I

2 Maccabees 7:1-2, 9-14 / 156

It happened that seven brothers with their mother were arrested and tortured with whips and scourges by the king, to force them to eat pork in violation of God's law. One of the brothers, speaking for the others, said: "What do you expect to achieve by questioning us? We are ready to die rather than transgress the laws of our ancestors."

At the point of death he said: "You accursed fiend, you are depriving us of this present life, but the King of the world will raise us up to live again forever. It is for his laws that we are dying."

After him the third suffered their cruel sport. He put out his tongue at once when told to do so, and bravely held out his hands, as he spoke these noble words: "It was from Heaven that I received these; for the sake of his laws I disdain them; from him I hope to receive them again." Even the king and his attendants marveled at the young man's courage, because he regarded his sufferings as nothing.

After he had died, they tortured and maltreated the fourth brother in the same way. When he was near death, he said, "It is my choice to die at the hands of men with the hope God gives of being raised up by him; but for you, there will be no resurrection to life."

RESPONSORIAL PSALM
Psalm 17:1, 5-6, 8, 15

Lord, when your glo-ry ap-pears, my joy will be full.

Hear, O LORD, a just suit;
    attend to my outcry;
    hearken to my prayer from lips
        without deceit. ℟.

My steps have been steadfast in your
    paths,
    my feet have not faltered.
I call upon you, for you will answer
    me, O God;
    incline your ear to me; hear my
        word. ℟.

Keep me as the apple of your eye,
    hide me in the shadow of your wings.
But I in justice shall behold your face;
    on waking I shall be content in your
        presence. ℟.

READING II
2 Thessalonians 2:16—3:5

Brothers and sisters: May our Lord Jesus Christ himself and God our Father, who has loved us and given us everlasting encouragement and good hope through his grace, encourage your hearts and strengthen them in every good deed and word.

Finally, brothers and sisters, pray for us, so that the word of the Lord may speed forward and be glorified, as it did among you, and that we may be delivered from perverse and wicked people, for not all have faith. But the Lord is faithful; he will strengthen you and guard you from the evil one. We are confident of you in the Lord that what we instruct you, you are doing and will continue to do. May the Lord direct your hearts to the love of God and to the endurance of Christ.

GOSPEL
Luke 20:27-38 or 20:27, 34-38

For short form read only the parts in brackets.

[Some Sadducees, those who deny that there is a resurrection, came forward] and put this question to Jesus, saying, "Teacher, Moses wrote for us, 'If someone's brother dies leaving a wife but no child, his brother must take the wife and raise up descendants for his brother.' Now there were seven brothers; the first married a woman but died childless. Then the second and the third married her, and likewise all the seven died childless. Finally the woman also died. Now at the resurrection whose wife will that woman be? For all seven had been married to her." [Jesus said to them, "The children of this age marry and remarry; but those who are deemed worthy to attain to the coming age and to the resurrection of the dead neither marry nor are given in marriage. They can no longer die, for they are like angels; and they are the children of God because they are the ones who will rise. That the dead will rise even Moses made known in the passage about the bush, when he called out 'Lord,' the God of Abraham, the God of Isaac, and the God of Jacob; and he is not God of the dead, but of the living, for to him all are alive."]

THIRTY-THIRD SUNDAY IN ORDINARY TIME / A   674

READING I   *Proverbs 31:10-13, 19-20, 30-31 / 157*

When one finds a worthy wife,
   her value is far beyond pearls.
Her husband, entrusting his heart to her,
   has an unfailing prize.
She brings him good, and not evil,
   all the days of her life.
She obtains wool and flax
   and works with loving hands.
She puts her hands to the distaff,
and her fingers ply the spindle.
She reaches out her hands to the poor,
   and extends her arms to the needy.
Charm is deceptive and beauty fleeting;
   the woman who fears the LORD is to
   be praised.
Give her a reward for her labors,
   and let her works praise her at the
   city gates.

RESPONSORIAL PSALM   *Psalm 128:1-2, 3, 4-5*

Bless - ed   are   those   who   fear   the   Lord.

Blessed are you who fear the LORD,
   who walk in his ways!
For you shall eat the fruit of your
   handiwork;
   blessed shall you be, and favored. ℟.

Your wife shall be like a fruitful vine
   in the recesses of your home;
your children like olive plants
around your table. ℟.

Behold, thus is the man blessed
   who fears the LORD.
The LORD bless you from Zion:
   may you see the prosperity of
   Jerusalem
all the days of your life. ℟.

READING II   *1 Thessalonians 5:1-6*

Concerning times and seasons, brothers and sisters, you have no need for anything to be written to you. For you yourselves know very well that the day of the Lord will come like a thief at night. When people are saying, "Peace and security," then sudden disaster comes upon them, like labor pains upon a pregnant woman, and they will not escape.

But you, brothers and sisters, are not in darkness, for that day to overtake you like a thief. For all of you are children of the light and children of the day. We are not of the night or of darkness. Therefore, let us not sleep as the rest do, but let us stay alert and sober.

GOSPEL   *Matthew 25:14-30 or 25:14-15, 19-21*

For short form read only the parts in brackets.

[Jesus told his disciples this parable: "A man going on a journey called in his servants and entrusted his possessions to them. To one he gave five talents; to another, two; to a third, one—to each according to his ability. Then he went away.] Immediately the one who received five talents went and traded with them, and made another five. Likewise, the one who received two made another two. But the man who received one went off and dug a hole in the ground and buried his master's money.

[After a long time the master of those servants came back and settled accounts with them. The one who had received five talents came forward bringing the additional five. He said, 'Master, you gave me five talents. See, I have made five more.' His master said to him, 'Well done, my good and faithful servant. Since you were faithful in small matters, I will give you great responsibilities. Come, share your master's joy.'] Then the one who had received two talents also came forward and said, 'Master, you gave me two talents. See, I have made two more.' His master said to him, 'Well done, my good and faithful servant. Since you were faithful in small matters, I will give you great responsibilities. Come, share your master's joy.' Then the one who had received the one talent came forward and said, 'Master, I knew you were a demanding person, harvesting where you did not plant and gathering where you did not scatter; so out of fear I went off and buried your talent in the ground. Here it is back.' His master said to him in reply, 'You wicked, lazy servant! So you knew that I harvest where I did not plant and gather where I did not scatter? Should you not then have put my money in the bank so that I could have got it back with interest on my return? Now then! Take the talent from him and give it to the one with ten. For to everyone who has, more will be given and he will grow rich; but from the one who has not, even what he has will be taken away. And throw this useless servant into the darkness outside, where there will be wailing and grinding of teeth.'"

675 THIRTY-THIRD SUNDAY IN ORDINARY TIME / B

READING I *Daniel 12:1-3 / 158*

In those days, I Daniel,
   heard this word of the Lord:
"At that time there shall arise
   Michael, the great prince,
   guardian of your people;
it shall be a time unsurpassed in distress
   since nations began until that time.
At that time your people shall escape,
   everyone who is found written in the
   book.

Many of those who sleep in the dust of
   the earth shall awake;
some shall live forever,
others shall be an everlasting horror
   and disgrace.

But the wise shall shine brightly
   like the splendor of the firmament,
and those who lead the many to justice
   shall be like the stars forever."

RESPONSORIAL PSALM *Psalm 16:5, 8, 9-10, 11*

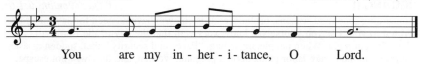

You are my in - her - i - tance, O Lord.

O LORD, my allotted portion and my cup,
   you it is who hold fast my lot.
I set the LORD ever before me;
   with him at my right hand I shall not
   be disturbed. ℟.

Therefore my heart is glad and my soul
   rejoices,
   my body, too, abides in confidence;

because you will not abandon my soul to
   the netherworld,
   nor will you suffer your faithful one
   to undergo corruption. ℟.

You will show me the path to life,
   fullness of joy in your presence,
   the delights at your right hand
   forever. ℟.

READING II *Hebrews 10:11-14, 18*

Brothers and sisters: Every priest stands daily at his ministry, offering frequently those same sacrifices that can never take away sins. But this one offered one sacrifice for sins, and took his seat forever at the right hand of God; now he waits until his enemies are made his footstool. For by one offering he has made perfect forever those who are being consecrated.

   Where there is forgiveness of these, there is no longer offering for sin.

GOSPEL　　　　　　　　　　　　　　　　　　*Mark 13:24-32*

Jesus said to his disciples: "In those days after that tribulation
　　the sun will be darkened,
　　　　and the moon will not give its light,
　　and the stars will be falling from the sky,
　　　　and the powers in the heavens will be shaken.
"And then they will see 'the Son of Man coming in the clouds' with great power and glory, and then he will send out the angels and gather his elect from the four winds, from the end of the earth to the end of the sky.

"Learn a lesson from the fig tree. When its branch becomes tender and sprouts leaves, you know that summer is near. In the same way, when you see these things happening, know that he is near, at the gates. Amen, I say to you, this generation will not pass away until all these things have taken place. Heaven and earth will pass away, but my words will not pass away.

"But of that day or hour, no one knows, neither the angels in heaven, nor the Son, but only the Father."

THIRTY-THIRD SUNDAY IN ORDINARY TIME / C　　　　676

READING I　　　　　　　　　　　　　　*Malachi 3:19-20a / 159*

Lo, the day is coming, blazing like an
　　oven,
　　when all the proud and all evildoers
　　　　will be stubble,
and the day that is coming will set them
　　on fire,

leaving them neither root nor branch,
　　says the LORD of hosts.
But for you who fear my name, there will
　　arise
　　the sun of justice with its healing
　　　　rays.

RESPONSORIAL PSALM　　　　　　　　　*Psalm 98:5-6, 7-8, 9*

The Lord comes to rule the earth with jus - tice.

Sing praise to the LORD with the harp,
　　with the harp and melodious song.
With trumpets and the sound of the horn
　　sing joyfully before the King, the
　　　　LORD. ℟.

Let the sea and what fills it resound,
　　the world and those who dwell in it;

let the rivers clap their hands,
　　the mountains shout with them for
　　　　joy. ℟.

Before the LORD, for he comes,
　　for he comes to rule the earth;
he will rule the world with justice
　　and the peoples with equity. ℟.

READING II　　　　　　　　　　　　*2 Thessalonians 3:7-12*

Brothers and sisters: You know how one must imitate us. For we did not act in a disorderly way among you, nor did we eat food received free from anyone. On the contrary, in toil and drudgery, night and day we worked, so as not to burden any of you. Not that we do not have the right. Rather, we wanted to present ourselves as a model for you, so that you might imitate us. In fact, when we were with you, we instructed you that if anyone was unwilling to work, neither should that one eat. We hear that some are conducting themselves among you in a disorderly way, by not keeping busy but minding the business of others. Such people we instruct and urge in the Lord Jesus Christ to work quietly and to eat their own food.

GOSPEL   *Luke 21:5-19*

While some people were speaking about how the temple was adorned with costly stones and votive offerings, Jesus said, "All that you see here—the days will come when there will not be left a stone upon another stone that will not be thrown down."

Then they asked him, "Teacher, when will this happen? And what sign will there be when all these things are about to happen?" He answered, "See that you not be deceived, for many will come in my name, saying, 'I am he,' and 'The time has come.' Do not follow them! When you hear of wars and insurrections, do not be terrified; for such things must happen first, but it will not immediately be the end." Then he said to them, "Nation will rise against nation, and kingdom against kingdom. There will be powerful earthquakes, famines, and plagues from place to place; and awesome sights and mighty signs will come from the sky.

"Before all this happens, however, they will seize and persecute you, they will hand you over to the synagogues and to prisons, and they will have you led before kings and governors because of my name. It will lead to your giving testimony. Remember, you are not to prepare your defense beforehand, for I myself shall give you a wisdom in speaking that all your adversaries will be powerless to resist or refute. You will even be handed over by parents, brothers, relatives, and friends, and they will put some of you to death. You will be hated by all because of my name, but not a hair on your head will be destroyed. By your perseverance you will secure your lives."

---

677   **LAST SUNDAY IN ORDINARY TIME**
CHRIST THE KING / A

READING I   *Ezekiel 34:11-12, 15-17 / 160*

Thus says the Lord GOD: I myself will look after and tend my sheep. As a shepherd tends his flock when he finds himself among his scattered sheep, so will I tend my sheep. I will rescue them from every place where they were scattered when it was cloudy and dark. I myself will pasture my sheep; I myself will give them rest, says the Lord GOD. The lost I will seek out, the strayed I will bring back, the injured I will bind up, the sick I will heal, but the sleek and the strong I will destroy, shepherding them rightly.

As for you, my sheep, says the Lord GOD, I will judge between one sheep and another, between rams and goats.

RESPONSORIAL PSALM   *Psalm 23:1-2, 2-3, 5-6*

The Lord is my shep-herd; there is noth-ing I shall want.

The LORD is my shepherd; I shall not
  want.
  In verdant pastures he gives me
    repose. ℟.

Beside restful waters he leads me;
  he refreshes my soul.
He guides me in right paths
  for his name's sake. ℟.

You spread the table before me
  in the sight of my foes;
you anoint my head with oil;
  my cup overflows. ℟.

Only goodness and kindness follow me
  all the days of my life;
and I shall dwell in the house of the
  LORD
    for years to come. ℟.

READING II
1 Corinthians 15:20-26, 28

Brothers and sisters: Christ has been raised from the dead, the firstfruits of those who have fallen asleep. For since death came through man, the resurrection of the dead came also through man. For just as in Adam all die, so too in Christ shall all be brought to life, but each one in proper order: Christ the firstfruits; then, at his coming, those who belong to Christ; then comes the end, when he hands over the kingdom to his God and Father, when he has destroyed every sovereignty and every authority and power. For he must reign until he has put all his enemies under his feet. The last enemy to be destroyed is death. When everything is subjected to him, then the Son himself will also be subjected to the one who subjected everything to him, so that God may be all in all.

GOSPEL
Matthew 25:31-46

Jesus said to his disciples: "When the Son of Man comes in his glory, and all the angels with him, he will sit upon his glorious throne, and all the nations will be assembled before him. And he will separate them one from another, as a shepherd separates the sheep from the goats. He will place the sheep on his right and the goats on his left. Then the king will say to those on his right, 'Come, you who are blessed by my Father. Inherit the kingdom prepared for you from the foundation of the world. For I was hungry and you gave me food, I was thirsty and you gave me drink, a stranger and you welcomed me, naked and you clothed me, ill and you cared for me, in prison and you visited me.' Then the righteous will answer him and say, 'Lord, when did we see you hungry and feed you, or thirsty and give you drink? When did we see you a stranger and welcome you, or naked and clothe you? When did we see you ill or in prison, and visit you?' And the king will say to them in reply, 'Amen, I say to you, whatever you did for one of the least brothers of mine, you did for me.' Then he will say to those on his left, 'Depart from me, you accursed, into the eternal fire prepared for the devil and his angels. For I was hungry and you gave me no food, I was thirsty and you gave me no drink, a stranger and you gave me no welcome, naked and you gave me no clothing, ill and in prison, and you did not care for me.' Then they will answer and say, 'Lord, when did we see you hungry or thirsty or a stranger or naked or ill or in prison, and not minister to your needs?' He will answer them, 'Amen, I say to you, what you did not do for one of these least ones, you did not do for me.' And these will go off to eternal punishment, but the righteous to eternal life."

LAST SUNDAY IN ORDINARY TIME
CHRIST THE KING / B
678

READING I
Daniel 7:13-14 / 161

As the visions during the night continued,
I saw
    one like a Son of man coming,
        on the clouds of heaven;
    when he reached the Ancient One
        and was presented before him,
    the one like a Son of man received
        dominion, glory, and kingship;

all peoples, nations, and
    languages serve him.
His dominion is an everlasting
    dominion
that shall not be taken away,
his kingship shall not be
    destroyed.

RESPONSORIAL PSALM
Psalm 93:1, 1-2, 5

The Lord is king; he is robed in maj-es-ty.

The LORD is king, in splendor robed;
    robed is the LORD and girt about
    with strength. ℟.

And he has made the world firm,
    not to be moved.

Your throne stands firm from of old;
    from everlasting you are, O Lord. ℟.

Your decrees are worthy of trust indeed;
    holiness befits your house,
    O Lord, for length of days. ℟.

READING II   *Revelation 1:5-8*

Jesus Christ is the faithful witness, the firstborn of the dead and ruler of the kings of the earth. To him who loves us and has freed us from our sins by his blood, who has made us into a kingdom, priests for his God and Father, to him be glory and power forever and ever. Amen.
    Behold, he is coming amid the clouds,
        and every eye will see him,
        even those who pierced him.
All the peoples of the earth will lament him.
    Yes. Amen.
"I am the Alpha and the Omega," says the Lord God, "the one who is and who was and who is to come, the almighty."

GOSPEL   *John 18:33b-37*

Pilate said to Jesus, "Are you the King of the Jews?" Jesus answered, "Do you say this on your own or have others told you about me?" Pilate answered, "I am not a Jew, am I? Your own nation and the chief priests handed you over to me. What have you done?" Jesus answered, "My kingdom does not belong to this world. If my kingdom did belong to this world, my attendants would be fighting to keep me from being handed over to the Jews. But as it is, my kingdom is not here." So Pilate said to him, "Then you are a king?" Jesus answered, "You say I am a king. For this I was born and for this I came into the world, to testify to the truth. Everyone who belongs to the truth listens to my voice."

679   LAST SUNDAY IN ORDINARY TIME
CHRIST THE KING / C

READING I   *2 Samuel 5:1-3 / 162*

In those days, all the tribes of Israel came to David in Hebron and said: "Here we are, your bone and your flesh. In days past, when Saul was our king, it was you who led the Israelites out and brought them back. And the LORD said to you, 'You shall shepherd my people Israel and shall be commander of Israel.'" When all the elders of Israel came to David in Hebron, King David made an agreement with them there before the LORD, and they anointed him king of Israel.

RESPONSORIAL PSALM   *Psalm 122:1-2, 3-4, 4-5*

Let us go re - joic - ing   to the house   of the Lord.

I rejoiced because they said to me,
    "We will go up to the house of the
        LORD."
And now we have set foot
    within your gates, O Jerusalem. ℟.

Jerusalem, built as a city
    with compact unity.
To it the tribes go up,
    the tribes of the LORD. ℟.

According to the decree for Israel,
to give thanks to the name of the
LORD.

In it are set up judgment seats,
seats for the house of David. ℟.

READING II   *Colossians 1:12-20*

Brothers and sisters: Let us give thanks to the Father, who has made you fit to share in
the inheritance of the holy ones in light. He delivered us from the power of darkness and
transferred us to the kingdom of his beloved Son, in whom we have redemption, the
forgiveness of sins.
He is the image of the invisible God,
the firstborn of all creation.
For in him were created all things in heaven and on earth,
the visible and the invisible,
whether thrones or dominions or principalities or powers;
all things were created through him and for him.
He is before all things,
and in him all things hold together.
He is the head of the body, the church.
He is the beginning, the firstborn from the dead,
that in all things he himself might be preeminent.
For in him all the fullness was pleased to dwell,
and through him to reconcile all things for him,
making peace by the blood of his cross
through him, whether those on earth or those in heaven.

GOSPEL   *Luke 23:35-43*

The rulers sneered at Jesus and said, "He saved others, let him save himself if he is the
chosen one, the Christ of God." Even the soldiers jeered at him. As they approached to
offer him wine they called out, "If you are King of the Jews, save yourself." Above him
there was an inscription that read, "This is the King of the Jews."
Now one of the criminals hanging there reviled Jesus, saying, "Are you not the
Christ? Save yourself and us." The other, however, rebuking him, said in reply, "Have
you no fear of God, for you are subject to the same condemnation? And indeed, we have
been condemned justly, for the sentence we received corresponds to our crimes, but this
man has done nothing criminal." Then he said, "Jesus, remember me when you come
into your kingdom." He replied to him, "Amen, I say to you, today you will be with me
in Paradise."

Seasons:
Weekday Psalm Responses

680 FIRST WEEK OF ADVENT

Monday / *175*
I rejoiced when I heard them say:
let us go to the house of the Lord.

Tuesday / *176*
Justice shall flourish in his time,
and fullness of peace for ever.

Wednesday / *177*
I shall live in the house of the Lord
all the days of my life.

Thursday / *178*
Blessed is he who comes in the
name of the Lord.

Or: Alleluia.

Friday / *179*
The Lord is my light and my
salvation.

Or: Alleluia.

Saturday / *180*
Happy are all who long for the
coming of the Lord.

Or: Alleluia.

681 SECOND WEEK OF ADVENT

Monday / *181*
Our God will come to save us!

Tuesday / *182*
The Lord our God comes in
strength.

Wednesday / *183*
O bless the Lord, my soul.

Thursday / *184*
The Lord is kind and merciful;
slow to anger, and rich in
compassion.

Friday / *185*
Those who follow you, Lord, will
   have the light of life.

Saturday / *186*
Lord, make us turn to you,
let us see your face and we shall be
   saved.

THIRD WEEK OF ADVENT 682

Monday / *187*
Teach me your ways, O Lord.

Tuesday / *188*
The Lord hears the cry of the poor.

Wednesday / *189*
Let the clouds rain down the Just
   One,
and the earth bring forth a savior.

Thursday / *190*
I will praise you, Lord,
for you have rescued me.

Friday / *191*
O God, let all the nations praise
   you!

LAST DAYS OF ADVENT 683

December 17 / *193*
Justice shall flourish in his time,
and fullness of peace for ever.

December 18 / *194*
Justice shall flourish in his time,
and fullness of peace for ever.

December 19 / *195*
Fill me with your praise
and I will sing your glory!

December 20 / *196*
Let the Lord enter;
he is king of glory.

December 21 / *197*
Cry out with joy in the Lord, you
   holy ones;
sing a new song to him.

December 22 / *198*
My heart rejoices in the Lord, my
   Savior.

December 23 / *199*
Lift up your heads and see;
your redemption is near at hand.

December 24 / *200*
Mass in the Morning
For ever I will sing the goodness of
   the Lord.

SEASON OF CHRISTMAS 684

December 29 / *202*
Let heaven and earth exult in joy!

December 30 / *203*
Let heaven and earth exult in joy!

December 31 / *204*
Let heaven and earth exult in joy!

January 2 / *205*
All the ends of the earth have seen
   the saving power of God.

January 3 / *206*
All the ends of the earth have seen
   the saving power of God.

January 4 / *207*
All the ends of the earth have seen
   the saving power of God.

January 5 / *208*
Let all the earth cry out to God
   with joy.

January 6 / *209*
Praise the Lord, Jerusalem.
Or: Alleluia.

January 7 / *210*
The Lord takes delight in his
   people.
Or: Alleluia.

685 **AFTER EPIPHANY**

Monday / *212*
I will give you all the nations for
   your heritage.

Tuesday / *213*
Lord, every nation on earth will
   adore you.

Wednesday / *214*
Lord, every nation on earth will
   adore you.

Thursday / *215*
Lord, every nation on earth will
   adore you.

Friday / *216*
Praise the Lord, Jerusalem.
Or: Alleluia.

Saturday / *217*
The Lord takes delight in his
   people.
Or: Alleluia.

686 **ASH WEDNESDAY**

READING I   *Joel 2:12-18 / 219*

Even now, says the Lord,
   return to me with your whole heart,
   with fasting, and weeping, and
      mourning;
Rend your hearts, not your garments,
   and return to the Lord, your God.
For gracious and merciful is he,
   slow to anger, rich in kindness,
   and relenting in punishment.
Perhaps he will again relent
   and leave behind him a blessing,
Offerings and libations,
   for the Lord, your God.
Blow the trumpet in Zion!
   Proclaim a fast,
   call an assembly;
Gather the people,
   notify the congregation;
Assemble the elders,
   gather the children
   and the infants at the breast;
Let the bridegroom quit his room,
   and the bride her chamber.
Between the porch and the altar
   let the priests, the ministers of the
      Lord, weep,
And say, "Spare, O Lord, your people,
   and make not your heritage a
      reproach,
   with the nations ruling over them!
Why should they say among the
      peoples,
   'Where is their God?'"
Then the Lord was stirred to
      concern for his
   land and took pity on his people.

RESPONSORIAL PSALM

Psalm 51:3-4, 5-6, 12-13, 14, 17

Be mer - ci - ful, O Lord, for we have sinned.

Have mercy on me, O God, in your
    goodness
  in the greatness of your compassion
    wipe out my offense.
Thorougly wash me from my guilt
  and of my sin cleanse me. ℟.

For I acknowledge my offense,
  and my sin is before me always:
"Against you only have I sinned,
  and done what is evil in your
    sight." ℟.

A clean heart create for me, O God,
  and a steadfast spirit renew within
    me.
Cast me not out from your presence,
  and your Holy Spirit take not from
    me. ℟.

Give me back the joy of your salvation,
  and a willing spirit sustain in me.
O Lord, open my lips,
  and my mouth shall proclaim your
    praise. ℟.

READING II

2 Corinthians 5:20—6:2

We are ambassadors for Christ, God as it were appealing through us. We implore you, in Christ's name: be reconciled to God! For our sakes God made him who did not know sin to be sin, so that in him we might become the very holiness of God.

As your fellow workers we beg you not to receive the grace of God in vain. For he says, "In an acceptable time I have heard you; on a day of salvation I have helped you." Now is the acceptable time! Now is the day of salvation!

GOSPEL

Matthew 6:1-6, 16-18

Jesus said to his disciples: "Take care not to perform righteous deeds in order that people may see them; otherwise, you will have no recompense from your heavenly Father. When you give alms, do not blow a trumpet before you, as the hypocrites do in the synagogues and in the streets to win the praise of others. Amen, I say to you, they have received their reward. But when you give alms, do not let your left hand know what your right is doing, so that your almsgiving may be secret. And your Father who sees in secret will repay you.

"When you pray, do not be like the hypocrites, who love to stand and pray in the synagogues and on street corners so that others may see them. Amen, I say to you, they have received their reward. But when you pray, go to your inner room, close the door, and pray to your Father in secret. And your Father who sees in secret will repay you.

"When you fast, do not look gloomy like the hypocrites. They neglect their appearance, so that they may appear to others to be fasting. Amen, I say to you, they have received their reward. But when you fast, anoint your head and wash your face, so that you may not appear to be fasting, except to your Father who is hidden. And your Father who sees what is hidden will repay you."

AFTER ASH WEDNESDAY

687

Thursday / 220

Happy are they who hope in the
  Lord.

Friday / 221

A broken, humbled heart, O God,
  you will not scorn.

Saturday / 222

Teach me your way, O Lord, that I
  may be faithful in your sight.

688 FIRST WEEK OF LENT

Monday / *224*
Your words, Lord, are spirit and
    life.

Tuesday / *225*
From all their afflictions
God will deliver the just.

Wednesday / *226*
A broken, humbled heart,
O God, you will not scorn.

Thursday / *227*
Lord, on the day I called for help,
you answered me.

Friday / *228*
If you, O Lord, laid bare our guilt
who could endure it?

Saturday / *229*
Happy are they who follow the law
    of the Lord.

689 SECOND WEEK OF LENT

Monday / *230*
Lord, do not deal with us as our
    sins deserve.

Tuesday / *231*
To the upright
I will show the saving power of
    God.

Wednesday / *232*
Save me, O Lord, in your steadfast
    love.

Thursday / *233*
Happy are they who hope in the
    Lord.

Friday / *234*
Remember the marvels the Lord has
    done.

Saturday / *235*
The Lord is kind and merciful.

690 THIRD WEEK OF LENT

Monday / *237*
My soul is thirsting for the living
    God:
when shall I see him face to face?

Tuesday / *238*
Remember your mercies, O Lord.

Wednesday / *239*
Praise the Lord, Jerusalem.

Thursday / *240*
If today you hear his voice,
harden not your hearts.

Friday / *241*
I am the Lord, your God:
hear my voice.

Saturday / *242*
It is steadfast love, not sacrifice,
that God desires.

691 FOURTH WEEK OF LENT

Monday / *244*
I will praise you, Lord, for you
    have rescued me.

Tuesday / *245*
The mighty Lord is with us;
The God of Jacob is our refuge.

Wednesday / *246*
The Lord is kind and merciful.

Friday / *248*
The Lord is near to broken hearts.

Thursday / *247*
Lord, remember us,
for the love you bear your people.

Saturday / *249*
Lord, my God, I take shelter in you.

FIFTH WEEK OF LENT 692

Monday / *251*
Though I walk in the valley of
     darkness,
I fear no evil, for you are with me.

Thursday / *254*
The Lord remembers his covenant
     for ever.

Friday / *255*
In my distress I called upon the
     Lord,
and he heard my voice.

Tuesday / *252*
O Lord, hear my prayer,
and let my cry come to you.

Wednesday / *253*
Glory and praise for ever!

Saturday / *256*
The Lord will guard us,
like a shepherd guarding his flock.

HOLY WEEK 693

Monday / *257*
The Lord is my light and my
     salvation.

Wednesday / *259*
Lord, in your great love, answer
     me.

Tuesday / *258*
I will sing of your salvation.

OCTAVE OF EASTER 694

Monday / *261*
Keep me safe, O God;
you are my hope.
Or: Alleluia.

Thursday / *264*
O Lord, our God,
how wonderful your name in all the
     earth!
Or: Alleluia.

Tuesday / *262*
The earth is full of the goodness of
     the Lord.
Or: Alleluia.

Friday / *265*
The stone rejected by the builders
     has become the cornerstone.
Or: Alleluia.

Wednesday / *263*
The earth is full of the goodness of
     the Lord.
Or: Alleluia.

Saturday / *266*
I praise you, Lord,
for you have answered me.
Or: Alleluia.

695 SECOND WEEK OF EASTER

Monday / *267*
Happy are all who put their trust in
the Lord.
Or: Alleluia.

Tuesday / *268*
The Lord is king;
he is robed in majesty.
Or: Alleluia.

Wednesday / *269*
The Lord hears the cry of the poor.
Or: Alleluia.

Thursday / *270*
The Lord hears the cry of the poor.
Or: Alleluia.

Friday / *271*
One thing I seek: to dwell in the
house of the Lord.
Or: Alleluia.

Saturday / *272*
Lord, let your mercy be on us,
as we place our trust in you.
Or: Alleluia.

696 THIRD WEEK OF EASTER

Monday / *273*
Happy are those of blameless life.
Or: Alleluia.

Tuesday / *274*
Into your hands, O Lord,
I entrust my spirit.
Or: Alleluia.

Wednesday / *275*
Let all the earth cry out to God
with joy.
Or: Alleluia.

Thursday / *276*
Let all the earth cry out to God
with joy.
Or: Alleluia.

Friday / *277*
Go out to all the world,
and tell the Good News.
Or: Alleluia.

Saturday / *278*
What return can I make to the Lord
for all that he gives to me?
Or: Alleluia.

697 FOURTH WEEK OF EASTER

Monday / *279*
My soul is thirsting for the living
God.
Or: Alleluia.

Tuesday / *280*
All you nations, praise the Lord.
Or: Alleluia.

Wednesday / *281*
O God, let all the nations praise
you!
Or: Alleluia.

Thursday / *282*
For ever I will sing the goodness of
the Lord.
Or: Alleluia.

Friday / *283*
You are my Son;
this day have I begotten you.
Or: Alleluia.

Saturday / *284*
All the ends of the earth have seen
the saving power of God.
Or: Alleluia.

FIFTH WEEK OF EASTER 698

Monday / 285
Not to us, O Lord,
but to your name give the glory.
Or: Alleluia.

Tuesday / 286
Your friends tell the glory of your
kingship, Lord.
Or: Alleluia.

Wednesday / 287
I rejoiced when I heard them say:
let us go to the house of the Lord.
Or: Alleluia.

Thursday / 288
Proclaim his marvelous deeds
to all the nations.
Or: Alleluia.

Friday / 289
I will praise you among the nations,
O Lord.
Or: Alleluia.

Saturday / 290
Let all the earth cry out to God
with joy.
Or: Alleluia.

SIXTH WEEK OF EASTER 699

Monday / 291
The Lord takes delight in his people.
Or: Alleluia.

Tuesday / 292
Your right hand has saved me, O
Lord.
Or: Alleluia.

Wednesday / 293
Heaven and earth are filled with
your glory.
Or: Alleluia.

Thursday / 294
The Lord has revealed to the nations
his saving power.
Or: Alleluia.

Friday / 295
God is king of all the earth.
Or: Alleluia.

Saturday / 296
God is king of all the earth.
Or: Alleluia.

SEVENTH WEEK OF EASTER 700

Monday / 297
Sing to God, O kingdoms of the
earth.
Or: Alleluia.

Tuesday / 298
Sing to God, O kingdoms of the
earth.
Or: Alleluia.

Wednesday / 299
Sing to God, O kingdoms of the
earth.
Or: Alleluia.

Thursday / 300
Keep me safe, O God;
you are my hope.
Or: Alleluia.

Friday / 301
The Lord has set his throne in
heaven.
Or: Alleluia.

Saturday / 302
The just will gaze on your face, O
Lord.
Or: Alleluia.

Ordinary Time: Psalm Responses

FIRST WEEK IN ORDINARY TIME

Monday / *305*

I   Let all his angels worship him.

II To you, Lord, I will offer a
sacrifice of praise.

   Or: Alleluia.

Tuesday / *306*

I   You gave your Son authority
over all creation.

II My heart rejoices in the Lord,
my Savior.

Wednesday / *307*

I   The Lord remembers his
covenant for ever.

   Or: Alleluia.

II Here am I, Lord; I come to do
your will.

Thursday / *308*

I   If today you hear his voice,
harden not your hearts.

II Save us, Lord, in your mercy.

Friday / *309*

I   Do not forget the works of the
Lord!

II For ever I will sing the
goodness of the Lord.

Saturday / *310*

I   Your words, Lord, are spirit
and life.

II Lord, your strength gives joy to
the king.

SECOND WEEK IN ORDINARY TIME

Monday / *311*

I   You are a priest for ever,
in the line of Melchizedek.

II To the upright I will show the
saving power of God.

Tuesday / *312*

I   The Lord will remember his
covenant for ever.

   Or: Alleluia.

II I have found David, my
servant.

Wednesday / *313*

I You are a priest for ever,
in the line of Melchizedek.

II Blessed be the Lord, my Rock!

Thursday / *314*

I Here am I, Lord;
I come to do your will.

II In God I trust;
I shall not fear.

Friday / *315*

I Kindness and truth shall meet.

II Have mercy on me, God, have
mercy.

Saturday / *316*

I God mounts his throne to
shouts of joy;
a blare of trumpets for the Lord.

II Let us see your face, Lord,
and we shall be saved.

THIRD WEEK IN ORDINARY TIME   703

Monday / *317*

I Sing to the Lord a new song,
for he has done marvelous
deeds.

II My faithfulness and love shall
be with him.

Tuesday / *318*

I Here am I, Lord;
I come to do your will.

II Who is the king of glory?
It is the Lord!

Wednesday / *319*

I You are a priest for ever,
in the line of Melchizedek.

II For ever I will keep my love for
him.

Thursday / *320*

I Lord, this is the people that
longs to see your face.

II God will give him the throne of
David, his father.

Friday / *321*

I The salvation of the just comes
from the Lord.

II Be merciful, O Lord, for we
have sinned.

Saturday / *322*

I Blessed be the Lord God of
Israel,
for he has visited his people.

II Create a clean heart in me, O
God.

FOURTH WEEK IN ORDINARY TIME   704

Monday / *323*

I Let your hearts take comfort,
all who hope in the Lord.

II Lord, rise up and save me.

Tuesday / *324*

I They will praise you, Lord,
who long for you.

II Listen, Lord, and answer me.

Wednesday / *325*

I The Lord's kindness is
everlasting to those who
fear him.

II Lord, forgive the wrong I
have done.

Thursday / *326*

I God, in your temple, we ponder
your love.

II Lord, you are exalted over all.

Friday / *327*

I   The Lord is my light and my
     salvation.

II Blessed be God my salvation!

Saturday / *328*

I   The Lord is my shepherd;
     there is nothing I shall want.

II Lord, teach me your decrees.

---

705 FIFTH WEEK IN ORDINARY TIME

Monday / *329*

I   May the Lord be glad in his
     works.

II Lord, go up to the place of
     your rest!

Tuesday / *330*

I   O Lord, our God,
     how wonderful your name in all
     the earth!

II How lovely is your dwelling
     place,
     Lord, mighty God!

Wednesday / *331*

I   Oh, bless the Lord, my soul!

II The mouth of the just man
     murmurs wisdom.

Thursday / *332*

I   Happy are those who fear the
     Lord.

II Lord, remember us,
     for the love you bear your
     people.

Friday / *333*

I   Happy are those whose sins are
     forgiven.

II I am the Lord, your God:
     hear my voice.

Saturday / *334*

I   In every age, O Lord, you
     have been our refuge.

II Lord, remember us,
     for the love you bear your
     people.

---

706 SIXTH WEEK IN ORDINARY TIME

Monday / *335*

I   Offer to God a sacrifice of
     praise.

II Be kind to me, Lord, and I
     shall live.

Tuesday / *336*

I   The Lord will bless his people
     with peace.

II Happy the man you teach,
     O Lord.

Wednesday / *337*

I   To you, Lord, I will offer a
     sacrifice of praise.

    Or: Alleluia.

II He who does justice shall live
     on the Lord's holy mountain.

Thursday / *338*

I   From heaven the Lord looks
     down on the earth.

II The Lord hears the cry of the
     poor.

Friday / *339*

I   Happy the people the Lord has
     chosen to be his own.

II Happy are those who do what
     the Lord commands.

Saturday / *340*

I   I will praise your name for
     ever, Lord.

II You will protect us, Lord.

SEVENTH WEEK IN ORDINARY TIME 707

Monday / *341*

I The Lord is king; he is robed in majesty.

II The precepts of the Lord give joy to the heart.

Tuesday / *342*

I Commit your life to the Lord, and he will help you.

II Throw your cares on the Lord, and he will support you.

Wednesday / *343*

I O Lord, great peace have they who love the law.

II Happy the poor in spirit; the kingdom of heaven is theirs!

Thursday / *344*

I Happy are they who hope in the Lord.

II Happy the poor in spirit; the kingdom of heaven is theirs!

Friday / *345*

I Guide me, Lord, in the way of your commands.

II The Lord is kind and merciful.

Saturday / *346*

I The Lord's kindness is everlasting to those who fear him.

II Let my prayer come like incense before you.

EIGHTH WEEK IN ORDINARY TIME 708

Monday / *347*

I Let the just exult and rejoice in the Lord.

II The Lord will remember his covenant for ever.

Or: Alleluia.

Tuesday / *348*

I To the upright I will show the saving power of God.

II The Lord has made known his salvation.

Wednesday / *349*

I Show us, O Lord, the light of your kindness.

II Praise the Lord, Jerusalem.

Or: Alleluia.

Thursday / *350*

I By the word of the Lord the heavens were made.

II Come with joy into the presence of the Lord.

Friday / *351*

I The Lord takes delight in his people.

II The Lord comes to judge the earth.

Saturday / *352*

I The precepts of the Lord give joy to the heart.

II My soul is thirsting for you, O Lord my God.

709   NINTH WEEK IN ORDINARY TIME

Monday / *353*

I   Happy the man who fears the Lord.

Or: Alleluia.

II   In you, my God, I place my trust.

Tuesday / *354*

I   The heart of the just man is secure, trusting in the Lord.

Or: Alleluia.

II   In every age, O Lord, you have been our refuge.

Wednesday / *355*

I   To you, O Lord, I lift my soul.

II   To you, O Lord, I lift up my eyes.

Thursday / *356*

I   Happy are those who fear the Lord.

II   Teach me your ways, O Lord.

Friday / *357*

I   Praise the Lord, my soul!

Or: Alleluia.

II   O Lord, great peace have they who love your law.

Saturday / *358*

I   Blessed be God, who lives for ever.

II   I will sing of your salvation.

710   TENTH WEEK IN ORDINARY TIME

Monday / *359*

I   Taste and see the goodness of the Lord.

II   Our help is from the Lord who made heaven and earth.

Tuesday / *360*

I   Lord, let your face shine on me.

II   Lord, let your face shine on us.

Wednesday / *361*

I   Holy is the Lord our God.

II   Keep me safe, O God; you are my hope.

Thursday / *362*

I   The glory of the Lord will dwell in our land.

II   It is right to praise you in Zion, O God.

Friday / *363*

I   To you, Lord, I will offer a sacrifice of praise.

Or: Alleluia.

II   I long to see your face, O Lord.

Saturday / *364*

I   The Lord is kind and merciful.

II   You are my inheritance, O Lord.

711   ELEVENTH WEEK IN ORDINARY TIME

Monday / *365*

I   The Lord has made known his salvation.

II   Lord, listen to my groaning.

Tuesday / *366*

I   Praise the Lord, my soul!

Or: Alleluia.

II   Be merciful, O Lord, for we have sinned.

Wednesday / *367*

I Happy the man who fears the Lord.

Or: Alleluia.

II Let your hearts take comfort, all who hope in the Lord.

Thursday / *368*

I Your works, O Lord, are justice and truth.

Or: Alleluia.

II Let good men rejoice in the Lord.

Friday / *369*

I From all their afflictions God will deliver the just.

II The Lord has chosen Zion for his dwelling.

Saturday / *370*

I Taste and see the goodness of the Lord.

II For ever I will keep my love for him.

TWELFTH WEEK IN ORDINARY TIME   712

Monday / *371*

I Happy the people the Lord has chosen to be his own.

II Help us with your right hand, O Lord, and answer us.

Tuesday / *372*

I He who does justice will live in the presence of the Lord.

II God upholds his city for ever.

Wednesday / *373*

I The Lord remembers his covenant for ever.

Or: Alleluia.

II Teach me the way of your decrees, O Lord.

Thursday / *374*

I Give thanks to the Lord for he is good.

Or: Alleluia.

II For the glory of your name, O Lord, deliver us.

Friday / *375*

I See how the Lord blesses those who fear him.

II Let my tongue be silenced, if I ever forget you!

Saturday / *376*

I The Lord has remembered his mercy.

II Lord, forget not the life of your poor ones.

THIRTEENTH WEEK IN ORDINARY TIME   713

Monday / *377*

I The Lord is kind and merciful.

II Remember this, you who never think of God.

Tuesday / *378*

I O Lord, your kindness is before my eyes.

II Lead me in your justice, Lord.

Wednesday / *379*

I   The Lord hears the cry of the poor.

II   To the upright I will show the saving power of God.

Thursday / *380*

I   I will walk in the presence of the Lord, in the land of the living.

    Or: Alleluia.

II   The judgments of the Lord are true, and all of them just.

Friday / *381*

I   Give thanks to the Lord for he is good.

    Or: Alleluia.

II   Man does not live on bread alone, but on every word that comes from the mouth of God.

Saturday / *382*

I   Praise the Lord for he is good!

    Or: Alleluia.

II   The Lord speaks of peace to his people.

714   FOURTEENTH WEEK IN ORDINARY TIME

Monday / *383*

I   In you, my God, I place my trust.

II   The Lord is kind and merciful.

Tuesday / *384*

I   In my justice, I shall see your face, O Lord.

II   The house of Israel trusts in the Lord.

    Or: Alleluia.

Wednesday / *385*

I   Lord, let your mercy be on us, as we place our trust in you.

II   Seek always the face of the Lord.

    Or: Alleluia.

Thursday / *386*

I   Remember the marvels the Lord has done.

    Or: Alleluia.

II   Let us see your face, Lord, and we shall be saved.

Friday / *387*

I   The salvation of the just comes from the Lord.

II   My mouth will declare your praise.

Saturday / *388*

I   Turn to the Lord in your need, and you will live.

II   The Lord is king; he is robed in majesty.

715   FIFTEENTH WEEK IN ORDINARY TIME

Monday / *389*

I   Our help is in the name of the Lord.

II   To the upright I will show the saving power of God.

Tuesday / *390*

I   Turn to the Lord in your need, and you will live.

II   God upholds his city for ever.

Wednesday / *391*

I   The Lord is kind and merciful.

II The Lord will not abandon his people.

Thursday / *392*

I   The Lord remembers his covenant for ever.

   Or: Alleluia.

II From heaven the Lord looks down on the earth.

Friday / *393*

I   I will take the cup of salvation, and call on the name of the Lord.

   Or: Alleluia.

II You saved my life, O Lord; I shall not die.

Saturday / *394*

I   His love is everlasting.

   Or: Alleluia.

II Do not forget the poor, O Lord!

SIXTEENTH WEEK IN ORDINARY TIME   716

Monday / *395*

I   Let us sing to the Lord; he has covered himself in glory.

II To the upright I will show the saving power of God.

Tuesday / *396*

I   Let us sing to the Lord; he has covered himself in glory.

II Lord, let us see your kindness.

Wednesday / *397*

I   The Lord gave them bread from heaven.

II I will sing of your salvation.

Thursday / *398*

I   Glory and praise for ever!

II You are the source of life, O Lord.

Friday / *399*

I   Lord, you have the words of everlasting life.

II The Lord will guard us, like a shepherd guarding his flock.

Saturday / *400*

I   Offer to God a sacrifice of praise.

II How lovely is your dwelling place, Lord, mighty God!

SEVENTEENTH WEEK IN ORDINARY TIME   717

Monday / *401*

I   Give thanks to the Lord for he is good.

   Or: Alleluia.

II You have forgotten God who gave you birth.

Tuesday / *402*

I   The Lord is kind and merciful.

II For the glory of your name, O Lord, deliver us.

Wednesday / *403*

I   Holy is the Lord our God.

II God is my refuge on the day of
     distress.

Thursday / *404*

I   How lovely is your dwelling
     place,
     Lord, mighty God!

II Blest are they whose help is the
     God of Jacob.

    Or: Alleluia.

Friday / *405*

I   Sing with joy to God our help.

II Lord, in your great love,
     answer me.

Saturday / *406*

I   O God, let all the nations praise
     you!

II Lord, in your great love,
     answer me.

718 EIGHTEENTH WEEK IN ORDINARY TIME

Monday / *407*

I   Sing with joy to God our help.

II Teach me your laws, O Lord.

Tuesday / *408*

I   Be merciful, O Lord, for we
     have sinned.

II The Lord will build up Zion
     again,
     and appear in all his glory.

Wednesday / *409*

I   Lord, remember us,
     for the love you bear your
     people.

    Or: Alleluia.

II The Lord will guard us,
     like a shepherd guarding his
     flock.

Thursday / *410*

I   If today you hear his voice,
     harden not your hearts.

II Create a clean heart in me, O
     God.

Friday / *411*

I   I remember the deeds of the
     Lord.

II It is I who deal death and give
     life.

Saturday / *412*

I   I love you, Lord, my strength.

II You will never abandon those
     who seek you, Lord.

719 NINETEENTH WEEK IN ORDINARY TIME

Monday / *413*

I   Praise the Lord, Jerusalem.

    Or: Alleluia.

II Heaven and earth are filled with
     your glory.

    Or: Alleluia.

Tuesday / *414*

I   The portion of the Lord is his
     people.

II How sweet to my taste is your
     promise!

Wednesday / *415*

I   Blessed be God who filled my
     soul with life!

II The glory of the Lord is higher
     than the skies.

    Or: Alleluia.

Thursday / *416*

I   Alleluia.

II Do not forget the works of the
     Lord!

Friday / *417*

I   His love is everlasting.

    Or: Alleluia.

II You have turned from your
     anger to comfort me.

Saturday / *418*

I   You are my inheritance, O
     Lord.

II Create a clean heart in me, O
     God.

TWENTIETH WEEK IN ORDINARY TIME   720

Monday / *419*

I   Lord, remember us,
    for the love you bear your
     people.

II You have forgotten God who
     gave you birth.

Tuesday / *420*

I   The Lord speaks of peace to his
     people.

II It is I who deal death and give
     life.

Wednesday / *421*

I   Lord, your strength gives joy to
     the king.

II The Lord is my shepherd;
    there is nothing I shall want.

Thursday / *422*

I   Here am I, Lord;
    I come to do your will.

II I will pour clean water on you
    and wash away all your sins.

Friday / *423*

I   Praise the Lord, my soul!

    Or: Alleluia.

II Give thanks to the Lord,
    his love is everlasting.

    Or: Alleluia.

Saturday / *424*

I   See how the Lord blesses those
     who fear him.

II The glory of the Lord will
    dwell in our land.

TWENTY-FIRST WEEK IN ORDINARY TIME   721

Monday / *425*

I   The Lord takes delight in his
     people.

    Or: Alleluia.

II Proclaim his marvelous deeds to
    all the nations.

Tuesday / *426*

I   You have searched me
    and you know me, Lord.

II The Lord comes to judge the
    earth.

Wednesday / 427
I   You have searched me and you know me, Lord.
II Happy are those who fear the Lord.

Thursday / 428
I   Fill us with your love, O Lord, and we will sing for joy!
II I will praise your name for ever, Lord.

Friday / 429
I   Let good men rejoice in the Lord.
II The earth is full of the goodness of the Lord.

Saturday / 430
I   The Lord comes to rule the earth with justice.
II Happy the people the Lord has chosen to be his own.

722 TWENTY-SECOND WEEK IN ORDINARY TIME

Monday / 431
I   The Lord comes to judge the earth.
II Lord, I love your commands.

Tuesday / 432
I   I believe that I shall see the good things of the Lord in the land of the living.
II The Lord is just in all his ways.

Wednesday / 433
I   I trust in the kindness of God for ever.
II Happy the people the Lord has chosen to be his own.

Thursday / 434
I   The Lord has made known his salvation.
II To the Lord belongs the earth and all that fills it.

Friday / 435
I   Come with joy into the presence of the Lord.
II The salvation of the just comes from the Lord.

Saturday / 436
I   God himself is my help.
II The Lord is near to all who call him.

723 TWENTY-THIRD WEEK IN ORDINARY TIME

Monday / 437
I   In God is my safety and my glory.
II Lead me in your justice, Lord.

Tuesday / 438
I   The Lord is compassionate to all his creatures.
II The Lord takes delight in his people.
    Or: Alleluia.

Wednesday / 439
I   The Lord is compassionate to all his creatures.
II Listen to me, daughter; see and bend your ear.

Thursday / 440
I   Let everything that breathes praise the Lord!
    Or: Alleluia.
II Guide me, Lord, along the everlasting way.

Friday / *441*

I   You are my inheritance, O Lord.

II How lovely is your dwelling place,
Lord, mighty God!

Saturday / *442*

I   Blessed be the name of the Lord for ever.

Or: Alleluia.

II To you, Lord, I will offer a sacrifice of praise.

TWENTY-FOURTH WEEK IN ORDINARY TIME   724

Monday / *443*

I   Blest be the Lord for he has heard my prayer.

II Proclaim the death of the Lord until he comes again.

Tuesday / *444*

I   I will walk with blameless heart.

II We are his people:
the sheep of his flock.

Wednesday / *445*

I   How great are the works of the Lord!

Or: Alleluia.

II Happy the people the Lord has chosen to be his own.

Thursday / *446*

I   How great are the works of the Lord!

Or: Alleluia.

II Give thanks to the Lord, for he is good.

Or: Alleluia.

Friday / *447*

I   Happy the poor in spirit;
the kingdom of heaven is theirs!

II Lord, when your glory appears,
my joy will be full.

Saturday / *448*

I   Come with joy into the presence of the Lord.

II I will walk in the presence of God,
with the light of the living.

TWENTY-FIFTH WEEK IN ORDINARY TIME   725

Monday / *449*

I   The Lord has done marvels for us.

II He who does justice shall live on the Lord's holy mountain.

Tuesday / *450*

I   I rejoiced when I heard them say:
let us go to the house of the Lord.

II Guide me, Lord, in the way of your commands.

Wednesday / *451*

I   Blessed be God, who lives for ever.

II Your word, O Lord, is a lamp for my feet.

Thursday / *452*

I   The Lord takes delight in his people.

II In every age, O Lord, you have been our refuge.

Friday / *453*

I   Hope in God; I will praise him, my savior and my God.

II Blessed be the Lord, my Rock!

Saturday / *454*

I   The Lord will guard us, like a shepherd guarding his flock.

II In every age, O Lord, you have been our refuge.

---

726 **TWENTY-SIXTH WEEK IN ORDINARY TIME**

Monday / *455*

I   The Lord will build up Zion again, and appear in all his glory.

II Lord, bend your ear and hear my prayer.

Tuesday / *456*

I   God is with us.

II Let my prayer come before you, Lord.

Wednesday / *457*

I   Let my tongue be silenced, if I ever forget you!

II Let my prayer come before you, Lord.

Thursday / *458*

I   The precepts of the Lord give joy to the heart.

II I believe that I shall see the good things of the Lord in the land of the living.

Friday / *459*

I   For the glory of your name, O Lord, deliver us.

II Guide me, Lord, along the ever-lasting way.

Saturday / *460*

I   The Lord listens to the poor.

II Lord, let your face shine on me.

---

727 **TWENTY-SEVENTH WEEK IN ORDINARY TIME**

Monday / *461*

I   You will rescue my life from the pit, O Lord.

II The Lord will remember his covenant for ever.

Or: Alleluia.

Tuesday / *462*

I   If you, O Lord, laid bare our guilt, who could endure it?

II Guide me, Lord, along the ever-lasting way.

Wednesday / *463*

I   Lord, you are tender and full of love.

II Go out to all the world, and tell the Good News.

Or: Alleluia.

Thursday / *464*

I   Happy are they who hope in the Lord.

II Blessed be the Lord God of Israel, for he has visited his people.

Friday / 465

I   The Lord will judge the world with justice.

II The Lord will remember his covenant for ever.

   Or: Alleluia.

Saturday / 466

I   Let good men rejoice in the Lord.

II The Lord remembers his covenant for ever.

   Or: Alleluia.

TWENTY-EIGHTH WEEK IN ORDINARY TIME 728

Monday / 467

I   The Lord has made known his salvation.

II Blessed be the name of the Lord for ever.

   Or: Alleluia.

Tuesday / 468

I   The heavens proclaim the glory of God.

II Let your loving kindness come to me, O Lord.

Wednesday / 469

I   Lord, you give back to every man, according to his works.

II Those who follow you, Lord, will have the light of life.

Thursday / 470

I   With the Lord there is mercy, and fullness of redemption.

II The Lord has made known his salvation.

Friday / 471

I   I turn to you, Lord, in time of trouble,
    and you fill me with the joy of salvation.

II Happy the people the Lord has chosen to be his own.

Saturday / 472

I   The Lord remembers his covenant for ever.

   Or: Alleluia.

II You gave your Son authority over all your creation.

TWENTY-NINTH WEEK IN ORDINARY TIME 729

Monday / 473

I   Blessed be the Lord God of Israel,
    for he has visited his people.

II The Lord made us, we belong to him.

Tuesday / 474

I   Here am I, Lord;
    I come to do your will.

II The Lord speaks of peace to his people.

Wednesday / 475

I   Our help is in the name of the Lord.

II You will draw water joyfully from the springs of salvation.

Thursday / 476

I   Happy are they who hope in the Lord.

II The earth is full of the goodness of the Lord.

Friday / *477*

I   Teach me your laws, O Lord.

II   Lord, this is the people that
longs to see your face.

Saturday / *478*

I   Lord, this is the people that
longs to see your face.

II   I rejoiced when I heard them
say:
let us go to the house of the Lord.

---

730   **THIRTIETH WEEK IN ORDINARY TIME**

Monday / *479*

I   Our God is the God of
salvation.

II   Behave like God as his very
dear children.

Tuesday / *480*

I   The Lord has done marvels for
us.

II   Happy are those who fear the
Lord.

Wednesday / *481*

I   All my hope, O Lord,
is in your loving kindness.

II   The Lord is faithful in all his
words.

Thursday / *482*

I   Save me, O Lord,
in your kindness.

II   Blessed be the Lord, my Rock!

Friday / *483*

I   Praise the Lord, Jerusalem.

II   How great are the works of the
Lord!

Or: Alleluia.

Saturday / *484*

I   The Lord will not abandon his
people.

II   My soul is thirsting for the
living God.

---

731   **THIRTY-FIRST WEEK IN ORDINARY TIME**

Monday / *485*

I   Lord, in your great love,
answer me.

II   In you, Lord, I have found my
peace.

Tuesday / *486*

I   In you, Lord, I have found my
peace.

II   I will praise you, Lord, in the
assembly of your people.

Wednesday / *487*

I   Happy the man who is merciful
and lends to those in need.

Or: Alleluia.

II   The Lord is my light and my
salvation.

Thursday / *488*

I   I believe that I shall see the
good things of the Lord in
the land of the living.

II   Let hearts rejoice who search
for the Lord.

Or: Alleluia.

Friday / *489*

I The Lord has revealed to the nations his saving power.

II I rejoiced when I heard them say:
Let us go to the house of the Lord.

Saturday / *490*

I I will praise your name for ever, Lord.

II Happy the man who fears the Lord.

Or: Alleluia.

THIRTY-SECOND WEEK IN ORDINARY TIME   732

Monday / *491*

I Guide me, Lord, along the ever-lasting way.

II Lord, this is the people that longs to see your face.

Tuesday / *492*

I I will bless the Lord at all times.

II The salvation of the just comes from the Lord.

Wednesday / *493*

I Rise up, O God, bring judgment to the earth.

II The Lord is my shepherd; there is nothing I shall want.

Thursday / *494*

I Your word is for ever, O Lord.

II Blest are they whose help is the God of Jacob.

Or: Alleluia.

Friday / 495

I The heavens proclaim the glory of God.

II Happy are they who follow the law of the Lord!

Saturday / *496*

I Remember the marvels the Lord has done.

Or: Alleluia.

II Happy the man who fears the Lord.

Or: Alleluia.

THIRTY-THIRD WEEK IN ORDINARY TIME   733

Monday / *497*

I Give me life, O Lord, and I will do your commands.

II Those who are victorious I will feed from the tree of life.

Tuesday / *498*

I The Lord upholds me.

II Him who is victorious I will sit beside me on my throne.

Wednesday / *499*

I Lord, when your glory appears, my joy will be full.

II Holy, holy, holy Lord, mighty God!

Thursday / *500*

I To the upright I will show the saving power of God.

II The Lamb has made us a kingdom of priests to serve our God.

Or: Alleluia.

Friday / *501*

I   We praise your glorious name,
    O mighty God.

II How sweet to my taste is your
    promise!

Saturday / *502*

I   I will rejoice in your salvation,
    O Lord.

II Blessed be the Lord, my Rock!

---

734   **THIRTY-FOURTH WEEK IN ORDINARY TIME**

Monday / *503*

I   Glory and praise for ever!

II Lord, this is the people that
    longs to see your face.

Tuesday / *504*

I   Give glory and eternal praise to
    him.

II The Lord comes to judge the
    earth.

Wednesday / *505*

I   Give glory and eternal praise to
    him.

II Great and wonderful are all
    your works,
    Lord, mighty God!

Thursday / *506*

I   Give glory and eternal praise to
    him.

II Blessed are they who are called
    to the wedding feast of the
    Lamb.

Friday / *507*

I   Give glory and eternal praise to
    him.

II Here God lives among his
    people.

Saturday / *508*

I   Give glory and eternal praise to
    him.

II Maranatha! Come, Lord Jesus!

Saints:
Weekday Psalm Responses

January 2 / *510*
**BASIL THE GREAT
AND GREGORY NAZIANZEN**
cf. 778 or 779

January 4
ELIZABETH ANN SETON
cf. 781

January 5
JOHN NEUMANN
Proclaim his marvelous deeds
to all the nations.

January 6
ANDRE BESSETTE
cf. 781

January 7 / *511*
RAYMOND OF PENYAFORT
cf. 778

January 13 / *512*
HILARY
cf. 778 or 779

January 17 / *513*
ANTHONY
cf. 781

January 20 / *514*
FABIAN
cf. 777 or 778

SEBASTIAN / *515*
cf. 777

January 21 / *516*
AGNES
cf. 777 or 780

January 22 / *517*
VINCENT
cf. 777

January 24 / *518*
FRANCIS DE SALES
cf. 778 or 779

January 25 / *519*
CONVERSION OF PAUL
Go out to all the world,
and tell the Good News.

Or: Alleluia.

January 26 / *520*
TIMOTHY AND TITUS
cf. 778

January 27 / *521*
ANGELA MERICI
cf. 780 or 781

January 28 / *522*
THOMAS AQUINAS
cf. 778 or 779

January 31 / *523*
JOHN BOSCO
cf. 778 or 781

736 FEBRUARY 2: PRESENTATION OF THE LORD

Forty days after the celebration of Christmas, this feast tells of how Mary and Joseph brought the child to the Temple. There the aged Simeon took the baby in his arms and proclaimed that Jesus would be "a light to the Gentiles, the glory of Israel." These words have been sung for centuries on February 2 as Christians have blessed and carried lighted candles in procession.

BLESSING OF CANDLES AND PROCESSION
As the candles are lighted, this antiphon (with optional verses) may be sung:

Antiphon

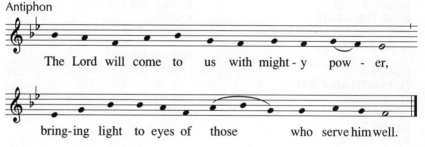

The Lord will come to us with might-y pow-er,

bring-ing light to eyes of those who serve him well.

Psalm (118)119, 105-108. 111-112

1. Your word is a lamp for my steps
2. I have sworn and made up my mind
3. Lord, I am deeply af - flict - ed;
4. Accept O Lord, the homage of my lips,
5. Your will is my heritage for ev - er,
6. I set myself to carry out your will

1. and a light for my path.
2. to o - bey your de - crees. ℟.
3. by your word give me life.
4. and teach me your de - crees. ℟.
5. the joy of my heart.
6. in full - ness for ev - er. ℟.

Music: Chant Mode VIII; setting by Richard Proulx, © 1985, GIA Publications, Inc.

When the candles have been blessed, the presider invites all: "Let us go forth in peace to meet the Lord." During the procession, the following may be sung:

Antiphon

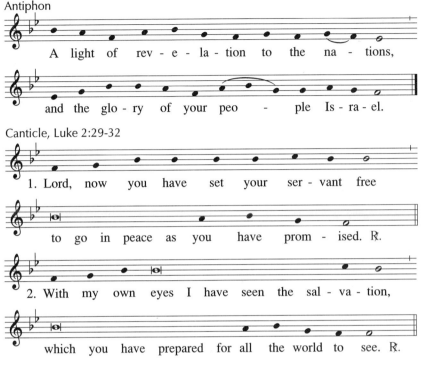

A light of rev - e - la - tion to the na - tions, and the glo - ry of your peo - ple Is - ra - el.

Canticle, Luke 2:29-32

1. Lord, now you have set your ser - vant free to go in peace as you have prom - ised. ℟.

2. With my own eyes I have seen the sal - va - tion, which you have prepared for all the world to see. ℟.

Music: Chant Mode VIII; setting by Richard Proulx, © 1985, GIA Publications, Inc.

READING I

Malachi 3:1-4 / 524

Thus says the Lord God:
Lo, I am sending my messenger
   to prepare the way before me;
and suddenly there will come to the
      temple
   the Lord whom you seek,
and the messenger of the covenant whom
      you desire.
   Yes, he is coming, says the Lord of
      hosts.
But who will endure the day of his
      coming?

And who can stand when he appears?
For he is like the refiner's fire,
   or like the fuller's lye.
He will sit refining and purifying silver,
   and he will purify the sons of Levi,
refining them like gold or like silver
   that they may offer due sacrifice to
      the Lord.
Then the sacrifice of Judah and Jerusalem
   will please the Lord,
   as in the days of old, as in years
      gone by.

RESPONSORIAL PSALM

Psalm 24:7, 8, 9, 10

Who is this king of glo-ry? It is the Lord!

Lift up, O gates, your lintels;
   reach up, you ancient portals,
   that the king of glory may come in! ℟.

Who is this king of glory?
   The Lord, strong and mighty,
   the Lord, mighty in battle. ℟.

Lift up, O gates, your lintels;
    reach up, you ancient portals,
    that the king of glory may come in! ℟.

Who is this king of glory?
    The LORD of hosts; he is the king of
    glory. ℟.

READING II   *Hebrews 2:14-18*

Since the children share in blood and flesh, Jesus likewise shared in them, that through death he might destroy the one who has the power of death, that is, the devil, and free those who through fear of death had been subject to slavery all their life. Surely he did not help angels but rather the descendants of Abraham; therefore, he had to become like his brothers and sisters in every way, that he might be a merciful and faithful high priest before God to expiate the sins of the people. Because he himself was tested through what he suffered, he is able to help those who are being tested.

GOSPEL   *Luke 2:22-40 or 2:22-32*

For short form, read only the part in brackets.

[When the days were completed for their purification according to the law of Moses, Mary and Joseph took Jesus up to Jerusalem to present him to the Lord, just as it is written in the law of the Lord, "Every male that opens the womb shall be consecrated to the Lord," and to offer the sacrifice of "a pair of turtledoves or two young pigeons," in accordance with the dictate in the law of the Lord.

Now there was a man in Jerusalem whose name was Simeon. This man was righteous and devout, awaiting the consolation of Israel, and the Holy Spirit was upon him. It had been revealed to him by the Holy Spirit that he should not see death before he had seen the Christ of the Lord. He came in the Spirit into the temple; and when the parents brought in the child Jesus to perform the custom of the law in regard to him, he took him into his arms and blessed God, saying:

"Now, Master, you may let your servant go
    in peace, according to your word,
for my eyes have seen your salvation,
    which you prepared in sight of all the peoples,
a light for revelation to the Gentiles,
    and glory for your people Israel."]

The child's father and mother were amazed at what was said about him; and Simeon blessed them and said to Mary his mother, "Behold, this child is destined for the fall and rise of many in Israel, and to be a sign that will be contradicted (and you yourself a sword will pierce) so that the thoughts of many hearts may be revealed." There was also a prophetess, Anna, the daughter of Phanuel, of the tribe of Asher. She was advanced in years, having lived seven years with her husband after her marriage, and then as a widow until she was eighty-four. She never left the temple, but worshipped night and day with fasting and prayer. And coming forward at that very time, she gave thanks to God and spoke about the child to all who were awaiting the redemption of Jerusalem.

When they had fulfilled all the prescriptions of the law of the Lord, they returned to Galilee, to their own town of Nazareth. The child grew and became strong, filled with wisdom; and the favor of God was upon him.

738

February 3 / *525*
BLASE
cf. 777 or 778

ANSGAR / *526*
cf. 778

February 5 / *527*
AGATHA
cf. 777 or 780

February 6 / *528*
PAUL MIKI AND COMPANIONS
cf. 777

February 8 / *529*
JEROME EMILIANI
cf. 781

February 10 / *530*
SCHOLASTICA
cf. 780 or 781

February 11 / *531*
OUR LADY OF LOURDES
cf. 776

February 14 / *532*
CYRIL AND METHODIUS
cf. 778 or 781

February 17 / *533*
**SEVEN FOUNDERS OF THE
ORDER OF SERVITES**
cf. 781

February 21 / *534*
PETER DAMIAN
cf. 778 or 779 or 781

February 22 / *535*
CHAIR OF PETER
The Lord is my shepherd;
there is nothing I shall want.

February 23 / *536*
POLYCARP
cf. 777 or 778

MARCH 739

March 3
KATHARINE DREXEL
cf. 780

March 4 / *537*
CASIMIR
cf. 781

March 7 / *538*
PERPETUA AND FELICITY
cf. 777

March 8 / *539*
JOHN OF GOD
cf. 781

March 9 / *540*
FRANCES OF ROME
cf. 781

March 17 / *541*
PATRICK
cf. 778

March 18 / *542*
CYRIL OF JERUSALEM
cf. 778 or 779

MARCH 19: JOSEPH, HUSBAND OF MARY 740

READING I *2 Samuel 7:4-5a, 12-14a, 16 / 543*

The Lord spoke to Nathan and said: "Go, tell my servant David, 'When your time comes and you rest with your ancestors, I will raise up your heir after you, sprung from your loins, and I will make his kingdom firm. It is he who shall build a house for my name. And I will make his royal throne firm forever. I will be a father to him, and he shall be a son to me. Your house and your kingdom shall endure forever before me; your throne shall stand firm forever.'"

RESPONSORIAL PSALM *Psalm 89:2-3, 4-5, 27, 29*

The son of Da-vid will live for ev - er.

The promises of the LORD I will sing
forever,
    through all generations my mouth
    will proclaim your faithfulness,

for you have said, "My kindness is
established for ever;"
    In heaven you have confirmed your
    faithfulness. ℟.

"I have made a covenant with my
chosen one;
I have sworn to David my servant:
forever will I confirm your posterity
and establish your throne for all
generations." ℟.

"He shall say of me, 'You are my father,
my God, the Rock my savior!'
Forever I will maintain my kindness
toward him,
my covenant with him stands
firm." ℟.

READING II   *Romans 4:13, 16-18, 22*

Brothers and sisters: It was not through the law that the promise was made to Abraham
and his descendants that he would inherit the world, but through the righteousness that
comes from faith. For this reason, it depends on faith, so that it may be a gift, and the
promise may be guaranteed to all his descendants, not to those who only adhere to the
law but to those who follow the faith of Abraham, who is the father of all of us, as it is
written, 'I have made you father of many nations.' He is our father in the sight of God,
in whom he believed, who gives life to the dead and calls into being what does not exist.
He believed, hoping against hope, that he would become "the father of many nations,"
according to what was said, "Thus shall your descendants be." That is why "it was
credited to him as righteousness."

GOSPEL   *Matthew 1:16, 18-21, 24a*

Jacob was the father of Joseph, the husband of Mary. Of her was born Jesus who is
called the Christ.

Now this is how the birth of Jesus Christ came about. When his mother Mary was
betrothed to Joseph, but before they lived together, she was found with child through the
Holy Spirit. Joseph her husband, since he was a righteous man, yet unwilling to expose
her to shame, decided to divorce her quietly. Such was his intention when, behold, the
angel of the Lord appeared to him in a dream and said, "Joseph, son of David, do not be
afraid to take Mary your wife into your home. For it is through the Holy Spirit that this
child has been conceived in her. She will bear a son and you are to name him Jesus,
because he will save his people from their sins." When Joseph awoke, he did as the angel
of the Lord had commanded him and took his wife into his home.

Or:

GOSPEL   *Luke 2:41-51a*

Each year Jesus' parents went to Jerusalem for the feast of Passover, and when he was
twelve years old, they went up according to festival custom. After they had completed
its days, as they were returning, the boy Jesus remained behind in Jerusalem, but his
parents did not know it. Thinking that he was in the caravan, they journeyed for a day
and looked for him among their relatives and acquaintances, but not finding him, they
returned to Jerusalem to look for him. After three days they found him in the temple,
sitting in the midst of the teachers, listening to them and asking them questions, and all
who heard him were astounded at his understanding and his answers. When his parents
saw him, they were astonished, and his mother said to him, "Son, why have you done
this to us? Your father and I have been looking for you with great anxiety." And he said
to them, "Why were you looking for me? Did you not know that I must be in my Father's
house?" But they did not understand what he said to them. He went down with them and
came to Nazareth, and was obedient to them.

741   **March 23** / *544*
       TURIBUS DE MOGROVEJO
       cf. 778

MARCH 25: ANNUNCIATION OF OUR LORD 742

READING I
Isaiah 7:10-14; 8:10 / 545

The LORD spoke to Ahaz, saying: Ask for a sign from the LORD, your God; let it be deep as the nether world, or high as the sky! But Ahaz answered, "I will not ask! I will not tempt the LORD!" Then Isaiah said: Listen, O house of David! Is it not enough for you to weary people, must you also weary my God? Therefore the Lord himself will give you this sign: the virgin shall conceive, and bear a son, and shall name him Emmanuel, which means "God is with us!"

RESPONSORIAL PSALM
Psalm 40:7-8, 8-9, 10, 11

Here am I, Lord; here am I, Lord; I come to do your will.

Sacrifice or offering you wished not,
  but ears open to obedience you gave
    me.
Holocausts and sin-offerings you sought
    not;
  then said I, "Behold, I come." ℟.

"In the written scroll it is prescribed for
    me.
To do your will, O God, is my delight,
  and your law is within my heart!" ℟.

I announced your justice in the vast
    assembly;
  I did not restrain my lips, as you, O
    LORD, know. ℟.

Your justice I kept not hid within my
    heart;
  your faithfulness and your salvation
    I have spoken of;
I have made no secret of your kindness
    and your truth
  in the vast assembly. ℟.

READING II
Hebrews 10:4-10

Brothers and sisters: It is impossible that the blood of bulls and goats takes away sins. For this reason, when Christ came into the world, he said:
  "Sacrifice and offering you did not desire,
    but a body you prepared for me;
  in holocausts and sin offerings you took no delight.
  Then I said, 'As is written of me in the scroll,
    behold, I come to do your will, O God.'"
First Christ says, "Sacrifices and offerings, holocausts and sin offerings, you neither desired nor delighted in." These are offered according to the law. Then he says, "Behold, I come to do your will." He takes away the first to establish the second. By this "will," we have been consecrated through the offering of the body of Jesus Christ once for all.

GOSPEL
Luke 1:26-38

The angel Gabriel was sent from God to a town of Galilee called Nazareth, to a virgin betrothed to a man named Joseph, of the house of David, and the virgin's name was Mary. And coming to her, he said, "Hail, full of grace! The Lord is with you." But she was greatly troubled at what was said and pondered what sort of greeting this might be. Then the angel said to her, "Do not be afraid, Mary, for you have found favor with God. Behold, you will conceive in your womb and bear a son, and you shall name him Jesus. He will be great and will be called Son of the Most High, and the Lord God will give him the throne of David his father, and he will rule over the house of Jacob forever, and of his kingdom there will be no end." But Mary said to the angel, "How can this be, since I have no relations with a man?" And the angel said to her in reply, "The Holy Spirit will come upon you, and the power of the Most High will overshadow you. Therefore the child to be born will be called holy, the Son of God. And behold,

Elizabeth, your relative, has also conceived a son in her old age, and this is the sixth month for her who was called barren; for nothing will be impossible for God." Mary said, "Behold, I am the handmaid of the Lord. May it be done to me according to your word." Then the angel departed from her.

743 APRIL

April 2 / 546
FRANCIS OF PAOLA
cf. 781

April 4 / 547
ISIDORE
cf. 778 or 779

April 5 / 548
VINCENT FERRER
cf. 778

April 7 / 549
JOHN BAPTIST DE LA SALLE
cf. 778 or 781

April 11 / 550
STANISLAUS
cf. 777 or 778

April 13 / 551
MARTIN I
cf. 777 or 778

April 21 / 552
ANSELM
cf. 778 or 779

April 23 / 553
GEORGE
cf. 777

ADALBERT
cf. 779

April 24 / 554
FIDELIS OF SIGMARINGEN
cf. 777 or 778

April 25 / 555
MARK
For ever I will sing the
goodness of the Lord.

Or: Alleluia.

April 28 / 556
PETER CHANEL
cf. 777 or 778

LOUIS DE MONTFORT
cf. 781

April 29 / 557
CATHERINE OF SIENA
cf. 780

April 30 / 558
PIUS V
cf. 778

744 MAY

May 1 / 559
JOSEPH THE WORKER
Lord, give success to the work of
our hands.

Or: Alleluia.

May 2 / 560
ATHANASIUS
cf. 778 or 779

May 3 / 561
PHILIP AND JAMES
Their message goes out through
all the earth.

Or: Alleluia.

May 12 / 562
NEREUS AND ACHILLEUS
cf. 777

PANCRAS / *563*
cf. 777

May 14 / *564*
MATTHIAS
The Lord will give him a seat with
    the leaders of his people.
Or: Alleluia.

May 15
ISIDORE
cf. 781

May 18 / *565*
JOHN I
cf. 777 or 778

May 20 / *566*
BERNARDINE OF SIENA
cf. 778

May 25 / *567*
VENERABLE BEDE
cf. 778 or 779

GREGORY VII / *568*
cf. 778

MARY MAGDALENE DE PAZZI / *569*
cf. 780 or 781

May 26 / *570*
PHILIP NERI
cf. 778 or 781

May 27 / *571*
AUGUSTINE OF CANTERBURY
cf. 778

May 31 / *572*
VISITATION
Among you is the great and Holy
    One of Israel.

**Saturday following the Second
Sunday after Pentecost** / *573*
IMMACULATE HEART OF MARY
cf. 776

JUNE

745

June 1 / *574*
JUSTIN
cf. 777

June 2 / *575*
MARCELLINUS AND PETER
cf. 777

June 3 / *576*
**CHARLES LWANGA AND
COMPANIONS**
cf. 777

June 5 / *577*
BONIFACE
cf. 777 or 778

June 6 / *578*
NORBERT
cf. 778 or 781

June 9 / *579*
EPHREM
cf. 779

June 11 / *580*
BARNABAS
The Lord has revealed to the
    nations his saving power.

June 13 / *581*
ANTHONY OF PADUA
cf. 778 or 779 or 781

June 19 / *582*
ROMUALD
cf. 781

June 21 / *583*
ALOYSIUS GONZAGA
cf. 781

June 22 / *584*
PAULINUS OF NOLA
cf. 778

JOHN FISHER / *585*
AND THOMAS MORE
cf. 777

READING I

Jeremiah 1:4-10 / 586

In the days of King Josiah, the word of the LORD came to me, saying:
Before I formed you in the womb I
        knew you,
    before you were born I
        dedicated you,
    a prophet to the nations I
        appointed you.
"Ah, Lord GOD!" I said,
    "I know not how to speak; I am
        too young."
But the LORD answered me,
Say not, "I am too young."
    To whomever I send you,
        you shall go;
whatever I command you,
        you shall speak.
Have no fear before them,
    because I am with you to
        deliver you, says the Lord.
Then the LORD extended his hand and
touched my mouth, saying,
    See, I place my words in your
mouth!
    This day I set you
        over nations and over kingdoms,
    to root up and to tear down,
        to destroy and to demolish,
        to build and to plant.

RESPONSORIAL PSALM

Psalm 71:1-2, 3-4, 5-6, 15, 17

Since my moth-er's womb,   you have been my strength.

In you, O LORD, I take refuge;
    let me never be put to shame.
In your justice rescue me, and deliver me;
    incline your ear to me, and save
        me. ℟.

Be my rock of refuge,
    a stronghold to give me safety,
    for you are my rock and my fortress.
O my God, rescue me from the hand of
    the wicked. ℟.

For you are my hope, O Lord;
    my trust, O Lord, from my youth.
On you I depend from birth;
    from my mother's womb you are my
        strength. ℟.

My mouth shall declare your justice,
    day by day your salvation.
O God, you have taught me from my
    youth,
    and till the present I proclaim your
        wondrous deeds. ℟.

READING II

1 Peter 1:8-12

Beloved: Although you have not seen Jesus Christ you love him; even though you do not see him now yet believe in him, you rejoice with an indescribable and glorious joy, as you attain the goal of your faith, the salvation of your souls.

Concerning this salvation, prophets who prophesied about the grace that was to be yours searched and investigated it, investigating the time and circumstances that the Spirit of Christ within them indicated when he testified in advance to the sufferings destined for Christ and the glories to follow them. It was revealed to them that they were serving not themselves but you with regard to the things that have now been announced to you by those who preached the good news to you through the Holy Spirit sent from heaven, things into which angels longed to look.

GOSPEL

Luke 1:5-17

In the days of Herod, King of Judea, there was a priest named Zechariah of the priestly division of Abijah; his wife was from the daughters of Aaron, and her name was Elizabeth. Both were righteous in the eyes of God, observing all the commandments and ordinances of the Lord blamelessly. But they had no child, because Elizabeth was barren and both were advanced in years. Once when he was serving as priest in his division's turn before God, according to the practice of the priestly service, he was chosen by lot to enter the sanctuary of the Lord to burn incense. Then, when the whole assembly of the people was praying outside at the hour of the incense offering, the angel of the Lord appeared to him, standing at the right of the altar of incense. Zechariah was troubled by what he saw, and fear came upon him. But the angel said to him, "Do not be afraid, Zechariah, because your prayer has been heard. Your wife Elizabeth will bear you a son, and you shall name him John. And you will have joy and gladness, and many will rejoice at his birth, for he will be great in the sight of the Lord. John will drink neither wine nor strong drink. He will be filled with the Holy Spirit even from his mother's womb, and he will turn many of the children of Israel to the Lord their God. He will go before him in the spirit and power of Elijah to turn their hearts toward their children and the disobedient to the understanding of the righteous, to prepare a people fit for the Lord."

JUNE 24: BIRTH OF JOHN THE BAPTIST / DURING THE DAY   747

READING I   *Isaiah 49:1-6 / 587*

Hear me, O coastlands
    listen, O distant peoples.
The LORD called me from birth,
    from my mother's womb he gave me
      my name.
He made of me a sharp-edged sword
    and concealed me in the shadow of
      his arm.
He made me a polished arrow,
    in his quiver he hid me.
You are my servant, he said to me,
    Israel, through whom I show my
      glory.

Though I thought I had toiled in vain,
    and for nothing, uselessly, spent my
      strength,

yet my reward is with the LORD,
    my recompense is with my God.
For now the LORD has spoken
    who formed me as his servant from
      the womb,
that Jacob may be brought back to him
    and Israel gathered to him;
and I am made glorious in the sight of
    the Lord,
    and my God is now my strength!
It is too little, he says, for you to be my
    servant,
    to raise up the tribes of Jacob,
    and restore the survivors of Israel;
I will make you a light to the nations,
    that my salvation may reach to the
      ends of the earth.

RESPONSORIAL PSALM   *Psalm 139:1-3, 13-14, 14-15*

I praise you, O Lord, for I am won-der-ful-ly made.

O LORD you have probed me and you
    know me;
    you know when I sit and when I
      stand;
    you understand my thoughts from
      afar.
My journeys and my rest you scrutinize,
    with all my ways you are familiar. ℞.

Truly you have formed my inmost being;

you knit me in my mother's womb.
I give you thanks that I am fearfully,
    wonderfully made;
    wonderful are your works. ℞.

My soul also you knew full well;
    nor was my frame unknown to you
when I was made in secret,
    when I was fashioned in the depths
      of the earth. ℞.

READING II   *Acts 13:22-26*

In those days, Paul said: "God raised up David as their king; of him he testified, 'I have found David, son of Jesse, a man after my own heart; he will carry out my every wish.' From this man's descendants God, according to his promise, has brought to Israel a savior, Jesus. John heralded his coming by proclaiming a baptism of repentance to all the people of Israel; and as John was completing his course, he would say, 'What do you suppose that I am? I am not he. Behold, one is coming after me; I am not worthy to unfasten the sandals of his feet.'

"My brothers, children of the family of Abraham, and those others among you who are God-fearing, to us this word of salvation has been sent."

GOSPEL   *Luke 1:57-66, 80*

When the time arrived for Elizabeth to have her child she gave birth to a son. Her neighbors and relatives heard that the Lord had shown his great mercy toward her, and they rejoiced with her. When they came on the eighth day to circumcise the child, they were going to call him Zechariah after his father, but his mother said in reply, "No. He will be called John." But they answered her, "There is no one among your relatives who has this name." So they made signs, asking his father what he wished him to be called. He asked for a tablet and wrote, "John is his name," and all were amazed. Immediately his mouth was opened, his tongue freed, and he spoke blessing God. Then fear came upon all their neighbors, and all these matters were discussed throughout the hill country of Judea. All who heard these things took them to heart, saying, "What, then, will this child be?" For surely the hand of the Lord was with him.

The child grew and became strong in spirit, and he was in the desert until the day of his manifestation to Israel.

---

748   **June 27** / *588*   **June 28** / *589*
        CYRIL OF ALEXANDRIA   **IRENAEUS**
        cf. 778 or 779   *cf. 777 or 779*

---

749   **JUNE 29: PETER AND PAUL / VIGIL**

READING I   *Acts 3:1-10 / 590*

Peter and John were going up to the temple area for the three o'clock hour of prayer. And a man crippled from birth was carried and placed at the gate of the temple called "the Beautiful Gate" every day to beg for alms from the people who entered the temple. When he saw Peter and John about to go into the temple, he asked for alms. But Peter looked intently at him, as did John, and said, "Look at us." He paid attention to them, expecting to receive something from them. Peter said, "I have neither silver nor gold, but what I do have I give you: in the name of Jesus Christ the Nazarene, rise and walk." Then Peter took him by the right hand and raised him up, and immediately his feet and ankles grew strong. He leaped up, stood, and walked around, and went into the temple with them, walking and jumping and praising God. When all the people saw the man walking and praising God, they recognized him as the one who used to sit begging at the Beautiful Gate of the temple, and they were filled with amazement and astonishment at what had happened to him.

RESPONSORIAL PSALM   *Psalm 19:2-3, 4-5*

Their mes - sage goes out through all the earth.

The heavens declare the glory of God,
and the firmament proclaims his
handiwork.
Day pours out the word to day,
and night to night imparts
knowledge. ℟.

Not a word nor a discourse
whose voice is not heard;
through all the earth their voice
resounds,
and to the ends of the world, their
message. ℟.

READING II   *Galatians 1:11-20*

I want you to know, brothers and sisters, that the gospel preached by me is not of human origin. For I did not receive it from a human being, nor was I taught it, but it came through a revelation of Jesus Christ.

For you heard of my former way of life in Judaism, how I persecuted the church of God beyond measure and tried to destroy it, and progressed in Judaism beyond many of my contemporaries among my race, since I was even more a zealot for my ancestral traditions. But when God, who from my mother's womb had set me apart and called me through his grace, was pleased to reveal his Son to me, so that I might proclaim him to the Gentiles, I did not immediately consult flesh and blood, nor did I go up to Jerusalem to those who were apostles before me; rather, I went into Arabia and then returned to Damascus.

Then after three years I went up to Jerusalem to confer with Cephas and remained with him for fifteen days. But I did not see any other of the apostles, only James the brother of the Lord. (As to what I am writing to you, behold, before God, I am not lying.)

GOSPEL   *John 21:15-19*

Jesus revealed himself to his disciples and, when they had finished breakfast, said to Simon Peter, "Simon, son of John, do you love me more than these?" He answered him, "Yes, Lord, you know that I love you." Jesus said to him, "Feed my lambs."

He then said to him a second time, "Simon, son of John, do you love me?" He answered him, "Yes, Lord, you know that I love you." He said to him, "Tend my sheep."

He said to him the third time, "Simon, son of John, do you love me?" Peter was distressed that Jesus had said to him a third time, "Do you love me?" and he said to him, "Lord, you know everything; you know that I love you." Jesus said to him, "Feed my sheep. Amen, amen, I say to you, when you were younger, you used to dress yourself and go where you wanted; but when you grow old, you will stretch out your hands, and someone else will dress you and lead you where you do not want to go." He said this signifying by what kind of death he would glorify God. And when he had said this, he said to him, "Follow me."

JUNE 29: PETER AND PAUL / MASS DURING THE DAY   750

READING I   *Acts 12:1-11 / 591*

In those days, King Herod laid hands upon some members of the church to harm them. He had James, the brother of John, killed by the sword, and when he saw that this was pleasing to the Jews he proceeded to arrest Peter also. (It was [the] feast of Unleavened Bread). He had him taken into custody and put in prison under the guard of four squads of four soldiers each. He intended to bring him before the people after Passover. Peter thus was being kept in prison, but prayer by the church was fervently being made to God on his behalf.

On the very night before Herod was to bring him to trial, Peter, secured by double chains, was sleeping between two soldiers, while outside the door guards kept watch on the prison. Suddenly the angel of the Lord stood by him and a light shone in the cell. He tapped Peter on the side and awakened him, saying, "Get up quickly." The chains fell from his wrists. The angel said to him, "Put on your belt and your sandals." He did so. Then he said to him, "Put on your cloak and follow me." So he followed him out, not realizing that what was happening through the angel was real; he thought he was seeing a vision. They passed the first guard, then the second, and came to the iron gate leading out to the city, which opened for them by itself. They emerged and made their way down an alley, and suddenly the angel left him.

RESPONSORIAL PSALM *Psalm 34:2-3, 4-5, 6-7, 8-9*

The an-gel of the Lord will res-cue those who fear him.

I will bless the LORD at all times;
    his praise shall be ever in my mouth.
Let my soul glory in the LORD;
    the lowly will hear me and be glad. ℟.

Glorify the LORD with me,
    let us together extol his name.
I sought the LORD, and he answered me
    and delivered me from all my
    fears. ℟.

Look to him that you may be radiant
    with joy,

and your faces may not blush with
    shame.
When the poor one called out, the LORD
    heard,
and from all his distress he saved
    him. ℟.

The angel of the LORD encamps
    around those who fear him, and
    delivers them.
Taste and see how good the LORD is;
    blessed the man who takes refuge in
    him. ℟.

READING II *2 Timothy 4:6-8, 17-18*

I, Paul, am already being poured out like a libation, and the time of my departure is at hand. I have competed well; I have finished the race; I have kept the faith. From now on the crown of righteousness awaits me, which the Lord, the just judge, will award to me on that day, and not only to me, but to all who have longed for his appearance.

The Lord stood by me and gave me strength, so that through me the proclamation might be completed and all the Gentiles might hear it. And I was rescued from the lion's mouth. The Lord will rescue me from every evil threat and will bring me safe to his heavenly kingdom. To him be glory forever and ever. Amen.

GOSPEL *Matthew 16:13-19*

When Jesus went into the region of Caesarea Philippi he asked his disciples, "Who do people say that the Son of Man is?" They replied, "Some say John the Baptist, others Elijah, still others Jeremiah or one of the prophets." He said to them, "But who do you say that I am?" Simon Peter said in reply, "You are the Christ, the Son of the living God." Jesus said to him in reply, "Blessed are you, Simon son of Jonah. For flesh and blood has not revealed this to you, but my heavenly Father. And so I say to you, you are Peter, and upon this rock I will build my church, and the gates of the nether world shall not prevail against it. I will give you the keys to the kingdom of heaven. Whatever you bind on earth shall be bound in heaven; and whatever you loose on earth shall be loosed in heaven."

751   **June 30 / 592**
      FIRST MARTYRS OF THE CHURCH OF ROME
      cf. 777

JULY

July 1
JUNÍPERO SERRA
cf. 778

July 3 */ 593*
THOMAS
Go out to all the world,
and tell the Good News.

July 4 */ 594*
ELIZABETH OF PORTUGAL
cf. 781

JULY 4: INDEPENDENCE DAY

RESPONSORIAL PSALM *Psalm 85:9-10, 11-12, 13-14*
℟. **The Lord speaks of peace to his people.**

I will hear what the Lord God has to say,
    a voice that speaks of peace,
peace for his people and his friends
    and those who turn to him in their
        hearts.
His help is near for those who fear him
    and his glory will dwell in our
        land. ℟.

Mercy and faithfulness have met;

justice and peace have embraced.
Faithfulness shall spring from the earth
    and justice look down from
        heaven. ℟.

The Lord will make us prosper
    and our earth shall yield its fruit.
Justice shall march before him
    and peace shall follow his steps. ℟.

July 5 */ 595*
ANTHONY ZACCARIA
cf. 778 or 781

July 6 */ 596*
MARIA GORETTI
cf. 777 or 780

July 11 */ 597*
BENEDICT
cf. 781

July 13 */ 598*
HENRY
cf. 781

July 14 */ 599*
KATERI TEKAKWITHA
cf. 780

CAMILLUS DE LELLIS
cf. 781

July 15 */ 600*
BONAVENTURE
cf. 778 or 779

July 16 */ 601*
OUR LADY OF MOUNT CARMEL
cf. 776

July 21 */ 602*
LAWRENCE OF BRINDISI
cf. 778 or 779

July 22 */ 603*
MARY MAGDALENE
My soul is thirsting for you, O
        Lord, my God.

July 23 / 604
BRIDGET
cf. 781

July 25 / 605
JAMES
Those who sow in tears, shall reap
with shouts of joy.

July 26 / 606
JOACHIM AND ANN
God will give him the throne of
David, his father.

July 29 / 607
MARTHA
cf. 781

July 30 / 608
PETER CHRYSOLOGUS
cf. 778 or 779

July 31 / 609
IGNATIUS OF LOYOLA
cf. 778 or 781

755 AUGUST

August 1 / 610
ALPHONSUS LIGUORI
cf. 778 or 779

August 2 / 611
EUSEBIUS OF VERCELLI
cf. 778

PETER JULIAN EYMARD
cf. 778

August 4 / 612
JOHN VIANNEY
cf. 778

August 5 / 613
**DEDICATION OF SAINT MARY
MAJOR**
cf. 775

756 AUGUST 6: TRANSFIGURATION

READING I   *Daniel 7:9-10, 13-14 / 614*

As I watched:
>   Thrones were set up
>   and the Ancient One took his throne.
>   His clothing was snow bright,
>   and the hair on his head as white as wool;
>   his throne was flames of fire,
>   with wheels of burning fire.
>   A surging stream of fire
>   flowed out from where he sat;
>   thousands upon thousands were ministering to him,
>   and myriads upon myriads attended him.
> The court was convened and the books were opened. As the visions during the night
>   continued, I saw
>   One like a Son of man coming,
>   on the clouds of heaven;
>   When he reached the Ancient One
>   and was presented before him,
>   The one like a Son of man received dominion, glory, and kingship;
>   all peoples, nations, and languages serve him.
>   His dominion is an everlasting dominion
>   that shall not be taken away,
>   his kingship shall not be destroyed.

RESPONSORIAL PSALM

Psalm 97:1-2, 5-6, 9

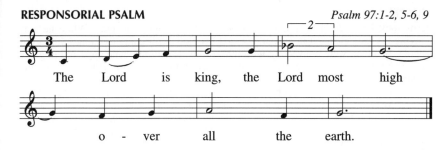

The Lord is king, the Lord most high
o - ver all the earth.

The LORD is king; let the earth rejoice;
let the many islands be glad.
Clouds and darkness are round about him;
justice and judgment are the
foundation of his throne. ℟.

The mountains melt like wax before the
LORD,

before the LORD of all the earth.
The heavens proclaim his justice;
all peoples see his glory. ℟.

Because you, O LORD, are the Most High
over all the earth,
exalted far above all gods. ℟.

READING II

2 Peter 1:16-19

Beloved: We did not follow cleverly devised myths when we made known to you the power and coming of our Lord Jesus Christ, but we had been eyewitnesses of his majesty. For he received honor and glory from God the Father when that unique declaration came to him from the majestic glory, "This is my Son, my beloved, with whom I am well pleased." We ourselves heard this voice come from heaven while we were with him on the holy mountain. Moreover, we possess the prophetic message that is altogether reliable. You will do well to be attentive to it, as to a lamp shining in a dark place, until day dawns and the morning star rises in your hearts.

GOSPEL / A

Matthew 17:1-9

Jesus took Peter, James, and his brother, John, and led them up a high mountain by themselves. And he was transfigured before them; his face shone like the sun and his clothes became white as light. And behold, Moses and Elijah appeared to them, conversing with him. Then Peter said to Jesus in reply, "Lord, it is good that we are here. If you wish, I will make three tents here, one for you, one for Moses, and one for Elijah." While he was still speaking, behold, a bright cloud cast a shadow over them, then from the cloud came a voice that said, "This is my beloved Son, with whom I am well pleased; listen to him." When the disciples heard this, they fell prostrate and were very much afraid. But Jesus came and touched them, saying, "Rise, and do not be afraid." And when the disciples raised their eyes, they saw no one else but Jesus alone.

As they were coming down from the mountain, Jesus charged them, "Do not tell the vision to anyone until the Son of Man has been raised from the dead."

GOSPEL / B

Mark 9:2-10

Jesus took Peter, James, and John and led them up a high mountain apart by themselves. And he was transfigured before them, and his clothes became dazzling white, such as no fuller on earth could bleach them. Then Elijah appeared to them along with Moses, and they were conversing with Jesus. Then Peter said to Jesus in reply, "Rabbi, it is good that we are here! Let us make three tents: one for you, one for Moses, and one for Elijah." He hardly knew what to say, they were so terrified. Then a cloud came, casting a shadow over them; from the cloud came a voice, "This is my beloved Son. Listen to him." Suddenly, looking around, they no longer saw anyone but Jesus alone with them.

As they were coming down from the mountain, he charged them not to relate what they had seen to anyone, except when the Son of Man had risen from the dead. So they kept the matter to themselves, questioning what rising from the dead meant.

GOSPEL / C   *Luke 9:28b-36*

Jesus took Peter, John, and James and went up a mountain to pray. While he was praying his face changed in appearance and his clothing became dazzling white. And behold, two men were conversing with him, Moses and Elijah, who appeared in glory and spoke of his exodus that he was going to accomplish in Jerusalem. Peter and his companions had been overcome by sleep, but becoming fully awake, they saw his glory and the two men standing with him. As they were about to part from him, Peter said to Jesus, "Master, it is good that we are here; let us make three tents, one for you, one for Moses, and one for Elijah." But he did not know what he was saying. While he was still speaking, a cloud came and cast a shadow over them, and they became frightened when they entered the cloud. Then from the cloud came a voice that said, "This is my chosen Son; listen to him." After the voice had spoken, Jesus was found alone. They fell silent and did not at that time tell anyone what they had seen.

757

August 7 / *616*
SIXTUS II
cf. 777

CAJETAN
cf. 778 or 781

August 8 / *617*
DOMINIC
cf. 778 or 781

August 10 / *618*
LAWRENCE
Happy the man who is merciful
and lends to those in need.

August 11 / *619*
CLARE
cf. 781

August 13 / *620*
PONTIAN AND HIPPOLYTUS
cf. 777 or 778

August 14
MAXIMILIAN MARY KOLBE
Precious in the eyes of the Lord
is the death of his faithful ones.

---

758   # AUGUST 15: ASSUMPTION / VIGIL

READING I   *1 Chronicles 15:3-4, 15-16; 16:1-2 / 621*

David assembled all Israel in Jerusalem to bring the ark of the LORD to the place that he had prepared for it. David also called together the sons of Aaron and the Levites.

The Levites bore the ark of God on their shoulders with poles, as Moses had ordained according to the word of the LORD.

David commanded the chiefs of the Levites to appoint their kinsmen as chanters, to play on musical instruments, harps, lyres, and cymbals, to make a loud sound of rejoicing.

They brought in the ark of God and set it within the tent which David had pitched for it. Then they offered up burnt offerings and peace offerings to God. When David had finished offering up the burnt offerings and peace offerings, he blessed the people in the name of the LORD.

RESPONSORIAL PSALM   *Psalm 132:6-7, 9-10, 13-14*

Lord,   go   up   to   the   place   of   your   rest,

you and the ark of your ho - li - ness.

Behold, we heard of it in Ephrathah;
we found it in the fields of Jaar.
Let us enter into his dwelling,
let us worship at his footstool. ℟.

May your priests be clothed with justice;
let your faithful ones shout merrily
for joy.
For the sake of David your servant,

reject not the plea of your
anointed. ℟.

For the LORD has chosen Zion;
he prefers her for his dwelling.
"Zion is my resting place forever;
in her will I dwell, for I prefer
her." ℟.

READING II
1 Corinthians 15:54b-57

Brothers and sisters: When that which is mortal clothes itself with immortality, then the word that is written shall come about:
"Death is swallowed up in victory.
Where, O death, is your victory?
Where, O death, is your sting?"
The sting of death is sin, and the power of sin is the law. But thanks be to God who gives us the victory through our Lord Jesus Christ.

GOSPEL
Luke 11:27-28

While Jesus was speaking, a woman from the crowd called out and said to him, "Blessed is the womb that carried you and the breasts at which you nursed." He replied, "Rather, blessed are those who hear the word of God and observe it."

AUGUST 15: ASSUMPTION / MASS DURING THE DAY   759

READING I
Revelation 11:19a; 12:1-6a, 10ab / 622

God's temple in heaven was opened, and the ark of his covenant could be seen in the temple.
A great sign appeared in the sky, a woman clothed with the sun, with the moon beneath her feet, and on her head a crown of twelve stars. She was with child and wailed aloud in pain as she labored to give birth. Then another sign appeared in the sky; it was a huge red dragon, with seven heads and ten horns, and on its heads were seven diadems. Its tail swept away a third of the stars in the sky and hurled them down to the earth. Then the dragon stood before the woman about to give birth, to devour her child when she gave birth. She gave birth to a son, a male child, destined to rule all the nations with an iron rod. Her child was caught up to God and his throne. The woman herself fled into the desert where she had a place prepared by God.
Then I heard a loud voice in heaven say:
"Now have salvation and power come,
and the kingdom of our God
and the authority of his Anointed One."

RESPONSORIAL PSALM
Psalm 45:10, 11, 12, 16

The queen stands at your right hand,   ar- rayed in gold.

The queen takes her place at your right
hand in gold of Ophir. ℟.

So shall the king desire your beauty;
for he is your lord. ℟.

Hear, O daughter, and see; turn your ear,
forget your people and your father's
house. ℟.

They are borne in with gladness and joy;
they enter the palace of the king. ℟.

READING II   *1 Corinthians 15:20-27*

Brothers and sisters: Christ has been raised from the dead, the first fruits of those who
have fallen asleep. For since death came through man, the resurrection of the dead came
also through man. For just as in Adam all die, so too in Christ shall all be brought to life,
but each one in proper order: Christ the first fruits; then, at his coming, those who belong
to Christ; then comes the end, when he hands over the kingdom to his God and Father,
when he has destroyed every sovereignty and every authority and power. For he must
reign until he has put all his enemies under his feet. The last enemy to be destroyed is
death, for "he subjected everything under his feet."

GOSPEL   *Luke 1:39-56*

Mary set out and traveled to the hill country in haste to a town of Judah, where she
entered the house of Zechariah and greeted Elizabeth. When Elizabeth heard Mary's
greeting, the infant leaped in her womb, and Elizabeth, filled with the Holy Spirit, cried
out in a loud voice and said, "Blessed are you among women, and blessed is the fruit of
your womb. And how does this happen to me, that the mother of my Lord should come
to me? For at the moment the sound of your greeting reached my ears, the infant in my
womb leaped for joy. Blessed are you who believed that what was spoken to you by the
Lord would be fulfilled."

And Mary said:
"My soul proclaims the greatness of the Lord;
my spirit rejoices in God my Savior
for he has looked upon his lowly servant.
From this day all generations will call me blessed:
the Almighty has done great things for me,
and holy is his Name.
He has mercy on those who fear him
in every generation.
He has shown the strength of his arm,
and has scattered the proud in their conceit.
He has cast down the mighty from their thrones,
and has lifted up the lowly.
He has filled the hungry with good things,
and the rich he has sent away empty.
He has come to the help of his servant Israel
for he has remembered his promise of mercy,
the promise he made to our fathers,
to Abraham and his children for ever."

Mary remained with her about three months and then returned to her home.

---

760   **August 16 / 623**
        STEPHEN OF HUNGARY
        cf. 781

        August 18
        JANE FRANCES DE CHANTAL
        cf. 780

August 19 / *624*
JOHN EUDES
cf. 778 or 781

August 20 / *625*
BERNARD
cf. 779 or 781

August 21 / *626*
PIUS X
cf. 778

August 22 / *627*
QUEENSHIP OF MARY
cf. 776

August 23 / *628*
ROSE OF LIMA
cf. 780 or 781

August 24 / *629*
BARTHOLOMEW
Your friends tell the glory of your
    kingship, Lord.

August 25 / *630*
LOUIS
cf. 781

JOSEPH CALASANZ / *631*
cf. 778 or 781

August 27 / *632*
MONICA
cf. 781

August 28 / *633*
AUGUSTINE
cf. 778 or 779

August 29 / *634*
BEHEADING OF JOHN THE BAPTIST
I will sing of your salvation.

FIRST MONDAY IN SEPTEMBER: LABOR DAY   761

RESPONSORIAL PSALM   *Psalm 90:2, 3-4, 12-13, 14, 16*
℟. **Lord, give success to the work of our hands.**

Before the mountains were born,
    the earth and the world brought
        forth,
from eternity to eternity you are God. ℟.

You turn man back to dust,
    saying, "Return, O children of men."
For a thousand years in your sight
    are as yesterday, now that it is past,
or as a watch of the night. ℟.

Teach us to number our days aright,
    that we may gain wisdom of heart.
Return, O Lord! How long?
    Have pity on your servants! ℟.

Fill us at daybreak with your kindness,
    that we may shout for joy and
        gladness all our days.
Show your deeds to your servants,
    your glory to their children. ℟.

SEPTEMBER   762

September 3 / *635*
GREGORY THE GREAT
cf. 778 or 779

September 8 / *636*
BIRTH OF MARY
With delight I rejoice in the Lord.

September 9
PETER CLAVER
cf. 778

September 13 / *637*
JOHN CHRYSOSTOM
cf. 778 or 779

763 SEPTEMBER 14: EXALTATION OF THE HOLY CROSS

READING I *Numbers 21:4b-9 / 638*

With their patience worn out by the journey, the people complained against God and Moses, "Why have you brought us up from Egypt to die in this desert, where there is no food or water? We are disgusted with this wretched food!"

In punishment the LORD sent among the people saraph serpents, which bit the people so that many of them died. Then the people came to Moses and said, "We have sinned in complaining against the LORD and you. Pray the LORD to take the serpents from us." So Moses prayed for the people, and the LORD said to Moses, "Make a saraph and mount it on a pole, and if any who have been bitten look at it, they will live." Moses accordingly made a bronze serpent and mounted it on a pole, and whenever anyone who had been bitten by a serpent looked at the bronze serpent, he lived.

RESPONSORIAL PSALM *Psalm 78:1-2, 34-35, 36-37, 38*

Do not for-get the works of the Lord!

Hearken, my people, to my teaching;
  incline your ears to the words of my
    mouth.
I will open my mouth in a parable,
  I will utter mysteries from of old. ℟.

While he slew them they sought him
  and inquired after God again,
remembering that God was their rock
  and the Most High God, their
    redeemer. ℟.

But they flattered him with their mouths
  and lied to him with their tongues,
though their hearts were not steadfast
    toward him,
  nor were they faithful to his
    covenant. ℟.

Yet he, being merciful, forgave their sin
  and destroyed them not;
often he turned back his anger
  and let none of his wrath be
    roused. ℟.

READING II *Philippians 2:6-11*

Brothers and sisters:
  Christ Jesus, though he was in the
      form of God,
    did not regard equality with God
      something to be grasped.
  Rather, he emptied himself,
    taking the form of a slave,
    coming in human likeness;
    and found human in appearance,
    he humbled himself,
    becoming obedient to the point
      of death,

    even death on a cross.
  Because of this, God greatly exalted
      him
    and bestowed on him the name
      which is above every name,
    that at the name of Jesus
    every knee should bend,
    of those in heaven and on earth
      and under the earth,
    and every tongue confess that
    Jesus Christ is Lord,
    to the glory of God the Father.

GOSPEL *John 3:13-17*

Jesus said to Nicodemus: "No one has gone up to heaven except the one who has come down from heaven, the Son of Man. And just as Moses lifted up the serpent in the desert, so must the Son of Man be lifted up, so that everyone who believes in him may have eternal life."

For God so loved the world that he gave his only Son, so that he who believes in him might not perish but might have eternal life. For God did not send his Son into the world to condemn the world, but that the world might be saved through him.

September 15 / *639*
OUR LADY OF SORROWS
Save me, O Lord, in your steadfast
   love.

September 16 / *640*
CORNELIUS AND CYPRIAN
cf. 777 or 778

September 17 / *641*
ROBERT BELLARMINE
cf. 778 or 779

September 19 / *642*
JANUARIUS
cf. 777 or 778

September 20
ANDREW KIM TAEGŎN,
PAUL CHŎNG HASANG,
AND COMPANIONS
Those who sow in tears shall sing
for joy when they reap.

September 21 / *643*
MATTHEW
Their message goes out through all
   the earth.

September 26 / *644*
COSMAS AND DAMIAN
cf. 777

September 27 / *645*
VINCENT DE PAUL
cf. 778 or 781

September 28 / *646*
WENCESLAUS
cf. 777

September 29 / *647*
MICHAEL, GABRIEL, AND RAPHAEL
In the sight of the angels
I will sing your praise, Lord.

September 30 / *648*
JEROME
cf. 778 or 779

OCTOBER

October 1 / *649*
THERESA OF THE CHILD JESUS
cf. 780 or 781

October 2 / *650*
GUARDIAN ANGELS
He has put his angels in charge of
   you,
to guard you in all your ways.

October 4 / *651*
FRANCIS OF ASSISI
cf. 781

October 6 / *652*
BRUNO
cf. 778 or 781

MARIE ROSE DUROCHER
cf. 780

October 7 / *653*
OUR LADY OF THE ROSARY
cf. 776

October 9 / *654*
DENIS AND COMPANIONS
cf. 777

JOHN LEONARDI / *655*
cf. 778 or 781

October 14 / *656*
CALLISTUS I
cf. 777 or 778

October 15 / *657*
TERESA OF JESUS
cf. 780 or 781

October 16 / *658*
HEDWIG
cf. 781

MARGARET MARY ALACOQUE / *659*
cf. 780 or 781

October 17 / 660
IGNATIUS OF ANTIOCH
cf. 777 or 778

October 18 / 661
LUKE
Your friends tell the glory of your
   kingship, Lord.

October 19 / 662
ISAAC JOGUES,
JOHN DE BRÉBEUF AND
COMPANIONS
cf. 777 or 778

October 20 / 663
PAUL OF THE CROSS
cf. 778 or 781

October 23 / 664
JOHN OF CAPISTRANO
cf. 778

October 24 / 665
ANTHONY CLARET
cf. 778

October 28 / 666
SIMON AND JUDE
Their message goes out through all
   the earth.

---

766   **NOVEMBER 1: ALL SAINTS**

READING I   *Revelation 7:2-4, 9-14 / 667*

I, John, saw another angel come up from the East, holding the seal of the living God. He
cried out in a loud voice to the four angels who were given power to damage the land
and the sea, "Do not damage the land or the sea or the trees until we put the seal on the
foreheads of the servants of our God." I heard the number of those who had been marked
with the seal, one hundred and forty-four thousand marked from every tribe of the
Israelites.

    After this I had a vision of a great multitude, which no one could count, from every
nation, race, people, and tongue. They stood before the throne and before the Lamb,
wearing white robes and holding palm branches in their hands. They cried out in a loud
voice:

    "Salvation comes from our God,
        who is seated on the throne,
    and from the Lamb."

All the angels stood around the throne and around the elders and the four living creatures. They prostrated themselves before the throne, worshipped God, and exclaimed:

    "Amen. Blessing and glory, wisdom and thanksgiving,
        honor, power, and might
        be to our God forever and ever. Amen."

Then one of the elders spoke up and said to me, "Who are these wearing white robes,
and where did they come from?" I said to him, "My lord, you are the one who knows."
He said to me, "These are the ones who have survived the time of great distress; they
have washed their robes and made them white in the blood of the Lamb."

RESPONSORIAL PSALM   *Psalm 24:1-2, 3-4, 5-6*

Lord, this is the peo - ple that longs to see your face.

The LORD's are the earth and its fullness;
    the world and those who dwell in it.
For he founded it upon the seas
    and established it upon the rivers. ℟.

Who can ascend the mountain of the
    LORD?
    or who may stand in his holy place?
One whose hands are sinless, whose

heart is clean,
    who desires not what is vain. ℟.

He shall receive a blessing from the
    LORD,
    a reward from God his savior.
Such is the race that seeks for him,
    that seeks the face of the God of
    Jacob. ℟.

READING II   *1 John 3:1-3*

Beloved: See what love the Father has bestowed on us that we may be called the
children of God. Yet so we are. The reason the world does not know us is that it did not
know him. Beloved, we are God's children now; what we shall be has not yet been
revealed. We do know that when it is revealed we shall be like him, for we shall see him
as he is. Everyone who has this hope based on him makes himself pure, as he is pure.

GOSPEL   *Matthew 5:1-12a*

When Jesus saw the crowds, he went up the mountain, and after he had sat down, his
disciples came to him. He began to teach them, saying:
    "Blessed are the poor in spirit,
        for theirs is the kingdom of heaven.
    Blessed are they who mourn,
        for they will be comforted.
    Blessed are the meek,
        for they will inherit the land.
    Blessed are they who hunger and
            thirst for righteousness,
        for they will be satisfied.
    Blessed are the merciful,
        for they will be shown mercy.
    Blessed are the clean of heart,
        for they will see God.
    Blessed are the peacemakers,
        for they will be called children of God.
    Blessed are they who are persecuted for the sake of righteousness,
        for theirs is the kingdom of heaven.
    Blessed are you when they insult you and persecute you and utter every kind of evil
against you falsely because of me. Rejoice and be glad, for your reward will be great in
heaven."

NOVEMBER 2: ALL SOULS   767

RESPONSORIAL PSALM   *Psalm 23:1-3a, 3b-4, 5, 6 / 668*

The Lord is my shep-herd; there is noth-ing I shall want.

or:

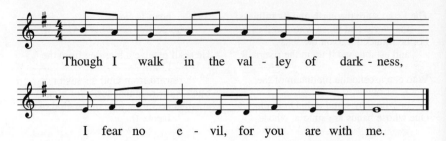

The LORD is my shepherd; I shall not
  want.
  In verdant pastures he gives me
    repose;
beside restful waters he leads me;
  he refreshes my soul. ℟.

He guides me in right paths
  for his name's sake.
Even though I walk in the dark valley
  I fear no evil; for you are at my side

with your rod and your staff
  that give me courage. ℟.

You spread the table before me
  in the sight of my foes;
you anoint my head with oil;
  my cup overflows. ℟.

Only goodness and kindness follow me
  all the days of my life;
and I shall dwell in the house of the Lord
  for years to come. ℟.

Or:

RESPONSORIAL PSALM   *Psalm 25:6 and 7b, 17-18, 20-21*

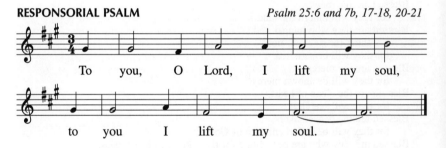

or:

Remember that your compassion, O
  LORD;
  and your love are from of old.
In your kindness remember me,
  because of your goodness, O LORD. ℟.

Relieve the troubles of my heart,
  and bring me out of my distress.
Put an end to my affliction and my
    suffering;
  and take away all my sins. ℟.

Preserve my life, and rescue me;
  let me not be put to shame, for I
    take refuge in you,
Let integrity and uprightness preserve
    me,
  because I wait for you, O LORD. ℟.

Or:

RESPONSORIAL PSALM   *Psalm 27:1, 4, 7 and 8b and 9a, 13-14*

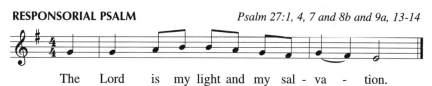

The Lord is my light and my sal - va - tion.

or:

I be - lieve that I shall see the good things of the
Lord in the land of the liv - ing.

The LORD is my light and my salvation;
  whom should I fear?
The LORD is my life's refuge;
  of whom should I be afraid? ℟.

One thing I ask of the LORD;
  this I seek:
to dwell in the house of the LORD
  all the days of my life,
that I may gaze on the loveliness of the
  LORD
  and contemplate his temple. ℟.

Hear, O LORD, the sound of my call;
  have pity on me and answer me.
Your presence, O LORD, I seek!
  Hide not your face from me. ℟.

I believe that I shall see the bounty of
  the LORD
  in the land of the living.
Wait for the LORD with courage;
  be stouthearted and wait for the
  LORD! ℟.

November 3 / *669*
MARTIN DE PORRES
cf. 781

November 4 / *670*
CHARLES BORROMEO
cf. 778

768

NOVEMBER 9: DEDICATION OF SAINT JOHN LATERAN   769

READING I   *Ezekiel 47:1-2, 8-9, 12 / 671*

The angel brought me back to the entrance of the temple, and I saw water flowing out from beneath the threshold of the temple toward the east, for the facade of the temple was toward the east; the water flowed down from the southern side of the temple, south of the altar. He led me outside by the north gate, and around to the outer gate facing the east, where I saw water trickling from the southern side. He said to me, "This water flows into the eastern district down upon the Arabah, and empties into the sea, the salt waters, which it makes fresh. Wherever the river flows, every sort of living creature that can multiply shall live, and there shall be abundant fish, for wherever this water comes the sea shall be made fresh. Along both banks of the river, fruit trees of every kind shall grow; their leaves shall not fade, nor their fruit fail. Every month they shall bear fresh fruit, for they shall be watered by the flow from the sanctuary. Their fruit shall serve for food, and their leaves for medicine."

RESPONSORIAL PSALM *Psalm 46:2-3, 5-6, 8-9*

The wa-ters of the riv - er glad - den the cit - y of God,

the ho - ly dwell - ing of the Most High.

God is our refuge and our strength,
an ever-present help in distress.
Therefore we fear not, though the earth
be shaken
and mountains plunge into the depths
of the sea. ℟.

There is a stream whose runlets gladden
the city of God,
the holy dwelling of the Most High.

God is in its midst; it shall not be
disturbed;
God will help it at the break of
dawn. ℟.

The Lord of hosts is with us;
our stronghold is the God of Jacob.
Come! behold the deeds of the Lord,
the astounding things he has wrought
on earth. ℟.

READING II *1 Corinthians 3:9c-11, 16-17*

Brothers and sisters: You are God's building. According to the grace of God given to me, like a wise master builder I laid a foundation, and another is building upon it. But each one must be careful how he builds upon it, for no one can lay a foundation other than the one that is there, namely, Jesus Christ.

Do you not know that you are the temple of God, and that the Spirit of God dwells in you? If anyone destroys God's temple, God will destroy that person; for the temple of God, which you are, is holy.

GOSPEL *John 2:13-22*

Since the Passover of the Jews was near, Jesus went up to Jerusalem. He found in the temple area those who sold oxen, sheep, and doves, as well as the money changers seated there. He made a whip out of cords and drove them all out of the temple area, with the sheep and oxen, and spilled the coins of the money changers and overturned their tables, and to those who sold doves he said, "Take these out of here, and stop making my Father's house a marketplace." His disciples recalled the words of Scripture, 'Zeal for your house will consume me.' At this the Jews answered and said to him, "What sign can you show us for doing this?" Jesus answered and said to them, "Destroy this temple and in three days I will raise it up." The Jews said, "This temple has been under construction for forty-six years, and you will raise it up in three days?" But he was speaking about the temple of his body. Therefore, when he was raised from the dead, his disciples remembered that he had said this, and they came to believe the Scripture and the word Jesus had spoken.

770

November 10 / 672
LEO THE GREAT
cf. 778 or 779

November 11 / 673
MARTIN OF TOURS
cf. 781

November 12 / 674
JOSAPHAT
cf. 777 or 778

November 13
FRANCES XAVIER CABRINI
cf. 780

November 15 / *675*
ALBERT THE GREAT
cf. 778 or 779

November 16 / *676*
MARGARET OF SCOTLAND
cf. 781

GERTRUDE / *677*
cf. 780 or 781

November 17 / *678*
ELIZABETH OF HUNGARY
cf. 781

November 18 / *679*
**DEDICATION OF THE CHURCHES
OF PETER AND PAUL**
The Lord has revealed to the
    nations his saving power.

ROSE PHILIPPINE DUCHESNE
cf. 780

November 21 / *680*
PRESENTATION OF MARY
cf. 776

November 22 / *681*
CECILIA
cf. 777 or 780

November 23 / *682*
CLEMENT I
cf. 777 or 778

COLUMBAN / *683*
cf. 778 or 781

MIGUEL AGUSTIN PRO
cf. 777

November 30 / *684*
ANDREW
Their message goes out through all
    the earth.

THANKSGIVING DAY   771

RESPONSORIAL PSALM I   *Psalm 67:2-3, 5, 7-8*
℟. **The earth has yielded its fruits; God, our God, has blessed us.**

May God have pity on us and bless us;
    may he let his face shine upon us.
So may your way be known upon earth;
    among all nations, your salvation. ℟.

May the nations be glad and exult
    because you rule the peoples in equity;

the nations on the earth you guide. ℟.

The earth has yielded its fruits;
    God, our God, has blessed us.
May God bless us,
    and may all the ends of the earth
    fear him! ℟.

Or:

RESPONSORIAL PSALM II   *Psalm 138:1-2, 2-3, 4-5*
℟. **I will give thanks to your name, because of your kindness and your truth.**

I will give thanks to you, O Lord, with
    all my heart,
    [for you have heard the words of my
        mouth;]
    in the presence of the angels I will
        sing your praise;
I will worship at your holy temple. ℟.

I will give thanks to your name,
    because of your kindness and your
        truth;

For you have made great above all things
    your name and your promise.
When I called, you answered me;
    you built up strength within me. ℟.

All the kings of the earth shall give
    thanks to you, O Lord,
    when they hear the words of your
        mouth;
And they shall sing of the ways of the
        Lord:
    "Great is the glory of the Lord." ℟.

772 DECEMBER

December 3 / 685
FRANCIS XAVIER
cf. 778

December 4 / 686
JOHN DAMASCENE
cf. 778 or 779

December 6 / 687
NICHOLAS
cf. 778

December 7 / 688
AMBROSE
cf. 778 or 779

773 DECEMBER 8: IMMACULATE CONCEPTION

READING I   *Genesis 3:9-15, 20 / 689*

After the man, Adam, had eaten of the tree, the LORD God called to the man and asked him, "Where are you?" He answered, "I heard you in the garden; but I was afraid, because I was naked, so I hid myself." Then he asked, "Who told you that you were naked? You have eaten, then, from the tree of which I had forbidden you to eat!" The man replied, "The woman whom you put here with me—she gave me fruit from the tree, and so I ate it." The LORD God then asked the woman, "Why did you do such a thing?" The woman answered, "The serpent tricked me into it, so I ate it."

Then the LORD God said to the serpent:
"Because you have done this, you shall be banned
    from all the animals
    and from all the wild creatures;
on your belly shall you crawl,
    and dirt shall you eat
    all the days of your life.
I will put enmity between you and the woman,
    and between your offspring and hers;
he will strike at your head,
    while you strike at his heel."
The man called his wife Eve, because she became the mother of all the living.

RESPONSORIAL PSALM   *Psalm 98:1, 2-3, 3-4*

Sing to the Lord a new song, for he has done marvelous deeds.

Sing to the LORD a new song,
    for he has done wondrous deeds;
his right hand has won victory for him,
    his holy arm. ℟.

The LORD has made his salvation known:
    in the sight of the nations he has
        revealed his justice.

He has remembered his kindness and his
        faithfulness
    toward the house of Israel. ℟.

All the ends of the earth have seen
    the salvation by our God.
Sing joyfully to the LORD, all you lands;
    break into song; sing praise. ℟.

READING II
Ephesians 1:3-6, 11-12

Brothers and sisters: Blessed be the God and Father of our Lord Jesus Christ, who has blessed us in Christ with every spiritual blessing in the heavens, as he chose us in him, before the foundation of the world, to be holy and without blemish before him. In love he destined us for adoption to himself through Jesus Christ, in accord with the favor of his will, for the praise of the glory of his grace that he granted us in the beloved.

In him we were also chosen, destined in accord with the purpose of the One who accomplishes all things according to the intention of his will, so that we might exist for the praise of his glory, we who first hoped in Christ.

GOSPEL
Luke 1:26-38

The angel Gabriel was sent from God to a town of Galilee called Nazareth, to a virgin betrothed to a man named Joseph, of the house of David, and the virgin's name was Mary. And coming to her, he said, "Hail, full of grace! The Lord is with you." But she was greatly troubled at what was said and pondered what sort of greeting this might be. Then the angel said to her, "Do not be afraid, Mary, for you have found favor with God. Behold, you will conceive in your womb and bear a son, and you shall name him Jesus. He will be great and will be called Son of the Most High, and the Lord God will give him the throne of David his father, and he will rule over the house of Jacob forever, and of his kingdom there will be no end." But Mary said to the angel, "How can this be, since I have no relations with a man?" And the angel said to her in reply, "The Holy Spirit will come upon you, and the power of the Most High will overshadow you. Therefore the child to be born will be called holy, the Son of God. And behold, Elizabeth, your relative, has also conceived a son in her old age, and this is the sixth month for her who was called barren; for nothing will be impossible for God." Mary said, "Behold, I am the handmaid of the Lord. May it be done to me according to your word." Then the angel departed from her.

774

December 9
BLESSED JUAN DIEGO
cf. 781

December 11 / *690*
DAMASUS I
cf. 778

December 12 / *691*
OUR LADY OF GUADALUPE
cf. 776

JANE FRANCES DE CHANTAL
cf. 781

December 13 / *692*
LUCY
cf. 777 or 780

December 14 / *693*
JOHN OF THE CROSS
cf. 778 or 779

December 21 / *694*
PETER CANISIUS
cf. 778 or 779

December 23 / *695*
JOHN OF KANTY
cf. 778

December 26 / *696*
STEPHEN
Into your hands, O Lord,
I entrust my spirit.

December 27 / *697*
JOHN
Let good men rejoice in the Lord.

December 28 / *698*
HOLY INNOCENTS
Our soul has escaped like a bird
    from the hunter's net.

December 29 / *699*
THOMAS BECKET
cf. 777 or 778

December 31 / *700*
SYLVESTER I
cf. 778

Commons: Psalm Responses

775   **DEDICATION OF A CHURCH** / *703*
1   We praise your glorious name, O mighty God.
2   How lovely is your dwelling place, Lord, mighty God!
    Or: Here God lives among his people.
3   Let us come before the Lord and praise him.
4   I rejoiced when I heard them say: let us go to the house of the Lord.
    Or: Let us go rejoicing to the house of the Lord.

776   **COMMON OF THE BLESSED VIRGIN MARY** / *709*
1   My heart rejoices in the Lord, my Savior.
2   You are the highest honor of our race.
3   Listen to me, daughter; see and bend your ear.
4   Blessed be the name of the Lord for ever.
    Or: Alleluia.
5   The Almighty has done great things for me and holy is his name.
    Or: O Blessed Virgin Mary, you carried the Son of the eternal Father.

777   **COMMON OF MARTYRS** / *715*
1   Into your hands, O Lord, I entrust my spirit.
2   The Lord set me free from all my fears.
3   Our soul has escaped like a bird from the hunter's net.
4   Those who sow in tears, shall reap with shouts of joy.

COMMON OF PASTORS / *721*   778

1   You are my inheritance, O Lord.

2   The Lord is my shepherd; there is nothing I shall want.

3   For ever I will sing the goodness of the Lord.

4   Proclaim his marvelous deeds to all the nations.

5   You are a priest for ever, in the line of Melchizedek.

6   Go out to all the world, and tell the Good News.
     Or: Alleluia.

COMMON OF DOCTORS OF THE CHURCH / *727*   779

1   The judgments of the Lord are true, and all of them just.
     Or: Your words, Lord, are spirit and life.

2   The mouth of the just man murmurs wisdom.

3   Lord, teach me your decrees.

COMMON OF VIRGINS / *733*   780

1   Listen to me, daughter; see and bend your ear.
     Or: The bridegroom is here; let us go out to meet Christ the Lord.

2   Alleluia.

COMMON OF SAINTS / *739*   781

1   Happy are they who hope in the Lord.
     Or: The just man will flourish like a palm tree in the garden of the Lord.

2   He who does justice shall live on the Lord's holy mountain.

3   You are my inheritance, O Lord.

4   I will bless the Lord at all times.
     Or: Taste and see the goodness of the Lord.

5   Oh, bless the Lord, my soul.

6   Happy the man who fears the Lord.
     Or: Alleluia.

7   Happy are those who fear the Lord.

8   In you, Lord, I have found my peace.

Seasonal Psalms

The psalm as a rule is drawn from the lectionary because the individual psalm texts are directly connected with the individual readings: the choice of psalm depends therefore on the readings.

Nevertheless, in order that the people may be able to join in the responsorial psalm more readily, some texts of responses and psalms have been chosen for optional use whenever the psalm is sung. These texts, chosen according to the different seasons of the year, may be used in place of the text corresponding to the reading.

These responsorial psalms are either printed below, or a reference is given to where they may be found elsewhere in the hymnal.

ADVENT SEASON
Psalm 25:4-5, 8-9, 10, 14 / 174
Use no. 479.

Or:

782 **RESPONSORIAL PSALM**   *Psalm 85:9-10, 11-12, 13-14*
℟. **Lord, show us your mercy and love.**

I will hear what God proclaims;
    the LORD—for he proclaims peace.
Near indeed is his salvation to those who
    fear him,
    glory dwelling in our land. ℟.

Kindness and truth shall meet;
    justice and peace shall kiss.

Truth shall spring out of the earth,
    and justice shall look down from
    heaven. ℟.

The LORD himself will give his benefits;
    our land shall yield its increase.
Justice shall walk before him,
    and prepare the way of his steps. ℟.

CHRISTMAS SEASON
Psalm 98:1, 2-3ab, 3cd-4, 5-6
Use no. 492.

EPIPHANY
Psalm 72:1-2, 7-8, 10-11, 12-13
Use no. 497.

LENTEN SEASON
Psalm 51:3-4, 5-6, 12-13, 14, 17
Use no. 502.

Or:

Psalm 91:1-2, 10-11, 12-13, 14, 16
Use no. 504.

Or:

Psalm 130:1-2, 3-4, 5-6, 7-8
Use no. 514.

HOLY WEEK
Psalm 22:8-9, 17-18, 19-20, 23-24
Use no. 521.

EASTER VIGIL

RESPONSORIAL PSALM

Psalm 136:1-3, 4-6, 7-9, 24-26 783
or 1, 3, 16, 21-23, 24-26

℞. **God's love is everlasting.**

Give thanks to the LORD, for he is good,
    for his mercy endures forever;
give thanks to the God of gods,
    for his mercy endures forever;
give thanks to the LORD of lords,
    for his mercy endures forever. ℞.

Who alone does great wonders,
    for his mercy endures forever;
who made the heavens in wisdom,
    for his mercy endures forever;
who spread out the earth upon the waters,
    for his mercy endures forever. ℞.

Or:

Give thanks to the LORD, for he is good,
    for his mercy endures forever;
give thanks to the LORD of lords,
    for his mercy endures forever;
who led his people through the
        wilderness,
    for his mercy endures forever. ℞.

Who made the great lights,
    for his mercy endures forever;
the sun to rule over the day,
    for his mercy endures forever;
the moon and the stars to rule over the
        night,
    for his mercy endures forever. ℞.

Who freed us from our foes,
    for his mercy endures forever;
who gives food to all flesh,
    for his mercy endures forever;
give thanks to the God of heaven,
    for his mercy endures forever. ℞.

Who made their land a heritage,
    for his mercy endures forever;
the heritage of Israel, his servant,
    for his mercy endures forever;
who remembered us in our abjection,
    for his mercy endures forever. ℞.

Who freed us from our foes,
    for his mercy endures forever;
who gives food to all flesh,

for his mercy endures forever;
give thanks to the God of heaven,
    for his mercy endures forever. ℟.

EASTER SEASON
Psalm 118:1-2, 16-17, 22-23
Use no. 551.

Or:

Psalm 66:1-3, 4-5, 6-7, 16, 20
Use no. 562.

ASCENSION
784 RESPONSORIAL PSALM   *Psalm 47:2-3, 6-7, 8-9*
℟. **God mounts his throne to shouts of joy.**

All you peoples, clap your hands,
    shout to God with cries of gladness,
for the LORD, the Most High, the
        awesome,
    is the great king over all the earth. ℟.

God mounts his throne amid shouts of
        joy;
    the LORD, amid trumpet blasts.

Sing praise to God, sing praise;
    sing praise to our king, sing praise. ℟.

For king of all the earth is God;
    sing hymns of praise.
God reigns over the nations,
    God sits upon his holy throne. ℟.

PENTECOST
Psalm 104:1, 24, 29-30, 31, 34
Use no. 570.

ORDINARY TIME
Psalm 19:8, 9, 10, 11
Use no. 509.

Or:

Psalm 27:1, 4, 13-14
Use no. 584.

Or:

785 RESPONSORIAL PSALM   *Psalm 34:2-3, 4-5, 6-7*
℟. **I will bless the Lord at all times.**
    or:
Taste and see the goodness of the Lord.

I will bless the LORD at all times;
    his praise shall be ever in my mouth.
Let my soul glory in the LORD;
    the lowly will hear me and be glad. ℟.

Glorify the LORD with me;
    let us extol his name.
I sought the LORD, and he answered me,
    and delivered me from all my fears. ℟.

Look to him that you may be radiant
with joy,
and your faces may not blush with
shame.
When the poor one called out, the LORD
heard
and from all his distress he saved
him. ℟.

The angel of the LORD encamps
around those who fear him, and
delivers them.
Taste and see how good the LORD is;
blessed the man who takes refuge in
him. ℟.

Or:

Psalm 63:2, 3-4, 5-6, 8-9
Use no. 613.

Or:

Psalm 95:1-2, 6-7, 8-9
Use no. 508.

Or:

Psalm 100:1-2, 3, 5
Use no. 558.

Or:

Psalm 103:1-2, 3-4, 8, 10, 12-13
Use no. 596.

Or:

Psalm 145:1-2, 8-9, 10-11, 13-14
Use no. 617.

LAST WEEKS
Psalm 122:1-2, 3-4, 4-5, 6-7, 8-9
Use no. 477.

Prayers of the Individual and Household

786   This book contains the texts and music which are used when the church assembles for the liturgy. With these pages members of the assembly may join fully in the Sunday eucharist, the liturgy of the hours, the celebration of the sacraments. All of these liturgies are, in fact, the work of the assembly, the work of Christians who gather to do those deeds—in word, in song, in gesture—which are the foundation and the strength of our lives. Over the years, the book itself becomes less and less necessary for we gradually learn many things by heart, making these words and tunes fully our own.

The texts in this section are not those of the assembly but those of the individual or household. They are included here because the daily prayer of Christians, prayers alone or in small groups, are part of our tradition, part of what we need for the daily expression of our faith. Many of the texts which follow have been the strength and sustenance of those who have walked the way of Jesus. Some of these prayers we already know by heart. Others will be learned with repetition. That is the intention, for most of these prayers are not meant to be read. They are words to be in the heart and on the lips at various times: by morning, by night, at table. Others are for special circumstances: when someone is ill, at the time of death, at times of thanksgiving.

Some of the prayers found in the liturgy itself are included or suggested here. When these become the regular prayer of an individual, the liturgy itself is the source of the Christian's spirit and life. This happens also when the scriptures read in the Sunday assembly are read and pondered again through the week. It happens when the verses of the psalm sung on Sunday become part of morning and evening prayer all week long. Such habits mean that we begin to come to the Sunday liturgy not as spectators but as celebrants, as the ones responsible for the liturgy.

The task of these prayers is to be with us day by day, over the years, to shape our lives. The prayers known by heart are a daily remembering and affirming of what became of us by baptism. Such prayers, coming day after day, in season and out, whatever the mood and circumstances, have us pray as the church. The individual becomes the voice of creation's praise, becomes the lament of the oppressed and suffering, becomes the whole world's giving of thanks.

MORNING PRAYERS

THE SIGN OF THE CROSS   787
This prayer is not the words but the sign itself. The cross is made on the whole upper part of the body, or simply on the forehead, or the lips, or the heart. By this gesture the Christian renews that baptism which plunged us into the death of the Lord so that we live now in Christ. The common words of the sign of the cross recall our baptism.

In the name of the Father,
and of the Son,
and of the Holy Spirit.

Or, when signing the lips:

Lord, open my lips and my mouth will proclaim your praise.

GLORY TO GOD   788
The strongest note of morning prayer is the praise of God who has kept us through the night and given us this new day. There are two common forms of the Gloria.

Glory to the Father, and to the Son, and to the Holy Spirit:
as it was in the beginning, is now, and will be forever. Amen.

Or:

Glory to God in the highest,
  and peace to his people on earth.

Lord God, heavenly King,
almighty God and Father,
  we worship you, we give you thanks,
  we praise you for your glory.

Lord Jesus Christ, only Son of the Father,
Lord God, Lamb of God,
you take away the sin of the world:
  have mercy on us;
you are seated at the right hand of the Father:
  receive our prayer.

For you alone are the Holy One,
you alone are the Lord,
you alone are the Most High,
  Jesus Christ,
  with the Holy Spirit,
  in the glory of God the Father. Amen.

789   THE LORD'S PRAYER

This prayer is used by many to mark not only the morning but several times of the day. The first translation is the one to which most Catholics are accustomed, the second is a translation used more and more by Christians of many churches.

Our Father, who art in heaven,
hallowed be thy name.
Thy kingdom come.
Thy will be done on earth
   as it is in heaven.
Give us this day our daily bread,
and forgive us our trespasses
as we forgive those who trespass against us;
and lead us not into temptation
but deliver us from evil. Amen.

Or:

790   Our Father in heaven,
   hallowed be your Name,
   your kingdom come,
   your will be done,
      on earth as in heaven.
Give us today our daily bread.
Forgive us our sins
   as we forgive those who sin against us.
Save us from the time of trial
   and deliver us from evil.
For the kingdom, the power
   and the glory are yours,
      now and for ever. Amen.

ANCIENT PRAYERS FOR MORNING

The first of these is the beginning of the "Hear, O Israel" prayer; this is the corner-stone of Jewish prayer and would have been the daily prayer of Jesus, his family and his disciples. The blessings which follow accompany some of the actions of early morning. The final text is from Psalm 95, long used at morning prayer.

Hear, O Israel: the Lord is our God, the Lord is One!
Blessed is his glorious kingdom for ever and ever!

Blessed are you, Lord our God, ruler of the universe,
opening the eyes of the blind.

Blessed are you, Lord our God, ruler of the universe,
clothing the naked.

Blessed are you, Lord our God, ruler of the universe,
setting captives free.

Blessed are you, Lord our God, ruler of the universe,
guiding our footsteps.

Blessed are you, Lord our God, ruler of the universe,
taking the sleep from my eyes and the slumber from my eyelids.

Come, let us sing to the Lord;   791
    and shout with joy to the Rock who saves us.
Let us approach him with praise and thanksgiving
    and sing joyful songs to the Lord.

Come, then, let us bow down and worship,
    bending the knee before the Lord, our maker.
For he is our God and we are his people,
    the flock he shepherds.

MORNING PSALMS   792

In addition to Psalm 95, above, the psalms of morning are the psalms of praise, especially Psalms 148, 149 and 150. Other morning prayers are Psalm 51 and Psalm 63.

MORNING HYMNS   793

Morning hymns are found at nos. 3 and 404.

THE BENEDICTUS   794

The Benedictus or Song of Zachary from Luke 1:68-69 is a morning prayer for the day when God's compassion like "the dawn from on high shall break upon us, to shine on those who dwell in darkness and the shadow of death, and to guide our feet into the way of peace." It is found at no. 6.

MORNING PRAYER OF ST. PATRICK   795

The Lorica or "Breastplate" is an ancient Celtic prayer attributed to St. Patrick.

I arise today
through the strength of heaven,
light of the sun,
radiance of the moon,
splendor of fire,
speed of lightning,
swiftness of the wind,
depth of the sea,
stability of the earth,
firmness of the rock.

I arise today
through God's strength to pilot me,
God's might to uphold me,
God's wisdom to guide me,
God's eye to look before me,
God's ear to hear me,
God's word to speak for me,
God's hand to guard me,
God's way to lie before me,
God's shield to protect me,
God's hosts to save me
from the snares of the devil,

from everyone who desires me ill,
afar and near,
alone or in a multitude.
Christ with me, Christ before me, Christ behind me,
Christ in me, Christ beneath me, Christ above me,
Christ on my right, Christ on my left,
Christ when I lie down, Christ when I sit down, Christ when I arise,
Christ in the heart of everyone who thinks of me,
Christ in the mouth of everyone who speaks of me,
Christ in the eye that sees me,
Christ in the ear that hears me.

DAYTIME PRAYERS

796 THE JESUS PRAYER

This is one of the most widely used of those prayers which are meant to be repeated over and over again so that the one praying becomes completely caught up in prayer. Often prayers like this one are intended to be in rhythm with one's breathing.

Lord Jesus Christ,
Son of the living God,
have mercy on me, a sinner.

797 THE ROSARY

The rosary is another prayer which in its repetition draws us into contemplation of the mysteries of our salvation. The rosary begins with the Apostle's Creed (no. 99) and consists of groups of ten Hail Marys, each group preceded by the Lord's Prayer and followed by the Glory to the Father. Each decade has traditionally been given to pondering one aspect of the paschal mystery:

The Joyful Mysteries
    1. The Annunciation (Luke 1:30-33)
    2. The Visitation (Luke 1:50-53)
    3. The Nativity (Luke 2:10-11)
    4. The Presentation (Luke 2:29-32)
    5. The Finding of Jesus in the Temple (Luke 2:48-52)

The Sorrowful Mysteries
    1. The Agony in the Garden (Matthew 26:38-39)
    2. The Scourging (John 19:1)
    3. The Crowning with Thorns (Mark 15:16-17)
    4. Jesus Carries His Cross (John 19:17)
    5. The Crucifixion (John 19:28-30)

The Glorious Mysteries
    1. The Resurrection (Mark 16:6-8)
    2. The Ascension (Acts 1:10-11)
    3. The Coming of the Holy Spirit (Acts 2:1-4)
    4. The Assumption (Song of Songs 2:3-6)
    5. The Coronation of Mary (Luke 1:51-54)

The prayer which makes up the rosary is the Hail Mary. Its words are drawn from the scriptures and the intercession of the church.

Hail Mary, full of grace,   798
the Lord is with you!
Blessed are you among women
and blessed is the fruit of your womb, Jesus.
Holy Mary, mother of God,
pray for us sinners,
now and at the hour of our death. Amen.

THE ANGELUS   799
This is the prayer prayed in early morning, at noon, and at the end of the work day. Through this constant presence in the midst of everyday, the Christian proclaims that all of our time and all of our human space is transformed by the incarnation, the presence of God with us.

The angel spoke God's message to Mary
and she conceived of the Holy Spirit.
Hail Mary...

"I am the lowly servant of the Lord:
let it be done to me according to your word."
Hail Mary...

And the Word became flesh
and lived among us.
Hail Mary...

Pray for us, holy Mother of God,
that we may become worthy of the promises of Christ.

Lord,
fill our hearts with your grace:
once, through the message of an angel
you revealed to us the incarnation of your Son:
now, through his suffering and death
lead us to the glory of his resurrection.

DIVINE PRAISES   800
These prayers may be used together, or each short line can be repeated over and over (as with the Jesus Prayer).

Blessed be God.
Blessed be his holy name.
Blessed be Jesus Christ, true God and true man.
Blessed be the name of Jesus.
Blessed be his most sacred heart.
Blessed be his most precious blood.
Blessed be Jesus in the most holy sacrament of the altar.
Blessed be the Holy Spirit, the Paraclete.
Blessed be the great mother of God, Mary most holy.
Blessed be her holy and immaculate conception.
Blessed be her glorious assumption.

Blessed be the name of Mary, virgin and mother.
Blessed be Joseph, her most chaste spouse.
Blessed be God in his angels and in his saints.

EVENING PRAYERS

801 **PRAISE OF GOD FOR CHRIST, OUR LIGHT**

The prayer as day ends has often begun with a verse or hymn in praise of God who has given us in Christ our true light. The ancient hymn Phos Hilaron, *"O Radiant Light," is a beautiful expression of this (no. 12). This praise is also contained in the simple invocation:*

Jesus Christ is the light of the world,
a light no darkness can overpower.

802 **EVENING PSALMS**

Psalm 141 prays:

Let my prayer arise before you like incense,
the raising of my hands like an evening oblation.

This is the primary psalm of evening prayer as it prays for God's protection. Other appropriate psalms of the evening are Psalm 23, Psalm 121 and Psalm 123.

803 **EVENING HYMNS**

Evening hymns are found at nos. 405 and 406.

804 **INTERCESSIONS**

At baptism the Christian receives the responsibility to intercede at all times, to be the voice of all creation and of all people before God. Each day we bring the needs and sufferings of our world. Such prayers are often made in the evening: our work is finished and we place all the world in God's care. The following prayers show how broad is the church's intercession. They may serve as an example for an individual's prayer.

For peace from on high and for our salvation, let us pray to the Lord. Lord, hear our prayer.

For the welfare of all churches and for the unity of the human family, let us pray...

For (name), our pope, (name), our bishop, and (name), our pastor, and for all ministers of the gospel, let us pray...

For nations and governments and for all who serve them, let us pray...

For this city and for every city and community and for all who live in them, let us pray...

For the good earth which God has given us and for the wisdom and will to conserve it, let us pray...

For the safety of travelers, the recovery of the sick, the care of the destitute and the release of prisoners, let us pray...

For an angel of peace to guide and protect us, let us pray...

For a peaceful evening and a night free from sin, let us pray...

THE MAGNIFICAT 805

The Song of Mary from Luke 1:46-55 has long been a part of evening prayer for Christians. It is strong in its praise and in its vision of justice brought by God. It is found at no. 48, with a metrical version at no. 15.

NIGHT PRAYERS

CONFESSION 806

Before sleep, the Christian recalls with sorrow the failures of the day and gives thanks to God for the love which surrounds us. Another prayer, the Act of Contrition, is found at no. 827.

I confess to almighty God,
and to you, my brothers and sisters,
that I have sinned through my own fault
in my thoughts and in my words,
in what I have done,
and in what I have failed to do;
and I ask blessed Mary, ever virgin,
all the angels and saints,
and you, my brothers and sisters,
to pray for me to the Lord our God.

SHORT PRAYERS 807

May the almighty Lord give us a restful night
and a peaceful death.

Keep us, Lord, as the apple of your eye
and shelter us in the shadow of your wing.

Protect us, Lord, as we stay awake;
watch over us as we sleep,
that awake, we may keep watch with Christ,
and asleep, rest in his peace.

Into your hands, Lord, I commend my spirit.
O Lord our God, make us lie down in peace
and raise us up to life.

Visit this house,
we beg you, Lord,
and banish from it
the deadly power of the evil one.
May your holy angels dwell here
to keep us in peace,
and may your blessing be always upon us.

Hear us, Lord,
and send your angel from heaven
to visit and protect,
to comfort and defend
all who live in this house.

808 NIGHT PSALMS

The traditional psalms of night are Psalm 4, Psalm 91 and Psalm 134.

809 CANTICLE OF SIMEON

The words spoken by Simeon in the Temple (Luke 2:29-32) are often used as a night prayer for the church. It is found at no. 737.

810 ANTHEMS OF MARY

The last prayer of night is addressed to our mother. The Salve Regina *(no. 415) is used throughout the year; during Eastertime it is replaced by the* Regina Caeli *(no. 265). Another appropriate prayer is the* Memorare.

Remember, most loving virgin Mary,
never was it heard
that anyone who turned to you for help
was left unaided.
Inspired by this confidence,
though burdened by my sins,
I run to your protection
for you are my mother.
Mother of the Word of God,
do not despise my words of pleading
but be merciful and hear my prayer.

MEAL PRAYERS

At table we learn to give God thanks and praise for all the fruit of the earth and work of human hands.

811 BEFORE MEALS

Bless us, O Lord, and these thy gifts
which we are about to receive
from thy bounty;
through Christ our Lord. Amen.

Or:

The eyes of all hope in you, Lord,
and you give them food in due season.
You open your hand,
and every creature is filled with your blessing.

Or:

Blessed are you, Lord our God, ruler of the universe,
for you bring forth bread from the earth.

AFTER MEALS 812

We give you thanks
for all your gifts,
almighty God,
living and reigning
now and for ever.

Or:

Blessed be the Lord
of whose bounty we have received
and by whose goodness we live.

SUNDAY PRAYERS 813

*Sunday is called by Christians "The Lord's Day." On this day Christians assemble,
listen to the scriptures, gather at the holy table and share in communion. Sunday
is the highest day in our calendar. It is appropriate to prepare for the eucharistic
assembly by reading and reflecting on the Sunday's scriptures. Week by week
these scriptures are read at the liturgy as a foundation for all our worship and all
our lives. In the eucharistic prayer and the holy communion, we "proclaim the
death of the Lord until he comes" (1 Corinthians 11:26). Thus each Sunday we
gather as the church "to praise and thank God, to remember and make present
God's great deeds, to offer common prayer, to realize and celebrate the kingdom
of peace and justice" (United States Bishops' Committee on the Liturgy,*
Environment and Art in Catholic Worship*). Some traditional prayers of preparation
for Mass and thanksgiving after Mass are found below. The eucharistic hymns of
Thomas Aquinas are fitting prayers both before and after communion: nos. 88 and
528. Among the psalms which have been used as communion prayers are Psalm
23, Psalm 34 and Psalm 147.*

HOW HOLY THIS FEAST 814

How holy this feast
in which Christ is our food:
his passion is recalled,
grace fills our hearts,
and we receive a pledge of the glory to come.

You gave them bread from heaven to be their food.
And this bread contained all goodness.

Lord Jesus Christ,
you gave us the eucharist
as the memorial of your suffering and death.
May our worship of this sacrament of your body and blood
help us to experience the salvation you won for us
and the peace of the kingdom
where you live with the Father and Holy Spirit,
one God, for ever and ever. Amen.

815 **ANIMA CHRISTI**

Soul of Christ, sanctify me.
Body of Christ, heal me.
Blood of Christ, drench me.
Water from the side of Christ, wash me.
Passion of Christ, strengthen me.
Good Jesus, hear me.
In your wounds shelter me.
From turning away keep me.
From the evil one protect me.
At the hour of my death call me.
Into your presence lead me,
to praise you with all your saints
for ever and ever. Amen.

816 **PRAYER TO THE VIRGIN MARY**

Mary, holy virgin mother,
I have received your Son, Jesus Christ.
With love you became his mother,
gave birth to him, nursed him,
and helped him grow to manhood.
With love I return him to you,
to hold once more,
to love with all your heart,
and to offer him to the Holy Trinity
as our supreme act of worship
for your honor and for the good
of all your children.
Mother, ask God to forgive my sins
and to help me serve him more faithfully.
Keep me true to Christ until death,
and let me come to praise him with you
for ever and ever. Amen.

817 **PRAYER FOR FRIDAYS**

In their 1983 letter, The Challenge of Peace, *the bishops of the United States called on Catholics to join them in fasting, prayer and charity on Fridays: "As a tangible sign of our need and desire to do penance we, for the cause of peace, commit ourselves to fast and abstinence on each Friday of the year... Every Friday should be a day significantly devoted to prayer, penance, and almsgiving for peace."*

All praise be yours, God our Creator,
as we wait in joyful hope
for the flowering of justice and the fullness of peace.
All praise for this day, this Friday.
By our weekly fasting and prayer
cast out the spirit of war, of fear and mistrust,
and make us grow hungry for human kindness,
thirsty for solidarity

with all the people of your dear earth.
May all our prayer, our fasting and our deeds
be done in the name of Jesus. Amen.

TIMES OF NEED

There are many scriptures, hymns and psalms in this book which give voice to our prayers for our own needs, for the needs of others and of the world. A familiarity with the psalms especially will lead the Christian to many prayers in troubled times.

IN TIMES OF SICKNESS 818

All-powerful and ever-living God,
the lasting health of all who believe in you,
hear us as we ask your loving help for the sick;
restore their health,
that they may again offer joyful thanks in your Church.

Or:

God of love,
ever caring,
ever strong,
stand by us in our time of need.
Watch over your child who is sick,
Look after him/her in every danger,
and grant him/her your healing and peace.

IN TIME OF SUFFERING 819

Lord Jesus Christ, by your patience in suffering you hallowed earthly pain
and gave us the example of obedience to you Father's will:
Be near me in my time of weakness and pain;
sustain me by your grace, that my strength and courage may not fail;
heal me, if it be your will;
and help me always to believe that what happens to me here
is of little account if you hold me in eternal life,
my Lord and my God.

WHEN DEATH IS NEAR 820

Go forth, Christian soul, from this world
in the name of God the almighty Father, who created you,
in the name of Jesus Christ, Son of the living God, who suffered for you,
in the name of the Holy Spirit, who has poured out upon you,
go forth, faithful Christian.
May you live in peace this day,
may your home be with God in Zion,
with Mary, the virgin mother of God,
with Joseph, and all the angels and saints.

Or:

Saints of God, come to his/her aid!
Come to meet him/her, angels of the Lord!

821 **WHEN SOMEONE HAS DIED**
Eternal rest grant to him/her/them, O Lord,
and let perpetual light shine upon him/her/them.

Or:

Loving and merciful God,
we entrust our brother/sister to your mercy.
You loved him/her greatly in this life:
now that he/she is freed from all its cares,
give him/her happiness and peace for ever.
The old order has passed away;
welcome him/her now into paradise
where there will be no more sorrow,
no more weeping or pain,
but only peace and joy
with Jesus, your Son,
and the Holy Spirit
for ever and ever. Amen.

Or:

822 God of all consolation,
in your unending love and mercy for us
you turn the darkness of death
into the dawn of new life.
Show compassion to your people in their sorrow.
Be our refuge and our strength
to lift us from the darkness of this grief
to the peace and light of your presence.
Your Son, our Lord Jesus Christ,
by dying for us, conquered death
and by rising again, restored life.
May we then go forward eagerly to meet him,
and after our life on earth
be reunited with our brothers and sisters
where every tear will be wiped away.
We ask this through Christ our Lord. Amen.

823 **PSALMS IN TIME OF NEED**
Among the psalms which are prayed in times of sickness and sorrow are the following: Psalm 6, Psalm 25, Psalm 42, Psalm 63, and Psalm 103.

824 **PRAYER TO MARY**
We turn to you for protection,
holy Mother of God.
Listen to our prayers
and help us in our needs.
Save us from every danger,
glorious and blessed Virgin.

PRAYER FOR PEACE 825

Lord, make me an instrument of your peace:
    where there is hatred, let me sow love;
    where there is injury, pardon;
    where there is doubt, faith;
    where there is despair, hope;
    where there is darkness, light;
    where there is sadness, joy.
O divine Master, grant that I may not so much seek
    to be consoled as to console,
    to be understood as to understand,
    to be loved as to love.
For it is in giving that we receive,
    it is in pardoning that we are pardoned,
    it is in dying that we are born to eternal life.

PENANCE AND RECONCILIATION 826

The rite of reconciliation for several penitents is at no. 66. When a person alone comes to celebrate the sacrament with a priest, the priest greets the penitent. Then the penitent makes the sign of the cross and the priest invites the penitent to have trust in God. A reading from scripture follows. After this, the penitent may say a prayer of confession (for example, "I confess to almighty God" no. 806). The penitent then makes a confession of sin and receives counsel from the priest. The penitent may then recite one of the following prayers or use some other way to express sorrow.

My God,
I am sorry for my sins with all my heart.
In choosing to do wrong
and failing to do good,
I have sinned against you
whom I should love above all things.
I firmly intend, with your help,
to do penance,
to sin no more,
and to avoid whatever leads me to sin.

Or:

Our Savior Jesus Christ
suffered and died for us.
In his name, my God, have mercy.

Or:

Lord Jesus, Son of God,
have mercy on me, a sinner.

The priest then extends hands over the penitent's head and speaks the absolution. The priest may then say: "Give thanks to the Lord, for he is good" and the penitent responds: "His mercy endures for ever." Then the priest dismisses the penitent in peace.

827 VARIOUS PRAYERS OF PENANCE AND RECONCILIATION

Lord,
turn to us in mercy,
and forgive all our sins
that we may serve you in true freedom.

828 Father of mercies
and God of consolation,
you do not wish the sinner to die
but to be converted and live.
Come to the aid of your people,
that they may turn from their sins
and live for you alone.
May we be attentive to your word,
confess our sins, receive your forgiveness,
and be always grateful for your loving kindness.
Help us to live the truth in love
and grow into the fullness of Christ, your Son,
who lives and reigns for ever and ever. Amen.

829 Father, all-powerful and ever-living God,
we do well always and everywhere to give you thanks.
When you punish us, you show your justice;
when you pardon us, you show your kindness;
yet always your mercy enfolds us.
When you chastise us, you do not wish to condemn us;
when you spare us, you give us time to amend for our sins
through Christ our Lord. Amen.

830 God and Father of us all,
you have forgiven our sins
and sent us your peace.
Help us to forgive each other
and to work together to establish peace in the world.

831 PSALMS OF PENANCE AND RECONCILIATION

Among the psalms which speak of sin, of sorrow and of forgiveness are the following: Psalm 51, Psalm 90, Psalm 123, Psalm 130 and Psalm 139.

VARIOUS PRAYERS

832 COME, HOLY SPIRIT

Come, Holy Spirit, fill the hearts of your faithful,
and kindle in them the fire of your love.
Send forth your Spirit and they shall be created,
and you will renew the face of the earth.

Lord, by the light of the Holy Spirit
you have taught the hearts of your faithful.
In the same Spirit
help us to relish what is right
and always rejoice in your consolation.

LITANY OF THE HOLY NAME 833

Lord, have mercy	Lord, have mercy
Christ, have mercy	Christ, have mercy
Lord, have mercy	Lord, have mercy
God our Father in heaven	have mercy on us
God the Son, Redeemer of the world	have mercy on us
God the Holy Spirit	have mercy on us
Holy Trinity, one God	have mercy on us
Jesus, Son of the living God	have mercy on us
Jesus, splendor of the Father	have mercy on us
Jesus, brightness of the everlasting light	have mercy on us
Jesus, king of glory	have mercy on us
Jesus, dawn of justice	have mercy on us
Jesus, Son of the Virgin Mary	have mercy on us
Jesus, worthy of our love	have mercy on us
Jesus, mighty God	have mercy on us
Jesus, father of the world to come	have mercy on us
Jesus, prince of peace	have mercy on us
Jesus, all-powerful	have mercy on us
Jesus, pattern of patience	have mercy on us
Jesus, model of obedience	have mercy on us
Jesus, gentle and humble of heart	have mercy on us
Jesus, lover of chastity	have mercy on us
Jesus, lover of us all	have mercy on us
Jesus, God of peace	have mercy on us
Jesus, author of life	have mercy on us
Jesus, model of goodness	have mercy on us
Jesus, seeker of souls	have mercy on us
Jesus, our God	have mercy on us
Jesus, our refuge	have mercy on us
Jesus, father of the poor	have mercy on us
Jesus, treasure of the faithful	have mercy on us
Jesus, Good Shepherd	have mercy on us
Jesus, the true light	have mercy on us
Jesus, eternal wisdom	have mercy on us
Jesus, infinite goodness	have mercy on us
Jesus, our way and our life	have mercy on us
Jesus, joy of angels	have mercy on us
Jesus, king of patriarchs	have mercy on us
Jesus, teacher of apostles	have mercy on us
Jesus, master of evangelists	have mercy on us
Jesus, courage of martyrs	have mercy on us
Jesus, light of confessors	have mercy on us
Jesus, purity of virgins	have mercy on us
Jesus, crown of saints	have mercy on us
Lord, be merciful	Jesus, save your people
From all evil	Jesus, save your people

From every sin	Jesus, save your people
From the snares of the devil	Jesus, save your people
From your anger	Jesus, save your people
From the spirit of infidelity	Jesus, save your people
From everlasting death	Jesus, save your people
From the neglect of your Holy Spirit	Jesus, save your people
By the mystery of your incarnation	Jesus, save your people
By your birth	Jesus, save your people
By your childhood	Jesus, save your people
By your hidden life	Jesus, save your people
By your public ministry	Jesus, save your people
By your agony and crucifixion	Jesus, save your people
By your abandonment	Jesus, save your people
By your grief and sorrow	Jesus, save your people
By your death and burial	Jesus, save your people
By your rising to new life	Jesus, save your people
By your return to the Father	Jesus, save your people
By your gift of the holy eucharist	Jesus, save your people
By your joy and glory	Jesus, save your people

834 LITANY OF LORETTO

Lord, have mercy	Lord, have mercy
Christ, have mercy	Christ, have mercy
Lord, have mercy	Lord, have mercy
God our Father in heaven	have mercy on us
God the Son, Redeemer of the world	have mercy on us
God the Holy Spirit	have mercy on us
Holy Trinity, one God	have mercy on us
Holy Mary	pray for us
Holy Mother of God	pray for us
Most honored of virgins	pray for us
Mother of Christ	pray for us
Mother of the Church	pray for us
Mother of divine grace	pray for us
Mother most pure	pray for us
Mother of chaste love	pray for us
Mother and virgin	pray for us
Sinless Mother	pray for us
Dearest of Mothers	pray for us
Model of motherhood	pray for us
Mother of good counsel	pray for us
Mother of our Creator	pray for us
Mother of our Savior	pray for us
Virgin most wise	pray for us
Virgin rightly praised	pray for us
Virgin rightly renowned	pray for us
Virgin most powerful	pray for us

Virgin gentle in mercy	pray for us
Faithful Virgin	pray for us
Mirror of justice	pray for us
Throne of wisdom	pray for us
Cause of our joy	pray for us
Shrine of the Spirit	pray for us
Glory of Israel	pray for us
Vessel of selfless devotion	pray for us
Mystical Rose	pray for us
Tower of David	pray for us
Tower of ivory	pray for us
House of gold	pray for us
Ark of the covenant	pray for us
Gate of heaven	pray for us
Morning star	pray for us
Health of the sick	pray for us
Refuge of sinners	pray for us
Comfort of the troubled	pray for us
Help of Christians	pray for us
Queen of angels	pray for us
Queen of patriarchs and prophets	pray for us
Queen of apostles and martyrs	pray for us
Queen of confessors and virgins	pray for us
Queen of all saints	pray for us
Queen conceived without sin	pray for us
Queen assumed into heaven	pray for us
Queen of the rosary	pray for us
Queen of peace	pray for us

Acknowledgments/*continued*

Acknowledgments/*continued*

Acknowledgments/*continued*

Please note: The Scripture Passages Related to Hymns Index, Liturgical Index, and Topical Index are found in the choir and accompaniment editions.

837   Suggested Hymns for the Church Year

The following hymns are suggested for the Sundays of the three-year lectionary cycle. Those with an asterisk (*) are directly related to the scriptures of the day, while the others are suggested because of their relationship to the predominant focus of the day's readings.

ADVENT I
A - Wait for the Lord 199
    Soon and Very Soon 409
B - Abba! Father! 308
    Wait for the Lord 199
C - Wait for the Lord 199

ADVENT II
A - On Jordan's Bank* 194
    Wait for the Lord 199
B - On Jordan's Bank* 194
    Like a Shepherd* 192
C - On Jordan's Bank* 194
    People, Look East* 191

ADVENT III
A - On Jordan's Bank* 194
    Wait for the Lord 199
B - On Jordan's Bank* 194
    You Have Anointed Me* 372
C - On Jordan's Bank* 194
    O Come, Divine Messiah 196

ADVENT IV
A - Savior of the Nations, Come 200
    Creator of the Stars of Night 195
B - Savior of the Nations, Come 200
    Creator of the Stars of Night 195
C - Savior of the Nations, Come 200
    O Come, O Come, Emmanuel 190

CHRISTMAS
see nos. 201-220

HOLY FAMILY
Sing of Mary, Meek and Lowly 417

MARY, MOTHER OF GOD
see nos. 414-422

EPIPHANY
see nos. 221-227

BAPTISM OF THE LORD
Songs of Thankfulness and Praise 227

Alternate readings
B - Come to the Water* 293
    Seek the Lord* 236
C - Like a Shepherd* 192
    God Is Here! As We His People 400

ASH WEDNESDAY
Again We Keep this Solemn Fast* 241
Parce Domine* 234
Deep Within 233

LENT I
A - Forty Days and Forty Nights 243
    The Glory of These Forty Days 239
    Tree of Life 242
B - Lord, Who throughout These Forty Days* 238
C - Forty Days and Forty Nights 243

LENT II
A - 'Tis Good, Lord, to Be Here* 413
    From Ashes to the Living Font 237
B - 'Tis Good, Lord, to Be Here* 413
    From Ashes to the Living Font 237
C - 'Tis Good, Lord, to Be Here* 413
    From Ashes to the Living Font 237

LENT III
A - I Heard the Voice of Jesus Say* 356
    From Ashes to the Living Font 237
    Tree of Life 242
B - Christ Is Made the Sure Foundation 363
    I Am the Bread of Life / Yo Soy el Pan de Vida 449
C - There's a Wideness in God's Mercy 348

LENT IV
A - Amazing Grace 342
    From Ashes to the Living Font 237
B - What Wondrous Love Is This 353
C - Amazing Grace 342
    Though the Mountains May Fall 347

LENT V
A - I Am the Bread of Life/Yo Soy el Pan de Vida* 449
    From Ashes to the Living Font 237
    Tree of Life 242
B - Tree of Life 242
    We Remember 330
C - Forgive Our Sins 465
    There's a Wideness in God's Mercy 348

PASSION SUNDAY
see nos. 244-246

HOLY THURSDAY
see nos. 247-248

GOOD FRIDAY
see nos. 249-251

EASTER VIGIL
see nos. 252-266

EASTER
see nos. 252-266

EASTER II
A - O Sons and Daughters* 260
    We Walk by Faith* 328
B - O Sons and Daughters* 260
    We Walk by Faith* 328
C - O Sons and Daughters* 260
    We Walk by Faith* 328

EASTER III
A - Shepherd of Souls 447
    In the Breaking of the Bread / Cuando Partimos el Pan del Señor 446
B - Shepherd of Souls 447
    That Easter Day with Joy Was Bright 263

Suggested Hymns for the Church Year/*continued*

C - Go* 270
   The Summons 375

EASTER IV
   A - You Satisfy the Hungry Heart 429
   B - What Wondrous Love Is This 353
      You Satisfy the Hungry Heart 429
   C - You Satisfy the Hungry Heart 429

EASTER V
   A - I Know That My Redeemer Lives* 259
      I Received the Living God 453
   B - We Have Been Told* 381
      Now We Remain 380
      Lord of All Nations, Grant Me Grace 350
   C - Lord of All Nations, Grant Me Grace 350
      They'll Know We Are Christians* 397

EASTER VI
   A - They'll Know We Are Christians 397
      If You Believe and I Believe 385
   B - No Greater Love* 753
      We Have Been Told* 381
      I Come with Joy 427
   C - Veni Creator Spiritus 273
      You Are Mine 357
      Come, Holy Ghost 276

ASCENSION
see nos. 267-270

EASTER VII
   A - Alleluia! Sing to Jesus 444
      At That First Eucharist 452
      Be Not Afraid 346
   B - Alleluia! Sing to Jesus 444
      At That First Eucharist 452
   C - Alleluia! Sing to Jesus 444
      Abba! Father! 308
      At That First Eucharist 452

PENTECOST
see nos. 271-277

TRINITY SUNDAY
see nos. 278-282
   A - What Wondrous Love Is This 353
      Come, Now Almighty King 280
   B - Go* 270
      Everyone Moved by the Spirit* 277
   C - Come, Now Almighty King 280
      O God, Almighty Father 279

BODY AND BLOOD
   A - I Am the Bread of Life/Yo Soy el Pan de Vida*
      449
      Look Beyond 442
      Eat This Bread 435
   B - Take and Eat* 441
      O Lord, with Wondrous Mystery 470
   C - Shepherd of Souls, in Love, Come* 432
      Now We Remain 380

ORDINARY TIME

SECOND SUNDAY
   A - Here I Am, Lord 373

B - Lord, When You Came / Pescador de Hombres
   378
   Here I Am, Lord 373
C - Songs of Thankfulness and Praise 227
   God, in the Planning 462

THIRD SUNDAY
   A - Two Fishermen* 376
      The Summons 375
   B - Two Fishermen* 376
      The Summons 375
   C - You Have Anointed Me* 372
      The Spirit of God 274

FOURTH SUNDAY
   A - Blest Are They* 359
      We Are the Light of the World 295
   B - There Is a Balm in Gilead 358
      The King of Glory 288
   C - May Love Be Ours* 354
      You Are Near 340

FIFTH SUNDAY
   A - Bring Forth the Kingdom* 360
      This Little Light of Mine 296
   B - There Is a Balm in Gilead 358
      There's a Wideness in God's Mercy 348
   C - Lord, When You Came/Pescador de Hombres*
      378
      Two Fishermen* 376

SIXTH SUNDAY
   A - Deep Within 233
      Eye Has Not Seen* 355
   B - We Remember 330
      There Is a Balm in Gilead 358
   C - Blest Are They* 359
      Be Not Afraid 346
      We Are the Light of the World 295

SEVENTH SUNDAY
   A - Lord of All Nations, Grant Me Grace* 350
      Jesu, Jesu 248
   B - I Danced in the Morning 382
      Now in This Banquet 448
   C - Lord of All Nations, Grant Me Grace* 350
      We Are Called 389

EIGHTH SUNDAY
   A - Seek Ye First the Kingdom of God* 335
      Lord of All Hopefulness 327
   B - Christ Is the King 284
   C - Make Me a Channel of Your Peace 392
      God, Whose Purpose Is to Kindle 388

NINTH SUNDAY
   A - Christ Is Made the Sure Foundation 363
      How Can I Keep from Singing 338
   B - Earthen Vessels* 230
      I Danced in the Morning 382
   C - O Lord, I Am Not Worthy 431
      We Walk by Faith 328

TENTH SUNDAY
   A - Lord, When You Came / Pescador de Hombres
      378
      Somebody's Knockin' at Your Door 232

Suggested Hymns for the Church Year/*continued*

B - The Master Came to Bring Good News 466
    In Christ There Is No East or West 395
C - Shepherd Me, O God 344

ELEVENTH SUNDAY
A - God's Blessing Sends Us Forth 369
    Lord, You Give the Great Commission 267
B - We Walk by Faith* 328
    Come, Ye Thankful People, Come 320
C - There's a Wideness in God's Mercy 348
    Sing of the Lord's Goodness 312

TWELFTH SUNDAY
A - Be Not Afraid 346
    Give Thanks and Remember 322
B - How Firm a Foundation* 345
    How Can I Keep from Singing 338
C - Take Up Your Cross* 384
    Only This I Want 379

THIRTEENTH SUNDAY
A - Take Up Your Cross* 384
    Whatsoever You Do 366
B - There's a Wideness in God's Mercy 348
    Jesus, Heal Us 464
C - Two Fishermen 376
    The Summons 375

FOURTEENTH SUNDAY
A - I Heard the Voice of Jesus Say* 356
    Like a Shepherd* 192
B - Praise to You, O Christ, Our Savior 298
C - Lord, You Give the Great Commission 267
    Go 270

FIFTEENTH SUNDAY
A - Come, Ye Thankful People, Come 320
    Bring Forth the Kingdom 360
B - Here I Am, Lord 373
    Lord, You Give the Great Commission 267
C - Lord of All Nations, Grant Me Grace* 350
    Jesu, Jesu 248

SIXTEENTH SUNDAY
A - Come, Ye Thankful People, Come* 320
    Bring Forth the Kingdom 360
B - There's a Wideness in God's Mercy* 348
    I Heard the Voice of Jesus Say 356
C - We Are Many Parts 396
    The Love of the Lord 377

SEVENTEENTH SUNDAY
A - Seek Ye First the Kingdom of God 335
    Bring Forth the Kingdom 360
B - Shepherd of Souls, in Love, Come* 432
    Shepherd of Souls 447
C - Seek Ye First the Kingdom of God* 335

EIGHTEENTH SUNDAY
A - Shepherd of Souls, in Love, Come* 432
    Come to the Water* 293
B - Look Beyond* 442
    All Who Hunger 436
C - One Bread, One Body* 433
    The Love of the Lord 377

NINTEENTH SUNDAY
A - How Firm a Foundation* 345
    O God, Our Help in Ages Past 343
B - I Am the Bread of Life/Yo Soy el Pan de Vida* 449
    Eat This Bread* 435
    Look Beyond* 442
C - A Living Faith 331
    For All the Saints 424

TWENTIETH SUNDAY
A - There Is a Balm in Gilead 358
    There's a Wideness in God's Mercy 348
B - I Am the Bread of Life/Yo Soy el Pan de Vida* 449
    Eat This Bread* 435
C - God, Whose Purpose Is to Kindle* 388

TWENTY-FIRST SUNDAY
A - The Church's One Foundation 362
    Beautiful Savior 329
B - Look Beyond* 442
    Father, We Thank Thee, Who Hast Planted 319
C - Hear Us, Almighty Lord / Attende Domine 229
    Seek the Lord 236

TWENTY-SECOND SUNDAY
A - Take Up Your Cross* 384
    Tree of Life 242
B - Deep Within 233
C - Gather Us In 403
    We Are Called 389

TWENTY-THIRD SUNDAY
A - Forgive Our Sins 465
    The Master Came to Bring Good News 466
B - Gather Us In 403
    Amazing Grace 342
    Now in This Banquet 448
C - Take Up Your Cross* 384
    The Summons 375

TWENTY-FOURTH SUNDAY
A - Forgive Our Sins* 465
    The Master Came to Bring Good News 466
B - Take Up Your Cross* 384
    Only This I Want 379
C - Amazing Grace 342
    There's a Wideness in God's Mercy 348
    Though the Mountains May Fall 347

TWENTY-FIFTH SUNDAY
A - Seek the Lord* 236
    Keep in Mind 368
B - We Are Called 389
    Let There Be Peace on Earth 391
C - The Love of the Lord 377
    God of Day and God of Darkness 405
    Two Fishermen 376

TWENTY-SIXTH SUNDAY
A - Jesus, the Lord* 249
    All Hail the Power of Jesus' Name 285
B - The Love of the Lord 377
    In Christ There Is No East or West 395
C - God, Whose Purpose Is to Kindle 388
    A Living Faith 331

Suggested Hymns for the Church Year/*continued*

TWENTY-SEVENTH SUNDAY
A - Christ Is Made the Sure Foundation 363
    We Have Been Told 381
B - When Love Is Found 461
C - We Walk by Faith 328

TWENTY-EIGHTH SUNDAY
A - Gather Us In* 403
    We Come to Your Feast 445
B - The Summons 375
    The Love of the Lord 377
C - Keep in Mind* 368
    Now Thank We All Our God 321

TWENTY-NINTH SUNDAY
A - Sing Praise to God Who Reigns Above 310
    Glory and Praise to Our God 299
B - 'Tis the Gift to Be Simple 367
    In Christ There Is No East or West 395
C - Sing Praise to God Who Reigns Above 310
    Seek the Lord 236
    Seek Ye First the Kingdom of God 335

THIRTIETH SUNDAY
A - Lord of All Nations, Grant Me Grace* 350
    Jesu, Jesu 248
    They'll Know We Are Christians 397
B - Amazing Grace 342
    We Walk by Faith 328
C - 'Tis the Gift to Be Simple 367
    Gather Us In 403

THIRTY-FIRST SUNDAY
A - 'Tis the Gift to Be Simple 367
    We Are the Light of the World 295
B - Lord of All Nations, Grant Me Grace 350
    Jesu, Jesu 248
C - Amazing Grace 342
    The Master Came to Bring Good News 466

THIRTY-SECOND SUNDAY
A - The King Shall Come When Morning Dawns
      193
    O Come, Divine Messiah 196
B - The Harvest of Justice 387
    The Love of the Lord 377
C - Come, Ye Faithful, Raise the Strain 252
    Soon and Very Soon 409

THIRTY-THIRD SUNDAY
A - City of God 371
    I Want to Walk as a Child of the Light 297
B - The King Shall Come When Morning Dawns
      193
    Sing a New Song to the Lord 307
C - Be Not Afraid 346
    How Can I Keep from Singing 338

CHRIST THE KING
see nos. 283-288
A - Whatsoever You Do* 366
    God of Day and God of Darkness 405
B - To Jesus Christ, Our Sovereign King 287
    All Glory, Laud, and Honor 244
C - Jesus, Remember Me* 246
    Were You There 251
    All Glory, Laud, and Honor 244

FEB. 2: PRESENTATION OF THE LORD
Canticle of Simeon 737

MARCH 19: JOSEPH, HUSBAND OF MARY
Of the Father's Love Begotten 211

MARCH 25: ANNUNCIATION OF OUR LORD
Immaculate Mary 421
Canticle of Mary / Luke 1:46-55 48
I Say "Yes," Lord / Digo "Sí," Señor 332

JUNE 24: BIRTH OF JOHN THE BAPTIST
Gospel Canticle (Now Bless the God of Israel) 6
O Come, Divine Messiah 196

JUNE 29: PETER AND PAUL
Beautiful Savior 329
How Firm a Foundation 345
For All the Saints 424

JULY 4: INDEPENDENCE DAY
see nos. 472-474

AUGUST 6: TRANSFIGURATION
'Tis Good, Lord, to Be Here* 413

AUGUST 15: ASSUMPTION
Hail, Holy Queen Enthroned Above 419
Sing We of the Blessed Mother 418
Canticle of Mary / Luke 1:46-55 48

LABOR DAY
Lord of All Hopefulness 327
Praise and Thanksgiving 407

SEPTEMBER 14: TRIUMPH OF THE CROSS
Lift High the Cross 423
Jesus, the Lord 249
How Great Thou Art 291

NOVEMBER 1: ALL SAINTS
Blest Are They 359
We Are the Light of the World 295

**NOVEMBER 9: DEDICATION OF
ST. JOHN LATERAN**
Come, Ye Thankful People, Come 320
The Church's One Foundation 362

THANKSGIVING DAY
see nos. 316-323

DECEMBER 8: IMMACULATE CONCEPTION
Immaculate Mary 421
I Say "Yes," Lord / Digo "Sí," Señor 332
Sing We of the Blessed Mother 418

Index of Composers, Authors and Sources/*continued*

Index of Composers, Authors and Sources/*continued*

Metrical Index of Tunes/*continued*

Metrical Index of Tunes/*continued*

A light of revelation to the nations, and the glory of your people Israel. 737

A light will shine on us this day: the Lord is born for us. 491

All the ends of the earth have seen the saving power of God. 34 492

Alleluia, alleluia, alleluia! 35 39 41 47 541

Arise, come to your God, sing him your songs of rejoicing. 35

Be merciful, O Lord, for we have sinned. 28 502

Be with me, Lord, when I am in trouble. 32 504

Blessed are they, blessed are they who hope in the Lord. 595

Blessed are they who dwell in your house, O Lord. 495

Blessed are they who follow the law of the Lord! 593

Blessed are those who fear the Lord. 674

Blessed are those who fear the Lord and walk in his ways. 493

Blessed the people the Lord has chosen to be his own. 573 634

Blessed the poor in spirit; the kingdom of heaven is theirs! 587

Blest are those who love you, happy those who follow you, blest are those who seek you, O God. 43

Create in me, create in me a clean heart, O God. 515 540

Cry out with joy and gladness: for among you is the great and Holy One of Israel. 485

Do not forget the works of the Lord! 763

Father, into your hands I commend my spirit. 529

Fill us with your love, O Lord, and we will sing for joy! 660

For ever I will sing the goodness of the Lord. 487 489 614

From the voices of children, Lord, comes the sound of your praise. 19

Give back to me the joy of your salvation. 68

Give thanks to the Lord, his love is everlasting. 612

Give thanks to the Lord for he is good, his love is everlasting. 552

Give the Lord glory and honor. 662

Glory and praise for evermore. 572

Go out to all the world, and tell the Good News. 604 640

God, in your goodness, you have made a home for the poor. 643

God mounts his throne to shouts of joy: a blare of trumpets for the Lord. 565

He who does justice will live in the presence of the Lord. 625

Here am I, Lord; here am I, Lord; I come to do your will. 581 582 742

Holy is God! Holy and strong! Holy and living for ever! 40

How great is your name, O Lord our God, through all the earth! 19

I believe that I shall see the good things of the Lord in the land of the living. 566 767

I love you, Lord, my strength, my strength. 665 669

I praise you, O Lord, for I am wonderfully made. 747

I shall live in the house of the Lord all the days of my life. 659

I turn to you, O Lord, in time of trouble, and you fill me with the joy of salvation. 594

I will praise you, Lord, for you have rescued me. 25 537 555 607 615

I will praise you, Lord, in the assembly of your people. 560

I will praise your name for ever, my king and my God. 46 561 617 670

I will rise and go to my father. 649

I will sing of your salvation. 589

I will take the cup of salvation, and call on the name of the Lord. 576

I will walk before the Lord in the land of the living. 506 648

If today you hear his voice, harden not your hearts. 33 508 588 631 644 658

In ev'ry age, O Lord, you have been our refuge. 646

In the morning I will sing, will sing glad songs of praise to you. 4

In the sight of the angels I will sing your praises, O Lord. 592

In you, O Lord, I have found my peace. 668

Justice shall flourish in his time, and fullness of peace for ever. 480

Let all the earth cry out to God with joy. 30 562 619

Let my tongue be silenced, if I ever forget you! 512

Let the Lord enter; he is king of glory. 486

Let us go rejoicing to the house of the Lord. 477 679

Let us sing to the Lord; he has covered himself in glory. 536

Like a deer that longs for running streams, my soul longs for you, my God, my soul longs for you, my God. 540

Lord, be my rock of safety. 602

Lord, come and save us. 483

Lord, come to my aid, Lord, come to my aid! 637

Lord, ev'ry nation on earth will adore you. 497

Lord, forgive the wrong I have done. 610

Lord, go up to the place of your rest, you and the ark of your holiness. 758

Lord, heal my soul, for I have sinned against you. 597

Lord, I love your commands. 626

Lord, in your great love, answer me. 611

Lord, it is good to give thanks to you. 601 609

Lord, let us see your kindness, and grant us your salvation. 481 621 632

Lord, let your face shine on us. 554

Lord, let your mercy be on us, as we place our trust in you. 505 559 663

Lord, make us turn to you; let us see your face and we shall be saved. 31 478 488

Lord, on the day I called for help, you answered me. 628

Lord, send out your Spirit, and renew the face of the earth. 38 534 569 570

Lord, this is the people that longs to see your face. 766

Lord, when your glory appears, my joy will be full. 673

Lord, you are good and forgiving. 623

Lord, you have the words of everlasting life. 20 509 539

Lord, you will show us the path of life. 553
Lord, your love is eternal; do not forsake the work of your hands. 638

May God bless us in his mercy, may God bless us in his mercy. 496
May the Lord bless and protect us all the days of our lives. 657
My God, my God, why have you abandoned me? 21 521
My prayers rise like incense, my hands like an evening offering. 13
My shepherd is the Lord, nothing indeed shall I want. 22
My soul is thirsting for you, O Lord, thirsting for you my God. 613 641 671
My soul rejoices in my God, my soul rejoices in my God. 48 484

No one who waits for you, O Lord, will ever be put to shame. 767

O bless the Lord, my soul, O bless the Lord. 500
O God, O God, let all the nations praise you! 564 635
O God, I seek you, my soul thirsts for you, your love is finer than life. 29
O Lord, our God, how wonderful your name in all the earth! 574
O praise the Lord, Jerusalem. 575
One who does justice will live in the presence of the Lord. 642
Our blessing cup is a communion with the blood of Christ. 526
Our eyes are fixed on the Lord, pleading for his mercy. 618
Our help is from the Lord, who made heaven and earth. 42 664

Praise the Lord, my soul! Praise the Lord! 645 655 672
Praise the Lord, praise the Lord, who heals the brokenhearted. 591
Praise the Lord, praise the Lord who lifts up the poor. 652
Proclaim his marvelous deeds to all the nations. 583

Remember your mercies, O Lord. 653
Rest in God alone, rest in God alone, my soul. 599

Since my mother's womb, you have been my strength. 746
Sing to the Lord a new song, for he has done marvelous deeds. 773
Sing with joy to God! Sing to God our help! 603

Taste and see the goodness of the Lord. 26 513 633 636 639
Teach me your ways, O Lord, teach me your ways. 585
The angel of the Lord will rescue those who fear him. 750
The earth is full of the goodness of the Lord, the goodness of the Lord. 534
The hand of the Lord feeds us; he answers all our needs. 627 629
The just man is a light in darkness to the upright. 590
The Lord comes to rule the earth with justice. 676

The Lord gave them bread from heaven. 630
The Lord has done great things for us; we are filled with joy. 482 516 666
The Lord has revealed to the nations his saving power, his saving power. 563 661
The Lord has set his throne in heaven. 567
The Lord hears the cry of the poor. 27 667
The Lord is kind and merciful, the Lord is kind and merciful. 37 510 596 598 600
The Lord is kind and merciful; slow to anger, and rich in compassion. 647
The Lord is king; he is robed in majesty. 678
The Lord is king, the Lord most high over all the earth. 568 756
The Lord is my light and my salvation. 24 58 507 584 767
The Lord is my shepherd; there is nothing I shall want. 22 511 556 580 624 677 67
The Lord is near to all who call on him. 650
The Lord remembers his covenant for ever. 494
The Lord upholds my life. 651
The Lord will bless his people with peace. 498
The Lord will come to us with mighty power, bringing light to eyes of those who serve him well. 736
The Lord's kindness is everlasting to those who fear him. 578
The precepts of the Lord give joy to the heart. 654
The queen stands at your right hand, arrayed in gold. 759
The seed that falls on good ground will yield a fruitful harvest. 620
The Son of David will live for ever. 740
The stone rejected by the builders has become the cornerstone. 557
The vineyard of the Lord is the house of Israel. 656
The waters of the river gladden the city of God, the holy dwelling of the Most High. 769
Their message goes out through all the earth. 749
This is the day the Lord has made; let us rejoice and be glad. 41 551
Though I walk in the valley of darkness, I fear no evil, for you are with me. 767
To the upright I will show the saving pow'r of God. 605
To you, O Lord, I lift my soul, to you I lift my soul. 23 479 767
Today, today, today is born our Savior, Christ the Lord. 490
Turn to the Lord in your need, and you will live. 622

We are his people: the sheep of his flock. 36 558 608
Who is this king of glory? It is the Lord. 737
With the Lord there is mercy, and fullness of redemption. 44 514 606

You are a priest for ever, in the line of Melchizedek. 577
You are my inheritance, O Lord. 535 616 675
You will draw water joyfully from the springs of salvation. 499 538 540 579
Your love is never ending. 45
Your ways, O Lord, are love and truth, to those who keep your covenant. 503
Your words, O Lord, are Spirit and life. 586 622

Index of First Lines and Common Titles/*continued*

Index of First Lines and Common Titles/*continued*

Index of First Lines and Common Titles/*continued*

Trilingual Intercessions

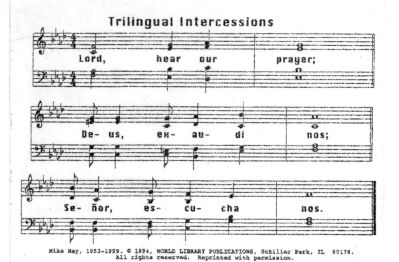

Lord, hear our prayer;

De- us, ex- au- di nos;

Se- ñor, es- cu- cha nos.

Jacob Bancks (b. 1982)

MASS OF THE
MOST
SACRED
HEART

in ENGLISH
According to the 2010 Translation
of the Roman Missal
and LATIN

Original artwork by
Daniel Mitsui

Mass of the Most Sacred Heart

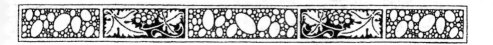

KYRIE

Or:

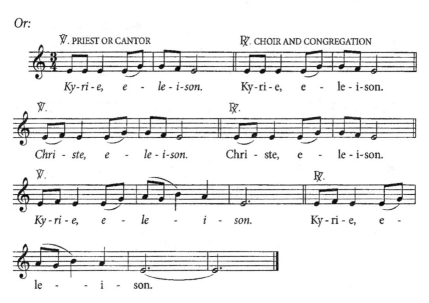

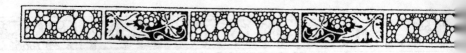

GLORIA

Glo-ry to God in the high-est, and on earth peace to

peo-ple of good will. We praise you, we bless you, we a-

dore you, we glo-ri-fy you, we give you thanks for your great glo-ry,

Lord God, heav-en-ly King, O God, al -

℣. CANTORS

migh-ty Fa - ther. *Lord Je - sus Christ, On - ly Be - got-ten*

℟. CHOIR AND CONGREGATION ℣.

Son, Lord God, Lamb of God, Son of the Fa - ther, *you*

℟.

take a - way the sins of the world, have mer - cy on us;

℣. ℟.

you take a - way the sins of the world, re - ceive our prayer;

℣. ℟.

you are seat-ed at the right hand of the Fa - ther, have mer -

℣. CANTORS

tens. Do-mi-ne Fi-li U-ni-ge-ni-te, Je-su Chri-ste,

℟. CHOIR AND CONGREGATION ℣.

Do-mi-ne De-us, Ag-nus De-i, Fi-li-us Pa-tris, qui

℟. ℣.

tol-lis pec-ca-ta mun-di mi-se-re no-bis; qui

℟.

tol-lis pec-ca-ta mun-di su-sci-pe de-pre-ca-ti-o-nem

℣.

nos-tram. Qui se-des ad dex-te-ram Pa-tris,

℟.

mi-se-re-re no-bis. Quo-ni-am tu so-lus San-ctus,

tu so-lus Do-mi-nus, tu so-lus Al-ti-si-mus, Je-su Chri-ste,

cum San-cto Spi-ri-tu: in glo-ri-a De-i Pa-

tris. A - men.

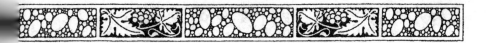

SANCTUS

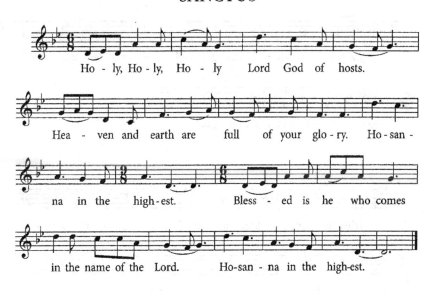

Ho - ly, Ho - ly, Ho - ly Lord God of hosts.

Hea - ven and earth are full of your glo - ry. Ho - san -

na in the high - est. Bless - ed is he who comes

in the name of the Lord. Ho - san - na in the high - est.

Or:

San - ctus, San - ctus, San - ctus Do - mi - nus De - us Sa - ba - oth.

Ple - ni sunt cae - li et ter - ra glo - ri - a tu - a. Ho - san -

na in ex - cel - sis. Be - ne - di - ctus qui ve - nit

in no - mi - ne Do - mi - ni. Ho - san - na in ex - cel - sis.

The Mystery of Faith

We pro-claim your Death, O Lord, and pro-fess your Re-sur-

rec-tion un-til you come a-gain.

Or:

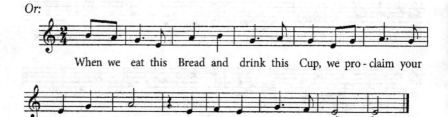

When we eat this Bread and drink this Cup, we pro-claim your

Death, O Lord, un-til you come a-gain.

Or:

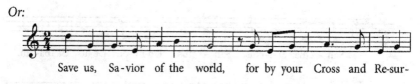

Save us, Sa-vior of the world, for by your Cross and Re-sur-

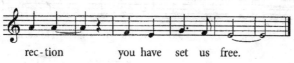

rec-tion you have set us free.

Amen of the Doxology

A - - - - men.

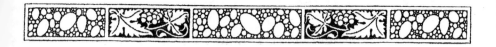

AGNUS DEI

Lamb of God, you take a - way the sins of the world, have mer - cy on us. Lamb of God, you take a - way the sins of the world, grant us peace.

Or:

Ag-nus De - i, qui to - lis pec - ca - ta mun - di, mi - se - re - re no - bis. Agnus De - i, qui to - lis pec - ca - ta mun - di, do - na no-bis pa-cem.

LITANY OF THE SACRED HEART OF JESUS

℣. Lord, have mercy on us.

℞. **Lord, have mercy on us.**

℣. Christ, have mercy on us.

℞. **Christ, have mercy on us.**

℣. Lord, have mercy on us.

℞. **Lord, have mercy on us.**

℣. Christ, hear us.

℞. **Christ, hear us.**

℣. Christ, graciously hear us.

℞. **Christ, graciously hear us.**

*After each invocation below, all respond, ℞. **have mercy on us.***

℣. God, the Father of Heaven, ℞.

℣. God, the Son, Redeemer of the World, ℞.

℣. God, the Holy Ghost, ℞.

℣. Holy Trinity, one God, ℞.

℣. Heart of Jesus, Son of the Eternal Father, ℞.

℣. Heart of Jesus, formed in the womb of the Virgin Mother by the Holy Ghost, ℞.

℣. Heart of Jesus, united substantially with the word of God, ℞.

℣. Heart of Jesus, of infinite majesty, ℞.

℣. Heart of Jesus, holy temple of God, ℞.

℣. Heart of Jesus, tabernacle of the Most High, ℞.

℣. Heart of Jesus, house of God and gate of heaven, ℞.

℣. Heart of Jesus, glowing furnace of charity, ℞.

℣. Heart of Jesus, vessel of justice and love, ℞.

℣. Heart of Jesus, full of goodness and love, ℞.

℣. Heart of Jesus, abyss of all virtues, ℞.

℣. Heart of Jesus, most worthy of all praise, ℞.

℣. Heart of Jesus, king and center of all hearts, ℞.

℣. Heart of Jesus, in whom are all the treasures of wisdom and knowledge, ℞.

℣. Heart of Jesus, in whom dwelleth all the fullness of the Divinity, ℞.

℣. Heart of Jesus, in whom the Father is well pleased, ℞.

℣. Heart of Jesus, of whose fullness we have all received, ℞.

℣. Heart of Jesus, desire of the everlasting hills, ℞.

℣. Heart of Jesus, patient and rich in mercy, ℞.

℣. Heart of Jesus, rich to all who invoke Thee, ℞.

℣. Heart of Jesus, fount of life and holiness, ℞.

℣. Heart of Jesus, propitiation for our sins, ℞.

℣. Heart of Jesus, saturated with revilings, ℞.

℣. Heart of Jesus, crushed for our iniquities, ℞.

℣. Heart of Jesus, made obedient unto death, ℞.

℣. Heart of Jesus, pierced with a lance, ℞.

℣. Heart of Jesus, source of all consolation, ℞.

℣. Heart of Jesus, our life and resurrection, ℞.

℣. Heart of Jesus, our peace and reconciliation, ℞.

℣. Heart of Jesus, victim for our sins, ℞.

℣. Heart of Jesus, salvation of those who hope in Thee, ℞.

℣. Heart of Jesus, hope of those who die in Thee, ℞.

℣. Heart of Jesus, delight of all saints, ℞.

℣. Lamb of God, who takest away the sins of the world,
   ℞. **spare us, O Lord.**

℣. Lamb of God, who takest away the sins of the world,
   ℞. **graciously hear us, O Lord.**

℣. Lamb of God who takest away the sins of the world,
   ℞. **have mercy on us.**

℣. Jesus, meek and humble of Heart.
   ℞. **Make our hearts like unto Thine.**

Let us pray.

Almighty and everlasting God, look upon the Heart of Thy well-beloved Son and upon the acts of praise and satisfaction which He renders unto Thee in the name of sinners; and do Thou, in Thy great goodness, grant pardon to them who seek Thy mercy, in the name of the same Thy Son, Jesus Christ, Who liveth and reigneth with Thee, world without end.

   ℞. **Amen.**